SHAKESPEARE SURVEY

ADVISORY BOARD

SHAKESPEARE SURVEY

AN ANNUAL SURVEY OF
SHAKESPEARE STUDIES AND PRODUCTION

49

Romeo and Juliet and its Afterlife

EDITED BY

STANLEY WELLS

CAMBRIDGE
UNIVERSITY PRESS

Published by the Press Syndicate of the University of Cambridge
The Pitt Building, Trumpington Street, Cambridge CB2 1RP
40 West 20th Street, New York, NY 10011–4211, USA
10 Stamford Road, Oakleigh, Melbourne 3166, Australia

First published 1996

Printed in Great Britain at the University Press, Cambridge

A cataloguing in publication record for this book is available from the British Library

ISBN 0 521 57047 6 hardback

Shakespeare Survey was first published in 1948. Its first
eighteen volumes were edited by Allardyce Nicoll.
Kenneth Muir edited volumes 19 to 33.

CE

EDITOR'S NOTE

Volume 50 of *Shakespeare Survey*, which will be at press by the time this volume appears, will be on 'Shakespeare and Language' and will include papers from the 1996 International Shakespeare Conference. The theme of Volume 51 will be 'Shakespeare in the Eighteenth Century'.

Submissions should be addressed to the Editor at The Shakespeare Institute, Church Street, Stratford-upon-Avon, Warwickshire CV37 6HP, to arrive at the latest by 1 September 1997 for Volume 51. Pressures on space are heavy; priority is given to articles related to the theme of a particular volume. Please either enclose postage (overseas, in International Reply coupons) or send a copy you do not wish to be returned. All articles submitted are read by the Editor and at least one member of the Editorial Board, whose indispensable assistance the Editor gratefully acknowledges.

Unless otherwise indicated, Shakespeare quotations and references are keyed to the modern-spelling Complete Oxford Shakespeare (1986).

Review copies of books should be addressed to the Editor, as above. In attempting to survey the ever-increasing bulk of Shakespeare publications our reviewers inevitably have to exercise some selection. We are pleased to receive offprints of articles which help to draw our reviewers' attention to relevant material.

S. W. W.

CONTRIBUTORS

MARY BLY, *Washingon University*
MARK THORNTON BURNETT, *The Queen's University, Belfast*
ANTHONY DAVIES, *Victoria College, Jersey*
LLOYD DAVIS, *University of Queensland*
PHILIP DAVIS, *University of Liverpool*
DAVID FARLEY-HILLS, *University of Wales, Lampeter*
R. A. FOAKES, *University of California, Los Angeles*
JAMES FOWLER, *The Theatre Museum*
REX GIBSON, *Cambridge Institute of Education*
ANDREW GURR, *University of Reading*
PETER HOLLAND, *Trinity Hall, Cambridge*
JOAN OZARK HOLMER, *Georgetown University*
JOHN JOWETT, *The Shakespeare Institute, University of Birmingham*
RONALD KNOWLES, *University of Reading*
JILL L. LEVENSON, *Trinity College, Ontario*
DAVID LINDLEY, *University of Leeds*
SUBHA MUKHERJI, *Gonville and Caius College, Cambridge*
EDWARD PECHTER, *Concordia University, Montreal*
NIKY RATHBONE, *Birmingham Shakespeare Library*
DOMINIC SHELLARD, *University of Sheffield*
SUSAN SNYDER, *Swarthmore College, Pennsylvania*
STANLEY WELLS, *The Shakespeare Institute, University of Birmingham*

CONTENTS

ILLUSTRATIONS

LIST OF ILLUSTRATIONS

THE CHALLENGES OF *ROMEO AND JULIET*

STANLEY WELLS

The story of Romeo and Juliet – one of the great myths of the Western world – first appeared fully formed in an Italian version of 1530, and since then has had a vigorous afterlife, not all of it deriving from Shakespeare. It has been frequently reincarnated and recollected in a multitude of forms and media – prose narratives, verse narratives, drama, opera, orchestral and choral music, ballet, film, television and painting among them. Besides being presented seriously it has been parodied and burlesqued; there are several full-scale nineteenth-century travesties of Shakespeare's play,[1] and its balcony scene in particular has often formed the basis for comic sketches. Romeo is a type name for an ardent lover, and Juliet's 'Romeo, Romeo, wherefore art thou Romeo?' is often jokily declaimed even by people who have never read or seen the play.

Already when, around 1594, Shakespeare decided to base a play on the story, he was able to consult more than one version. He worked closely from *The Tragical History of Romeus and Juliet*, by Arthur Brooke (who, like the hero and heroine of the story, himself died young), first published in 1562 and reprinted in 1587. Brooke had used a moralistic French adaptation, by Pierre Boaistuau, of a story by the Italian Matteo Bandello, and Shakespeare probably also read William Painter's translation of Boaistuau in his *Palace of Pleasure*, of 1567.

Brooke's style is, to say the best, uninspired, but he provided Shakespeare with both a well laid-out story and much valuable detail. Brooke treated the events as historical, ending his poem with the statement that

The bodies dead removed from vault where they
  did die
In stately tomb on pillars great of marble raise they
  high.
On every side above were set and eke beneath
Great store of cunning epitaphs in honour of their
  death.
And even at this day the tomb is to be seen,
So that among the monuments that in Verona
  been
There is no monument more worthy of the sight
Than is the tomb of Juliet, and Romeus her
  knight.

These lines clearly influenced the end of Shakespeare's play, in which the effect of the lovers' deaths is to some extent alleviated by the consequent reconciliation of their feuding families; and the alleged historicity of the tale continues to be of value to the Veronese tourist industry.

For most people at the present time Shakespeare's play embodies the classic version of the story. But, although it is widely read and frequently performed, it has itself undergone adaptation, sometimes slight, sometimes substantial, in ways that are implicitly critical of the

---

[1] Nineteenth-century burlesques and travesties are reprinted in *Shakespeare Burlesques*, ed. Stanley Wells, 5 vols. (London, 1977). One of the best is Andrew Halliday's *Romeo and Juliet Travestie, or, The Cup of Cold Poison*, first performed in 1859, in which Romeo and Juliet catch cold in the balcony scene: 'Swear not by the boon – the inconstant boon'.

original. The play's ending has proved especially subject to alteration. In a lost version by James Howard performed shortly after the restoration of the monarchy in 1660, the tragedy was endowed with a happy ending (or perhaps one should say an even happier ending: one of my old professors, responding to a lady who said, after seeing a performance of Shakespeare's play, that she wished it ended happily, mischievously asked 'O, don't you think it does?') The result was that (as the prompter Downes wrote) 'when the tragedy was revived again 'twas played alternately, tragical one day and tragi-comical another for several days altogether'.[2] Not long after this, in 1680, Thomas Otway wrote a new play, *Caius Marius*, borrowing much of Shakespeare's dialogue. Apparently Otway was dissatisfied with Shakespeare's conclusion, in which Romeo dies before Juliet recovers from the sleeping potion given to her by the Friar. Otway, clearly – and perhaps rightly – thinking that Shakespeare had missed a good opportunity for an affecting passage of dialogue, conceived the notion of causing his heroine to wake before her lover expired, and gave them a touching duologue. When Theophilus Cibber came to adapt Shakespeare's play, in 1744, he incorporated passages from Otway, including the death scene, with only minor changes, and around the same time David Garrick, in a version that follows Shakespeare's text more closely, nevertheless seized upon Otway's basic idea, while writing a new duologue for the lovers in which they go successively mad. This was accepted into the theatrical tradition, and although the American Charlotte Cushman (playing Romeo) returned to Shakespeare in the mid-nineteenth century, Garrick's version appears not to have been completely abandoned until Henry Irving put on the play in 1882.

Garrick's death scene is easily guyed: 'Bless me! how cold it is!' says Juliet on waking, and later, 'And did I wake for this!'; yet Francis Gentleman, writing in 1770, praised it highly: 'no play ever received greater advantage from

alteration than this tragedy, especially in the last act; bringing Juliet to life before Romeo dies, is undoubtedly a change of infinite merit. The whole dying scene does Mr Garrick great credit.'[3] In its day, and for long afterwards, it must have been highly actable – and it gave the performer of Romeo a stronger death scene than Shakespeare had provided. Bernard Shaw, writing in 1894, described his first experience of the play, 'in which Romeo, instead of dying forthwith when he took the poison, was interrupted by Juliet, who sat up and made him carry her down to the footlights, where she complained of being very cold, and had to be warmed by a love scene, in the middle of which Romeo, who had forgotten all about the poison, was taken ill and died'.[4] No modern director would be likely to interpolate Garrick's words into Shakespeare's text, but in more than one production the terrible irony of the situation has been pointed by Juliet's showing signs of life as Romeo dies which are visible to the audience though not to him.[5]

In the twentieth century English-speaking productions have at least taken Shakespeare's original text as their point of departure, though the dénouement was radically altered in one of Stratford's more iconoclastic versions, the one directed by Michael Bogdanov in 1986. This modern-dress production came to be known as the *Alfa-Romeo and Juliet* because of the presence on stage during part of the action of a bright red

---

[2] John Downes, *Roscius Anglicanus* (London, 1708; Facsimile Reprint, Augustan Reprint Society no. 134, Los Angeles, 1969), sig. C3v.

[3] Cited in G. C. D. Odell, *Shakespeare from Betterton to Irving*, 2 vols. (New York, 1920), 1.347.

[4] From an article called 'The Religion of the Pianoforte' (*The Fortnightly Review*, February 1894), reprinted in part in *Shaw on Shakespeare*, edited by Edwin Wilson (London, 1962), p. 246.

[5] See for example Peter Holding, *Romeo and Juliet: Text and Performance* (London, 1992), pp. 61–2 for a description of the scene in a 1976 Stratford production directed by Trevor Nunn and Barry Kyle. In Adrian Noble's 1995 Stratford production, too, Juliet showed signs of life before Romeo died.

sports car. Characteristically of this director, it had a strong political slant which manifested itself especially in his handling of the ending. Academic critics have suggested that when Montague and Capulet say that they will 'raise the lovers' statues in pure gold' they are revealing false, materialistic values.[6] Bogdanov translated this suggestion into theatrical terms. His text came to a halt with Juliet's death; the dead lovers were covered with golden cloths and then, during a brief blackout, they sprang to attention and stood as their own statues; the final episode became a wordless media event, as reporters and photographers flooded the scene, the survivors posed in attitudes suggestive rather of a desire to have their photographs published in *Hello!* magazine than of either true grief or reconciliation, and the Prince spoke part of the prologue – omitted at the start – transposed to the past tense.

In this essay I want to concentrate on the text as it has come down to us in editions based normally on the 'good' Quarto of 1599 (though often incorporating stage directions, and occasionally other readings, from the 'bad' Quarto of two years before) and on some of the challenges faced by directors who try to translate this text into terms of modern theatre. I do not intend to be judgemental about this text; indeed, I shall deliberately refrain from expressing my own opinions about its theatrical viability. Theatre history clearly shows that lines, speeches, whole episodes that were unacceptable in other ages, and in other theatres than those of today, have been restored to theatrical life in more recent productions. Even so, the programme for Adrian Noble's, in 1995, admitted to the omission of about 564 lines – getting on for twenty per cent of the complete text. That presumably represented Noble's judgement of what could be made to work by his particular actors in the Royal Shakespeare Theatre before the audiences going to that theatre in the theatrical conditions pertaining in 1995. It did not, I take it, claim to present an absolute judgement on the text's theatrical vi-

ability. Different textual cuts might be made in different circumstances even at the present time; it will be interesting to see if a full text will be presented in the new Globe, and if so, how it will work.

As I have said, twentieth-century productions, at least since John Gielgud's of 1935, in which he and Laurence Olivier successively played Romeo and Mercutio, and which also had Peggy Ashcroft as Juliet and Edith Evans as the Nurse, have tended to play fuller and purer texts than those of earlier ages; the BBC radio production by the Renaissance Theatre Company, available on audio cassette, uses a full text, but that is a special case, and it has to be admitted that even in our time some of the most theatrically exciting productions, including those of Peter Brook at Stratford in 1947 and Franco Zeffirelli at the Old Vic in 1960, have cut and otherwise altered the text extensively, presenting their vision of it in terms of the theatre of their time rather than offering text-centred performances. Indeed, both the directors I have named explicitly rejected engagement with the text's literary values; Brook declared that 'To come to the theatre merely to listen to the words was the last decadence', and Zeffirelli is reported to have 'said repeatedly that he had no use for [the play's] verse'.[7] And even directors who have been less radical in their treatment of the text than Brook and Bogdanov have made extensive cuts. Later I shall try to identify some of the main areas that have presented problems, and to suggest some reasons why they have done so.

The modern director's task is complicated by the fact that, since Shakespeare wrote, the story of the fated lovers has attracted many other

---

6 For example, Marjorie Garber, '*Romeo and Juliet*: Patterns and Paradigms', in *The Shakespeare Plays: A Study Guide* (San Diego, 1979), pp. 50–63; reprinted in '*Romeo and Juliet': Critical Essays*, edited by John F. Andrews (New York and London, 1993), pp. 119–31; p. 131. See also Susan Snyder, p. 96, below.
7 Jill L. Levenson, '*Romeo and Juliet': Shakespeare in Performance* (Manchester, 1987), pp. 66 and 97.

creative artists, some of whom have drawn exclusively on Shakespeare, some on other versions of the tale, and others who have mixed the traditions. There is no reason, for instance, to suppose that Tchaikovsky went beyond Shakespeare for his immensely popular fantasy overture of 1869 (later revised), or Prokofiev and his choreographers for their ballet, first performed in 1938; on the other hand, Bellini's opera *I Capuleti ed i Montecchi* (1830) appears to owe nothing to Shakespeare (though its double death scene bears a suspicious resemblance to Garrick's), and the librettists of the only other successful opera based on the story, Gounod's *Roméo et Juliette* (1867), incorporated Garrick's tomb scene into their work, as does Berlioz (wordlessly) in his dramatic symphony of 1839.

The existence and popularity of symphonic, operatic, balletic, filmic, and other offshoots is relevant to the performance history of the play itself because they create images that superimpose themselves on the Shakespearian text, forming expectations in the imaginations of the play's interpreters and audiences which subtly affect our response to efforts to translate that text into performance. In the wonderful *scène d'amour* in Berlioz's work, long-breathed phrases accompanied by rhythmical pulsations speak eloquently of passionate yearning in a manner that would not lead listeners to expect the humour that also lies latent in Shakespeare's dialogue; and Berlioz's musical depiction of the gradual dispersal of the masquers into the night, apparently strumming their guitars and humming snatches of half-remembered song, is not only theatrical as well as musical in its effect but appeared to be reflected, whether consciously or not, in one of the more sensitively directed episodes of Michael Bogdanov's production with the dying away of the sounds of motor bikes as revellers left the Capulets' ball. In a different way, the long tradition of scenically spectacular productions, aided and abetted by the popularity of Zeffirelli's film (discussed in later essays in this volume), with its beautiful

Tuscan settings, may lead theatregoers to expect visual splendours.

Also relevant to modern theatrical interpretations is the play's complex literary background. Although the often incandescent quality of its verse is responsible for much of the admiration that the play has evoked, at the same time its self-conscious literariness has repeatedly been implicitly or explicitly criticized as detrimental to its theatrical effectiveness. 'It is a dramatic poem rather than a drama', wrote Henry Irving, 'and I mean to treat it from that point of view.'[8] For all that, he omitted a lot of its poetry while succeeding, according to Henry James, only in making 'this enchanting poem' 'dull … mortally slow' and 'tame' by 'smothering' it 'in its accessories'.[9] The history of critical and theatrical reactions to the play demonstrates the fact that Shakespeare worked in a far more literary mode than has been fashionable in the theatre of later ages, and that its literariness has often been regarded as a theatrical handicap.

In a memorable tribute, T. J. B. Spencer wrote that 'Nothing in European drama had hitherto achieved the organisation of so much human experience when Shakespeare, at the age of about thirty, undertook the story of Juliet and Romeo.'[10] The manner in which the play organizes experience is highly self-conscious and deeply indebted to a variety of literary traditions. Many devices of parallelism and repetition create an almost architectural sense of structure. This structure is defined by the appearances of the Prince of Verona. Some productions bring him on to speak the Prologue, appropriately enough since his three appearances within the action have something

---

[8] Cited in Alan Hughes, *Henry Irving, Shakespearean* (Cambridge, 1981), p. 160.

[9] Henry James, in an article, 'London Plays', originally published in the *Atlantic Monthly*, August, 1882, and reprinted in *The Scenic Art*, edited by Allan Wade (London, 1949), pp. 162–7; p. 164.

[10] T. J. B. Spencer, ed., *Romeo and Juliet*, New Penguin Shakespeare (Harmondsworth, 1967 etc.), p. 7.

of a choric function. We first see him in his own right as he enters to exercise his authority at the height of the brawl between the followers of Montague and Capulet in the opening scene; he makes one formal though impassioned speech, and his departure marks a turning point from the public to the private action of the play as Benvolio, after recapitulating what has happened in lines that are usually abbreviated, describes the symptoms of Romeo's love-sickness for Rosaline. The Prince's second appearance comes at the climax of the play's second violent episode, culminating in the killing of Tybalt and Mercutio, which provokes him to another display of authority as he banishes Romeo, the principal turning point of the action; and he reappears in the final scene to preside over the investigation into the lovers' deaths and to apportion responsibility. His are the closing lines which round off the play, returning it to the condition of myth:

> For never was a story of more woe
> Than this of Juliet and her Romeo.

The formality evident in the appearances of the Prince recurs in many other aspects of the play's design. Shakespeare is still sometimes regarded as an inspired improviser, and perhaps in some plays he was, but it is impossible not to feel that before he started to write the dialogue of this play he worked out a ground plan as carefully as if he had been designing an intricate building. One could point, for example, to the parallels in function between Mercutio and the Nurse, both of whom are almost entirely of Shakespeare's creation: he a companion and foil to Romeo, she to Juliet, he consciously mocking Romeo's romanticism with high-spirited, bawdy cynicism, she no less earthy but less aware of the sexual implications of much of what she says, each of them involuntarily failing their companion in their greatest need, he through his accidental death which turns the play from a romantic comedy into a tragedy, she because of the limitations in her understanding of the depths of Juliet's love which

leave Juliet to face her fate alone. There are parallels too in the design of scenes: the Capulets' bustling preparations for the ball (1.5) are echoed in those for Juliet's marriage to Paris (4.4); and each of the play's three love duets — one in the evening, at the ball, the second at night, in the garden and on its overlooking balcony, the third at dawn, as the lovers, now married, prepare to part — is interrupted by calls from the Nurse.

These features of the play's structure create an impression of highly patterned formality; they may be regarded as dramatic strengths; and in any case a director can scarcely avoid them without rewriting the play, but there are others that have often suffered under the blue pencil. For example, at a number of points characters recapitulate action that has already been enacted before us. In the opening scene, Benvolio spends ten lines satirically describing Tybalt's intervention in the fray between the servants of the Montagues and Capulets; later, after the fight in which both Mercutio and Tybalt are killed, Benvolio again recapitulates what has happened, this time in twenty-three lines of verse; and in the closing scene the Friar, notoriously, after claiming 'I will be brief', recapitulates the full story of the lovers in one of the longest speeches of a play that is not short of long speeches. 'It is much to be lamented' wrote Johnson, 'that the poet did not conclude the dialogue with the action, and avoid a narrative of events which the audience already knew.'[11]

This technique of recapitulation can be, and has been, defended; for example, Bertrand Evans remarks that, 'far from being a repetitious exercise best deleted on the stage, the Friar's speech is an indispensable part of the total experience of the tragedy; not to be present when some key participants learn how their acts resulted in the pile of bodies in the Capulet

---

[11] *Johnson on Shakespeare*, edited by Arthur Sherbo, The Yale Edition of the Works of Samuel Johnson (New Haven, 1968), vol. 8, p. 976.

tomb – Romeo's, Juliet's, Tybalt's, Paris's – would be to miss too much'.[12] Certainly these speeches constitute a challenge that should be accepted by directors concerned to present the text in its integrity; for the actors, I take it, the challenge is to seek out a psychological subtext that will help them to deliver the lines not merely as a summary of what has gone before but as utterances emanating naturally and spontaneously from the characters as they have conceived it. Performers of Benvolio can portray his summaries of the action as the reactions of a well-meaning but puzzled man desperately attempting to make sense of what has happened; the Friar's long speech has been played in more than one production less as a judicial apportioning of blame (which it unequivocally is in Berlioz, where the role of the Friar encompasses some of the functions of Shakespeare's Prince) than as the frightened reactions of a man who fears he has betrayed his responsibility; the reactions of the other onstage characters as he reveals the secrets, previously unknown to them, of the marriage and the potion are no less important than his own state of mind as he speaks. Nevertheless the speech has been implicitly criticized by directors concerned to streamline the action; Peter Brook and Michael Bogdanov omitted it altogether,[13] and all twelve of the Stratford productions since Brook's have shortened it, some considerably.

The deliberation of the play's structure is of a piece with its self-conscious, even ostentatious literariness and intellectualism. 'Now is he for the numbers that Petrarch flowed in. Laura, to his lady, was a kitchen wench', says Mercutio of Romeo whom he believes to be still in love with the 'pale, hard hearted wench' Rosaline, as if to draw attention to Shakespeare's indebtedness to the Petrarchan tradition, well established in England at the time he was writing, of the besotted lover sighing in vain for an unresponsive beloved – a situation that he was to dramatize directly in the figures of Silvius and Phoebe in *As You Like It* and that is also related to that of the chaste young man with no interest

in ensuring his own posterity who is addressed in the first seventeen of Shakespeare's sonnets. The explicit reference to a major literary influence on the play – also omitted in most modern performances – is a counterpart to the appearance on stage of a volume of Ovid in *Titus Andronicus*.

The literary form most strongly associated with Petrarchism was the sonnet. The Argument to Brooke's poem is in sonnet form, and *Romeo and Juliet*, written during the ten or so years when the amatory sonnet cycle was enjoying a vogue greater than ever before or since, makes direct use of the complete form in the Prologue, in the rarely performed Chorus to Act 2, and, famously, in the shared sonnet spoken between the lovers on their first meeting. At a number of other points, too, such as the speech by the Prince that ends the play, Shakespeare uses the six-line rhyming unit ending in a couplet that forms the final part of the sonnet form as used by Shakespeare and which is also the stanza form of his narrative poem *Venus and Adonis*, of 1593. Other well established literary conventions, less obvious to the modern playgoer, that influence the play include the epithalamium, reflected in Juliet's great speech beginning 'Gallop apace, you fiery-footed steeds', and the dawn-parting, or 'alba' – one of the most universal of poetic themes – which provides the basic structure for the entire scene of dawn-parting between Romeo and Juliet.[14]

---

[12] Bertrand Evans, *Shakespeare's Tragic Practice* (Oxford, 1979), p. 51.

[13] Judging by the prompt book held in the Shakespeare Centre, Stratford-upon-Avon, Brook originally omitted all the text after Juliet's death (like Bogdanov after him) except for the addition of 'Brother Montague give me thy hand' from Capulet and the Prince's concluding six lines spoken by the Chorus, but restored some of the omitted dialogue, including part of the Friar's long speech, in later performances.

[14] The theme is studied in its multiple international manifestations in *Eros: An Enquiry into the Theme of Lovers' Meetings and Partings at Dawn in Poetry*, edited by Arthur T. Hatto (London, The Hague, Paris, 1965); the

The play's creative use of conventions of lyric poetry is responsible for much of its enduring popularity as perhaps the greatest of all expressions of romantic love; it is complemented and to some extent counterbalanced by an intellectualism manifesting itself especially in complex wordplay that has stood the passage of time less well and has often been censured (and, in recent times, defended) by literary critics as well as being subjected to the more practical criticism of being excised from acting texts. David Garrick, in the Advertisement to his 1748 adaptation, states his 'design . . . to clear the original as much as possible from the jingle and quibble which were always thought the great objections to reviving it'. 'Jingle' refers to Shakespeare's extensive use of rhyme, regarded by neoclassical critics as indecorous in tragedy; Garrick's modifications – which included reducing the sonnet form of the lovers' declaration to two quatrains – reduced the play's range of poetic style.

'Quibble' is, if anything, even more integral than rhyme to the effect of the play as Shakespeare wrote it. Wordplay extends from the bawdy of the servants' comic opening dialogue, through the self-conscious jesting of Mercutio and the often involuntary *double entendres* of the Nurse, up to passages of quibbling wordplay spoken in wholly serious, even tragic circumstances by Romeo and Juliet themselves. Modern performers and audiences have been educated into an easier acceptance of wordplay than Garrick, partly as a result of its serious use in post-Freudian literature, above all by James Joyce (whose 'stream of consciousness' technique is anticipated by the Nurse), and also by studies encouraging an historical awareness of its prevalence in uncomic writings by Shakespeare and his contemporaries, such as John Donne. Even so, cuts made in acting versions of the present day suggest that the quibble is still more easily regarded as an ingredient of comedy than as a vehicle of tragic effect. This springs, perhaps, from too limited a notion both of what Shakespeare may encompass within the port-

manteau definition of tragedy, and of the language appropriate to the form – if, indeed, it can properly be called a form. It has often been observed that for much of its considerable length *Romeo and Juliet* – especially if, as in Bogdanov's production, the Prologue is omitted – comes closer to our expectations of romantic comedy than of such a tragedy as the one that immediately precedes it in Shakespeare's output, *Titus Andronicus*, to which *Romeo and Juliet* might be regarded as a deliberately contrasting companion piece. If directors are to realize this script in its full richness they need to free themselves of the conventional connotations of tragedy and to play each episode in its own terms. And if audiences are to meet Shakespeare on his own terms they must find room in their responses not only for the direct if poetically heightened expression of heartfelt emotion that has caused the balcony scene to be valued as perhaps the most eloquent of all depictions of romantic love, but also for the contrived artificiality with which Shakespeare endows even the lovers' language at some of the most impassioned points of the play's action. This is not only a 'most excellent and lamentable tragedy', as the title page of the 1599 quarto puts it, it is also, in the terms of the title page of the 'bad' quarto of 1597, 'an excellent conceited tragedy' – which I suppose might be paraphrased as a tragedy notable for the ingenuity of its verbal expression. Under the surface of the play's poetry lies a complicated network of rhetorical figures (examined in Jill Levenson's essay, pp. 44–55) that are rarely recognized by even the more erudite among the play's modern readers. This poses great problems for the actors, as Bernard Shaw recognized when he wrote 'It should never be forgotten in judging an attempt to play Romeo and Juliet that the parts are made almost impossible except to actors of positive genius, skilled to the last degree in metrical declama-

section on English, by T. J. B. Spencer, includes discussion of Shakespeare's use of the motif.

tion, by the way in which the poetry, magnificent as it is, is interlarded by the miserable rhetoric and silly lyrical conceits which were the foible of the Elizabethans.'[15] The conceit with which Juliet imagines her and her lover's fate after death, with its hidden wordplay on the sexual sense of 'die', is as extreme as anything in metaphysical poetry:

> when I shall die
> [or 'he shall die', according to the unauthoritative
>   fourth quarto and some later editors]
> Take him and cut him out in little stars,
> And he will make the face of heaven so fine
> That all the world will be in love with night
> And pay no worship to the garish sun.   (3.2.21–5)

Even more difficult, I take it, are the play's several extended passages of dialogue in which characters are required, on the basis of misunderstanding or of false information, to act out emotions that, as the audience knows, the true situation does not justify. One such passage comes just after the lines I have quoted. Juliet's Nurse enters with the cords designed to make a rope ladder to give Romeo access to Juliet at night. 'Wringing her hands', as the bad quarto's direction and the good quarto's dialogue tell us, she bemoans Tybalt's death, of which Juliet has not heard, but in such a way that Juliet thinks Romeo, not Tybalt, is dead. In a sense the episode is an extended piece of wordplay on the pronoun 'he':

> Ah, welladay! He's dead, he's dead, he's dead!
> We are undone, lady, we are undone.
> Alack the day, he's gone, he's killed, he's dead!
>   (3.2.37–9)

So says the Nurse, speaking of Tybalt, but Juliet takes her to refer to Romeo, and even when the Nurse speaks directly of Romeo –

>   O Romeo, Romeo,
> Who ever would have thought it Romeo?
>   (3.2.41–2)

Juliet takes her to mean that Romeo is the victim, not the killer. The misunderstanding continues through a long episode in which Juliet again resorts to complex wordplay:

> Hath Romeo slain himself? Say thou but 'Ay',
> And that bare vowel 'I' shall poison more
> Than the death-darting eye of cockatrice.
> I am not I if there be such an 'Ay',
> Or those eyes shut that makes thee answer 'Ay'.
> If he be slain, say 'Ay'; or if not, 'No'.
> Brief sounds determine of my weal or woe.
>   (3.2.45–51)

Not until the Nurse resorts to plain statement is the misunderstanding clarified:

> Tybalt is gone and Romeo banishèd.
> Romeo that killed him – he is banishèd.
>   (3.2.69–70)

And even then Juliet launches into a highly mannered lament, full of the oxymorons that are a conspicuous feature of this play's style. This scene has regularly been abbreviated in post-war Stratford productions, every one of which has omitted or shortened the wordplay on 'I', and most of which have abbreviated the oxymorons.

The artifice both of situation and of style in this scene is bound to have a distancing effect; it displays wit on the part of both Shakespeare and Juliet, yet for Juliet the situation is tragic. She needs to speak her lines with a high degree of intellectual control which may seem at odds with the spontaneous expression of deeply felt emotion. But perhaps this is the point: M. M. Mahood regards the puns on 'I' as 'one of Shakespeare's first attempts to reveal a profound disturbance of mind by the use of quibbles'[16] and Jill Levenson too regards Juliet's withdrawal from emotional expression as psychologically plausible: 'Juliet's prothalamium quickly shrinks to mere word-play and sound effects as she glimpses calamity in the Nurse's report, the swift reduction implying that absolute grief has arrested Juliet's imagination.'[17] Those are, I

---

[15] From a review of Forbes-Robertson's production, *The Saturday Review*, 28 September 1895; reprinted in *Shaw on Shakespeare*, pp. 168–74; p. 173.
[16] M. M. Mahood, *Shakespeare's Wordplay* (London, 1968), p. 70.
[17] Levenson, *Romeo and Juliet*, p. 7.

think, subjectively interpretative rather than objectively descriptive comments, but they suggest ways in which the performer may face the need to hold emotion in suspense, as it were, so that we appreciate the paradox of the situation while retaining sympathy with Juliet's plight.

Juliet faces a rather similar situation a little later, when her mother mistakes her grief at Romeo's banishment for mourning for her cousin Tybalt's death combined with anger at his killer, Romeo. She dissembles her true feelings in a series of quibbles and paradoxes:

> Indeed, I never shall be satisfied
> With Romeo till I behold him, dead,
> Is my poor heart so for a kinsman vexed.
> Madam, if you could find out but a man
> To bear a poison, I would temper it
> That Romeo should, upon receipt thereof,
> Soon sleep in quiet. O, how my heart abhors
> To hear him named and cannot come to him
> To wreak the love I bore my cousin
> Upon his body that hath slaughtered him!
>
> (3.5.93–102)

Johnson comments that 'Juliet's equivocations are rather too artful for a mind disturbed by the loss of a new lover',[18] and they are shortened or cut in the promptbooks of all the productions I have mentioned except one;[19] but perhaps the cleverness of style here is more encompassable than that in the previous scene as an expression of Juliet's bewilderment as she tries to respond to her mother's misplaced sympathy without actually perjuring herself; perhaps, indeed, it should teach us that wit is not incompatible with tragic effect.

The play's most notorious instance of discrepancy between what characters can be expected to be feeling and the manner in which it is expressed is the scene of mourning following the discovery of Juliet's supposedly dead body. The keening starts with the Nurse's words 'O lamentable day!', and is taken up successively by Lady Capulet, Paris, and Old Capulet in a formalized liturgy of grief whose repetitions culminate in the Nurse's

> O woe! O woeful, woeful, woeful day!
> Most lamentable day! Most woeful day
> That ever, ever, I did yet behold!
> O day, O day, O day, O hateful day,
> Never was seen so black a day as this!
> O woeful day, O woeful day! (4.4.80–5)

These lines take us into the world of Pyramus and Thisbe; indeed, one of the reasons for the hypothesis that *A Midsummer Night's Dream* dates from later than *Romeo and Juliet* (about which I am doubtful) is the suggestion that Bottom's expressions of grief over the corpse of Thisbe burlesque the Nurse's over Juliet. But it is all too easy for the lines to burlesque themselves. The classic objections to the passage were put by Coleridge:

As the audience knows that Juliet is not dead, this scene is, perhaps, excusable. But it is a strong warning to minor dramatists not to introduce at one time many separate characters agitated by one and the same circumstance. It is difficult to understand what effect, whether that of pity or of laughter, Shakespeare meant to produce; – the occasion and the characteristic speeches are so little in harmony![20]

Over a century later Granville Barker remarked that 'even faithful Shakespeareans have little good to say of that competition in mourning between Paris and Capulet, Lady Capulet and the Nurse. It has been branded as deliberate burlesque.' He attempts a defence, but admits that 'The passage does jar a little.'[21] Most attempts to justify the scene have proposed that the blatant artificiality of the mourners' expressions of grief represents a deliberate distancing effect, forcing the audience to recall that Juliet is not actually dead even though these people believe her to be so. These defences tend to seem half-hearted and lame.[22] Scholarship came

---

[18] *Johnson on Shakespeare*, vol. 8, p. 951.

[19] David Leveaux's, in 1991.

[20] Quoted from *The Romantics on Shakespeare*, ed. Jonathan Bate (Harmondsworth, 1992), p. 519.

[21] Harley Granville Barker, *Prefaces to Shakespeare*, Second Series (London, 1930), p. 26.

[22] See, for example, Evans, *Shakespeare's Tragic Practice*, pp. 42–3.

to the aid of criticism when Charles Lower, observing that the passage is particularly inadequately reported in the first quarto, proposed that this is because the lines were delivered simultaneously in the performance on which that text is putatively based: in other words, that the speeches were intended to convey a generalized impression of mourning, not be listened to in their own right.[23] The Oxford editors, while not accepting that this was Shakespeare's original intention as represented in the 'good' quarto, nevertheless (in keeping with their aim of representing the plays so far as possible as they were acted) print the direction '*Paris, Capulet and his Wife, and the Nurse all at once wring their hands and cry out together.*' Whether this represents Shakespeare's own solution of a problem with which he had presented himself, or merely an evasion of it, we can't tell. The scene of mourning, and the episode with the Musicians that follows, have often been omitted and, I think, always abbreviated, even in recent times. Nevertheless, at least one director had anticipated the editors: Peter Holding records that in Terry Hands's 1973 Stratford production this episode, so far from being ridiculous, was

Perhaps the most affecting ... successive speakers picked up the tone of lament from their predecessor, overlapping with some of the final phrases and then developing the cry with appropriate personal embellishments. The emotion of the lament was sincere but kept at a certain distance, while allowing the audience simultaneously to enjoy the fact that of course Juliet was still alive.[24]

The scene was handled in similar fashion in Adrian Noble's production.

Holding's comment reminds us that these texts, for all their undoubted literary quality, are, fundamentally, scripts for performance, and that at too many points we simply lack information about how their author intended them to be realized on the stage. A successful surmounting in any given production of problems that have previously seemed acute may vindicate Shakespeare's judgement, but equally may

simply demonstrate the ingenuity of the interpreter. All criticism must be provisional.

Although there are uncertainties about tone in various passages of the play, perhaps its greatest glory is the wide range of its literary style in both prose and verse, encompassing the vivid, frequently obscene colloquialisms of the servants in the opening scene and elsewhere, the more elegant witticisms of the young blades, the fantasticalities of Mercutio, the controlled inconsequentialities of the Nurse, the humane sententiousness of the Friar, the dignified passion of the Prince, the lyricism of the lovers and also the increasing intensity of their utterance as tragedy overcomes them. Even as one attempts to characterize the play's stylistic range one is conscious of the inadequacy of the attempt to do so within a brief compass, but it may at least be worth insisting that the play is not simply, as the novelist George Moore described it, 'no more than a love-song in dialogue'.[25] No play that Shakespeare – or anyone else – had written up to this date deploys so wide a range of literary expressiveness, and very few later plays do so, either. And it is partly as a result of this stylistic diversity and richness that the play offers so wide a range of opportunities to actors. Performers of minor roles such as Samson and Gregory, Peter, and even the Apothecary – who speaks only seven lines, though he is also picturesquely described by Romeo in lines that provide a challenge to

[23] Charles Lower, '*Romeo and Juliet*, IV.v: A Stage Direction and Purposeful Comedy', *Shakespeare Studies* 8 (1975), 177–94.

[24] Holding, *Romeo and Juliet*, p. 56. Richard David also praises this device as 'a brilliant solution and one that was genuinely faithful to Shakespeare's intention': Richard David, *Shakespeare in the Theatre* (Cambridge, 1978), p. 113.

[25] *Confessions of a Young Man* (1888); edited by Susan Dick (Montreal and London, 1972), p. 143; Moore was responding to Irving's spectacular production, which made him long for 'a simple stage, a few simple indications, and the simple recitation of that story of the sacrifice of the two white souls for the reconciliation of two great families'.

the make-up department – can create a strong impression within a short space. On the other hand, some of the more important characters may seem, at least on the printed page, to lack individuality – by which I suppose I mean that their speeches seem more important for what is said than for who says them. Obviously this is true of the two speeches given to the anonymous Chorus, in which the authorial voice is most apparent. Johnson regarded the second chorus as pointless: 'The use of this chorus is not easily discovered, it conduces nothing to the progress of the play, but relates what is already known, or what the next scene will show; and relates it without adding the improvement of any moral sentiment',[26] and it has almost always been omitted in performance. The obvious functionality of the speeches of the Prince puts them in a similar category, which no doubt is why some directors have had him speak the opening Chorus while, conversely, Peter Brook gave his closing lines to the actor who had spoken the Chorus (who also played Benvolio). The prince is an authority figure who quells the opening brawl with passionate indignation, exiles Romeo for killing Tybalt, and takes command in the final scene; but we know nothing about him personally except that he is a kinsman of both Mercutio and Paris, and feels some responsibility for their deaths:

> And I, for winking at your discords, too
> Have lost a brace of kinsmen.　　(5.3.293–4)

It is just enough to create a sense of personal involvement, and his response – 'We still have known thee for a holy man' – to the Friar's offer of himself as a sacrifice can be moving, but does not invite detailed characterization. Paris is a relatively undercharacterized role, hard to bring to life, and Benvolio – who is more interesting as satirized by Mercutio (3.1.5–33) than in his own right – vanishes without trace soon afterwards. Tybalt is potentially more interesting – in Bogdanov's production he was having an intralineal affair with Lady Capulet – in spite of Shaw's view that 'Tybalt's is such an

unmercifully bad part that one can hardly demand anything from its representation except that he should brush his hair when he comes to his uncle's ball (a condition which he invariably repudiates) and that he should be so consummate a swordsman as to make it safe for Romeo to fall upon him with absolute abandonment ...'.[27] If these roles constitute challenges to their performers, it is in remaining content with being cast as lay figures: 'don't do something, just stand there'. The composition of the play requires relative colourlessness from some of its constituent parts.

In other roles the challenge lies mainly in suggesting that the lines of the play have not been just learned by the actor, but spring spontaneously from the character he is playing. Friar Laurence has some characteristics in common with the Prince in the relative impersonality of his many sententious, generalizing remarks, but he has a longer role, plays a crucial part in the play's action, and is far more personally involved with a number of the characters. Though the role is not an obvious gift to an actor, it offers opportunities for suggesting a warmly human, compassionate, and even vulnerable man beneath the clerical garb, as Robert Demeger showed in the Bogdanov production when, looking exhausted after his efforts to rouse Romeo out of his almost suicidal depression, he watched Romeo go off and then, sighing with relief, produced a cigarette from beneath his scapular and took a quick drag on it. And in Adrian Noble's 1995 production Julian Glover virtually stole the show as a Friar who kept a chemistry set on a bench in his cell and, as Michael Billington wrote, "work[ed] up Juliet's death potion from old chemistry books to her fascination'.[28]

If the challenge to the actor in the role of the Friar is to seek out a humanizing subtext, with other roles the problem lies rather in discrepan-

---

[26] *Johnson on Shakespeare*, vol. 2, p. 944.
[27] *Shaw on Shakespeare*, p. 171.
[28] *Guardian*, 7 April 1995.

cies of behaviour or of style which the actor may leave unresolved but, at least if he has been trained in the school of Stanislavski, may otherwise seek to reconcile into some semblance of psychological consistency. For much of the action Capulet seems an amiable old buffer genuinely fond of his daughter; when we first see him he expresses the fear that she is too young to be married and declares

> But woo her, gentle Paris, get her heart;
> My will to her consent is but a part,
> And, she agreed, within her scope of choice
> Lies my consent and fair-according voice.
>
> (1.2.14–17)

Yet when it comes to the point he reacts with uncontrolled violence to Juliet's prayers that she be not forced into a marriage which we know would be bigamous, in a display of angry indignation that culminates in threats of physical violence.

> An you be mine, I'll give you to my friend.
> An you be not, hang, beg, starve, die in the
>   streets,
> For, by my soul, I'll ne'er acknowledge thee,
> Nor what is mine shall never do thee good.
>
> (3.5.191–4)

Is Shakespeare simply careless of consistency, providing his actor here with a strong set piece, regardless of what has come before? Or is he expecting his actor to lead up to this passage by making what he can of earlier signs of tetchiness in Capulet, as for instance in his harsh words to Tybalt at the dance (1.5.75–87), or even by suggesting, as Bogdanov did, that Capulet is more concerned that his daughter should advance his family's social status than achieve personal happiness? Perhaps modern audiences are more conscious of inconsistency of characterization than those of Shakespeare's time; although I found Bogdanov's capitalist monster a caricature, I was also disturbed by the absence of transition in the Adrian Noble production.

If Capulet's rage is a concerted set piece such as might form the basis for an impressive bass aria in an opera by Handel or Rossini, Mer-

cutio's Queen Mab speech is a solo set piece that actually forms the basis of a tenor aria in Berlioz's dramatic symphony; in fact his scherzetto is Mercutio's only verbal contribution to the work, and – along with the Friar's impressive concluding exordium – the only part of it to use words at all close to Shakespeare's; Berlioz apparently regarded the speech as so important, or at least so appealing, that he also composed an orchestral scherzo, 'Queen Mab, the spirit of dreams', which opens Part 4. Within the play it complicates the role of Mercutio in a way that may help to account for the fascination that it has held for actors, audiences, and readers. Mercutio's role – like Shylock's, which also encompasses elements so diverse that they have sometimes been held to be incompatible – has been accused of having taken on a life of its own that endangers the dramatic balance; indeed, according to Dryden Shakespeare 'said himself that he was forced to kill him in the third act, to prevent being killed by him'.[29] This is nonsense, I think; Shakespeare developed the role from a hint in his sources as a foil to Romeo and a counterpart to the Nurse, and Mercutio's death is an essential element in the plot. But the Queen Mab speech has been regarded as a charming excrescence, a piece of self-indulgence on Shakespeare's part that is difficult to integrate into both the play and the role – to Granville Barker, 'as much and as little to be dramatically justified as a song in an opera is';[30] and more recently Edward Pearlman has proposed that Shakespeare interpolated the speech after completing his first version of the play, remarking that 'without the Queen Mab speech, Mercutio is consistent and coherent; once the speech is added, his character is incoherent on the page and must be reinvented by the collaboration of performer and audience or by the ingenuity and faith of stage-

[29] John Dryden, 'Of Dramatic Poesy' and other Essays, ed. George Watson, Everyman's Library, 2 vols. (London, 1962), vol. 1, p. 180.
[30] Granville Barker, Prefaces to Shakespeare, p. 7.

literate readers.'[31] It has also, of course, been defended.[32] Richard David wrote that 'its main purpose ... is to create a gossamer sense of uneasy mystery so that Romeo's supernatural forebodings do not fall on altogether unprepared ground'.[33] That may be true in terms of the play but probably would not be of much use to an actor trying to reconcile its fancifulness with Mercutio's mocking obscenity elsewhere. But audiences rarely feel it as a problem – or even actors, because for all the accusations of irrelevance this speech generally survives the blue pencil. Mercutio's wordplay, bawdy as it is, marks him as a clever man, and there is a cerebral quality to Queen Mab that is in line with this. In any case the speech is moving into obscenity in its closing lines, when Mercutio's fancy seems in danger of getting out of hand and Romeo halts him in his tracks as if to save him from his over-heated imaginings, provoking Mercutio to deny their validity:

> I talk of dreams,
> Which are the children of an idle brain,
> Begot of nothing but vain fantasy,
> Which is as thin of substance as the air,
> And more inconstant than the wind ...
>
> (1.4.96–100)

in terms that demonstrate the very 'fantasy' that he is denigrating. The role seems to me to be one of fascinating complexity rather than of irreconcilable discrepancies; but it certainly faces the actor with challenges in the handling of verse. In recent times it has become complicated by psychological interpretations of subtext proposing that the evident homosociality of the young men verges on, or even merges into, homosexuality. In Terry Hands's Swan Theatre production of 1989 the actor conveyed in both gesture and body language an intense but undirected sexuality that motivated the bawdy; a sense of male bonding not quite amounting to direct homosexuality was conveyed in one of the character's bawdiest passages (2.1), full of fantasies about Romeo's sexuality, in which he leapt on Benvolio's back and groped his crotch

as if impelled to mock the absent Romeo by the pressure of repressed impulses within himself. Later he kissed Romeo on the lips, heartily if not lingeringly.

Perhaps the most complete character in the play as written is that of the Nurse, one of Shakespeare's few (if unknowing) gifts to actresses who are no longer able to play young women. The main danger here, in my experience, is sentimentalization. I remember a production at Stratford by John Barton and Karolos Koun in 1965 in which the role was sensitively played by a deeply sympathetic actress, Elizabeth Spriggs, but in which she made what seemed to me to be the mistake of suggesting that the Nurse's attempts to reconcile Juliet to the thought of marrying Paris went against the grain, as if she was doing her duty by the parents while identifying with the desires of the daughter. It was interesting but implausible.

The roles of which I have spoken so far are all ones that can be played by what are known as character actors. Romeo and Juliet themselves come firmly into the category of romantic lead, with all the challenges and problems that the term implies. For one thing, there is the matter of age. Juliet is emphatically and repeatedly stated to be not yet fourteen. This may not have caused difficulties when the role was played by a highly trained boy; now that women have taken over, it is often said that actors with the experience to encompass the technical difficulties of the part will inevitably be too old to look it. But recent directors seem to have more difficulty in casting plausible Romeos than Juliets. His exact age is not given, but too many actors, Ian McKellen among them, in 1976, when he was, I believe, thirty-five, – and, I should say, Kenneth Branagh in the sound

---

[31] E. Pearlman, 'Shakespeare at Work: *Romeo and Juliet*', *English Literary Renaissance*, 24.2 (Spring 1994), pp. 315–42; p. 336.

[32] Pearlman summarizes arguments for the speech's relevance in his footnote 20.

[33] David, *Shakespeare in the Theatre*, p. 115.

recording – try too hard to look and/or sound younger than their years. Henry James wrote that 'it is with Romeo as with Juliet; by the time an actor has acquired the assurance necessary for playing the part, he has lost his youth and his slimness'.[34] Though the role is a passionate one it is not heroic, which may explain why it has appealed to women. By all accounts the most successful Romeo of the nineteenth century was Charlotte Cushman, playing to the Juliet of her sister Susan. Admittedly the text was tailored to emphasize the role. And I think this is a crucial pointer to the principal challenges offered by the title roles. *Romeo and Juliet* does not accord such prominence to its tragic lovers as Shakespeare's other double tragedy, *Antony and Cleopatra* does to its, especially at its end. Even more to the point, Romeo and Juliet are not as vividly characterized as the later pair, or, still more importantly, as other roles in the same play, notably Mercutio and the Nurse. Though I spoke of these characters as foils to the lovers, there are times when the actors playing the lovers may feel that it is they who are acting as foils to the supposedly subsidiary characters: Peter Holding remarks that 'Productions have occasionally been dominated by Mercutio or the Nurse.'[35] This no doubt helps to explain why actors go to some pains to find comic touches in the lovers' verse: in the balcony scene, for instance, Peggy Ashcroft got a laugh on 'I have forgot why I did call thee back,'[36] and in Bogdanov's production there was comedy in the lovers' self-absorption, their wonder at each other – 'She speaks', said Romeo, as if it was a remarkable achievement for Juliet to have acquired the skill at such an early age. This is entirely legitimate, but theatrical changes that have been made at the end of the play, and indeed some critical reactions to it, betray a dissatisfaction with the original script that seems designed to make it conform to expectations that may derive from conceptions

of tragedy other than those that were in Shakespeare's mind as he wrote. Garrick, we have seen, expanded the lovers' death scene; Peter Brook, like most directors, severely shortened the last scene; in some performances he even went so far (like Gounod's librettist) as to omit the reconciliation of the houses.[37]

In part the alterations to the last scene result from practical considerations of staging; it is (as Andrew Gurr notes, pp. 20–5) notoriously difficult to work out exactly how it would have been played in the theatres of Shakespeare's time. Perhaps Shakespeare was not in this play a complete master of practical stagecraft. Perhaps too some of what I have, somewhat neutrally, described as challenges to be faced might more properly be regarded as weaknesses that have to be overcome. I don't want to imply that *Romeo and Juliet* is in every respect a perfect specimen of dramatic craftsmanship. But I find it interesting that many of the criticisms and alterations to which the play has been subjected over the centuries bring it closer in line with expectations of romantic tragedy, perhaps derived in part from Shakespeare's own practice in later plays; they do not face up to the challenge of interpreting the text as written. They suggest, in short, that perhaps the play's greatest challenge is to our notions of genre. The script can be interpreted in all its richness and diversity only if we abandon the idea that because it is called a tragedy it must centre on the fate of individuals, and accept its emphasis on the multifarious society in which these individuals have their being.

---

[34] First published in 'Notes from Paris, 1876', in the *New York Tribune*, 5 February 1876; reprinted in *the Scenic Art*, pp. 51–4; p. 54.
[35] Holding, *Romeo and Juliet*, p. 44.
[36] Levenson, *Romeo and Juliet*, p. 53.
[37] Ibid., p. 67.

THE DATE AND THE EXPECTED VENUE OF *ROMEO AND JULIET*

ANDREW GURR

Titus Andronicus and *Romeo and Juliet* share some staging features that in the original performances laid quite distinct demands on their venues: a large balcony, a trapdoor, separate entry doors, and a sufficiently ample opening for 'discoveries' to admit the use of a curtained bed. The playwright when writing these plays must either have chosen to be exceptionally demanding over what the playing-places he expected to be used for the play could provide, or have been confident that the plays would be performed only at places which had these resources. They are features that so far as we know all of the suburban open-air theatres of the time, even the Swan, could offer without difficulty. *Titus* was performed at the Rose up to 1594, and *Romeo* at the Theatre and from 1597 at the Curtain, so the facilities the plays demand must have been available there. The company or companies that staged these two plays did not, however, have any fixed venue for playing until after the establishment of the two leading companies as a 'duopoly' after May 1594.[1] If either play was written before that development, we ought to wonder why their author should have laid such substantial demands on the then-expected venues.

Titus certainly pre-dates 1594, and very possibly *Romeo* does as well. The demands on the staging of these plays therefore raise the question of what the playing companies would have done with them up to the time when the Theatre and the Rose became the places designated by the Privy Council for the two compa-

nies to use when in London. Up to then, the plays might have been performed at the city's inns, or taken on tour to venues where the staging resources were markedly limited. Equally, it raises the question why such heavy demands should have been written into these plays, and the others like them that were beginning to burgeon on the London stages in the late 1580s,[2] if the predominant expectation was not that their main venue would be the new amphitheatres in London's suburbs. These plays lack the kind of provisionality that Robert Greene signalled some time before his death in 1592 in *Alphonsus of Aragon*, when he gave Venus her final exit either on foot or '*if you can conveniently, let a chaire come downe from the top of the stage, and draw her up.*'[3] Convenience clearly was a limiting factor in the minds of at least some of the early authors.

The use of traps and balconies indoors, whether at guildhalls in the towns that the companies habitually visited on their travels, or at inns either in the towns or the city of

---

[1] See Gurr, 'Three Reluctant Patrons and Early Shakespeare', *Shakespeare Quarterly*, 44 (1993), 159–74, esp. p. 164.

[2] Between the late 1580s and 1594 several plays, including *The Spanish Tragedy, Faustus,* and *The Jew of Malta,* began to lay demands on the players for more complex staging, along with uniquely large casts of actors. See Gurr, 'The Chimera of Amalgamation', *Theatre Research International* 18 (1993), 85–93.

[3] *Alphonsus King of Aragon*, 1599, Malone Society Reprints, 1926, 2109–10.

London, is something we have to accept if we believe the expectation of travelling to be predominant when these plays were composed. It is just possible that the upper chambers of large inns, like the larger guildhalls, might once in a while have been fitted with raised galleries, though none of the surviving ones has any. Neither the guildhall-builders nor the town inn-keepers had any reason to build one in their upper rooms, unless they were specifically designing them for the acting of plays like *Romeo and Juliet* or for the rare travelling company that might carry a consort of musicians along with it. The inns that were converted into indoor playhouses early in James's reign, at Bristol and at York, may have been supplied with such features.[4] But that such venues would also have had trapdoors or other openings, such as those needed for the Senate at the opening of *Titus*, or the Capulet monument, is highly unlikely. The largest and most privileged room in such buildings was always on the upper floor, and the installation of a trapdoor, besides seriously weakening the floor, could only give access to the floor below, not to the fairly shallow space that the Capulet monument requires under the stage.

Robert Tittler's study of the Tudor guildhall[5] identifies two main types of building, varying chiefly in the traditional market function that the ground floor of such structures commonly supplied. With a weighty symbolic role as the focus for the newly acquired local authority of Tudor times, supplanting the pre-Reformation manorial and church authorities, they were built by local craftsmen, on sites restricted in scale and scope because they had to be financed by the municipality and located in the centre of town. They filled many functions besides the most usual one of providing a sheltered marketplace or shops at ground level. They had to include several facilities that were not easy to overlap in one space. Their uses included courtrooms for the assizes and quarter sessions, the town gaol, usually located either in a cellar or an attic, and sometimes lesser courtrooms,

together with storage for official documents, perhaps an office for the clerk and recorder, and above all a main hall for the meetings of the mayor and burgesses. Only this latter might duplicate any of the other functions, perhaps doubling as the courtroom.

Some town halls had an external balcony, to facilitate the overseeing of the market, but none of them had a musician's gallery or internal balcony inside the main meeting hall. Nor was their structure suited to the cutting of trapdoors in the main hall floor. The evidence of the 31 guildhalls surviving from the 202 of the Tudor period and after, and the 27 others illustrated in pictures, makes it clear that none of them could have had a trapdoor in its main flooring, and none show any sign of ever including a balcony or raised gallery in their main hall.[6] There is some evidence that on occasions stages or 'scaffolds' were built specially in the halls for performances by the visiting players, and such constructions might have included some provision for a trapdoor, although the only stage mentioned in any detail, at Norwich, specifies no more than planks laid on barrels for the occasion. Local carpenters made scaffolds for plays in the town hall at different times in towns such as Exeter, Gloucester, Stafford and Shrewsbury.[7] Such specially constructed stages conceivably might have included a trapdoor if the plays that the players were travelling with demanded them. It is always possible that the players supplied their own 'booth' or curtaining

---

[4] See Pilkington, Mark C., 'The Playhouse in Wine Street, Bristol', *TN*, 37 (1983), 14–21, and *Records of Early English Drama: York*, edd. Alexandra F. Johnston and Margaret Rogerson, 2 vols., Toronto, 1979, 1.530–1.

[5] Robert Tittler, *Architecture and Power: The Town Hall and the English Urban Community, c. 1500–1640* (Oxford, 1991).

[6] Tittler, *Architecture and Power*, has a list (pp. 162–8) of the guildhalls, moot halls, and town halls of the period, with notes of those which survive either in some version of their original form or in pictures.

[7] Tittler, *Architecture and Power*, pp. 144–5.

to stand on the temporary stage scaffold so that they could make their entries and exits from a tiring-house. Whether such a booth could have been made to serve the additional function of providing for 'discoveries', as well as the height and strength needed for Juliet's and the Roman Senate's balcony, is a question that depends on how confident, how resourceful and how adaptable we consider the playing companies to have been. There is still a very large discrepancy between what the basic travelling venues seem to have offered and what the playwrights in London, even in the early 1590s, seem to have expected to be available for the staging of the new plays they were writing.

The use of guildhalls for plays was banned in Norwich in 1589, in Great Yarmouth in 1595, Durham in 1608, and Chester in 1614. At Bristol an order of 1585 banning plays from the guildhall was sternly renewed eleven years later, though even then the order was not firmly observed. This tendency to shut the players from the central town venues may have led by the beginning of the 1590s to a growing preference among the professional companies for alternative venues, places with nearly as ample space as the town halls, and with the same advantage of being enclosed spaces which allowed the players to control access for the audiences. These may have been custom-built, or houses especially adapted for players, like the inns that were turned into playhouses at Bristol and York. Both of those venues, however, provided indoor places for playing, not inn-yards, and in consequence are unlikely to have had the balconies that plays such as *Romeo and Juliet* and *Titus Andronicus* require. Raising a stage above the level of the main floor in a hall or upper room would have made it possible to fit in a trapdoor, though the low height of Tudor ceilings must have meant that any players using the trap would have had to squirm on their stomachs to reach it. A stage at a maximum of four feet high seems to have been normal for indoor venues with an all-seated clientele. That is the height of the stage in the Inigo Jones drawings for his putative theatre of 1616.[8]

Such minimal provision for travelling players must have meant that they came to regard the large London amphitheatres as infinitely more ample for performing in as well as in their far more generous audience capacity. Only in such custom-built places was there any guarantee that the resources demanded for the staging of *Romeo* and *Titus* would be on hand. None the less, it is not really likely that *Romeo and Juliet* was composed principally in the expectation that it would be staged only or even chiefly at James Burbage's Theatre. Until 1594 no playing company and no playwright had any reason to expect a play to be staged exclusively at any one playhouse. Companies expected to travel, and even when enjoying an extended stay, as they tried to do in London up to 1594, they usually hoped to play at venues inside the city rather than in the more welcoming suburbs. We know that *Romeo and Juliet* was not performed at the Rose from the time Henslowe's records begin early in 1592, and whereas before 1594 Burbage's Theatre was the chief alternative to the Rose as a custom-built playhouse, it was still only one among several possible places available for playing in London, before the reorganization of May 1594 that confined playing to those two places and stopped playing in the city inns altogether.

The versatility of the professional companies over their playing-places up to 1594 is shown most clearly by the Queen's Men, who in their first ten years used every venue available to them, both inside the city and in the suburbs. The Privy Council's negotiations on their behalf with the Lord Mayor produced an order of November 1583 from the Guildhall granting permission for them to play 'at the Sygnes of the Bull in Busshoppesgatestreete, and the sygne

---

8 See John Orrell, *The Theatres of Inigo Jones and John Webb* (Cambridge, 1985), Chapter 3, especially p. 51. The use of floor joists to support the stage planking would have restricted head-height under the stage still more.

of the Bell in gratiousstreete and nowheare els within this Cyttye'.[9] The Bull in Bishopsgate Street was an inn like the Bel Savage, with a square of galleries open to the sky. The Bell in Gracechurch Street, by contrast, seems to have been an inn with a large upstairs hall available for playing. The Lord Mayor's designation of these two gave the company access to one large open-air and one smaller-capacity roofed venue, both inside the city. Outside in Middlesex they had the Theatre and the Curtain, and they are subsequently reported as using both of them. *Tarlton's Jests* has anecdotes about their clown which tell of him playing at the Bull, the Bel Savage and the Curtain, and Nashe's *Pierce Penilesse* says he played at the Theatre.[10] Henslowe records a group from the Queen's Men playing at the Rose in early 1594. If such versatility over the possible venues was routine for the Queen's Men, not just when travelling the country but also in London, a similar versatility must have been standard for every playing company and all their early playwrights up to May 1594.

One of the more striking features of many of the new plays that started to appear in the late 1580s and the early 1590s was the remarkable size of their demands on staging, and especially for the staging of large spectacles in special features of the stage. The smoking hell's-mouth for *Faustus* and *The Jew of Malta*, along with Barabbas's scaffold that plummets him into his hell's-mouth cauldron and the balcony which Abigail uses for the retrieval of his gold from the new-made convent: such features in the plays laid down ample precedents for the equivalent demands that Shakespeare laid down for the staging of his early plays. Few plays in later years made such demands. *The Jew of Malta* and *Titus Andronicus* are only two of the seven or eight or more ambitiously 'large' plays of the early 1590s that have survived. The implications of this innovation are radical. Large casts and demanding staging were far more suitable for performing in London than for travelling the country. What is odd is that these demanding

plays were composed at a time when it was so much more difficult to stage the plays in the London venues for which they appear to have been written than it became after 1594.

Where does this put *Romeo and Juliet*? It does not demand an exceptionally large cast of players, but it does lay heavy demands on the stage's resources for its finale. Whether we think *Romeo and Juliet* was written before or after 1594, and what we consider the precise nature of its demands on stage resources was, depends in part on what we make of that feature of playwriting in the early 1590s, and whether the reduction in the demands on staging for the plays written by Shakespeare in later years involved a personal or a company shift in policy and expectation. The allocation of the Theatre to Shakespeare's company in May 1594 seems paradoxically to have reduced the demands he made on the company's staging resources. A date for *Romeo and Juliet* pre-1594 would place it with the 'large' plays and their exceptionally demanding staging. A date after 1594 places it amongst the plays that appear to make far more modest demands on staging than it does.

The effect on the two leading companies of being allocated to two of the chief suburban playhouses raises a question that needs answering by close study of the surviving playtexts. That the Privy Council joined forces with the Lord Mayor in banning any more playing in city inns and innyards as part of the establishment of the two duopolizing companies in May of 1594 is nowhere stated explicitly, either in the Council's or in the city's records. But it was certainly a policy that was maintained from then on. It must have been the product of a verbal agreement between the two Councillors who set up their pair of companies as replacements

---

[9] From a licence of the Court of Aldermen, dated 28 November 1583. Printed in *Malone Society Collections*, II.3 (1931), 314.

[10] *Tarlton's Jests*, ed. J. O. Halliwell, London, 1844, pp. 13, 16, 24; Nashe, *Pierce Penilesse*, in *Works*, ed. R. B. McKerrow, 5 vols., London, 1904–10, I.197.

for the Queen's Men, and the Lord Mayor. Its effect was immediate. The two suburban playhouses, the Rose and the Theatre, were protected as the venues for the two companies, a provision which subsequent Privy Council orders acknowledged, and no city inns were approved. What happened subsequently provides an ample demonstration of the effects of this agreement between the two London authorities. The companies' dislike of the ban on access to the city's roofed playing places led first to the Lord Chamberlain having to appeal to the Lord Mayor for his company to have access through the winter of 1594 to the Cross Keys inn, a breach of the agreement apparently not allowed by the city; and secondly it led to James Burbage's plan in 1596 to build a new roofed playhouse in the Blackfriars precinct as a replacement for his Theatre. Francis Langley, a sharp speculator, most likely built his Swan in 1595, upriver of the Rose and the Bear Garden, in order to cash in on the new restriction on the places for playing in London and the opportunity that it seemed to offer for new venues in the suburbs.

The only version of *Romeo and Juliet* that we have, whether in the 1597 or the 1599 Quarto, must date from after 1594, since it specifies a part for the clown Will Kemp, who did not join the company that Shakespeare was writing for until the Chamberlain's Men were set up in May of that year. It would be easy to assume that the highly specific demands it lays on its stage, for a balcony, a trap and an opening for the Capulets' monument, meant that its author knew the company now had a specific playhouse to use, and chose to exploit its main fixtures. None of the later plays makes so much explicit use of all these stage features. That makes it tempting to fix the date of the play to some time after May 1594. But the extremely close match of its staging demands to those of *Titus Andronicus*, and the generally less demanding nature of the plays such as *Richard II* written after 1594, makes that a fragile case indeed.

Internal evidence from *Romeo and Juliet* has

been used to fix its composition to anywhere between 1592 and 1596.[11] It is quite possible that Shakespeare was working at the Theatre more or less throughout those years. He was certainly working for the company that used the Theatre between June 1594 and April 1597, when the lease expired and it was closed. He may have been working there previously, between 1592 and 1593, as a member of the breakaway group that parted company with Strange's in 1591 when it went with Alleyn, leaving the Theatre for the Rose, and instead formed the new Pembroke's company to take its place at the Theatre. The ascription of the later *Henry VI* plays and *The Taming of the Shrew* to Pembroke's does strongly suggest that their author was working for Pembroke's up to its collapse in the autumn of 1593, and the Theatre was at that time the most profitable London alternative to the Rose,[12] quite apart from the likelihood that the Theatre's owner had a son playing in Pembroke's. So, against all the evidence for the versatility of the companies over their likely venues up to 1594, it does seem most likely that if Shakespeare did have any specific playhouse in mind when he wrote *Romeo and Juliet*, at pretty well any point between 1592 and 1596, it would have been Burbage's Theatre, which was to provide the Globe's skeleton for the performances of the play through its subsequent years with the King's Men.

The transition in company thinking from

---

[11] G. Blakemore Evans, in the New Cambridge *Romeo and Juliet* (Cambridge, 1984), says that while a date later than May 1596 is attractive and 1594–6 is likely, the evidence both internal and external is inconclusive, and any date between 1592 and 1596 is possible. The editors of the Oxford *Textual Companion* (Oxford, 1987), p. 106, incline towards 1595 or just after.

[12] At 3,000 or so, the Theatre had the largest capacity of any of the London venues, with the possible exception of the Bel Savage, until the Swan was built in 1595. Its near neighbour the Curtain is the only other venue that might have matched its capacity. The smaller Rose's capacity from 1592 was roughly 2,400.

habitual travelling to habitual residence in London was a slow process. Travelling must have been pervasive up to 1594, and it persisted with the greatest companies in the Stuart years. There are records of the companies travelling through every year, including all the long periods after 1603 when there were no closures for plague. All three of the leading companies selected by King James for his family's patronage continued to travel every year. None the less, the first period when the Admiral's and the Chamberlain's had designated places to play in London's suburbs proved to be a unique period in their history. It was the time when they clung most consistently to London, and travelled least. Between the end of the Privy Council's ban in October 1597 and late 1602 or 1603, for all its troubles with the loss of the Theatre and the related loss of its intended replacement the Blackfriars, the Chamberlain's company appears to have worked exclusively in London.[13] From early 1596 until March 1603 there were no closures for plague, and the company was evidently happy to exploit its new and quasi-unique right to perform in London's suburbs to the full. This, in fact, is the longest period without any travelling to be found in the records for any of the major London companies. The Admiral's company is also totally absent from the provincial records from August 1597 until late 1599.[14] Neither of the duopoly companies travelled nearly as much between 1594 and 1603 as they did both before and after. The principal reason was obviously the Privy Council's innovation of granting exclusive rights for the use of the two authorized London playing-places to this pair of companies, and in the case of the Chamberlain's from early 1597 the pressing need to maximize its income in order to help it secure a new London playhouse.

So the likelihood that the Theatre was in Shakespeare's mind as the main if not the only venue for *Romeo and Juliet* does have some force, a little for the years up to May 1594 and a lot thereafter. Conceivably the analogous requirements for staging *Titus* before 1594 might incline the evidence to the earlier period. But there is nothing conclusive in any of the evidence, and even the apparent specificity of the staging requirements is not so clear as we might like it to be. Whether the last scene was conducted around a trapdoor as the Capulet 'grave' or in front of an opening in the *frons scenae* as a 'monument', both of which are named in the dialogue, indicates one possible economy that might have been exercised in the staging, if the *frons* could be made to provide both a balcony and a space behind the hangings for a monument. Careful and sceptical analysis of this and the other evidence, for all the attention they have been given in the past, may still throw a little more light on the issue.

It is in no way a simple question, of course. The emphasis given to staging features in the dialogue must always be suspect, since a verbal reference to any demanding element on stage, whether a window or a tomb, might equally signify that it needed attention calling to it because the author wanted it noted, or that he expected that some of the spectators might not be able to see it properly, or because it was a fiction which needed emphasis precisely because it was not actually visible or available on stage. Stage directions are more reliable than

---

[13] The provincial records show them at Cambridge in 1594–5, Ipwich in 1595, Faversham in Kent at 'about Lamas' (1 August) 1596, and Dover at a similar time, in Marlborough, Faversham, and Bath through 1596–7, at Rye in Sussex in August 1597 and Bristol in September 1597, while the London theatres were closed by Privy Council order. There are then no records of any travels until 1602–3, when they went to Shrewsbury and Ipswich.

[14] They were recorded at Oxford, Faversham, Maidstone and Bath in 1594–5, at Gloucester, Bath, Oxford and Ipswich in 1595–6, at Faversham on 21 February 1596, at Dunwich in Suffolk in August 1596, at Coventry some time in the same years, and at Ipswich on 27 August 1597, during the London closure prompted by the *Isle of Dogs* prohibition. They were then in London until they appeared at Bristol, Coventry and Leicester in the autumn of 1599. In 1599–1600 they appeared at Canterbury and Bath, and in November 1600 they were received by the Cavendishes at Hardwick in Derbyshire.

dialogue as indicators of the planned staging.[15] In fact *Romeo and Juliet*, like *Titus*, supplies ample evidence that some distinctive features were needed on the stage.

The two quartos of *Romeo and Juliet* are distinct in more than the quality of the verse they transmit. It is usually agreed that Q2 was printed from a set of author's papers, since it includes sections which seem to be rough drafting, with false starts such as 5.3.102–3: 'Why art thou yet so fair? I will beleeue, / Shall I beleeue that vnsubstantiall death is amorous ...',[16] where editors follow the ten-syllable principle, cancelling the last three words of the first line and using the first three words of the second line to fill their place. Its stage directions, as in other pre-theatre manuscripts or texts printed from 'foul papers', are minimal and some way from complete. The stage directions in Q1, on the other hand, are elaborate to the point of being descriptive. At 2.5.15, the bald Q2 direction '*Enter* Juliet' becomes '*Enter Juliet somewhat fast, and embraceth Romeo*' in Q1. This is fictional rather than theatrical to use Richard Hosley's distinction between directions intended for practical use in the theatre and those designed to catch the reader's imagination.[17] It may of course reflect what the transcriber of the manuscript used for Q1 remembered seeing in the theatre at some point of the early staging up to 1597. If so, it has considerable value as evidence of the early staging. Editors have never hesitated to make use of the Q1 stage directions to augment Q2's. We could do with more of the descriptive stage directions, if we could be sure of distinguishing the evocative fictional from the routine theatrical.

There has been some debate about the different character of the two texts, and what might have helped to generate them before they entered the printing house. I can find little indication that the staging of the play was expected to be in any way significantly different in either text. Q1's descriptive stage directions show signs that the play was known from

performance, which is much less evident in Q2. But the properties and the main features of the stage indicated either in the stage directions or in the dialogue are substantially the same in both quartos.

The original staging of *Romeo and Juliet* was quite demanding of properties and attendants. It required musicians for the dancing at 1.5 and 4.4, and a fairly large number of portable properties: swords and bucklers, clubs and partisans in 1.1, masks and torches in 1.4, napkins and food-serving gear in 1.5, a fan for the Nurse in 2.3, the rope climbing-ladder ordered in 2.3 for 3.2, rapiers for 3.1, spits, logs and a basket for 4.4, a bunch of herbs including rosemary for 4.4 (specified in Q1), Balthazar's travelling boots (Q1) and the poison for 5.1, and for the finale two more torches, flowers, a mattock, a spade, and a crowbar. The more substantial features needed as part of the stage design and furniture are the balcony or 'window' in 2.1 and 3.5, Q1's

---

[15] The choice between realistic or symbolic staging is invoked all too often when a reference in the text specifies something on stage. Does, for instance, the pair of references to the greenness of the ground in *The Tempest*'s masque (*TLN*, 1741, 1795: Ceres: 'this short gras'd Greene'; Iris: 'this green-Land') really mean that the stage was visibly strewn with green rushes, or that it was not, and hence the words were needed to invoke the imaginary existence of a greensward? It is certainly possible to be too literal-minded. The Drawer's reference to Ancient Pistol being 'below' in the Eastcheap tavern scene of *2 Henry IV* (2.4.76) has been used to argue that the whole scene must have been played on the stage balcony. This ignores the fact that the best drinking rooms in any tavern, like the main living rooms of any house up to the nineteenth century, were always upstairs, so the Drawer was merely announcing a new arrival, not his physical position in relation to the on-stage characters.

[16] The texts quoted are from quarto facsimiles, Q1: *Shakespeare's Plays in Quarto*, edd. Michael J. B. Allen and Kenneth Muir, Berkeley, 1981; Q2: the Shakespeare Association Facsimiles, 1949. The line numbering used here is from the Oxford *Complete Works*, edd. Stanley Wells, Gary Taylor et al.

[17] See 'The Gallery over the Stage in the Public Playhouse of Shakespeare's Time', *Shakespeare Quarterly*, 8 (1957), 16–17.

'*bed within the Curtaines*' for 4.3 and 4.4, and the monument for 5.3. In addition, Paris's sending his page off to put his ear to the ground 'under yond trees', which later become 'this yew tree here', might call either for a stage post, or more simply for a removed place and a limited supply of audience imagination.

These specifications, besides indicating rather firmly that the author expected a London base with more ample resources than were usual on a company's travels, raise considerable questions of interpretation. Were the '*curtaines*' the same as the stage 'hangings', or were they specific curtains around a canopied stage bed that was 'put out' especially for the apparent death of Juliet? The entry of Desdemona '*in her bed*' at the beginning of 5.2 in the Folio *Othello* evidently left her fully visible, because Othello is given no words to make him pull back any curtains before he addresses her. Still, it was a curtained or canopied bed, because after he has killed her he says he must draw the 'curtaines' to conceal the body from Emilia. Such a bed could well have done a similar service for Juliet.[18]

Whether the bed itself was behind the stage hangings, which were sometimes called a 'curtain', is the chief uncertainty here. It has been considered an attractive idea provided that the same central opening would later become the Capulet monument, on the grounds that the marriage bed aptly becomes the funeral bed.[19] Symbolic symmetry, entailing the use of the central opening for major events such as royal entries and funeral exits, including perhaps the final exit hand in hand of the Capulets with old Montague, has considerable appeal, but there is all too little explicit external evidence to support it. The best evidence is a material point, that each of the flanking entry doors was usually named as a single '*dore*', which does not indicate great width, while the central opening must have been wide enough to admit the largest of the standard properties, the dais holding the royal or judicial throne, often a pair of thrones, as well as the bed which was '*put out*'. How far

Juliet's bed was put out, and whether its curtains or the stage hangings were what she fell through, is not an easy point to decide. My preference would be, on the grounds of the plural use, and with *Othello*'s support, for the bed to have its own curtains which were distinct from the stage hangings.

What was needed for the Capulet monument has been debated at length, and the conclusions have varied according to what features it was thought the Elizabethan theatre ought to have had. Malone thought it most likely that the trap would have been employed.

Though undoubtedly Shakespeare's company were furnished with some wooden fabrick sufficiently resembling a tomb, for which they must have had occasion in several plays, yet some doubt may be entertained whether any exhibition of Juliet's monument was given on the stage. Romeo, perhaps, only opened with his mattock one of the stage trapdoors (which might have represented a tombstone), by which he descended to a vault beneath the stage, where Juliet was deposited. Juliet, however, after her recovery, speaks and dies on the stage. If, therefore, the exhibition was such as I have supposed, Romeo must have brought her up in his arms from the vault beneath the stage, after he had killed Paris.[20]

There have been many readings of the evidence since then. One of the best of the modern scholars, Richard Hosley, whose study of the evidence from stage directions and from playhouse design is rigorous and thorough,[21] has been broadly supported in his conclusion that three main areas were required. In addition to

---

18 Leslie Thomson makes some useful comments on these questions. See Thomson, ' "With patient ears attend": *Romeo and Juliet* on the Elizabethan Stage', *Studies in Philology*, 92 (1995), 230–47.
19 Leslie Thomson, ' "With patient ears attend" ', lays stress on this as a feature of the play's language which dictates the form of the staging. She sees the oxymoronic equation of bed and bier as demanding (p. 241) that the 'discovery space' was the location for both Juliet's curtained bed and the Capulet tomb.
20 Edmond Malone, *A History of the English Stage*, p. 90.
21 'The Use of the Upper Stage in *Romeo and Juliet*', *SQ* 5 (1954), 371–9.

the main stage, there was for most plays an upper stage in the form of a 'tarras' or balcony, and below that a 'discovery space'. This term, invoked by Hosley as a replacement for the older 'inner stage', is also known, in respect for the hangings that covered it, as an 'alcove'. My own more neutral term would be 'central opening', since it begs fewer questions. The question of the balcony or space signalled in many plays as 'above' is important both for Juliet's balcony, and for Q1's '*window*'. Whether the Theatre or any other playhouse of the time had any sort of supplement to the upper space used by such figures as King Richard at Flint Castle before he descended to the 'base court', or the Governor of Harfleur standing on Harfleur's walls over the town gates in *Henry V*, that might have been identifiable as a window rather than a balcony, is another of those chimeras generated by the use of terms in the dialogue which are specific precisely because the objects referred to are not visible on the stage. The argument is nicely balanced: it could equally well be argued that an object was specified because it was there and because it was not.

Walter Hodges, in his drawings for the New Cambridge edition,[22] provides what appear to be the two main alternatives in modern thinking about the staging of the play's most demanding scene, the finale. One uses the trapdoor, while the other two of the three pictures, showing the positions rather later in the sequence of events, show the use of a 'discovery space'. Captioned in the plural as 'Possible ways to stage the churchyard sequence', in the first, Romeo is levering up the stage trapdoor, which is located in front of the curtained central opening or 'discovery space'. The middle picture shows Romeo pulling back the curtain to 'discover' a tomb with two tiers of bodies above stage level, one Juliet's, in her normal clothes, and one Tybalt's, in a shroud (a difference specified by the Friar at 4.1.110, and by Juliet at 4.3.42). Paris's body is left lying on the ground beside the trapdoor, near the central

opening. The third picture shows a similar scene, with the bodies of Romeo and Juliet adjacent, Juliet still on her raised level and Romeo on the ground beneath her. The editor, G. Blakemore Evans, ignores the alternative of the trapdoor and states only that 'the simplest and most probable solution, as in 4.3–5, is to postulate the use of the discovery space, centre rear, below the upper stage' (p. 33). He accounts for Romeo levering open a pair of curtains by adding 'Whether something more realistic than the usual traverse curtain (used, we have argued, in 4.3–5) was employed for the doors of the monument which Romeo breaks open with his mattock and wrenching iron after line 48 (*Romeo opens the tomb*, Q1) must remain conjectural, but the introduction of framed wooden doors, slipped across the discovery space during 5.2 (on the main front stage) would not present any special difficulty.'[23]

Alan C. Dessen in chapter 9 of *Recovering Shakespeare's Theatrical Vocabulary*, entitled '*Romeo opens the tomb*', identifies the choice as between Hosley's 'theatrical' or 'fictional' readings, and invokes the evidence of word-usage in other stage directions to establish as much as can be identified with confidence about what the author expected the players to use the stage's features for in the final scene. He notes Q1's use of 'Tomb', and such features of other plays as the stage direction in *James IV*, which prescribes '*a Tomb, placed conveniently on the Stage*', and the notes of three tombs amongst Henslowe's properties, and that thirty plays have references to tombs, a few of which relate them to the trapdoor. He notes the potential incongruity of 'real' tools like crowbars and mattocks being used on a 'fictional' tomb. He is inclined to conclude (pp. 190–5) that whether positioned in the central opening or in the stage floor the tomb was most likely not 'verisimilar' but

---

[22] *Romeo and Juliet*, ed. G. Blakemore Evans (Cambridge, 1984), p. 32.

[23] Ibid., p. 33.

fictional, with a minimal number of real features other than the tools used to open it.

Fictional or 'real', for all the symbolic attractiveness of making the marriage bed into the funeral bier, my own inclination is towards the trapdoor. Given Romeo's mattock, an instrument for digging in the ground, and the crowbar or 'wrenching Iron' (5.3.22), which are matched by the Friar's tools for the same purpose, described in the Q2 stage direction as '*Lanthorne, Crowe, and Spade*' (120), provided in response to his demand for an 'Iron Crow' at 5.2.21, the marble which is said to be so blood-stained (another fictional rather than literal direction?) was most likely the stage floor, and it was there that Romeo used the crowbar to lever up the trapdoor. A tomb in the lowest position on the stage floor would give the best final representation of the play's emphasis on the vertical, noted by David Bevington and Leslie Thomson.[24] If so, the bodies of Tybalt and Juliet which Romeo uncovers (Q1: '*Romeo opens the tomb.*') were under the trapdoor. The 'vault' which Malone conceives need not have had any depth. When the watch enters at line 170, their leader's words indicate a search of the stage, not of the tiring-house opening:

> The ground is bloudie, search about the
>   Churchyard.
> Go some of you, who ere you find attach.
> Pittifull sight, heere lies the Countie slaine,
> And *Juliet* bleeding, warme, and newlie dead:
> Who heere hath laine this two daies buried.

The officer of the watch orders his men to scatter, presumably standing where the page had set him while they do so. The boy takes him to the place 'there where the torch doth burne', and which the officer says is bloody. He, placed at the centre of the action, is the one to find the bodies. That it is a 'sight', and that Juliet has been buried 'heere', by where Paris is lying, argues for a real presence, most likely in centre-stage, that needs some garnishing with verbal description.

Romeo's own explanation makes him say

'Why I descend into this bed of death' (28). He also calls it a 'detestable mawe' with rotten jaws that he prises open with his crowbar. It is a 'wombe of death' (45), an oxymoron that more readily fits a flat opening in the floor than a hole in the stage wall. The descriptive language used fits a horizontal structure more easily than a wall. Spades and mattocks are tools 'fit to open / These dead mens Tombes' (199–200). Monuments did not have to be tall structures to be set in churchyards. Paris at first calls the tomb 'thy grave' (5.3.17), saying 'thy Canapie is dust and stones' (13). Romeo echoes him at 83–4, following it with 'this Vault' (86). When he is dying and asks to be laid alongside Juliet Paris calls it 'the Tombe' (73). Friar Lawrence is the first to call it a monument. He sees Romeo's torch, and exclaims 'It burneth in the *Capels* monument' (127). He also calls it 'the Vault' twice, and 'this Sepulchre', with its 'stony entrance' (131, 253, 141), and 'the Tombe' (261). Lady Capulet calls it 'our Monument' (192), and Balthazar in his report starts with 'this same monument' (273), adding that he saw Romeo 'going in the Vault' (275). In all, through the finale it is called a 'Vault' or a 'grave' seventeen times, against six when it is called a 'monument' or 'Sepulchre', and six when it is the more neutral 'tomb'.

The choice whether a stage direction is fictional or theatrical becomes more difficult to establish when a reference is in the text itself. It might be possible, for instance, to take the metaphorical literally, and conclude that when the Duke says 'Seale up the mouth of outrage for a while' (215) we should think that to be the moment when the trap is shut and the bodies concealed. He speaks to quieten old Montague, who is protesting that his son has gone to his grave before himself, and in full knowledge of the lengthy choruses of outrage voiced by the Capulets and Montagues. Such a literal

---

24 David Bevington, *Action is Eloquence* (Cambridge, MA, 1984), p. 111; Leslie Thomson, '"With patient ears attend"', pp. 235–6, 237.

reference to closing the trap on the bodies might well prove bathetic. On the other hand, with the living and the dead already assembled in the churchyard, there can be no funeral procession to carry the bodies off at the end of this tragedy. The general rule, firmly identified by Michael Neill,[25] that tragedies commonly closed with a funeral procession that took the corpses offstage, cannot be applied in this play. Such an ending would not serve the closure of *Romeo and Juliet*. You do not take corpses away when the scene is already set in a graveyard. Interring them afresh in the existing graves, whether to be covered by the trapdoor or closed off by a curtain, was a simple solution to tragedy's chronic problem of removing the bodies. If all the bodies were expected to be lying inside the trap already, clearing the stage would have been exceptionally easy.

To take this just a little further, the central position of both trap and 'discovery space' or opening on the stage raises a further implication for 'symbolic' staging. Most entrances and exits in the course of the play would normally have been made through a flanking door, assuming that the Theatre was designed with three openings in the *frons*, and not the Swan's two. In the usual symbolic patterning of entrances and exits, it would be normal to expect the Capulets and old Montague to have entered for the finale by different flanking doors. Then, if the central opening were free, the neatest and clearest mark of the reconciliation between the two families would be if they were to depart together, escorted by the Duke, through the central

opening. But if it was used for that symbolic purpose it could not have been encumbered with the corpses that would have filled it if it served as the Capulet tomb.

Romeo and Juliet is an extreme case of the play which seems to have made demands for its staging which the conditions of the time made it difficult to meet. The centuries of disputes over the staging of Juliet's balcony, bed and tomb may signal something that was in the minds of the playwrights and that our own scrupulousness over the terminology of writing and especially of stage directions has obscured. Alan Dessen's attempts to identify a standardized theatrical language used in stage directions and (for the familiar) in some dialogue may end in finding only an overlay on top of a morass of deliberately vague language, where terms like 'tomb', 'grave' and 'monument' were intentionally non-specific, explicitly fictional configurations designed to allow the players to use whatever resources that day's venue could afford. If such a loosely metaphorical allusiveness was a feature of the specifications laid down in the texts for the staging of *Titus* and *Romeo*, then Greene's '*if you can conveniently*' is the kind of let-out that must have accompanied every playbook the players ever bought at this time from their authors.

---

[25] Michael Neill, ' "Exeunt with a Dead March": Funeral Pageantry on the Shakespearean Stage', in *Pageantry in the Shakespearean Theater*, ed. David Bergeron (Athens, GA, 1984), pp. 153–93.

THE 'BAD' QUARTO OF *ROMEO AND JULIET*

DAVID FARLEY-HILLS

The view that the first quarto of *Romeo and Juliet* (1597) is a memorial reconstruction of Shakespeare's play, published by the printer, John Danter, without the authority of its owners, is still the current orthodoxy. It has had the sanction (*mutatis mutandis*) of such distinguished scholars as E. K. Chambers and W. W. Greg and it is endorsed widely in modern scholarship, by Brian Gibbons, for instance, in the Arden edition (1980), and in the Oxford *Complete Works* edited by Stanley Wells and Gary Taylor (1986). One of the most recent endorsements comes in a detailed study, supported by computer analysis, of the so-called 'bad' quartos by Kathleen Irace.[1] The most detailed account of how such a text might have come into being is to be found in H. R. Hoppe's *The Bad Quarto of Romeo and Juliet, A Bibliographical and Textual Study*, and this account is the foundation on which modern orthodoxy is largely based. Similar assumptions about other so-called 'bad' quartos have recently come under scrutiny, notably the recent stylometric study by Thomas Merriam and Robert Matthews of the 'bad' quartos of *2* and *3 Henry VI*[2] and the doubts expressed about the origins of the first quarto of *Hamlet* by some of the contributors to the collection of essays, *The Hamlet First Published*.[3] It seems worthwhile, therefore, to re-examine the *Romeo and Juliet* first quarto to see how secure the foundations of the orthodox view are. Alternative explanations of the state of these Q1 texts have been mooted in the past. In the nineteenth century a promi-

nent view was that they originated from earlier sketches by Shakespeare himself of plays he went on to revise. More recently it has been argued that these plays are simply shortened versions of Shakespeare's originals prepared by a redactor for provincial performance. This is the position taken on the six 'bad' quartos by Robert Burkhart in his short book *Shakespeare's Bad Quartos*,[4] which my own argument will tend to support insofar as it affects *Romeo and Juliet*, though I think it unlikely that all six 'bad' quartos have similar origins.

Burkhart is principally concerned with the provincial staging of Q1 and in particular the way the casting list is reduced by eliminating dispensable walk-on parts. My own argument is primarily concerned with the relation of Q1 to Q2 and what it tells us of the genesis of Q1. The most notable feature of the 'bad' quarto is how

---

1. Kathleen O. Irace, *Reforming the 'Bad' Quartos, Performance and Provenance of Six Shakespearean First Editions* (London and Toronto, 1994), pp. 120, 126–31, 141.

2. Thomas Merriam and Robert Matthews, 'Neural Computation in Stylometry II: An Application to the Works of Shakespeare and Marlowe', *Literary and Linguistic Computing*, 9, 1, 1994, pp. 1–6.

3. *The Hamlet First Published (Q1, 1603) Origins, Form, Intertextualities*, edited by Thomas Clayton (University of Delaware, London and Toronto, 1992). See, for instance, A. C. Dessen, 'Weighing the Options in *Hamlet* Q1' and Steven Urkowitz, 'Back to Basics, Thinking about the *Hamlet* First Quarto'.

4. Robert E. Burkhart, *Shakespeare's Bad Quartos, Deliberate Abridgements Designed for Performance by a Reduced Cast* (Mouton, The Hague, Paris, 1975).

good it is as an acting text, and how close are the 2215 (or so) lines of Q1 to the equivalent lines in Q2 (of around 2986 lines overall). I shall base my argument principally on Alfred Hart's analysis of the play in his book *Stolne and Surreptitious Copies*,[5] which argues that some 2058 lines of Q1 can be regarded as close to their equivalent in Q2 (i.e. some 92 per cent of Q1's lines). This is a very high figure, made even more remarkable if we suppose (as most textual critics do) that Q1 represents an original that has been reduced by about 26 per cent overall by a redactor, for any redaction would probably involve the writing of some bridging passages. Although Hart supports the memorial reconstruction theory, the implication must be that the text of Q1 is closer to the text we now have as Q2 than can easily be explained by such an hypothesis. Whether the redaction took place after the putative memorial reconstruction or before, we should have to assume the reconstruction of the original was at least 92 per cent accurate in Hart's terms, a figure so high, in either case, that memorial reconstruction would seem on the face of it highly unlikely, for the feat of memory involved, unless virtually the whole cast got together for the piracy, would be phenomenal. In other words, unless there are very compelling reasons for assuming a memorial reconstruction took place (which there are not) such an hypothesis looks scarcely credible.

Hoppe's case for regarding *Romeo and Juliet* Q1 as a reported text rests on a number of related hypotheses

(i) That Q1 derives indirectly from a shortened version of Shakespeare's original text, a fuller and more correct version of which was published in the second quarto of 1599.

(ii) That the copy for Q1 was reconstructed from memory by two actors who had played in a performance (or performances) of the original text as prepared for the stage. (Hoppe suggests these actors played the parts of Romeo and Paris.)

(iii) That this memorial reconstruction was itself either devised from an adaptation or was itself adapted for stage performance.

(iv) That the copy for Q1 was 'stolne and surreptitious', that is, that the publication was unauthorized by the rightful owners of the authentic text and that Danter, the printer, issued a pirated edition of the play.[6]

There is general agreement that the version of *Romeo and Juliet* represented by Q1 is a version intended for the stage. As a shorter version of the text it was presumably intended for performance by a touring troupe in the provinces. It shares the major characters of Shakespeare's play as represented in Q2, and the action and plotting are generally similar, but, as it is Burkhart's main purpose to show, there is a marked reduction in the number of walk-on parts.[7] The main difference, however, is in the language, which, compared to Q2, is considerably less poetic; it relies for effect more on the speed of the action.

A clear indication of Q1's status as an acting text is in the stage directions, which are generally more elaborate than in Q2 and, as Hoppe points out, often require action to substitute for lines that in Q2 explain the action. Many of

5   Alfred Hart, *Stolne and Surreptitious Copies, a Comparative Study of Shakespeare's Bad Quartos* (Melbourne University Press, 1942, reprinted 1970), p. 72, Table xii, c.

6   John Jowett, *William Shakespeare, A Textual Companion*, by Stanley Wells, Gary Taylor, with John Jowett and William Montgomery (Oxford, 1987), p. 288, interprets Hoppe as showing 'that it [Q1] was not published surreptitiously'. That is not my reading of Hoppe. See *The Bad Quarto of Romeo and Juliet*, Ithaca, N.Y.: Cornell University Press (1948), pp. 16–17: 'Danter has often been singled out as a particularly notorious printer of surreptitious play-texts; ... his record is not so scandalous as Burby's ... There remains only *Romeo and Juliet*, the most notable and notorious of Danter's productions. This is certainly a bad Quarto; it is, moreover, the only one about which we can say that on the available evidence the burden of guilt rests on Danter for bringing it before the public'.

7   *Shakespeare's Bad Quartos*, pp. 19, 56–65.

these stage directions add considerably to the information of the staging given in Q2. Hoppe argues that in many instances they derive from Shakespeare's original dialogue, which presupposes either that the redactor was using a fairly accurate memorial reconstruction or, as Hoppe argues, that the memorizers could remember the action better than the words that explained it. One could equally conclude, however, that the stage directions of Q1 are authorial in the sense that they instruct the players how the action is to be presented. Whoever wrote them had a good practical knowledge of the stage and Hart's comment seems justified: 'they are written with more intelligence and in better style than those in the other bad quartos'.[8] The use of stage directions in place of dialogue might well be explained as a convenient way of reducing the play's length.

Take, for instance, the stage direction in scene 12 (3.2)[9] 'Enter Nurse wringing her hands, with the ladder of cordes in her lap', which Hart calls 'ridiculous'[10] and Hoppe derides as requiring the actor to be 'something of a prestidigitator'.[11] Q2 has at the same point *'Enter Nurse with cords'*. The stage direction of Q1 either anticipates or reflects the line of Juliet's speech in Q2 where she asks the Nurse: 'why dost thou wring thy hands?' Q1 thus presents in action what Q2 presents in both the action and the dialogue. There is nothing ridiculous about combining this instruction with the reminder that the Nurse must bring 'the ladder of cordes in her lap' when we consider that the 'lap' here refers to 'the skirt or apron pocket', as it frequently does in Elizabethan English (see *OED*, lap, sb.4). This almost certainly reflects the intention of Q2 as well, for there would not be much point in Juliet asking 'what hast thou there?', if the Nurse was holding the cords for all to see. Both texts are probably indicating the action that actually took place on stage. It is worth noting that the Arden editor amends the Q2/F stage direction at this point to 'enter Nurse with cords, wringing her hands' (though this *does* give the unfortunate

impression that the Nurse has to achieve a feat of prestidigitation).

Q1 can on occasions give the sharper and more satisfactory stage action. At 3.1.77 (scene 11), for instance, the scene in which Mercutio is fatally wounded, Q1 gives a detailed stage direction describing what happens, 'Tybalt under Romeos arme thrusts Mercutio, in and flyes', where Q2 simply has 'Away Tybalt' followed by a rather fuller dialogue. Both versions include Mercutio's comment 'I was hurt under your arme', but the Q2 dialogue is rather clumsy, with Mercutio crying 'I am hurt' and then Benvolio repeating lamely, 'What, art thou hurt?' where Q1 has curt and effective dialogue:

MERCUTIO Is he gone, hath hee nothing? A poxe on your houses.
ROMEO What art thou hurt man, the wound is not deepe.
MERCUTIO Noe not so deepe as a Well ...
(Q1 scene 11, lines 5–8)

'A poxe on your houses' is perhaps not as good as Q2's 'A plague a both houses', and certainly not as good as Dyce's emendation (now widely accepted) 'A plague o'both your houses'. The Arden editor remarks that the copy for Q2 was probably difficult to read at this point (note to 3.1.90) and one possible explanation of the difference between the two texts here is that both are derived directly from a messy holograph (but more of that later).

Hoppe argues, I think rightly, that Q1 represents an abridgement of Shakespeare's original and not a first draft by Shakespeare or some other playwright (as *3 Henry VI* would seem to be a revision of a play by Marlowe if Merriam

---

8   Hart, *Stolne and Surreptitious Copies*, p. 421.
9   References to the Quartos are to the facsimile edition prepared by Michael Allen and Kenneth Muir, *Shakespeare's Plays in Quarto* (Berkeley, Calif., 1981). I have followed Alfred Hart's division of scenes in Q1, as presented in table xii,c of *Stolne and Surreptitious Copies*.
10   Hart, *Stolne*, p. 423.
11   Hoppe, *The Bad Quarto*, p. 88.

and Matthews prove to be correct in their analysis).[12] We can conclude this from a closer look at the differences between the two versions of *Romeo and Juliet*. For instance at 3.2.89–108 (scene 12) Q2 has Juliet in confusion on hearing the news of Tybalt's murder:

NURSE Shame come to *Romeo*.
JULIET Blistered be thy tongue
  For such a wish, he was not borne to shame:
  Vpon his brow shame is asham'd to sit:
  For tis a throane where honour may be crownd
  Sole Monarch of the vniuersal earth.
  O what a beast was I to chide at him:
NURSE Wil you speak wel of him that kild your
  cozin;
JULIET Shall I speak ill of him that is my husband?
  Ah poor my lord, what tongue shal smooth thy
    name,
  When I thy three houres wife haue mangled it?
  But wherefore villaine didst thou kill my Cozin?
  That villaine Cozin would haue kild my husband:
  Backe foolish teares, backe to your natiue spring,
  Your tributarie drops belong to woe,
  Which you mistaking offer vp to ioy,
  My husband liues that *Tybalt* would haue slaine,
  And *Tybalts* dead that would haue slain my
    husband:
  All this is comfort, wherefore weepe I then?
  Some word there was, worser then *Tybalts*
    death. . .

Q1's version is as follows:

NURSE Shame come to *Romeo*.
JULIET A blister on that tung, he was not borne to
    shame:
  Vpon his face Shame is ashamde to sit.
  But wherefore villaine didst thou kill my Cousen?
  That villaine Cousen would haue kild my
    husband.
  All this is comfort. But there yet remaines
  Worse than his death, which faine I would forget.

Here the cutting has been drastic, some 19 lines of Q2 reduced to six lines, a 68 per cent reduction, compared to a 26 per cent reduction overall between the two texts. The difference seems more like cutting than faulty memory, for what remains is quite close to the Q2 text, and this closeness of the surviving lines is highly characteristic of Q1 as a whole. That this *is* deliberate cutting at work is surely confirmed by the isolated and illogical phrase in Q1 'All this is comfort', which only makes sense when we turn to Q2 to find out what 'all this' stands for. Not only does this indicate clearly that Q1, at least at this point, is a cut down version of a text similar to Q2, but also, and equally importantly, that the cutting is more likely to be derived from a written than a spoken text. An actor who remembers the surviving lines so well would certainly have remembered some of the connecting link to the isolated phrase; moreover, this is not simply rote learning of lines, because some minimal attempt at adaptation has been made here and there. On the other hand anyone hurriedly going through the *text* of the play with the Elizabethan equivalent of a blue pencil might well slash out lines that would leave such an isolated phrase as 'All this is comfort.' Such a process would surely produce just such a mosaic of near verbatim lines and isolated mosaic fragments, whereas memory where it fails tends to fudge and blur rather than leave clear edges. If we assume (as Hoppe does) that both memorial reconstruction *and* a redactor are at work we could only conclude on this evidence that the slashed lines would have been close to the original. Kathleen Irace, who follows Hoppe in arguing that Q1 is both a memorial reconstruction and a redacted text, is forced into the most convoluted hypotheses to justify her assumption, such as, that the 'Romeo' actor reported only the redacted version, while the 'Mercutio' actor, the other reporter, knew the longer version.[13] But this is surely a case where Occam's razor needs to be applied, for what need is there to postulate a memorizer *and* a redactor if the state of the text can be explained in terms of a redactor? The cutting in this particular passage is unusually clumsy, although an audience would have no difficulty following the progress of the passage.

---

12 'Neural Computation', p. 6.
13 Irace, *Reforming the 'Bad' Quartos*, p. 130.

Such clumsiness would argue strongly against Shakespeare as the redactor. Hoppe's complaint (p. 107) that an audience would assume the nurse is being addressed as 'villain' is surely quite unfounded, however, for little acting skill would be needed to show that Juliet's tergiversations are addressed to the absent Romeo. Even the abrupt and inconsequential 'All this is comfort' would be easily understandable as the words of a distraught wife. So here we appear to be seeing a redactor at work on a text close to the text represented in Q2 (though not identical with it) and one moreover where he needs to do little re-writing as he slashes his way towards the 26 per cent reduction or so he is looking for overall. His method is designed to do the job with the minimum of disruption, and as quickly as possible, with the emphasis on producing a text that is effective on stage. This picture conforms with the nature of the Q1 text throughout (with one minor exception) as can be illustrated with a further example.

Act 4 scene 1 (scene 16) shows a very high correlation of lines common to Q1 and Q2. Alfred Hart finds only two lines out of Q1's 92 lines that are substantially different from those of Q2 (I think four lines would be a more accurate figure).[14] In Q2 this scene runs to 126 lines and the difference is largely accounted for by Q1's omitting most of the very long speech of Friar Laurence (32 lines) at the end of the scene. In Q1 this speech and the six lines of dialogue that conclude the scene are reduced to 15 lines. In spite of the drastic cutting of this speech Q1 still manages to retain 13 lines of the original (as represented in Q2) in fairly close approximation. The bulk of the cutting affects the second half of the Friar's speech, where he gives Juliet an account of what he hopes will happen after she has taken the potion he offers her. She will appear to be dead and will be taken to the tomb where Romeo, warned in a letter what to expect, will arrive and with the Friar await her wakening, when he will return with her to Mantua. Q1 opens this passage with two lines taken from the original:

> And in this borrowed likenes of shrunke death,
> Thou shalt remaine full two and fortie houres...

compare Q2:

> And in this borrowed likenese of shrunke death
> Thou shalt continue two and fortie houres ...
>
> (4.1.104–5)

Then in Q1 comes the excision of 15 lines followed by four lines to conclude the scene:

> And when thou art laid in thy Kindreds Vault,
> Ile send in hast to *Mantua* to thy Lord,
> And he shall come and take thee from thy graue.
> JULIET Frier I goe, be sure thou send for my deare *Romeo*.

Of these four lines, the first three make use of lines present in Q2:

> Be borne to buriall in thy kindreds graue:
> Thou shall be borne to that same auncient vault,
>
> (Q2 4.1.111–12)

and

> To *Mantua*, with my Letters to thy Lord
>
> (Q2 4.1.124)

Juliet's riposte, we can be sure, was entirely the redactor's work, and we can be equally sure (again) that Shakespeare was not the redactor.

Once again the redactor has gone about his task with great economy. He has kept the bulk of the scene as he found it in his source, and has left it to the end of the scene to get his quota of cut lines. What he has cut he summarizes with reasonable competence (apart from the calamitous last line). Juliet's speech at 4.1.77f. exhibits a more complicated version of the same kind of piecing together of near-verbatim lines (six out of Q1's eleven lines) with five lines of summary. One interesting sign of visual transmission here in a near-verbatim line is the spelling of the much more usual 'yellow' as 'yealow' in Q2, coming through as 'yeolow' in Q1. It is difficult to see how such a result overall could have been obtained by memorial reconstruction unless we make the otiose assumption that the memorial reconstruction was virtually identical with the

---

[14] Hart, *Stolne*, p. 72, table XIIC.

original. A similar process is repeated scene by scene (with the one exception of the highly anomalous 2.6).

It has recently been suggested that the memorizing of *Hamlet* which produced the bad quarto took place after the redactor did his work.[15] In the case of that text, which is much less close to its original than in the case of *Romeo and Juliet*, the suggestion is plausible. In *Romeo and Juliet*, however, the places where cutting has occurred stand out so clearly that there is no sign of the fudging that might be expected if memorizing as inefficient as must be postulated occurred, as the two examples I have given illustrate.

Hart's statistical analyses of Q1 show that the patterns we have so far examined recur with only the one exception I have mentioned (2.6). Hart divides the lines of Q1 into five categories (Table XIIc, p. 72):

1 Q1 prose
2 Verse lines substantially identical in Q1 and Q2 (col. B)
3 Verse lines substantially identical in Q1 and Q2 except for one key word (col. C).
4 Verse lines substantially identical in Q1 and Q2 except for two key words (col. D).
5 Verse lines of Q1 not in Q2.

The total in this last category is only 157. A summary column (A) shows the total number of lines in Q1 close to those in Q2 as defined in columns B–D. In one of the scenes where there is a substantial amount of prose in one text compared to the other (Q1 scene 11; Q2 3.1) column A turns out to be misleading, for there is considerably less correlation than Hart implies – I shall therefore omit this scene from statistical analysis at this stage. There are also columns showing the total number of lines in each scene of Q1 and Q2. In 1.1 for instance, 236 lines of Q2 becomes 141 in Q1, of which all can be defined as close on Hart's terms. The same one hundred per cent near-correlation, in Hart's terms, between those lines of Q2 found in Q1 and the total lines of Q1 is repeated in 1.2 and 1.3 while 1.4 shows two lines of verse in Q1

unrelated to lines of verse in Q2 out of a total of 94 lines in Q1. 1.5 shows just one line of verse unrelated to Q2. Although these figures must be regarded as approximate, the implication is clear: the differences in Act 1 between Q1 and Q2 are largely a matter of cuts by the redactor. The very high verbal correlation between Q1 and Q2 continues into Act 2 (93 per cent in spite of the one anomalous scene, Q1 scene 10/Q2 2.6.) and Act 3 (97 per cent, omitting Q1 scene 11 / Q2 3.1). There is some, but not that much, falling off in Acts 4 and 5 at 83 per cent and 81 per cent respectively. The falling off in Acts 4 and 5 is ascribed by Hoppe to the fatigue of the memorizers, but redactors might equally be supposed to suffer from fatigue, especially if they are in a hurry, as this one clearly was. Indeed if we suppose that the redactor was using the author's 'foul papers' we might posit double fatigue (the author's and the redactor's) as the reason for the falling off. If systematic memorial reconstruction were to achieve such an accurate reflection of the original as we see in Q1, once the cutting is taken into account, virtually the whole cast would have to be involved in the process, for it is inconceivable that any two actors could have remembered parts other than their own so accurately, especially when no part can be singled out as consistently better than the others. Hart estimates that Mercutio's lines are best represented (he of course doesn't suffer from the late fatigue) followed closely by Romeo, Benvolio, Capulet and Friar Laurence.[16] The Nurse's part is reproduced more patchily and Juliet's part is both patchily reproduced and cut more heavily. Patchy reproduction would tell against memorial reconstruction unless it could be shown to relate to who was on stage when the lines were spoken, which in the case of Q1 of *Romeo and Juliet* it cannot. The reduction of Juliet's part

[15] K. Irace, 'Origins and Agents of Q1 *Hamlet*', in *The Hamlet First Published*, edited by Thomas Clayton (University of Delaware, 1992), p. 91.
[16] Hart, *Stolne*, p. 347.

can most readily be explained by assuming the travelling troupe did not want boys with them. Not surprisingly Hart concludes that no actor or group of actors can be identified as carrying out the memorizing process[17] and Hoppe's attempt to identify them as Paris and Romeo is wholly unconvincing. Apart from anything else it would be difficult to understand why the principal actor of a troupe should want to act against the troupe's interest, as Hart remarks. But unless the mechanism by which memorial reconstruction was effected can be demonstrated the theory can have no standing in the absence of any other evidence that it occurred.

Not all the verbal differences between the two texts can be explained by the summarizing process I described earlier. This is clearly not the reason for such differences as that illustrated in my last quotation between Q2's

Thou shalt continue two and fortie houres.

and Q1's

Thou shalt remaine full two and fortie houres.

If we postulate that the copy for both the redactor of Q1 and the compositor of Q2 was the author's 'foul papers', differences between the two texts must be the result of one of three causes (or their combination): the process of redaction, error or disagreement between the copyists, or change in the copy text between the two readings. There are other possibilities, such as, that the redactor's copy text was the prompt copy prepared for the London stage by the Company's 'book-keeper'. I think this is less likely (though certainly not impossible), because there are times when the muddle in the text behind Q2 (as for instance in Mercutio's Queen Mab speech) seems to be reflected in Q1. Another possibility is that a quick copy from the 'foul papers' was made (inevitably involving some guessing in difficult passages) specifically for the redaction, and in terms of the logistics of the operation, this might seem the most likely.

That Q2 was printed mostly from Shakespeare's 'foul papers' is now (I think) universally agreed and that these were not always easy to decipher is clear from such muddles as the version of the Queen Mab speech in Q2 (1.4) which modern editors correct by reference to Q1. The obvious superiority of Q1 over Q2 in this case has led one commentator[18] to suggest that here Q2 exhibits the memorial reconstruction, on the grounds that mishearing is the most likely explanation of 'ottamie' (for 'Atomi') 'the lash of Philome' (for 'the lash of filmes') and 'tith-pigs tale' (for 'tith-pigs taile'), but given a messy enough holograph (perhaps made easier by later revision), the simpler explanation of misreading is to be preferred to the complex hypothesis involved in supposing the Q2 speech memorially reconstructed. If the compositor was setting type from a very difficult holograph he would presumably need someone to read out the text to him, at least in the most difficult passages, and this could account for some element of mishearing in transmission.[19] In any case one likely source of difference between the redactor's version of Q1 and the printer of Q2 is the difficulty of reading a MS where, textual scholars agree, Shakespeare did not always make his intentions clear. Brian Gibbons gives some examples of this in the introduction to his Arden edition (pp. 13–17). For instance, he points out that at 3.5.177–9 in Q2 Shakespeare seems to be trying to decide between alternative phrases:

CAPULET   Gods bread, it makes me mad,
  Day, night, houre, tide, time, worke, play,
  Alone in companie, still my care hath bene
  To haue her matcht . . .

Gibbons comments: 'Here it seems probable that Shakespeare first wrote "Day, night", then considered in turn "houre", "tide", and "time",

[17] Ibid., p. 346.
[18] Sidney Thomas, 'The Queen Mab Speech in *Romeo and Juliet*', *Shakespeare Survey 25* (1972), pp. 73–80.
[19] Professor John Manning, University of Wales, Lampeter, informs me that he has clear evidence that this has occurred in a number of continental Latin publications in this period.

discarded them, and then wrote "worke, play"; but he did not score out the discarded words, or if he did, it was too lightly for the Q2 compositor' (p. 15). If we assume that the hurried redactor was faced with this problem, then he did rather well, as appears in the Q1 version:

CAPULET Gods blessed mother wife it mads me,
  Day, night, early, late, at home, abroad,
  Alone, in company, waking or sleeping,
  Still my care hath beene to see her matcht

The rhythms (although still irregular) have been brought under effective control and sense has been made by recasting the second line (if rather lamely). In situations like this it is likely that different copyists will come to different conclusions. Ernst Honigmann remarks that Q2 is riddled with 'false starts' and that these are often 'quite trivial variants'.[20] The modern scholar tries to recover the author's intention in such difficult passages, or at least to record the important variants, whereas the aim of the redactor was, it seems, to prepare a shorter acting version that was more concerned with action than with verbal niceties, as quickly as possible for his troupe. Confronted with a messy manuscript, he would surely tend to rewrite what he took to be the gist of the difficult passage rather than attempt the painstaking process of reconstructing the author's verbal intentions.

In addition to the difficulties in interpreting the 'foul papers', however, it is not improbable (as Honigmann has argued)[21] that Shakespeare might make some changes between the time when the redactor was at work for the copy of Q1 in 1597 and the appearance of Q2 in 1599. That Shakespeare frequently revised his texts, and that *Romeo and Juliet* in particular was revised, has been persuasively argued by Grace Ioppolo in her book *Revising Shakespeare*. Ioppolo argues that the Q2 title page may imply that Shakespeare revised his play after the printing of Q1 and suggests as plausible that certain 'duplicated' passages (at the end of 2.2 / beginning of 3.1; at 3.3.39/41 and in the Queen

Mab speech) also point to subsequent revision. She suggests that either Shakespeare revised these passages during composition, except perhaps for the revisions of the Queen Mab speech, which he added after the shortened version had ceased to be acted, or, 'more plausible':

Shakespeare composed the play and his first version was transcribed and perhaps abridged for performances by Hunsdon's Men, and subsequently reported and printed in Quarto 1 in 1597; Shakespeare revised several passages in his foul papers, including the 'duplicated' passages and the Queen Mab speech, perhaps when the play ceased to be acted in an abridged version by the Chamberlain's Men; a new prompt-copy was transcribed from the revised foul papers, either with or without the old versions of the revisions cancelled; once the new version had been successfully recopied, the uncorrected and unedited foul papers were released to the printer in 1599 for an edition that would supersede the reported one.[22]

It is possible that passages were revised both before and after the publication of Q1, and I hope to show some evidence of this. Ioppolo, it will be noted, supports the theory of memorial reconstruction.

A prompt copy must have been made for the London stage (assuming that the shorter version was made for provincial touring) and there is some evidence, as we have seen in examining the stage directions, that the redactor of Q1 had seen the full play acted, presumably in the prompt copy version, before he began his alterations. The redactor might well have been a member of the original cast or the company book keeper. Further evidence that the redactor had seen the full play acted is contained in the anomalous scene I mentioned earlier (2.6., scene 10). The anomaly here is that only one of the thirty lines of the scene in Q1 bears a substantial likeness (in Hart's terms) to any of

---

[20] E. A. J. Honigmann, *The Stability of Shakespeare's Text* (London, 1965), pp. 129, 130.

[21] *Stability*, p. 43 *et passim*.

[22] Grace Ioppolo, *Revising Shakespeare* (Cambridge, Mass. and London, 1991), p. 93.

those of Q2, even though the length (37 lines in Q2), the action and the characters are similar in both texts. Verbally the scene is either largely the redactor's invention or Shakespeare re-wrote the scene for the publication of Q2. The former is the more probable for there are some signs of the verbal influence of the Q2 scene on Q1 (influence the other way round can probably be discounted). For instance, in Q2, 2.6.14–15, Friar Laurence warns the lovers:

Therefore love moderately, long loue doth so,
Too swift arriues, as tardie as too slowe.

In Q1 the redactor also uses a rhymed couplet at this point (admittedly at the end of a scene in this case) to express similar sentiments, but in different words:

O, soft and faire makes sweetest worke they say.
Hast is a common hindrer in crosse way.

(Q1 scene 10, 26–7)

It is as if the redactor remembers there to have been a sententious couplet at this point and can remember its purport, but can't remember the words that expressed it. This would be a level of memory of a much lower order than anything shown in the other scenes of the play, if we were to postulate a memorial version overall, and such a difference would be extremely difficult, if not impossible, to explain. It should be noted, too, that Romeo, one of Hoppe's designated memorizers, is on stage throughout the scene. The most likely explanation is that a page of the redactor's copy text had gone missing. This copy text could have been a page of the memorial reconstruction, but equally it could have been a sheet of Shakespeare's 'foul papers', and we know that a page of Shakespeare's holograph went missing when the type was set up for Q2 because part of scenes 1.2 and 1.3 were set up from Q1, a fact pointed out by Robert Gericke in 1879.[23] The supposition that a sheet of the redactor's copy was missing is supported by the fact that the only line shared substantially by Q1 and Q2 in this scene is the last line of the scene, which could well have been the first line of a new sheet. The very fact

that the printers of Q2 were willing to use Q1 to provide readings for their supposedly authorized text, incidentally, suggests a level of trust that would hardly be justified for a memorized and pirated text, especially with an author available to provide missing copy.

The evidence so far better suggests that Q1 is a redaction of a copy text, which was probably substantially the same as the holograph MS from which the Q2 compositors set up their text, than that it is memorially reconstructed. This view also has the advantage that it is a simpler hypothesis than supposing the intrusion of a memorial reconstruction between Shakespeare's text and the redactor or between the redactor and the compositor, and is therefore to be preferred on the Occamite principle that the fewer the hypotheses the stronger the supposition. The case for memorial reconstruction seems weak not only because of the consistent coincidence between Q1 and Q2, but also because the mechanics of such a memorial process has so far defied convincing explanation. Hoppe suggests that the reporting was done by the actors of Romeo and Paris (a suggestion supported, with some modification, by Kathleen Irace)[24] but such a supposition bristles with difficulties. Any one who has acted, even under leisurely amateur conditions, will know that it is more than enough to remember one's own part. The memorizing at a good level of accuracy of most of the lines of the play would seem a super-human task, though not absolutely impossible if the two actors set out to steal the play right from the beginning of their acquaintance with the text. But why should such anomalies arise as the catastrophic failure of memory in just one scene (2.6) or the wide variations within scenes from very accurate to garbled? And there are no parts in the play that do not exhibit this contradictory mixture. Even a comparatively badly reported part like that of Juliet varies between the very

---

[23] Robert Gericke, '*Romeo and Juliet* nach Shakespeares Manuskript', *Shakespeare Jahrbuch*, 14 (1879), pp. 270–2.
[24] *Reforming the 'Bad' Quartos*, pp. 118, 120.

close correspondence of the two texts in 2.1 and the highly variable, as in 4.1, which ranges from accurate to garbled.

We have yet to consider the mechanical details Hoppe gathers in chapters 3 and 4 in defence of his thesis. He argues that Q1 exhibits some of the typical signs of memorized transmission, such as faulty metre, transposition of lines or phrases either in anticipation of lines that appear later in Q2 or recollections of earlier lines, borrowings from other plays, repetition, mishearing and what Hoppe describes collectively as 'paraphrase, summary, and expansion' (pp. 181f.); other headings include 'non-Shakespearean verse' (p. 184) and 'equivalent expressions'. Several of these categories need not detain us long. Hoppe himself admits that 'paraphrase, summary, and expansion' are, taken by themselves, 'without significance as evidence of reporting' (p. 181). Any redactor, of course, might well engage in such practices. Indeed all of these categories could be explained as part of a process of authorial composition, redaction and printing, for even mishearing might occur in the process of reading out difficult copy in the printing house, as I mentioned earlier. In any case, Hoppe is again forced to admit that, of the examples he gives, 'few ... may be true mishearings, most of them can be just as well explained on other grounds' (p. 179) and goes on to admit that 'unlike so many of those instanced from other bad quartos, none strikes one with the force of immediate conviction as being indisputable mishearings' (in other words in this respect at least Q1 is not a bad quarto).

Borrowing from other plays in *Romeo and Juliet* is equally untypical of 'bad' quartos and again Hoppe is forced to admit that the play 'does not contain any transferred passages that are so extensive or so spectacular as many that have been found in other bad quartos' (p. 160). This, we shall see, also applies to the other kinds of transposition. The 24 examples Hoppe gives of borrowings from other plays turn out to be single line comparisons including: *Hamlet* 2.2.256 'O what a rogue and peasant slave am I'

/ Q1 *Romeo*, scene 11, line 70 'Some peasantly rogue ... some base slaue' (this 'remembered' in some way before *Hamlet* had yet been written). An example that carries rather more conviction is the comparison with *Titus* 1.1.388 'Till we with trophies do adorn thy tomb' and *Romeo* Q1 scene 22 line 11 'With funerall praises doo adorne thy Tombe' – it would not be the only time, however, if Shakespeare were here echoing himself. It would not be surprising, either, if he subsequently revised the self-plagiarism out. The same explanation might also apply to the most convincing of the echoes cited: *Richard III* 1.3.271 'Peace, peace, for shame, if not for charity' / Q1 *Romeo* sc. 19 line 50 'O peace for shame, if not for charity'. There seem to be very few (if any) echoes of non-Shakespearian plays, although (as Hoppe says) such echoes are common in other 'bad' quartos (p. 160). There is a possible echo of *Faustus* at Q1 sc. 6 lines 22–3 'What must be shal be. / Thats a certaine text', but that this is Shakespearian is confirmed by its occurrence at the same point in Q2 (4.1.22–3). Marlowe is almost the only playwright Shakespeare quotes elsewhere other than himself.

So far, then, the evidence adduced for memorial reconstruction makes *Romeo* Q1 atypical of 'bad' quartos. Nor is the rest of the evidence any more conclusive. That the language of Q1 strikes the reader sometimes as un-Shakespearian is indisputable, but this is what we might expect if a redactor other than Shakespeare was supplying summarizing and link passages. There are some passages (for example, Paris's speech at 5.3.12–17, which contains the supposed *Titus* echo) where the variant lines look like authorial rewriting, for the passage in Q1 here (scene 22 lines 5–11) has an eloquence that one would be reluctant to ascribe to any ordinary redactor, though even less to a memorial reconstruction. A possible explanation for the difference in the two texts is that Shakespeare revised the original (represented in Q1) because it sounded too eloquent for the rejected Paris.

The case for memorial reconstruction is no stronger when we turn to metrical matters. Hoppe lists a variety of metrical irregularities such as the use of prose in one text where the other has verse. Here the evidence is as strongly against Q2 as Q1. In Q1, for instance, the first half of scene 11 (3.1) is presented as prose and changes to verse only after Mercutio is taken off-stage mortally wounded. In Q2 the verse begins before Romeo's entry at 3.1.58, but reverts to prose (mostly) for Mercutio's dying speeches. Some of Q1's prose lines here are simply mislineated verse, but all this might mean is that the foul papers failed to indicate the lineation clearly. It is generally remarkable that, in spite of the cutting, which might have been expected to cause considerable verse dislocation, the redactor seems to have managed to keep much of the verse more or less intact. Sometimes, indeed, it is Q2 that seems to be the less satisfactory, as, for instance, in Romeo's paradoxical speech on the nature of love (1.1.177–89). Here the two texts are close, but there are significant differences. For Q1's metrical couplet:

> Why then, O brawling loue, O louing hate,
> O anie thing, of nothing first create!

Q2 has:

> Why then ô brawling loue, o louing hate,
> O any thing of nothing first created ...

If faulty memory is to be evoked here, it would have to be assigned to Q2, but the much more likely explanation is compositorial carelessness. There is an interesting sign of authorial revision, I think, in the opening lines of this speech where Q1 reads:

> Alas that loue whose view is muffled still,
> Should without lawes giue path-waies to our
> will ...

Q2 has:

> Alas that loue, whose view is muffled still,
> Should without eyes, see pathwaies to his will ...

Both readings play on the paradox that the blind Cupid takes on the role of guide, but in Q1 the

paradox is that the *lawless*, blind Cupid (continuing the image of love as tyrant in the previous speech) can guide the lover's will (with a characteristic Shakespearian bawdy pun on 'will'), while Q2 simplifies and weakens by otiosely repeating the image of blindness. It is impossible to believe the superior reading could have been hit upon by a reporter's failure of memory. But why did Shakespeare revise it for the worse? A possible explanation is that the foul papers left the alternatives side by side (lawes give/eyes see; our/his) without making a choice between them and that the editors have gone for different alternatives (the Oldham holograph in the Bodleian adopts this method when Oldham wants to leave his options open).[25]

Hoppe lists only eight examples in Q1 where metrically correct lines in Q2 appear shortened and twelve where extra syllables are found in Q1. The first example (p. 113) shows a missing foot at 2.1.42–3:

Q1 MERCUTIO Come, lets away, for tis but vaine,
Q2 MERCUTIO Come shall we go?
BENVOLIO   Go then, for tis in vaine

Hoppe comments: 'A play-adapter might have reason to join the two speeches and omit "Go then" even at the expense of an incomplete verse, but not substitute words from another part of the play.' The words Hoppe considers borrowed from an earlier scene are the Nurse's 'Come, lets away' (1.5.146). As such phrases are standard line fillers I think we should not take too seriously the suggestion that the adapter (or memorizer) harks back to an earlier scene. Hoppe has been disingenuous here, for Q2 at this point is far from orthodox, presenting the lines as:

MERCUTIO Come shall we go?
BENVOLIO Go then, for tis in vaine to seeke him
here
That means not to be found.

---

25 See my review of *The Poems of John Oldham* edited by Harold Brooks and Ramon Selden, *Review of English Studies*, n.s. 39, 1988, p. 445.

If this is mislineation (as Hoppe tacitly indicates), we must assume that the underlying manuscript was unclear about the metrical division at this point. The most likely explanation of the metrical irregularity of Q1 then, is that the redactor, confronted with a MS muddle, simply took a quick way out by allowing two octosyllabic lines at the point where stage action would mask any irregularity, but then made sure of a correct metrical line at the end of Mercutio's speech, so that it could be picked up as part of a rhymed couplet at the beginning of Romeo's soliloquy, 'He jests at scars that never felt a wound.'[26] It is worth noting that Mercutio's speech up to this point has been virtually identical in the two versions except for a line in Q2 that is deficient (2.1.37-8):

> O *Romeo* that she were, ô that she were
> An open, or thou a Poprin Peare.

This is not only metrically defective, it is nonsensical. Q1 on the other hand has an extra syllable in the defective line:

> O *Romeo* that she were, ah that she were
> An open *Et caetera*, thou a poprin Peare.

Here at least Q1 makes sense, for the *et caetera* is meant to stand for some such indecency as 'arse'. It is more than likely that Q1 rather than Q2 represents the manuscript reading here.

It is at least as easy to find metrical irregularities at random in Q2 as in Q1, and often when Q1 exhibits satisfactory metre. Take, for example, the opening lines of 1.5 (scene 6) where each of the first five lines in Q2 is irregular:

> Welcome gentlemen, Ladies that haue their toes
> Vnplagued with Cornes, will walke about with
>   you:
> Ah my mist[r]esses, which of you all
> Will now denie to daunce, she that makes daintie,
> She Ile swear hath Corns: am I come neare ye
>   nowe?

On the other hand, Q1 here, apart from the wild third line, is the more regular metrically (even down to recording the elision in 'plagud'):

> Welcome Gentlemen, welcome Gentlemen,
> Ladies that haue their toes vnplagud with Corns
> Will haue about with you, ah ha my Mistresses,
> Which of you all will now refuse to dance?
> Shee that makes daintie, shee Ile sweare hath
>   Corns.

Again this suggests the muddle of a common manuscript source, which the two editors have sorted out as best they can, the Q1 redactor doing rather better (as perhaps we might expect of a more literary man) than the Q2 compositor.

Turning now finally to examples of passages in Q1 allegedly transposed from one part of the play (as represented in Q2) to another, and of other kinds of substitution: here the evidence is potentially strongest for the theory of memorial reconstruction. Hoppe gives a number of sub-headings in analysing these, starting with intra-linear substitutions. For example, no. 5 (p. 131) is:

3.5.131 Q1 thou resemblest a sea, a barke, a storme
          Q2 Thou countefaits. A Barke, a Sea, a Wind

Here the redactor is summarizing a twelve-line speech in Q2 in seven lines, partly by piecing together phrases found in Q2 and partly by using phrases of his own. Such variations as the example shows can be illustrated throughout the speech. For instance, the two following lines in Q2 are:

> For still thy eyes, which I may call the sea,
> Do ebbe and flowe with teares, the Barke thy
>   body is ...

which is represented in Q1 as:

> For this thy bodie which I tearme a barke,
> Still floating in thy euerfalling teares ...

The speech is just such a wordy passage in Q2 as the redactor might be expected to cut back by

---

[26] For sound/wound as rhymed words see E. J. Dobson, *English Pronunciation, 1500–1700*, 2 vols. (Oxford, 1957), 2, p. 687.

summary. Hoppe comments on a similar example of transposition and substitution (example 7, 4.4.7–8) 'Since this passage appears in a Q1 speech which is a mere prose summary of Q2, this transposition is doubtless the reporter's work' – but to summarize lines you had largely forgotten as coherently as this would be an even more remarkable feat than the act of memory represented by Q1 overall. It is surely much more likely that the redactor is paraphrasing passages either to reduce them in length (as in example 5) or because the manuscript is difficult to sort out and paraphrasing what he *can* read is the best option (possibly in example 7).

Under the sub-heading 'anticipations' Hoppe first gives a list of minor variations between Q1 and Q2 that could again be as readily explained by the summarizing process of the redactor and/or the difficulties of reading the manuscript from which he was working. A list of more widely spaced anticipations has rather greater weight for his argument (pp. 144–50) and will need to be looked at in some detail. All, however, suggest other explanations than faulty memory. The first example notes that the third line of the Q1 prologue has 'ciuill broyles' where Q2 has 'auncient grudge'. Hoppe suggests this may be an anticipation in Q1 of the line at 1.1.96 printed in Q1 as 'Three Ciuell brawles bred of an airie word' and repeated in substance in Q2. I give reasons at the end of this article for regarding the Q1 prologue as a special case, but in any event, it is difficult to understand why a Q1 reporter should get the phrase right in one place and wrong in the other. Example 2 involves the substitution of *'Well goe thy waies'* for Q2 1.3.59 *'Peace I haue done'*, in which Hoppe thinks Q1 may be anticipating 'go thy wayes wench' at 2.5.45. This is too trivial a phrase to make much of and was no doubt often used as a tag; it might as easily have been introduced by a speeding redactor as by a reporter. Similarly the third example, the substitution of 'I cannot stir' for 'I cannot moue' at

Q2 1.4.16 is more likely to be either a manuscript alternative which the redactor has picked up or the redactor's error, rather than the memorial anticipation of 2.1.15 'he stirreth not' suggested by Hoppe. The next two examples show anticipations from within the Queen Mab speech, another special case, which E. Pearlman describes as a later interpolation[27] and which would seem to involve considerable manuscript muddle. As the muddle in Q2 is considerably worse than that of Q1 at this point some explanation of both texts other than faulty memory is required. The next example (6, p. 146) is the most interesting of the passages cited, as it involves the transposition of two lines, reproduced verbatim, from 3.4.6–7 in Q2 to 1.5.128–9 (scene 5) in Q1: 'I promise you, but for your companie, / I would haue bene a bed an houre ago' (Q1 'company', 'bin', 'agoe'). Not surprisingly these words of Capulet have been made much of by those arguing for memorial reconstruction. Yet other explanations are possible and indeed more probable. One consideration that works against the theory that memory is involved is the very precise nature of the duplication. A memory that had put the lines into the wrong scene might be expected to make some mistake in reproducing the lines; a visual element in the transmission on these grounds seems more likely. There are several possible ways in which this could have happened. One possibility is that Shakespeare may have decided to transfer the lines to Act 3, where they make rather more appropriate sense (one usually resists the temptation to tell one's guests they've been keeping one up beyond one's usual hours) at a post-Q1 stage of revision. There is also, of course, the possibility of Shakespearian duplication, later revised, that the redactor has resolved either intentionally or by accident. Yet another possibility is that the memory of the actor-redactor is involved. For instance, if the re-

[27] E. Pearlman, 'Shakespeare at Work: *Romeo and Juliet*', *English Literary Renaissance*, 24 (1994), 332–40.

dactor had been the actor playing Capulet it would be possible to account for both the accuracy of the duplication and the wrong positioning. My purpose, however, is not to attempt a solution to what is insoluble, but merely to point out that even in this instance alternatives to the theory of systematic memorial reconstruction can be found. A less verbally precise duplication can be found between Q2 1.3.1f. and Q1 1.3.1f. (scene 3) and Q1 3.5.65 (scene 15 line 56f.). Here the transposition is easier to explain in terms of Shakespearian revision of duplication, but again the recollections of the actor-redactor may have played a part. These are in any case isolated, minor examples of repetition that could not possibly sustain a theory of systematic memorial reconstruction, more especially, in this last example, because the three actors on stage, Juliet, Lady Capulet and Nurse, could not have been the principal reporters. None of the further passages that Hoppe cites as anticipation or (in the next sub-section) recollections has greater force than those already discussed, so we can reasonably conclude that there is no example of either anticipation or recollection for which an explanation other than systematic memorial reconstruction cannot be made.

Confronted with all these problems, how, then, did the theory of memorial reconstruction become the orthodox theory for explaining the state of the text of Q1? To answer this we need to examine the two hypotheses with which Hoppe and Hart support their theories: the related suppositions that the copy for Q1 was 'stolne and surreptitious' and that Q1 itself was published piratically. The two hypotheses are closely related because any theory of systematic memorial reconstruction must presuppose an inability to obtain an authorized copy and in this case the original had certainly not been lost. Hoppe makes it clear, however, that there is no positive evidence that the play was published without the permission of its rightful owners, who were presumably the company that had first performed the full play. We have the authority of Shakespeare's colleagues Hemminge and Condell for assuming such stealing went on, although their claim that the Folio has not only supplied the true versions of the 'stolne and surreptitious copies' but supplied the texts of all the others 'absolute in their numbers, as he [Shakespeare] conceived them'[28] is (to put it mildly) some exaggeration. The whole of this address to the readers, we need to remember, is a blatant case of advertising hype, intended, as is disarmingly admitted, to get people to buy the product ... 'what ever you do, Buy'. There is some corroboration from elsewhere (in for instance Thomas Heywood's preface to his tragedy *The Rape of Lucrece*) that such stealing went on, and indeed it would hardly be consistent with human nature to assume it didn't. On the other hand, there is very little evidence (if any) that rival companies took advantage of this nefarious activity by producing the plays of their rivals. The evidence, on the contrary, suggests that usually each playhouse attempted to find its own distinctive niche in the theatrical market. Very occasionally we find plays being adapted from the boys' theatres to the adult players, such as Webster's adaptation of Marston's Blackfriars play *The Malcontent* for the Globe, or Dekker's *Satiromastix* at both the Globe and Paul's. But this seems to have caused no friction between the companies involved. The transfer of *Satiromastix* seems to have been part of an arrangement of mutual support between Paul's Boys and the Globe in their rivalry with Blackfriars, as Shakespeare and Dekker seem to have teamed up in the 'War of the Theatres' to give Ben Jonson a purge (as *The Second Return from Parnassus* has it). However none of this proves anything about the particular case of *Romeo and Juliet* four or five years earlier.

The current wisdom on these 'stolne and surreptitious copies' is that in several instances, including the 'bad' quartos of *2* and *3 Henry VI*,

---

[28] 'To the Great Variety of Readers', *Mr William Shakespeare's Comedies, Histories, and Tragedies* (London, 1623).

unauthorized publishers obtained mangled versions of the Shakespeare plays from disaffected actors who had played a part in the authorized versions. In the case of *Romeo and Juliet* (1597) and *Hamlet* (1603) the theory goes, the rightful owners of the play responded by producing an authorized text. The title page of the second quarto of *Romeo and Juliet* (1599) is described as a version 'newly corrected, augmented, and amended'. It is worth comparing the relationship between Q1 and Q2 of *Hamlet* where the second edition (1604/5) is described on the title page as 'Newly imprinted and enlarged to about as much againe as it was, according to the true and perfect Coppie.' The second part of this statement implies that the printers have gone back to an authoritative copy; the absence of such a statement on the title page of *Romeo and Juliet* Q2 is worth remarking, even though it is clear that Q2 derives in large part from authorial copy. It suggests that the publishers of *Romeo and Juliet* Q2 (unlike the publishers of the second quarto of *Hamlet*) were willing to acknowledge a relationship with the earlier printed text. It is usually assumed that the holding company would be anxious to retain its copies of successful plays for as long as possible without publication, to prevent other companies using their products. The facts, however, do not support this assumption. *Hamlet* was by all accounts one of the most successful plays of the Elizabethan theatre, for as early as 1604 Anthony Scoloker advises authors that they 'should please all, like Prince Hamlet'.[29] It would therefore seem odd that in 1604 Shakespeare's company should authorize a copy of the full text to be published to counter the publication of so mangled a surreptitious copy as the first quarto *Hamlet* – indeed it would surely have been a shrewd move to let rival companies perform so botched a job and hold on to the real thing. Much of what we know about Shakespeare suggests his business calculations would generally be shrewd and profitable. It seems at least as likely, therefore, that Q1 was seen as a useful, if unauthorized, trailer and that

the publication of the second quarto of *Hamlet* was not felt likely to affect the size of the audiences. In the case of *Romeo and Juliet* we may have rather a different story, in which the first quarto was not unauthorized, but a shrewd off-loading of a provincial acting text that had been sufficiently popular on the stage to justify the cost of printing. Certainly the Q1 title page would allow such an assumption, announcing as it does that it is presenting the play 'As it hath been often (with great applause) plaid publiquely'. The motive for the publication of *Romeo and Juliet* Q2 (as with *Hamlet* Q2) is also likely to have been sound commercial considerations. In both cases Shakespeare had, it seems, achieved outstanding success on the stage and it would surely be a reasonable calculation that the market would comfortably sustain *both* a continuing flow of visitors to the playhouse *and* a sizeable reading public for the text. Certainly modern publishers would not consider these two aims incompatible. There is (as I have said) no evidence that rival companies would take advantage of this by putting on rival productions, for it would not make much commercial sense to try to split the market (especially when your rivals had Richard Burbage playing Romeo and the Prince of Denmark). When in the 1690s two rival *Hamlets* were scheduled for performance on the same evening, it was entirely as a spoiling tactic; moreover, one of the companies cried off at the last minute and produced Congreve's *Old Bachelor* instead.[30]

When we look at the details of the publication of the first quarto of *Romeo and Juliet* as Hoppe presents them, we get little indication that the publication was surreptitious. It is true that there is no entry in the Stationers' Register by the publisher, but that is not directly relevant to the question of the relationship between the

---

[29] *Shakespeare Allusion Book*, re-edited, revised, and re-arranged by John Munro, 2 vols. (London and New York, 1909), vol. 1, p. 133.

[30] See Colley Cibber, *An Apology for his Life* (Dent, Everyman, London, 1914), pp. 106–7.

owners of the copy and the printer. In any case, no Stationers' Register entry is to be found claiming publishing rights for Q2, which is generally regarded as being set up from Shakespeare's 'foul papers' and presumed to have been authorized. Moreover, of the two publishers, Cuthbert Burby, who was responsible for the publication of Q2, would seem to have had considerably the worse record as pirate.[31] It is also the opinion of at least one modern editor that Q2 'is on the whole less carefully printed than Q1'.[32] Interestingly, there seems to have been a trade relationship between Danter and Burby going back to at least 1592 and involving 'at least six extant books whose entry or imprint involves Danter and Burby'.[33] It is not impossible therefore that Danter was acting as printer for Burby in the publication of Q1. As the second quarto of *Romeo and Juliet* was published after Danter's death we might speculate that the publication of an 'amended' text after the sale of Q1 had run its course was part of the original deal Danter (or Burby) had arranged with Shakespeare's company. Danter's earlier publications had included the first quarto of *Titus Andronicus* (1594), which was very probably printed from Shakespeare's 'foul papers' and presumably authorized by its owners. Its most recent editor compares it favourably with the general run of quarto play texts, describing it as 'a strikingly well laid out text' ... 'with far fewer blunders than most'.[34] Of the eight play texts printed by Danter, Hoppe maintains that the first quarto of *Romeo and Juliet* is the only 'bad' text that can be laid fairly at his door.[35] It looks more probable that it was published as a money-spinner and trailer for Q2 by arrangement with Shakespeare's company at a time when the play itself was still being presented, at least in its fuller form, in the playhouse.

Burkhart points to evidence that links the first quarto versions of *Romeo* to Shakespeare's company. The title page of Q1 tells us that the version being offered is 'As it hath been often (with great applause) plaid publiquely, by the right Honourable the L[ord] of Hunsdon, his

Seruants', and Burkhart reminds us that the company went by that title for only the eight months or so between the death of the Lord Chamberlain, Henry Carey, on 22 July 1596 and the appointment of his son, George Carey, Lord Hunsdon, as Lord Chamberlain on 17 March 1597. Burkhart also shows that 'Lord Hunsdonns Players' are recorded as playing in Faversham, Kent, on 1 August 1596 at a time when playing in London, Middlesex and Surrey had been prohibited because of the plague. The shortened form of the London 'hit', with a reduced cast to cut down the cost and complications of travelling into the provinces, would be a highly suitable (and profitable) offering at the Lammas-tide fair in Faversham.[36]

I have suggested the possibility that one cause of different readings between Q1 and Q2 might be that Shakespeare made some alterations to his 'foul papers' after the redactor had used them to produce his shortened version. It would be difficult, if not impossible, to distinguish such alterations from differences caused by the re-writing of the redactor or difficulties in reading the original. But one possible indication of later authorial revision is in the prologue. The usual view is that the Q1 prologue is simply a misremembered attempt to reproduce the Shakespearian sonnet that appears in Q2 as prologue, but this is a very unconvincing explanation in view of the remarkable feat of memory (if that's what it is) represented by Q1 as a whole. It would be the only example where cutting could not convincingly be ascribed to the general aim of reducing the play's length. There is too the curious fact that the reference

[31] See Hoppe, *The Bad Quarto*, pp. 16–17.
[32] *Romeo and Juliet*, edited by G. Blakemore Evans (Cambridge, 1984), p. 208.
[33] Hoppe, *The Bad Quarto*, p. 10.
[34] *Titus Andronicus*, edited by Jonathan Bate (The Arden Shakespeare, Third Series, London and New York, 1995), p. 111.
[35] Hoppe, *The Bad Quarto*, p. 17.
[36] *Shakespeare's Bad Quartos*, pp. 65–7.

to 'the two houres traffique of our Stage' (which appears in both versions of the prologue) applies with reasonable accuracy to the length of Q1, but not to the longer version of Q2, which takes (and presumably did take) something nearer three hours to act. It is true there are other references to long plays taking two hours to play, for instance, in the prologues of *Henry VIII* (3463 lines) and *Alchemist* (3010 lines), while the Induction to *Bartholomew Fair* refers to 'two hours and an half and somewhat more' for a play that has 3912 lines. We should hardly expect scientific measurements from Elizabethan playwrights, but Jonson, at least, seems to be attempting some degree of *relative* accuracy, even though *Alchemist* (slightly longer than *Romeo* Q2) must have taken considerably longer than two hours to play. Steven Urkowitz points out that 'there are many … contemporary citations of three-hour and longer performance times in English Renaissance theaters'[37] and comes to the conclusion that the playing time of the Elizabethan stage was highly variable. If we assume, then, that the playwright tried to make a rough estimate, in referring to his own play, of how long he expected the play to take to act then we would seem to need to give priority to the Q1 prologue of *Romeo and Juliet* over Q2 as the more accurate. This would suggest that the reference in the Q2 prologue to two hours' playing time derives from Q1. This would further require us to suppose that the Q2 prologue is Shakespeare's re-writing of what in this instance was a redactor's interpolation. There is a snippet of textual evidence to support this supposition, for Q1 has, in one scene (scene 4, lines 4–6), one of its rare additions to the Q2 original, where a joking reference is made to the last minute addition of a prologue. In this scene in Q2 Romeo and Benvolio are discussing whether they should introduce themselves with some sort of speech as they arrive for the Capulet masked ball. Q1 has a similar passage, but introduces two lines into an otherwise virtually identical version of the Q2 speech. Q2's lines read:

> Weele haue no *Cupid*, hudwinckt with a
>   skarfe,
> Bearing a Tartars painted bow of lath,
> Skaring the Ladies like a Crowkeeper.
> But let them measure *vs* by what they will,
> Weele measure them a measure and be gone.
>
> (Q2 1.4.4–8)

Q1 adds two lines as follows:

> Weele haue no *Cupid*, hudwinckt with a
>   Skarfe,
> Bearing a *Tartars* painted bow of lath,
> Scaring the Ladies like a crow-keeper:
> Nor no withoutbooke Prologue faintly spoke
> After the Prompter, for our entrance.
> But let them measure *vs* by what they will,
> Weele measure them a measure and be gone.
>
> (Q1 scene 4, lines 4–10)

The Arden editor explains the missing lines in Q2 as compositorial carelessness, but the punctuation does not support this suggestion. The redactor's addition of these lines, completely unnecessary to the scene and running counter to his general purpose of abridgement, can best make sense as a kind of in-joke for the cast, in which he recalls what actually happened when the added prologue was supplied for the touring version. Moreover the verbal coincidence of these two passages, apart from the two extra lines, extending as it does even to spelling for the most part, makes it far more likely that both the redactor and the Q2 compositor were using the same copy text (presumably fairly clear at this point) than that memorial reconstruction is intruding between them. To account for the similarities in terms of the actors' memories is hardly credible. Nor in this instance can the similarity be accounted for by supposing the Q2 compositor is consulting Q1 at this point, for if he had, he would surely have included the two extra lines. On this evidence the theory that Q1 derives from Shakespeare's 'foul papers' not only has the advantage of involving one

---

[37] 'Back to Basics', *The Hamlet First Published*, edited by Thomas Clayton, 1992, p. 268.

hypothesis less than Hoppe thinks necessary, but accounts more convincingly for the characteristics of the Q1 texts.[38]

---

[38] Jay L. Halio's article 'Handy-Dandy: Q1/Q2 *Romeo and Juliet*' also argues that Q1 is an abridged version of Shakespeare's original and not a reported text. Halio, however, argues that the redaction is in great part likely to be authorial. The article, from *Shakespeare's 'Romeo and Juliet': Texts, Contexts, and Interpretation* (Newark: University of Delaware Press; London: AUP, 1995), pp. 123–50, appeared too late to be considered in the preparation of this article.

SHAKESPEARE'S *ROMEO AND JULIET*: THE PLACES OF INVENTION

JILL L. LEVENSON

[R]hetoric is like the air which ... exceeds and penetrates ... and transforms itself into all things created here.

  Joan de Guzman, *Primera Parte de la Rhetorica* (1589)[1]

Shakespeare's *Romeo and Juliet* not only dramatizes a fiction but also transforms its rhetoric. In the process it reopens a book which writers of the previous generation had apparently closed. By the 1560s, when Brooke and Painter translated Boaistuau, the Romeo and Juliet narrative had become fixed in more than one way. Luigi da Porto's *Historia novellamente ritrovata di due nobili amanti, ...* (*c.* 1530) set its format: a dozen events and as many characters organized in a tragic action. Matteo Bandello's version in his *Novelle* (1554) established its style, which invited the audience to judge the story as if they were participating in a rhetorical occasion.[2] Typical of the period, this fiction depends on the forms of oration and dispute. Figures of repetition ornament the narrative while securing each event firmly in place.

Although numerous studies have traced Shakespeare's changes to the narrative's plot and characters, they have not examined his alterations of style. Yet analysis of the play's rhetoric in relation to that of the established fiction reveals an unexplored dimension of the later work; it brings the tragedy into focus like a print from a negative. In particular it shows how *Romeo and Juliet* deliberately complicates rhetoric by neutralizing argument and combining figures of ambiguity with other schemes.

As a result it clarifies a dramatic text which calls attention to its own display of rhetoric, questioning oratorical strategies and objectives, engaging critically with the art of persuasion and inquiry.[3]

I

The Romeo and Juliet narrative assumed its most popular non-dramatic form in the middle decades of the sixteenth century; Bandello's novella was translated into French and English between 1559 and 1567. As rhetoric flourished, 'polymorphous and ubiquitous',[4] the novellas took shape as rhetorical compositions based on the story as da Porto had arranged it. They used each of the dozen plot elements as a *res* or subject-matter, amplifying episodes through

---

1 Translated and quoted by Wayne A. Rebhorn, *The Emperor of Men's Minds: Literature and the Renaissance Discourse of Rhetoric* (Ithaca, N.Y., 1995), p. 5.

2 Arthur F. Kinney gives this description for the writing of Renaissance fiction generally in 'Rhetoric and Fiction in Elizabethan England', in *Renaissance Eloquence: Studies in the Theory and Practice of Renaissance Rhetoric*, ed. James J. Murphy (Berkeley, Los Angeles, and London, 1983), p. 388. For a study of the lineage and style of the Romeo and Juliet narrative, see my 'Romeo and Juliet before Shakespeare', *Studies in Philology*, 81 (1984), 325–47.

3 Rebhorn argues that all Renaissance literature, from the fourteenth to the seventeenth centuries and throughout Western Europe, has 'an active and critical relationship' with rhetoric, pp. 18–19 and *passim*.

4 Rebhorn, *The Emperor of Men's Minds*, p. 6.

the larger processes of rhetoric and, more specifically, through a limited number of figures. Uniform in tone, they advance through the narrative-speech-narrative-speech pattern which Richard A. Lanham defines as a staple of Western literary expression: narrators argue their interpretations of events; 'lovers orate spontaneously', engaging in debate with themselves and others; and rhetorical figures ornament each fiction from beginning to end.[5] In Arthur Brooke's *Tragicall Historye of Romeus and Juliet*, generally accepted as Shakespeare's immediate source, the narrator occasionally evaluates the suasion in rhetorical terms:

> Oh how we can perswade, our self to what we
>   like,
> And how we can diswade our mynd, if ought our
>   mynd mislyke.
> Weake arguments are stronge, our fansies streyght
>   to frame
> To pleasing things, and eke to shonne, if we
>   mislike the same.[6]

Of course these novellas, like other Renaissance literature, adapted rhetorical discourse for use in their fictions. Among other borrowings, for example, they incorporated features from the three kinds of orations: demonstrative or epideictic, when the narrator praises Verona or attributes of the characters, or when the characters praise or dispraise one another or their circumstances; judicial or forensic, when Friar Laurence defends himself in open assembly before a judge; and, most frequently, deliberative, 'wherby we do perswade, or disswade, entreate, or rebuke, exhorte, or dehorte, commende, or côforte any man'.[7] When Juliet discovers who Romeo is, she sounds like this in Bandello:

Now let us assume that he really loves me, as I am ready to believe he does, and that he wants me as his legitimate wife: should I not be reasonable and consider the fact that my father will never agree to it? And yet, is it just possible that this union could bring the two families together again in peace and harmony? I have heard it said many times that such marriages have brought about peace not only

between private citizens and gentlemen, but that often times true peace and amity ensued between the greatest princes and kings engaged in the cruelest wars. Perhaps I shall be the one to bring peace to these two households by such means.[8]

Boaistuau and Painter shorten this argument; Brooke lengthens it, particularly with allusions to 'sage writers' (line 409), and condemns it outright (lines 429–32, quoted above). Yet the discussion remains essentially logical in each version, a deliberation which finally calms Juliet and supplies her with an objective. It is typical of these fictions where everyone deliberates, resolves, and argues, from Juliet herself to Juliet's nurse.

If the novellas seem copious, oratory supplies the abundance: the details which crowd the narrative constitute evidence for the many arguments. If the novellas generated emotion for their original audiences, rhetorical figures of pathos must have heightened the story's mythological and romantic elements. These figures are especially prominent in the complaints which punctuate the sequence, in the lovers' exchanges, and in the narrators' appeals for empathy:

> [Juliet] in so wondrous wise began her sorowes to
>   renewe
> That sure no hart so hard, (but it of flint had byn,)

---

5 Lanham defines the pattern and describes the lovers in *The Motives of Eloquence: Literary Rhetoric in the Renaissance* (New Haven and London, 1976), p. 9.

6 *The Tragicall Historye of Romeus and Juliet written first in Italian by Bandell, and nowe in Englishe by Ar. Br.*, in Geoffrey Bullough, ed., *Narrative and Dramatic Sources of Shakespeare*, vol. 1 (London and New York, 1957), lines 429–32. Further references to Brooke's poem will appear parenthetically in my text.

7 Thomas Wilson, *The Arte of Rhetorique* (1553), Theatrum Orbis Terrarum (Amsterdam and New York, 1969), D4. Kinney quotes this passage in his *Humanist Poetics: Thought, Rhetoric, and Fiction in Sixteenth-Century England* (Amherst, Mass., 1986), p. 10.

8 *Novelle*, ed. Giuseppe Guido Ferrero, Classici Italiani (Turin, 1974), p. 447. I am grateful to Professor Anne Paolucci for this translation from the Italian.

But would have rued the pitious plaint that she
did languishe in.   (lines 1092–4)[9]

But figures of pathos make up only about ten per cent of the two hundred or so devices catalogued by Sister Miriam Joseph; and those cited in her larger grammatical category, the orthographic/syntactical schemes, play a modest role in Bandello, Boaistuau, and Painter.[10] Yet the figures of grammar also provide a source of emotional power in rhetorical speech. According to Brian Vickers, who identifies these figures and three kinds of word-play (figures of logos) as the most important group, they serve as 'representations of human emotional and psychological states', or 'little reservoirs of energy'.[11] Bandello and his translators, depending on the simplest devices of repetition, often produce stylistic languor.

The English translations frequently expand the French novella with rhetorical figures; they rarely enhance it. After the death of Thibault, for instance, Boaistuau's Juliette apostrophizes the window through which Romeo entered her chamber in a moment of prosopopoeia anticipating Chekhov:

'O malheureuse fenestre, par laquelle furent ourdies les ameres trames de mes premiers malheurs! si par ton moyen j'ay receu autresfois quelque leger plaisir ou contentement transitoire, tu m'en fais maintenant payer un si rigoureux tribut que mon tendre corps … ne le [peut] plus supporter, …'[12]

Painter's Julietta makes the same speech with more repetition:

'Oh vnhappy Windowe, oh entry most vnlucky, wherein were wouen the bitter toyle of my former mishaps, if by thy meanes I have receyued at other tymes some light pleasure or transitory contentation, thou now makest me pay a tribute so rigorous and paynefull, as my tender body [is] not able any longer to support the same, …'[13]

As this brief passage illustrates, Painter favours a device which hovers at the edge of tautology and has no other name in Joseph's exhaustive study: he links synonymous terms which neither build to a climax nor otherwise add force to the

passage. No other device occurs as consistently, or relentlessly, in his text; others appear sprinkled on the prose, here and there, like seasoning. Painter reiterates words and units of syntax, balances phrases and contrasts ideas, plays on terms from the same root and introduces hyperbole, but these diffuse figures produce no sustained effect. Finally it is the pairs of synonyms which make a lasting impression of narrative proof against surprises.

Brooke's version, the play's direct source, makes the same impression more emphatically. Reinforced by poulter's measure, its elaborate repetitions predetermine the narrative. The effect can be heard early in the poem, as the narrator appeals for inspiration through anaphora:

Helpe learned Pallas, helpe, ye muses with your
    arte,
Helpe all ye damned feendes to tell, of joyes
    retournd to smart,
Helpe eke ye sisters three, my skillesse penne
    t'indyte
For you it causd which I (alas) unable am to
    wryte.

                                    (lines 21–4)

Immediately Brooke stresses the cause of rancour between the families by using the word *envy* three times in three lines, once as a verb

---

9 For the corresponding passage in Painter's version see William Painter, 'The goodly Hystory of the true, and constant Loue between Rhomeo and Ivlietta, …' in Joseph Jacobs, ed., *The Palace of Pleasure*, vol. 3 (London, 1890), p. 97.

10 *Shakespeare's Use of the Arts of Language* (New York, 1947). For this paper I have adopted Sister Miriam Joseph's organization of the figures into four groups (grammar, logos, pathos, ethos) and the names which she has assigned to the schemes.

11 *Classical Rhetoric in English Poetry* (London, 1970), chapters 3 and 4 (quotations from pp. 121, 122). See also Vickers's essay on 'Shakespeare's Use of Rhetoric' in *A New Companion to Shakespeare Studies*, ed. Kenneth Muir and S. Schoenbaum (Cambridge, Eng., 1971), pp. 83–98.

12 Pierre Boaistuau, *Histoires tragiques*, ed. Richard A. Carr, Société des textes français modernes (Paris, 1977), p. 85.

13 Painter, 'The goodly Hystory', p. 97.

and twice as a noun (lines 32–4). These verses set the tone for Brooke's *Historye*, a conscientious reflection of his rhetorical training: anaphora and polyptoton will recur frequently until the end of the narrative, when they play a significant part in Friar Laurence's self-defence (lines 2837–970).

In addition, Brooke combines devices in a straightforward way. Lines arranged by anaphora usually include another device or two; often they contain antithesis (as in line 22, quoted above), a figure of logos on which the poem relies. Other verses mix antimetabole with diacope, or antimetabole with diacope and polyptoton, or asyndeton with synonymia. Despite Brooke's efforts, the resulting compounds are simple:

> But she espyd straight waye ... chaunging of his
>   hewe
> From pale to red, from red to pale, and so from
>   pale anewe, ...   (lines 271–2)

> The world is always full of chaunces and of
>   chaunge,
> Wherfore the chaunge of chaunce must not seeme
>   to a wise man straunge.
> For tickel Fortune doth, in chaunging but her
>   kind,
> But all her chaunges cannot chaunge a steady
>   constant minde.   (lines 1403–6)

> My Juliet, my love, my only hope and care, ...
>   (line 1543)

Sometimes the figures seem pointless, a habit which the writer cannot break (e.g., lines 1729–30). Like the other Romeo and Juliet narratives, this poem lacks word-play: a few puns (e.g., line 1169) almost disappear among more than three thousand lines.

Yet Brooke's rhetoric acquires a degree of complexity from Petrarchan conventions: his awareness of the Italian sonnet is declared not only by 'The Argument', which takes that form, but also through recurrent antitheses (sweet/sour, freedom/bondage, life/death) and tropes (beleaguered ships, returning Phoebus, fire). Of the fictions, his poem also has the most

elaborate prefatory material to link romance with teaching literature: '*Hereunto if you applye it* [i.e., this precedent], *ye shall deliver my dooing from offence, and profit your selves*' (p. 285). The young poet tries to present the love-story as a controversial issue, matching his rhetorical devices to the task at hand. In the end his project lacks conviction, tragedy sinks *controversia*, and his rhetoric gives the romantic narrative a sense of closure.

II

Some time in the 1590s the young dramatist chose the young poet as his model: Shakespeare takes details from Brooke and at points quotes his very words. Obviously the playwright broke with tradition in his rendering of the narrative with comic infusions and sonneteering.[14] The comedy threatens to upset the sequence but never does; the Petrarchism, a nuance in Brooke, gives the legend contemporary relevance.[15] Perhaps less obviously, Shakespeare broke with tradition in his treatment of the rhetoric inevitably attached to this narrative. Brooke's exaggerated use of figures may have invited him to revise the typical presentation; and the tragic story offered an appropriate means to investigate the weaknesses or potential failure of an art which had infiltrated so many areas of sixteenth-century life. Whatever the cause, this version reinvents the medium through which the story had been transmitted.

---

[14] The most thorough treatment of the comedy is the second chapter of Susan Snyder's *The Comic Matrix of Shakespeare's Tragedies: 'Romeo and Juliet', 'Hamlet', 'Othello', and 'King Lear'* (Princeton, N.J., 1979); the first influential comments on the sonneteering appear in the fourth section of Nicholas Brooke's *Shakespeare's Early Tragedies* (London, 1968).

[15] For the connection between writing sonnets and seeking patronage in Queen Elizabeth's court, see my essay '*Romeo and Juliet*: Tragical-Comical-Lyrical History', in *Proceedings of the PMR* [Patristic, Mediaeval, and Renaissance] *Conference*, vol. 12/13 (Villanova, Pa., 1990 for 1987/8), pp. 31–46.

In the first place, *Romeo and Juliet* cuts and reallocates deliberative argument, assigning most of what remains to characters other than the protagonists: Friar Laurence and Benvolio do most of the lecturing; the Capulets, the Nurse, and Prince Escalus also advise and exhort. Their counsel, which frequently halts rash action, more often accelerates disaster and gives rise to irony. At the centre of the play Friar Laurence has the most extensive speech of disputation. This passage of fifty-one lines, 3.3.107–57, illustrates one of Shakespeare's straightforward techniques for calling rhetoric into question: setting an accomplished performance into a context which reduces its effect.[16]

Robert O. Evans, who analyses a number of rhetorical passages in the text, thoroughly explicates Friar Laurence's speech as a premier specimen of rhetoric, 'a brilliant example both of argumentation and of the use of figures'.[17] From the opening of this argument to the close, he identifies various figures organized to enhance the reasoning: enthymeme, the device which 'combines antithesis with inference and works out two opposing arguments in a small space'; anamnesis, a recital of past happenings, usually woes or injuries; philophronesis, a form of mitigation. Friar Laurence focuses on the idea of self-defence: Tybalt would have killed you; you killed Tybalt.[18]

Certainly this long speech displays a panoply of figures, especially figures of repetition: it repeats words to link the end of one clause to the beginning of the next (anadiplosis) and to link clauses by concluding them with the same term or phrase (epistrophe); it incorporates polyptoton, diacope, and epizeuxis. It may also employ two figures of word-play: antanaclasis, where a word shifts from one meaning to another when repeated (*shape*, lines 121–9); and syllepsis, when a single word has more than one meaning (*wax*, line 125).[19] Moreover, the speech carefully refines and consolidates an argument in Brooke, more than twice as long (lines 1353–480), which starts to ramble after beginning with the same enthymeme.

Brooke's version of this passage draws attention not only to Shakespeare's skill but also to his ambivalence: it leaves no doubt that the Friar's rhetoric has the desired effect on Romeus. Even before the argument begins, the narrator states: 'So wisely did the fryre unto his tale replye, / That he straight cared for his life, that erst had care to dye' (lines 1351–2). When it ends he devotes sixteen lines to a description of the lover's response, an appreciation of the Friar's reasoning and persuasiveness (lines 1481–96). Significantly changed, the context of the dramatic passage suggests that suasion has no such effect. Romeo has already damned philosophy (lines 57–60), and he provokes the speech with a desperate question (itself rhetorical):

> O, tell me, friar, tell me,
> In what vile part of this anatomy
> Doth my name lodge? Tell me, that I may sack
> The hateful mansion.   (lines 104–7)

After Friar Laurence concludes we hear not Romeo but the Nurse, who exclaims 'O, what learning is!', and perhaps counteracts the audience's perception of tediousness by (unintentionally) expressing it: 'O Lord, I could have stayed here all the night / To hear good counsel!' (lines 158–60). Romeo acts in response not to the argument but to the promise of seeing Juliet.

Friar Laurence's rhetoric seems even more questionable in 4.4; and the figures of pathos which become so prominent during this scene have led critics to suspect the dramatist of either bad taste or travesty. In the source the Friar plays no part in this episode; Lady Capulet alone grieves in a lament; sorrow makes Capulet and the Nurse speechless; and rhetorical figures

---

[16] References to the play come from John Jowett's edition in *William Shakespeare: The Complete Works* (Oxford, 1986).

[17] *The Osier Cage: Rhetorical Devices in 'Romeo and Juliet'* (Lexington, Ky., 1966), p. 55.

[18] For Evans's analysis, see pp. 54–60. On p. 55 he quotes the definition of enthymeme from Joseph, p. 179.

[19] Evans, *The Osier Cage*, p. 57.

occur only in narration and one complaint (lines 2421–72). Shakespeare seems deliberately to have realized the awkwardness latent in this incident, which arises from a false premise and therefore centres on what Thomas Moisan calls a 'non-event'.[20] In a theatrical setting the audience remains keenly aware of Juliet's actual condition: the actor lies on a bed somewhere on the stage, a physical reminder that this rhetoric has no point. At the same time the idea of death, a continuous presence which materializes in 3.1, evokes a style so exaggerated that it seems to avoid the issue: 'the "instruments of ornament" become instruments for denying and evading the experience of death that they are so ostensibly employed to acknowledge and confront'.[21] As a result of this style and a stage direction in Quarto 1, Charles B. Lower has argued that Shakespeare intended the lamentation as 'purposeful comedy'.[22] Jowett, acting on this interpretation, has *all at once wring their hands and cry out together* in his edition (4.4.67.1–2). Clearly this passage skirts the edge of decorum at every turn.

Apostrophe sets the key of lamentation, and exergasia amplifies the theme. Rephrasing the same idea, distancing it, figures of repetition and prosopopoeia insistently personify both death and time. Although asyndeton gives the lists of adjectives a pronounced sense of rhythm, synonyms accumulate in no particular order: 'Accursed, unhappy, wretched, hateful day!' (line 74). When Capulet and Paris catalogue indignities, modifiers lack a clearly defined object; they shift between the speaker and Juliet: 'Beguiled, divorcèd, wrongèd, spited, slain!' (line 70; cf. line 86). Lady Capulet use antimetabole with a twist that diminishes Juliet (line 77); Paris reaches for synoeciosis, or oxymoron, and misses (line 73); and the recurring epizeuxis – 'cruel, cruel', 'woeful, woeful, woeful', 'ever, ever', 'murder, murder' – suggests characters at a loss for words. Delivering one of the four complaints, the Nurse introduces pleonasmus, empty repetition and a vice of language which accentuates stylistic idiosyncrasies in the other speeches.

As he tries to bring order to this chaos, Friar Laurence gives another well-disposed speech which echoes the prosopopoeia of the laments: 'Confusion's cure lives not / In these confusions'; 'Yet nature's tears are reason's merriment' (lines 92–3, 110). This time he begins with epanalepsis, repetition at the end of a clause of the word with which it began; and he concludes with onedismus, upbraiding those addressed for ingratitude and impiety. In the middle he depends on antanaclasis, a somewhat ponderous repetition of *heaven* five times in nine lines. Sententiae, a character note since his soliloquy in 2.2, again represent experience in binary terms. Along with the other devices they prove effective in this uneasy context: Capulet, chastened and reorganized, applies the Friar's advice with synecdoche and balanced antitheses adapted from Brooke's narrator (lines 2507–14).[23] Finally one rhetoric contains the other; dissimulation limits excess.

Ambivalence, which accompanies disputation and some of the pathos in *Romeo and Juliet*, assumes most importance in the figures of ambiguity which complicate the narrative. As M. M. Mahood has shown in her seminal book, word-play begins with the Prologue and never disappears from the text.[24] Like other rhetorical devices, it interacts with different kinds of figures. Friar Laurence's staid arguments, cited above, include word-play. Often it destabilizes equilibrium, disrupts order, or baffles predictability. It opens a familiar story to new interpretations while making the familiar devices seem inadequate, in themselves, to the demands

[20] 'Rhetoric and the Rehearsal of Death: The "Lamentations" Scene in *Romeo and Juliet*', *Shakespeare Quarterly*, 34 (1983), 391.
[21] Moisan, 'Rhetoric and the Rehearsal of Death', pp. 389–90.
[22] '*Romeo and Juliet*, IV.v.: A Stage Direction and Purposeful Comedy', *Shakespeare Studies*, 8 (1975), 177–94.
[23] This speech is discussed in some detail by both Evans, *The Osier Cage*, pp. 162–4, and Moisan, 'Rhetoric and the Rehearsal of Death', pp. 399–401.
[24] *Shakespeare's Wordplay* (London, 1968), chapter 2.

of narration. It raises many and various questions about rhetoric through techniques that range from blatant to subtle.

The first notable instance of this dynamic occurs in the fourth line of the opening sonnet, 'Where civil blood makes civil hands unclean'. Here the Prologue introduces a rhetorical feature which Harry Levin has identified as a component of the play's symmetry: a form of diacope or ploce which stresses a word by repeating it within a line; a device which will balance more than one hundred verses of the text.[25] In this case the repeated term helps to define contradictions in Verona; it produces an antithesis of concepts, a kind of synoeciosis or oxymoron. The word *civil* applies first to citizens living together in a community (*OED a.*1 quotes this line as its first illustration of the current usage); it refers as well to sharing the advantages of that social condition; and it may also mean 'non-military'. Of course the rest of the line subverts these definitions, the literal and figurative senses of the words denoting violence, disorder, absence of civility. It makes *civil* a more complex word, a type of antanaclasis or syllepsis with more than one meaning.

With the next line ambiguity begins to take the form of identifiable puns: strong alliteration draws attention to *fatal*, which means both 'fateful' and 'deadly'. This key word introduces the idea of destiny, linking it simultaneously with the lovers' experience and the disastrous anger of their fathers. Then the star-crossed pair 'take their life' from fatality, deriving or destroying it in a skewed antithesis, fusing the opening of their love-story with its conclusion. In the ninth line, which joins quatrains through figures of repetition, Mahood locates six puns which 'pose the play's fundamental question at the outset: is its ending frustration or fulfilment? Does Death choose the lovers or do they elect to die?' *Fearful* can mean 'frightened', applying to the lovers' helpless responses, or 'fearsome', indicating the spectators' awed reactions. *Passage* denotes both 'course of events' and 'voyage', its second definition anticipating *traffic* in line 12

and the Petrarchan motif of sea-journey which runs through Romeo's speeches. In addition *passage* means 'death' and enhances the wordplay in *death-marked*, which signifies not only 'marked out for (or by) death', 'foredoomed', but 'having death as their objective'.[26]

With the entrance of Samson and Gregory, parts of the Chorus's narrative materialize on stage in a comic mode. The serving-men caricature not only the content of the Prologue but also its rhetoric. Evans finds 'rhetorical display' in their opening ten lines, devices of logos pushed to the extremities of logical reasoning.[27] Figures of repetition drive the exchange, making each point equally emphatic. Even more striking, the puns which constitute the dialogue reintroduce motifs of anger and violence in another key. Mahood's assessment of them as 'heavy-witted' is, perhaps, misleading.[28] However indelicate, the quibbles derive from a significant word in the Prologue. They translate *rage* to *choler*, multiplying definitions of the latter term which give it concreteness: 'I mean', Samson explains, 'an we be in choler, we'll draw' (line 3). When Gregory says, 'Ay, while you live, draw your neck out of collar', his obvious pun on 'hangman's noose' alludes to the ultimate punishment for indulgence of choler. Using a proverbial expression[29] and blunt paradox, he advises Samson to avoid such a death as long as he lives. At the same time his gallows-joke introduces the legal and retributive components of the plot. When Samson

25 'Form and Formality in *Romeo and Juliet*', *Shakespeare Quarterly*, 11 (1960), rpt. *Shakespeare and the Revolution of the Times* (New York, 1976), pp. 112–13.

26 Mahood, *Shakespeare's Wordplay*, pp. 56–7.

27 Evans, *The Osier Cage*, pp. 19–21.

28 Mahood, *Shakespeare's Wordplay*, p. 60. Evans thinks the pun on *collar* 'trite' but points out that Shakespeare uses it again in *1 Henry IV* 2.5.327–8 (p. 19; line numbers from Jowett's Oxford edition).

29 R. W. Dent, *Shakespeare's Proverbial Language: An Index* (Berkeley, Los Angeles, and London, 1981), compares 'After a collar comes a halter' (c513) and 'To slip (one's neck out of) the collar' (N69).

answers, 'I strike quickly, being moved', he links choler with bawdy, warfare with sex, in banter which will continue to burlesque Petrarchan conceits. At the start of the action, anger and violence occupy more than thirty lines of word-play, as if Shakespeare had combed the places of invention to amplify his subject with humour. He organizes the word-play as a contest which postpones the love-story. In this instance the contest takes place between two men of low order.

This format, word-play as contest, recurs frequently and involves the protagonists. It captures in rhetorical figures a competitive element in the social exchange of Verona. It interferes with the progress of the sequence, delaying the action as it enlarges upon one of its themes or motifs. Often it correlates with invention of another kind: new characters, episodes, or speeches. On their way to the Capulet party at the start of 1.4, Romeo and Mercutio share a series of puns which Evans calls 'a hot, fast match of wits'.[30] An addition to the narrative, this dialogue is less a hot, fast match than an uneven contest: Mercutio repeatedly deflates Romeo's clichés, amplifying love as Samson and Gregory elaborated anger. Again the puns sound obvious and ribald. At times they echo the earlier quibbles on the mechanics of sex:

ROMEO

          You have dancing shoes
With nimble soles; I have a soul of lead
So stakes me to the ground I cannot move.
MERCUTIO
You are a lover; borrow Cupid's wings,
And soar with them above a common bound.
                    (lines 14–18)

When the young men meet the next day in 2.3, they begin an exchange which both recognize as a match. Mercutio appeals to Benvolio as his second in a duel: 'Come between us, good Benvolio. My wits faints' (line 63). Romeo encourages Mercutio to keep up the contest as if he were racing a horse: 'Switch and spurs, switch and spurs, or I'll cry a match' (lines

64–5). With these breaks the dialogue continues for almost fifty lines, often cut in performance, interrupted by the entrance of the Nurse. It returns to words and devices which appeared before in a Petrarchan context: a quibble on *sole*, the antithesis bitter/sweet, the personifying of infatuation. Ultimately it returns to the subject of love, becoming more and more obscene until it stops. Mercutio views this exchange, a concentrated display of rhetorical figures, as the most accomplished kind of social discourse: 'Now art thou sociable, now art thou Romeo, now art thou what thou art by art as well as by nature' (lines 82–3). In his terms the art which complements nature in Romeo may be understood not only as skill but also as rhetoric (*OED sb.* 2a, 3a). Yet this conversation spins words so fast and automatically that it threatens to empty them of meaning:

MERCUTIO Sure wit, follow me this jest now till thou hast worn out thy pump, that when the single sole of it is worn, the jest may remain, after the wearing, solely singular.
ROMEO O single-soled jest, solely singular for the singleness!   (lines 58–62)

In this episode word-play and other figures, agents of sociability, flirt with nonsense. They also create an interlude in the sequence of the love-story.

As a medium of social exchange in *Romeo and Juliet,* this combination of figures resembles other kinds of play: it has a precarious edge where a speaker may lose control of the game; it licenses players to court disaster or mask deception. During a new episode in 3.1 Mercutio challenges Tybalt in rhetorical terms: 'Will you pluck your sword out of his pilcher by the ears? Make haste, lest mine be about your ears ere it be out' (lines 79–80). Tybalt, who never responds to Mercutio's verbal sparring, takes this dare literally. Mercutio dies in character, famously, with a series of puns and other figures. No longer part of a competition,

---

[30] Evans, *The Osier Cage*, p. 71

the devices now convey disbelief and outrage. In the aftermath of this scene word-play will fuse with various schemes to negotiate risky situations through subterfuge. Juliet in particular depends on equivocation to communicate with her family and with Paris.

When Lady Capulet condemns 'that same villain Romeo' in 3.5, Juliet both agrees and disagrees with her. Brooke has Juliet confuse her mother with a single enigma (lines 1802–8); Shakespeare creates a new version of this exchange through the figure asteismus: 'the answerer catches a certain word and throws it back to the first speaker with an unexpected twist, an unlooked for meaning. It usually has a mocking or scoffing character, ...'[31] In the drama Juliet plays a one-sided game which continues until her mother, oblivious, changes the topic. Romeo will receive 'an unaccustomed dram', promises Lady Capulet, 'And then I hope thou wilt be satisfied' (lines 90–2). Juliet answers:

> Indeed, I never shall be satisfied
> With Romeo till I behold him, dead,
> Is my poor heart so for a kinsman vexed.
>
> (lines 93–5)

Mahood points out a triple ambiguity in these lines, 'with one meaning for Juliet, another for her mother and a third for us, the audience: Juliet will never in fact see Romeo again until she wakes and finds him dead beside her'.[32] For us *dead* connects with both *him* and *heart*, word-play that most editors since Pope heighten by setting it off with dashes (Quarto 2 has a period after *him*). In addition, as Brian Gibbons demonstrates, Juliet's quibbles on *satisfied* and *kinsman* permit these lines five different readings.[33]

A short time later, in an encounter invented for the next scene, Juliet engages Paris in almost twenty lines of stichomythia which keep him at a distance until he prepares to leave Friar Laurence's cell. Again she relies on asteismus, combining it with devices such as sententia, antithesis, and paradox:

JULIET
> That is no slander, sir, which is a truth,
> And what I spake, I spake it to my face.

PARIS
> Thy face is mine, and thou hast slandered it.

JULIET
> It may be so, for it is not mine own. — (lines 33–6)

In this passage, as in 3.5, the context turns this form of word-play into other figures: noema, an obscure or subtle speech; and schematismus, circuitous speech.[34] For a while Juliet manages to hold events in check, moment by moment and tenuously, by rhetorical means.

Clearly rhetorical figures in *Romeo and Juliet* not only amplify the narrative but also call attention to the processes of amplification. Like the playwright's exploration of the sonnet, this focus on his medium seems deliberate, self-conscious. Several well-known passages labour devices as if they were inviting a critical assessment of both the schemes and their effects. What strikes modern sensibility as sheer flamboyance is probably a figure stretched beyond its usual range, performing a more complex function. At 3.2.45–50, Juliet's frenzied series of puns on aye/i/I/eye produces three effects: the sound of high-pitched keening; the sustaining of eye imagery from the prothalamium just delivered; and the manifestation of profound psychological disturbance.[35] In this scene, lines 73–85, and 1.1.173–8, extended passages of synoeciosis, condensed paradox or oxymoron, project confused emotions and points of view: Romeo's about Rosaline; Juliet's about Romeo, who has just killed Tybalt. The formal, imprecise figures express what the speakers feel but fit their subjects awkwardly.

Perhaps Mercutio's Queen Mab speech at

---

[31] Joseph, *Shakespeare's Use of the Arts of Language*, p. 167.

[32] Mahood, *Shakespeare's Wordplay*, p. 71.

[33] Brian Gibbons, ed., *Romeo and Juliet*, The Arden Shakespeare (London and New York, 1980), 3.5.94n.

[34] Jane Freeman, a Ph.D. student at the University of Toronto, showed me how the figures work in 4.1.

[35] Mahood, *Shakespeare's Wordplay*, p. 70.

1.4.56–96 offers the most elaborate array of rhetorical devices in a passage invented for the text. It stands far enough apart from the sequence that E. Pearlman considers it an interpolation: 'Mercutio's excursus is not articulated with the remainder of *Romeo and Juliet* in terms of plot, content, language, or intellection. There is no overlap between the realist, materialist Mercutio and the Mercutio who celebrates Queen Mab in elaborate, imaginative, and romantic terms'.[36] His conclusions about Mercutio notwithstanding, Pearlman raises an important issue by emphasizing the singularity of the speech: Mercutio takes up the subject of dreams, introduced by Romeo but absent from the other narratives at this point, and amplifies it for forty lines.

Evans calls Mercutio's performance 'a demonstration of rhetorical fireworks', and he claims that no Elizabethan writer would employ so many figures without intending to make the passage conspicuous.[37] From the start Shakespeare extends the use of anaphora and zeugma (one verb serving more than one clause), outdoing the illustrations in contemporary textbooks. These grammatical devices frame other kinds of schemes from apostrophe to figures of ambiguity and ominatio, or prognostication of evil. At the end Romeo's interruption results in an ellipsis which may be more abrupt than a modern audience realizes. Mab was known for bringing young women dreams of their future husbands or lovers; Mercutio never reaches this climactic stage in his portrayal of her.

Scattered through the text, a number of passages seem to reflect explicitly on the play's use of rhetoric. The first and most obvious follows Romeo's apostrophe to love in a burst of contradictions. 'Dost thou not laugh?', he asks Benvolio. The answer, 'No, coz, I rather weep', compounds the deflation even as it directs the exchange towards more derivative paradoxes (1.1.180). In the wedding scene Juliet makes a comment about decorum which applies not only to Romeo's language but also to the play's:

Conceit, more rich in matter than in words,
Brags of his substance, not of ornament.

(2.5.30–1)

However the audience interprets *conceit* – as idea, understanding, imagination, or device – Juliet rejects Romeo's invitation to verbalize their experience in formal terms. Of course she does so rhetorically, in a speech which elaborates its subject through word-play, polyptoton, and an epigram. At the end of 4.4. Peter and the musicians provide a more extensive commentary. As Moisan explains this episode, these characters subject the operations of rhetoric to common sense, take amplification literally, and deconstruct a phrase from Richard Edwardes's *Paradyse of Daynty Devises* (1576), 'a compendium of the lachrymose rhetoric we have heard *fortissime* throughout the mourners' speeches'.[38] Juliet's famous (and vexed) question in 2.1 may also refer to the medium she speaks:

What's in a name? That which we call a rose
By any other word would smell as sweet.

(lines 85–6)

In *Shakespeare and the Rhetoricians*, Marion Trousdale makes a distinction which states what these lines imply:

Shape is something absolute and suggests parts whose functions, once determined, are irrevocably fixed. A rose in that sense is a rose. But one cannot say the same thing about its name, which, like language itself, is artificial. A name can, at will, both define and embellish, and, unlike the rose, it can divide 'one thing entire to many objects' (*Richard II*, 2.2.17).[39]

---

36 E. Pearlman, 'Shakespeare at Work: *Romeo and Juliet*', *English Literary Renaissance*, 24 (1994), 332. See note 20 on 332–3 for a summary of criticism which argues that the speech is relevant.

37 Evans, *The Osier Cage*, pp. 81, 86. My paragraph on Mercutio's Queen Mab speech condenses Evans's detailed analysis, pp. 73–86.

38 Moisan, 'Rhetoric and the Rehearsal of Death', p. 402.

39 (Chapel Hill, N.C., 1982), p. 157.

Romeo and Juliet allows its audience to measure the advantages of such embellishment against its limitations.

That kind of engagement animates other literary works of the late sixteenth century, as critics like Altman, Kinney, and Rebhorn have demonstrated.[40] It informs Shakespeare's Sonnets and narrative verse as well as his early plays: Lanham shows how it affects *Venus and Adonis*, *Lucrece*, and the Sonnets; Trousdale analyses *Love's Labour's Lost*.[41] In most of these texts rhetoric, vigorous and accomplished, comes up against barriers of its own making, rigidities inherent in language. Its processes expose the sources of intractableness: the inability of words, even large numbers of words, to express for their speakers the real conditions of their lives; the potential for amplification to grow out of control.[42] According to Altman, Renaissance tragedy takes a particularly dim view of rhetoric: '... invention fails, as in comedy, because it cannot transcend man's epistemological condition and attain to truth – and it fails because it deals with a world in which will, not reason, determines human actions'.[43] All of these texts exploit and doubt rhetoric at the same time, raising questions not only about the art itself but also about rhetoricians and the culture that fosters them.[44]

In *Romeo and Juliet* Shakespeare worked at rhetoric; there is evidence of revision in extravagant passages like Juliet's extended synoeciosis in 3.2.[45] Schemes appear everywhere until the end: they are heard in the speeches of the Chief Watchman (5.3.178–9), the prelude to Friar Laurence's self-defence (5.3.222–34), and Prince Escalus's closing words. Just as the play tests the flexibility and compass of sonnet conventions, it explores the capacity of rhetoric to rationalize human conduct in moving terms. It pursues this investigation with the ambivalence that Kenneth Muir has recognized in Shakespeare's early works.[46] Argument inevitably leads to error, accident, and death, as it did in the Romeo and Juliet fictions. Rhetorical schemes may interrupt the sequence but they fail to change it in any substantive way. While figures amplify events, da Porto's plot and characters move inexorably towards their tragic conclusion. Rhetoric cannot overcome necessity or describe it with precision. Yet it can present the full range of ambiguities that surround every human act. Despite its limitations, rhetorical virtuosity in *Romeo and Juliet* allows more than one interpretation of both events and the verbal medium through which they travel. It releases the old narrative to tell a new story.

---

[40] See Joel B. Altman, *The Tudor Play of Mind: Rhetorical Inquiry and the Development of Elizabethan Drama* (Berkeley, Los Angeles, and London, 1978), and the books by Kinney and Rebhorn.

[41] Lanham, *The Motives of Eloquence*, chapters 4 and 5; Trousdale, *Shakespeare and the Rhetoricians*, pp. 95–113.

[42] Rebhorn, *The Emperor of Men's Minds*, makes these points on p. 235.

[43] Altman, *The Tudor Play of Mind*, p. 230.

[44] See Rebhorn, *The Emperor of Men's Minds*, especially chapter 2.

[45] See Pearlman's article, 'Shakespeare at Work', pp. 317–21, for the connection between rhetoric and revision in Quarto 2.

[46] 'Shakespeare and Rhetoric', *Shakespeare Jahrbuch*, 90 (1954), 46–68.

'DEATH-MARKED LOVE': DESIRE AND PRESENCE IN *ROMEO AND JULIET*

LLOYD DAVIS

I

The action of *Romeo and Juliet* occurs between two speeches proclaiming the lovers' deaths – the prologue's forecast of events and the prince's closing summary. The vicissitudes of desire take place in this unusual period, after life yet before death. It is a kind of liminal phase in which social and personal pressures build to intense pitch before they are settled. Such liminal tension, as Victor Turner suggests, is the very stuff of which social dramas are made.[1] It figures a mounting crisis that envelops those observing and taking part in the unfolding action. At the same time, this temporal setting has a range of interpretative implications.

With the lovers' deaths announced from the start, audience attention is directed to the events' fateful course. The question is less what happens than how it happens. By framing the action in this way, the prologue triggers various generic and narrative effects. First, it establishes the play as 'a tragedy of fate' similar to Kyd's *The Spanish Tragedy*, which gives 'the audience a superior knowledge of the story from the outset, reducing the hero's role to bring into prominence the complex patterns of action'.[2] In turn, this generic marker initiates a compelling narrative, poised between prolepsis and analepsis, as opening portents of death are played off against background details and further intimations in the following scenes.[3] The tension between these hints and flashbacks fills the narrative with foreboding. The breakneck speed

of events (in contrast to the extended time frame of Arthur Brooke's version, a few days as opposed to nine months)[4] sees the ordained end bear relentlessly on the lovers. They are caught between a determining past and future.

The narrative has a further generic analogue. Gayle Whittier suggests that the play develops through a contrast between sonnet lyricism and tragedy that is finally reconciled in death: 'the "spoken lines" of the Prologue predestine the plot of the play to be tragic from without, even as the spirit of Petrarchan poetry spoken by Romeo to Juliet finally necessitates their tragic deaths from within'.[5] What first appears as thematic conflict between two of the period's key literary modes makes way for a troubling similarity. The spirit of Petrarchism is revealed as tragically fatal and idealized romance collapses.

In this view, *Romeo and Juliet* stages the outcome of unfulfillable desire. Although it appears to reverse the erotic story told in the Sonnets, the dramatic narrative ends up

---

1   *Drama, Fields, and Metaphors: Symbolic Action in Human Society* (Ithaca, 1974), pp. 40–1 and *passim*.

2   Brian Gibbons, Introduction, in *Romeo and Juliet* (London, 1980), p. 37.

3   On analepsis and prolepsis, see Shlomith Rimmon-Kenan, *Narrative Fiction: Contemporary Poetics* (London, 1983), pp. 46ff.

4   Gibbons, Introduction, p. 54.

5   Gayle Whittier, 'The Sonnet's Body and the Body Sonnetized in *Romeo and Juliet*', *Shakespeare Quarterly*, 40 (1989), 27–41; p. 40.

57

LLOYD DAVIS

paralleling the failing course of identity and desire which can be traced through those poems. There the poet reluctantly finds his desire shifting from the self-gratifying potential figured by the youth to the disarming dark lady, who offers instead 'a desire that her very presence at the same time will frustrate'.[6] This pattern initially seems to be inverted in the play – Romeo willingly renounces self-centred longing for Rosaline, Juliet tests and proves her self-reliance, both find true love in each other. However, their love ends in reciprocal death, with the Petrarchan images fatally embodied and materialized. The links between love and death unveil a dark scepticism about desire, despite bursts of romantic idealism. They convey a sense of futility and ironic fate which Romeo momentarily feels but is able to forget for a time, 'my mind misgives / Some consequence yet hanging in the stars / Shall bitterly begin his fearful date / With this night's revels' (1.4.106–9).

Such scepticism appears in many subsequent literary and psychoanalytic conceptions, where possibilities of romantic union are queried.[7] These questions carry implications about selfhood and desire and about ways of representing them. In theories and stories of divorce or isolation, selfhood is not effaced but conceived as incomplete; as Barbara Freedman puts it, 'The denial of self-presence doesn't negate presence but redefines it as a distancing or spacing we always seek but fail to close'.[8] Characters cannot attain their goals, and the inability to claim satisfaction affects desire as much as selfhood. Proceeding from an uncertain source, desire remains 'predicated on lack, and even its apparent fulfilment is also a moment of loss'.[9] In this view, desire and presence are forever intertwined: 'Differantiated [sic] presence, which is always and inevitably differed and deferred, and which in consequence exceeds the alternatives of presence and absence, is the condition of desire'.[10] They forestall each other's wholeness yet continue to provide the self with images of consummation, contentment and victory – the

curtsies, kisses, suits, livings and battles which Mercutio's dreamers envisage but cannot clasp, 'Begot of nothing but vain fantasy, / Which is as thin of substance as the air, / And more inconstant than the wind' (1.4.98–100).

The recurrence of this viewpoint in fiction and theory suggests that *Romeo and Juliet* stages a paradigmatic conflict between ways of representing and interpreting desire. The play affects these possibilities by placing idealized and tragic conceptions of desire and selfhood in intense dialogue with each other. This dialogue continues to be played out in literary and theoretical texts since, as Alan Sinfield notes, notions of sexuality and gender are 'major sites of ideological production upon which meanings of very diverse kinds are established and contested'.[11] *Romeo and Juliet* informs and illustrates a cultural history of desire in which images of romantic fulfilment or failure carry great importance.

As well as being part of this history, Shakespeare's play has two other distinctive temporal

---

6 Joel Fineman, *Shakespeare's Perjured Eye: The Invention of Poetic Subjectivity in the Sonnets* (Berkeley, 1986), p. 24.
7 Two of the primary psychoanalytic texts are *Civilization and Its Discontents*, and *Beyond the Pleasure Principle*. A clear reading of this direction in Freud is offered by Jean Laplanche, *Life and Death in Psychoanalysis*, trans. Jeffrey Mehlman (Baltimore, 1976): 'the death drive is the very soul, the constitutive principle of libidinal circulation' (p. 124). Related scepticism underlies Lacan's view of the link between desire and demand. Desire is dependent on demand, but demand, 'by being articulated in signifiers, leaves a metonymic remainder that runs under it … an element that is called desire': desire leads only to desire. See *The Four Fundamental Concepts of Psycho-Analysis*, trans. Alan Sheridan (New York, 1981), p. 154; compare Catherine Belsey's gloss of Lacan's view – 'desire subsists in what eludes both vision and representation, in what exceeds demand, including the demand for love' – in *Desire: Love Stories in Western Culture* (Oxford, 1994), p. 139.
8 *Staging the Gaze: Postmodernism, Psychoanalysis, and Shakespearean Comedy* (Ithaca, 1991), p. 110.
9 Belsey, *Desire*, pp. 38–9.
10 Ibid., p. 70.
11 *Faultlines: Cultural Materialism and the Politics of Dissident Reading* (Oxford, 1992), p. 128.

features. First, as noted above, it unfolds over a charged time span. Time allows desire to be acted out but also threatens its fulfilment, by either running out or not stopping. This equivocal link affects desire's tragic course in *Romeo and Juliet*, 'as the time and place / Doth make against' the characters (5.3.223–4).

Secondly, its depiction of desire reverberates with erotic tropes from earlier traditions – Platonic, Ovidian, Petrarchan, as well as popular sayings. These tropes are used by the characters to talk and think about relationships, but they are also challenged for not allowing the gap between self and other to be bridged. They are unfulfilling since it feels as if they belong to someone else; as Astrophil puts it, 'others' feet still seemed but strangers in my way'.[12] The lovers are often dissatisfied with or unsure about the words of others. Their discontent grows from early dismissals such as Romeo's 'Yet tell me not, for I have heard it all' (1.1.171) and 'Thou talk'st of nothing' (1.4.96), or Juliet's 'And stint thou, too, I pray thee, Nurse' (1.3.60), to deeper disquiet over the inability of this language to match their experience: 'Thou canst not speak of that thou dost not feel' (3.3.64); 'Some say the lark makes sweet division; / This doth not so, for she divideth us' (3.5.29–30). The corollary of their frustration with the language of others and of the past is the value they put on their own: 'She speaks. / O, speak again, bright angel' (2.1.67–8); 'every tongue that speaks / But Romeo's name speaks heavenly eloquence' (3.2.32–3).

Like the lovers, the play also seeks to revise existing rhetorical conventions. It reworks these tropes into personal, tragic terms which underlie later literary and psychological conceptions. Hence, in addition to exemplifying Stephen Greenblatt's point that 'psychoanalysis is the historical outcome of certain characteristic Renaissance strategies',[13] *Romeo and Juliet* shows that these strategies develop in response to earlier discourses. The play's pivotal role in later depictions of desire stems from the way it juxtaposes historical and emergent conceptions.

These complex temporal and rhetorical effects are hinted at in the Prologue, which repeatedly sets past, present and future against each other. 'Our scene' is initially laid in a kind of continuous present, yet one that remains hanging between 'ancient grudge' and 'new mutiny'. Likewise, the 'star-crossed lovers take their life' in a present whose intimations of living and loving are circumscribed by 'the fatal loins' of 'their parents' strife'. As the birth-suicide pun on 'take their life' hints, sexuality is already marked by violence and death, its future determined by the past's impact on the present. The Prologue ends by anchoring the staging of 'death-marked love' in the here and now of the audience, who attend 'the two-hours' traffic of our stage'. It anticipates a successful theatrical conclusion, with the play's performance 'striv[ing] to mend' what the lovers 'shall miss' – a kind of closure that their desire cannot realize. In contrast to the simple linear Chorus to Act 2, which culminates in the lovers' union, the rebounding moments of the Prologue displace consummation with death.[14]

A complicity between sex and death is well known in Renaissance texts. Its function in *Romeo and Juliet* is, however, distinguished by temporal shifts which define the characters' relations. While the lovers in a poem such as Donne's 'The Canonization' exceed worldly time and place, and their post-coital condition is eternally celebrated, in Shakespeare's play the links between past and present, social and personal, cannot be transcended. The intense

---

[12] *Sir Philip Sidney: Selected Poems*, ed. Katherine Duncan-Jones (Oxford, 1973), p. 117. As discussed below, this first sonnet's turn to a seemingly authentic self is also made in *Romeo and Juliet*.

[13] Stephen Greenblatt, 'Psychoanalysis and Renaissance Culture', in *Literary Theory / Renaissance Texts*, ed. Patricia Parker and David Quint (Baltimore, 1986), 210–24; p. 224.

[14] 'But passion lends them power, time means, to meet, / Tempering extremities with extreme sweet' (2 Chor. 13–14). The Chorus, not included in first Quarto, is reprinted in the Arden edition (see n. 2).

oneness felt by the lovers appears to signify mutual presence, but such intersubjective moments are overlaid with social and historical pressures. The drama alternates between instants of passion, when time seems to stand still, and inevitable returns to the ongoing rush of events. This contrast is manifested not only in the characterization and plot but in the interplay of underlying traditions, sources and tropes. The play reiterates and revises these conventions, confirming a conception of desire that speeds not to its goal but its end. In this conception personal presence can exist only as a transient, illusory sign of desire.

II

One of the main influences *Romeo and Juliet* has had on later depictions of love lies in its celebration of personal desire. The force of this celebration comes partly from its dramatic mode, staging the lovers' experiences for a 'live' audience. In the decades after the play was first performed, poetry (till then, the key romantic discourse) was changing from oral to written modes. Until the rise of the novel, drama remained the pre-eminent form for presenting love stories, and stage performance could give these tales the confessional tones which earlier forms of poetic recitation doubtless achieved. The Prologue enacts this shift by relocating the love sonnet in the drama, a move again underlined by the verse which the lovers will soon share in Act 1, scene 5.

On stage, the impact of the 'personal' can come across in different ways – through physical, verbal, even interpersonal performance. In *Romeo and Juliet* these forms of presence concentrate in the protagonists' unshakeable love. It seems to assume an essential quality which captures the 'diachronic unity of the subject'.[15] This unity underwrites numerous adaptations of and responses to the play, from elaborate stage productions, operas and ballets, to more popular versions such as the American musical *West-Side Story* or the Australian narrative verse of C. J.

Dennis's *A Sentimental Bloke*, whose colloquial tones add to the impression of true romance. For many audience groups, each of these transformations once again discovers the play's 'spirit', which surpasses local differences to reveal truths about desire and 'ourselves'.

The director's programme notes to a recently well-received production in Australia illustrate this kind of response. The mixed tones of confession and authority sway the audience to accept his views:

My fascination with this play continues. Considerable research over the years has taken me twice to Verona and Mantua, but the conflict in Bosnia has brought the work urgently closer. I first considered a Muslim-Christian setting several months before the tragedy of Bosko and Admira ... A study of the text supplies no religious, class, nor race barriers between the 'two households' and this makes Shakespeare's vision all the more powerful. When differences are minimal, ancient grudges seem the more difficult to understand. Yet they remain with us today, passed on by our parents. It seems the one thing we teach the next generation is how to maintain rage and other forms of prejudices. Thus this work is as much about young people in the Brisbane Mall today as it is about the hot days in medieval Verona ... The human spirit, as portrayed by the 31 year old playwright, is a thing of wonder to be nurtured and treasured.[16]

The paradoxical effects of citing 'real' personal and political situations are first to detach the drama from its own historical concerns and then to efface the ideological grounds of the current crisis. The revelation of 'human spirit' triumphs over any tragic significance. Indeed, the play's freedom from material contexts testifies to its, its author's, and our affirming 'vision'. This viewpoint recalls Coleridge's claim that Shakespeare is 'out of time', his characters 'at once

---

15 Catherine Belsey, *The Subject of Tragedy: Identity and Difference in Renaissance Drama* (London, 1985), p. 34.

16 Aubrey Mellor, 'From the Artistic Director', in Queensland Theatre Company Program for *Romeo and Juliet* (Brisbane, 1993), p. 3.

true to nature, and fragments of the divine mind that drew them'.[17]

Because it hides sexual, class and ethnic factors behind archetypal human experience, this sort of perception of Shakespeare's work becomes a target of materialist criticism:

Idealised and romanticised out of all dialectical relationship with society, it [Shakespeare's work] takes on the seductive glamour of aestheticism, the sinister and self-destructive beauty of decadent romance ... this 'Shakespeare myth' functions in contemporary culture as an ideological framework for containing consensus and for sustaining myths of unity, integration and harmony in the cultural superstructures of a divided and fractured society.[18]

In relation to sexual issues, universal images of the personal in *Romeo and Juliet* can be seen as helping to naturalize notions of desire which reinforce an 'ideology of romantic love' in terms of 'heterosexualizing idealization' and the 'canonization of heterosexuality'.[19] Personal romance and desire are revealed as authoritative codes which conceal and impose official sexuality.

The kinds of ideological impacts that the 'personal' registers may be intensified *or* interrogated by the generic effects of 'Excellent conceited Tragedie', as the Quarto titles announce. The combination of personal experience and tragic consequence can turn *Romeo and Juliet* into an account of contradictory notions of desire and identity, in line with Jonathan Dollimore's recognition that, notwithstanding traditions of celebration 'in terms of man's defeated potential', tragedy questions ideological norms.[20] The genre's ambiguous drift to 'radical' or cathartic ends sees the play assume a kind of meta-textual disinterestedness, distanced from final interpretations as it seems to reflect on how desire may be conceived and staged. This distance can be observed in the play's citing and reworking of tropes and conventions from existing discourses of love and romance. The intertextual traces reveal continuities and changes in the depiction of desire, keyed to social and historical notions of the personal and interpersonal.

Platonism is traditionally seen as offering a set of tropes that affirm selfhood and desire as forms of true being despite possibilities of loss.[21] In the *Symposium*, for instance, Socrates defines love as desire for what one lacks, either a specific quality or a lost or missing element of the self. Aristophanes goes so far as to image love as a 'longing for and following after [a] primeval wholeness ... the healing of our disseuered nature'. The *Symposium* deals with this incipiently tragic situation by redirecting desire to the heavens; in a comedic resolution, love's lack is fulfilled by catching sight of 'the very soul of beauty ... beauty's very self'.[22] Such vision provides the model for Renaissance Petrarchism.

This model is famously reproduced in Pietro Bembo's Neoplatonic paean to divine love at the close of Castiglione's *The Courtier*. He recounts 'a most happie end for our desires', as the courtier forsakes sensual desire for a wiser

---

[17] Samuel Taylor Coleridge, *Lectures on Shakespeare and Other Poets and Dramatists*, Everyman's Library (London: Dent, 1914), p. 410.

[18] Graham Holderness, Preface: 'All this', in *The Shakespeare Myth*, ed. Graham Holderness (Manchester, 1988), pp. xii–xiii.

[19] See Dympna Callaghan, 'The Ideology of Romantic Love: The Case of *Romeo and Juliet*', in Dympna Callaghan, Lorraine Helms and Jyotsna Singh, *The Weyward Sisters: Shakespeare and Feminist Politics* (Oxford, 1994), pp. 59–101; Jonathan Goldberg, '*Romeo and Juliet*'s Open Rs', in *Queering the Renaissance*, ed. Jonathan Goldberg (Durham, 1994), 218–35; p. 227; and Joseph A. Porter, 'Marlowe, Shakespeare, and the Canonization of Heterosexuality', *South Atlantic Quarterly*, 88 (1989), 127–47.

[20] *Radical Tragedy: Religion, Ideology and Power in the Age of Shakespeare and His Contemporaries* (Chicago, 1984), p. 49.

[21] Cf. Michel Foucault, *The Use of Pleasure*, vol. 2 of *The History of Sexuality*, trans. Robert Hurley (New York, 1990), p. 5 and *passim*.

[22] *Symposium*, in *The Collected Dialogues of Plato*, ed. Edith Hamilton and Huntington Cairns (Princeton, 1985), 193a–c, 211d–e.

love that guides the soul: 'through the particular beautie of one bodie hee guideth her to the universall beautie of all bodies ... Thus the soule kindled in the most holy fire of true heavenly love, fleeth to couple her self with the nature of Angels'. This 'most holy love' is 'derived of the unitie of the heavenly beautie, goodnesse and wisedom', and in narrating its course Bembo himself undergoes an ecstatic loss of identity. He speaks as if 'ravished and beside himselfe', and emphasizes that 'I have spoken what the holy furie of love hath (unsought for) indited to me'.[23] Speaking and experiencing true desire are related forms of self-transcendence, and Bembo can rejoice in the loss of selfhood.

Similar experience underpins the double structure of Edmund Spenser's *Fowre Hymnes*, first published in 1596, around the time *Romeo and Juliet* was written. The hymn in honour of earthly love characterizes the lover as Tantalus, feeding 'his hungrie fantasy, / Still full, yet neuer satisfyde ... For nought may quench his infinite desyre'. This figure is recast in the corresponding hymn of heavenly love, where the poet renounces his earlier poems – 'lewd layes' which showed love as a 'mad fit' – for a lover linked to 'high eternall powre'.[24] In these instances, the lack or absence which motivates love is conceived positively, part of a spiritual response which lifts the lover beyond temporal identity. Through its philosophic or poetic utterance, the self is not destroyed but surpassed.

However, the link between lack and love can also affect selfhood less positively, even fatally. Classical texts again offer tropes and characters to Renaissance authors. Ovid depicts less drastic versions of desire and self-loss in the changes that Jove makes to pursue various nymphs. These can be read in varying ways – on the one hand, a carnivalesque switching of sexual roles for the sake of pleasure; on the other, a sequence of illusory identities that offers no final fulfilment. Though Jove's transformations bring different degrees of satisfaction, none is tragi-

cally oriented (at least for himself). In contrast, the tale of Narcissus sets desire and selfhood in irresolvable conflict. In Arthur Golding's 1567 translation of the *Metamorphoses*, Narcissus gazes into the pond to find that 'He knowes not what it was he sawe. And yet the foolishe elfe / Doth burn in ardent love thereof. The verie selfe same thing / That doeth bewitch and blinde his eyes, encreaseth all his sting'.[25] His desire cannot be satisfied, and the attempt to do so pains and then destroys selfhood.

Opposing notions of genre, time and character underlie these figures of ecstasy and loss. Platonic and Neoplatonic transcendence is marked by timelessness and selflessness. It brings narration and character to an end, as the self enjoys eternal fusion with the other. In comparison, Ovidian images of disguised or deluded self-loss entail conflict within or between characters. These interactions rely on distinct, often opposed, figures who respond to each other through time. Their fates frequently impose eternities of lonely, unfulfilled selfhood.

Platonic images of true desire and identity are invoked in Shakespeare's comedies during the 1590s; but even there, as characters move to romantic union, they are usually questioned. The disguises, confusions and mistakes through which love's destiny is reached may suggest random or enforced effects that unsettle 'nature's bias'. In a less equivocal way, Shakespeare's use of Ovidian images of desire and selfhood tends to limit or foreclose positive readings, especially where narcissistic traces are discerned. This tendency takes place in both comic and tragic genres: 'Like Ovid's tales, Shakespeare's comedies never lose sight of the

23 Baldassare Castiglione, *The Book of the Courtier*, trans. Sir Thomas Hoby (London, 1948), pp. 319–22.
24 *Fowre Hymnes*, 'A Hymne in Honovr of Love' (lines 197–203) and 'A Hymne in Honovr of Heavenly Love' (lines 8–28), in *Spenser: Poetical Works*, ed. J. C. Smith and E. de Selincourt (Oxford, 1979).
25 *Shakespeare's Ovid: Being Arthur Golding's Translation of the 'Metamorphoses'*, ed. W. H. D. Rouse (Carbondale, 1961), book 3: lines 540–2.

painfulness and the potential for the grotesque or for disaster wrought by love's changes ... If part of the Ovidianism of the comedies is their potential for violence and tragedy, it would seem logical to expect that Ovidianism to be developed in the tragedies'.[26] In *Venus and Adonis*, for example, the humour of the goddess's overweening desire and her beloved's petulance changes to grim consequence. 'The field's chief flower' (line 8) is mournfully plucked, recalling Narcissus's end, 'A purple flower sprung up, chequered with white, / Resembling well his pale cheeks, and the blood / Which in round drops upon their whiteness stood' (lines 1168–70). The characters have shared an ironic desire whose deathly goal was unwittingly imaged by Venus, 'Narcissus so himself himself forsook, / And died to kiss his shadow in the brook' (lines 161–2). As noted earlier, comparable effects occur throughout *Romeo and Juliet*, where moments of romantic union are disrupted by ongoing events that undercut their idealism. The mixed genres in these tales represent desire as a hybrid of the comic, tragic and ironic.[27]

Related images of threatening or incomplete desire and self-transformation are repeated through many sixteenth- and seventeenth-century texts, from the angst of sonneteers to Montaigne's musings in the *Apologie of Raymond Sebond* on 'The lustfull longing which allures us to the acquaintance of women, [and] seekes but to expell that paine, which an earnest and burning desire doth possesse-us-with, and desireth but to allay it thereby to come to rest, and be exempted from this fever'.[28] As most of these references suggest, this notion of erotic jeopardy is almost always tied to masculine conceptions of desire and selfhood. The pains of desire are indulged if not celebrated, and they may convert to misogyny, as in Hamlet's tirade against Ophelia or Romeo's charge that Juliet's beauty 'hath made me effeminate' (3.1.114).

This attitude echoes through Romeo's early laments about Rosaline. As Coleridge noted, he is 'introduced already love-bewildered':[29] 'I

have lost myself. I am not here. / This is not Romeo; he's some other where' (1.1.194–5). Amid these tones of despair a self-satisfied note can be heard. The early Romeo is a 'virtual stereotype of the romantic lover',[30] whose role-playing brings a kind of egotistic reassurance. The lament for self-loss becomes proof of self-presence, a 'boastful positiveness',[31] with Romeo still to know the unsettling force of desire.

From this point, the play proceeds by exploring the limits of the Platonic, Ovidian and Petrarchan tropes. The seriousness of narcissistic absorption is questioned (underlined by Mercutio's quips at romantic indulgence);[32] yet the full consequence of desire is not realized in Platonic union but deferred to its aftermath. None of the conventional models can quite convey what is at stake in the lovers' story, and the discourse of desire must be revised.

III

Clearly, then, *Romeo and Juliet* invents neither tragic nor personal notions of desire. Both are strongly at work in Shakespeare's direct source, Brooke's *The Tragicall Historye of Romeus and Juliet* (1562): the threats to selfhood caused by

[26] Jonathan Bate, *Shakespeare and Ovid* (Oxford, 1993), p. 173. Bate emphasizes Actaeon as another figure of self-consuming desire (p. 19 and *passim*).

[27] Cf. George Bataille's conceptions of eros as 'laughable', tragic and 'arousing irony', and of 'The complicity of the tragic – which is the basis of death – with sexual pleasure and laughter': *The Tears of Eros*, trans. Peter Connor (San Francisco, 1990), pp. 53 and 66.

[28] Michel de Montaigne, *Essays*, trans. John Florio (London, 1980), vol. 2, pp. 192–3.

[29] Coleridge, *Lectures*, p. 103.

[30] Harry Levin, 'Form and Formality in *Romeo and Juliet*', in *Twentieth-Century Interpretations of 'Romeo and Juliet': A Collection of Critical Essays*, ed. Douglas Cole (Englewood Cliffs, N.J., 1970), 85–95; p. 86.

[31] Coleridge, *Lectures*, p. 103.

[32] Joseph A. Porter emphasizes that Mercutio's opposition is to romantic love not to sex: *Shakespeare's Mercutio: His History and Drama* (Chapel Hill, 1988), p. 103.

love; the workings of 'False Fortune' and 'wavering Fortunes whele'; an intense desire that can be quenched 'onely [by] death and both theyr bloods'; time as tragic and ironic, first intimated in woe at Juliet's 'untimely death' and then gaining full significance as Romeus's man tells him 'too soone' of her end.[33]

While it reiterates these ideas, Shakespeare's play also develops and sharpens the connections among desire, the personal and the tragic. The lovers create new images of individuality and of togetherness in order to leave their worldly selves behind. Yet their efforts remain circumscribed by social forces. The ironic result is that the ideal identities the lovers fashion in order to realize their desire become the key to its tragic loss. Self-transcendence can be experienced but not as a kind of timeless ecstasy; instead it becomes entwined with unfulfilled desire.

The play personalizes desire in ways which constantly alternate between idealism and failure. As Kay Stockholder notes, threats to desire are 'externalized' and the lovers consciously create 'a radiant world apart by attributing all inimical forces to surrounding circumstance'.[34] In this reordering of reality, desire becomes part or even constitutive of private, individual identity. Romeo and Juliet's love is secret from others and transgresses the roles imposed by their families. In *The Petite Pallace of Pettie his Pleasure* (1576), George Pettie considered this opposition the key to the story: 'such presiness of parents brought Pyramus and Thisbe to a woful end, Romeo and Julietta to untimely death'.[35] In *A Midsummer Night's Dream* and *Romeo and Juliet*, resisting or contesting patriarchal authority allows a temporary move towards selfhood.

Through this contest, love appears to be one's own, yet both plays show the impossibility of holding onto it. The personal is as elusive as it is idealized, destined to slip back into constraining and distorting social forms. In retrospect, we may see this elusiveness prefigured in the lovers' first meeting, an intense bonding that occurs amid an elaborate ritual of masks and misrecognition. The symbolic means through which love must be expressed will prevent its consummation.[36] For the moment, however, love beholds a single object of desire, whose truth authenticates the lover and recreates both their identities: 'Deny thy father and refuse thy name, / Or if thou wilt not, be but sworn my love, / And I'll no longer be a Capulet ... Call me but love and I'll be new baptized. / Henceforth I never will be Romeo' (2.1.76–93).

The nexus between identity and desire is strengthened by the need for secrecy. Hidden and equivocated as the lovers move between private and public realms, secret desire endows selfhood with interiority and intention. It grants a depth of character, and even if its longings are not fulfilled inner experience is confirmed. Juliet's cryptic replies to her mother's attack on Romeo reveal private pleasure couched in pain: 'O, how my heart abhors / To hear him named and cannot come to him / To wreak the love I bore my cousin / Upon his body that hath slaughtered him!' (3.5.99–102). Like secret desire, the obstacles to fulfilment sharpen internal experience and give it a kind of sensuous reality: 'runaways' eyes may wink, and Romeo / Leap to these arms untalked of and unseen. / Lovers can see to do their amorous rites / By their own beauties' (3.2.6–9).

---

[33] Geoffrey Bullough, *Narrative and Dramatic Sources of Shakespeare*, vol. 1 (London, 1966), lines 114, 210, 935, 2420 and 2532.

[34] Kay Stockholder, *Dream Works: Lovers and Families in Shakespeare's Plays* (Toronto, 1987), p. 30. In *Love's Argument: Gender Relations in Shakespeare* (Chapel Hill, 1984), Marianne Novy sees that the lovers' private world crystallizes in the aubade of Act 2, scene 1 (p. 108).

[35] Bullough, *Sources*, vol. 1, p. 374.

[36] On the interplay among misrecognition, desire and the symbolic, see Catherine Belsey, 'The Name of the Rose in *Romeo and Juliet*', *Yearbook of English Studies*, 23 (1993), 126–42; on the significance of the lovers being masked from each other, see Barbara L. Parker, *A Precious Seeing: Love and Reason in Shakespeare's Plays* (New York, 1987), p. 142.

This deep desire and selfhood develop in terms of intentionality – desire *for* someone, effected through imagination, speech and action. Desire marks the self as agent, and tragic desire portrays the onus of agency. It is felt sharply by Juliet before she takes the friar's potion, 'My dismal scene I needs must act alone' (4.3.19), and by Romeo as he enters the Capulet tomb 'armed against myself' (5.3.65). In this sense, the play's depiction of desire is linked to representations of subjectivity that emerge during the sixteenth century. It reflects the important role that tropes such as the secret, with its social and personal disguises, have in discourses which are starting to inscribe both an inner self and the individual as agent.

Even as it invests in such notions of selfhood, at its most intense desire in *Romeo and Juliet* surpasses individual experience and realizes an intersubjective union. The lovers re-character-ize each other as much as themselves: 'Romeo, doff thy name, / And for thy name – which is no part of thee – / Take all myself' (2.1.89–91). Again this effect has generic analogues, as we see the lovers' discourse moving beyond single-voiced Petrarchism. They share exchanges which reveal 'not only the other's confirming response, but also how we find ourselves in that response'.[37] Unlike contemporary sonnet sequences, which portray the poet by stifling the woman's voice (just as Romeo invokes and silences Rosaline), the play is marked by the lovers' dialogues. This reciprocity is epitomized by the sonnet they co-construct and seal with a kiss at their first meeting (1.5.92–105).[38] It is a highly suggestive moment, capturing the separateness of the lovers' world and speech from others, and also rewriting the dominant 1590s genre for representing desire. The sonnet is re-envoiced as dialogue, its meanings embodied in the climactic kiss. At the same time, the heightened artifice of the scene intimates its transience. The lovers start another sonnet but are interrupted by Juliet's garrulous nurse, who foreshadows the dire interventions of others. A further irony is also implied – as noted earlier,

their union will be ended by events that literal-ize poetic tropes of love and death: Romeo really does die 'with a kiss' (5.3.120), and Juliet falls in eternal sexual embrace, 'O happy dagger, / This is thy sheath! There rust, and let me die' (5.3.168–9).[39]

The deaths verify the Prologue's vision of inescapable ties between sex and violence. Not only can the lovers not escape the eternal feud that frames them, they even play parts in it, responding impulsively, at the threshold of nature and nurture, to news of Mercutio's and Tybalt's deaths. For a moment their union bows under its violent heritage as each impugns the other: 'O sweet Juliet, / Thy beauty hath made me effeminate, / And in my temper softened valour's steel' (3.1.113–15); 'did Romeo's hand shed Tybalt's blood? ... O serpent heart, hid with a flow'ring face!' (3.2.71–3)

Other characters also link sex and violence, suggesting that the connection has become naturalized and accepted. The Capulet servants joke aggressively about raping and killing the Montague women (1.1.22–4). The friar parallels birth and death, 'The earth, that's nature's mother, is her tomb. / What is her burying grave, that is her womb' (2.3.9–10), and is later echoed by Romeo, who calls the Capulet crypt a 'womb of death' (5.3.45). The friar also connects 'violent delights' to 'violent ends' (2.5.9), and the lovers' suicides suggest a final fusing of love and death. Yet as different inter-pretations maintain, this fusion's meaning may

---

[37] Jessica Benjamin, *The Bonds of Love: Psychoanalysis, Feminism, and the Problem of Domination* (New York, 1988), p. 21.

[38] Edward Snow suggests that the sonnet registers 'an intersubjective privacy' that subdues 'sexual difference and social opposition': 'Language and Sexual Difference in *Romeo and Juliet*', in *Shakespeare's 'Rough magic': Renaissance Essays in Honor of C. L. Barber*, ed. Peter Erickson and Coppélia Kahn (Newark, 1985), pp. 168–92; p. 168; Novy contrasts this scene with the sticho-mythic exchange between Juliet and Paris at 4.1.18–38 (*Love's Argument*, p. 108).

[39] On the love-death oxymoron, cf. Whittier, 'Sonnet's Body', p. 32.

be tragic, romantic, or both. The lovers are 'consumed and destroyed by the feud' and seem to rise above it, 'united in death'.[40]

The final scene thus accentuates the connections among selfhood, death and desire. It caps off the discourse of tragic desire announced by the Prologue – a tradition of failed love known through numerous European novellas, the second volume of *The Palace of Pleasure* (1567), and two editions of Brooke's *Tragicall Historye* (1562, 1587). The action has thus had a doubly repetitive stamp, not only replaying this oft-told tale but restaging what the Prologue has stated. Foreknowledge of the outcome plays off against moments of romantic and tragic intensity, and triggers a kind of anxious curiosity that waits to see the details of the deaths – the near misses of delayed messages, misread signs, plans gone awry.

Through this repetitive structure, the play affirms precedents and conditions for its own reproduction as if anticipating future responses. Before ending, it even shows these possibilities being realized. The grieving fathers decide to build statues of the lovers, and the prince's final lines look forward to 'more talk of these sad things', in an effort to establish once and for all what desire's tragic end might mean (5.3.306). As Dympna Callaghan observes, the play not only 'perpetuates an already well-known tale', but its closure is predicated on 'the possibility of endless retellings of the story – displacing the lovers' desire onto a perpetual narrative of love'.[41]

Patterns of repetition weave through the play as well as framing it. Characters constantly restate what has previously been staged – in the first scene Benvolio explains how the opening brawl started, and later he recounts details of Mercutio's and Tybalt's deaths and Romeo's involvement; the Chorus to the second act reiterates the lovers' meeting; the Nurse tells Juliet of Tybalt's death; the Capulets and Paris echo each other's lamentations over Juliet's apparent death;[42] and lastly the Friar recaps the whole plot to the other characters after the

bodies are found. These instances are part of the effort to explain the violent meaning of events, but as the prince's closing words suggest, something extra needs to be told, 'never was a story of more woe / Than this of Juliet and her Romeo' (5.3.308–9). There is a sense that 'this' version of the story exceeds earlier ones. For all its repetition of tropes and narratives, in closing the play recognizes and stresses a difference from precursors.

Other repetitive designs through the play are used to underline the tension between desire and death. Four meetings and kisses shared by Romeo and Juliet structure the romance plot. They are in counterpoint to four violent or potentially violent eruptions that occur between the male characters, especially involving Tybalt. A muted fifth interruption is provided by the presence of Tybalt's corpse in the Capulet crypt where Juliet and Romeo finally meet and miss each other. These turbulent scenes frame the romantic ones, unsettling the lyric and erotic essence which they seem to capture.

The repetitions and retellings connect with the representation of time in the play, imposing a destructive pressure between the weight of social and family history and personal longings. Social and personal time are opposed, and desire is caught between these conflicting time frames. Social time is frequently indexed through the play, in general terms such as the 'ancient grudge' and through the scheduling of specific events such as Capulet's banquet and Juliet's

---

40 Coppélia Kahn, 'Coming of Age in Verona', in *The Woman's Part: Feminist Criticism of Shakespeare*, ed. Carolyn Ruth Swift Lenz, Gayle Greene and Carol Thomas Neely (Urbana, 1980), pp. 171–93; p. 186. Marilyn Williamson regards the deaths as alienating rather than uniting, 'Romeo's suicide fulfills a pattern to which Juliet is both necessary and accidental': 'Romeo and Death', *Shakespeare Studies*, 14 (1981), 129–37; p. 132.
41 Callaghan, 'Ideology', p. 61.
42 See Thomas Moisan, 'Rhetoric and the Rehearsal of Death: the "Lamentations" Scene in *Romeo and Juliet*', *Shakespeare Quarterly*, 34 (1983), 389–404.

wedding to Paris. Against this scheme, the lovers' meetings seem to dissolve time, making it speed up or, more powerfully, stop and stand still, as the present is transformed into 'the time of love'.[43] The lovers seek to disregard time and death in their union, 'Then love-devouring death do what he dare – It is enough I may but call her mine' (2.5.7–8). Yet this passionate energy also drives the drama to its finale, and Romeo's words link their union and separation with death. The time of love confronts the passing of its own presence.

In various ways, then, *Romeo and Juliet* renovates tragic desire for the Elizabethans and for subsequent periods. In early scenes it evokes a narcissistic poetics of desire as self-loss and death but moves beyond that to stage a dialogic reciprocal presence. The reappearance of death then inscribes ineluctable external influences – the determinations of time and history which frame desire – and the impossible idealization of self and other which passion seeks but fails to find. In this sense, Shakespeare's play marks a complex intersection between historical and emergent discourses of desire. First, in a period when modern institutions of family, marriage and romance are starting to appear, it translates Platonic, Ovidian and Petrarchan tropes of ecstasy and love into personal notions of desire. Next, it conceives desire as the interplay between passion, selfhood and death. And thirdly, its equivocal staging of love's death anticipates the tension between romantic and sceptical visions of desire that runs through many later literary and theoretical works.

It could be said that the play's symbolic bequest to these works is a notion of desire as lost presence. Though love continues to be celebrated as present or absent or present-in-absence in many texts (in different ways, Herbert's poetry and Brontë's *Wuthering Heights* come to mind), a significant line of literary works explores the interplay among desire,

death and selfhood. Like *Romeo and Juliet*, these texts place desire in conflict with time, recounting moments of ideal presence whose future reveals they could never have been. This revision of desire begins with Shakespeare's later tragedies – *Hamlet*, *Othello*, *Macbeth* and *Antony and Cleopatra* – where one lover survives, though briefly, to feel the other's loss. It runs from the fallen lovers of *Paradise Lost* ('we are one, / One flesh; to lose thee were to lose myself' [9.958–9]), to the equivocal pairings at the end of Dickens's great novels or the images of foreclosed desire in Henry James's major phase. Its most poignant statement comes at the close of Scott Fitzgerald's *The Great Gatsby*:

the green light, the orgiastic future that year by year recedes before us. It eluded us then, but that's no matter – to-morrow we will run faster, stretch out our arms farther ... And one fine morning –

So we beat on, boats against the current, borne back ceaselessly into the past.

If *Romeo and Juliet* helps to initiate this tradition, it does so as the last tragedy of desire. For in these later texts the note is of melancholic rather than tragic loss: what hurts is not that desire ends in death but that it ends before death. The present then becomes a time for recounting lost desire, and the self's task is to try to hold the story together. 'The subject's centre of gravity is this present synthesis of the past which we call history', writes Lacan.[44] Like Romeo's last letter, this history reveals the 'course of love' (5.3.286) to those who remain.

---

[43] Julia Kristeva, *Tales of Love*, trans. Leon S. Roudiez (New York, 1987), p. 213.

[44] *The Seminar of Jacques Lacan*, Book 1, *Freud's Papers on Technique 1953–1954*, trans. John Forrester (New York, 1991), p. 36. On literature and psychoanalysis as twin discourses of mourning and melancholia, see Julia Reinhard Lupton and Kenneth Reinhard, *After Oedipus: Shakespeare in Psychoanalysis* (Ithaca, 1993), esp. pp. 32–3.

CARNIVAL AND DEATH IN *ROMEO AND JULIET*: A BAKHTINIAN READING

RONALD KNOWLES

The significance of festivity in Shakespeare's work has always been recognized. Incidentally, or centrally, allusions to the ritual of the liturgical year and seasonal folk custom are found throughout the plays. Recently François Laroque's study *Shakespeare's Festive World* (1991)[1] has examined in great detail the inter-relationship between the patterned cycle of calendar festival, Elizabethan society and Shakespeare. In the 1950s Northrop Frye drew on Frazerian anthropology and fertility myth to suggest the regenerative 'green world', as he calls it, of Shakespeare's comedy, which symbolizes the conflict between court and country, culture and nature.[2] However, since 1959, the best-known study in this area has been C. L. Barber's *Shakespeare's Festive Comedy*, the subtitle of which stresses the fundamental concern, 'A Study of Dramatic Form and its Relation to Social Custom'.[3] In the concept of 'clarification' Barber suggests a kind of comic catharsis in festivity by which the individual experiences a heightened awareness between man and nature. In effect this hypostasis of nature depoliticizes the festive, displacing the social by something vaguely spiritual.

In great contrast is the idea of the carnivalesque as espoused by Mikhail Bakhtin in his now famous study *Rabelais and his World*.[4] Here the festive is deeply political since it always gives expression to a populist culture that contests the official ideology of Church and aristocracy. Carnival subverts hegemony by travesty, parody and inversion, but it is not merely anarchic. Its positive life force insists on a Nietzschean counter-culture challenging the death-ridden ethos of the later Middle Ages. As his title indicates, Bakhtin is primarily concerned with medieval culture, but he does offer many fascinating asides on the carnivalesque in the early modern world, and in Shakespeare particularly. 'Shakespeare's drama', he writes, 'has many outward carnivalesque aspects: images of the material body lower stratum, of ambivalent obscenities, and of popular banquet scenes.' He also suggests that 'the analysis we have applied to Rabelais would also help us to discover the essential carnival element in the organization of Shakespeare's drama. This does not merely concern the secondary clownish motives of his plays. The logic of crownings and uncrownings, in direct or indirect form, organises the serious elements also' (p. 275). In retrospect, the primitivist idealism of Bakhtin's text as a covert anti-Stalinist critique is not difficult to see. Again, many would question the class polarization of 'official' and 'popular'; and the separation of popular from learned humanist elements in

---

[1] Cambridge. Originally published as *Shakespeare et la fête* (Paris, 1988). The Cambridge edition is revised and enlarged.

[2] 'The Argument of Comedy', in *Shakespeare, Modern Essays in Criticism*, ed. L. F. Dean (Oxford, 1957).

[3] Princeton, N.J.

[4] Bloomington, 1984. Page references in the text are to this edition (translated by Hélène Iswolsky and originally published by The Massachusetts Institute of Technology in 1968).

Rabelais, with almost complete relegation of the latter, severely qualifies Bakhtin's appraisal of *Gargantua and Pantagruel*.[5] But Bakhtin's interpretation of carnival remains vividly provocative and provides the means to reassess large aspects of Renaissance culture and Shakespeare in particular.

This essay will argue that Shakespeare's inheritance of carnival or festive culture finds expression in *Romeo and Juliet* by means of the three Bakhtinian categories indicated above, the body, bawdy and the banquet.[6] I shall argue that the complex figure of Juliet's Nurse can be seen beyond her obvious comic realism as representing something much larger, the Bakhtinian 'grotesque body' as well as 'mock' Fortune. Secondly, Capulet's 'old accustom'd feast' (1.2.20),[7] though not a public carnival, has carnivalesque elements, along with the highly structured comedy of the servants and musicians, generally. Thirdly, there are the many instances of proverbs and bawdy wit in the play. Together these three elements contribute to much of the comedy, but this comedy has a profound cultural ambivalence. The issue is ultimately not so much Carnival versus Lent, as life versus death. For Bakhtin the triumph of life is always expressed by the laughter of the people.

In most discussions of *Romeo and Juliet* Shakespeare's most radical carnivalesque innovation usually goes unacknowledged. In drama, romantic love was commonly the subject of comedy. Shakespeare challenges the worlds of myth and legend which conventionally provided tragic heroes and heroines by introducing the first romantic tragedy. Critics have indeed always recognized the preponderance of comic materials in *Romeo and Juliet* though nearly all modern productions severely cut the carefully placed comic scenes of Act 4. A carnivalesque critique of Petrarchan love in the play is found in several forms, but perhaps most tellingly in the technique of burlesque juxtaposition in scenic structure. The subjective world of idealized love is seen to resist the social world of festival and to succumb to 'star-cross'd' fate in spite of all the ministrations of an earthly Fortune which is benignly represented in the domesticated and naturalized figure of Juliet's Nurse. The tragedy of Romeo and Juliet will always remain the fulcrum but the cultural dimensions of the play reach back to the collectivity of joyous carnival on the one hand, and on the other look forward to what Bakhtin calls 'the interior infinite' (p. 44), the capitalist culture of individualism which developed out of the Middle Ages.

For Bakhtin the ideology which carnival challenged derived from the dogma of Catholicism. In *Romeo and Juliet* the ideology of romantic love is conjoined with that of the death cult of the second half of the fifteenth century which persisted into the Renaissance, particularly in painting, illustrations and emblems linking love, festivity and death, as we shall see.

5 Simon Dentith's *Bakhtinian Thought. An Introductory Reader* (London and New York, Routledge, 1995) provides several useful references: see Peter Stallybrass and Allon White, *The Politics and Poetics of Transgression* (London, 1986), pp. 6–28; Richard M. Berrong, *Rabelais and Bakhtin* (Lincoln and London, 1986), *passim*. An authoritative appraisal is Michael Holquist, *Dialogism: Bakhtin and His World* (London, 1990). Michael D. Bristol draws on Bakhtin's thought in his *Carnival and Theater. Plebeian Culture and the Structure of Authority in Renaissance England* (New York and London, 1985).

6 This essay has benefited from comments on readings of preliminary drafts at the Reading Renaissance Research Seminar, and the 'Shakespeare, Carnival and Society' wing of Reading's Literature and History Conference, 1995. At the former my attention was drawn to Kent Cartwright's extensive and subtle chapter 'Theater and Narrative in *Romeo and Juliet*' in his *Shakespearean Tragedy and Its Double: The Rhythms of Audience Response* (Pennsylvania, 1991). In his concentration on the central topic of 'spectatorial distance' he alludes several times to the Bakhtinian carnivalesque functioning within the play in ways close to my own, but we differ fundamentally concerning Romeo and Juliet's love. He sees it as *part* of, I see it as *opposed* to, the carnivalesque.

7 All references are to Brian Gibbons (ed.), *Romeo and Juliet*, The Arden Shakespeare (London and New York, 1980).

Three associated ideas underpin Bakhtin's theory of carnival culture: 'the material bodily principle', 'the concept of grotesque realism' and 'the collective ancestral body' (pp. 18–19). Abundance, fertility, growth and regeneration characterize the festive and utopian ethos of carnival. 'Degradation' and 'debasement' are the translator's words for the material principle of lowering all that is 'high, spiritual, ideal and abstract' (p. 19). Unfortunately these words suggest the pornographic in modern English. On the contrary, Bakhtin's focus on the organic functions of the body is celebratory and life-affirming in the face of the official ideology of the ascetic and life-denying church. Bakhtin expounds most of his carnival theory within his introduction, and in one paragraph epitomizes much of his thought:

Degradation here means coming down to earth, the contact with earth as an element that swallows up and gives birth at the same time. To degrade is to bury, to sow, and to kill simultaneously, in order to bring forth something more and better. To degrade also means to concern oneself with the lower stratum of the body, the life of the body and the reproductive organs: it therefore relates to acts of defecation and copulation, conception, pregnancy and birth. Degradation digs a bodily grave for new birth; it has not only a destructive, negative aspect, but also a regenerating one.

(p. 21)

The occasion of carnival itself makes apparent the relationship of the materialist principle with the pattern of the cyclical year in which the ecclesiastical is naturalized by seasons, in contrast to the eschatological rigours of linear time, from creation to doomsday. All these ideas are implied in the Nurse's speech in her first appearance on stage (1.3.2ff.).

Juliet's Nurse is a metamorphosis of Bakhtin's material bodily principle. Lower-class comic garrulity, taken from a hint in the source, always runs the risk of critical condescension – perhaps nowhere more so than in Coleridge's reference to the Nurse's 'uncultivated understanding'[8] – but the discernible carnivalesque pattern of the Nurse's references transcends critic, character

and caricature. The boy actor or actress of the Nurse should appear aged. Shakespeare made the disparity in age between Juliet and the Nurse even greater than in his source by lowering Juliet's age from sixteen to thirteen while following the original reference to the Nurse as an 'ancient dame'.[9] Her senility is indicated by her relative toothlessness, 'I have but four' (line 13) she says, and her physical appearance should be consonant with this.

The Nurse's first words in response to Lady Capulet's 'where's my daughter' (line 1), 'Now by my maidenhead at twelve year old, / I bade her come' (lines 2–3) ironically parallel her with Juliet who will also lose her maidenhead at thirteen in the course of the play. Youth, puberty, virginity and the onset of sexual life are evoked as part of a pattern of natural human growth. The religious imprecation 'God forbid' (line 4) follows the endearments 'What, lamb. What, ladybird' (line 3), thus aligning human and divine affection and concern in terms of the natural world. Following her first query concerning 'Lammas-tide' (line 5) the Nurse embarks on what has become known as 'the Nurse's speech', which includes two more references to 'Lammas Eve' (lines 17, 21), Juliet's birthday. These are the only references to this festival in Shakespeare's works. This, again, aligns the religious with the natural; Lammas, or loaf-mass day, with old age and birth. Lammas day is the first of August, a harvest festival at which loaves of bread made from the first ripe corn were consecrated. Harvest is often found as a metaphor or analogy for death (for example 'all flesh is grass', Isaiah 40.6) but here death is transformed into life in the provision of sustaining food. Ominously, Juliet is to be cut down by death before Lammas eve, pre-empting the natural harvest of her body in the fructification

8 Terence Hawkes (ed.), *Coleridge on Shakespeare* (Harmondsworth, 1969), pp. 87–8.
9 Geoffrey Bullough, *Narrative and Dramatic Sources of Shakespeare*, vol. I (London and New York, 1964), p. 295, line 344.

of marriage. Juliet is paralleled with the Nurse's daughter: 'Susan and she – God rest all Christian souls – / Were of an age' (lines 18–19). The phrase 'Well, Susan is with God' (line 19) is free from regret or sadness and the recollection of the earthquake in the same context as Susan's death and Juliet's weaning suggests again both death and birth, disaster and generation, as natural occurrences, just as 'Shake! quoth the dovehouse' (line 33) converts danger and death to laughter and life. (The weaning is important for the iconography of the Nurse as Fortune and will be returned to shortly.) The established pattern of the naturalization of the religious, a carnivalesque inversion, is extended in the juxtaposition of 'by th' rood' (line 36), 'God be with his soul' (line 39), and 'by my holidame' (line 43) with the Nurse's recollection of her husband picking up Juliet after an accident: '"Yea", quoth he, "dost thou fall upon thy face? / Thou wilt fall backward when thou hast more wit, / Wilt thou not, Jule?"' (lines 41–3). A dead man is brought to life in comic anticipation of young Juliet eventually fulfilling her sexual nature, a cyclic continuity of life emphasized by the Nurse's hyperbolic vindication of the triumph of nature over time. 'The pretty wretch left crying and said "Ay" ... / I warrant, and I should live a thousand years / I never should forget it.' (lines 44, 46–7).

Remembered as a toddler, Juliet is then anticipated as a bride: 'And I might live to see thee married once' (line 61). After Lady Capulet's literary conceit on 'the volume of young Paris' face' (line 81) concluding 'By having him, making yourself no less' (line 94), the Nurse roundly adds 'No less, nay bigger. Women grow by men' (line 95), thereby completing the cyclic pattern of her speech with yet further generation. This sense of cyclic generation is continued within a festive setting when old Capulet exchanges reminiscences with his cousin at the revels, looking on the young masquers, recalling their youthful masking, weddings and birth (1.5.16–40). But as we shall

see, this carnivalesque dance of life is haunted by the late medieval dance of death.

In the Nurse and Juliet we have in emergent realism a splitting of the image of the grotesque body. Bakhtin remarks that 'in the seventeenth century some forms of the grotesque began to degenerate into static "character" presentation and narrow "genrism"' (p. 52). In earlier culture the images of the 'real grotesque ... present simultaneously the two poles of becoming: that which is receding and dying, and that which is being born; they show two bodies in one'. Elsewhere Bakhtin points out terracotta figures from antiquity, of 'senile pregnant nags ... laughing ... it is pregnant death, a death that gives birth' (p. 25). As an example of an image of the duality of the body surviving but only as 'a pale reflection of its former dual nature' Bakhtin cites the suckling of a child (p. 322), and refers to Eckermann's *Conversations with Goethe* in which the German poet speculates that in a lost painting called 'The Weaning of a Child', then attributed to Correggio, 'the sacred becomes all-human' (p. 252). Unfortunately, in his consideration of *Romeo and Juliet*, this carnival inversion of Goethe's views did not extend to the Nurse and Mercutio, for 'these two figures, and what surrounds them, come in only as farcical interludes, and must be as unbearable to the minds of the lovers on the stage as they are to us'.[10] Carnival laughter, central to Bakhtin's theory, annoys Goethe as merely 'farcical interludes', but Shakespeare's mixture of comedy and tragedy may be seen as an insistent festive laughter resisting the prescriptions of neo-classicism, though to some extent compromising with genre by giving a certain kind of comedy to the lower orders. The Nurse's laughter echoes a whole culture, not simply a character from below stairs. In Bakhtin's terms, Rabelais, Cervantes and Shakespeare embodied the Renaissance conception of laughter in its 'deep philosophical meaning',

---

[10] 'Shakespeare ad Infinitum' in Oswald Le Winter, *Shakespeare in Europe* (Harmondsworth, 1963), p. 66.

affording 'one of the essential forms of truth concerning the world', when 'the world is seen anew, no less (and perhaps more) profoundly than when seen from the serious standpoint' (p. 66). In the Nurse's speech and laughter life-affirming joyousness subsumes the metaphysics of religion and death, banishes fear, and celebrates the regenerative cycle of organic being – the essence of carnival.

As the Nurse represents a certain kind of love and life which is contrasted in the play with romantic love and death, so at a conscious level, probably taking a few hints from Chaucer, Shakespeare seems to have contrasted malign fate with the Nurse as benign fortune. The Nurse, like Friar Laurence, has several functions within the play beyond the limitations of naturalist character furthering plot. In his ramified presentation Shakespeare includes both pragmatic carnivalesque and human limitation. Howard R. Patch's *The Goddess Fortuna in Medieval Literature*[11] still remains one of the best sources of information on the subject and the following references are indebted to this study. In one of the seminal works of western culture, Boethius's *The Consolation of Philosophy*, Fortune as nurse says, in Chaucer's translation, 'Whan than nature brought the foorth out of thi modir wombe, I resceyved the nakid and nedy of alle thyngs, and I norissched the with my richesses.'[12] In Renaissance iconography Fortune is consequently depicted with the right breast exposed and bearing a cornucopia.[13] Changeable Fortune laughs and cries, we have heard the Nurse laughing and she later weeps.[14] Perhaps the most common attributes of Fortune are her fickleness and the idea of her as a strumpet. 'O Fortune, Fortune! All men call thee fickle' Juliet cries, and later in the same scene the Nurse declares 'Romeo's a dishclout to him' (3.5.219), fickly transferring her allegiance to Paris. Earlier the Nurse approaches Romeo seeking 'some confidence', upon which Mercutio exclaims 'A bawd! A bawd! A bawd!' (2.4.128). To add physical emphasis to this symbolic incrustation on realist character,

Shakespeare has Juliet insist, impatient of the Nurse's return from Romeo, 'O, she is lame' (2.5.4). This echoes a detail of Chaucer's depiction of Fortune in *The Book of the Duchess*, 'she goth upryght and yet she halt'.[15] Shakespeare's allusion is in direct contrast to the source in Brooke where at one point the Nurse rushes home 'with spedy pace'.[16] This is made into a rather blatant joke immediately after by Juliet who responds to the Nurse's 'Hie you to the cell' with 'Hie to high fortune! Honest Nurse, farewell' (2.5.78–9). In contrast to the comedy of the Nurse and Fortune's hobbling, Fate and death will strike with tragic haste.

However, it is in the evocation of the Nurse weaning Juliet that Shakespeare most finely balances traditional iconography and dramatic character: 'When it did taste the wormwood on the nipple / Of my dug and felt it bitter, pretty fool, / To see it tetchy and fall out with the dug' (1.3.30–2). Patch comments, 'As we thirst for her gifts, so Fortune gives us sweet and bitter to drink, by turns honey and gall.'[17] Romeo, as yet in thrall to Rosaline, invokes this commonplace: 'A madness most discreet, / A choking gall, and a preserving sweet' (1.1.191–2). It is repeated by Tybalt when restrained by Capulet at the feast: 'but this intrusion shall / Now seeming sweet, convert to bitt'rest gall' (1.5.90–1). Finally, the Nurse is linked to nature herself on whom 'divers kind / We sucking on her natural bosom find' (2.3.7–8). Like the Nurse and Fortune, nature provides honey or gall, or, in Friar Laurence's words, 'poison' or

---

[11] Cambridge, Mass., 1927.

[12] Patch, *The Goddess Fortuna*, p. 56. F. N. Robinson (ed.), *The Complete Works of Geoffrey Chaucer* (Oxford, 1957), p. 330.

[13] Ibid., p. 56. Achille Bocchi, *Symbolicarum Quaestionum de Universo Genere* (Bologna, 1574). Stephen Orgel (ed.), New York and London, 1979, G1r.

[14] Patch, *The Goddess Fortuna*, p. 44.

[15] Ibid., p. 37; F. N. Robinson, *Complete Works*, p. 273, line 622.

[16] Bullough, *Sources*, vol. I, p. 303, line 673.

[17] *The Goddess Fortuna*, p. 52.

'medicine'. The friar's speech here (2.3.1–26) espouses a concept central both to Bakhtin's thought and to Shakespeare's representation of death and carnival, and will be returned to. The nurse's love and comedy provides a carnivalesque contrast with romance and tragedy, but mock-Fortune is no match for blind Capid, blindfold Fortune and masked Death.

Bakhtin sees carnival as a cultural form of opposition, subversion and liberation from what he terms the 'official' ideology propounded by the ecclesiastical orthodoxy of the Middle Ages, whereas Shakespeare's use of the carnivalesque in *Romeo and Juliet* provides a contrastive frame for the inherent values of romantic love as it had developed in literature by the late sixteenth century into an amalgam of courtly love, Petrarchism and neoplatonism. Many critics have looked at those elements variously considering them as comic, satirical or burlesque. They have primarily looked at the first half of the play, often without giving due weight to the later comic scenes of the Nurse's response to Juliet's seeming 'death' and the festive-funeral musicians (4.5). More broadly considered, comedy can be seen to draw on the carnivalesque and to become something of a touchstone in a cultural critique of romantic tragedy.

Firstly, it might be said that it is difficult to understand how, if Shakespeare had intended to present only a poignant tragedy of ideal love, he chose to emphasize Romeo's first love, Rosaline, who is swiftly passed over in the source. Garrick dropped all references to her, entirely. In the early exchanges between Benvolio and Montague, Romeo is pictured as having ostracized himself for love, and his behaviour is explained in heavily parodic Petrarchan language (1.1.116ff.). Having discovered the identity of Romeo's lover who is included in the list of Capulet's guests, Benvolio challenges Romeo with, 'Go thither and with unattainted eye / Compare her face with some that I shall show / And I will make thee think thy swan a crow' (1.22.87–9). Immediately on entering the Capulet festivity, with a single glance at Juliet and without any prompting whatsoever from his friend, Romeo confirms Benvolio's scepticism:

> So shows a snowy dove trooping with crows
> As yonder lady o'er her fellows shows ...
> Did my heart love till now? Forswear it, sight.
> For I ne'er saw true beauty till this night.
>
> (1.5.47–8, 51–2)

This change happens without any such externalized agency as the magic potion of love-in-idleness administered to the lovers by Puck in *A Midsummer Night's Dream*. The paradox of love as both arbitrary and absolute creates a richly comic moment which is developed in the scene and in what follows not least when Mercutio unwittingly echoes Romeo's words, 'Romeo! Humours! Madman! Passion! Lover! / ... Cry but "Ay me!" Pronounce but "love" and "dove"' (2.1.7, 10), and then goes on, unaware of Romeo's new love, to evoke the chaste Rosaline in comically inappropriate erotic terms. Again, Friar Laurence assumes that Romeo has been with Rosaline. This Romeo hastily denies with 'I have forgot that name, and that name's woe' (2.3.42), but his language inadvertently recalls Juliet's 'What's in a name?' (2.2.43) and their amorous wordplay on 'forgetting' (2.2.170–5). Little wonder that the friar continues to chide: 'Is Rosaline, that thou didst love so dear, / So soon forsaken? Young men's love then lies / Not truly in their hearts but in their eyes' (2.3.62–4). The dramatic interplay of such references serves to compromise, if not undermine, the evident partiality of a purely romantic response created by traditions of performance from Garrick to Franco Zeffirelli, in which most of the comedy was cut to emphasize romance and pathos.[18] Moreover, if we return to the Capulet festival aspects of the staging suggest a further comedic dimension.

As the young men make their way to the Capulet house visors are distributed. Most likely

[18] See Jill L. Levenson, *Shakespeare in Performance: Romeo and Juliet* (Manchester, 1987).

these would have been full-face visors, like those in *Much Ado About Nothing* (2.1), of a grotesque nature, and attention is specifically drawn to this detail in Mercutio's dialogue:

> Give me a case to put my visage in:
> A visor for a visor. What care I
> What curious eye doth quote deformities?
> Here are the beetle brows shall blush for me.
>
> (1.4.29–32)

For Bakhtin the mask reveals 'the essence of the grotesque' (p. 40) in the carnivalesque conversion of the fearful into the funny, an analogue to carnival death in which the hideous becomes humorous. Tybalt identifies Romeo by his voice since his visage is 'cover'd with an antic face' (1.5.55); Capulet restrains Tybalt from violence; and Romeo plays court to Juliet with a quatrain which develops into a sonnet in an exchange on the Petrarchan commonplace of the lover as pilgrim worshipping at the shrine of his 'saint'.

In the source 'All dyd unmaske'[19] but Shakespeare does not indicate any unmasking in an explicit stage direction. (In fact the stage directions *He kisses her* at lines 105, 109 were provided by Rowe and Capell in response to the cue lines 'Thus from my lips' (line 106) and 'You kiss by th' book' (line 109).) Romeo has seen Juliet's beauty so she is not wearing a lady's half-mask. Harley Granville Barker simply assumed that 'Romeo, his mask doffed, moves towards her.'[20] This is far from certain. Although recognized by Tybalt and identified to Capulet, for Romeo to have unmasked would surely have given such provocation as to have cancelled the hospitality which initially admitted the masked revellers. But if Romeo remains masked until the kiss, it means that Juliet has instantly fallen in love with a visor and a quatrain. If Romeo unmasked at the beginning of the 'sonnet', then Juliet falls for someone she doesn't know, albeit handsome, who recites modish love verses. However it is seen, idealized romance is rather undermined in contrast with the source which stresses that

Romeo's love-lorn complexion convinces Juliet of his devotion.[21] The prologue to Act 2 may imply something less than ideal in the comment that both were 'Alike bewitched by the charm of looks' (line 6).

The Arden editor, Brian Gibbons, points out that the Act 2 scene division inaugurating the famous balcony exchange between Romeo and Juliet is traditional and convenient for reference though, in fact, Romeo's first line – 'He jests at scars that never felt a wound' – rhymes with the preceding line of Benvolio, 'Go then, for 'tis in vain / To seek him here that means not to be found'. More significantly, given this fluidity of the Elizabethan stage, is the fact that one of the most celebrated scenes in romantic literature begins with the grossest example of explicit bawdy in the play echoing in the audience's ears, Mercutio's 'O Romeo, that she were, O that she were / An open-arse and thou a poperin pear!' (2.1.37–8). Surprisingly, Bakhtin only touches on bawdy in passing, though he recognizes that it is fundamental to the carnivalesque acceptance of life in its derisive 'degradation' of high to low: 'mockery and abuse is almost entirely bodily and grotesque. The body that figures in all the expressions of the unofficial speech of the people is the body that fecundates and is fecundated, that gives birth and is born, devours and is devoured, drinks, defecates, is sick and dying' (p. 319). Bawdy can give expression to revulsion and lead to pornographic hatred as in *Othello*, *Hamlet* and *Troilus and Cressida*. On the other hand, almost throughout *Romeo and Juliet* bawdy is used not only for structural and thematic contrast, but for something larger and more positive – the carnivalesque embrace of existence.

Bawdy reduces passion to the lower bodily stratum. It demystifies the romantic with the physical. Romantic love privatizes passion by

---

[19] Bullough, *Sources*, vol. 1, p. 290, line 169.

[20] *Prefaces to Shakespeare*, Second Series (London, 1930), p. 8.

[21] Bullough, *Sources*, vol. 1, p. 297, lines 413ff.

subjectifying experience, and excludes life by claiming all existence. Somewhat compromising Brian Gibbons' belief that the sonnet form of Romeo and Juliet's dialogue in 1.5 creates 'an experience equivalent to that ... in the imagination of the solitary reader', the dramatized contrasts of comedy and burlesque introduce an element of relative travesty into the artificiality of the genre when exposed to an audience. Love's private worship is revealed to the laity, reversing John Donne's succinct and ironic exclusiveness in the political metaphor of 'She is all states, all Princes, I, / Nothing else is'.[22] The literary imagery of Petrarchan love alienates further with its elitist cult of suffering and isolation, and in the excesses of poets like Marino and Serafino subjectivity becomes merely a reified rococo artefact. Shakespeare sees both the comic and tragic implications of dramatizing Petrarchan conceits in contrast with bawdy.[23] Bawdy reflects the collective levelling culture of carnival. Sex is part of life and bawdy imagery reflects not sonnet sequences but the market place, the tavern, the kitchen, the farm yard, and so on – nature and society as one. However vulgar, bawdy is social in its humorous relation, person to person, in anecdote, proverb or joke, and this is duplicated in the theatre with the collectivity of laughter.

Mercutio's vulgarism, though characteristic of his bawdy wit, here draws on folk culture in the dialect names for fruits popularly considered to resemble in shape the male and female sexual organs. Sex and fruit compound the carnival images of earth and body mutually sustaining and reproducing. From such a point of view this is not obscene but a comic affirmation shared by 'maids ... when they laugh alone' (2.1.36), that is, amongst themselves. In contrast to such earthiness Romeo's romantic expostulation invokes the celestial: 'It is the east and Juliet is the sun!' (2.2.3). Juliet's eventual interjection in what has been appropriated as one of the most celebrated of love overtures, again adding a touch of burlesque, is merely 'Ay me' (line 25), precisely fulfilling Mercutio's parodic prediction

of fifty-six lines earlier. The staging here indicates that Juliet cannot see Romeo, who is listening – 'Shall I hear more' (line 37) – 'bescreen'd in night' (line 52), but she eventually recognizes his voice: 'Yet I know the sound' (line 59). Instead of romantic union in love, at this point the lovers are spatially, psychologically and socially separated from each other and others. Thus it is rather difficult to accept the idea of maturity accorded the thirteen-year-old Juliet in this scene. Later, awaiting fulfilment of 'amorous rites' Juliet's language of love (3.2.1–30) converts the physicality of orgasm – '... come Romeo ... when I shall die' – into the poetic transcendence of passion. Yet as we shall see the literalness of death once more is anticipated. Here, in the balcony scene the Nurse's calling voice (lines 149, 151) is like the voice of reality, structurally placed in answer to Romeo's 'I am afeard, / Being in night, all this is but a dream, / Too flattering sweet to be substantial' (lines 139–41).

The social mode of bawdy is perhaps nowhere better seen in the play than in Mercutio's ribald chiding later in the act in which he effects a carnivalesque rescue of Romeo, a rescue albeit like carnival itself, only temporary. As we have seen in the alternating structure so far, after the balcony exchange Romeo has to endure Friar Laurence's sober criticism, and on entering in the following scene he faces Mercutio's welcoming witty play on his name:

Without his roe, like a dried herring.   O flesh, flesh, how art thou fishified.   Now is he for the numbers that Petrarch flowed in.   Laura, to his lady, was a

---

22 Gibbons, *Romeo and Juliet*, p. 43. A. J. Smith, ed. *John Donne. The Complete English Poems* (Harmondsworth, 1971). See 'The Sun Rising' p. 80, lines 21–2. Romeo exclaims 'Turn back, dull earth, and find thy centre out' (2.1.2), cf. 'The Sun Rising', line 30 – 'This bed thy centre is, these walls thy sphere'.

23 For an argument opposite to that made here, see Ann Pasternak Slater, 'Petrarchism Come True in *Romeo and Juliet*' in *Images of Shakespeare*, ed. Werner Habicht, D. J. Palmer and Roger Pringle (Newark, 1988), pp. 129–50.

kitchen wench – marry, she had a better love to berhyme her – Dido a dowdy, Cleopatra a gypsy, Helen and Hero hildings and harlots, Thisbe a grey eye or so ...   (2.4.38–44)

Early in his introduction Bakhtin hints at the 'comic crownings and uncrownings' (p. 11) of carnivalesque inversion in Shakespeare and others. This is the case with Petrarch throughout the first half of *Romeo and Juliet* and here, in particular, the laureate poet is 'uncrowned'. Seizing on the anomaly of Petrarch's chaste love, Mercutio laughs at the metamorphosis of carnival sex, 'flesh', into Lenten 'dried herring', as if this love was actually life-denying.[24] Brian Gibbons points out that the *OED* cites this passage as an illustration of 'roe' as the sperm of male fish.[25] Conversely the romantic heroines of legend and history are travestied in a mode anticipating a figure frequently referred to by Bakhtin – Scarron. Romeo responds with extensively witty word play culminating in Mercutio's bawdy capitulation – 'I was come to the whole depth of my tale and meant indeed to occupy the argument no longer' (lines 98–9) – which, in fact, is a victory, 'Now art thou sociable, now art thou Romeo' (line 89).

Mercutio's laughter at Petrarch's Laura as a kitchen maid has been anticipated earlier in a carefully structured scenic interpolation which is a perfect cameo of Shakespeare's carnivalesque method in *Romeo and Juliet*, and has a specifically Rabelaisian echo. This is 1.5 where the stage directions *They march about the stage, and* Servingmen *come forth with napkins* indicate the entry of Romeo's group into the Capulet household. Immediately preceding this is Romeo's speech of foreboding which recalls the tragic motif of the prologue:

> ... my mind misgives
> Some consequence yet hanging in the stars
> Shall bitterly begin his fearful date
> With this night's revels, and expire the term
> Of a despised life clos'd in my breast
> By some vile forfeit of untimely death.
>   (1.4.106–11)

As the servants enter a question immediately introduces a Rabelaisian note: 'Where's Potpan' (1.5.1). Amongst the sixty-four cooks of book 4 of *Gargantua and Pantagruel* is 'Pudding-pan' in Urquhart's translation, 'Piepan' in the modern Penguin edition.[26] Whereas Romeo has a fated assignation at the revels, the servants are arranging their high jinks below stairs.

> Away with the joint-stools, remove the court-cupboard, look to the plate.   Good thou, save me a piece of marchpane, and as thou loves me, let the porter let in Susan Grindstone and Nell – Antony and Potpan!   (1.5.6–10)

It seems unlikely that these lovers will exchange Petrarchan conceits – Susan Grindstone's carnivalesque surname says it all, alluding to motion in coition and an avid sexuality wearing out the male. Yet, as we have seen above, sex and the body are also combined with nature and sustenance in a regenerative cycle. All harvest corn will be threshed and the seed ground for flour to make bread to feed people. The servants and their girlfriends will enjoy food and sex with their own banqueting and revels while 'the longer liver take all' (1.5.15), a proverbial relegation of death, in direct contrast to Romeo's apprehension of 'some vile forfeit of untimely death' (1.4.111). Carnival death is subsumed into the social and natural cycle in which human and harvest seed ensures life, whereas Romeo and Juliet are singled out by another kind of death for extinction.

It has been argued, with some justification, that *Romeo and Juliet* in large part dramatizes the proverb *festina lente*, hasten slowly.[27] But much more central than this cautionary morality is the

---

[24] For a parallel interpretation see François Laroque, *Shakespeare's Festive World* (Cambridge, 1991), p. 210.

[25] Gibbons, *Romeo and Juliet*, p. 144.

[26] *The Works of Francis Rabelais* by Sir Thomas Urquhart and Peter Motteux (London, 1849), vol. 2, p. 311. *The Histories of Gargantua and Pantagruel* translated by J. M. Cohen (Harmondsworth, 1965), p. 535.

[27] Marjorie Donker, *Shakespeare's Proverbial Themes* (Westport and London, 1992), ch. 2.

philosophy of nature as espoused by Friar Laurence drawing on proverbial knowledge encapsulating the carnivalesque. From this point of view the play dramatizes a dialogism between high and low cultures – between the Renaissance philosophy of love and proverbial folk wisdom, between emergent subjective individualism and communal consciousness. At the centre of the play we hear from the friar

> The earth that's nature's mother is her tomb:
> What is her burying grave, that is her womb;
> And from her womb children of divers kind
> We sucking on her natural bosom find.
>
> (2.3.5–8)

This proverbial knowledge gains particular force in English with the rhyming agnomination of 'womb' and 'tomb', a rhetorical figure at the heart of the play and a figure which both unites and divides the later Middle Ages and the Renaissance. In his lengthy chapter on 'The Grotesque Image of the Body' we find in Bakhtin:

Death, the dead body, blood as a seed buried in the earth, rising for another life – this is one of the oldest and most widespread themes. A variant is death inseminating mother earth and making her bear fruit once more ... Rabelais speaks elsewhere of the 'sweet, much desired embrace of ... Mother Earth, which we call burial' ... This image of burial is probably inspired by Pliny, who gives a detailed picture of the earth's motherhood and of burial as a return to her womb. (p. 327)

In a speech combining the rhythm of the seasons, human growth, and social festivity, Capulet explains of Juliet to Paris that 'Earth hath swallow'd all my hopes but she; / She is the hopeful lady of my earth' (1.2.14–15). Carnival and capitalist notions seem to be played against each other here if the second 'earth' is taken as referring ambiguously to either Capulet's body, alive and dead, or to his lands. Given the prevalent references to age and youth, summer and winter, the cyclic carnival element is to the fore, earth as womb and tomb.

The design of *Romeo and Juliet* does not fall into a simple division of a tragic following upon a comic movement, and neither is there an unbridgeable dichotomy between the language of romantic love and sexuality, as we have seen above. Until Act 5 comedy and tragedy alternate. 'My grave is like to be my wedding bed' (1.5.134), Juliet remarks, while Romeo later declares, 'Then love-devouring death do what he dare' (2.6.7). Many proleptic notes like this are sounded throughout the play. In contrast the carnival world persists in the midst of death; Menippus laughing in the underworld is a favourite image for Bakhtin (see p. 69), whereas in *Romeo and Juliet* Mercutio jests at death, 'you shall find me a grave man' (3.1.99). But carnival surrenders to tragedy at the close. More precisely, the reversals in Capulet's 'festival'/ 'funeral' speech (4.5.84–90), agnomination again, pattern Act 4 as a whole. In 4.1 Juliet evokes the horrors of the charnel house and death-shrouds, whereas 4.2 opens with proverbial jokes about cooks licking their fingers. In 4.3 just before taking the potion the horrors of being entombed are vividly before Juliet. And then the carnivalesque world of food and the body is heard once more – 'more spices', 'They call for dates and quinces', 'Look to the bak'd meats' (4.4.1, 2, 5). The nurse as weeping Fortune discovers Juliet's body in 4.4, and the festive musicians decide to stay on for a funereal free meal. The homiletic association of death and musicians is of great importance and will be touched on shortly. Suffice it here to note how the social festive world vies with the medieval horrors of death, and eventually with the development of death as lover.

In Act 5, in Capulet's tomb, the festive is finally superseded by the counter-carnival triumph of death, and carnival day and festive light are extinguished by tragic darkness. Capulet's feast was to 'make dark heaven light' (1.2.25), but Montague had acknowledged that his son 'locks fair daylight out / And makes himself an artificial night', a 'black ... humour' that indeed proves 'portentous' (1.1.137–9). Yet 'night' also gives expression to the most potent love language in the play, touched on above: 'Come gentle night, come loving black-brow'd night, / Give me my Romeo; and when I shall die / Take him and cut him out in little stars ...' (3.2.20–2). The orgasmic reading of 'die' is now commonplace and the proleptic punning equally so, but 'black-brow'd night' bears re-examination in a context in which Juliet recalls her first meeting with the masked Romeo on a festive occasion, 'So tedious is this day / As is the night before some festival' (3.2.28–9). The speech is remarkable for its affirmation and conversion of sexuality to poetry, and in effect offers an inherent rebuff to bawdy, but this in turn is severely qualified, yet again, by 'death-mark'd love'. 'Black-brow'd night' recalls the 'beetle [i.e. overhanging] brows' of Mercutio's grotesque visor and anticipates the 'overwhelming brows' (5.1.39) of the death-like apothecary who delivers the deadly potion. 'Black-brow'd night' seems part of a half-realized metaphor of night as a masquer at the revels. Romeo the antic masquer brings both love and death. In this the iconographic complex of death, festivity and romance in fifteenth and sixteenth-century graphic art is recalled, par-ticularly that of the 'Dance of Death'.

Shakespeare would have first encountered the iconography of the 'Dance of Death' as a child. John Stow noted in his copy of Leland's *Itinerary* that this imagery, common to all Europe by the beginning of the sixteenth century, was found on the wall of the parish church of Stratford-upon-Avon.[28] The 'Dance of Death' was otherwise known as the 'Danse Macabre' from its original attribution as 'The Dance of Machabree', as it appears in John Lydgate's translation.[29] The original fifteenth-century French poem with accompanying illustrations adorned the walls of the Church of the Holy Innocents in Paris. Lydgate's version was similarly used with illustrations in old St Paul's cathedral where it became an object of devotion for Sir Thomas More contemplating death without us, and within us.[30] Holbein's forty-one woodcuts for his work, commonly

referred to as *The Dance of Death*, are well known and they became the basis for the psaltery of Queen Elizabeth's *Book of Common Prayer* (1569) with the number of border illustrations of *The Dance of Death* expanded to seventy-one.[31]

The Dance of Death might well have arisen in response to the horrors of the Black Death, but from a larger perspective it was a development of the death obsession of the Middle Ages as exemplified in Pope Innocent III's *De Miseria Condicionis Humane* (1195) which was circulated all over Europe in manuscripts and books and translated by George Gascoigne in his *The Droomme of Doomes Day* (1576).[32] This literature focused on bodily corruption, death, burial and decomposition, with Death the leveller used to reinforce the hierarchy of the church. In *The Dance of Death* the estates of man, and eventually women, are led off to their inevitable end. Tomb sculpture often reflected this worm-ridden fate.[33]

The Dance of Death strikes at the heart of carnival since it concentrates on final bodily putrefaction, whatever might await the soul,

---

[28] J. M. Clark, *The Dance of Death* (Glasgow, 1950), p. 15.

[29] Two manuscript versions of Lydgate's poem, with further collation, edited by Florence Warren and Beatrice White, are published as *The Dance of Death* (The Early English Text Society, no. 181, London, 1931).

[30] 'The Four Last Things', *The English Works of Sir Thomas More* (London and New York, 1931), vol. 1, p. 468.

[31] See Francis Douce, *Holbein's Dance of Death* (London, 1898). The Queen Elizabeth prayer book reproduced on p. 83 is the version by William Pickering, London, 1853. See Ruari McLean *Victorian Book Design* (London, 1963), pp. 10–12. The woodcuts were by Mary Byfield. I am indebted to Christopher and Phillipa Hardman for help with this reference.

[32] Robert E. Lewis (ed.), *De Miseria Condicionis Humane* (Athens, 1978), pp. 3–5 survey the transmission of manuscripts. John W. Cunliffe (ed.), *The Complete Works of George Gascoigne* (Cambridge, 1910), vol. 2, *The Glasse of Government and Other Poems and Prose Works*, pp. 209–450.

[33] See 'The Vision of Death', ch. XI of J. Huizinga, *The Waning of the Middle Ages* (New York, 1954).

1 'The Triumph of Death' by Breugel (detail).

whereas carnival celebrates bodily regeneration on earth. As the word 'dance' implies, music and dancing reflect the festive world of carnival, banqueting and romance. Throughout *Romeo and Juliet* Capulet's household reflects both this revelry, and impending death. As we have seen with the old Capulets looking on at the revels (1.5) the carnivalesque is affirmed in spite of Romeo's foreboding. Acts 4 and 5 with the preparations for the wedding feast, festive musicians and so on, reverse this, finally succumbing to death, tragedy and the tomb. *Romeo and Juliet* was performed within a culture in which the iconography of death had persisted, yet with some degree of development in which moral censure of the carnivalesque and festive partly displaced the homiletic corpse or skeleton. All this is reflected in the design of the play.

Arthur Brooke's source had provided the commonplace from which Shakespeare developed. In Brooke Romeo pursues his love 'till Fortune list to sawse his sweete with sowre', until 'all his hap turnes to mishap, and all his myrth to mone'.[34] *Romeo and Juliet*'s 'womb'/'tomb', 'festival'/'funeral' have been touched on. Brooke's figure of agnomination, 'myrth'/'mone', echoes what seems to have been a source for English Renaissance rhetoric, St Gregory the Divine (Gregorius Nazianzen). In his translation of Innocent III, Gascoigne cites St Gregory on the contrasts to joy in a heavenly Creator; 'all other myrth is mournyng, all other pleasure is payne, all sweete soure, all leefe lothsome, and all

---

[34] Bullough, *Sources*, vol. I, p. 310, lines 932–46.

2   From 'The Dance of Death' by Holbein.

3   From 'The Dance of Death' by Holbein.

delyghtes are dollorous'. John Lyly's Euphuism would appear to owe something to church fathers like St Augustine and St Gregory as John Hoskins notes, while providing his own carnival-esque–lenten example in 'feasting'/'fasting'.[35] The conflation of antitheses in the iconography of death partly developed from this homiletic rhetoric, and particularly seized on images of the carnival and festive, above all music, masks and dancing. In Thomas Nashe's diatribe *Christ's Teares Over Jerusalem* (1593), just a few years before *Romeo and Juliet*, we find 'Your morne-like christall countenances shall be netted over and (Masker-like) cawle-visarded with crawling venomous wormes.'[36] An indicative dramatic example is, of course, Vindice in Middleton's *The Revenger's Tragedy* (1607) holding a skull and declaring 'It were fine, methinks / To have thee seen at revels, forgetful feasts', to 'put a reveller / Out of his antic amble' (3.5.89–93). This is precisely what the illustrations of death did.

In Breugel's still harrowing painting 'The Triumph of Death', which included several motifs from the 'Dance of Death' sequences, we see in the lower right-hand corner a cloaked and masked death overturning flagons of wine, disrupting feasting and gaming as a jester tries to hide, while two lovers, blithely unaware, sing and play music accompanied by another unseen death (fig. 1).[37] Similarly, in a Dürer woodcut a shrouded figure introduces a corpse into a banquet. Most of the guests, including two lovers, are too engrossed to notice.[38] In Ripa's

[35] *Directions for Speech and Style* (1599), ed. Hoyht H. Hudson (Princeton, 1935), pp. 16, 37. Gascoigne, *Works*, vol. 2, p. 398.

[36] Ronald B. McKerrow, *The Works of Thomas Nashe* (London, 1904), vol. 2, pp. 138–9.

[37] See Walter S. Gibson, *Breugel* (London, 1977), p. 116.

[38] Dr Willi Kurth, *The Complete Woodcuts of Albrecht Dürer* (New York, 1963), illustration 15. I am indebted to Pat Righelato for this reference.

4 'Dance aux aveugles'.

Iconologia (1603) Death is masked and in a burden carries 'musical instruments ... of worldly joys' along with symbols of power and pleasure.[39]

Shakespeare's musicians in Act 4 do not convert festival to funeral, mirth to moan, but persist in a carnival humour with Peter, the Capulet servant. The carnivalesque element is uppermost as, before their actual entry, the musicians' festive music is heard even as Juliet's 'dead' body is discovered. The original stage direction at 4.4.20 is *Play music*, as Capulet says, 'The County will be here with music straight, / For so he said he would. I hear him near' (4.4.21–2). As the Nurse, Capulet and Lady Capulet heavily bemoan death, comedy supervenes since the audience knows that Juliet is drugged, not dead – in the midst of death we are in life, the reverse of the iconographic tradition.

In at least nine of Holbein's woodcuts for *The Dance of Death* death and music are associated, nearly always with death as a musician. Number thirty-five shows newlyweds seemingly engrossed in each other while Death dances before them striking a festive tabor (fig. 2), an image reflected in the Breugel painting. The fifth illustration shows the entrance to a tomb with half a dozen partially clothed skeletons playing instruments which compound festival with funeral – crumhorns, kettle drums, a hurdy-gurdy, a shawm, and so on (fig. 3). There is an apocalyptic element here whereas some earlier sequences, such as the 1491 *La grande Danse macabre* had included 'The Orchestra of

39 Hildesheim and New York, 1970, '... istromenti de l'allegrezze mondane', p. 340.

5 From Queen Elizabeth's *Book of Common Prayer*
and *Psaltery*.

Death'.[40] A variant of this tradition is found in
Pierre Michault's fifteenth-century poem *Dance
aux aveugles* which in an illustrated Geneva
manuscript shows the three 'blind' – or blind-
folded – ones, Cupid, Fortune and Death,
disposed in a triptych. At the foot of each panel
seated musicians look on awaiting those led to
this dance of death (fig. 4).[41] *Romeo and Juliet*
reflects Michault's structure as the lovers move
from Cupid's blind, or masked, passion through
fatal misfortune to death with, at one point,
musicians in attendance. Queen Elizabeth's
prayer book separates the musicians from death.
As they play a skeleton looms behind (fig. 5).
And in contrast to the carnivalesque death–

birth, tomb–womb cycle we have seen in the
Nurse's speech particularly, one of the woodcuts shows Death behind a nurse cradling her
charge, with the words 'give suck no more; for
I am at the door' (fig. 5).

Emblems and paintings not directly concerned with eschatological death nevertheless
endorsed an anti-carnivalesque view of music,
dancing and love. Joos van Winghe's *Nocturnal
Party* (1588) depicts masked musicians joining in
with dancers before a statue of Venus.[42]
Drunken abandon makes the moral implications
quite clear. More directly pertinent to *Romeo
and Juliet* is Otto van Veen's emblem entitled
'Voluptatum Usurae, Morbi et Miseriae'
(Pleasure's Usury, Sickness and Misery) in his
Horatii Emblemata, 1612 (fig. 6).[43] Masked
dancers accompanied by a masked musician
with a drinker and a venal couple looking on
dominate the foreground. In the background
gamblers play, an old man grasping a cupid-
putto is admitted, while at the rear on a
darkened sickbed reclines a figure whose urine
is being examined in a glass bottle by a physi-
cian. Arthur Brooke's source for *Romeo and
Juliet* indirectly provides a comment since precisely at that point quoted above where he
considers 'myrth' and 'mone', he draws on the
same moral commonplace which gave van
Veen his title, the metaphor of usury for
pleasure; Fortune 'payd theyr former greefe
with pleasures doubled gayne, / But now for
pleasures usery ten folde redoubleth payne'.[44]
In the polyglot verses beneath several lines from
Latin sources once again we find predictable

---

40 *Le Sentiment de la Mort au Moyen Age* (Montreal, 1979),
p. 199.

40 *Le Sentiment de la Mort au Moyen Age* (Montreal, 1979),
p. 199.

41 Bruno Roy, 'Amour, Fortune et Mort: La danse des
trois aveugles' in *Le Sentiment de la Mort au Moyen Age*,
pp. 121–37. The illustration is reproduced in Erwin
Panofsky's seminal chapter 'Blind Cupid; in *Studies in
Iconology* (New York, 1962), plate XLVI.

42 *Masters of Seventeenth-Century Dutch Genre Painting*
(Philadelphia 1984), p. 177.

43 New York and London, 1979, pp. 38–9.

44 Bullough, *Sources*, vol. I, p. 310, lines 953–4.

6   From Otto van Veen *Horatii Emblemata*.

antitheses of pleasure and pain, joy and tears, glossing van Veen's picture. Van Veen and Brooke both share a common moralizing outlook. Sickness and death follow upon indulgence of vice. Shakespeare's comparable scene, the revels with the aged Capulets looking on, affirms the carnivalesque by including age with youth suggesting a triumph of life. But this is not to be. As James Black has noted of the repeated stage picture of the prince of Verona and his feuding subjects, with youth killed off and the aged solemnly gathered; it 'is made progressively tragic as it becomes more and more a pageant of death'.[45]

On entering the tomb Romeo's language recalls the carnivalesque death-earth-womb but transforms it into death as a ravenous monster, a traditional hell-mouth.

> Thou detestable maw, thou womb of death
> Gorg'd with the dearest morsel of the earth,
> Thus I enforce thy rotten jaws to open,
> And in despite I'll cram thee with more food.
>
> (5.3.45–8)

Inside, the sight of Juliet's beauty transforms her surroundings. Complementing her earlier speech when she had related night, death, and festival, Romeo says, 'her beauty makes / This vault a feasting presence, full of light' (5.3.85–6). As his first glimpse of Juliet was in the midst of revels and banqueting, an image as we have seen associated with the entrance of death, so the tomb scene inverts this and festival enters into the midst of death. Analogously, as he was lover at the festival, so death is lover here:

> Shall I believe
> That unsubstantial Death is amorous,
> And that the lean abhorred monster keeps
> Thee here in dark to be his paramour?
>
> (5.3.102–5)

And so Romeo rivals death who can only be the final triumpher as Breugel rehearsed in a title which Petrarch bequeathed to the Renaissance in *The Triumph of Death* from his *Trionfi*.[46] In carnival there can be no triumph of death, only a triumph of life in human generation. Echoing the sonneteers, Romeo had said that Rosaline's chastity 'Cuts beauty off from all posterity' (1.1.218). Romeo and Juliet were briefly lovers but now it is her beauty which is cut off from all posterity. This is the larger, more inclusive sense of tragedy, from a carnivalesque perspective: not simply the poignancy of their deaths, but that only death came from their love, not the renewal and thus reaffirmation of life. When Capulet follows Juliet to the tomb, that will be the end of his line. And the same for the Montagues since Brooke included the detail that Romeo's 'parentes have none other heyre, thou art theyr onely sonne'.[47] The funereal gold statues are no substitute for the warmth of new life. But carnival can never really be defeated. It finds new life in new forms as long as there is comedy. It is said that *The Dance of Death* itself arose partly as a homiletic reaction to a peasant custom – of dancing in graveyards.[48]

---

[45] 'The Visual Artistry of *Romeo and Juliet*', *Studies in English Literature*, vol. 15, 1975, p. 250.

[46] D. D. Carnicelli in his edition of *Lord Morley's Tryumphes of Frances Petrarcke* (Cambridge, Mass., 1971) provides much useful introductory material, pp. 1–74.

[47] Bullough, *Sources*, vol. I, p. 289, line 120.

[48] See Lydgate, *The Dance of Death*, p. xiii.

IDEOLOGY AND THE FEUD IN *ROMEO AND JULIET*

SUSAN SNYDER

Romeo and Juliet are very young. They are young to be married, and also young to be protagonists in a tragedy. Shakespeare made a special point of Juliet's extreme youth, first subtracting two years from the already tender age of Arthur Brooke's heroine (instead of sixteen, just under fourteen), and then having the characters disagree more than once over whether she is old enough to marry.[1] Romeo, presumably somewhat older than Juliet, is nevertheless not yet grown up: still in the family home, fussed over by his parents, free to roam about with his friends but apparently not seen as ready for adult responsibility.

Why did Shakespeare insist on his tragic lovers as adolescents? To be sure, their youthfulness accentuates the generational conflict implicit in the story, the tragic disjunction that Franco Zeffirelli exploited so well in his compelling film version. But the extreme youth of Romeo and Juliet opens up a possibility beyond the traditional clashes of young and old. The very embeddedness in family that signals their tender years may itself be the point. It is surely significant that each of the two protagonists is introduced to us first as the object of parental concern. In the opening scene the Montagues worry about Romeo's solitary moping, fearing that some secret sorrow may blight their promising son before he ever arrives at maturity.[2] In the scene directly following, Capulet is busy providing for his daughter's future by negotiating her marriage with Paris. It is important that each of these parental discussions takes place before we even meet the young person being discussed. Our initial view is of Romeo as a son, Juliet as a daughter.

Juliet as daughter of the house continues a prominent emphasis. Even her love scenes with Romeo are played out inside the Capulet enclave, with one family member or another always threatening to intrude. Romeo is seen in the streets rather than enclosed in Montague domesticity, in the company of his friends rather than his parents. This reflects, of course, the relative freedom accorded to young males as opposed to young females. But the difference in terms of family embeddedness may be more apparent than real. Romeo's peer group is not separate from kinship structure but a kind of extension of it, in that his habitual companions are Montague allies.

All of us are always being shaped into our ways of being and knowing by extensive social processing, but the lives of the young make this process especially visible. Romeo and Juliet do not necessarily have less autonomy than adults who have undergone the full ideological conditioning afforded by society's institutions. Yet their subordinate situation as children, acted on

---

[1] Arthur Brooke, *The Tragicall Historye of Romeus and Juliet* (1562), fol. G4. Her mother says that most of the girl's friends are already married. In Painter's version Juliet is almost eighteen: *The Palace of Pleasure* (1567), Nnn2r.

[2] Montague likens him to 'the bud bit with an envious worm / Ere he can spread his sweet leaves to the air / Or dedicate his beauty to the sun' (1.1.148–50).

(cajoled, lectured, ordered, modelled) by the parents who in effect own them, makes that lack of autonomy more apparent. And the major constituting force that operates in their society is the feud between Montagues and Capulets.

At first glance this would seem too comprehensive a claim for the feud's reach and impact. The quarrel involves only two families, and it is not always taken seriously even by Montagues and Capulets. H. B. Charlton finds the family feud unsatisfactory as Fate's instrument in *Romeo and Juliet*, 'unsubstantial', because it is sometimes treated comically and does not consistently inform the feelings and actions of most characters. In any case, thinks Charlton, such barbaric mores are not realistic in the civilized Verona the play depicts.[3] (On this last point, one wonders how a study published soon after World War II could ignore such abundant evidence in the recent history of civilized Western Europe of resurgent group hatreds and the barbaric behaviour they generated.) Critics in their own time have less trouble seeing the destructive dimensions in Veronese civility. Marilyn Williamson, for example, points to the violent atmosphere of the play's society.[4] For Coppélia Kahn, the feud is 'an extreme and peculiar expression of patriarchal society'.[5] I agree that informing social institutions are the play's major tragic force, though I would quarrel with Kahn's term 'peculiar' if it is meant to characterize the feud as uncommon, individual rather than general. The dramatic *expression* of dynastic hostility may seem extreme and eccentric, but the feud in its operations acts like any ideology, indeed offers a model of how ideology works.

Like ideology in Althusser's classic formulation, the feud has no obvious genesis that can be discerned, no history. It pervades everything, not as a set of specific ideas but as repeated practices. The feud-system is not in fact predicated on any substantive difference between Montagues and Capulets. A Jerusalem production which presented Montagues as Arabic-speaking Palestinians and Capulets as Hebrew-speaking Jews had its own political point to make about the clash of rival cultures.[6] Shakespeare, though, with his 'two households both alike in dignity', seems to be creating a different sort of division, one that is obviously arbitrary and artificial. The members of his rival houses belong to the same culture, use the same verbal and behavioural languages. When Montagues intrude on the Capulet festivities, only their faces have to be covered; nothing else in their bearing or manners marks them as outsiders. What's in a name? Everything, it would seem. One thinks of Lacan's two identical doors with *Ladies* over one and *Gentlemen* over the other.

Shakespeare also emphasizes the artificial nature of the feud by suppressing the account of its origins given in this source. Brooke explains that it was their very equality of station that gave rise to enmity between the two families, breeding envy and hatred which in time became 'rooted'.[7] Shakespeare says only that the quarrel is 'ancient'.[8] The first scene subtly enacts this 'always already' quality of the feud, when a question of origins is raised only to fall short of an answer. The elder Montague asks Benvolio what started the latest round of hostilities – asks,

---

[3] H. B. Charlton, *Shakespearian Tragedy* (Cambridge, 1948), pp. 59–60.

[4] Marilyn Williamson, 'Romeo and Death', *Shakespeare Studies*, 14 (New York, 1981), 129–37; pp. 135–6. Her main point is Romeo's bent to self-destruction, which she sees as expressing his society's pervasive violence.

[5] Coppélia Kahn, 'Coming of Age in Verona', *Modern Language Studies*, 8 (1978), repr. *'Romeo and Juliet': Critical Essays*, ed. John F. Andrews, Garland Shakespearean Criticism Series, 10 (New York, 1993), 337–58; p. 337.

[6] Reported on *All Things Considered*, National Public Radio, 27 July 1994.

[7] *Romeus and Juliet*, A2r.

[8] Prol. 3; 1.1.101. G. K. Hunter points to the lack of content in the enmity between Capulets and Montagues when he observes that the feud has 'little political reality' and exists to put pressure on the love of Romeo and Juliet: 'Shakespeare's Earliest Tragedies: *Titus Andronicus* and *Romeo and Juliet*', *Shakespeare Survey* 27 (Cambridge, 1974), pp. 1–9; p. 5.

we should note, only *after* both of them have automatically taken part in the fighting. Benvolio can't give a good explanation because the clash was already under way when he entered. The audience has been on the scene longer than he has, but any answer spectators can give to 'how did this start?' is no more definitive than Benvolio's. We have seen the Capulet servants come on already primed to fight, as if they need contrary Montagues to define their manhood. Or rather, this has been Sampson's stance, while Gregory twits him and plays generally with words. But the feud, like ideology, flattens out personal differences, slotting individuals into predetermined roles; after some actual Montagues arrive on the scene, Gregory quickly falls into line with Sampson's pugnacity – just as Benvolio, whose natural bent is to peacemaking and who a few minutes later tries to stop the servants' scrap, must nevertheless slide into his appointed slot to cross swords with Tybalt. The dominance of an 'assigned form of subjectivity'[9] over individual temperament or initiative is evident in the exaggerated symmetry of the whole sequence: servants matched by opposing servants, nephew of one house paired off against nephew of the other, Capulet patriarch answered by Montague patriarch, all entering as if on cue and doing the same thing.

The Montague–Capulet feud may be like ideology in having no apparent beginning, but is it not different in coming to a publicly announced end in the last moments of the play? I shall delay addressing this somewhat problematic issue till the end of my essay, and consider here another question that has probably occurred to more than one reader already. Is it legitimate to see the feud as shaped by Shakespeare enacting the workings of ideology as conceived by modern theorists? Where we may accept without difficulty readings that discern in his plays and poems the features of specific ideological systems, explore their contradictions, and trace their transmutations, the assumption in these cases is that Shakespeare need have made no conscious effort to delineate these

systems, which rather inscribe themselves through us without our awareness or cooperation. But doesn't taking the feud as a metaphor for ideology in general imply some conscious intent on Shakespeare's part?

Yes, it does, and the assumption is not unwarranted. Without precognizing Althusser, Shakespeare nevertheless displays in *Romeo and Juliet* a very conscious concern with society's impact on the individual, especially in the characters' meditations on names and their power. Names define us as individuals, announce who we are. Yet no name is unique to one person. It has been attached to others in the society, blood kin in the case of the surname, saints or leaders or forebears in the case of the given name. Names are imposed on infants before they are individuals, by society and its central unit the family. The considerable dynastic and cultural freight they carry begins the child's constitution as a subject. 'Romeo Montague' inscribes the young man who is called that into a particular subject-position. (We tend to see this dimension mainly in the family name, but Juliet laments over the given name as well: 'Deny thy father and refuse thy name' is preceded by 'Wherefore art thou Romeo?' And her lover, invited to doff his offending name, responds 'Henceforth I never will be Romeo.')

Juliet's familiar 'what's in a name?' meditation shows up the power of ideology by signally underestimating its force. She and Romeo have met unlabelled, as it were, a faceless youth and an anonymous girl at a party. They have not encountered each other before in the usual contextual way because of the enmity between their families. Each asks for the name of the other, and discovers conflict:

ROMEO   Is she a Capulet?
O dear account! My life is my foe's debt ...

---

[9] This term, preferred by Goran Therborn over role (*The Ideology of Power and the Power of Ideology* [London, 1981]), better emphasizes inward conditioning along with the behaviour it generates.

JULIET My only love sprung from my only hate!
  Too early seen unknown, and known too late![10]

In soliloquy later, Juliet convinces herself that *seeing*, responding to individual looks and attitudes, can blot out *knowing*, which acknowledges the social context. She tries to separate her lover's name from his essential properties.

> 'Tis but thy name that is my enemy.
> Thou art thyself, though not a Montague.
> What's Montague? It is nor hand, nor foot,
> Nor arm, nor face, nor any part
> Belonging to a man.   (2.1.80–4)

Name and self are not so easily divisible, though. While Romeo immediately disavows his name, Juliet even here goes on calling him 'Romeo' and 'Montague', and worries about the danger of his staying with her, 'considering who thou art' (2.1.106). A name may not be a body part, but Romeo will soon feel it to be just as intrinsic. Fearing that Juliet hates him for killing her cousin Tybalt, he attributes the act to 'that name's cursed hand'. The contorted phrase makes manifest the social construction of his agency. Contradicting Juliet's earlier optimism, he feels 'Romeo' as something so enmeshed with his being that it needs to be forcibly ripped out of his body (3.3.101–7). What has happened to change his perception from 'Henceforth I never will be Romeo' to 'In what vile part of this anatomy / Doth my name lodge?' is the reactivation of the feud: the need to avenge Mercutio, who died taking Romeo's own place against Tybalt, by killing in turn the enemy Capulet. Romeo's name has turned out to be a part of his self after all, directing his actions and defining his responses.

Juliet's hopeful separation of essence from what seems to her an external label – 'Thou art thyself, though not a Montague' – is soon shown to be wrong, then. Even the supporting argument that she uses at the time is suspect. 'That which we call a rose / By any other word would smell as sweet' (2.1.85–6) sounds self-evidently true. But would that flower really retain its full sweetness in our subjective

judgement if we were not conditioned to think of the rose as the best, the most worthy? The blossom itself retains its natural properties under any name, but our use and valuation of it must alter. The name 'rose' carries with it considerable cultural baggage, suggesting surpassing beauty combined with difficulty of access (surrounded by thorns), hence something supremely precious, as well as the paragon, the ideal. What Ophelia means when she calls Hamlet 'th' expectancy and rose of the fair state' (*Hamlet* 3.1.155) would be significantly altered if she talked of 'th' expectancy and lilac', even though lilacs smell sweet too – especially since the 'fair state' of the audience for whom Shakespeare wrote this line had a rose as its familiar symbol.

Shakespeare did not need Althusser's analysis in order to grasp the workings of interpellation or to feel the force of the dual meaning of *subject*, the 'autonomous' agent who is formed by and in a social formation to which he is subjected. Jonathan Dollimore approaches the same question through parallels between Montaigne's 'custom' and Althusser's 'ideology', concluding that 'the Renaissance possessed a sophisticated concept of ideology if not the word'.[11] The preoccupation with names in *Romeo and Juliet* points directly to the most basic function of ideology, central also to the feud: identifying, hailing or interpellating into predetermined subject-positions. The feud operates in the classic way of language, and of ideology: it creates meaning by differentiating. Terry Eagleton, following Jameson, finds the opposition between self/familiar/good on the one hand and non-self/alien/bad on the other 'the fundamental gesture of all ideology'.[12] Capulets

---

[10] 1.5.116–38. For the formality of the lovers' rhymed couplets here as an expression of the feud mentality, see below, pp. 94–5.

[11] Jonathan Dollimore, *Radical Tragedy: Religion, Ideology and Power in the Drama of Shakespeare and his Contemporaries*, 2nd edn (Durham, N.C., 1993), pp. 17–18; the idea is developed in ch. 10.

[12] Terry Eagleton, *Ideology: An Introduction* (London and

define who they are against Montagues, Montagues against Capulets. 'This' can only be distinguished when set against 'that', however arbitrary such distinctions are in language and other social constructions.[13] The feud is not a matter of contrary ideas, not a matter of ideas at all, but of repeated, habitual actions that keep reasserting the defining distinctions between 'us' and 'them'.

Ideology is what constructs our consciousness and makes sense of our world. It is pervasive, working everywhere. Can this be said of the feud? After all, not everyone in Verona is a Montague or a Capulet. We get fleeting glimpses of some nameless citizens, and various members of another family come in for more extended attention as individual characters: Prince Escalus, and especially his two kinsmen Mercutio and Paris. But on scrutiny the Montague–Capulet hostility can be seen to gather in and organize these third parties as well as the two central clans. The feud exemplifies the workings of any ideology, of Ideology itself, but the specifics of its enactment express their historical moment.[14] The Veronese discourse of family division thus embraces some important social imperatives of early modern élite culture in Western Europe: the obligation to maintain one's honour by avenging insults, the obligation to contract a suitable marriage and adapt appropriately to the married state.

To some extent these were gendered. It was men who were bound in this way by the code of honour. Marriage, though expected of both sexes, was more central and defining for women, since a wife took on the loyalties as well as the status of her new family along with its name. In *Romeo and Juliet* Lady Capulet not only makes the case for marriage to her young daughter but also demonstrates her own thorough conditioning as a wife. Presumably not a Capulet by birth, she nevertheless has committed herself totally and fervently to the family feud. Her husband, born into the anti-Montague faith, can be easygoing about it at times, as when he accepts Romeo's presence at the party. His wife, a typical convert, is possessed by her acquired faith. She is not on hand to comment on this first occasion, but after Romeo has killed Tybalt she fills the air with cries of grief and demands for revenge. Indeed, it is presumably her role as chief mourner for Tybalt in 3.1, as contrasted with her husband's silence, that led Malone and subsequent editors to list Tybalt in the Dramatis Personae as the nephew of *Lady* Capulet, not Capulet himself.[15] But family titles like *nephew* and *brother* routinely included in-laws as well as blood relatives,[16] and Tybalt's own deep investment in Capulet family values, not to speak of his interment in the family tomb, strongly suggests that he is a Capulet born. While a woman's transfer of loyalties to her husband's kin was fitting, a man's proper adherence was to his own clan. Lady Capulet's extreme sorrow for Tybalt, then, and her murderous designs on his slayer convey not special concern for her own family of birth but complete interpellation as a Capulet

---

New York, 1991), p. 126; cf. Fredric Jameson, *The Political Unconscious* (Ithaca, N.Y., 1981), pp. 114–15. Althusser came close, in his essays on Freud and Lenin and in *Lenin and Philosophy*, to equating language and the symbolic order with ideology as agents constructing the subject. Catherine Belsey completes the connection in *Critical Practice* (London and New York, 1980), ch. 3.

13 The lack of real difference between Montagues and Capulets (see above, p. 88) illustrates Saussure's central dictum that language is a system of differences with no positive terms, a system which creates meaning rather than discovers a pre-existing one. For the inextricable relation of language and ideology, see Rosalind Coward and John Ellis, *Language and Materialism: Developments in Semiology and the Theory of the Subject* (London, 1977). Erik Erikson in *Identity and the Youth Cycle* (New York, 1980) discusses (pp. 97–8) the function of group identification and exclusion in the adolescent years, the founding of identity on difference.

14 'Existential ideologies always exist in concrete historical forms, but are never reducible to them': Therborn, *The Ideology of Power*, p. 44.

15 Eighteenth-century editions before Malone's of 1790 list Tybalt as Capulet's kinsman.

16 Both Capulet and Lady Capulet refer to Tybalt as the son of 'my brother' (3.5.127; 3.1.146).

by marriage.[17] To Juliet as a prospective bride she lays out the same course, inviting her to be the decorative cover to the book that is Paris – in other words, to take her meaning from her husband. 'So shall you share in all he doth possess / By having him, making yourself no less' (1.3.81–96). Paris himself, like Juliet initially, gives docile heed to the imperative of suitable alliance; indeed, this is his sole motive for action in the play. The marriage of Paris and Juliet never takes place, but it is his moves towards that union that involve him fatally in the bloodshed of the feud.

Like his kinsman Paris, Mercutio gets entangled in the feud and dies in consequence. By his intervention in the fight to uphold Romeo's masculine good name when Romeo himself refuses to rise to Tybalt's insulting provocations, Mercutio brings out the other specific historical face of ideology in this play, the masculine code of honour. Mercutio presents himself as a scorner of codes and conventions. He shows no sign of negotiating like Paris for a bride, he delights in recasting Romeo's Petrarchan metaphors of adoration for Rosaline into leering physicality. He mocks standard beliefs like the power of dreams to prognosticate, and standard practices like the formulas of fencing. Yet Mercutio is as deeply implicated in ideology as anyone else. His reduction of woman to a set of sexual parts to be attacked is not really his own, but derives from another ideological strain, as extreme as Petrarchan adoration and even hoarier as a cultural tradition. And for all his disdain of the *duello*, he hurls himself with no question at all into the duel proposed by Tybalt. His response is as mechanical as any we have witnessed in the opening Montague–Capulet brawl. Mercutio himself attributes his death to the family feud, obsessively repeating through his last moments 'A plague o' both your houses ... A plague o' both your houses! ... A plague o' both your houses ... Your houses!' (3.1.91–108).

When these specific ideological ramifications thus draw in the two chief 'outsiders' in the play, and the third 'outsider' finally reads his

own implication in theirs ('And I, for winking at your discords, too / Have lost a brace of kinsmen', 5.3.293–4), the feud does appear all-pervasive. No part of society that we see can escape from its influence.[18] Romeo and Juliet themselves are deeply conditioned by it, although they also, necessarily, transcend the family division. I call this movement beyond the feud necessary not only because it allows their love for each other to begin and develop, but also because their venture outside the circumscribing feud-ideology makes that ideology visible, as it would never be if everyone continued to operate inside its unspoken premises.

Transcendence is perhaps a misleading term for the lovers' attempted isolation of themselves from the feud. Enclosed by Veronese social formations, they do not rise above so much as withdraw inward. Romeo and Juliet have no space of their own. Their love scenes are all played out inside the Capulet establishment, constantly impinged upon by Tybalt, or the Nurse, or Lady Capulet. The closest the lovers come to a shared private space is Friar Laurence's cell, where they met in 2.5 to be married. But that encounter is brief and driven (Friar Laurence feels it necessary to 'make short work' of the marriage ceremony, line 34). Moreover,

---

[17] Lady Capulet demonstrates that one of Juliet's propositions about names is not naive wish but fact. Her assertion that in union with Romeo she would 'no longer be a Capulet' (2.1.78) has the whole weight of contemporary theory and practice of marriage to support it.

[18] The feud is an example of Althusser's ideology of the ruling class, as that class is embodied in the three élite clans on view. The potentially opposing interests of the lower classes are not thematized: Capulet and Montague servants are instead shown as interpellated by their masters' feud, identified with the interests of the houses they serve. Althusser's formulation is not completely appropriate here, however, since the *cui bono* question – whose interests are served by the constituting force? – is not relevant to the feud as presented by Shakespeare. Ideology in *Romeo and Juliet* is not analysed structurally but experienced from the subject's point of view; its origins and purposes are not visible.

this respite from the feud is granted not by escape from ideology but by the temporary ascendancy of a rival one, the Friar's Christian agenda of reconciling the two warring houses. Nor does a freer space seem to be imaginable for Romeo and Juliet somewhere else. A milieu less insistently enclosing might make visually possible the option of leaving the city together and finding a new life somewhere else. Instead, the play's physical dimensions only confirm that 'there is no world without Verona walls' (3.3.17). Verona, constituted by the feud, asserts itself like any ideology as the only reality there is.[19] Even as they die, another Capulet enclave surrounds the young pair, the family tomb.

Hemmed in as they are, how can Romeo and Juliet constitute even an inner space in terms different from the all-powerful norm? As is suggested by Friar Laurence's transgression of the feud's dictates to sanction their love, opportunity arises through the presence of rival ideologies coexisting with and sometimes challenging the dominant one. For example, Romeo and Juliet can initially meet and talk as they do not only because they are momentarily free of family-name labels but because Juliet's father is for once tolerating the presence of a Montague. He restrains the angry Tybalt, swayed by imperatives other than the feud:

> Content thee, gentle coz, let him alone.
> A bears him like a portly gentleman,
> And, to say truth, Verona brags of him
> To be a virtuous and well-governed youth.
> I would not for the wealth of all this town
> Here in my house do him disparagement.
>
> (1.5.64–9)

Such indulgence at first glance seems to support Charlton's dismissal of the feud as too lightweight to sustain its role in the tragic structure, let alone to express the central shaping force of any culture. If the family enmity can be so easily set aside by the leader of one faction, how can it nevertheless represent the all-powerful operations of ideology? But one can see in Capulet's attitude not a casual shedding of the feud but an internal disruption in the social ideology, as the dominant discourse is crossed by other, locally influential ones. Montagues are to be spurned, yet good cheer must be fostered at social gatherings, especially by the host. Categorically, a Montague is an enemy, yet a particular young man's good behaviour and reputation make it hard to treat him rudely. For convivial Capulet, whose favourite activity is preparing and presenting feasts, the primary value at this moment of cross-purposes is surely hospitality. '*Here in my house*', whatever you do, don't spoil the party.

Normally kept apart by the reigning ideology, Romeo and Juliet can thus come together in a kind of aporia created by ideological contestation, which in turn enables them to find in their sonnet-exchange discourses that they can share, of romantic courtship and religion. Religion will continue as a common discourse embodied in Friar Laurence. The commonality has in fact preceded this first meeting: it is another sign of crossed ideologies that these two young people so firmly separated by the feud can nevertheless share without any special dispensation the same confessor. His cell is another aporia, or a version of the first, the (only) place where hereditary enemies can meet and formally unite.

The discourse of romantic courtship presents a more complicated picture. The first exchange between Romeo and Juliet is in some ways highly conventional, grounded in a familiar cultural master-script. Their dialogue falls neatly into the standard sonnet's three quatrains and a couplet, and in typical sonnet fashion elaborates a conceit, the lover as pilgrim. In showing so clearly the impress of literary tradition, this

---

[19] Here again Shakespeare departs significantly from earlier versions of the story, in which Juliet begs to accompany her lover into exile, either openly as his wife or in disguise. Brooke has Romeus refuse for fear that Capulet will pursue and harm them, but in the world Shakespeare has created, to leave the city together is not even conceived as possible.

wooing passage may remind us of Romeo a few scenes before, expounding his hopeless love for Rosaline in Petrarchan clichés. If that earlier love-talk nevertheless feels more artificial, it is partly because the speaker's diligence in piling up the conceits and oxymora suggests a scholar's zeal rather than a lover's;[20] but partly because, with the other party to the courtship not even present, Romeo's one-sided romance acquires the flavour of rhetorical exercise. The passage between Romeo and Juliet at the Capulet party moves more naturally: proposition, response, adjustment and further proposition, new response. Here Romeo's speech has a real purpose, pleading for a kiss. And they do kiss, twice. Juliet breaks off the second sonnet begun by Romeo with 'You kiss by th' book' (1.5.109). While the latter part of her teasing complaint underlines how the impersonal discourse of literary love has written itself through their exchange, the first part nevertheless acknowledges real physical contact between them. The later love-speech of Romeo and Juliet uses rhyme much less and highly wrought form not at all. Their language cannot of course completely escape tradition – no language can. But in subsequent dialogue between the lovers convention is not prominent as such, and familiar materials are reworked to flow, with the verse, more freely.[21]

This often-noted evolution, from romantic discourse shaped by convention to a more direct lyricism that seems to override form, enacts through language the withdrawal of Romeo and Juliet from the defining difference imposed on them by the feud, into immediate, fervent engagement with each other. Perhaps their very youthfulness, which on the one hand highlights the social processing they are undergoing, on the other hand makes that withdrawal more possible in that the processing is not complete. They are less fixed by constant conditioning than their elders, less habituated to their social roles as Montague and Capulet. Even so, the grip of ideology is tenacious, and apt to tighten in moments of emotional crisis.

Both lovers offer examples of this tenacity, and both temporary re-conformings are accentuated by a lapse into 'speaking by the book'. Trying to deal with Tybalt's rage right after his marriage to Juliet, Romeo has been unconventional in both action and speech: 'I do protest I never injured thee, / But love thee better than thou canst devise ... good Capulet – which name I tender / As dearly as mine own – be satisfied' (3.1.67–71). But when Mercutio takes up Tybalt's challenge on Romeo's behalf and is mortally wounded as a result, conventional reactions and conventional language suddenly reclaim Romeo. Now, not before, he worries about his 'reputation stained / With Tybalt's slander' (lines 111–12). The news that Mercutio is dead completes Romeo's total absorption into the avenger-role prescribed for him in the code of honour, the role from which he had earlier distanced himself so carefully.

> He gad in triumph, and Mercutio slain?
> Away to heaven, respective lenity,
> And fire-eyed fury be my conduct now.
> Now, Tybalt, take the 'villain' back again
> That late thou gav'st me.   (lines 122–6)

The style of his speech as well as its substance belongs to revenge tragedy. In the scene following, Juliet in her turn is repossessed by ideology. She has begun this sequence in soliloquy, wishing impatiently for night and her

---

[20] Feather of lead, bright smoke, cold fire, sick health,
Still-waking sleep, that is not what it is! ...
Love is a smoke made with the fume of sighs,
Being purged, a fire sparkling in lovers' eyes,
Being vexed, a sea nourished with lovers' tears.
   (1.1.177–89)

[21] Several critical studies chart the lovers' shift out of conventional speech: perhaps the best known of these is Harry Levin, 'Form and Formality in *Romeo and Juliet*', *Shakespeare Quarterly*, 11 (1960), 3–11. Kiernan Ryan applies Romeo's line 'Love goes toward love as schoolboys from their books' (2.1.201) to this movement beyond the 'prescribed texts': '*Romeo and Juliet*: The Language of Tragedy', *The Taming of the Text: Explorations in Language, Literature, and Culture*, ed. Willie van Peer (London and New York, 1988), pp. 106–21; p. 116.

bridegroom, her speech hastening along with her desire and overflowing the artificial pentameter bounds. Now the Nurse tells her that Tybalt her cousin is dead by the hand of that same bridegroom.

> O serpent heart, hid with a flow'ring face!
> Did ever dragon keep so fair a cave?
> Beautiful tyrant, fiend angelical!
> Dove-feathered raven, wolvish-ravening lamb!
> Despisèd substance of divinest show!
> Just opposite to what thou justly seem'st –
> A damnèd saint, an honourable villain.
>
> (3.2.73–9)

When Juliet lapses into her feud-assigned form of subjectivity as outraged Capulet, her speech changes. All at once, she is speaking in hackneyed images and formally balanced end-stopped lines. Her shock at suddenly having to superimpose Romeo the murderer on Romeo the lover is certainly real, but its articulation through neat oxymora (reminiscent of Romeo's own conventional language of emotion before his meeting with Juliet) makes clear that she is speaking as a generic Capulet.[22] As Orwell might say, feudthink generates bookspeak.

Yet if the language of Romeo and Juliet, apart from these lapses, hints at a journey beyond the prevailing ideology, the constraints implicit in the play's action leave them with nowhere to go, nothing to do except die. For individuals who try to advance beyond their ideology but cannot undo its constitutive influence, there is no feasible way to live. The deaths of Romeo and Juliet can be seen as the final expression of a process of excommunication that was adumbrated earlier when Romeo was banished from Verona. Exclusion, as Goran Therborn reminds us, is the main form of sanction invoked by ideology against those who transgress its barriers and definitions.[23] The crime that cut Romeo off from his social existence came about through acts of ideological rebellion: crossing over the feud-barrier to love an 'enemy', refusing (as a result) a challenge in violation of the code of honour. The lovers' deaths look avoidable on the plot level, a matter

of misunderstanding and bad timing, but from this perspective that tragic finale inside the family tomb (a setting that visibly manifests the weight of past practices) is all too inevitable. Laurence Stone thinks that an Elizabethan audience would have understood the tragedy of Romeo and Juliet as self-inflicted: their destruction came about because, by placing personal passion before obedience to family imperatives, they violated the norms of their society.[24] I have been arguing that, on the contrary, the norms themselves bring about the tragedy. One could go further and propose that the tragic predicament – possibilities for human development narrowed down and cut off – is built into the operations of ideology. That which is necessary to give us a stable identity and a consistent view of the world is by the same token what limits and distorts us. The suicides of Romeo and Juliet represent one version of ideology's destructive power. An alternative outcome to the action, less dramatic but just as tragic in its own way, would portray the two young people as recaptured for good by their social conditioning. Romeo would become the Tybalt of the Montagues, challenging Capulets on cue and advancing his manly reputation. Juliet would have an elaborate church wedding and afterward live comfortably in her different sphere as the rich and decorative cover to Paris's book.

---

22 W. H. Auden notes the radical disparity between this conventional speech and the one that opened the scene, without suggesting any function for the difference: 'Commentary on the Poetry and Tragedy of *Romeo and Juliet*', *Romeo and Juliet*, Laurel edn (New York, 1988), p. 26.

23 The victim of this process 'is excluded from further meaningful discourse as being insane, depraved, traitorous, alien, and so on. The excommunicated person is condemned, temporarily or forever, to ideological non-existence ... Usually ideological excommunication is connected with the material sanctions of expulsion, confinement, or death' (Therborn, *The Ideology of Power*, p. 83).

24 Lawrence Stone, *The Family, Sex, and Marriage 1500–1800* (New York, 1977), p. 87.

Does the destruction of this young pair do anything to transform the feud and ideological force it represents? Certainly Capulet and Montague join hands in their mutual grief at the very end of the play, initiating what the Prince calls 'a glooming peace'. Taking the hopeful view, we might conclude that the union of Romeo and Juliet, born in the contradictions of ideology that open up possibilities for change and development, signals even in their death the end of the old system and the beginning of a new phase. But the hopeful view has to ignore or discount the ironies that hedge that reconciliation of the patriarchs. The fathers propose to seal their peace by erecting gold statues to their children, an image that not only suggests vulgar show but also resonates disturbingly with Romeo's recent diatribe against gold as a poison, a murderer (5.1.81–5). Memorializing the feud's victims in a medium that is synonymous with corruption and death makes at best an inauspicious beginning for a new era of peace. What is more, as many readers have observed, the proposals of Montague and Capulet suggest in their form renewed competition rather than cooperation.

CAPULET O brother Montague, give me thy hand.
This is my daughter's jointure, for no more
Can I demand.
MONTAGUE But I can give thee more,
For I will raise her statue in pure gold,
That whiles Verona by that name is known,
There shall no figure at such rate be set
As that of true and faithful Juliet.
CAPULET As rich shall Romeo's by his lady lie . . .
(5.3.295–302)

Both fathers speak the language of commercial rivalry as they strive not to be outdone in conspicuous display. If mercantile competition played a part in their feud, it has never been so noticeable as in this moment of supposed reconciliation.[25]

Traditional productions of Romeo and Juliet, while often cutting or omitting entirely Friar Laurence's lengthy explanations in the last scene, usually present the reconciliation to be taken at face value. Directors more inclined to social criticism interrogate it. Viewers of Michael Bogdanov's 1986–7 RSC production, for example, could have little assurance of a brave new world in Verona when they witnessed the actual unveiling of those golden statues, staged as an empty public relations event with the Prince speaking from cue cards and papparazzi photographing all the surviving principals in appropriate poses. The handshake of Capulet and Montague became a photo op.[26] In any case, even the most optimistic reading or staging of the final exchange between Capulet and Montague as marking a definitive social change leaves unaltered the larger tragic script of ideology. If this particular instrument of forming subjectivities becomes outmoded, a new system of distinctions and codes will replace it as the 'ancient' order of things that divides and excludes in order to define.

[25] Among critics who have found irony in the final rapprochement of Capulet and Montague, see Clifford Leech, 'The Moral Tragedy of Romeo and Juliet', English Renaissance Drama, ed. Standish Henning et al. (Carbondale, Ill., 1976), pp. 59–75, p. 70; on the competitive nature of their speeches, Nathaniel Wallace, 'Cultural Tropology in Romeo and Juliet', Studies in Philology, 88 (1991), 329–44; p. 342; Thomas Moisan, '"O Any Thing, of Nothing First Create!": Gender and Patriarchy in the Tragedy of Romeo and Juliet', In Another Country: Feminist Perspectives on Renaissance Drama, ed. Dorothea Kehler and Susan Baker (Metuchen, N.J., and London, 1991), pp. 113–36; p. 125; Greg Bentley, 'Poetics of Power: Money as Sign and Substance in Romeo and Juliet', Explorations in Renaissance Culture, 17 (1991), 145–66; pp. 163–4.
[26] For an account of several stagings of the final scene, see Barbara Hodgdon, 'Absent Bodies, Present Voices: Performance Work and the Close of Romeo and Juliet's Golden Story', Theatre Journal, 41.3 (October, 1989), repr. Andrews, pp. 243–65. Bogdanov's is discussed pp. 252–4.

BAWDY PUNS AND LUSTFUL VIRGINS: THE LEGACY OF JULIET'S DESIRE IN COMEDIES OF THE EARLY 1600s

MARY BLY

Romeo and Juliet is a play crowded with lewd puns. Mercutio, Benvolio and Romeo toy with bawdy innuendoes; Gregory, Peter and Sampson delight in the proximity of maidenheads and their own naked weapons; the Nurse both puns and is punned about. The play's lyricism contends with language intoxicated by carnality. Even Juliet, the romantic centre of the play, quibbles with erotic meaning, most notably in her epithalamium of 3.2. Juliet is chaste and desirous, a unique combination in plays of the early 1590s. This essay argues that Juliet's erotic fluency had a marked influence on the shaping of comic heroines in the four to five years after the play's first performances. I look first at Juliet's language, and then at two parodic versions of Shakespeare's heroine, written between 1598 and 1607. *Romeo and Juliet* was often imitated; what interests me are those balcony scenes in which pseudo-Juliets express erotic desire in clever puns. These imitative plays are among the very few extant Renaissance comedies portraying virginal heroines who make self-referential bawdy jokes. It seems that the act of parodying the enormously popular Shakespeare play created an odd sub-genre, that of romantic comedies whose heroines display a ribald humour.[1]

Balcony scenes litter Renaissance plays; the popularity of *Romeo and Juliet* has caused most amorous balcony exchanges to be labelled imitative. I limit my discussion to Henry Porter's *The Two Angry Women of Abington* (1598) and Thomas Dekker's *Blurt, Master Constable* (1607)

because these two playwrights explicitly borrow language as well as plot devices from Shakespeare's play.[2] I also look more briefly at the balcony scene in an anonymous play, *The Puritan* (1607). *Romeo and Juliet* was an enduring favourite with Elizabethan audiences; its language apparently filtered into normal conversation. Several works written after 1600 mock those who borrow its verse. For example, Gullio, the foolish courtier of *1 Return from*

---

[1] Since I spend most of this paper discussing bawdy puns, I want to address a problem with terminology. The puns I discuss are difficult to label. 'Bawdy' is a word used by Shakespeare, and it carries a definition, according to Webster's, of humorously coarse. On the other hand, it also has connotations of obscenity and Victorianesque naughtiness. Other adjectives tend to be more pejorative (licentious, lewd, indecent, obscene); I use 'ribald' or 'bawdy' because of the implication of humour as well as sexual reference.

[2] Another play which exhibits a similar combination of *Romeo and Juliet* tags, desirous virgins, and ribald jokes is Edward Sharpham's *Cupid's Whirligig* (1607). Sharpham borrows Shakespearian metaphors, describing the court, for example, as a place where 'so many earth-treading starres adornes the sky' (see Capulet's description of his dance, 1.2.22–3). Marston's *Jack Drum's Entertainment* (1600) also stages a parodic balcony scene. Marston satirizes cloying love language, but his Katherine offers no sexual puns. Michael Scott, while making a claim for a parody of Shakespeare's balcony scene in *The Insatiate Countess*, argues that *Romeo and Juliet* was at a height of popularity around 1600. See 'Marston's Early Contributions to "The Insatiate Countess"', *Notes and Queries*, n.s. 24, 222 (1977), 116–17, and Andrew Gurr, for a discussion of the play's influence on Henslowe's repertory. *Shakespeare Quarterly*, 38 (1987), pp. 189–200.

Parnassus (1606), imitates Mercutio: 'the moone in comparison of thy bright hue a meere slutt, Anthonies Cleopatra a blacke browde milkmaide, Hellen a cowdie.' But Ingenioso (an impoverished scholar) leaps on the theft: 'Marke Romeo and Iuliet: o monstrous theft.'[3] *Romeo and Juliet*'s popularity suggests that the dual presence of a balcony scene and 'monstrous theft' would make the connection immediately apparent to a contemporary audience.

Porter and Dekker make two fundamental revisions of *Romeo and Juliet*: their plays end with marriage rather than death, and their heroines display skill at erotic innuendo in conversation, rather than in soliloquy. Punning duels are, of course, found in other Shakespeare plays. Berowne's and Beatrice's witty exchanges are sexually charged, if not explicitly sexually allusive. Yet virginal heroines rarely make bawdy jokes. In the context of romance, heroines tend to stay within conventional lyric guidelines.[4] In *Much Ado About Nothing* (1598), for example, Hero's maid Margaret tries to cheer up the heavy-hearted bride by joking that she will 'be heavier soon by the weight of a man'; Hero scolds her for immodesty: 'Fie upon thee, art not ashamed?' (3.4.25–6). For the most part, erotic innuendo in drama remains the province of marginal characters. Old women, clowns, malcontents and male sidekicks, Parolles, Pandarus, Iago, lewdly mock and are mocked, but it is hard to find a young heroine referring even indirectly to copulation.

Why, then, should these two plays be among the very few whose heroines are ribald jokers? Significantly, the plays are not simple burlesques; they are romantic comedies in their own right, and their connection to *Romeo and Juliet* has so far been considered merely a matter for footnotes. If a blunt expression of lust is an inappropriate statement for a virginal heroine, what is the position of a witty expression of desire? The nature of the expression is clearly important. Porter's and Dekker's heroines are not straightforwardly lustful; they speak in puns.

If desire is revealed in clever puns, does that wit protect the heroine from a charge of immodesty? Certainly, the very elaboration of rhetoric involved in puns removes them from clear revelation. Puns impose an order on speech: face-value relinquishes its place to paradox, plain definition to the imagination. For example, Porter's Mall's 'quarterly I must receive my rent' plays on secondary meanings: 'rent' does not, in itself, carry an erotic meaning, although the sexual reference is easily surmised from her definition of 'income' as 'kisses and embraces every day'.[5] Puns, Walter Redfern writes, 'are a means of circumventing taboos, as are euphemisms, which play a similar hide-and-seek game with the listener/reader'.[6] The audience's attention may be redirected from the titillating *double entendre* to admiration of rhetorical cleverness. This argument assumes that erotic puns act as a masking device for desire, that Porter and Dekker are able to circumvent cultural restrictions on female speech by clever phrasing. However, I would argue that bawdy puns do not mask desire but flaunt it.

A bawdy pun is a word placed in such a context that it points to a secondary, sexual, reference, as in Juliet's 'Give me my Romeo, and when I shall die ...' (3.1.21). Juliet's 'death' is both ceasing to be and erotic ecstasy. The sexual innuendo Juliet uses was a common

---

3 *1 Return from Parnassus*, *The Three Parnassus Plays*, ed. J. B. Leishman (London, 1949), 3.1.988–92. In another example, John Marston's 10th satire mocks the play's followers: '*Luscus*, what's play'd to-day? Faith now I know / I set thy lips abroach, from whence doth flow / Naught but pure Juliet and Romeo.' 'Satire XI', *The Scourge of Villainie*, *Works*, vol. 3, ed. A. H. Bullen (London, 1887), pp. 37–9.

4 See Linda Woodbridge's discussion of dramatic treatments of female desire, *Women and the English Renaissance: Literature and the Nature of Womankind, 1540–1620* (Urbana, 1984), especially pp. 244–63.

5 Henry Porter, *The Two Angry Women of Abington*, ed. Marianne Brish Evett (N.Y., 1980). Modern editors have divided the play into thirteen scenes. 8.150–2.

6 Walter D. Redfern, *Puns* (Oxford, 1984), p. 91.

one in Renaissance literature.[7] It is important to recognize that in the case of a pun as ordinary as this, a Renaissance audience would definitely grasp its double meaning. As James Brown says of puns, 'When we know enough ... failure to perceive a pun is impossible; we cannot wilfully suspend our ability to see puns.'[8] Obviously, seemingly non-sexual speech often carries an inference of carnal desire, as when Miranda calls Ferdinand a 'thing divine' (1.2.422). But if Miranda had been conscious enough of that carnality to construct a witty play with words, had she offered a bawdy pun, the effect of her statement would have been radically different and quite surprising. Miranda's innocence is stressed throughout *The Tempest*, and her explicit lack of knowledge is echoed in her speech. As an audience grasps the *double entendre* behind Juliet's 'die', they grasp her sexual knowledge and her consciousness of carnal desire at the same time. That sexual knowledge was a dubious virtue in light of Elizabethan conceptions of a chaste young woman's education; it may explain why witty heroines in Renaissance plays rarely offer immodest puns.

It is common for female characters' rhetoric to produce an inadvertent sexual reference, as in Juliet's Nurse's protest: 'thou must stand by, too, and suffer every knave to use me at his pleasure'. Peter replies: 'I saw no man use you at his pleasure. If I had, my weapon should quickly have been out' (2.3.145–8). Eyre's wife Margery in Dekker's *The Shoemaker's Holiday* (1599) provides a similar example. Her robust tone leads to puns – when her husband swears to 'firke' her if she doesn't stop quarrelling, she responds: 'Yea, yea man, you may vse me as you please.'[9] The prolonged scenes between Margery, Firke, and Hodge, in which the servants slyly mock her wrinkles, aged body and social ambition, are typical. These two female characters, the Nurse and Margery, are laughable precisely due to their age, sexual unattractiveness and inadvertent sexual references. It is their choice of words – 'use' interpreted as 'copulate with' – that creates a bawdy in-

nuendo. The sexual pun arises from the word's two interpretations, not from the women's deliberate command of those two meanings.

On the other hand, Juliet's invitation to Romeo in 3.2 – to 'Hood my unmanned blood' – offers an elaborately rhetorical, self-consciously erotic image. Juliet's long soliloquy strings together six separate invocations, each specifically alluding to the physical pleasure she expects that night. The epithalamium's metaphorical flourishes allow her desire to be latent and yet obvious; they are particularly surprising in view of the dense Petrarchan rhetoric of the play.[10] Romeo first loves Rosaline who, in a fine Petrarchan tradition, 'hath forsworn to love' (1.1.220). She is invulnerable to Cupid's arrow, 'in strong proof of chastity well armed' (1.1.207). To Romeo, both Juliet and the absent Rosaline are archetypal Petrarchan mistresses: chaste, undesirous and beautiful. Certainly Romeo believes Juliet and Rosaline to be untouched by desire:

---

7 'Die' is frequently used by female characters, as in Marston's and Barksted's *The Insatiate Countess* (1610). Isabella goes to her nuptial bed reluctantly: 'When my loath'd mate / Shall struggle in due pleasure for his right, / I'll think't my love, and die in that delight!' John Marston and others, *The Insatiate Countess*, ed. Giorgio Melchiori (Manchester, 1984), 1.2.259–61. For further examples, see James Henke, *Courtesans and Cuckolds: A Glossary of Renaissance Dramatic Bawdy (Exclusive of Shakespeare)* (N.Y., 1979), p. 67.

8 James Brown, 'Eight Types of Pun', *PMLA*, 71 (1956), pp. 15–16.

9 Thomas Dekker, *The Shoemaker's Holiday, The Dramatic Works*, vol. 1, ed. Fredson Bowers (Cambridge, 1953), 2.3.39. Firke and Hodge view the Wife as a natural butt of sexual innuendo. For example, Hodge: 'Maister I hope yowle not suffer my dame to take downe your iourneymen.' Firke: 'If she take me downe, Ile take her vp, yea and take her downe too, a button-hole lower.' 2.3.29–32.

10 See Gayle Whittier's definitive study of Petrarchan conceits in the play, 'The Sonnet's Body and the Body Sonnetized in *Romeo and Juliet*', *Shakespeare Quarterly*, 40 (1989), pp. 27–41. Also M. M. Mahood, *Shakespeare's Wordplay* (London, 1957), p. 61, and Jill Levenson, 'The Definition of Love: Shakespeare's Phrasing in *Romeo and Juliet*', *Shakespeare Studies*, 15 (1982), pp. 21–3.

She will not stay the siege of loving terms,
Nor bide th'encounter of assailing eyes,
Nor ope her lap to saint-seducing gold.
O she is rich in beauty ...   (1.1.209–12)

Romeo's construction of Rosaline's beauty ties it directly to her chastity. He also sees Juliet's beauty as ensuring her chastity: 'Beauty too rich for use, for earth too dear' (1.5.46). The energy of Romeo's Petrarchan rhetoric is bound up in fruitless pursuit, rather than in an anticipation of lovers' meeting.

It is Mercutio who envisions union: 'O Romeo, that she were, O that she were / An open-arse, and thou a popp'rin' pear' (2.1.37–8). Mercutio speaks of sex only in puns. Erotic humour predominates. Love, for him, is a chase towards copulation: 'this drivelling love is like a great natural that runs lolling up and down to hide his bauble in a hole' (2.3.84–5). Romeo's solemn poetry sits uneasily in a play where it is ridiculed by Mercutio's banter ('Laura to his lady was a kitchen wench ... Dido a dowdy, Cleopatra a gypsy, Helen and Hero hildings and harlots' (2.3.37, 39–40)) and mocked by Friar Laurence: 'Thy love did read by rote, that could not spell' (2.2.88). Even Juliet offers a mild rebuke: 'You kiss by th'book' (1.5.109).

Juliet is unsuited to the role of Romeo's Petrarchan mistress. She is desirous, and more-over, she is long-winded in anticipation: 'O, I have bought the mansion of a love / But not possessed it, and though I am sold, / Not yet enjoyed' (3.2.26–8). Juliet is not precisely bawdy – but neither is she modest.[11] Remark-ably, Shakespeare gives her the epithalamium traditionally spoken by a bridegroom. Act 3 scene 2 opens with her invocation to the night: 'Gallop apace, you fiery-footed steeds', an in-version of Ovid's 'lente currite, noctis equi'.[12] Juliet's soliloquy is a mixture of plainly ex-pressed invitations and artfully phrased metaphors. Her initial call to Romeo, 'Leap to these arms untalked of and unseen' (3.2.7), echoes one of the most beautiful passages in Marlowe's *Tragedy of Dido* (1587):

If thou wilt stay
Leap in mine arms; mine arms are open wide;
If not, turn from me, and I'll turn from thee ...[13]

The passage comes from Dido's final plea to Aeneas to remain in Carthage; it is spoken by a sexually knowing woman, intoxicated with love.

Juliet turns from Marlovian invitation to a lengthy series of sexual metaphors: 'Come, civil night ... And learn me how to lose a winning match / Played for a pair of stainless maiden-hoods' (3.2.10, 12–13). This is a good example of the complexity of Juliet's speech.[14]

---

[11] Juliet's erotic epithalamium has distressed many critics, particularly those from the nineteenth century. I quote from the appendix to the Variorum edition: N.J. Halprin argued in 1845 that bridal ceremonies must have been common in the 1590s: 'hence may be inferred her familiarity with thoughts and expressions not likely in any other way to have obtained entrance into the mind of an innocent and unsophisticated girl of fourteen' (374); Massey in 1866 argues for emendation of the speech, or 'the sole incentive of this appeal for night to come was Juliet's eagerness for the perfecting of her marriage. It is not so. That would make of Juliet a forward wanton, and of her speech an invocation most immodest' (392); and A. de Lamartine rants in 1865: 'the most scandalous obscenity usurps the place of that virgin purity' (440). *A New Variorum Edition of Romeo and Juliet*, vol. 1, ed. Horace Furness (Philadelphia, 1871).

[12] Noted by Harry Levin, 'Form and Formality in *Romeo and Juliet*', *Romeo and Juliet: Critical Essays*, ed. John F. Andrews (N.Y., 1993), p. 49. See Gary McCown's thorough study of the genre of epithalamium in terms of Juliet's speech. McCown points out that the bride-groom should speak the epithalamium and the bride, like Junia in Catullus 61, is supposed to be afraid and weep to demonstrate modesty. '"Runnawayes Eyes" and Juliet's Epithalamium', *Shakespeare Quarterly*, 27 (1976), pp. 150–76.

[13] Christopher Marlowe, *The Tragedy of Dido Queen of Carthage*, *Works*, vol. 1, ed. C. F. Tucker Brooke (London, 1933), 5.1179–81.

[14] I have tried to limit my discussion of sexual puns to those I think audiences would readily grasp. Frankie Rubinstein finds a more obscure series of puns in the following line from Juliet's epithalamium: 'Spread thy close curtain, love-performing night' (3.2.5): 'Juliet's amorous impatience is conveyed in (1) the spreading of the "close" (genitals) curtain; (2) the love-performing

'Winning' is turned to a pun meaning both victorious and appealing. Moreover, the 'match' Juliet hopes to lose and win is, at once, a wedding and an erotic game. At the pun's heart, obviously, is the fate of her virginity: it is a match in which she will lose a 'stainless' maidenhead, while she gains a 'match' or marriage with Romeo.[15]

The rest of her speech is similarly full of *doubles entendres*:

Hood my unmanned blood, bating in my cheeks,
With thy black mantle, till strange love grow bold,
Think true love acted simple modesty.

(3.2.14–16)

Talking to her Nurse, Juliet's linguistic stress turns from sex itself ('true love acted') to Romeo's beauty. Romeo has a 'flow'ring face'; he is a 'gorgeous palace', a 'mortal paradise of such sweet flesh' (3.2.73, 85, 82). But the epithalamium itself stands as a lyric anticipation of erotic pleasure:

Come night, come Romeo; come, thou day in
    night,
For thou wilt lie upon the wings of night
Whiter than new snow on a raven's back.

(3.2.17–19)

I would suggest that Juliet's cleverly phrased desire for consummation acts as a bridge between desirous, tragic heroines and comic plots. Shakespeare bestowed sexual metaphors on a young heroine; Porter and Dekker follow his example, moving into comedy. They use *Romeo and Juliet* as a distant subtext, fashioning heroines who are virginal and wittily desirous. Like Juliet, these heroines are intensely interested in the fate of their maidenheads, and their wit similarly reveals a specific understanding of sexual congress.

Henry Porter's *The Two Angry Women of Abington* turns *Romeo and Juliet* into a subtext for a comedy. Porter appropriates Juliet's wit; at the same time he manipulates famous bits of the play (such as the balcony scene) to jest at Romeo's lyric dedication. Juliet's nimble metaphors are turned wholly to sexual puns. Porter

shapes his heroine, Mall, around the epithalamic Juliet. Mall speaks only in erotic quibbles and sexual metaphors.

The Two Angry Women is constructed around a breach between two neighbouring families, which the fathers hope to patch by marrying their son and daughter. The young couple, Frank and Mall, are introduced, woo and agree to marry in a bare three minutes. Although the plot summary seems in line with conventional romantic comedies, Mall's character is radically opposed to Petrarchan idealization. She is, her brother says, 'a wicked wench to make a jest' (8.25). She is not merely witty, like Rosaline or Beatrice, but lusty, and her jokes are overtly sexual. For example, Mall opens the ninth scene by musing on conies – rabbits but also slang for women:

Good Lord, what pretty things these conies are;
How finely they do feed till they be fat!
And then what a sweet meat a coney is,
And what smooth skins they have, both black and
    gray.
They say they run more in the night than day ...
But when that Francis comes, what will he say?
'Look, boy, there lies a coney in my way.'

(9.7–11, 24–5)[16]

Mall's sexual bravado extends past sly puns. When her father asks Mall if she has a mind to marry, she points out that since she is a maid, she ought to 'blush, look pale and wan, / And then look pale again' (3.124–5). However, she decides to 'speak truth and shame the devil' (3.133). In fact, she has lately 'let restrained

---

... "night", her "knight", as she calls Romeo in the last line of the scene.' *A Dictionary of Shakespeare's Sexual Puns and their Significance* (London, 1984), p. 251.
[15] See Brown, 'Eight Types of Pun', pp. 20, 22.
[16] In John Day's *Isle of Gulls*, Dametas uses 'coney' with a similar implication: 'I would thou shouldst know, we olde Courtiers can hunt a Cony, and put her to the squeake, & make her cry out like a young married wife of the first night.' *The Isle of Gulls*, ed. Raymond S. Burns (N.Y., 1980), 1.4.16–19. For an extended discussion of the sexual implications of 'coney', see James Henke's glossary, *Courtesans and Cuckolds*.

fancy loose, / And bade it gaze for pleasure' (3.158–9). Mall urges her father to a quick match: 'If I shall have a husband, get him quickly / For maids that wears cork shoes may step awry' (3.163–4). The scene ends with her blunt summary of the evils of letting maids lie alone:

> Lying alone they muse but in their beds
> How they might lose their long-kept
>   maidenheads.
> This is the cause there is so many scapes . . .
> Therefore, come husband, maidenhead adieu!
>
> (3.205–7, 10)

Her mother bitterly labels her 'lusty guts'; certainly Mall's forthright acknowledgement of her own physical desire is extraordinary. I would argue that Porter is deliberately abrogating romantic ideals – perhaps most clearly in his veiled mockery of *Romeo and Juliet*.

At various points in *The Two Angry Women of Abington*, *Romeo and Juliet* is invoked as a romantic model, and then burlesqued by Porter's rewriting.[17] We can see an echo of Juliet above, in Mall's response to her father's query: 'hast thou a mind to marry?' (3.120). Lady Capulet asks Juliet a similar question: 'How stands your dispositions to be married?' and Juliet responds 'It is an honour that I dream not of' (1.3.67–8). Mall lampoons Juliet's answer on two levels: she announces that she does dream of marriage, and she rejects a modest answer as dishonest. The textual crux behind the Shakespearian line (Q2 reads 'It is a houre that I dream not of') creates an even sharper counterpart, since Mall specifically alludes to maidens dreaming of that hour:[18]

> How many maids this night lies in their beds
> And dream that they have lost their maidenheads.
> Such dreams, such slumbers I had, too, enjoyed . . .
>
> (12.13–15)

Considering that the balcony scene (in which Juliet initiates the idea of marriage) supposedly occurs only a few hours after the scene between Juliet and her mother, Juliet's demure answer does appear conventional rather than truthful.

In the balcony scene Juliet actually emphasizes the cultural restrictions on her speech: 'For that which thou hast heard me speak tonight. / Fain would I dwell on form, fain, fain deny / What I have spoke; but farewell, compliment' (2.1.129–31). Mall's refusal to respond with 'close-clipped civility' may also point to Juliet:

> With true-faced passion
> Of modest maidenhead I could adorn me,
> And to your question make a sober cursey,
> And with close-clipped civility be silent;
> Or else say 'No, forsooth,' or 'Aye, forsooth.'
> If I said 'No, forsooth,' I lied, forsooth.
>
> (3.126–31)

Mall's emphasis on maidenheads is characteristic of Porter's humour: marriage is seen as consummation, not ceremony. Mall and the other characters often conflate the two.

Mall and Frank meet and woo in a balcony scene which apes the parallel scene in *Romeo and Juliet*. Both balcony scenes involve rapid wooing between near strangers. Juliet takes no joy in a contract 'too rash, too unadvised, too sudden' (2.1.160); Frank's reaction is more confident: 'Now in good faith, Phillip, this makes me smile, / That I have wooed and won in so small while' (8.135–6). The scenes are remarkably similar in concept and choreography, but quite different in language, a difference which I would

---

17 One of the most exact borrowings occurs between Lady Capulet's 'I would the fool were married to her grave' (3.5.140) and Mistress Barnes's 'I'll rather have her married to her grave' (8.175). R. W. Dent lists Porter and Shakespeare as the only users of the phrase until Fletcher's *The Night Walker* in 1611. See *Proverbial Language in English Drama Exclusive of Shakespeare 1495–1616* (Berkeley, 1984). For a list of all verbal parallels between the two plays, see Evett, *The Two Angry Women*, pp. 51–4. An unlikely argument has been made that Porter's play was written earlier than 1597 and that Shakespeare looked to his play, rather than the reverse. See J. M. Nosworthy, 'The Two Angry Families of Verona', *Shakespeare Quarterly*, 3 (1952), pp. 219–26.

18 The generally accepted reading of this line (an 'honour') is taken, in fact, from Q1 (the 'bad' Quarto). The 'newly corrected' Q2, Q3 and Q4 all read 'It is an houre that I dreame not of.'

suggest grows from the dominant topic of conversation in each scene. Romeo and Juliet, famously, talk of love; Mall and Frank, of sex.

Mall's brother Phillip brings Frank to her bedroom window. Phillip calls up: ''Tis I.' Mall's response is raucously far from Juliet's dignified 'What man art thou that, thus bescreened in night, / So stumblest on my counsel?' (2.1.94–5). Mall shouts back: ''Tis I? Who I? "I, quoth the dog", or what?' (8.45). Romeo and Juliet speak in verse strewn with loving metaphors: 'thou art / As glorious to this night, being o'er my head, / As is a wingèd messenger of heaven' (2.1.68–70). Their conversation moves adroitly between lyrical metaphors and conventional phrases. Romeo, in particular, strikes extravagant chords in his praise: Juliet is a sun; her eyes are stars; her cheeks are brighter than starlight.

Mall's and Frank's dialogue is diametrically opposed to Romeo and Juliet's balcony scene, in that they fall into metaphors of sexual innuendo, not those of romantic love. They begin by talking of Venus's chariot, punning on the similarity of couch and coach, a joke which also alludes to the 'carting' of prostitutes:

MALL I pray, sir, tell me, do you cart the Queen of
   Love?
FRANK Not cart her, but couch her in your eye,
   And a fit place for gentle love to lie.
MALL Aye, but methinks you speak without the
   book.   (8.61–4)

Mall's 'methinks you speak without the book' is a mocking rewriting of Juliet's 'You kiss by th' book' (1.5.109). Whereas Juliet chides Romeo for his ready command of conventional sonnet conceits, Mall's retort to Frank's play on 'couch' is a direct recognition of the unconventional manner of their conversation. To woo 'by th' book' is to gild one's language with sonnet rhymes and conceits: Romeo and Frank are quite opposite in this respect. Frank does speak 'without' the book. Mall's brother Phillip had earlier advised Frank to woo her by setting 'such painted beauty on thy tongue / As it shall ravish every maiden sense', a neat summary of sonneteers' ornate love language (8.10–11). Phillip himself speaks in Romeo-esque metaphors. He opens scene 10, one of the nocturnal scenes, with a soliloquy on the night:

> The sky that was so fair three hours ago
> Is in three hours become an Ethiope,
> And, being angry at her beauteous change,
> She will not have one of these pearlèd stars
> To blab her sable metamorphesy.   (10.3–7)

Phillip is faintly echoing Romeo's praise of Juliet:

> O, she doth teach the torches to burn bright!
> It seems she hangs upon the cheek of night
> As a rich jewel in an Ethiope's ear –
> Beauty too rich for use, for earth too dear.
>   (1.5.43–6).[19]

Porter's use of Romeo's famous speech (also adapted by Dekker in *Blurt, Master Constable*) plays to the audience's theatrical knowledge: much of the humour in this play depends on acquaintance with the language of *Romeo and Juliet*. Phillip's echoing of Romeo refers not only to the play, but to the convoluted phrasing of stately love language in general. However, Frank discards Phillip's advice to use 'painted beauty' in wooing.

Mall's retort to Frank's superficially gallant wish to 'couch' Venus in her eye leads to an even more explicit dialogue:

MALL Where will you have room to have the
   coachman sit?
FRANK Nay, that were but small manners and not
   fit.
   His duty is before you bare to stand,
   Having a lusty whipstock in his hand.
MALL The place is void. Will you provide me one?
FRANK And if you please, I will supply the room.
MALL But are you cunning in the carman's lash?

                                         (8.66–72)

---

[19] See Shakespeare's sonnet 27: 'Which like a jewel hung in ghastly night / Makes black night beauteous and her old face new' (27:11-12).

The kind of metaphor by which Mall and Frank build a conversation is very different from the parallel set of metaphors which Romeo and Juliet build between them (their play on 'tassel-gentle', for example). Romeo's and Juliet's conceits are elaborately matched: she wears a 'mask of night', he has 'night's cloak'.[20] Mall and Frank build a series of metaphors which point not to conventional conceits but to sexual metaphors. Romantic love, and the metaphors of romantic love, are here replaced by puns of sexual wit. Porter's lovers manipulate a rhyming exchange to create not a sonnet, but an extended set of bawdy riddles about Mall's virginity:

MALL Nun, votary, stale maidenhead, seventeen-and-upward?
  Here be names! What, nothing else?
FRANK Yes, or a fair built steeple without bells.
MALL Steeple, good people? Nay, another cast.
FRANK Aye, or a well-made ship without a mast.
MALL Fie, not so big, sir, by one part of four!
FRANK Why, then ye are a boat without an oar.
MALL O, well rowed, wit! (8.102–9)

The relentless puns on male sex organs – or the lack thereof – are helped by the fact that the dialogue falls into couplets. If puns rely on displacement of face-value meanings, rhyming puns allow an even greater disjuncture from apparent sense, and rhyming puns characterize the entire balcony scene. 'I had both wit to grant when he did woo me' Mall says, 'And strength to bear what ere he can do to me' (8.209–10). Frank later echoes her: 'Well, I must bear with her – she'll bear with me' (9.65). I would argue that Mall and Frank are able to dance further into obscenity because their puns tumble onto each other, delighting the ear before comprehension strikes. Gillian Beer writes that the second rhyme word moves in on the first and tricks it into rhyme, 'sound dominates sense'.[21] In one sense a pun is itself a compressed rhyme; fixing one or the other possible definition as correct is less important than grasping the contexts linked together in one syntactic unit.

This joining of contexts makes puns vulnerable to the passing of time. If Mercutio's quibbles with 'prick' are still understood, it is only because of the durability of that particular reference. Mall's joke about the danger of wearing cork heels is a case in point. Many such puns are understandable only with a dictionary in hand. The problematics of phallic references in the language of female characters and, therefore, of boy actors point to another context which may be missed by a modern reader. Porter's *The Two Angry Women of Abington* was written for Henslowe's (adult) company at the Rose; the Admiral's Men is not a company generally discussed as employing *doubles entendres* which reference the boy behind the female role.[22] But Mall's and Frank's exchange, quoted above, certainly raises the possibility:

FRANK Aye, or a well-made ship without a mast.
MALL Fie, not so big, sir, by one part of four!
FRANK Why, then ye are a boat without an oar.

On one hand, Frank's jokes refer to Mall as a virgin in need of an oar. At the same time, the dialogue could be construed as a pointed reference to the boy actor's smaller sex organ: 'not so big, sir, by one part of four!' Thus Porter's

---

20 See Edward Snow for an intricate analysis of the gender differences in Romeo's and Juliet's use of matched metaphors. 'Language and Sexual Difference in *Romeo and Juliet*', *Shakespeare's 'Rough Magic': Essays in Honor of C.L. Barber*, ed. Peter Erickson and Coppélia Kahn (Newark, 1985), pp. 168–92.
21 Gillian Beer, 'Rhyming as Comedy: Body, Ghost and Banquet', *English Comedy*, eds. Michael Cordner, Peter Holland and John Kerrigan (Cambridge, 1994), p. 181.
22 Boys' companies are generally singled out as prone to boy-actor innuendo, a fact often attributed to a more exaggerated acting style. On the other hand, considerable work has been done on proposed *doubles entendres* in Shakespeare's plays. Many studies of the erotic potential of transvestism have been recently published: see, for example, Susan Zimmerman's claim that Jacobean playwrights deliberately privileged transvestism for purposes of erotic titillation. 'Disruptive Desire: Artifice and Indeterminacy in Jacobean Comedy', *Erotic Politics: Desire on the Renaissance Stage*, ed. S. Zimmerman (N.Y., 1992), p. 39.

puns link three contexts: literal meaning, erotic innuendo, and extra-textual, actorial reference.

When Mall descends from the bedroom she defines the contract between them in rhyming puns:

MALL Francis, my love's lease I do let to thee,
    Date of my life and thine. What sayest thou to me?
    The entering fine or income thou must pay
    Are kisses and embraces every day,
    And quarterly I must receive my rent.
    You know my mind.
FRANK   I guess at thy intent.
    Thou shalt not miss a minute of thy time.
                                        (8.148–54)

The difference between the two romances is encapsulated in Juliet's wish for marriage ('thou wilt perform the rite, / And all my fortunes at thy foot I'll lay, / And follow thee, my lord, throughout the world' (2.1.188–90)) and Mall's demand of 'rent'. In the majority of Renaissance comedies, well-born heroines speak in Petrarchan measures; low-born females speak a kind of rolling dialect, marked by indecorous jokes and coinages. It is a source of extra dramatic interest if a low-born woman is able to use Petrarchan metaphors. The protagonist of Thomas Heywood's *I The Fair Maid of the West* (1610), for example, is a barmaid and later a tavern owner who loves chastely and expresses herself in Petrarchan hyperboles. The entire play revolves around this social anomaly. It is similarly remarkable when well-born heroines play with erotic puns.[23] By Elizabethan standards, Mall's punning banter with Frank sails dangerously close to shameful. I would suggest that the popularity of *The Two Angry Women of Abington* came at least partially from its heroine's defiance of the conventions prescribing a well-born maiden's concerns and behaviour.[24] Wit here is not merely verbal dexterity but the daring involved in staging a virgin's expression of sexual desire.

In this regard, the discrepancies between the bad quarto (Q1) of *Romeo and Juliet* [1597] and the 'newly corrected, augmented, and amended' Q2, published in 1599, are interesting. Q1 retains

only the first four lines of the epithalamium. The Arden editor, Brian Gibbons, suggests the lines may have been cut in anticipation of a provincial audience, and there is some evidence that travelling versions of plays were deliberately shortened in such a way as to tone down sexual content.[25] I would suggest that the excised epithalamium points to the fact that Juliet's expression of erotic desire represented a breach of cultural expectation. Mall's transgressive speech is acknowledged in the play itself: her suitor says her wit is 'held a wonder,' and her brother acknowledges that she can 'make blush / The boldest face of man that ere man saw' (8. 127, 5.10–11). The heroine of the anonymous play *The Puritan* has similarly impressed her suitor: 'th'art a mad wench *Moll*'.[26]

---

23 Puns and malapropisms, writes William C. Carroll, 'offer the sexual low road, the eruption of the carnival-esque sexual into high discourse ...' 'The Virgin Not: Language and Sexuality in Shakespeare', *Shakespeare Survey 46* (1994), p. 109.

24 *The Two Angry Women of Abington* is surmised to have been popular, considering Henslowe paid the sum of £7 (as against a standard £6) for its sequel. The sequel went into production in February 1598, and Porter was paid the final £2 on 12 February. There was apparently a third sequel planned (*The Two Merry Women of Abington*); on 28 February Henslowe records the following payment: 'Lent unto harey porter at the Requeste of the company in earnest of his boocke called ij mery women of abenton the some of forty shellyngs & for the Resayte of that money he gave me his fayfthulle promysse that I shold have alle the boockes wch he writte ...' Qtd. Evett, *The Two Angry Women*, p. 5. The only comparable arrangement was made with Chettle. While the entry indicates Porter's desperate financial straits, it also points to the popularity of his first two plays.

25 See *Romeo and Juliet*, ed. Brian Gibbons (London, 1980), p. 8. The British Library owns a copy of the first quarto of Edward Sharpham's *The Fleire*, bowdlerized some time in the seventeenth century with cuts congruent with a provincial performance of the play. Apparently many bawdy jokes, in particular, were cut. See Clifford Leech, 'The Plays of Edward Sharpham: Alterations Accomplished and Projected', *Review of English Studies*, 11 (1935), 70–4.

26 W. S., *The Puritan, or the Widow of Watling Street*, ed. John S. Farmer (London, 1911), p. H2r, line 3.

If *Romeo and Juliet* influenced Porter's creation of a bawdy heroine, Porter's play, in turn, seems to have garnered an imitator. *The Puritan* was printed in 1607 as having been acted by the Children of Paul's. The play involves foolery plotted by a witty scholar and his nefarious compatriots, who pretend to raise both the devil and a man from the dead, in order to wrangle freedom from prison and the hands of a rich widow and her eldest daughter, Franke. The younger daughter, Moll, is in love with Sir John Penny-dub, and is fluently bawdy: 'Ide as soone vow neuer to come in Bed. / Tut? Women must liue by th'quick, and not th'dead' (A4r, lines 6–7).

The heroine is known as Moll, basically the same name as Porter's Mall, and at various points the *Puritan* Moll appears to echo the earlier character. In *The Two Angry Women*, for example, Mall is agonized by the frustration of her wedding plans: 'A starved man with double death doth die / To have the meat might save him in his eye / And may not have it – so am I tormented' (12.17–19). When the *Puritan* Moll's marriage plans are thwarted, she is similarly wrought: 'A double torment ... a double curse' (D2r, lines 3, 27). The most notable parallel between the plays is found in *The Puritan*'s balcony scene. Sir John appears below: 'Whewh Mistris Mol, Mistris Mol.' Moll appears above, 'lacing of her clothes'. Like the earlier Mall, she calls 'Who's there?' And just as does Phillip in Porter's play, Penny-dub replies, 'Tis I' (H2, lines 26–7). What ensues is a wild series of puns, instigated solely by Moll, *not* by Penny-dub. In *The Two Angry Women of Abington*, Mall generally answers Frank's sallies with a rhyming couplet; but this Moll is bolder than her predecessor: 'O you'r an early cocke ifayth, who would haue thought you to be so rare a stirrer' (H2r, lines 28–9). Penny-dub offers to climb into Moll's bed-chamber, but she refuses. 'No by my faith Sir Iohn, Ile keepe you downe, for you Knights are very dangerous if once you get aboue' (H2r, lines 31–32). She explains her refusal by a bawdy quibble: 'Sir Iohn you must

note the nature of the Climates your Northen wench in her owne Countrie may well hold out till shee bee fifteene, but if she touch the South once, and come vp to *London*, here the Chimes go presently after twelue' (H2, lines 34–6 – H2r, lines 1–2).

One subject which seems to mark the group of heroines I discuss in this paper is an anxious regard for their virginity. Porter's Mall is a gentlewoman who three times explains her urgent desire to lose that virginity. Her own family jokes about her maidenhead: 'by my troth, my sister's maidenhead / Stands like a game at tennis: if the ball / Hit in the hole or hazard, fare well all' (3.327–9). Juliet's epithalamium speaks to the same issue; hearing Romeo is banished she takes to her bed: 'I, a maid, die maiden-widowèd. / Come, cords; come, Nurse; I'll to my wedding bed, / And death, not Romeo, take my maidenhead!' (3.2.135–7). Her maidenhead is a topic of conversation, notably of the Nurse, but also of her mother. Quibbles about virginity are common throughout Renaissance drama, particularly when spoken boastfully by male characters (Sampson's vow that he will cut off the heads of Montague's maids is a good example). But in these plays virginity skips from the provenance of Sampson and the Nurse, to that of the upper classes: Juliet's despairing attention to her maidenhead, Mall's dreams of her wedding night.

Thomas Dekker's *Blurt, Master Constable* (1602) is another play which exploits the ribald potential of a desirous virgin. Like Porter, Dekker borrows both plot and language from *Romeo and Juliet*. The main plot grows from the love of Violetta and Fontinelle, who meet at a ball. Fontinelle is a member of the enemy (France) and is later thrown into prison by Violetta's aristocratic suitor, Camillo. In Act 4, the lovers are secretly married by a friar. Thus marked parallels exist between the two plays: a ball-room scene depicting instantaneous love between members of warring factions, a secret marriage, even borrowed language. Violetta's admirer, Camillo, adapts Romeo's praise of Juliet:

And of Beautie what tongue would not speake the best, since it is the Jewell that hangs upon the brow of heaven, the best cullor that can be laide upon the cheeke of earth?[27]

Fontinelle also adopts Romeo's language. He refuses to dance: 'bid him whose heart no sorrow feeles / Tickle the rushes with his wanton heeles' (1.1.181–2), as does Romeo, who lets 'wantons light of heart / Tickle the sense-less rushes with their heels' (1.4.35–6). Romeo characterizes himself as having a 'soul of lead' (1.4.15); Fontinelle declares he has 'too much lead' in his heart (1.1.183). Falling in love at the ball, Fontinelle is as bombastic and Petrarchan as Romeo: 'Oh what a heaven is love! oh what a hell!' (1.1.212).

The last act appears to offer a startling reversal of Shakespeare's play: Fontinelle falls in love with another woman, a prostitute, and Violetta is forced to arrange a bed-trick to consummate her marriage. Yet one of the aspects of Romeo's character that has interested many commentators is the passion of his initial love for Rosaline, instantly displaced by an equal ardour for Juliet. Fontinelle shows that same inconstancy, and makes a similar use of Petrarchan rhetoric to describe both women. In the last act he defends his (supposed) night with the courtesan, Imperia: 'who dyes / For so bright beauty, is a bright Sacrifice', and returns to language nearly identical to that which he applied to Violetta in the first act: 'She is my heaven; she from me, I am in hell' (5.3.77–8, 183).

If Fontinelle is a Romeo pushed to the extremes of Petrarchan shallowness, Violetta is also a parodied version of Juliet. In the ballroom scene of *Blurt, Master Constable*, Fontinelle dances with another woman, while Violetta watches: 'In troth a very pretty French man; the carriage of his bodie likes me well; so does his footing, so does his face, so does his eye above his face, so does himselfe, above all that can bee

above himselfe' (1.1.187–90). Violetta repeatedly swears by her maidenhead and answers respectful questions with bawdy puns: 'What breeds that desire?' asks Camillo when she ends their dance. 'Nay I hope it is no breeding matter: tush, tush, by my maiden-head I will not …' (1.1.173–5). As a whole, the play is bawdier than *Romeo and Juliet*; jokes to do with maidenheads embellish virtually every scene, and many of these scenes burlesque Shakespeare's play. In 4.1, for example, a would-be lover tries to climb a rope to his mistress's window, borrowing Romeo's phrasing – 'Ile hang a Jewell at thine eare, sweet night' – but he is doused with urine when he pulls the cord (4.1.20).

The balcony scene in *Blurt, Master Constable* takes place in 3.1, between Violetta, her suitor (but not beloved) Camillo, and her brother Hippolito. Camillo, in response to Fontinelle's presumption in loving Violetta, has thrown the Frenchman into prison. Camillo and Hippolito are accompanied by musicians singing in an effort to 'pleade to a stonie heart' (3.1.120). The scene which ensues is marked by Violetta's lusty wit. She baits the anger of Camillo by risqué references to her desire for Fontinelle: 'Let him pleade your love for you; / I love a life to heare a man speake French / Of his complection' (3.1.164–6). She uses Fontinelle's nationality as a metaphor for consummation: 'I would undergoe / The instruction of that language rather far, / Than be two weekes unmaried (by my life)' (3.1.166–8). Like Mall, she ties a wish for marriage specifically to a desire for sex: 'Because Ile speake true French, Ile be his wife' (3.1.169). Her defiance is underlined by the boldness of her expression: 'the French-man's mine, / And by these hands Ile have him' (3.1.157–8). After Camillo and Hippolito leave, Violetta receives a letter from the imprisoned Fontinelle. Her response evokes Juliet's wish that night come with

---

27 *A Critical Old-Spelling Edition of Thomas Dekker's Blurt, Master Constable*, ed. Thomas Leland Berger (Salzburg, Austria, 1979), 1.1.90–3. See *Romeo* 1.5.44–6.

her 'black mantle': 'Blest night, wrap *Cinthia* in a sable sheete, / That fearefull lovers may securlie meete' (3.1.188–9).

One very important shift has occurred between Shakespeare's play and its parodic siblings. When Mercutio juggles puns, as in his 'Prick love for pricking, and you beat love down' (1.4.28), he does so to display his wit. He relies for humour on the fact that he has wrangled three priapic references into one sentence. But Juliet's erotic puns and metaphors are not directed, for the most part, at a display of her wit. Eroticized humour does steal into the balcony scene. Romeo cries 'O, wilt thou leave me so unsatisfied?' and Juliet responds 'What satisfaction canst thou have tonight?' (2.1.167–8). Satisfaction, in her hands, becomes a demure play on the sating of desire. But in general Juliet's wordplay does not demand laughing applause. Mall's and Violetta's puns, on the other hand, are spoken in joking exchanges, similar to those Shakespeare gives to Romeo and Mercutio. In fact, Mall's quibbles about Venus's coach can be matched to Mercutio's jokes about Queen Mab's chariot. The Queen Mab speech ends in a bawdy pun: 'This is the hag, when maids lie on their backs, / That presses them and learns them first to bear, / Making them women of good carriage' (1.5.93–5). Yet Mall is not simply a female Mercutio. Her puns, like Juliet's, are self-referential. Juliet's epithalamic images of Romeo lying on her, like snow on a raven, like day on night, are personally referent. Mercutio does not address his own desire; Juliet, Mall and Violetta do. Thus while Mercutio jokes about maids being taught 'to bear', Mall makes the same joke about herself, boasting she has 'strength to bear what ere he can do to me' (8.210).

These women offer self-referential sexual puns, not bawdy quibbles which rise solely from the punning potential of the English language. I would argue that Mercutio's delight in ribald double meanings leads to a different kind of banter than that which Mall and Frank engage in. If Mercutio's quibbles are funny, bawdy puns spoken by virgins are both comic and transgressive. The woman's revelation of desire may strengthen the audience's belief in the romantic relationship being staged, but it also violates a fundamental convention regarding the behaviour of a marriageable young female.

Puns desert surface rationality, turning instead to an emphasis on linguistic cleverness. I would argue that it is this emphasis on cleverness which precludes them from the language of virginal heroines in the majority of romantic comedies. Puns challenge a claim to chastity; the speaker is too knowledgeable. To understand the connotation of 'die' is to reveal carnal knowledge. To apply such a pun to one's own desire is even more damning. Thus these puns cannot operate as a mask, using ambiguity of interpretation to allow transgression of cultural expectations regarding virginal female speech. Not only does the commonplace nature of puns such as Mall's on 'oars' and Juliet's on 'die' preclude a censorious audience member from mistaking them, but the particular parallelism involved in a romantic balcony scene also operates to dispel the necessary ambiguity. The puns of parodic Juliets bring together more contexts than surface meaning and erotic implication. The audience sees yet another balcony scene, yet another desirous 'Juliet'.

I would suggest that the sexual jesting of Porter's and Dekker's heroines certainly looks in part to Juliet's remarkable epithalamium. She expresses, if in metaphor, a joyful anticipation of sexual pleasure not found in the language of a virginal heroine preceding her in English drama. Imitation of this aspect of Juliet's character seems to be divided: on the one side, a few Renaissance balcony scenes stage outspoken, lustful pseudo-Juliets, and on the other, there are the punning pseudo-Juliets I have discussed in this essay. The balcony scene in Jonson's *Poetaster* (1601), for example, takes place between Caesar's daughter, Julia, and the newly banished Ovid. Julia's wrath at Ovid's banishment grows from anticipated celibacy: 'Let me vse all my pleasures: vertuous loue / Was neuer scandall to a Goddesse state.'[28] Notably, *Poeta-ster* is no romance. Parody traditionally attacks the ideals of a famous predecessor: when Julia hysterically invites Ovid to climb up to her room ('enioy me amply, still' (4.9.691)), Jonson burlesques Juliet's chastity at the same time as he mocks her sexual desire. Both types of balcony scenes involve a brutalizing of the passion that permeates the Shakespeare play, but Porter's and Dekker's emphasis on punning wit creates a very different kind of burlesque.

In the punning balcony scenes, Juliet's deeply felt sexual metaphors are turned to shallow banter, but the emphasis on wordplay as an appropriate vehicle for a female revelation of desire remains. Shakespeare used puns in two ways in *Romeo and Juliet*: as witty conversation (between Mercutio and Romeo, for example) and as a device by which Juliet expresses erotic anticipation. Dekker and Porter conflate the two. Bawdy conversation turns to self-referential sexual wit, an important shift.

When Porter and Dekker move Mercutio's decorative puns to the central female figure of a romance, the playwrights explicitly renounce the lyric concept of wooing. Their lovers speak 'without the book' as Mall observes. Romantic hyperbole is abandoned for a heady acknowledgement of sexual interest. Petrarchan idealization is mocked as representative of blind foolishness, and desire that grows from bodily appreciation is contrasted to insincere similes comparing eyes to suns. That alteration is certainly foreshadowed in Shakespeare's play. It is Juliet – so adroit at wordplay that reveals carnal desire – who tells Romeo that he kisses 'by th' book,' and begs him not to make empty vows. Perhaps the presence of that distant subtext, *Romeo and Juliet*, can explain why Mall and Violetta are practically unique among Renaissance heroines in their use of bawdy puns. If puns themselves cannot operate as an excuse for the expression of female desire, the faint burlesque of Juliet may. In this case, parody offers protection.

---

[28] *Poetaster, Ben Jonson*, vol. 4, ed. C. H. Herford and Percy Simpson (Oxford, 1952), 4.9.63–4.

PICTURING *ROMEO AND JULIET*

JAMES FOWLER

From the eighteenth century to the present *Romeo and Juliet* has ranked among the most frequently illustrated of all Shakespeare's plays.[1] The sheer number and diversity of the pictures it has generated explains why Henry Irving believed that '*Hamlet* could be played anywhere on its acting merits. It marches from situation to situation. But *Romeo and Juliet* proceeds from picture to picture. Every line suggests a picture. It is a dramatic poem rather than a drama, and I mean to treat it from that point of view.'[2] So rich is the subject that one could write at length about the illustration of *Romeo and Juliet* in books, acting, stage designs, photographs or film and video. In the space provided here the focus will be mainly on paintings and prints of the play and their relationship to the theatre.

The earliest illustrations are in editions of Shakespeare dating from the first half of the eighteenth century when Thomas Otway's adaptation *Caius Marius* (1679) still held the stage. Shakespeare's text had been performed soon after the Restoration in competition with James Howard's tragicomic version where the lovers survived.[3] Both were ousted by Otway who cut Shakespeare heavily and set the story of the couple – renamed Marius and Lavinia – in classical Rome.[4] They met a tragic end after bidding each other farewell in the tomb. In 1744 Theophilus Cibber rescued the original title in an amalgamation of Shakespeare and Otway that included the lovers' farewell. His version was superseded in 1748 by that of David Garrick who restored most of Shakespeare's text

but wrote his own version of the lovers' farewell. This proved so successful that it kept Shakespeare's ending off the London stage until 1845 and lingered on until at least 1875.

In his text of 1750 Garrick introduced a funeral procession at the beginning of Act 5, an elaborate stage picture with music by William Boyce which rivalled a similar scene with Thomas Arne's music at Covent Garden.[5] Set in a church with clergy, singing choir and tolling bells, it showed Juliet lying 'on a state bed with a canopy over her, guarded by girls who strew flowers and by torch-bearers with flaming torches'.[6] The funeral procession realized an opportunity for spectacle in Shakespeare, and, despite carping from critics, remained a favourite attraction well into the nineteenth century. Although a few later illustrations of it exist, for example on six sheets in a juvenile drama

---

1   Richard D. Altick, *Paintings from Books: Art and Literature in Britain 1760–1900* (Columbus, 1985), p. 259.

2   As quoted in Alan Hughes, *Henry Irving, Shakespearean* (Cambridge, 1981), p. 160.

3   Kalman Burnim, *David Garrick Director* (1961; reprinted Carbondale and Edwardsville, 1973), pp. 127ff.

4   Charles Beecher Hogan, *Shakespeare in the Theatre 1701–1800*, 2 vols. (Oxford, 1952), vol. I, pp. 404–5.

5   See *Shakespeare in Music. A Collection of Essays*, edited by Phyllis Hartnoll (London, 1966), p. 62.

6   From an eyewitness account of 1761 quoted in Burnim, *David Garrick*, p. 136. (For a description by the Drury Lane prompter of *c.* 1776 see Edward A. Langhans, *Eighteenth Century British and Irish Promptbooks: A Descriptive Bibliography* (New York, 1987), pp. 188–9.)

7 Juliet in the Tomb scene, probably by Elisha Kirkall after François Boitard, 1709.

version published by Hodgson in 1823,[7] artists do not appear to have illustrated it during the eighteenth century. As it was essentially a creation of the stage, they presumably saw no point in translating it into another medium. Rather, it was the Tomb scene (5.3) which proved equally popular with eighteenth-century audiences, painters and illustrators of Shakespeare's text. For example, 'Juliet's tomb' featured in the procession of Shakespeare characters in Garrick's *The Jubilee* from 1770,[8] and the tomb scene was chosen to represent the virtue of Love when episodes from Shakespeare were staged at the Haymarket in 1781.[9]

The very first illustration of *Romeo and Juliet*, in Nicholas Rowe's 1709 edition of Shakespeare, anticipates the popularity of the Tomb scene (5.3) in later eighteenth-century illustration. The engraving, believed to be by Elisha Kirkall after François Boitard, shows Juliet beside the bier between Romeo and Paris stabbing herself by torchlight as the Page and Watch arrive in the background. Since other prints in this edition show evidence of contemporary staging,[10] it is possible that the lofty vault interior reflects Otway's 'Temple and Monument' setting. But it more likely derives from Shakespeare as the men's costumes are in Renaissance not Roman style. The image was re-used with slight alterations in Rowe's second edition of 1714,[11] and again in Pope's edition of 1728 which was reprinted in 1733 and 1735.[12]

It was superseded in 1740 by a print in Theobald's (second) edition of Shakespeare engraved by G. Vandergucht after Hubert Gravelot, who did much to introduce French rococo drawing into England. Illustrating an earlier moment within the vault, Gravelot gives Friar Laurence a 'crow and spade' (5.3.120 s.d.) and lantern that shines on the dead Romeo as Juliet wakes on her bier. Behind Paris's body through the doorway is a shadowy figure, perhaps Balthasar or the Watch, lit by a crescent moon. Like its predecessor of 1709, Gravelot's design gained wide circulation, Theobald's edition being reprinted five times from 1752 to 1773.

Gravelot also engraved Francis Hayman's design for Romeo entering the vault (5.3) in Thomas Hanmer's edition of Shakespeare published in 1743–4 and reprinted in 1770–1. It is the first image of the play by an easel artist who trained and practised as a scene painter.[13] Unfortunately, Hayman had little scope for artistic or theatrical licence as he was bound by the instructions of Hanmer, a scholarly editor with 'a profound loyalty to Shakespeare's text' in which he was 'deeply immersed'.[14] These stipulate for *Romeo and Juliet*:

a church yard spread over with graves and gravestones. Among the rest and near the church (one small part of which may be shewn) must be raised a handsome entrance as leading down into a Vault (like that in St Paul's Church yard). The door to be open and the steps leading down to appear in view. Near the door Paris a young man lies just slain in a duel by Romeo, and Romeo is going towards the door as in purpose of descending into the Vault.[15]

Hayman adds details such as a 'wrenching iron', two swords and full moon, and heightens the

---

7   The Theatre Museum, London has four of the six sheets showing eight sections of the procession including Juliet's bier.

8   Johanne H. Stochholm, *Garrick's Folly* (London, 1964), p. 164. Compare Hazlitt's description of the Tomb scene business in a Drury Lane revival of *The Jubilee* on 28 April 1816 in *A View of the English Stage*, edited by W. Spencer Jackson (London, 1906), pp. 197–8.

9   On 17 August for Bannister's benefit. See also Hogan, *Shakespeare*, vol. 2, pp. 73, 602.

10   W. Moelwyn Merchant, *Shakespeare and the Artist* (London, 1959), p. 49.

11   The changes include making Juliet more decolleté and substituting a sword for the bones lying beside the dead Paris.

12   Merchant, *Shakespeare*, p. 52 and plate 11(b) which reproduces P. Fourdrinier's engraved version of 1728 with further alterations.

13   Brian Allen, *Francis Hayman* (London, 1987), pp. 11–15.

14   Marcia Allentuck, 'Sir Thomas Hanmer Instructs Francis Hayman: An Editor's Notes to his Illustrator (1744)', *Shakespeare Quarterly*, 27 (1976), 288–315; p. 290.

15   As quoted in Allentuck, 'Sir Thomas Hanmer ...', pp. 314–15, which also reproduces Hayman's illustration engraved by Gravelot.

8   David Garrick as Romeo and George Anne Bellamy as Juliet in the Tomb scene, by Benjamin Wilson.

dramatic effect by having the door off its hinges and Romeo actually stepping down into the vault (5.3.28). Although it has been argued – before the discovery of Hanmer's instructions – that Hayman's monument resembles that later used by Garrick (see below),[16] its influence upon or derivation from the stage is uncertain, as it may simply be modelled on an actual vault as Hanmer suggests.

It was, however, the theatre that caused *Romeo and Juliet* to be painted for the first time around 1752 and led to an extraordinary burst of interest in illustrating the play in its own right. In 1750 Garrick's star Romeo, Spranger Barry, deserted Drury Lane with Mrs Cibber – his Juliet – for the rival Covent Garden, a defection that occasioned the topical print titled *The Theatrical Steelyards*.[17] Not to be outdone, Garrick played Romeo opposite George Anne Bellamy as Juliet for twelve nights in direct competition with Barry and Mrs Cibber at Covent Garden until the latter conceded defeat on the thirteenth. Barry, with melting look and plaintive tones, won the plaudits in the first three acts, while Garrick excelled in the last two, raising terror and pity when he used the crowbar to kill Paris and break open the monument, and in his final farewell to Juliet. Indeed, Romeo's forcing of the monument with 'extravagant attitudes'[18] remained standard business

---

[16] W. Moelwyn Merchant, 'Francis Hayman's Illustrations of Shakespeare', in *Shakespeare Quarterly*, 9 (1958), 141–7; p. 145.

[17] By Patrick O'Brian, 1751 (reproduced in Iain Mackintosh and Geoffrey Ashton, *The Georgian Playhouse Actors, Artists, Audiences and Architecture 1730–1830*, catalogue entry no. 66).

[18] A phrase used of Garrick in 1757 quoted in Arthur Colby Sprague, *The Stage Business in Shakespeare's Plays: A Postscript* (1954, repr. London, 1995), pp. 28–9.

for many years. Isaac Cruikshank caricatured it in 1797 in *An Itinerant Theatrical Sketch* (etching by Woodward; Harvard Theatre Collection).[19]

As the rivalry of the Romeos continued through 1751–2 Benjamin Wilson saw a commercial opportunity in painting his theatrical conversation piece *David Garrick as Romeo and George Anne Bellamy as Juliet in the Tomb Scene from 'Romeo and Juliet'* (versions at Theatre Museum, London (n.d.); Yale Center for British Art, 1753; and at Stourhead).[20] Romeo – in contemporary dress – stands amazed in the monument as Juliet wakes upon her bier, a moment for which both actors won praise. Mrs Bellamy, in contrast to the rival Mrs Cibber, 'rises more gradually; she keeps the audience longer in amazement, while the astonishment of *Romeo* rises in proportion, and is finely heightened and wonderfully affecting as perform'd by Mr *Garrick*, whose attitudes through the whole play are so inimitably excellent, as to bid defiance to the other *Romeo*'.[21]

Wilson's painting celebrates both the actors' performances and Garrick's success as an adaptor. His heightening of the scene's emotional impact was realized through pictorial acting. As Francis Gentleman observed in 1774: 'The waking of *Juliet* before *Romeo's* death, is exceedingly judicious; it gives an opportunity of working the pathos to its tenderest pitch, and shows a very fine picture, if the performers strike out just and graceful attitudes. What Mr GARRICK has wrote of this scene, does him and the stage great credit, as it affords a fine and extensive scope for capital powers.'[22] Wilson's tomb with its shattered door in the moonlit churchyard probably represents the actual staging, making it 'one of the first pictorial records of practical double doors in a backscene',[23] although it must not be forgotten that such paintings sought to evoke performance rather than reproduce it in photographic detail.[24] The painting was engraved by François-Simon Ravenet and successfully published[25] on 25 April 1753 shortly before Garrick and Mrs Bellamy ceased their partnership,

though which version it is based on is not known for certain. Enamel pictures after the engraving, which was republished by John Boydell in 1765, testify to the popularity of the image.[26] Wilson's later paintings of Garrick as Hamlet and King Lear were engraved in mezzotint by James McArdell and published in 1754 and 1761 respectively. These helped cultivate the taste for the theatrical conversation piece in the 1760s with which Wilson's assistant Johann Zoffany made his name under Garrick's patronage.[27]

A rare mezzotint possibly after Benjamin Wilson depicting a later moment in the Tomb scene (collection of the Hon. Christopher Lennox-Boyd)[28] was published at some time before the death of the engraver James McArdell in 1765. Juliet kneels over Romeo's body before the monument and is caught in the lantern beam of a very dark Friar Laurence,

[19] Reproduced by Colin Visser, 'Scenery and Technical Design' in *The London Theatre World 1660–1800*, edited by Robert D. Hume (Carbondale and Edwardsville, 1980), pp. 66–118; p. 81.
[20] Iain Mackintosh, 'David Garrick and Benjamin Wilson', *Apollo*, 121 (May 1985), pp. 314–20; see also Geoffrey Ashton, *Catalogue of Paintings at the Theatre Museum, London* (London, 1992), pp. 13–15.
[21] As quoted in Burnim, *David Garrick*, p. 132.
[22] In his commentary to the text in *Bell's Edition of Shakespeare's Plays*, 9 vols. (London, 1773–4), vol. 2, p. 148n.
[23] Burnim, *David Garrick*, p. 137. See also Sybil Rosenfeld, *Georgian Scene Painters and Scene Painting* (Cambridge, 1981), p. 43.
[24] Shearer West, *The Image of the Actor: Verbal and Visual Representation in the Age of Garrick and Kemble* (London, 1991), p. 2.
[25] According to Wilson the engraving 'sold very well; and brought me in some money', quoted from his unpublished memoir by Mackintosh, 'David Garrick', p. 317.
[26] See Mackintosh, 'David Garrick', p. 315, and Christie's London sale catalogue of *Fine English Enamels* (18 March 1987), lot no. 492.
[27] West, *The Image*, pp. 29–30ff.
[28] Reproduced in Christopher Lennox-Boyd, Guy Shaw and Sarah Halliwell, *Theatre in the Age of Garrick* (London, 1994), p. 49.

while an observer, possibly Balthasar, lurks in the background. It is not clear if it depicts Shakespeare's or Garrick's version, or portrays an actual performer such as Miss Nossiter as Juliet. The atmosphere is reminiscent of Wilson's painting despite differences in detail such as the less ornate tomb and a sunken moon on the other side of the monument which gives a much darker and grimmer effect. If Wilson is not the source then it may independently reflect similar staging in the theatre.

Wilson's painting of Garrick prompted other scenes in the play to be illustrated for the first time. On 1 March 1753 an etching was published of *Mr Woodward in the Character of Mercutio in 'Romeo and Juliet'* – just two days before Ravenet's print of Garrick was first advertised to potential subscribers.[29] Henry Woodward was feted in the role[30] and, as he had remained loyal to Garrick at Drury Lane, the near coincidence in date probably reflects opportunism on the part of the print publisher, W. Herbert. Dressed as an eighteenth-century gentleman, Woodward delivers the 'Queen Mab' speech as in Garrick's text (inscribed beneath) against a sylvan background representing Garrick's setting of a 'Wood near Verona'. With his forefinger he touches his nose at the lines 'Sometimes she gallops o'er a lawyer's nose, / And then dreams he of smelling out a suit:' (Garrick version of 1.4.77–8) – a clear use of pictorial gesture to illustrate the lines.[31]

When Mrs Cibber returned to Garrick and Drury Lane in the autumn of 1753, Barry countered by successfully bringing out Maria Nossiter, his eighteen-year-old protégée and lover, as Juliet. They were painted performing the balcony scene together (2.1) by Robert Pyle (formerly Marina Henderson Gallery)[32] which must date from 1753 if the engraving of it in reverse by William Elliott was published in the same year.[33] It depicts a stage setting complete with overhead chandelier with Barry as Romeo in eighteenth-century dress addressing Juliet in the balcony against a backscene of moonlit

pointed trees possibly meant to represent Italian cypresses.

The staging of *Romeo and Juliet* in 1753 may have inspired Anthony Walker to illustrate five different scenes – the first series to be devoted to the play in its own right. Four drawings, three of them dated 1753, are in the Henry E. Huntington Library. Engravings after them by Walker, one of which has the publication date 15 January 1754, plus another of the Apothecary scene (5.1) for which no drawing is known, are in the Folger Shakespeare Library, Washington D.C.[34] Walker's balcony scene (2.2)[35] resembles the engraving after Pyle in composition and detail such as the pointed trees, but Romeo – unlike Barry – is dressed in Elizabethan style. Three other scenes by Walker had not been illustrated before: a lively version of the masquerade scene (1.5) which was invariably trumpeted in playbills; the departure of Romeo and Juliet with Friar Laurence in 2.6; and Romeo with the Apothecary (5.1).[36] Walker's last drawing shows the horrified Friar discovering Romeo's body inside the vault in 5.3, but at a later moment than Gravelot since Juliet leans on

[29] Mackintosh, 'David Garrick', p. 316.

[30] Burnim, *David Garrick*, p. 133.

[31] Compare Herbert Standing's use of 'pantomimic gesture' in the same speech in Mary Anderson's 1884 production, cited in Russell Jackson, 'The Shakespearian Productions of Lewis Wingfield (1883–90), *Theatre Notebook*, 31 (1977), 28–41; p. 33.

[32] Reproduced in Mackintosh, 'David Garrick', p. 318.

[33] Philip H. Highfill Jr, Kalman A. Burnim and Edward A. Langhans, *A Biographical Dictionary of Actors, Actresses, Musicians, Dancers, Managers and Other Stage Personnel in London, 1660–1800*, vol. 11 (Carbondale and Edwardsville, 1987), p. 67.

[34] William L. Pressly, *A Catalogue of Paintings in the Folger Shakespeare Library* (New Haven and London, 1993), pp. 101–2. A set of five prints is also held by the Boston Public Library according to William Jaggard, *Shakespeare Bibliography* (Stratford-upon-Avon, 1911), p. 444.

[35] Reproduced in Robert R. Wark, *Drawings from the Turner Shakespeare* (San Marino, 1973), p. 66.

[36] A photographic reproduction is in the Witt Library, Courtauld Institute, University of London.

9 Juliet and the Friar in the Tomb scene, by Anthony Walker, 1754.

Romeo with dagger poised. Beneath are inscribed lines from Garrick's text.[37] Walker's illustrations may have been intended for a quarto edition of the play, like other drawings he made of 1 *Henry IV* and *King John*, that never materialized. Whether Walker exhibited the *Romeo and Juliet* among his scenes from Shakespeare at the Society of Artists in 1760 is not known, but one engraving was certainly published in 1795.[38]

David Garrick elevated acting to the rank of a liberal profession, and championed Shakespeare on stage and through his immensely influential Jubilee of 1769. He also encouraged many artists to paint him in role in theatrical conversation pieces which were widely published as prints.[39] Yet, curiously, his genius hardly impinged on the illustration of Shakespeare's text until the 1770s.[40] The turning point was John Bell's attractive and affordable edition of Shakespeare of 1773–4 which aimed at 'classical, theatrical, and general readers', like its successor *Bell's British Theatre* of 1776.[41] Dedicated to Garrick, Bell's Shakespeare combined acting texts where available (e.g. Garrick's version of *Romeo and Juliet*) with literary illustrations by recognized artists. Edward Edwards's design for *Romeo and Juliet* (engraved by William Walker) shows the Apothecary outside his shop with Romeo in Elizabethan-style costume with Shakespeare's text (5.1.83) inscribed beneath. To this was added in 1775 a portrait engraving by Charles Grignion after Parkinson of *Mr DOD[d], in the Character of MERCUTIO* – a role he first played at Drury Lane in 1768. Wearing contemporary dress he speaks Garrick's text 'See where he steals –'. As Bell explained elsewhere in 1776, 'animated' portraits of actors that accompany the playtext 'aid the audiences of the present excellent performers to recall at any time during life, the pleasures they have received'.[42]

Bell's second edition of 1785–7 used even more distinguished artists as illustrators while replacing the acting versions with Johnson and Steevens's text. Johann Ramberg portrayed the actress Mrs Kemble as Juliet on the point of

suicide in the Tomb – 'be brief / O Happy dagger ...' (5.3.168), while De Loutherbourg drew an earlier moment: 'Poison I see, hath been his timeless end' (5.3.162), and both were engraved by Charles Sherwin. Although De Loutherbourg had designed scenes for Garrick and his successors from the early 1770s, this is a literary interpretation of Shakespeare's text.

Bell's combination of literary and theatre-based images straddles a growing interest in Shakespeare on page and stage during the 1770s and 1780s. As public and private theatricals became increasingly fashionable, so artists turned more frequently to the plays for subjects to illustrate. In 1778 Benjamin West completed a 'history' (i.e. narrative) painting of Romeo's farewell (3.5) in *Romeo and Juliet* (New Orleans Museum of Art).[43] Viewing the scene from within the balcony West brilliantly conveys both the romance and the tension in the situation by showing Romeo trying to depart but still embraced by Juliet as the Nurse presses his hand in her agitation at Lady Capulet's imminent arrival (3.5.37–40).

Three years later John Pine advocated Shakespeare as a fit subject for a series of history paintings from which engravings were to be published: 'These subjects, having hitherto been

37 See Pressly, *A Catalogue*, pp. 101–2.

38 Wark, *Drawings*, p. 49.

39 Iain Mackintosh and Geoffrey Ashton, *Thirty Different Likenesses: David Garrick in Portrait and Performance* (Buxton, 1981).

40 Geoffrey Ashton, 'The Boydell Shakespeare Gallery: Before and After' in *The Painted Word: British History Painting: 1750–1830*, edited by Peter Cannon-Brookes (London, 1991), pp. 37–43; p. 42.

41 Vol. 1, p. 2.

42 *Bell's British Theatre*, vol. 1, p. 4.

43 Reproduced in *A Brush with Shakespeare: The Bard in Painting 1780–1910* (Montgomery, Alabama, 1985), p. 91. Although the date on the painting is 1778, West must have begun it three or four years earlier since the figures of Romeo and Juliet were engraved by G. Scorodonow in 1775 (see Helmut von Erffa and Allen Staley, *The Paintings of Benjamin West* (New Haven and London, 1986), p. 276).

unattended to, but for frontispieces to the plays; it may be proper to observe, that the pictures proposed are not meant to be representations of stage scenes, but will be treated with the more unconfined liberty of painting, in order to bring those images to the eye, which the writer has given to the mind; and which, in some instances, is not within the power of the Theatre.'[44]

During 1783–7 Thomas Stothard and Robert Smirke published scenes from Shakespeare without accompanying play texts in *The Picturesque Beauties of Shakespeare*. Stothard shows Juliet conversing with Romeo not from a stage balcony[45] but a window as in Shakespeare (2.1.44), and her refusal to marry Paris in 3.5. These together with Smirke's images of the Nurse's discovery of Juliet (4.4) and Paris slain by Romeo (5.3)[46] are among the first illustrations of these particular scenes. In 1785 William Hamilton romantically portrayed the lovers' 'palmer's kiss' encounter in the Ball scene (1.5) in an engraving by Francesco Bartolozzi[47] published on 15 June. While these show little influence of the theatre, Mather Brown portrayed in 1786 the Covent Garden stars Joseph George Holman and Anne Brunton life-size as Romeo and Juliet emerging from the monument in Garrick's version (Mander and Mitchenson Collection, London; engraved Thomas Park, 1787). The generalized pathos, neo-classical architecture and large-scale canvas (201 × 130 cms) aspire to the grandeur of history painting and look forward to Thomas Lawrence's monumental portraits of John Philip Kemble in leading Shakespearian roles.[48] Curiously, Brown used a fussy, late rococo style to depict Friar Laurence taking away Romeo and Juliet to be married (2.5) (date unknown, RSC Collection, Stratford-upon-Avon), the Friar's cell being set in woodland outside Verona, not in a monastery as in the acting text.

All the artists just mentioned contributed to Boydell's Shakespeare Gallery which grew out of the ambition of the leading printseller John Boydell to found a British school of history painting, long regarded as the highest form of art.[49] As the work of the national poet, Shakespeare's plays were an ideal subject for history paintings that Boydell commissioned from the best artists of the day. These were exhibited in a special Pall Mall gallery and published in a series of large engravings in addition to smaller ones that illuminated a special new edition supervised by Steevens. Boydell's Shakespeare Gallery was immediately successful on opening in 1789 and spawned several rivals such as Woodmason's Shakespeare Gallery, the Irish Shakespeare Gallery and the 'Poets' Gallery' of Thomas Macklin[50] – who from 1792–6 published engravings after pen and ink and wash drawings by Henry William Bunbury including *Romeo and Juliet and Friar Laurence* in 2.6 (The Shakespeare Birthplace Trust, Stratford-upon-Avon).[51] But war with France in the 1790s disrupted the foreign print trade, undermined Boydell's business and led to the closure of his Shakespeare Gallery in 1805. Although the paintings were sold off and dispersed they enjoyed a phenomenally successful after-life through being

44 As quoted in David Alexander, 'Print Makers and Print Sellers in England, 1770–1830' in *The Painted Word*, pp. 23–9; p. 27.
45 Juliet's balcony was a purpose-built scenic piece certainly at the Crow Street Theatre in Dublin by 1776, see Sybil Rosenfeld, *Georgian Scene Painters*, p. 26.
46 Reproduced in Pressly, *A Catalogue*, p. 64.
47 The lines inscribed beneath – 'Good pilgrim, you do wrong your hand too much / For palm to palm is holy palmer's kiss. vide Shakespeare' are actually from Garrick's text.
48 Shearer West, 'Thomas Lawrence's 'Half-History' Portraits and the Politics of Theatre', *Art History*, 14 (1991), 225–49.
49 Winifred Friedman, *Boydell's Shakespeare Gallery* (New York and London, 1976); *Alderman Boydell's Shakespeare Gallery*. Introduction by Richard W. Hutton and catalogue entries by Laura Nelke (Chicago, 1978); Richard D. Altick, *The Shows of London* (Cambridge, Mass. and London, 1978), pp. 106–9.
50 Ashton, 'The Boydell Shakespeare Gallery', p. 39.
51 Reproduced in John Christian, *Shakespeare in Western Art* [Tokyo Shimbun exhibition catalogue] (Tokyo, 1992), pp. 58, 168.

10 *'Romeo and Juliet*: The Tomb Scene' by Joseph Wright of Derby, 1790/91.

reproduced in many Shakespeare editions during the nineteenth century.

Boydell commissioned five paintings, one for each act of *Romeo and Juliet*, that reflect late eighteenth-century taste while anticipating interests of the nineteenth. William Miller's painting of the Ball scene (1.5) (engraved by G. S. and J. G. Facius, 1792) shows Romeo about to kiss Juliet's hand with musicians and swirling dancers beyond – a fateful moment rather obviously underlined by the glowering figure of Tybalt to the right. Robert Smirke's *Juliet and the Nurse* (engraved by James Parker, 1797) anticipates a subject which became very popular in the 1820s and 1830s. Setting the scene indoors he shows Juliet coaxing the grim-acing Nurse who sits on a sofa with her fan.[52]

John Francis Rigaud's *Romeo, Juliet and the Nurse* (engraved by James Stow, 1797) depicts Romeo's farewell (3.5) as the Nurse rushes in. But his portrayal of contrasting emotion is not so finely balanced as West's. The rococo use of colour, such as Romeo's apricot-coloured suit and carmine cloak,[53] emphasizes romance at the

---

[52] A larger fan had long been popular on stage, see illustration of 1770 of *The Jubilee* procession in Stochholm, *Garrick's Folly*, p. 155.

[53] Friedman, *Boydell's Shakespeare Gallery*, p. 168. While Friedman reproduces the Boydell paintings and prints, larger versions of the latter can be consulted in *The Boydell Shakespeare Prints*, with an introduction by A. E. Santaniello (New York, repr. 1979).

11 Romeo and the Apothecary, by William Blake after Henry Fuseli, 1804.

Blake, was later issued of the first version of the painting.

Some critics doubted the capacity of Boydell's artists to portray Shakespeare's characters, arguing that this was the province of actors requiring special talent and lifelong study ('the intense application of a KEMBLE or HARLEY'). As Horace Walpole observed: 'Pray who to give an idea of Falstaff, now Quin is dead?'[54] Other critics who sought the Grand Style were relieved to find the paintings showed no dependence on the stage: 'there was some reason to fear a representation of all that extravaganza of attitude and start which is tolerated, nay in a degree demanded, at the playhouse. But this has been avoided, the pictures in general give a mirror of the poet.'[55] Nevertheless, the influence of actors is occasionally felt. James Northcote, for example, altered his *Meeting of the Princes from 'Richard III'* to include a portrait of J. P. Kemble as Richard.[56] The same artist's *A Monument Belonging to the Capulets. Romeo and Paris dead; Juliet and Friar Lawrence* (1789, formerly Heim Gallery, London; engraved P. Simon 1792)[57] is believed to reflect the actors Joseph George Holman and Anne Brunton as portrayed by Mather Brown.[58] As the Friar descends into the vault his torch reveals Juliet starting up with arm outstretched, Romeo slumped on the bier and Paris lying by. The painting relies heavily on facial expression and large size (276 × 335 cms) for its effect but was highly sought after when the Gallery was sold off.[59]

In complete contrast is Joseph Wright of Derby's depiction of a later moment in 5.3 '*Romeo and Juliet'. The Tomb Scene. "Noise*

expense of the danger heralded by the Nurse. John Opie depicts the 'dead' Juliet on her bed in a crowded room (4.4) with the Friar trying to calm the Capulet household. Winifred Friedman describes how the first engraving of 1791 by G. S. and J. G. Facius is crowded with figures including musicians who disappear from the smaller plate engraved by Jean Pierre Simon in 1792. Opie may have had second thoughts about removing figures to simplify the composition since another small engraving, by William

54 As quoted in Friedman, *Boydell's Shakespeare Gallery*, pp. 81, 69.
55 As quoted in Friedman, *Boydell's Shakespeare Gallery*, p. 75.
56 West, *The Image*, pp. 116–17.
57 Reproduced in *The Painted Word*, p. 84.
58 Friedman, *Boydell's Shakespeare Gallery*, p. 165; West, *The Image*, p. 116.
59 See *The Painted Word*, p. 85.

again! then I'll be brief" (1790/1, Derby Art Gallery) which views Juliet from behind kneeling by Romeo, and conveys her extreme tension through her back and uplifted arm. Holding the dagger ready behind her, she starts with arm and fingers outstretched in the gloom at the shadow of the approaching Watch. Rejected by Boydell,[60] this painting was exhibited at the Royal Academy in 1790 and again (re-worked) the following year. The Reverend Matthew Peters, however, painted the same moment from the front with uncharacteristic power in *The Death of Juliet* (1793, Folger Shakespeare Library, Washington D.C.),[61] though not in this case for Boydell's Shakespeare Gallery. Juliet's monumental pose and intense, saint-like gaze as she holds the dagger at full stretch movingly combines pathos with the female beauty Peters was famous for portraying.

Henry Fuseli came late to *Romeo and Juliet* having painted major works for Boydell's Shakespeare Gallery. He illustrated Romeo and the Apothecary inside his shop (5.1), engraved by Blake,[62] for Rivington's 1805 Shakespeare edition, and over the next decade executed major paintings which profoundly explore the relationship of love and death in *Romeo and Juliet* through contrasts of light and darkness. *Romeo Stabs Paris at the Bier of Juliet* (c. 1809, Folger Shakespeare Library, Washington D.C.)[63] presents a double image in 5.3, with Paris in the background being transfixed by Romeo's sword as Romeo darkly lunges in front of the white figure of the reclining Juliet. His *Romeo at Juliet's Bier* shows an ensuing moment (1809, Richard Dreyfus collection, Basle)[64] suggesting Juliet's death through her ashen features and sunken eyes as absolutely as Romeo, who lifts her shroud, imagines it to be. Fuseli returned to the play in 1814 with *Queen Mab* (Carl Laszlo collection, Basle)[65] who hovers with a whip of cricket's bone and moth-like attendants over a bare-breasted young woman who dreams of love in her boudoir (1.4.71–2). In *Romeo and Juliet* (1810–15, private collection (sold Sothe-

by's London, 12 April 1995)) the viewer looks down on Romeo slipping away into darkness as Juliet turns her head in a premonition of his death. Catalogued as Romeo's farewell (3.5.54–7),[66] it also appears to suggest at the same time Romeo's arrival in 2.1 with Juliet in the balcony leaning her head on her arm while musing on her lover. Fuseli's subject matter may reflect his known admiration for Eliza O'Neill[67] who made her celebrated debut as Juliet at Covent Garden on 6 October 1814. Early in 1815 he drew three versions of Romeo on the rope ladder in 3.5 (Weimar, Staatliche Kunstsammlungen;[68] private collection, London[69]) in

---

[60] Friedman, *Boydell's Shakespeare Gallery*, p. 133, and Judy Egerton, *Wright of Derby* (London, 1990), pp. 123–4 who reproduces the work in colour and also quotes a letter from Wright to William Hayley of 23 December 1786. Wright found an engraving after Benjamin Wilson – presumably the one featuring Garrick – hard to keep out of his mind when deciding on the composition of the present painting: 'When I think of the subject, a print after Ben: Wilson, which you have seen I suppose, crosses my imagination – I sometimes fancy there is no way so good of telling the story.'

[61] Reproduced in Pressly, *A Catalogue*, plate 8; p. 100.

[62] Reproduced in W. Moelwyn Merchant, 'Blake's Shakespeare', *Apollo*, special Shakespeare number, April 1964, 318–25; p. 323. Merchant also illustrates Blake's vignette of Juliet with a cup, probably in 4.3, and his engraving *Jocund Day* based on 3.5.9–10 (dated 1780 but probably engraved *c.* 1793) on pp. 319–20.

[63] Reproduced in Pressly, *A Catalogue*, plate 12, pp. 63–4. See also Gert Schiff, *Johann Heinrich Füssli 1741–1825*, 2 vols. (Zurich and Munich, 1973), plates vol. p. 365, text vol. p. 563.

[64] Reproduced in Schiff, *Füssli*, plates vol. p. 366, text vol. 563.

[65] Reproduced in Schiff, *Füssli*, plates vol. p. 488, text vol. p. 603.

[66] Reproduced in Schiff, *Füssli*, plates vol. p. 562, text vol. pp. 641–2.

[67] See letter of 15 December 1815 from William Roscoe to Dawson Turner, about how Miss O'Neill had inspired a Fuseli drawing of Juliet in the Balcony scene, in David H. Weinglass, *The Collected English Letters of J. H. Fuseli* (New York and London 1982, p. 415).

[68] Reproduced in Schiff, *Füssli*, plates vol. p. 510, text vol. p. 610.

passionate embrace with Juliet who leans over the Balcony.[70]

Miss O'Neill was portrayed by George Dawe (c. 1816, oil study in the Folger Shakespeare Library, Washington D.C.)[71] as Juliet pensively leaning her cheek on her hand in the Balcony (2.1.65) – the scene which became most popular of all during the nineteenth century. This was a distinguished addition to an ever-growing number of theatrical portraits of actors in role. These include watercolours by Samuel De Wilde of William Lewis as Mercutio (1809, Garrick Club, London), and the Romeos of young William Charles Macready (1810, private collection)[72] and of Robert Coates (c. 1812, Garrick Club).[73] Among the many paintings of Juliets are those of Sarah Booth (n.d., RSC Collection, Stratford-upon-Avon) and later, Fanny Kemble, daughter of the celebrated Romeo, Charles Kemble. Among the illustrations inspired by Fanny's legendary 1829 debut is John Hayter's series of lithographs of her various 'attitudes', and a charming watercolour by Frederick Tayler showing her first encounter with Romeo (1.5) who hides behind a comic mask (1830, Theatre Museum, London). The most unusual tribute, however, is Henry Perronet Briggs's off-stage painting of Fanny Kemble in a Covent Garden dressing room about to make her first appearance as Juliet (location unknown).[74] Among the most attractive thespian paintings is Wilhelm Lehmann's portrayal of Helen Faucit (1873, RSC Collection, Stratford-upon-Avon) on a balcony as if she were Juliet – a role she made her own from 1833 to 1871.[75]

During the nineteenth century imaginary studies of individual characters continued to be illustrated as interest began to be shown in the Nurse stimulated partly by the success of Mary Ann Davenport in the role in 1829, and later in the Apothecary.[76] The great favourite was Juliet who won the hearts of all as a 'keepsake beauty' in books such as *The Heroines of Shakespeare* so beloved of the Victorians. Though cloyingly pretty, John Hayter's ideal picture of Juliet in the balcony (2.1) is, however, unusual in striving to portray her as a fourteen-year-old girl. The grand 'Boydell' style was succeeded by more intimate scenes and moods. Henry Perronet Briggs's painting of *Juliet and her Nurse* (2.5.18–19) (1827, Tate Gallery, London) humorously contrasts the beautiful heroine with the less slender Nurse who has a crutch and fan (carried by Peter), properties which were traditional on stage.[77] While scenes of Juliet and the Nurse remained more popular, no little interest was shown in those featuring Juliet and Friar Laurence, notably by John Pettie, E. M. Ward and others.[78]

By far the most extraordinary version of *Juliet and her Nurse* is Joseph Mallord William Turner's painting of 1836 (collection of Mrs Flora Whitney Miller).[79] It depicts a minuscule Nurse and Juliet, cheek on hand, on a balcony in the bottom corner of a bird's-eye view of the crowded Piazza San Marco. Venice glows beyond by the light of lamps and fireworks.

---

[69] Reproduced in Schiff, *Füssli*, plates vol. p. 510, text vol. p. 610; and in *Henry Fuseli* (London, 1975), p. 68.
[70] Compare Hazlitt's review of Miss O'Neill's Juliet at Covent Garden on 16 October 1814 when he criticized her in 2.1 for hanging 'in a fondling posture over the balcony', see *A View*, p. 35.
[71] Pressly, *A Catalogue*, pp. 194–6.
[72] Reproduced in Ian Mayes, *The De Wildes* (Northampton, 1971), illus. no. 6, catalogue no. 16.
[73] Reproduced in *A Brush with Shakespeare*, p. 50.
[74] Reproduced in Dorothy Marshall, *Fanny Kemble* (London, 1977). Formerly exhibited in the Picture Gallery of the Shakespeare Memorial Theatre, see *Illustrated Catalogue of the Pictures &c in the Shakespeare Memorial at Stratford-upon-Avon* (Stratford-upon-Avon, 1911), no. 59.
[75] Reproduced in Geoffrey Ashton, *Shakespeare's Heroines in the Nineteenth Century* (Buxton, 1980), p. 35.
[76] Altick, *Paintings from Books*, pp. 295–7.
[77] Arthur Colby Sprague, *Shakespeare and the Actors* (Cambridge, Mass., 1944), p. 304.
[78] Ashton, *Shakespeare's Heroines*, p. 24.
[79] Reproduced in Martin Butlin and Evelyn Joll, *The Paintings of J. M. W. Turner*, 2 vols. revised edition (New Haven and London, 1984), plate vol. no. 369; and in John Walker, *Joseph William Mallord Turner* (London, 1989), p. 107.

12 'Love – Romeo and Juliet' by Richard Dadd, 1853.

124

Turner's preference for Venice over Verona incensed critics unwilling to tolerate such artistic licence.[80] Yet his concern to create an 'authentic' Italian setting for his subject from a topographical and architectural point of view heralds later interest in contextualizing the play. For example, Charles Edouard Delort's *Romeo and Juliet – Capulet's Garden* painted probably after 1866 (Mr and Mrs E. Hal Dickson, Mr and Mrs James R. Duncan, Mr and Mrs Frank W. Rose, San Angelo, Texas)[81] features an Italianate building with Gothic-style pediment in full sunlight which almost dwarfs Juliet at a window (2.1.44), and Romeo holding a lute below.

The growing realism of such settings can be detected in later nineteenth-century paintings of the balcony scene.[82] Those portraying Juliet alone in 2.1 range from Daniel Hartington's *Juliet on the Balcony* (1857, National Academy of Design, New York)[83] to Thomas Francis Dicksee's work of the same title (1875, City of Dundee Museums and Art Galleries Dept.), to William Hatherell's *Juliet* (c. 1912, Tate Gallery) discussed below.[84] Notable romantic paintings of Romeo's farewell in 3.5 include Eugène Delacroix's *Les Adieux de Roméo et Juliette* (1845, Christie's New York, 26 October 1988), and the elaborate balcony architecture of Frank Dicksee's *Romeo and Juliet* (1884, Southampton City Art Gallery).

Richard Dadd's watercolour sketch, *Sketch for the Passions. LOVE: Romeo and Juliet* (1853, Yale Center for British Art),[85] shows Romeo standing on the rope ladder outside the balcony embracing Juliet who is wrapped in a counterpane, while the Nurse, fearful of Lady Capulet's approach, bites her nails behind. Yet two faces sculpted on the balcony – one a lecherous satyr, the other more serene – appear to comment on Romeo's look of satisfaction suggesting the transforming power of love or, perhaps, more cynically, the post-coital escape of a sated lover. Ford Madox Brown paints the same moment (1870, Delaware Art Museum)[86] as a scene of pure passion – unqualified by agitated Nurse or satyr faces – except for a sinister crow that lurks

in apple blossom by the balcony. Here the focus is on Juliet's rapturous look – erotically reinforced by her deshabillé. Gorgeously dressed in red, Romeo has his arm and leg over the balcony, but Juliet clasps him so tightly that he cannot leave. John Roddam Spencer Stanhope features medieval details in the interior setting of his painting *Juliet and the Nurse* (1863, Pre-Raphaelite Inc.).[87] It realizes an 'off-stage" moment by showing Juliet deep in thought near the window apparently waiting for Romeo to arrive before 3.5 begins, with the rope ladder lying by on the floor and the Nurse observing her closely.[88]

The aftermath of the lovers' tragedy – a far less popular subject – was painted by John Everett Millais (1848, Manchester City Art Galleries)[89] and features the Prince bringing together Montague and Capulet in the crowded vault. John Christian describes it as 'an essentially private picture in which everything is sacrificed to emotional intensity' compared to Frederick Leighton's watercolour of *The Reconciliation of the Montagues and the Capulets* (1854, Yale Center for British Art)[90] which presents 'a highly romanticized image of "the Italian Middle Ages", full of rhetorical gestures, elabo-

---

80 Butlin and Joll, *Turner*, text vol. pp. 215–17; and Walker, *Turner*, pp. 24–6.
81 Reproduced in *A Brush with Shakespeare*, p. 48.
82 Ashton, *Shakespeare's Heroines*, p. 12.
83 Reproduced in Richard Stading, *Shakespeare in American Painting: A Catalogue from the late Eighteenth Century to the Present* (London and Toronto, 1993), no. 403.
84 The latter two are reproduced in Ashton, *Shakespeare's Heroines*, pp. 13, 29.
85 Reproduced in Geoffrey Ashton, *Shakespeare and British Art* (New Haven, 1981), p. 123.
86 Reproduced in colour in Jan Marsh, *Pre-Raphaelite Women* (London, 1987), p. 59. A version in pen and black chalk dated 1876 in Bradford Art Galleries and Museums is reproduced and discussed in Christian, *Shakespeare*, pp. 122, 185.
87 Reproduced in Christian, *Shakespeare*, p. 136.
88 Christian, *Shakespeare*, p. 188.
89 Reproduced in Christian, *Shakespeare*, p. 130.
90 Reproduced in Christian, *Shakespeare*, p. 142; quotations from p. 190.

rate costumes and picturesque decor'. Leighton, however, later expressed his concerns about illustrating such a comprehensive soul as Shakespeare's: 'I must candidly confess that I cannot agree about a complete illustration of the Shakespearian plays, those masterpieces already in existence as *exhaustively finished* works of art; it seems to me that in literature only those subjects lend themselves to pictorial representation which stand in written work more as *suggestion*.'[91]

The striving for greater authenticity in paintings and watercolours was paralleled by an innovation in the illustration of Shakespeare's text. Tallis's edition of 1850 returned to the stage for inspiration by featuring engravings based on photographs of costumed actors and actresses.[92] These included Miss Vandenhoff as Juliet, and the celebrated Charlotte Cushman as Romeo playing opposite her sister Susan as Juliet. At his New York theatre in 1869 Edwin Booth emulated Charles Kean by staging *Romeo and Juliet* with lavish settings: Juliet's balcony, an exquisite and faithful bit of architecture, sat in 'an Italian garden surrounded by brick and marble walls . . . The facade of a Romanesque church, at least forty feet high, backs the square upon which Mercutio meets his death'.[93]

In 1882 at the Lyceum in London, Henry Irving seized on the pictorial potential of the play as quoted earlier. Rich costumes, eighteen settings by Hawes Craven, Telbin, Cuthbert and Hann, and complex crowd scenes – inspired by the Duke of Saxe-Meiningen's company which had visited London the previous season – made *Romeo and Juliet* Irving's most ambitious and spectacular production to date.[94] Clement Scott extolled the splendour of scenes such as the hall in Capulet's house ('a glorious picture'), Juliet on her marble balcony terrace with a lily bed beneath, and the 'pinks and oranges and purples of a sunrise' in Romeo's farewell – even though the profusion of colour and detail distracted from the acting.[95] But, as Alan Hughes observes, 'under the pretty surface, the city was a hell of vendetta and sordid murder where

tempers boiled over in the Mediterranean sun',[96] particularly in 1.1 when the deadly riot shattered the tranquillity of the market place. This realization of Latin violence in the play was foreshadowed – albeit less spectacularly – from the 1820s when interest was already being shown in the thumb-biting Abraham/Samson confrontation (1.1.42–3), for example in H. Mayer's engraving (1822, Witt Library, Courtauld Institute) after Henry Perronet Briggs. The riot itself was later illustrated in full blown form by Ludovic Marchetti in a Shakespeare edition of 1892.[97] Edwin Austin Abbey depicted the moments following the slaughter in 3.1 in his watercolour *The Death of Mercutio* (1902, Yale University Art Gallery) in a fully realized Veronese street.

Irving's real triumph, however, came in the Tomb scene which he set below ground as suggested in 5.3.28. This allowed him to pull the body of Paris down no fewer than forty steps with macabre effect, as Shaw recalled: 'One remembers Irving, a dim figure dragging a horrible burden down through the gloom "into the rotten jaws of death".'[98] The subterranean setting was an innovation on stage though not in art – compare Northcote's 1789 Boydell painting above. It replaced the conventional Gothic monument on stage, of which there is a sketch *c*. 1840 drawn by H. Scharf in Covent Garden Theatre (Theatre Museum, London), and influenced succeeding theatre productions.

Apart from large engravings of this scene and

[91] As quoted in Lucy Oakley's introduction to *A Brush with Shakespeare*, p. 19.

[92] Ashton, 'The Boydell Shakespeare Gallery', in *The Painted Word*, p. 43.

[93] See Charles H. Shattuck, *Shakespeare on the American Stage* (Washington D.C., 1976), pp. 137–9.

[94] Hughes, *Henry Irving*, pp. 160–6.

[95] Clement Scott, *From 'The Bells' to 'King Arthur'* (London, 1897), pp. 236ff.

[96] Hughes, *Henry Irving*, p. 162.

[97] Reproduced in *The Annotated Shakespeare*, edited by A. L. Rowse (London, 1984), p. 1614.

[98] George Bernard Shaw, *Our Theatres in the Nineties*, 3 vols. (London, 1932), vol. 1, p. 202.

13   'Juliet and the Nurse' by Walter Sickert, *c.* 1935–6.

Romeo's farewell which appeared in publications such as *The Illustrated London News*, very few illustrations of Irving's decor survive.[99] Anna Lea Merritt continued a long-established tradition by painting Ellen Terry as Juliet and the inimitable Mrs Stirling as the Nurse in 2.5. (1883, Garrick Club, London). More unusual are three portraits by the distinguished caricaturist William Giles Baxter (published prints in Theatre Museum, London) which show Irving and Terry separately in the Balcony scene and together on Juliet's bier.

In 1884 Mary Anderson, assisted by Lewis Wingfield, tried to outdo Irving's production by experiencing Verona for herself, and by hiring as scenic artist John O'Connor, who had just completed a series of topographical views of the city.[100] But her opening riot scene was criticized on the grounds that the victims displayed no obvious wounds, and that Wingfield's costumes were historically inaccurate. A funeral procession was also planned but cut because it made the play too long. The décor of Johnston Forbes-Robertson's 1895 production of *Romeo and Juliet* aroused considerable expectation since he had trained at the Royal Academy Schools and exhibited as a painter before turning actor-manager. Shaw, however, found the dresses too 'chastened by the taste of a British gentleman', the Veronese sky 'too cold, and the cypresses too pale' but praised the scene in Mantua as surpassing the real thing 'in respect of its freedom from the atrocious Mantuan stenches and huge mosquitos from the marshes'.[101] The aesthetic staging is most beautifully captured in photographs of the Tomb scene (5.3) where Forbes-Robertson as Romeo leans across Juliet (Mrs Patrick Campbell) as she lies on the flower-garlanded bier.[102]

Romeo and Juliet continued to be illustrated in the early years of the twentieth century by distinguished artists such as Dudley Hardy who depicted very youthful lovers in Romeo's farewell scene (3.5.42) in 1902, and Arthur Rackham whose *At the Cell of Friar Lawrence* (2.5) illuminated an 1899 edition of Charles

and Mary Lamb's *Tales from Shakespeare* (revised in an edition of 1909; reprinted, New York, 1995). William Hatherell executed twenty-two colour designs for a luxury edition of the play published in 1912 by Hodder and Stoughton. Among the scene represented is a Juliet strikingly reminiscent of Ellen Terry on her balcony, and a rare depiction of Romeo's tantrum at 3.3.82 *Where's Romeo?* (watercolour, Birmingham Museums and Art Gallery).[103]

After the first World War, Laura Knight pursued her lifelong interest in portraying performers on and off the stage, catching Gwen Ffrangçon Davies dressing for Juliet at the Birmingham Repertory Theatre in 1922 in the watercolour *Fastening her dress* (Theatre Museum, London). But it was John Gielgud's landmark 1935 production in which he and Laurence Olivier successively played the roles of Romeo and Mercutio opposite Peggy Ashcroft which caught the painters' imagination. Harold Knight exhibited his portrait of Olivier as a smouldering young lover at the Royal Academy in 1936 (The Royal National Theatre, London), while Ethel Gabain painted the lovely Peggy Ashcroft as Juliet (1935, RSC Collection, Stratford-upon-Avon). Walter Sickert depicted her being comforted by Edith Evans as the Nurse, probably at the end of 3.5. The painting may be based on a photograph as were many of Sickert's late works. However, Dame Peggy later recalled in interview how Sickert was

a tremendous Shakespearean … He'd very often come at matinées when there wasn't a very large

[99] See George Rowell, 'William Terriss in *Romeo and Juliet*', in *Shakespeare and the Victorian Stage*, edited by Richard Foulkes (Cambridge, 1986), pp. 87–96, which reproduces one extant Hawes Craven setting.
[100] Jackson, 'The Shakespeare Productions', pp. 31ff.
[101] Shaw, *Our Theatres*, vol. 1, pp. 198–9.
[102] Reproduced in Robert Speaight, *Shakespeare on Stage* (London, 1973), p. 120.
[103] Ashton, *Shakespeare's Heroines*, p. 28; Christian, *Shakespeare*, pp. 155, 193.

audience there and you would find that some line that never got a laugh ordinarily, there would be a gust of laughter from this one solitary person – even a tremendous burst of applause ... I think this was probably less from a dramatic point of view than from a painter's point of view – he would suddenly see something in a scene which to him was very pictorial ...[104]

Since 1945 publishers have explored ways of illustrating Shakespeare which break down the old tradition of adding plates of paintings or actors' photographs into the text. The Folio Society's edition of *Romeo and Juliet* (London, 1950) features costume and set designs by Jean Hugo for Jean Cocteau's 1924 production at the Théâtre de la Cigale, Paris.[105] Paul Hamlyn published *Romeo and Juliet* as part of *Shakespeare Ten Great Plays* (London, 1962) with illustrations in contemporary style by Alice and Martin Provensen that break up the monotony of double-columned text. More recently academic editions in paperback have featured cover designs by distinguished living artists. These

include the lovers in Milton Glaser's Tomb setting (5.3) (*c.* 1963–4, The Signet Classic Shakespeare) and in David Gentleman's Balcony scene (2.1) (*c.* 1967, New Penguin Shakespeare), the latter being replaced by Paul Hogarth's mix of symbols – lute, swords and behatted skull. David Inshaw, a member of the Brotherhood of Ruralists, appealed to the young of the day by portraying Juliet in *c.* 1980 for The Arden Shakespeare as a solitary, contemporary girl of fourteen, a tender age which Shakespeare was at pains to emphasize.

---

104 From the quotation in Patrick O'Connor, '"The Reunion of Stage and Art": Sickert and the theatre between the Wars', in *Sickert Paintings*, edited by Wendy Baron and Richard Schone (New Haven and London, 1992), pp. 25–32; p. 30. This painting is reproduced with catalogue entry by R. Schone on pp. 326–7.
105 Arthur King Peters, *Jean Cocteau and his World* (London, 1987), pp. 84–5.

NINETEENTH-CENTURY JULIET

PHILIP DAVIS

Spread thy close curtain, love-performing night
That runaways' eyes may wink and Romeo
Leap to these arms untalked of and unseen.
Lovers can see to do their amorous rites
By their own beauties; or, if love be blind,
It best agrees with night. Come, civil night,
Thou sober-suited matron all in black,
And learn me how to lose a winning match
Played for a pair of stainless maidenhoods.
Hood my unmanned blood, bating in my cheeks,
With thy black mantle till strange love grown bold
Think true love acted simple modesty.
Come night, come Romeo; come, thou day in night
  . . .
O, I have bought the mansion of a love
But not possessed it, and though I am sold,
Not yet enjoyed. So tedious is this day
As is the night before some festival
To an impatient child that hath new robes
And may not wear them.   (*Romeo* 3.2.5–17, 26–31)

In Liverpool University in 1899, Kenneth Muir reports, Dr Friedel, a lecturer in French, was denied an extension to his appointment, much to the dismay of the then Professor of English, Sir Walter Raleigh.[1] The main charge against Friedel was that he had set for translation into French prose Juliet's soliloquy, as she awaited the consummation of her marriage.

In 1817, in contrast, Hazlitt had deliberately cited the soliloquy precisely in the teeth of the ethos of Thomas Bowdler:

We the rather insert the passage here, inasmuch as we have no doubt it has been expunged from the Family Shakespeare. Such critics do not perceive that the feelings of the heart sanctify, without disguising, the impulses of nature. Without refinement themselves, they confound modesty with hypocrisy.[2]

Here 'heart' and 'nature', the feelings of love and the impulses of sex, are consummated in each other.

Between these two responses, seemingly reinforcing the popular stereotypes of Romantic and Victorian attitudes, comes a further complicating case – that of Anna Jameson writing of Juliet in *Shakespeare's Heroines: Characteristics of Women, Moral, Poetical, and Historical*, 1852. Mrs Jameson refers to the passage in question but does not cite it, although she does defend it:

Let it be remembered, that in this speech Juliet is not supposed to be addressing an audience, nor even a confidante; and I confess I have been shocked at the utter want of taste and refinement in those who, with coarse derision, or in a spirit of prudery yet more gross and perverse, have dared to comment on this beautiful 'Hymn to the Night' breathed out by Juliet in the silence and solitude of her chamber. She is thinking aloud; it is the young heart 'triumphing to itself in words'. In the midst of all the vehemence with which she calls upon the night to bring Romeo to her arms, there is something so almost infantine in her perfect simplicity, so playful and fantastic in the imagery and language, that the charm of sentiment

---

[1] Kenneth Muir, 'Raleigh's Tragedy', *Essays on Sir Walter Raleigh 1988*, ed. A. A. Ansari (Aligarh Muslim University Press, 1988), pp. 10–21.

[2] *Complete Works* of William Hazlitt, ed. P. P. Howe, 21 vols. (London and Toronto: J. M. Dent, 1932), vol. 4 (*Characters of Shakespeare's Plays*), p. 253. Hereafter cited as 'Hazlitt'.

and innocence is thrown over the whole; and her impatience, to use her own expression, is truly that of 'a child before a festival, that hath new robes and may not wear them'.[3]

Although she subsumes 'innocence' within the term 'infantine', the comparison with the child before a festival is more playful or more dangerous than Mrs Jameson allows, even though she acknowledges Juliet's 'bold and beautiful' language. What she prefers to call a 'Hymn to the Night' is really a cry to that 'matron' Night that this young virgin should be no longer 'unmanned' but husbanded, winning full womanhood in the loss of her maidenhead. Elsewhere, Mrs Jameson takes fully enough Hazlitt's point when he says that the play 'presents a beautiful *coup d'oeil* of the progress of human life':

In thought it occupies years, and embraces the circle of the affections from childhood to old age.

(Hazlitt, 4, p. 251)

Juliet has become 'a young woman', notes Hazlitt, 'since we first remember her a little thing in the idle prattle of the nurse'. In this play, the lovers themselves help Shakespeare to make minutes into years, because to them, as they keep saying, minutes feel like years when they are apart and must be in lieu of years when they are together. Thus, when Juliet is shocked by the Nurse's time-serving proposal that she should take Paris in place of banished Romeo, Mrs Jameson comments:

This scene is the crisis in the character; and henceforth we see Juliet assume a new aspect. The fond, impatient, timid girl puts on the wife and the woman. (*Shakespeare's Heroines*, p. 114)

'Puts on' would be a more frank and bold description in the context of Juliet's soliloquy of 3.2 than the remark that 'the charm of sentiment and innocence is *thrown over* the whole' – the language of veils and drapes. What Shakespeare manages for Juliet, in her sexual transition to the putting on of the name of woman, is something almost precisely in between Donne's 'What needst thou have more covering than a man?' in 'To his Mistress Going to Bed' and Yeats's 'from meagre girlhood's putting on / Burdensome beauty' in 'Broken Dreams'.

Yet at least when Mrs Jameson confesses 'I have been shocked', it is emphatically not Juliet who shocks her but those apparent opposites, prudes or cynics, who are alike in disbelieving in innocence. Juliet's sexual feelings are emphatically part of her and her love, not something which undermines that love. Only the world's Iagos think otherwise, like envious worms in the bud 'ere he can spread his sweet leaves to the air' (*Romeo* 1.1.148–9). 'For observe, Iago's disbelief in the virtue of Desdemona is not pretended, it is real. It arises from his total want of faith in all virtue; he is no more capable of conceiving goodness than she is capable of conceiving evil' (*Shakespeare's Heroines*, p. 25).

Yet although Mrs Jameson speaks best of Juliet when she says that 'the Passion is her state of being, and out of it she has no existence' (*Shakespeare's Heroines*, p. 97), she cannot write of Juliet for long without giving her the existence of a character embodying an abstraction. The male speaker in the introductory dialogue to *Shakespeare's Heroines* asks whether a character of passion and imagination such as Juliet is meant as an example or a warning to modern youth. The female speaker replies guardedly that there might be a few who are 'in danger of being misled by an excess of generous impulses of fancy and feeling' but for most young women in these days of heartless expediency, 'there is no such thing as youth':

The bloom of existence is sacrificed to a fashionable education, and where we should find the rosebuds of the spring, we see only the full-blown, flaunting, precocious roses of the hot-bed.

(*Shakespeare's Heroines*, p. 27)

Not for such, Juliet's 'This bud of love by summer's ripening breath / May prove a beau-

3 Jameson, *Shakespeare's Heroines*, revised edition, Bohn's Standard Library (London: George Bell, 1891), pp. 117–18.

teous flower when next we meet' (2.1.163–4). *Romeo and Juliet* is, as Hazlitt above all makes clear, Shakespeare's great play of natural youthfulness, where 'Passion ... is infinite, extravagant, inexhaustible, till experience comes to check and kill it' (Hazlitt, 4, p. 249). Helped by the example of Juliet's bounty, *Shakespeare's Heroines* was written as a reminder 'that the condition of women in society, as at present constituted, is false in itself, and injurious to them' (p. 5). Drawing upon the Romantic interpretation of Shakespeare as one whose imagination takes any shape or form, male or female, it is a book that uses Shakespeare 'to illustrate the various modifications of which the female character is susceptible' (p. 4), as though Shakespeare offered a more *natural* variety of possibilities than those contained and constrained in the current monolithic shape and wrenched ordering of society. Marian Evans, about to become 'George Eliot', wrote to similar purpose in 1855 in a review for the *Leader*, with whose co-founder G. H. Lewes she was already living outside wedlock:

Shakespeare's women have no more decided characteristic than the frankness with which they avow their love, not only to themselves but to the men they love.

She thinks of Juliet's 'Or, if thou think'st I am too quickly won, / I'll frown and be perverse and say thee nay, / So thou wilt woo; but else, not for the world. / In truth, fair Montague, I am too fond' (2.1.137–40), and adds more boldly in her notebook:

It is remarkable that Shakespear's women almost always *make love*, in opposition to the conventional notion of what is fitting for woman.

In chapter 22 of *Daniel Deronda*, the heiress Catherine Arrowpoint finds herself saying to her beloved but socially unsuitable Klesmer, 'Why should I not marry the man who loves me? ... I am afraid of nothing but that we should miss the passing of our lives together'; and George Eliot says that the desperate effort 'was something like the leap of a woman from the deck into the lifeboat'. 'Feminine frankness', Marian Evans went on in her review, 'must be simply a natural manifestation which has only been gradually and partially repressed by the complex influences of modern civilization.'[4]

George Eliot finally met Mrs Jameson through their mutual friend Barbara Bodichon. But for Mrs Jameson the natural, frank and witty activeness that Marian Evans found most congenial in Shakespeare's women was just one element. Mrs Jameson uses Shakespeare to chart all the possible elements and compounds of female combination, imagining, for example, how any of the other heroines would have responded to Hamlet: 'Juliet would have pitied him; Rosalind would have turned him over with a smile to the melancholy Jaques; Beatrice would have laughed at him outright ... but Ophelia loves him' (p. 161). As Nina Auerbach explains, Mrs Jameson was involved in a project of her own even in relation to the more passive of Shakespeare's women – a project more to do with freedom than with action: 'Jameson's colony of mythic women frees its heroines from the plays in which they are generally subordinate to the heroes and to the demands of the plot ... Living a larger life than their plays allow, these heroines and the womanhood they exemplify are granted by this freedom of the conditional tense a mobility and spaciousness that exist only in the domain of myth.'[5]

At the beginning of 3.2 Juliet, insists Mrs Jameson, is not immodestly addressing the audience or a confidante: it truly makes a difference – the sort of difference in which Mrs Jameson is most interested – that Juliet is on her own now, vulnerably addressing herself. These are the moments from which *Shakespeare's Heroines* extrapolates, till it turns the plays into their own

---

4 George Eliot, *A Writer's Notebook, 1854–1879, and Uncollected Writings*, ed. J. Wiesenfarth (Charlottesville: University of Virginia, 1981), p. 255 (review), 11 (notebook).
5 Nina Auerbach, *Woman and The Demon* (Cambridge, Mass.: Harvard University Press, 1982), p. 211.

separated and finished characters, using language even as Shakespeare does not – to convert what is passing into what may be statically painted.

It is not always so, for Mrs Jameson can end her account of Juliet's 'Hymn to the Night' with a properly dramatic point about the configurations of time in the play: 'It is at the very moment too that her whole heart and fancy are abandoned to blissful anticipation, that the Nurse enters with the news of Romeo's banishment; and the immediate transition from rapture to despair has a most powerful effect' (*Shakespeare's Heroines*, p. 118) Hazlitt himself would have appreciated the stress laid on transition there. For to Hazlitt, where painting gives the solid object and the finished event, poetry gives something more dynamic in concentrating itself upon the very midst of life in transition. 'It is ... in the interval of expectation and suspense, while our hopes and fears are strained to the very highest pitch of breathless agony, that the pinch of the interest lies':[6]

> till strange love grown bold,
> Think true love acted simple modesty.

What moves Hazlitt is that 'fearful passage' from one state of being into another ('strange, bold, true, simple'): the entry of girl into woman, sexually; 'the feelings of the heart' not 'thrown over' or 'disguising' but actually going *into* 'the very impulses of nature' and 'sanctifying' them from *within*.

Romeo and Juliet is a rapid as well as a young play: the two go together – 'like the lightning, which doth cease to be / Ere one can say it lightens' (2.1.161–2). Writes Hazlitt of the lovers' vitality, 'All that was to come of life was theirs': their very inexperience drives them forward to the future in the instant, filling 'the void to come with the warmth of desires' (4, p. 250). But Victorian critics with a social mission such as Mrs Jameson often tend to seek greater space, less speed, and more time than Shakespeare allowed, as if increased room might mean more freedom. Their model is the spaciousness that the Victorian novel offers for

characterization. 'It has been said,' wrote Peter Bayne in an essay for *Blackwood's Magazine* in 1883 entitled 'Shakespeare and George Eliot', 'that if Shakespeare had lived in the Victorian age, he would have written novels', where 'a good novel' means 'a good drama writ large'. 'The dramatist must put into an hour what the novelist spreads out in a volume.'[7] The novel is taken as realistically expanding what Shakespeare's 'coup d'œil' contracts:

> For in a minute there are many days.
> O, by this count I shall be much in years
> Ere I again behold my Romeo.   (3.5.45–7)

But the issue is whether this Victorian critical method, taken at second hand from what is assumed to be the discourse provided by the realist novel, truly offers 'a larger life' than Hazlitt's way of reading. It is worth recording that George Eliot herself did not finally endorse such a method. In Book 6 chapter 6 of *The Mill on the Floss* she explicitly contests Novalis's dictum 'Character is destiny', insisting on the inter-relation of circumstance and temperament in Hamlet himself.

'By writing character studies and inventing biographies, Jameson, Cowden Clarke, and such actresses as Ellen Terry *liberate* Shakespeare's women from the confines of their plots.'[8] I want to suggest that, for all the good social intentions and the incidentally useful critical insights displayed in this liberal Victorian method, it is not a true freedom that is thereby

---

6 'On Poetry in General', Hazlitt, vol. 5, p. 10, after which Hazlitt quotes from *Julius Caesar*. 'Between the acting of a dreadful thing / And the first motion, all the interim is / Like a phantasma or a hideous dream.'
7 Peter Bayne, 'Shakespeare and George Eliot', *Blackwood's Magazine*, April 1883, vol. 133, p. 524. Thomas Hardy read and made notes on this article – see *The Literary Notebooks of Thomas Hardy*, ed. Lennart A. Bjiork, 2 vols. (London: Macmillan, 1985), I pp. 152, 1297.
8 Marianne Novy, *Engaging with Shakespeare: Responses of George Eliot and Other Women Novelists* (Athens: University of Georgia, 1994), p. 18, emphasis mine. I am indebted to this work for note 4 above.

offered. The best Victorian accounts of Juliet are not those which *extract* her from her specific situation but which return her to it, with all the more imaginative power in proportion to the very confinement and loneliness. Helena Faucit Martin can write of *Romeo and Juliet* with both sentimentality and prudery, but when she writes as an actress rather than a pseudo-novelist, she can produce a powerful sense of the sheerly practical context surrounding the opening of 4.3:

Lady Capulet, who sees nothing in her daughter's change of manner but what she considers natural in the situation – wrought in her, doubtless, by the good Friar's spiritual advice and counsel – bids her 'good night' in the usual way, only adding, as she knew Juliet had been waking and weeping all the previous night, 'Get thee to bed, and rest; for thou hast need.'

With what awe, with what dread fascination, I used to approach what follows! I always felt a kind of icy coldness and stillness come over me after leaving the Friar's cell which lasted until this moment. The 'Farewell!' to Lady Capulet, – 'God knows when we shall meet again,' – relaxed this state of tension. When I knelt to my father, I had mutely, in kissing his hand, taken leave of him; but now my mother – the mother whose sympathy would have been so precious – was leaving me to my lonely despair. This breaking up of all the natural ties of youth and home, the heart-sick feeling of desolation, overpowered me, and sobs came against my will. The very room looked strange, larger, darker, with but the faint light of the lamp, which threw the recesses of the windows and the heavy furniture into deeper shade. I used to take up the lamp and peer into the shadows, to try to take away their terror. Already I could fancy I had descended into the vault.

    I have a faint cold fear thrills through my veins,
      That almost freezes up the heat of life.

There was no enduring it: 'I'll call them back to comfort me; – Nurse!' No! I have forgot. 'What should she do here?' No one must know, – 'my dismal scene I needs must act alone.' ... Now Juliet stands, for the first time, alone, to think over and to face what is to follow. She does not waver, but she has to put before herself the dread realities which must be encountered in the way of the escape

devised for her. The hush of the unaccustomed solitude is strange ...[9]

What is crucial here is that Juliet's speech of farewell is paradoxically inseparable from her own consciousness that mother and Nurse do not know it to *be* farewell. Character in Shakespeare's 'coup d'oeil' is not simply something given as separate, detachable and finished, shown most of all in set explanatory soliloquies. Rather there, as Lady Martin sets the scene, character is something that *happens* in the very interchange with circumstance, something that is in the very act of still being youthfully created and realized as such in the play's own process – even by Juliet wanting to call the Nurse back and then realizing that she cannot do that any more, that she is past that in the speed of this play. Earlier, in the balcony scene, she could twice call back her Romeo after she in turn had been twice called back inside by her Nurse. At first she comes back to him with a tone of caution that she seems to have caught from inside the house: 'If that thy bent of love be honourable', 'But if thou mean'st not well' (2.1.185, 192); but beautifully that fear disappears again in the renewed context of new love. Now in 4.3 time and events push on harder and are less to be recalled, as Lady Martin helps us see. For no sooner does Juliet find herself emotionally separate from father and mother and Nurse, and left almost spatially withdrawn from home and her own youth, than external space itself begins to turn, inside her very thoughts, to future time and the confinement in the vault to come. 'The very room looked strange, larger, darker ... I used to take up the lamp and peer into the shadows, to try to take away their terror. Already I could fancy I had descended into the vault. "I have a faint cold fear thrills through my veins."' These are changes in the very dimensions of being.

---

[9] Helena Faucit, Lady Martin, *On Some of Shakespeare's Female Characters* (Edinburgh and London: William Blackwood and Sons, 1885), pp. 178–9.

To Ellen Terry an actress must be 'in a state of grace' to surrender herself to Juliet's 'complete abandonment to passion'. But as with Lady Martin, the spiritualizing of Shakespeare is less telling than the sheer practical acting of him. Ellen Terry is at her best when she puts together her general thought that a fourteen-year-old girl matured earlier when the average age of human life was shorter, with the specific dramatic consideration that the 'swiftness' of Juliet's sexual 'surrender' is also governed by her finding that her sudden beloved is, already before she knows it, a Montagu.[10] 'Too early seen unknown, and known too late' (1.5.138). Juliet rushes at the primary human feeling to keep ahead of the surrounding family story: 'What's in a name?' (2.11.85). Ellen Terry loved that sense of vital swiftness and is said to have felt 'sexual as well as artistic frustration' at Henry Irving's slow classical delivery, not least in their ill-received performance of *Romeo and Juliet*. 'Pace is the soul of comedy,' she wrote in her *Memoirs*, 'and to elaborate lines at the expense of pace is disastrous ... Of course, it is not a question of swift utterance only, but of swift thinking.'[11] Indeed the pace of *Romeo and Juliet*, as Peggy Ashcroft later declared in the long line of commentaries by great women actors, is testimony to its being fundamentally a comedy, in the sheer joy of the lovers, itself overtaken by a catastrophe.[12]

The temptation to slow down the drama and take the characters out of their stories is emotional: it arises out of sympathy with the sheer natural force of the lovers' passion, which wants to ignore the life-story surrounding them. Again Hazlitt, writing in his essay 'On the Feeling of Immortality of Youth', best understands this:

It is the simplicity and, as it were, abstractedness of our feelings in youth that (so to speak) identifies us with Nature and (our experience being weak but our passions strong) makes us fancy ourselves immortal like it ... We know our existence only by ourselves, and confound our knowledge with the objects of it. We and Nature are therefore one ... Objects in youth, from novelty, etc., are stamped upon the brain with such force and integrity that one thinks nothing can remove or obliterate them. They are riveted there, and appear to us as an element of our nature. It must be a mere violence that destroys them, not a natural decay. In the very strength of this persuasion we seem to enjoy an age by anticipation. We melt down years into a single moment of intense sympathy.[13]

This is what Friar Laurence had to deal with. Lady Martin reports what a difference it made to her understanding of the play when instead of the mutilated copy adapted for the stage, she first read the play as a whole and saw the wider context of bloody feuds surrounding the love-story that goes on within them.[14] The story is not to be separated. For as Hazlitt sees, it is as though one natural force – the force of the young lovers – goes on unknowingly within a wider scene of Nature as well as society. The lovers, as so often, try to make *one* out of what is really *two*. 'Their souls can accomplish this,' writes the neo-platonist Leone Ebreo, 'for they are spirits, and incorporeal spirits can interpenetrate, unite and come together as one':

But in their bodies which are distinct, each with a spatial location of its own, there remains after such union and interpenetration – by contrast with what it is that they both desire – an even more avid longing for that union which they can never achieve.[15]

---

[10] See Ellen Terry, *Four Lectures on Shakespeare* (London: Martin Hopkinson, 1932), pp. 151, 138–9.

[11] Nina Auerbach comments on Ellen Terry's frustration in *Ellen Terry: Player in her Time* (London: J. M. Dent, 1987), p. 225, where the *Memoirs* are quoted thus.

[12] Quoted in Judith Cook, *Women and Shakespeare* (London: Harrap, 1980), p. 91.

[13] The text here cited is from the original version published in *Monthly Magazine*, March 1827, reprinted in *Hazlitt: Selected Essays*, ed. G. Keynes (London: Nonesuch Press, 1970), pp. 312, 314, 316.

[14] See *On Some of Shakespeare's Female Characters*, p. 134.

[15] Leone Ebreo, *Dialoghi d'amore*, in *Renaissance Philosophy vol. 1: The Italian Philosophers*, ed. A. B. Fallico and H. Shapiro (New York: The Modern Library, 1967), pp. 223–4.

Thus Juliet tries to ignore the almost physically surrounding story at the beginning of 3.5 when, after the night of consummation, she cries emotionally for continuous re-union – despite day, despite the family feud, despite the very impossibility of their forever avoiding the necessity of being separate characters:

> Wilt thou be gone? It is not yet near day.
> It was the nightingale, and not the lark,
> That pierced the fearful hollow of thine ear.

To which Romeo replies (6–7): 'It was the lark ... No nightingale'; but then again, at Juliet's renewed insistence: 'Let me be ta'en, let me be put to death. / I am content, so thou wilt have it so' (17–18). Yet no sooner does he conclude by taking her view:

> Come, death, and welcome; Juliet wills it so.
> How is't, my soul? Let's talk. It is not day.

than, by a form of serious handy-dandy or just exchange, Juliet returns to his:

> It is, it is. Hie hence, begone, away.
> It is the lark that sings so out of tune ...
>
> (3.5.24–7)

The rhyme between the two lovers is itself no longer in love's tune. It bespeaks the pressure of space, the lack of room for manoeuvre, whichever way they try to turn. As soon as Romeo leaves a mental space by lovingly agreeing to Juliet's attempt to pretend that it is not day, so Juliet, out of equivalent love, must fill that space he has vacated, by taking his part for his sake. Shakespeare, like Aristotle's Nature, abhors a vacuum. It is a serious version of Benvolio's commonplace: 'one fire burns out another's burning, / One pain is lessened by another's anguish' (1.2.44–5) or in Brooke's *Romeus and Juliet*, 'as out of a planke a nayle a nayle doth drive' (line 207). Even this, replacing the to-and-fro of kisses when first they met, is what ages Juliet; years put on in a second's change to felt responsibility. The void that Hazlitt said was previously filled with present emotions so large as to seem to offer a limitless future is now filled instead from different directions and by different pressures:

> a kind of hope
> Which craves as desperate an execution
> As that is desperate which we would prevent.
> If, rather than to marry County Paris,
> Thou hast the strength of will to slay thyself,
> Then is it likely thou wilt undertake
> A thing like death to chide away this shame,
> That cop'st with death himself to scape from it.
>
> (4.1.68–75)

Instead of the attraction of love with love, now they must meet fire with fire, one nail displacing another. This situation has come out of the suddenness of Tybalt's untimely death, followed all too swiftly by the wish of Juliet's parents to replace her apparent mourning-sorrow with marriage to Paris. Now the older generation urges speed, while Juliet begs her father for delay, distorting Hazlitt's sense of the natural law of life in the play: 'Thus one period of life makes way for the following, and one generation pushes another off the stage' (Hazlitt, 4, p. 252). And again this whole knock-on process resulting from the failure of complete freedom in the world of space and time is something Hazlitt understands. For Hazlitt recognizes Shakespeare's denser medium of mixed life in which the later nineteenth-century alternatives of character versus story or freedom as opposed to determinism must seem clumsy over-simplifications:

> In Shakspeare there is a continual composition and decomposition of [the character's] elements, a fermentation of every particle in the whole mass, by its alternate affinity or antipathy to other principles which are brought into contact with it. Till the experiment is tried, we do not know the result, the turn which the character will take in its new circumstances.
>
> (5, p. 51)

As his 1812 lecture 'On Liberty and Necessity' makes clear, for Hazlitt there are primary forces in the experimental chemistry of the world's composition which mean that a human agent can never be more than a possible *second* cause of change and action. That is not, however, completely to destroy any useful distinction between being active and passive. By passiveness, Hazlitt understands 'an indifference in the agent to this or that motion, except as it is acted upon by, and transmits the efficacy of other causes'; but anything is active 'in so far as it modifies and reacts upon the original impulse rather than receiving and continuing it' (2, pp. 268–9). There is no entirely separate freedom: we are either transmitters, merely passing on the pressures around us, or reactors, who, as the external pressures bear in upon us, employ such inner resources as those pressures call forth in order to modify them. When the Nurse says to Juliet that Romeo banished is no more good to her than Romeo dead, and that she should therefore turn instead to Paris as his successor, then the Nurse only transmits and passes on the world's pressure and is not truly a real person. In contrast, we realize through Juliet's almost silent external reaction to this, that Juliet does have and increasingly will have to have within her a separate heart and mind:

JULIET Speak'st thou from the heart?
NURSE And from my soul, too, else beshrew them both.
JULIET Amen. (3.5.226–8)

'I have often been startled', reported Lady Martin, 'at the sad solemnity of my own tones, as I put the question, "Speakest thou from thy heart?"' (On Some of Shakespeare's Female Characters, p. 173). And it is as though that is what the character is like – in the midst of being appalled to hear what others say, surprised to hear her own quiet voice and find it is deeply hers. That is how character is called into being in Shakespeare's plays in a way not consonant with either Liberalism's desire for freedom or vulgar Marxism's belief in determinism. For when Juliet says to Romeo after all, 'It *is* the lark', or thinking to call back the Nurse, instead says to herself 'What should she do here? / My dismal scene I needs must act alone', she is finding something in herself which will re-act and not merely transmit. 'Each Agent must

suffer in acting and act in suffering.'[16] This is the very making of her adult character in the Shakespearian experiment: 'the endeavour in the patient to restore itself to that situation from which it was forced by the agent'.[17] In Shakespeare's double perspective, humans are no more than mere secondary parts in the composition of the world and the play, yet at the selfsame time parts that matter so much, separately, to themselves in their own terms. But that 'separately' is still re-actively felt *within* the world that impinges upon it.

Hazlitt's is a profounder and more intrinsically dramatic sense of nature than that offered for polemical and political purposes by liberal Victorians trying to adjust the arrangements of contemporary society.[18] He has a philosophy of energetic nature that brings him close to the

---

[16] Kenelm Digby, *Two Treatises* (1644) quoted in John L. Russell, 'Action and Reaction Before Newton', *British Journal for the History of Science*, 9 (1976), 32.

[17] Thomas Hobbes, *Elementiae philosophiae: De corpore* (1655) quoted in Russell, p. 34. Hazlitt quotes Hobbes in his lecture on liberty and necessity.

[18] In 'On Liberty and Necessity' Hazlitt also refers to Spinoza. Marian Evans was reading *Romeo and Juliet* amongst other Shakespeare plays whilst she was translating Spinoza (who himself was influenced by Ebreo, note 15). It may have been her reading of Spinoza that helped keep George Eliot in implicit relation to Renaissance dynamics, such that James Sully could write of her work that in it character is not shown as determined but 'in the making': 'I have observed that the distinction between the characters and the plot of a novel is only a rough distinction. This remark applies with special force to George Eliot's stories. These appear in a remarkable degree, when regarded from one point of view, as the outcome of her characters, from another point of view, as the formation of those characters.' ('George Eliot's Art', *Mind*, 6 (1881), 384–5). Whereas Shakespeare achieves this effect of 'life in the making' through speed, George Eliot, as Bayne notes (pp. 535–6), works more slowly and minutely through the signalization of 'the neutral, the indirect influences', vis inertiae, gradual evolution, and 'the impalpable, inaudible, invisible action of ten thousand circumstances'. Hence her crucial remark in chapter 15 of *Middlemarch*: 'Character too is a process and an unfolding. The man was still in the making...'

Renaissance dynamics behind and around Shakespeare, and the relation of that philosophy to Shakespeare himself first becomes clear to Hazlitt in his study of *Romeo and Juliet*. For when he writes of the powerful innocence of desire in that play, he explicitly writes against modern philosophy which 'reduces the whole theory of mind to habitual impressions, and leaves the natural impulses of passion and imagination out of the account' (4, p. 250).

What Hazlitt in 1817 is recalling through such a comment is his own youthful essay 'On The Principles of Human Action' (1805). For it is significant in relation to his later Shakespearian studies that Hazlitt himself as a young man wrote this essay in defence of something fundamentally more dynamic and more innocent in human thought and action than the prudential considerations of the Lockeian or Hobbesian man measuring his own present self-interests. Identity, says Hazlitt, is made up in retrospect, is a thing of memory. Deeper than that, because prior to it, is a passional dynamic more innocent and instantaneous than sheer ego. In the original function of action, Man when he acts is not in the present or the past, is not prudentially conscious, but, in sheer imaginative thought of a future in which he does not yet exist, seeks to bring that future into immediate existence in the very micro-second of action. Thus when Romeo requests 'th'exchange of thy love's faithful vow for mine', Juliet at once responds:

I gave thee mine *before* thou didst request it.
(2.1.170)

Hazlitt's model writer is not Wordsworth but Shakespeare, for the heaven that lies about the lovers is not for Hazlitt some neo-platonic memory of a mystical pre-existent state from which we grow away in time, as in Wordsworth's great Ode; on the contrary, it is a world new to the young not through knowledge of the past but ignorance of the future: 'a new world, of which we know nothing but what we wish it to be, and believe all that we wish'

(4, p. 250). In the micro-seconds of movement registered in Shakespeare's verse, 'there is a continual composition and decomposition of the characters' elements'. Juliet steps back into convention for a moment when she offers to 'frown and be perverse', lest she seems too light or too 'quickly' won – provided Romeo will woo her a second time round. But more *primary* is her:

but else, not for the world.
In truth, fair Montague, I am too fond.

It is that innocent primary form of being, prior to habit, ego, self-interest and calculation, that Hazlitt hates to see killed by experience. It is only later, after the associations of ideas about our selves have built up, that a sense of a future self does become steadily present to us, says Hazlitt in 'On The Principles of Human Action', and that self is really the past self transferred forward. We create a secondary conscious idea of ourselves, back-to-front, from our memory. And even so this second-stage, second-order self forgets the dynamic of human nature by which he previously lived. It is that slower idea of a macro-self, in lieu of a micro-process, that dominates Victorian character studies of Shakespeare.

Yet, sixteen years later, in writing 'On Living to One's-self' in 1821, Hazlitt reports himself stuck with just such a later self:

Woe be to him when he first begins to think what others say of him ... when he undertakes to play a part on the stage, and to persuade the world to think more about him than they do about themselves.
(8, p. 92)

Hazlitt had begun to become socially conscious of himself, to be a mind aware of itself as confined within the limitations of its own body and personality, and operating inside the competitive pressures of the world's sense of time. He had had to develop his own aggressive and defensive interests as a self, prudential interests that narrowed the very definition of self even as it sought to extend its power. Something primary has gone, and in thinking about the fate of Keats as an example of the destruction of a force of being prior to the idea of the conventional self, Hazlitt again naturally thinks in terms of Shakespeare and, in particular, *Romeo and Juliet*:

Poor Keats! What was sport to the town was death to him. Young sensitive, delicate, he was like

> 'A bud bit by an envious worm,
> Ere he could spread his sweet leaves to the air
> Or dedicate his beauty to the sun;'

and unable to endure the miscreant cry and idiot laugh, withdrew to sigh his last breath in foreign climes.   (8, p. 99)

What happened to Hazlitt himself lies in the story of *Liber Amoris* (1823), the story of how the feelings of Romeo and Juliet became those of Othello.[19] In 'On the Fear of Death', one of the essays written in the midst of that humiliating experience of love disabused by experience, Hazlitt laments 'the effeminate clinging to life' that results from living in 'a highly civilized and artificial society'. In ancient days, neither men *nor* women needed to be 'effeminate' like that, but staked their lives on passions and beliefs:

Every thing else is dross. They go to death as to a bridal bed, and sacrifice themselves or others without remorse at the shrine of love, of honour, of religion, or any other prevailing feeling. Romeo runs his 'seasick, weary bark upon the rocks' of death, the instant he finds himself deprived of his Juliet; and she clasps his neck in their last agonies, and follows him to the same fatal shore. One strong idea takes possession of the mind, and overrules every other; and even life itself, joyless without that, becomes an object of indifference or loathing.   (8, p. 329)

This is life in the 'instant', such as Hazlitt in his depressed and humiliated survival felt he could never know again. Thomas Hardy's brief re-writing of *Romeo and Juliet* in *The Well Beloved* is virtually the consequence of what *Liber Amoris* has sceptically to make of love in the light of a

later self's sense of experience.[20] But for Hazlitt, the word is finally Romeo's, still living life *forwards* (5.3.102, 94): 'Why art thou *yet* so fair?'

Thou art not conquer'd.

Yet, vigilant as ever to the simply circumstantial, Lady Martin notes how even now, unknown to Romeo, Juliet's abiding beauty is also, simultaneously, ironic evidence of the potion wearing off and life itself returning.[21] Even thus she bears witness to Shakespeare's double perspective, at once inside and outside the human character.

Even with just such corrective modifications of his Romanticism, it remains true that Hazlitt is the nineteenth-century critic who best understands the meaning of Shakespeare's kinetic story of life. For Hazlitt that Shakespearian story was told first of all in the sheer drama of *Romeo and Juliet*. When nineteenth-century actors and commentators respond to *Romeo and Juliet* as drama rather than as novel, they come closest to Hazlitt's dynamic model of understanding.

---

[19] In *Liber Amoris* the play to which the protagonist takes his beloved and her mother is, ironically enough, *Romeo and Juliet* (Hazlitt, vol. 9, p. 114); nothing better illustrates the disturbed ending of the love-affair than Hazlitt's deliberately modified quotation from *Othello*: 'she's gone, I am abused, and my revenge must be to *love* her!' (Hazlitt, vol. 9, p. 132).

[20] See chapter viii of the first part of Hardy's *The Well-Beloved* (1897), where Marcia Bencomb, the equivalent Juliet, says bitterly: 'It was a fortunate thing for the affections of those two Veronese lovers that they died when they did. In a short time the enmity of their families would have proved a fruitful source of dissension; Juliet would have gone back to her people, he to his; the subject would have split them as much as it splits us. . . . They saw their recent love as what it was: "Too rash, too unadvised, too sudden; Too like the lightning . . ."' Hardy had read in Bayne's article (6, p. 259) the view that Shakespeare's was still an age of faith, George Eliot's an age of scepticism.

[21] See *On Some of Shakespeare's Female Characters*, p. 188.

'O, WHAT LEARNING IS!' PEDAGOGY AND THE AFTERLIFE OF *ROMEO AND JULIET*

REX GIBSON

One of the curiosities about the afterlife of *Romeo and Juliet* – or any other Shakespeare play – is the scholarly neglect of one area of great activity and importance: school Shakespeare. Jonathan Miller roots his discussion of afterlife firmly in performance.[1] Critical dialogue extends the concept to include its own transformative contribution, as it implicitly and explicitly records its own role in establishing, interpreting and evaluating the Shakespeare canon.[2] But that substantial fraction of the afterlife: how Shakespeare is studied by students under nineteen years of age, goes largely unremarked in the major journals. When 'teaching Shakespeare' is addressed, the focus of attention is undergraduate level or higher. In the past dozen years, *Shakespeare Quarterly* has devoted two issues to the topic, but only three out of thirty-two articles concern schools.[3] *Shakespeare Survey* is innocent of any direct address to pedagogy or to schools: the articulation of 'Shakespearian studies and production' with teaching is left for readers to infer.

Yet patently, school Shakespeare is an activity of major significance. The numbers involved are huge. Currently, in England and Wales alone, the National Curriculum requires that each year at least half a million fourteen year-olds must study, and be tested on, one of three plays: *Romeo and Juliet, A Midsummer Night's Dream, Julius Caesar*. World-wide the numbers can only be guessed at. Some commentators identify sinister hegemonic or intellectually malign elements in the process. One critic suspects variously that school Shakespeare inculcates 'the two fundamental mystifications of bourgeois ideology' and 'seems designed to construct a petty bourgeoisie'.[4] Another fears that much American school teaching of *Romeo and Juliet* promotes 'not only casually cynical indifference to truth but thoughtlessness'.[5]

Whatever truth lies in these views or in more benign perceptions of school Shakespeare, what cannot be gainsaid is that for the majority of people, school will have been their first and only sustained engagement with a Shakespeare play. In that youthful encounter, attitudes are conditioned and shaped by the experience afforded in classrooms. The ways in which the plays are taught will influence whether school students choose to maintain their acquaintance with Shakespeare as they grow older.

---

[1] Jonathan Miller, *Subsequent Performances* (London, 1986), pp. 19–72.

[2] See, as an example of explicit discussion of the role of scholarship in shaping Shakespearian afterlife: Gary Taylor, *Reinventing Shakespeare: A Cultural History from the Restoration to the Present* (London, 1990).

[3] *Shakespeare Quarterly*, 35 (1984), 515–656; 41 (1990), 139–270.

[4] Alan Sinfield, 'Give an account of Shakespeare and Education, showing why you think they are effective and what you have appreciated about them. Support your comments with precise references', in Jonathan Dollimore and Alan Sinfield, eds. *Political Shakespeare: New Essays in Cultural Materialism* (Manchester, 1985), pp. 134–57; pp. 138 and 142.

[5] Stephen Booth, 'The Function of Criticism at the Present Time and All Others', *Shakespeare Quarterly*, 4 (1990), 262–8; p. 267.

Pedagogy, then, is crucial, and in recent years in Britain the method of teaching Shakespeare in schools has undergone a sea-change. What might be called a pedagogy of explanation is being replaced, or greatly augmented, by a pedagogy of performance, or active methods. The rhetoric of those active methods, in which the play is taught as a play, rather than as a literary text, is not new, but practice was rare. Occasional anecdotal accounts recall 'the wrong way and the right' of the 1920s, contrasting unfavourably the 'barbarous methods' of grinding through the Notes with the greater understanding yielded by rehearsing and acting out the play.[6] One exceptional school made such rehearsal methods its curriculum policy, with 'English through Drama' as its conventional pedagogy.[7]

But only quite recently have active methods been widely adopted in practice. In 1984 John Andrews commented

A decade ago 'performance-oriented' pedagogy was relatively unfamiliar among Shakespeareans and was anything but universally accepted as the wave of the future. Now it is difficult to find a dissenting voice.[8]

Many accounts of the use of such methods in schools have been documented in the following decade,[9] but it is only very recently that an active pedagogy has been embodied in editions of the plays used by students. This paper considers one such edition of Romeo and Juliet in order to identify issues raised by that change in publishing practice.

Today, most British school students studying the play will see part or whole of a video (the Zeffirelli or BBC version). A much smaller number will make a theatre visit to see a stage version. Fewer will experience a visit to their school of a TIE (Theatre in Education) company and may have the opportunity to join in a workshop on the play. Only a tiny handful will act out the play in a public performance (in the 'School Play'). The one constant presence of Romeo and Juliet for the students will be the edition they use. School editions play a crucial

part in shaping students' perception of, and attitudes towards, Shakespeare. They embody assumptions about the 'nature' of Shakespeare, and about how legitimate knowledge (that is, esteemed and desired by 'experts') should be held and demonstrated. Some assumptions about what knowledge is suitable for school students have bizarre results. An American Standard School Abridgement version of Romeo and Juliet:

is deprived of all references to parts of the body including feet, legs, wombs, bones, hams, bosom; all references to God, Jesus, religion, heretics, liars, hell, fiend; all the obvious bawdy and sexual words such as prick, flesh, maidenhood, Cupid, Venus ... half of Friar Laurence's speech about Nature, as it is couched in the extended metaphor of Nature as a woman.[10]

Such censorship of Romeo and Juliet, more after-death than afterlife, seems widespread in America. James Andreas reports that of six literature textbooks he examined, published 1984–7, 'five used mutilated texts of the play'.[11] School editions published in Britain around the same period reject such Bowdlerization. But by taking scholarly editions as their model they promoted a pedagogy of explanation. The

---

6 Kenneth Muir, 'The Wrong Way and the Right', Shakespeare Quarterly, 35 (1984), 642–3.
7 Christopher Parry, English through Drama (Cambridge, 1972).
8 John F. Andrews, 'From the Editor', Shakespeare Quarterly, 35 (1984), 515–16; p. 515.
9 See examples in: Shakespeare and Schools, vols. 1–24 (1986–94); Susan Leach, Shakespeare in the Classroom: What's the Matter? (Buckingham 1992); Lesley Aers and Nigel Wheale, eds., Shakespeare in the Changing Curriculum (London, 1991). In America the active methods approach to teaching Shakespeare in schools is exemplified in Peggy O'Brien, ed., Shakespeare Set Free (New York, 1993, 1994).
10 Leach, Shakespeare in the Classroom, p. 55. Leach reports that this version 'is enforced in some states; it is the version which you must do if you wish to study the play with high school students'.
11 James Andreas, 'The Neutering of Romeo and Juliet', in Robert P. Merrix and Nichola Ranson, eds., Ideological Approaches to Shakespeare: the Practice of Theory (Lewiston, 1992), pp. 229–42; p. 229.

implied reader was a passive, isolated school student whose task was to absorb an authoritative and relatively unambiguous account of language, character, plot and themes. The status of the play was that of a literary text rather than a drama; knowledge of it to be tested by written examination. Some editions included sample examination questions, hints for candidates on constructing answers, and occasionally, model answers. The clear implication was that Shakespeare was to be studied in order to gain an academic qualification; some editions paraded their editors' qualifications to add authority. The mimicry of critical editions resulted in extensive glossing, giving the impression that Shakespeare was truly a foreign language.

There was little acknowledgement of the play as a drama whose birthright is development through successive re-creation,[12] including active re-creation by the students themselves. As school editions endeavoured to assume a similar authority to the critical editions that have been their model,[13] there was seldom recognition that a class of students studying a play are similar in one respect to an audience watching a performance: they all 'see' the same thing (the words on the page, the actors on stage), but they perceive, understand, interpret and value what they see in sometimes very different ways. Interpretative possibilities were excluded or restricted. A combination of the compulsion to explain and the consensual imperialism of the use of the first person plural implies to students that Shakespeare is a matter of learning the right answer. An edition 'designed especially for school students' exemplifies the style:

Romeo strikes us as a generous person ... [Tybalt] despises his enemies and makes us therefore dislike him ... The language makes us see Lady Capulet as the empty, cold and selfish person she is ... we are meant to contrast their [the servants' and Mercutio's] lecherous and cynical attitude to sex with the purity of love of Romeo and Juliet ... the language of old Capulet shows that he is not just a fussy and harmless old man. Shakespeare shows that he is a violent and nasty old man.[14]

What has only recently become apparent is that an editor of a school edition must more self-consciously address matters of pedagogy than the editor of an edition not aimed primarily at school students. Other editions have wider purposes loosely caught in the expressions 'scholarly' or 'critical'. But all editors consider their likely readers; and even those who include that elusive animal 'the general reader' among their intended audience, keep their peers, other professional Shakespearians, firmly in mind. There is a strong sense in which such editions are written by Shakespearian scholars for other Shakespearian scholars. School editions have in focus a quite different audience and very different aims.

For a school edition to take over the 'scholarship model' is to forget that a hawk is different from a handsaw. A school edition must take full account of its intended readership and the school settings in which the edition will be used. For example, editors of scholarly editions take 'establishing the text' as a central task. No school editor today can make serious claims to perform such a function.

'School students' may be a very specific audience, but they are by no means a homogeneous readership. Just as a theatre audience comprises very differently perceiving individuals, so too school students are similarly (or even more) various. Culture and background

---

12 Miller, *Subsequent Performances*, p. 23.

13 The expression 'watered-down Arden' to characterize school editions has been variously used by British teachers to denote approval, neutral description and opprobrium.

14 W. Shakespeare, *Romeo and Juliet*, ed. Roderick Wilson (London, 1983), pp. 8–10. The longstanding critical use of 'we', 'our' and 'us', implicitly denying and disqualifying alternative interpretations, dies hard at all levels: 'the little we are told of the largely silent Antony induces us to consider him a trivial irresponsible character'. John Wilders, 'Dramatic Structure and Dramatic Effect in *Julius Caesar*', in Bruce McIver and Ruth Stevenson, eds., *Teaching with Shakespeare: Critics in the Classroom* (Newark, London and Toronto, 1994), p. 149. Wilders's 'we' is unexceptionable; his 'us' provokes dissent.

apart, most are studying Shakespeare because they have no choice in the matter. A minority will go on to study the plays in higher education. A tiny number will become professional Shakespearians. The ability range of school students is that of the population as a whole. The editor of a school edition must have that heterogeneous readership in mind, together with the duty that all must be offered Shakespeare in ways that possess integrity and validity.

Such obligations mean that an editor of a school edition must consider pedagogy in the light of certain key questions. What text, and what account of the text should be given? What help is appropriate in those staples of school Shakespeare: story, character, themes, language, dramatic structure? What place has criticism in such an edition, whether traditional or derived from literary theory of more recent years? What accounts of context are needed: historical, social, literary and dramatic, political and ideological? How should questions of sources, dating and textual history, stage history be addressed?

Simply to pose these questions is to demonstrate the need for due humility on the part of any editor. They are also a reminder that answers will be different for each class of students, and that the person best placed to answer them is the individual class teacher. Any school edition must, can only, trust the professionalism of the teachers whose students use it. They best know the particularities of their students, the aims of the course and other 'local' matters. The task of a school edition is to resource the teachers' professional knowledge and expertise (in which the degree of acquaintance with Shakespeare will vary widely). Unlike the editor of a scholarly edition, the school editor has an additional responsibility: to turn the rhetoric of active methods into practical activities firmly and organically linked to the play.

The Cambridge School Shakespeare series grew out of the work of the Shakespeare and Schools Project.[15] As Director of that project, and series editor, my role has been to ensure that each edition embodies an active pedagogy that reflects and resources the paradigm shift in school Shakespeare teaching methods. In what follows I draw upon the edition of *Romeo and Juliet* I edited in order to demonstrate in detail the radically changed nature of school editions. The principles and practice described raise issues that have application beyond school Shakespeare. The edition's opening statement, addressed directly to students, illustrates key principles:

This *Romeo and Juliet* aims to be different from other editions of the play. It invites you to bring the play to life in your classroom, hall or drama studio through enjoyable activities that will increase your understanding. Actors have created their different interpretations of the play over centuries. Similarly you are encouraged to make up your own mind about *Romeo and Juliet*, rather than having someone else's interpretation handed down to you.[16]

How is the claim to difference redeemed? A small but symbolic sign is the presentation of the List of Characters. The long tradition, still dominant, of ordering by status and gender, is rejected. Escales no longer heads the list; Juliet and the other women are not relegated to the foot of the page below such characters as the Apothecary and the Musicians.

Instead, characters are grouped (Capulets, Montagues, the Court, the Church, the City, Mantua). Juliet and Romeo jointly head the list and other characters are defined by their relationship to the young lovers ('her father', 'her mother' and so on).

Such grouping is not an act of political correctness, but an acknowledgement of the characters' dramatic status. Rather than observing the conventions of scholarship or pub-

[15] Based at the University of Cambridge Institute of Education, the Project began its work in 1986. See Rex Gibson, *Teaching Shakespeare* (Cambridge, forthcoming 1996/7).
[16] W. Shakespeare, *Romeo and Juliet*, ed. Rex Gibson (Cambridge, 1992), prelim page. To highlight the importance of the play over editorial comment, such matter is placed in the end pages.

lishing practice, such presentation makes conflict and tension structurally apparent, signifying that this is a play for dramatic enactment. It reflects a practice increasingly common in the cast lists of theatre programmes. Here, it is a pedagogic decision, choosing a form more helpful to students' understanding.

The text is that of the New Cambridge Shakespeare.[17] Its use signifies that school students are entitled to a text that is neither cut nor superficially simplified as in the examples given above (see notes 10 and 11). But in a marked and deliberate departure from conventional practice, throughout the edition 'script' is substituted for 'text'. The insistence on 'script' signifies a commitment to the play as an allographic work of art[18] demanding completion, or rather re-creation, in performance.

The decision to use 'script' is controversial. 'Text' is deeply engrained in Shakespearian study at all levels, and carries greater implied status and authority. Scholarship accepts that modern playwrights produce scripts, but any classical author is deemed to have written a text (it is time to drop the inverted commas). The issue is not a trivial semantic one. A script declares that it is writing to be brought to life in performance. It suggests a provisionality and incompleteness that anticipates and demands imaginative, dramatic enactment. A text makes no such demand (and 'playtext' in use quickly dwindles to text). The privileged taken-for-grantedness bestowed upon text conceals its social construction behind a mask of naturalness.

Further, the notion of a script more fully emphasizes the collaborative nature of an active pedagogy. School Shakespeare is, like a group of actors in rehearsal, a social experience. In contrast, text implies the solitary, individual, desk-bound scholar. A script, like a rehearsal, implies that learning about and enacting drama arises from shared experience. Insisting upon script is not to devalue personal study, merely to redress a traditional school imbalance of individual versus social approaches to Shakespeare. Script also signifies that group activity extends

beyond discussion, the characteristic form of group work in education. It gives due weight to the recognition of the physical dimension in the social experience of enacting a play.

For school students embarking on their study of Shakespeare, script presents no problems. To those steeped in Shakespearian studies, it is uncongenial. Readers of *Shakespeare Survey* are invited to examine their response to the word script each time it is used in this paper.

The paramount importance in traditional scholarship of establishing the script is symbolized in the current Arden *Romeo and Juliet*.[19] It opens with twenty-six closely argued and scrupulously evidenced pages which assume readers' familiarity with the historical process of publishing Shakespeare's plays. Collations are given on each script page. For school editions, such issues must be decided play by play. With *King Lear* and *Hamlet*, Quarto/Folio problems are central and might be deemed an integral part of a school edition. But with *Romeo and Juliet* such questions are surely of much lower priority for school students. Problems of textual instability can be addressed in other ways. For example students are invited to make considered judgements about cuts or word choices (e.g. at the end of 4.5 or with Juliet's final line):

What's the purpose of this scene of the musicians? Sometimes these lines (100–38) are cut from performances. Talk together about whether you would cut the musicians and Peter from your production.

No one really knows whether Shakespeare wrote 'rest' or 'rust' at line 170. Which word do you think is most appropriate and why?[20]

Scholarly editions give the impression that the layout of any script page is determined by the length of footnotes and collations. In contrast

---

[17] W. Shakespeare, *Romeo and Juliet*, ed. G. Blakemore Evans (Cambridge, 1984). All quotations that follow are from this New Cambridge edition.

[18] Miller, *Subsequent Performances*, p. 32.

[19] W. Shakespeare, *Romeo and Juliet*, ed. Brian Gibbons (London, 1980).

[20] Shakespeare, *Romeo and Juliet* (Gibson), pp. 166 and 188.

the Cambridge school edition presents only the script on each right-hand page with all editorial apparatus on the facing left-hand page. Two controversial decisions, both arising from pedagogic considerations, challenge conventional practice.

First, a sustained attempt is made to present, as an unbroken sequence on a single right-hand page, units of speech that are likely to be the focus of classroom work: the Prologue, Juliet's 'Gallop apace' (3.2.1–31), the whole of the two-Friars scene (5.2) and so on. Where a speech is too long for the forty-line page, the page break is made at what is usually the 'classroom focus' point. Thus script pages begin with Juliet's 'What if it be a poison' (4.3.24), Romeo's 'How oft when men are at the point of death' (5.3.88), and Friar Lawrence's 'I married them' (5.3.233). The remainder of each speech occupies the whole page. Such practice obviously makes arguable prejudgements, but it has been found helpful to students and is an organic part of the activities strategy, discussed below.

The second controversial decision harks back to, and revives, a tradition firmly rejected by modern scholarship: an emphasis on act and scene divisions and locations. Wherever possible, each scene begins on a fresh page, the act and scene number is firmly signalled in capitals (rather than being typographically unobtrusive),[21] and scene locations are given. Critical editions generally frown on such practice, seen as disrupting the flow of stage action:

> Locations are not given in the stage directions, since they are the invention of editors and often obscure or contradict the principles and practices of the Elizabethan stage.[22]

Such exclusive insistence on conventions of Elizabethan staging seems inappropriate to school Shakespeare. Scenes *do* possess their own distinctiveness, a singularity (of which place is an element) which contributes to the coherence of the whole play. As Emrys Jones remarks 'Plays are made of scenes before they are made of words ... the scene is the primary dramatic

unit'.[23] In schools, lessons are commonly structured in scene 'units'. What is more at issue is that students recognize the dramatic fluidity of stage action as scenes change from place to place. Students, like directors and designers, can exercise their imagination to define locations and to ensure dramatic flow:

> At the beginning of each scene, a location is given (for example 'Verona A public place'). But no one can be sure of the precise location Shakespeare had in mind. So, don't be afraid to suggest, with reasons, alternative places where each scene could be set.

> Modern productions are always concerned to avoid lengthy breaks for scene-shifting. Even though the locations shift from place to place, the flow of action is continuous ... Work out how each scene can flow swiftly into the next.[24]

Act divisions are also emphasized by the two editorial pages that follow each act: 'Looking back at Act 1' and so on. These pages attempt to help students grasp the structural significance of the Act. Some activities put the onus on the student:

> Imagine you are a newspaper sub-editor. Is your paper a tabloid or 'heavy'? Your job is to write brief memorable headlines for each of the five scenes of Act 1. Make your headlines as accurate as possible. Try to use some of Shakespeare's own words.

Some direct attention to aspects of Shakespeare's craftsmanship:

> Single line sentences. Go through the whole of Act 2 but only read aloud sentences that occupy one line. Don't read any sentence that is longer than one line. How much of the sense and feeling of the act comes through from this 'single line reading'?

---

21 Rather than being 'typographically unobtrusive', regarded as a 'necessary evil': Stanley Wells, *Re-Editing Shakespeare for the Modern Reader* (Oxford, 1984), p. 64.

22 Shakespeare, *Romeo and Juliet* (Gibbons), p. 26.

23 Emrys Jones, *Scenic Form in Shakespeare* (Oxford, 1971), p. 3.

24 Shakespeare, *Romeo and Juliet* (Gibson), pp. 4 and 217. All other examples of student activities that follow appear on the left-hand page of the edition facing the script to which it refers.

Sentences in single syllables. Now repeat the activity, but this time read aloud only one-line sentences that have only single syllable words in them [example given] ... Talk together about how Shakespeare uses these monosyllabic sentences to create feeling and atmosphere. How do they give insight into character?

Others draw attention to a major feature of the act and invite students to speculate:

Shakespeare keeps Romeo off stage throughout this act. Talk together about some of the reasons for his absence.

Yet other interact activities have an openendedness that different teachers will deem peripheral or necessary depending on their own experience and the needs of their students. For example a 1756 Drury Lane playbill is reproduced. It promises 'the additional scene representing the funeral procession to the monument of the Capulets'. Students are invited to devise and show their own dramatic presentation of Juliet's funeral, using some of the 'mourning language' from 4.5.

The most radical break with tradition, signalling a new development in the educational afterlife of the play, occurs on each left-hand page that faces a forty-line unit of script. Here the shift from an explanation centred pedagogy to active and dramatic methods is most evident. The editorial apparatus comprises three elements: a running head, glosses and activities.

A running head of not more than three lines summarizes the action of the script lines: Facing 4.3.24–58 ('What if it be a poison ... I drink to thee'):

Juliet is filled with fearful thoughts. Is the Friar honest? Will she awake in the tomb before Romeo comes? Will she go mad with dread? She drinks the potion.

At the foot of the page, six lines are available for glosses, set as half lines. For Juliet's lines 24–58 only six words are glossed (ministered, tried, conceit, mandrakes, environed, spit). Conventional editions give more glosses, but here glossing decisions are strongly influenced by the principle that certain words or phrases are likely

to be understood by students when they speak the lines aloud. Elsewhere for example 'slug-a-bed' (4.5.2) is deliberately left unglossed. Alternative meanings are given where possible to avoid ironing out ambiguities. Special difficulties are acknowledged as for example at 3.2.6 with Juliet's 'that runaways' eyes may wink':

over forty different meanings have been suggested. No one can be certain what it means. What do you think?

The major departure from conventional practice is in the activities that occupy the bulk of each left-hand page. These activities focus on the language of the script, because it is Shakespeare's language, more than anything else, with which students need help. For Juliet's speech students are invited to work together in groups of various sizes and choose from five activities: to present the lines for radio; as an atmospheric choral speaking exercise by the whole class (a learned shared-line activity); by sections to show the progress of Juliet's fears; how it might be played on an Elizabethan or modern stage; or an echoing activity in pairs designed to identify vocabulary choice:

One person reads the lines. The other echoes every word to do with fear or death. What does this activity tell you about Juliet's feelings?

Such activities expand the conventional practice of performance-oriented school Shakespeare which allows only a few students in a class to perform whilst the others watch. Active methods, aimed to increase understanding of language, seek to involve all students, usually through small group work in which all students have the opportunity of speaking or acting out lines in some way. This expanded notion of performance methods supplements the common, but more numerically restricted, 'acting out' pedagogy. In a quite different context, and as a springboard for a lecture, it is exemplified in Marvin Rosenberg's invitation[25]

---

[25] Marvin Rosenberg, 'Sign Theory and Shakespeare', *Shakespeare Survey 40* (1988), pp. 33–40; p. 33.

to over one hundred members of the 1987 International Shakespeare conference to each demonstrate Hamlet's gesture that Ophelia describes:

And with his other hand thus o'er his brow   (2.1.89)

Rosenberg's invitation is a tiny but significant example of a method in which a teacher endeavours to involve every member of the class in an active role other than watching or listening. Such activity is remembered by participants as both motivating and an aid to learning.

Rosenberg's practice also exemplifies the principle that activity must have a clear purpose. Even the most free-ranging exploratory methods require this justification. The teacher must have the expectation and the confidence that such activity will enhance students' understanding of language or situation or some necessary question of the play. That same requirement applies to the editor of an edition that embraces an active pedagogy. Each activity must have an aim that relates in some way to the object of study. Activity, exploration, play, is undertaken not for itself alone, but for how it can facilitate students' imaginative, emotional and intellectual habitation of *Romeo and Juliet*.

Just as a director in rehearsal endeavours to ensure that the spontaneity and individuality of each actor interact in creative reciprocity with the discipline of the language of the script, so too the editor of a modern school edition has in mind similar intentions for each activity set. Some aims will be very specific, others much more general. Criteria for assessing success are similarly extensive (and, in the nature of matters Shakespearian, often contentious).

A central activity for all school students is the obvious one: how might this line, speech or scene be spoken and acted? It is the staple question of any performance-oriented pedagogy, and the teacher's role is to alert students to the multiplicity of choices embodied in the script. Because most school students will rarely have seen more than one production of the play, reminder of the plurality of possibilities is

necessarily direct, even prescriptive. The few school students who had the opportunity in 1995 to see the two very different Juliets of Emily Woof and Lucy Whybrow[26] will not need the following suggestion on the parting at 3.5, but most students will:

How should the lines be spoken? (in pairs)
Try different ways of speaking lines 1–25 (e.g. Juliet as loving, or impatient, or bossy, or sleepy, or ... Romeo as loving, or afraid, or secretly desiring to go, or irritable ...) Can you agree on how you think the lines should be delivered?

Such activities can go well beyond questions of how a character speaks, and can challenge critical convention or pose questions about Shakespeare's craftsmanship. Are Paris' lines (5.3.12–17) 'Sweet flower ... weep', artificial or do they seem to come from his heart? The question is left open for students to decide for themselves rather than emphasizing the weight of critical judgment of the formality of the lines. In the same scene students are invited to experiment with speaking Paris' and Friar Lawrence's sentences in lines 54–7 ('Stop thy unhallowed toil ... die') and 151–9 ('I hear some noise ... stay') in different order to that of the script. The question is posed:

Do you think anything is gained by changing the order?

Student judgement is similarly encouraged in the invitation to challenge longstanding stage conventions. For example, facing an exchange in 5.3.129–31, an activity describes custom, but leaves acceptance open:

BALTHASAR It doth so, holy sir, and there's my master,
  One that you love.
FRIAR LAWRENCE   Who is it?
BALTHASAR   Romeo.
FRIAR LAWRENCE How long hath he been there?
BALTHASAR   Full half an hour.
FRIAR LAWRENCE Go with me to the vault.
BALTHASAR   I dare not, sir.

---

26 At the Lyric Theatre, Hammersmith and The West Yorkshire Playhouse, Leeds (Woof), and the Royal Shakespeare Theatre, Stratford upon Avon (Whybrow).

How should lines 129–31 be spoken? These are shared between Friar Lawrence and Balthasar. There's a theatrical convention that when a line is shared, there should be no pauses between the speakers. From your own experience of speaking the words, do you agree?

Language activities are not confined to speech styles, but extend into active methods that seek both to acquaint students with certain language characteristics and to deepen their understanding of the play. Obvious examples are the many 'echoing' activities that give students access to how Shakespeare's lexical and image choices create and heighten atmosphere. As one student reads, the other echoes such 'atmospheric' words: for example those evoking 'movement' in 2.5.1–19, 'time' in 3.4, urgency and fear in Friar Lawrence's language in 5.3 and so on.

In more physical activities, groups of students are invited to enact, incident by incident, the different 'stories' that are told in the play: Benvolio's accounts of the first riot and of Mercutio's death; Friar Lawrence's long recapitulation in 5.3 (and his 'borrowed likeness of shrunk death' plan of 4.1.89–117); the Prologue:

The Prologue gives an outline of the play. Work out your own short play to show all the actions described. One person reads the Prologue aloud, a line at a time. The others mime what is described in each line.

There are all kinds of ways of sectioning such stories for acting out. In practice students often reject the method suggested (for example line by line) and present longer or shorter units. Friar Lawrence's explanation (5.3.231–64) contains at least thirty incidents that can be shown in group enactment. Another activity on the same lines demonstrates the kind of language learning activity that is common in schools, but in higher education is undertaken as an analytic exercise in deixis. Students work in groups of eight or more:

Each person takes a part (Friar, Romeo, Juliet,

Tybalt, Paris, Friar John, the Nurse, Capulet). Stand in a circle. The Friar slowly reads the lines. Every one points to whoever is mentioned, e.g. to the Friar on 'I', to Romeo and Juliet on 'them' and 'their' and so on. You'll find it fun, and it will vividly remind you of the story. If you want a technical word for this pointing activity, it's 'deixis', pronounced deyesis or dakesis.

Such physical activity dramatically and freely extends Hamlet's advice to the Players. It suits the action to the word, the word to the action, in ways that Shakespeare did not intend, but which releases the physical energy of the language. School students are thus encouraged to act out the six or more actions that Juliet declares she would do 'rather than marry Paris', leaping 'From off the battlements of any tower / Or walk in thievish ways' and so on (4.1.77–86). Clearly, such portrayals do not translate into stage action, but an alternative set of activities invite students to take on the role of the director to advise on particular speeches or moments of theatre, for example:

How does Romeo react to hearing Rosaline's name? (1.2.69)
How do Juliet and Lady Capulet behave during the Nurse's story?
Would you wish to get a laugh on 'I have forgot why I did call thee back'? (2.2.170)
How to play Mercutio's death?
Would you play the fight between Romeo and Tybalt in a formal way or brutally realistically?

Even seemingly tiny points can help students to think about characters' motivations. Asking students to think about who Capulet addresses as Angelica at 4.4.5, students are reminded:

No one is quite sure whether Angelica is the Nurse's name or Lady Capulet's. In the 1992 production by the Royal Shakespeare Company, Angelica was a young serving woman with whom Capulet was obviously having an affair.

In such cases students require little or no additional knowledge other than having read the play. Elsewhere the question of prior knowledge is clearly an issue for students, teachers and editors alike. What does a student need to know to make sense of Mercutio's greeting of Romeo?

Now is he for the numbers that Petrarch flowed in. Laura to his lady was a kitchen wench (marry, she had a better love to berhyme her), Dido a dowdy, Cleopatra a gypsy, Helen and Hero hildings and harlots, Thisbe a grey eye or so.

(2.4.34–7)

Here every editor must make a judgement about the appropriate nature and length of explanation. For a school edition, that explanation must be brief but should identify how Mercutio's list of ladies has some crucial relevance (greater than alliteration) to the play itself:

Mercutio teases Romeo, accusing him of writing love poetry (numbers) to Rosaline, like that of the fourteenth century Italian poet Petrarch to his love, Laura. But all the examples he gives are ominous, because all ended tragically:

Dido queen of Carthage. When her lover Aeneas deserted her, she killed herself
Cleopatra queen of Egypt, loved by both Julius Caesar and Mark Antony. She and Antony committed suicide
Helen wife of Menelaus, King of Sparta, was stolen by the Trojan Paris. Her abduction led to the siege and destruction of Troy
Hero Every night her lover Leander swam across the Hellespont (the Dardanelles) to meet her. He drowned.
Thisbe loved Pyramus. Their families were bitter enemies. She could only speak to him through a chink in the wall between their houses.

For some students, the explanation is sufficient. Others respond to the opportunity for active work: 'Work out a short mime showing all the love stories.' Every teacher makes a decision about how worthwhile it is to divide the class into groups of six or more, each of which, on the basis of the information given, prepares and presents its mime. Those teachers who have given time to such an activity claim it as valuable in reinforcing their students' awareness of the theme of doomed lovers.

But centrally, the task of an editor of a school edition is to help students perceive how the deep structure of a play is evidenced in its particularities. *Pace* the wilder shores of theory, every play has its quiddities, and every school edition must address those distinctive characteristics, essences (or however they may be described), aware that every teacher will put different emphasis on each.

For example, it is trite (to Shakespeare scholars) but true to say that *Romeo and Juliet* is much concerned with oppositions and conflict (Montagues versus Capulets, youth versus age, life versus death and so on). Shakespeare's usual linguistic embodiment of conflict is in antithesis, but in *Romeo and Juliet* his use of oxymorons at 1.1.167–72 and 3.2.75–9 instantiates the conflicts of the play.

A school edition must necessarily explain the construction of an oxymoron, but an active pedagogy suggests that students physically embody one or more in a tableau or mime for other students to identify ('brawling love', 'beautiful tyrant', 'damned saint' and so on). Some students occasionally attempt the difficult task of enacting 'Misshapen chaos of well-seeming forms' or 'Just opposite to what thou justly seem'st', displaying a grasp of the deep structure of oxymoronic form and insight into how Shakespeare's language embodies theme.

Direction can be found out by indirection. Two examples suggest how both modern relevance and freewheeling imagination can develop school students' understanding. First, the familiar request to seek modern parallels includes such activities as suggesting settings for the feud other than Verona (*West Side Story* provides the obvious and available example), or improvising contemporary versions of father–daughter conflict, or of falling in love at first sight. The second, less familiar, but in practice a potent motivator, is the activity presented opposite the Prologue:

What began the feud?
But *why* were the Montagues and Capulets such bitter enemies? Shakespeare never tells us and no one really knows. Talk together about why you think

these families should have been at each others' throats for so long. Prepare a short scene to show what long ago incident sparked off the hatred between two of Verona's leading families.

Every group of students presents a different, usually modern, version of the origins of the ancient grudge. In practice all enactments invariably demonstrate historic and universal preoccupations with sex, money, territory and honour (in current student-speak 'respect').

To mention universals is to bring me necessarily to theory. What account should school editions of Shakespeare take of the scholarly ferment of recent years? For the Cambridge series the same principle applies to both recent and traditional criticism: students must be made aware of different approaches and interpretations, and be encouraged to make their own judgements on those viewpoints.

Concepts and assumptions in appropriate form, rather than label- or name-dropping, underpin activities and editorial comment (in which experienced Shakespearians can easily detect the influence of, say, both cultural materialism and Bradley). For example in some editions students are invited to enact or interpret a scene from the standpoint of Marxist, feminist, psychoanalytic, historical or some other 'theoretical' perspective. In *Hamlet* four editorial pages interpret the play from a committed neo-Marxist standpoint, but students are urged to argue with that interpretation. In *Romeo and Juliet* such criticism is addressed through a variety of activities which for example resist liberal humanism's interpretative inclination towards fulfilment and harmony.

Students are encouraged to adopt the viewpoint of the play's lower status characters, women and servants, e.g. telling their own story in letter or diary form. An invitation to stage alternative versions of the ending, one showing that the feud will continue, declares its roots not simply in Michael Bogdanov's 1986 RSC staging but in the power-seeking and structural inequalities that cultural materialists see as denying hopes of reconciliation.

Elsewhere, students role-play an enquiry into the causes of the tragedy, examining evidence for alternative explanations (couched for example in the language of feminism: 'Verona is a patriarchal city. Fathers hold virtually absolute sway over their daughters ...'). The instabilities of post-structuralism, the problematics of language and reference, naming and identity, underlie an activity on 'What's in a name?' where students speculate on what would happen if they habitually 'misnamed' either themselves or conventionally accepted signifieds.

Jonathan Miller offers his own answer to that abiding and contentious question 'But is it Shakespeare?' (which usually carries its own implied firm denial). Miller requires that the afterlife of a play should be organic development, an 'emergent evolution' that displays 'topological decorum': the form of the original should be discernible in subsequent productions.[27] How far does an edition for schools which incorporates an active pedagogy represent an afterlife of organic development? This paper concludes by identifying certain issues that inhere in such an edition:

How much does it matter that young, inexperienced students are invited to make their own decisions on questions of language, interpretation and staging that have long perplexed professional Shakespearians?

---

[27] Miller, *Subsequent Performances*, pp. 35–7. But such well-expressed and convincing principles are just that: principles. In practice discordant voices lay claim to similar principled criteria. I must declare an interest. At the 1994 'Shakespeare for All' season at the Barbican, London, I found the Dusseldorfer Schauspielhaus' *Romeo and Juliet*, the Suzuki Company of Toga's *The Tale of Lear*, and Chicago's Goodman Theatre's *The Merchant of Venice*, admirable productions of Shakespeare, re-thought and imaginatively expressed through cultures other than my own. Most reviews of all three productions were vituperatively hostile; this was not 'Shakespeare'. Miller's evolutionary analogies, used without due respect for cultural creativity, naturalize and universalize particular evaluations, privileging text over script.

Is *Romeo and Juliet* in schools more than a vehicle for addressing matters of contemporary relevance, moral and political issues, language learning? What is that 'more': the specific Shakespearian quiddities of the play?

How is criticism, past and present, most appropriately presented to school students?

What judgements are appropriately made on students' enactments? What criteria are involved in assessing and evaluating the transient, evanescent processes and outcomes of student activities other than writing?

What, for school students, is an appropriate balance between explanation and activity, direction and openness, acceptance and discovery?

How important is presentation in a school edition: page units of script, scene locations, act/scene division, use of illustrations, positioning and nature of editorial matter?

What are the relationships of school editions and critical editions?

In practice, many of these questions, and the way in which any edition is used in school, are determined by each particular teacher's judgement of local circumstance and his or her view of 'Shakespeare'. That local determination is not simply part of the afterlife of *Romeo and Juliet*; for school students it is *Romeo and Juliet* itself. The way the play is taught is an integral constituent of students' perception of *Romeo and Juliet*.[28]

---

[28] Since this paper was written, the Summer 1995 issue of *Shakespeare Quarterly* again addresses pedagogy (46,2). Once more the focus is on college and university teaching of Shakespeare (see note 3), but two articles concern schools. Peggy O'Brien provides a literature review ('"And Gladly Teach": Books, Articles and a Bibliography on the Teaching of Shakespeare', pp. 165–72). Russ McDonald presents school teachers' experience of classroom practice ('Shakespeare goes to High School: some current practice in the American Classroom', pp. 145–56). It is significant that McDonald begins his article with 'It is probably fair to say that most regular readers of *Shakespeare Quarterly* are unfamiliar with the way Shakespeare is now being taught in the American Secondary School' (p. 145).

THE FILM VERSIONS OF *ROMEO AND JULIET*

ANTHONY DAVIES

I

Many of Shakespeare's plays have inspired music written subsequently, either as full opera scores or as incidental music to accompany theatre productions. But it is difficult to call to mind a play whose musical associations have become so well known in their own right as Tchaikovsky's *Romeo and Juliet* Fantasy Overture, originally written in 1869, or Prokofiev's ballet score completed in 1936, the year which saw the release of George Cukor's film. And since film, from its early days, has leaned heavily upon music as a commentary on dramatic action, it is not surprising that snatches of Tchaikovsky's *Romeo and Juliet* music have been woven into the sound tracks of George Cukor's film adaptation of the play as well as other films of the 1930s and 1940s at a clear remove from Shakespeare where love is thwarted by uncontrollable circumstance. Prokofiev's music has remained more firmly tied to the ballet stage, but its musical and choreographic dramatization has the rare distinction of having twice been filmed for cinema.

In their selected filmography Holderness and McCullough list twenty-three film adaptations of the play, the earliest (1900) made in France by Clement Maurice. Its frequency is bettered only by films of *Hamlet*, the earliest made, again by Clement Maurice, in 1900.[1] Rothwell and Meltzer in a more comprehensive listing record sixty-one film versions of *Romeo and Juliet*, including Bernstein's modern musical adaptation of the play into *West Side Story*.[2] The play

would seem, then, to have put down deep roots into our consciousness and to have flowered successfully in both musical and photographic dramatization since the late nineteenth century. The films through which it will be most helpful to trace the play's life in cinema and television are the films directed by Cukor (1936), Renato Castellani (1954), Zeffirelli (1968) and the BBC Television film (1978) directed by Alvin Rakoff.

1936 was an exceptionally fertile year for the cinematic dramatization of Shakespeare. Not only did there emerge vigorous discussion of the medium's suitability for Shakespeare's plays, but in this year, both Paul Czinner's *As You Like It* and Cukor's *Romeo and Juliet* were released. Unlike Czinner who chose a burgeoning stage actor, Laurence Olivier, for his romantic lead, Cukor gave his film a distinct Hollywood resonance by casting Leslie Howard and Norma Shearer in the lead parts with John Barrymore as Mercutio and Basil Rathbone as Tybalt. While a 1995 viewer may find the relatively advanced ages of the players, the emotional restraint in the speaking of the dialogue and the romantic style of the visual treatment insurmountable barriers to serious involvement with the issues of the play, the film reflects in an engaging way priorities which were conceived as proper in Hollywood's presentation of classic drama. The characters were

---

[1] Anthony Davies and Stanley Wells (eds.), *Shakespeare and the Moving Image* (Cambridge, 1994), pp. 42–4.

[2] Kenneth Rothwell and Annabel Henkin Melzer (eds.), *Shakespeare on Screen* (London, 1990), pp. 245–66.

played by well-known film actors of the day, love was portrayed as essentially a-sexual, women were waiting to be rescued and men were agile, athletic and handsome. The characters were governed by – or they reacted against – restraints and forces imposed from outside; there were no psychological complexities, no interior conflicts which might make of each individual character as difficult a field of battle as the world of social interests in which each was placed. Not unlike the Victorian melodrama – or, for that matter, the basic 'Western' film formula – Cukor's *Romeo and Juliet* was more the drama of situation than of character.

Critical response at the time dealt not at all with the lack of subjective depth – which is unsurprising since the impulses which have prompted later analytical approaches to character were hardly obsessive – but rather with the visual presentation of the young lovers. Paul Dehn considered Rathbone's Tybalt 'with a white-hot, whipping elegance of diction that matches his sword-play', and Barrymore's Mercutio 'in ... "old-style" Shakespearean fashion at its finest' the chiefly memorable features of the film. He found Howard's Romeo with its combination of the actor's grasp of the role and a camera treatment 'which made him look young enough' more believable than Norma Shearer's Juliet in which she 'gives the impression of being no longer young enough to remember how Juliet must have felt, and a little too old to be able to simulate (even with the camera's help) what she must have looked like'.[3]

Yet it would be wrong to dismiss the film too lightly. There was, in the making of it, a striving for academic respectability. A published script exists with the verse printed as prose, and in the interests of giving some scholarly authority to the medium's treatment of the material, Professor William Strunk from Cornell University was appointed literary consultant. There was, too, an expensively pursued desire for geo-historical authenticity. The Hollywood set was designed in detail from carefully selected photo-graphs of Italian Renaissance architecture, the shift from picture to three-dimensional set becoming clear to a modern viewer in the early sequence with the frame enclosing first an aerial view of the city and then people in medium-shot moving in spaces bounded by extensive replicated facades. It is an establishing technique foreshadowing that used by Olivier in his *Henry V* and *Hamlet*.

The introduction to the film not only lists the credits by name, but also presents framed head-and-shoulder portraits of the characters, so linking the film actor's image with the character, and enforcing the implicit shift from page to picture. The characters are placed, too, with little dramatic subtlety, in clear categories coloured by the musical accompaniment, Escalus, Tybalt, Montague and Capulet attended by dark, brassy staccato motifs while Benvolio, Romeo, Paris, the Nurse and Juliet are characterized by a lyrical rather tuneless theme played in unmistakable Hollywood sound on high strings. The next shot is of a triptych fresco, held for some seconds in stillness to establish it as a picture, before one figure comes to life and reads the prologue.

By the time we are brought to the opening action of the play, the audience has been taken through a number of transitional processes: from word to picture, from picture to framed action, and then from picture to reconstructed three-dimensional place, the city's theatre for social interaction. In addition we have had presented to us two groups of characters towards whom our responses have been partially primed. It is a conventional cinematic device to enable both the cinematic transposition and the action to function within an aesthetic and historical context. The cinematic conventions here tend to prepare us for a sad love story set against an inflexibility which is

---

[3] Paul Dehn, *Talking of Shakespeare*, edited by John Garrett (London, 1954), p. 59. (See also Rothwell and Melzer, *Shakespeare on Screen*, p. 249).

only remotely credible rather than for a dramatic tragedy.

Juliet is established framed by arches, hand-feeding a deer when the Nurse summons her for her mother's initial announcement of the planned marriage to Paris. Her subsequent run forward through the arch and down the steps to her mother is in essence the start of her journey from a childhood harmony with nature to the world of manipulated relationships which sets out to tame Juliet. Mercutio's Queen Mab narration is delivered with the camera centring him in the frame throughout with Romeo the only persistent listener. It is framing with dialogue in mind, an understandable priority within the idiom of the film, but for a modern viewer it makes for a predictability of camera technique, and a certain rigidity of style. We miss, too, the opportunity here for a meta-theatrical effect with Mercutio holding in thrall an audience. Romeo's 'Thou talkest of nothing' is delivered as something of a 'throw-away' line, a jocular means of terminating the visual sequence rather than a poignant comment on the relationship between the teller of stories and the listener. There is some attempt to exploit the metatheatrical potential of Mercutio's natural histrionics in his endeavour to 'conjure' Romeo, 'That in thy likeness thou appear to us', (2.1) and in his description of Tybalt as 'More than the Prince of Cats ... the courageous captain of compliments' for which he has an audience of women on a balcony above him, but his double-edged toying with his process of dying after his duel with Tybalt is contained with Benvolio and Romeo as confidential listeners.

The festivities at the Capulet house are varied and combine shots of robust male activity followed by slow willowy dancing and unison singing by groups of women, very much a Hollywood style of the period, and affording an extensive opportunity for the visual language of cinema to follow the shift in Romeo from his obsession with Rosaline to his awakening love for Juliet. Romeo's mask is cleverly used, not merely to hide his identity as a Montague, but its removal during the ball suggests the emergence of his more serious emotions, so that in revealing his feelings to Juliet across the hall he also reveals his identity to Tybalt. Capulet's restraint of Tybalt's impulse to challenge the uninvited Montague is in line with the attempts by older Capulets and Montagues to restrain their young from giving or responding to provocation in the opening tense encounter in the city square.

The absence of deeper complexities in the character relationships in the film is chiefly evident in Juliet's scenes with the Nurse, especially in the early scene where Lady Capulet initially excludes the Nurse from her proposal that Juliet prepare to marry Paris and later, where the Nurse finally colludes with the family to persuade Juliet of Paris' superior eligibility as a husband. In the former of these scenes, the Nurse retires with an inaudible grumble, but without a hint of any privileged closeness with her charge. In the latter, Juliet's bewildered 'Speak'st thou from thy heart?' and her disappointment at the Nurse's 'And from my soul, too, else beshrew them both' is plain enough but her dignity is sought in restrained acceptance rather than in any flash of anger. Indeed anger – for which there is some legitimate room in the play – seems not to be seemly in the young. Even Romeo's 'Then I defy you, stars' is pronounced with quiet, inner reflective resignation. Where anger is expressed by Capulet in his exasperation with Juliet's refusal to agree with the marriage plans, it is expressed vocally in his speaking of the lines rather than in any articulate movement of the camera or of the actor in the frame.

The balcony scenes are imaginatively shot, with an awareness of the vertical distance being sustained in the high- and low-angle shooting, sometimes over Romeo's and Juliet's shoulders, and with an unexpected framing of the two from the side, fragments of the set being finally placed in a composite image with the whole elevation shown. While the placing of massive potted plants momentarily suggests a garden centre, the longer shots of the surrounding greenery reinforce without crudeness the nature imagery with which the poetry of the play is so finely woven.

Cukor's decision to film Juliet's drinking of the 'distilling liquor' supplied by the Friar in close-up was once recalled by Olivier to give point to his sureness that climactic moments in Shakespeare should be filmed at greater distance in order not to reduce the scale of the actor's projection. Cukor's camera

crept right up to a huge head, the ordinary film climax. But it was in fact a mistake ... At the moment of climax she was acting very smally, because the camera was near. That was not the way it should have been.[4]

But the moment is not without its power as Cukor filmed it, suggesting a depth to Juliet's grasp of the essential privacy of her action and to her sober confrontation of its uncertain consequences.

There is much more that one could write about this film. These sequences are selected to illustrate some of the challenges that were felt at the time to exist in making Shakespeare's *Romeo and Juliet* into a Hollywood movie and to suggest that neither the performances nor the direction were without intelligence. Despite the many moments which strike a modern viewer as unsubtle, over simplified and dramatically flattened, there is an honesty and a humility about the film and, at the same time, a firm belief in the style which Hollywood at that period handled with assurance. And for all its emotional restraint there are benefits in leaving the lines to carry their meaning, for the poetic images of day, night, life, death and nature come over with a surprisingly memorable impact. In Kenneth Rothwell's words, 'The film should be cherished as a masterwork from antiquity: a bit archaic, a little rigid, slightly overdone, but, yes, still withal warm and good.'[5]

II

In all likelihood, it is not so great a film as Olivier's *Henry V* or Mankiewicz's *Julius Caesar*, both of which are faithful to the text as well as the spirit of Shakespeare. But it is certainly a much better film than Orson Welles's *Macbeth* and probably a much better one than Olivier's *Hamlet*, both of which it significantly surpasses in fidelity to *Romeo*'s *intentions*.[6]

The film assessed in these rather attenuated terms is Renato Castellani's 1954 *Romeo and Juliet*. While its availability appears now to be very limited, and while it has drawn little favourable − or even penetrating − critical response in the intervening years, it did win the 1954 Venice Film Festival Grand Prix and it has become historically interesting for the way in which Italian neo-realism brought its particular cinematic emphases to bear on the filming of the play. Roger Manvell maintained that the acclaim with which the film was received at the Venice Film Festival was a response to 'a splendidly colourful reincarnation of fifteenth-century Italy in Technicolour ... and there were few present in the audience at Venice who cared one way or the other whether the film kept reasonable faith with Shakespeare'.[7]

As well as insistently filling the frame with authentic architectural and artistic detail, the film set a clear trend in the casting of young actors (Laurence Harvey and Susan Shentall) as the two young lovers and in doing so encountered, in reverse, the incongruity remarked on in Cukor's film. In meeting cinema's demand for visual credibility, Castellani considered the capacity of his young actors for carrying conviction in the dialogue as relatively unimportant.

---

4   Laurence Olivier in Roger Manvell, *Shakespeare and the Film* (London, 1971), pp. 37–8.
5   Rothwell and Melzer, *Shakespeare on Screen*, p. 249.
6   Paul A. Jorgensen, 'Castellani's Romeo and Juliet: Intention and Response', *Film Quarterly*, 10, no. 1 (Autumn, 1955), 1–10.
7   Roger Manvell, *Shakespeare and the Film* (London, 1971), p. 97.

Manvell is uncharacteristically deprecating about the obvious priorities in the film, and draws interestingly on Meredith Lillich's observations as evidence of Castellani's obsession with spatial detail, and his choice of specific locations in Venice, Siena and Montagnana as well as paintings by Uccello, Piero, Botticelli and Raphael used for camera set-ups, Capulet in his study, for instance, replicating 'Raphael's portrait of the Pope'.[8] Such care in the selection of spatial detail and in the pursuit of historical authenticity need not of themselves negate the impact of a Shakespeare film, but Castellani's locations too often amount to a displacement rather than a dramatization of the issues, the action and the poetry of the play. The film suffers, too, from a clash of styles, Castellani's thrusting of the play into cinematic realism being radically at odds with the heightened dialogue of Shakespeare's poetry.

For all that, it is a film which should be rescued from oblivion in the interests of its historical and documentary value. Writing for the *New York Times*, Bosley Crowther saw it as 'a film drama in the violent, smashing, uncompromising style of the Italian neo-realist school' with its most striking feature as 'the dramatic realism and sensuousness of its Renaissance *mise-en-scène* and the headlong impulsiveness and passion with which it is artfully played'.[9]

III

'Headlong impulsiveness and passion' are terms which have been applied also to Franco Zeffirelli's 1968 film. Like Castellani, Zeffirelli sought to stress the generation gap in the social world of the play, and to make cinematically believable the characters and the perpetuation of the violence amidst which they live. In seeking to set the entrenched values of an older generation against a youthful, physically beautiful and naive innocence, Zeffirelli was riding the wave of the time. The young whose voices echo through the stone-walled streets of Zeffirelli's Verona are as much the children of the

bloody feud between Montagues and Capulets as they are the children of America's Vietnam turbulence.

Zeffirelli sought also to present the feud as an outlet for repressed aggression within the families themselves. The Capulet marriage is clearly one in which the veneer of respectability masks conflicts which have hardened with age into resentment. Lady Capulet's embittered face and her closing of the window against her husband's glance prompts his wry 'And too soon marred are those so early made' in response to Paris' protest that Juliet is old enough to marry. And Lady Capulet's capacity to control the blaze of Tybalt's urge to challenge Romeo at the Capulet ball suggests that there is more than a blood relationship between them. She is given Capulet's 'Well said, my hearts', and 'You are a princox', said to Tybalt with more admiration in it than rebuke. Her passionate plea in the public square to the Prince for just retribution on Romeo comes from a woman devastated by the death of a lover rather than a nephew. On the other hand there is a remoteness in her dealings with her daughter. In approaching the prospect of Juliet's marriage to Paris, her false start and calling back the Nurse reflect her own lack of confidence, and the Nurse's close relationship with Juliet is nicely pointed in the differing reactions of mother and daughter to the Nurse's bawdy joke.

Most successful of Zeffirelli's psychological structures is the development of Mercutio. He is a compulsive performer, and Zeffirelli exploits the metatheatrical opportunities in such a way that, more convincingly than for anyone else in the film, character becomes destiny. His Queen Mab speech, delivered in the dark with the faces of his listeners lit to show the magnetism of the performer who speaks momentarily through a dancing torch flame, is given an impressive

---

[8] Ibid., p. 100.
[9] Bosley Crowther, *New York Times* (22 December, 1954), p. 28. See also Rothwell and Melzer, *Shakespeare on Screen*, p. 253.

spatial breadth as he moves away and becomes an isolated figure continuing his act surrounded in the darkness by stone. Like an actor 'drying', Mercutio falters into silence and Romeo's tender 'Peace, peace, Mercutio, peace: / Thou talk'st of nothing' is spoken as their foreheads meet in close-up. Not only does this give Romeo's character depth, but it establishes the loving relationship between the two men, and it foreshadows effectively the later fatal closeness when Mercutio is 'hurt under [Romeo's] arm'.

Mercutio's 'Nay I'll conjure, too' performance is severely cut, the camera's concentration moving in on Romeo's approach to the Capulet garden, and like many lines in the dialogue, Romeo's 'He jests at scars that never felt a wound' loses its impact and seems undirected. But Mercutio's duel with Tybalt is superbly consistent with what has been established in Mercutio's characterization, the mercurial unpredictability, the neurotic compulsion to play to the crowd, the miraculous improvisation that keeps him balanced on the tight line between life and death; and then his being trapped in the web of his own making, his audience refusing to believe in a real man dying a real death. It is arguably the high point of the film. Convincing as this sequence is of Mercutio, it is more questionable of Tybalt. Would the man who says, 'What, drawn and talk of peace? I hate the word / As I hate hell, all Montagues and thee' play games with weapons? Would Tybalt feel remorse at the sight of blood on his blade? Zeffirelli seems to have introduced a wilful inconsistency here.

The balcony scene is visually captivating, but more noticeable here is the lost impact of the poetic imagery. This is partly due to the close-up action in the frame. In his pursuit of an authentic expression of youthful love, Zeffirelli clearly stressed physicality as central to their relationship. But it is the poetry that makes this relationship something more than just any adolescent love relationship, and while many of the best known poetic lines remain in the film's dialogue, they come across with a puzzling

superficiality. The poetic images do not register a meaning in the consciousness of the characters. 'Speak again, bright angel' does not belong in the contemplative or rhetorical world of the young lovers as Zeffirelli has presented them. In emphasizing their adolescence, in making the film 'a young person's *Romeo and Juliet*', in insisting that 'the kids in the story are like teenagers today', Zeffirelli has cultivated a disappointing legitimacy for making the poetry inconsequential.[10] Juliet's giggling laugh is given the same weight in the scene as 'th'inconstant moon / That monthly changes in her circled orb'. Similarly lacking in dramatic resonance is Juliet's

> And all my fortunes at thy foot I'll lay
> And follow thee, my lord, throughout the world

partly because of the frenetic activity which precedes it – Juliet's rushing along the balcony's considerable length to answer the Nurse's call and Romeo's arboreal gymnastics as he descends from the balcony parapet – but largely because the Juliet that Zeffirelli presents is as unaware of her 'fortunes' as she is of 'the world', and if these lines are without meaning to her, then both she and the poetry at this point are rendered insubstantial. All, indeed, are punished.

Much has been written of the effectiveness with which Zeffirelli has replaced the poetic imagery of the play's dialogue with a visual eloquence. Most convincing of those who have analysed this 'poetry of human relationships'[11] is Jorgens who – rightly, it seems to me – stops short of championing Zeffirelli's achievement, but who relates the film's emphasis on body language among the young to the very rift which divides the two generations.

Like the lovers, the young bloods of the square 'speak' with their bodies and their 'weapons'. The young distrust the rhetoric of the old: Juliet asks

---

[10] Zeffirelli in *The Liverpool Echo*, 9 March 1968.
[11] Zeffirelli in Toby Cole and Helen Crich Chinoy (eds), *Directors on Directing* (Indianapolis, 1963), p. 440.

'what's in a name?' Mercutio responds to Benvolio's echoing of parental cautions with 'blah, blah, blah', and Romeo is so impatient with Friar Laurence's tired saws while awaiting Juliet that he fills in the next word each time the holy man pauses. The impotent old, on the other hand, talk and talk ... They seem overly deliberate, unspontaneous, slow compared with the young.[12]

There is, however, a cost in establishing the 'generation gap' in this way, for there is wonderful poetry in the lines spoken by the young lovers, and it is not simply bardolatry to recognize with regret its debasement or its excision. Another sense in which Zeffirelli's keenness to make of his film 'a "youth movie" of the 1960s' limits the development of character is evident in Juliet's final dismissal of the Nurse. The camera faces the Nurse as she holds the kneeling Juliet to her, and after her advice that Juliet should 'marry with the County', the camera shoots Juliet's reaction from behind the Nurse's shoulder as she turns her eyes up to confront her former confidante. The Nurse turns three times in the hope of a reprieve, but while Juliet's 'Go' is both direct and final, it would seem to emerge from a petulant anger at being betrayed by yet another adult rather than from a growing understanding of the lonely decision that her commitment demands of her.

It is in the crowd scenes and especially the fights rather than the intimate character relationships that the film carries most conviction. The initial brawl in the square, the Tybalt/Mercutio duel and the Romeo/Tybalt fight are each infused with an authenticity, partly by the camera's closeness to the action where it is seemingly jostled as it frames parts of bodies in hectic movement, but largely because Zeffirelli exploited the dynamics of adolescent peer pressure to trap the participants in asserting their masculinity. Heat, dust and the frenzied loss of control give to the Romeo/Tybalt clash both the unleashed blaze of a playground fight and the inevitability of a death.

Structurally, too, the film's achievement is not inconsiderable. Jorgens finds a clear

relationship of the early morning mist which shrouds Verona at the film's opening and sun which fills the frame at moments and shines on the young lovers in bed and at their funeral. The white shroud motif is taken up in Mercutio's handkerchief, the needlework and sewing, the bandage which hides Mercutio's fatal wound, the Nurse's veil and the winding sheets in Juliet's funeral sequence and the coverings of the corpses in the vault. The sun, Jorgens suggests, becomes 'the symbol [which] captures the underlying unity of emotions which come together dialectically at the end of the play.'[13]

Zeffirelli's *Romeo and Juliet* must stand as one of the most vigorous forms in which Shakespeare's play has been brought to twentieth-century audiences. Its accessibility to the young audiences of the late 1960s and 1970s, its commercial success and the colourful vigour of its action sequences tend to impose upon its critics an uneasiness in making an unequivocal judgement. Those who do feel obliged to relate it to Shakespeare's play are interestingly divided. Jill Levenson has claimed it to be 'a version of the famous legend more uniform in tone, beautiful in conception, and passionate in mood than Shakespeare's'.[14] Ace Pilkington in a carefully considered assessment maintains that 'Zeffirelli has created a film which provides at once a respectable critical interpretation and a believably fiery incarnation of Shakespeare's text.'[15] Jack Jorgens found 'this *Romeo and Juliet*, transforming tragedy into a story of sentiment and pathos, [to be] a less mature work than Shakespeare's ... The clear-sighted calm and sense with which Shakespeare's tragic hero and heroine greet their end have disappeared.'[16]

[12] Jack Jorgens, *Shakespeare on Film* (Bloomington, 1977), p. 85.
[13] Ibid., p. 82.
[14] Jill Levenson, *Romeo and Juliet* (Shakespeare in Performance series, Manchester, 1987), p. 123.
[15] Ace Pilkington, 'Zeffirelli's Shakespeare' in Davies and Wells, *Moving Image*, p. 173.
[16] Jorgens, *Shakespeare on Film*, p. 91.

IV

Television Shakespeare – which looked for a time, for both economic and social reasons, as though it would displace cinema Shakespeare – has generally disappointed its most optimistic proponents. There are doubtless many reasons for this, but among them are shifts in the language of television itself, and changes in the receptivity and nature of the domestic audience. When John Wilders wrote of television viewers as 'an audience as varied as the one for which Shakespeare originally wrote, and far more numerous',[17] he seemed to imply that 'television viewers' constituted *one* audience, and his assumptions about the structure and predilections of that audience suggested that if Shakespeare was available it would be chosen.

Paradoxically, the sequence and framing of Zeffirelli's images are much closer to the fare that television viewers take for granted than those through which televised theatre is presented. Where Zeffirelli used real locations and filmed action with a *cinéma-vérité* realism, the framed images of Alvin Rakoff's BBC TV *Romeo and Juliet* are spatially confined, predictable, poorly lit and awkward in attempting to match stylized sets with spatially conceived action. For all that, the production is thematically more satisfying in its subtlety than the Zeffirelli film. One is quickly aware of the greater complexity of characterization among the older generation of Montagues and Capulets, Capulet himself finding some difficulty in being both the gracious host becoming expansive in the warmth of his assembled guests and one who imposes his will on the young. Michael Hordern's Capulet is authoritarian but his threats carry no menace; he is socially incompetent but also likable; he occupies a position of power, yet he is a ditherer; he heads one of the feuding families but he is, in a military sense, impotent. The commands he gives even in his own house are neither received nor carried out by anyone. 'What, ho!' he calls

after Juliet's apparent agreement to marry Paris: and then with a self-deprecating shrug,

> They are all forth. Well, I will walk myself
> To County Paris to prepare up him
> Against tomorrow.

Lady Capulet, far from being embittered by a marriage that has lost its excitement, is able to respond to the world around her with graciousness and intelligent humour. Unshocked by the Nurse's recollection of Juliet's infant fall, she enjoys, without loss of dignity, both the Nurse's presence and her moment of earthy humour. And when she finds Juliet weeping for Romeo's banishment (though she takes it to be for Tybalt's death), her 'We will have vengeance for it, fear thou not' emerges more from a mother's urge to console her daughter – and from an inherited sense of the Capulet–Montague feud – than from her own rancour against Tybalt's killer. Her grief at the discovery of Juliet's apparent death is genuine and desperate. Indeed, in confronting the silent unresponsive body of their daughter on her wedding morning, both Capulet and his wife grow into the realities of parenthood, Capulet helping his wife to stand as he now draws clear distinctions between celebration and mourning: between 'ordained festival' and 'black funeral'. Where once his life oscillated between impetuosity and distraction, it is now borne in upon him that 'all things change them to the contrary'.

Celia Johnson's Nurse is a consistent and credible character whose dignity is never lost. Her relationship with Juliet, her complicity in advancing the secret marriage and her final dismissal by Juliet are presented without overblown comedy or sentimentality. Like all the characters in this production, she is called upon to play more roles than she can competently manage. Ultimately she is nothing more than a Capulet household employee. Similarly, Joseph O'Connor's Friar Laurence comes across as a

---

[17] John Wilders, *New Prefaces to Shakespeare* (Oxford, 1988), p. vii.

man of more profound integrity than Milo O'Shea's somewhat shallow and plaintive characterization for Zeffirelli, and his capacity for philosophical inquiry is clearly established on his initial entrance where he holds before him a small yellow flower. His recognition of its dual components, 'poison' and 'medicine' and his 'Two such opposèd kings encamp them still / In man as well as herbs' suggests that the fate of the young lovers is determined not merely by the feud-ridden society in which they are held, but by the nature of humankind. The conflict is not *between*, but *within*. His intellectualism – a dimension lacking in Zeffirelli's film – makes sense, too, of the Nurse's

> O Lord, I could have stayed here all the night
> To hear good counsel! O, what learning is!

The younger Capulets and Montagues, indeed, the younger generation in general are not projected with as much subtlety. Their lives are not so private nor their poetry so reflective. The fight scenes in the square are carried through with energy and theatrical conviction, but they lack a sense of happening in public. Despite the killing of an infant in the opening brawl, there is not, as there is in Zeffirelli's film, that awesome awareness of chaos poised to destroy the whole community in a frenzy of killing. It is, of course, arguable that the very localized outbursts of violence and the shocked paralysis of those who appear in the background as by-standers mirror a more apathetic political and social response than that which characterized the 1960s.

While both Patrick Ryecart's Romeo and Rebecca Saire's Juliet are weightier characters than Zeffirelli's young lovers, the power of their poetry is vitiated by uninspired and predictable camera work. The night which cloaks their brief and secret meetings and the opposition of light and darkness which resounds through their poetry are given no effective visual dramatization in the frame. In the balcony scene, while it endeavours to give due weight to the development of what John Wilders has identified as

central to the play, 'the attempt and tragic failure of the two young people to "deny their names" and thereby to become exclusively themselves',[18] the framing tends to fragment the flow in the spoken verse and to work against its natural rise and fall of intensity.

It is as she confronts the double disaster of Tybalt's death and Romeo's banishment that Juliet's capacity for growth in awareness is made clear. As she pieces together the truth from the confused lamentations of the Nurse, her face registers her apprehension of the start of her journey to isolation. As her natural alliances, first with her mother and then with the Nurse, collapse – not merely because she cannot agree to marry Paris but because she is no longer the submissive child she was – Juliet is brought closer to us, the viewers, her profile later framed in close-up as she recognizes the uncertainties of a world in which she must deceive in order to defend her own truth. Her 'Farewell', to her mother and the Nurse, indeed to the relationships of childhood, has both courage and trepidation in it:

> God knows when we shall meet again.
> I have a faint cold fear thrills through my veins
> That almost freezes up the heat of life.

Alvin Rakoff's 1978 *Romeo and Juliet* is a daring successor to the much acclaimed Zeffirelli film. If it lacks the passionate, compulsive energy with which the earlier film is charged, it responds with more sensitivity to the thematic complexities of Shakespeare's play. At its centre is the domestic life of the Capulet household, united in 'the bond of intending only Juliet's best interests'.[19] In charting an appropriate growth in both Juliet and the older Capulets Rakoff stands clear of cheapening the family's relationships. Lady Capulet's 'Do as thou wilt, for I have done with thee' after Capulet's

---

[18] Wilders, 'Preface to *Romeo and Juliet*', *New Prefaces*, p. 80.

[19] Charles B. Lower, 'Romeo and Juliet', *Shakespeare on Film News Letter*, vol. 3, no. 2 (1979), p. 6.

furious rejection of his daughter carries the pain of a mother's hopes rejected. Life is no less difficult for the old than for the young.

V

In looking at four versions of *Romeo and Juliet* as samples of its afterlife on film, one becomes aware of particular features in this play's construction which make it both a powerful attraction and an unusually daunting challenge for the film maker. In the first place, both cinema and television depend upon a greater degree of visual credibility than does theatre. Actors who can bring to the play's language a maturity of understanding will look too old on the screen, and those who are convincingly youthful to the eye will have difficulties in giving the verse appropriate authority. Secondly, the play strikes a balance between athletic outdoor action leading to deaths on the one hand and fervent inner poetic action of the mind on the other. The pace of the play's overall thrust is insistently driven, but the theatre can accommodate both physical and poetic action in a way which film finds much less easy. The flow of visual images through which film dramatizes the kind of action which this play affords is likely to be halted with much awkwardness in the interests of dense poetic imagery, an aesthetic problem which both Castellani and Zeffirelli recognized. Finally, in its projection of love and hate spread across two generations, the play will tempt directors – in film and theatre – to tilt it towards social and political commentary and away from dramatic tragedy. This is more dangerous for film than for theatre, for while social attitudes are fickle film is fixed, both as text and interpretation.

THE POETICS OF PARADOX: SHAKESPEARE'S VERSUS ZEFFIRELLI'S CULTURES OF VIOLENCE

JOAN OZARK HOLMER

Shakespeare's drama has proved the most popular theatrical afterlife of the time-honoured story of Romeo and Juliet, and Franco Zeffirelli's film (1968) continues to be its most popular filmic afterlife.[1] Zeffirelli's film deserves its success, especially for its cinematic brilliance in capturing the colourful and passionate intensity of Verona and its legendary lovers. However, Zeffirelli's version does not fully succeed in rendering Shakespeare's emphasis on moral philosophy and the rhetoric of paradox for the genre of tragedy. Shakespeare greatly improved upon these elements in his main literary source, Arthur Brooke's poem *The Tragicall Historye of Romeus and Juliet* (1562), for his own staging of the uses and abuses of human nature.[2] As a result, Zeffirelli lessens Romeo's stature as a tragic protagonist and underestimates the importance of Friar Lawrence's philosophical role in the play's competing definitions of manhood in relation to the problem of violence. Shakespeare's creation of Romeo as his tragic protagonist is a bit of a paradox in itself. He is arguably the least responsible of all Shakespearian tragic heroes in the canon. Yet Shakespeare also altered Brooke's poem in ways that complicate and heighten Romeo's role of tragic responsibility. For example, Brooke's Romeus fights Tybalt in self-defence, after trying to be a peacemaker on behalf of God and the commonwealth; his stated reasons for intervention are religious and political, making no mention of his personal love for Juliet (lines 999–1034). But Shake-speare's Romeo is confronted with a highly personal dilemma of having to choose between his love for Juliet and his desire to revenge his friend's death as well as his own slandered reputation (3.1.100–20). Even in his final hour, Romeo, despite the intensity of his emotional agony, can self-reflectively beg Paris: '... tempt not a desp'rate man, / ... Put not another sin upon my head, / By urging me to fury' (5.3.59, 62–3), although the duel that occasions these lines is absent from both Brooke's and Zeffirelli's versions.

Many of Zeffirelli's omissions tend to oversimplify the play's complexly tragic texture, a texture Shakespeare seems determined to fashion given his new dramaturgical challenge of composing romantic tragedy that is in itself somewhat paradoxical. Shakespeare takes the typical matter of comedy, young love, and transforms it stylistically and thematically for the

---

1   In this essay quotations from the play follow the New Cambridge Shakespeare *Romeo and Juliet*, ed. G. Blakemore Evans (Cambridge, 1984). Quotations of all other Shakespearian plays follow *William Shakespeare: The Complete Works*, ed. Stanley Wells, Gary Taylor, John Jowett, and William Montgomery (Oxford, 1986). For a fine study of the play's realization in performance, including Zeffirelli's stage and film productions, see Jill L. Levenson, *Romeo and Juliet* (Manchester, 1987), pp. 82–126.
2   Quotations from this poem, cited parenthetically, are from Geoffrey Bullough, *Narrative and Dramatic Sources of Shakespeare*, vol. 1 (London, Henley, and New York, 1977), pp. 284–363.

genre of tragedy.[3] Since the death of the lovers is announced in the opening Chorus, the audience will be less preoccupied with the product than the process, that is, the means by which that end is to be achieved, both the *how* and the *why* of it. Shakespeare's artistic changes of what he finds in Brooke's poem reveal much about the play's conceptualization of human potential so that Shakespeare ultimately does succeed in writing 'the *tragedy*' of Romeo and Juliet, as the play's title indicates, and not merely the *pathos* of Zeffirelli's more melodramatic rendition of this famous love legend. The greater the degree of personal responsibility, the more 'tragic' the emphasis; the greater the degree of victimization, the more 'pathetic' the emphasis.[4] Shakespeare combines both emphases through his pervasive trope of paradox and his dilemmas involving the difficulty of knowing and doing the good. This essay will explore the significance of several of Zeffirelli's crucial changes that undercut Shakespeare's own innovations on Brooke's poem. Despite the overall technical brilliance of the film, at times the film ironically comes closer to Brooke's poem than to Shakespeare's script, especially regarding Shakespeare's greater enhancement of the Romeo–Friar Lawrence relationship.

Zeffirelli's deletions from the play's text might be questioned for their quantity as well as their quality. He retains only about a third of the play's lines, and what he chooses to delete involves not only obscure language (e.g., the opening 'colliers'/'choler'/'collar'/ puns), which is easier to justify, but also philosophical passages, much more difficult to justify. True to his bias for avoiding rhetorical difficulty and for emphasizing passionate feeling at the expense of philosophical thought, Zeffirelli cuts Friar Lawrence's opening soliloquy and thereby undercuts the symbolic significance and tragic potential of the Friar's as well as Romeo's entrances for this scene, sacrificing the paradoxical imagery and themes that Shakespeare *created* for this moment. This soliloquy might justly be called the play's 'philosophical centrepiece', yet critics tend to

overlook that the Friar's speech is not to be found in any of Shakespeare's literary sources. There are, of course, plenty of scattered lines in the many speeches of Brooke's friar that emphasize the commonplace importance of manly reason over 'witles will' (line 1400), and critics have identified much of the proverbial wisdom as well as Christian theology that inform this speech.[5] But Shakespeare's crystallization of ideas and images through analogy and paradox, his emphasis on the doctrine of proper use, and his dramaturgical integration of this speech as a touchstone for the play's dilemmas have not been fully appreciated. A comparison of Shakespeare's and Zeffirelli's versions of this juncture in the play underscores the gap between their understanding of the human condition.

After Zeffirelli's Romeo leaves Juliet with 'such sweet sorrow' (2.2.184), he runs jubilantly

[3] In Brooke's preface 'To the Reader', he refers to an excellent stage play on this story, but he says he has penned 'the same argument' in his poem (p. 285). We can, therefore, reasonably assume Shakespeare's differences are his own inventions on the same matter shared by Brooke and the no longer extant play to which he alludes. Shakespeare's play appears to be our first extant example of romantic tragedy as well as the most famous example.

[4] For the idea of responsibility as central to a definition of tragic heroism, see Robert W. Corrigan, *Tragedy: Vision and Form* (2nd edn, New York, 1981), pp. 10–12; *A Handbook to Literature*, ed. C. Hugh Holman and William Harmon (6th edn, New York and London, 1992), 'Pathos', p. 348; 'Hamartia', p. 222; 'Melodrama', p. 285. Corrigan, however, seems to overstate his case for a difference of 'kind and not degree' regarding the merits of the tragic and the pathetic (p. 11). For the complexity of literary theory regarding definitions of tragedy, see *Princeton Encyclopedia of Poetry and Poetics*, ed. Alex Preminger, Frank J. Warnke, and O. B. Hardison, Jr, enl. edn (Princeton, 1974), 'Tragic Flaw', pp. 864–5; 'Tragedy', pp. 860–4.

[5] See Evans, pp. 101–2. Cf. *Romeo and Juliet*, ed. Brian Gibbons (New Arden Shakespeare) (London, 1980), pp. 137–8. For Saviolo's possible influence on Shakespeare's analogous imagery of plants and men, see my essay, '"Draw, if you be men": Saviolo's Significance for *Romeo and Juliet*', *Shakespeare Quarterly*, 45 (1994), 163–89; pp. 179–80.

through a verdant Italian landscape to seek the help of his surrogate 'father', his spiritual adviser and chosen sole/soul confidant. The film then presents a panoramic view of the dawn's illumination of a monastery suitably situated in a pastoral setting. The camera zooms in to focus blankly on some tall, flowering bushes, until the viewer, puzzled about this particular visual viewpoint, descries motion in the bushes and the head of someone moving among them. Enter Friar Lawrence. This entrance is at best somewhat comical, and the film will reinforce this impression with the Friar's stumbling exit from this scene.

However, Shakespeare's version of the Friar's entrance, as well as Romeo's, is a masterful revision of what he found in Brooke's poem. Because this long soliloquy strikes the modern ear as platitudinous, Shakespeare's originality in crafting this speech tends to be overlooked. It addresses the correspondence between Nature and human nature in relation to good and ill as well as life and death. Shakespeare carefully integrates the language and ideas of the Friar's soliloquy within this scene as well as the rest of the play. What are some aspects of this speech that we should attend to? Depending on the decision of the play's textual editor,[6] the soliloquy can open with images aptly descriptive for the macrocosmic–microcosmic analogy to follow, the image of intermingled light and dark as smiling dawn displaces 'frowning night' and the images of excess and speed as 'fleckled darkness like a drunkard reels / From forth day's path and Titan's fiery wheels' (2.3.1, 3–4). Much criticism has been devoted to the numerous patterns of opposition (such as love and hate, light and dark, life and death) in this play; however, the contrasts are not simply opposed but rather paradoxically interrelated, as Caroline Spurgeon keynoted in her analysis of the 'lightning' imagery in the play as light-in-darkness.[7] The earth is not simply Nature's womb or tomb, but both. Although this idea is classical in origin and even proverbial in the sixteenth century,[8] the womb/tomb rhyme is Shake-

speare's. Furthermore, the natural and specifically horticultural imagery to analogize Nature and human nature is Shakespeare's careful addition to Brooke's poem, as is his cultivation here of paradox coupled with the idea of Nature's proper use.

Shakespeare's analogy between Earth and man's earth pervades the language of the play's fathers and children, which is not surprising given the biblical genesis of man's formation from earth, into which God breathed His spirit for the soul, and the return of dust to dust at the body's death.[9] Shakespeare has partially prepared us for the spiritual father's earthy imagery in the early comments of the physical fathers, Montague and Capulet. Montague's cankered bud image for his son (1.1.142–3) is followed in the next scene with Capulet's similar imagery when he tells Paris about his only child: 'Earth hath swallowed all my hopes but she; / She's the hopeful lady of my earth' (1.2.14–15); his horticultural image of beautiful young women as 'fresh fennel buds' (1.2.29) likewise anticipates the Friar's more developed plant imagery for humans who, like the earth's *children of divers kind*' have 'powerful grace' in 'their true qualities' or 'true birth' (2.3.10, 15–16, 20; my italics). Romeo refers to his body as 'dull earth' (2.1.2); Juliet refers to hers as 'vile earth' (3.2.59); and the Friar images Romeo's soul as 'heaven' and his body as 'earth' (3.3.120). Romeo describes his supposedly dead Juliet as 'the dearest morsel of the earth' devoured by

6 See *William Shakespeare: A Textual Companion*, ed. Stanley Wells, Gary Taylor, John Jowett, and William Montgomery (Oxford, 1987), p. 295.

7 See Spurgeon, *Shakespeare's Imagery and What It Tells Us* (Cambridge, 1935), pp. 213, 315.

8 For the allusion to Lucretius, see Steevens, cited by Evans, 2.3.9n. See also the proverb, 'The Earth produces all things and receives all again' (E32), in Morris Palmer Tilley, *A Dictionary of Proverbs in England in the Sixteenth and Seventeenth Centuries* (Ann Arbor, Michigan, 1950).

9 See *The Geneva Bible* (a facsimile of the 1560 edition), intro. Lloyd E. Berry (Madison, Wisconsin, 1969), Genesis 1.26–7, 2.7, 22 and Ecclesiastes 12.7 as well as the accompanying marginal glosses on these passages.

the 'womb of death' he calls the Capulets' burial vault (5.3.45–6). Unlike the film, which ends with a funeral procession in the town square, Shakespeare's play ends appropriately in this 'womb of death' with its earthen 'canopy' of 'dust and stones' (5.3.12) and also ends with tragic irony on 'bloody' earth (5.3.172) that should be a 'place of peace' (5.3.143).

Shakespeare's introduction of Friar Lawrence demonstrates daring but successful dramaturgy because a choric voice is wedded to a character who is not a Chorus but rather a *dramatis persona* who, like the others, is fully integrated within the play's dominant pattern of good intentions gone awry. Romeo's complaint, 'I thought all for the best' (3.1.95), would make an appropriate subtitle for the play's tragic ironies. The Friar's herbal entrance transcends the function of plot preparation for his later use of the remarkable sleeping potion, which is all that is accomplished in both Brooke's and Zeffirelli's versions. In several ways Shakespeare uses this soliloquy to lay the groundwork for the audience's judgements of those causes of human tragedy that can be attributed to the use of will. The Friar's on-stage action of gathering plants lends itself naturally to his meditation on the paradox of creation with its intertwinings of good and ill:

> For nought so vile, that on the earth doth live,
> But to the earth some special good doth give;
> Nor ought so good but, strained from that fair use,
> Revolts from true birth, stumbling on abuse.
>
> (2.3.17–20)

Adding his own verbal embellishments (e.g., 'earth', 'special', 'strained', 'fair use', 'true birth', and 'stumbling'), Shakespeare combines here two opposite proverbs in order to underscore the proper use of Nature.[10]

The paradoxical conclusion of vicious virtue and virtuous vice is Shakespeare's own: 'Virtue itself turns vice, being misapplied, / And vice sometime by action dignified' (2.3.21–2). Shakespeare specifies the language of virtue and vice that looks back to the powers of plants and simultaneously forward in the language of usage ('misapplication' and 'action') to the powers of humans in the Friar's singular flower analogy. These lines haunt the audience's auditory imagination because the play is full of such dilemmatic examples, e.g., the virtue of Escalus' past clemency to the feudists is misapplied – 'Mercy but murders, pardoning those that kill' (3.1.188) – or the painful deception of the sleeping potion stratagem is dignified by the prevention of bigamy: 'To live an unstained wife to my sweet love' (4.1.88). Although virtually every character in the play is challenged in varying degrees by this dilemma of how to use virtue and vice properly, I suggest that Shakespeare attempts to develop the stature of Romeo as a tragic protagonist by reserving the most difficult decisions for his lead. At the same time Shakespeare maximizes audience sympathy for such a *young* protagonist by constantly stressing his youthfulness as an extenuating excuse for his mistakes, by poignantly juxtaposing momentous events of emotional impact (both joyful and sorrowful), and by drastically compressing the time scheme (the action opens Sunday morning and ends Thursday morning) so that time's pressures also prompt untimely death. Shakespeare, moreover, raises the stakes of fate by supplementing Brooke's reiterative insistence on Fortune with his own emphasis on the greater power of heaven and the

---

10 See Tilley, *Proverbs*; for lines 17–18, see the proverbs, 'There is Nothing but is good for something' (N327) and 'There is Nothing so bad in which there is not something of good' (N328); for lines 19–20, see 'Nothing so good but it (The best things, Everything) might be abused' (N317). Evans overlooks the last proverb but notes the influential opening of Brooke's preface 'To the Reader' (p. 284). The difference is that Brooke has none of Shakespeare's rhetorical use of analogy, paradox, and specific imagery, and his passage reflects the general idea of another proverb, 'The earth that yields food yields also poison' (see Tilley, E32). I suggest that Shakespeare took a hint for his use/abuse motif from Brooke's justification of the friar's knowledge of nature: 'For justly of no arte can men condemne the use / But right and reasons lore crye out agaynst the lewd abuse' (lines 573–4).

stars, heavenly imagery that complements the emphasis on a retributive heaven that lowers if its 'high will' is continually crossed (see 4.5.94–5).[11] Such a change commingles the motif of tragic human ignorance with the motif of mystery that enshrouds heavenly power.

After the Friar announces the paradoxical use of virtue and vice and the governing idea of true use or right action, Romeo enters. It is precisely at this juncture that the early printed editions of the text, except for the First Quarto, present the stage direction, '*Enter* ROMEO'. For the audience he symbolically stands on stage as the human emblem of the Friar's 'weak flower', with its inner potential for good and ill. Being 'weak' or 'frail' not only suits the idea of fallen man as frail, but particularly suits Romeo's greater fragility because of his youthful or bud-like stage of development that worries his father. Expressing his deep concern for his son's potentially 'black and portentous' humour that needs 'good counsel', Montague initially describes his recently much changed son in imagery that anticipates the Friar's: 'But to himself so secret and so close, ... / As is the bud bit with an envious worm / Ere he can spread his sweet leaves to the air' (1.1.132–3, 140, 142–4). Zeffirelli omits these lines as well as Montague's hinted direction to Benvolio (1.1.145–6); Romeo is first glimpsed as a lovesick youth sniffing a flower. The film's beautiful theme song does incorporate the play's analogical imagery of flower and person to lament the fragility of earthly beauty: 'A rose will bloom; it then will fade. So does a youth, so does the fairest maid'.[12] By the play's end five representatives of Verona's youth are cropped in a premature harvest a fortnight before Lammas-tide, in England the feast offering of the earth's first fruits. However, Zeffirelli's deletion of Romeo's opening speeches about Rosaline as well as the Friar's soliloquy with its 'weak flower' analogy misses an opportunity to capitalize on this image and the issue of 'violence' as it is philosophically developed in Shakespeare's text for Romeo as well as the rest of the cast. Zeffirelli's image

presents the flower's beauty but not also its poison; the rose blooms before naturally fading, but Shakespeare's youthful flowers are prematurely nipped in the bud.

The Friar's soliloquy is dramatically contextualized for Romeo's affairs of the heart. Such a philosophical piece one might expect to find juxtaposed with the feud, placed near one of the three stage fights to comment on destructive male violence. Instead, the speech is placed within the story of Romeo's loves and their significance. With a single 'weak flower' functioning as an important stage prop, Shakespeare blends analogical and allegorical modes of presentation as the Friar now concretely explicates the more abstractly stated wisdom of his preceding six lines in order to clarify the life-or-death correspondence between Nature and human nature:

Within the infant rind of this weak flower
Poison hath residence, and medicine power:
For this, being smelt, with that part cheers each
    part,
Being tasted, stays all senses with the heart.
Two such opposèd kings encamp them still
In man as well as herbs, grace and rude will;
And where the worser is predominant,
Full soon the canker death eats up that plant.
                  (2.3.23–30)

---

[11] Brooke's poem neither emphasizes the heavens or heaven as fate. Its opening sonnet (p. 286) perfunctorily relates the main events of the lovers' lives, but it does not frame those 'star-crossed' (apparently Shakespeare's coinage) lives within the larger context of costly reconciliation, as Shakespeare's sonnet does. At the end the families are moved to tears by 'the straungenes of the chaunce' (line 3004), and Brooke inserts one parenthetical reference to Jove's will: 'At length (so mighty Jove it would) by pitye they are wonne' (3010). Neither Brooke's friar nor prince indicates a role for heavenly fate.

[12] Shakespeare specifically associates the three lovers with flowers: Capulet calls his supposedly dead Juliet 'the sweetest flower of all the field' (4.5.29); praising Paris, Lady Capulet exclaims, 'Verona's summer hath not such a flower' (1.3.78); and in his final entry Paris will carry flowers with which to keep a mourning vigil for Juliet whom he calls 'sweet flower' (5.3.12).

Within the same individual, either plant or human, exists the potential for both good and ill. Whether one is poisoned or healed depends on how one *uses* this flower, whether one tastes it or smells it. Whether one dies or lives, depends on how one uses one's own nature, whether grace or rude will predominates in sovereign sway over the battle. As John Milton's Adam cogently reminds Eve, '... within himself [humankind] / The danger lies, yet lies within his power: / Against his will he can receive no harm'.[13] Later that very afternoon the Friar will admonish Romeo as a 'usurer' of his natural gifts because he shamefully misuses his shape, love, and wit, perverting these riches from their 'true use' (3.3.122–5). If love is Romeo's lord, directing him to find Juliet (2.2.80–4), then we should recall Thomas P. Roche's observation about the *use* of love in the literary tradition of Petrarch and the English sonnets, a tradition widely acknowledged as very influential for this tragedy: 'Love, whether it be cupidinous or charitable, springs from the same God-given gift of creation and creativity. All love is one ... It is how we use this impulse that determines whether we are to be trapped or cured'.[14] The blessing of Romeo's and Juliet's faithful love shines all the brighter against the foil of Verona's benighted feud, but how should it be used?

Despite the apparently even opposition of two kingly powers, 'grace' and 'rude will', conventional Renaissance hierarchy governs the favoured victor. In a monistic Christian view of creation, good is primary, and evil results as the perversion of good; for example, God created Lucifer, but Lucifer created Satan. The various editorial glosses for 'grace' and 'rude will' are all similar in according to 'grace' a better power, one that encourages life, and in granting to 'rude will' a worser power, one that fosters death. 'Grace' is so positive a term that it needs no qualifier. 'Will', however, can be positive or negative, depending on whether or not it functions to maintain the proper marriage of soul and body so that right reason guides fleshly appetites and not the rebellious reverse. 'Rude', therefore, is a necessary qualifier to signify 'unbridled', as George Lyman Kittredge suggests, or 'unruly', as G. Blakemore Evans suggests.[15] Shakespeare's choice of 'rude' complements the play's preoccupation with what is 'violent', one of the meanings of 'rude'.[16] The *Oxford English Dictionary* cites some of the etymological meanings for 'violent' as 'forcible, impetuous, vehement'.

For moderns, 'violence' tends to be limited to the idea of 'force' in a physical sense, but for Elizabethans 'violence' embraces the physical sense as well as an emotional sense ('passionate') and a moral sense ('excessive' or 'extreme').[17] Hence, for Elizabethans, 'violence' could characterize either human love or hate, whereas moderns would tend to link it to the latter.[18]

---

13 See Milton, *Paradise Lost*, ed. Merritt Y. Hughes (New York, 1962), Book IX, lines 348–10, p. 212.

14 Roche, *Petrarch and the English Sonnet Sequences* (New York, 1989), p. 438.

15 See Kittredge, ed. *The Tragedy of Romeo and Juliet* (Boston, 1940), 2.3.28n, p. 148; Evans, 2.3.28n.

16 See the *Oxford English Dictionary*, 2nd edn, 'rude', adj., 5; cf. 6. Is it merely coincidental that 'rude' (in its various meanings) appears five times in the play, all instances explicitly involving Romeo to a greater or lesser degree? See '... [love] is too rough, / too rude, too boist'rous, and it pricks like thorn' (1.4.25–6); 'And touching hers, make blessèd my rude hand' (1.5.50); 'grace and rude will' (2.3.28); 'My blood for your rude brawls doth lie a-bleeding' (3.1.180); 'O deadly sin! O rude unthankfulness!' (3.3.24).

17 See the *OED*, 'violence', sb., 1.; 5, and 'violent', adj., 1d., 3., 4b., and 8b. and c.

18 See, e.g., Coppélia Kahn, 'Coming of Age: Marriage and Manhood in *Romeo and Juliet* and *The Taming of the Shrew*', in *Man's Estate: Masculine Identity in Shakespeare* (Berkeley, 1981), pp. 82–118. Marianne Novy insightfully discusses male violence in both bellicosity and sexuality, but she argues that Romeo's love for Juliet is not violent, as was his love for Rosaline, except from the Friar's 'conventional' view of manhood as 'emotional control'. See *Love's Argument: Gender Relations in Shakespeare* (Chapel Hill and London, 1984), pp. 99–108; quotations are from p. 107. It is not a matter of simple control, as if the Friar disapproves of sexual love within marriage, which he does not, but rather understanding the 'true qualities' (2.3.14), 'fair use' (2.3.19),

Although the second Chorus stresses the passionate power of Romeo's and Juliet's 'extreme sweet' (1.5.157), it nonetheless sounds strange to us to hear the Friar describe Romeo's love for Juliet as 'violent delights' in his premarital warning to Romeo about the combustible danger of such intense love: 'These violent delights have violent ends, / And in their triumph die like fire and powder, / Which as they kiss consume' (2.6.9–11). From a modern viewpoint, the Friar seems less prudent and more a prude.[19] But Milton's sociable angel Raphael similarly warns Adam about the difference between passion and love: true love refines the mind and enlarges the heart, having its seat in reason, and it 'is the scale / By which to heav'nly Love' a person may ascend.[20] Unlike our modern bias favouring the intensity of extremely passionate love as an indicator of true love, Elizabethans tended, at least in theory, to distrust 'violence' and to see it as indicative of mutability. Their proverbial wisdom insisted that extremes do not hold, that nothing violent, including love, could be permanent.[21] Shakespeare complicates this notion with a paradoxical twist by having the intense love of Romeo and Juliet prove constant but their own earthly lives extinct. With an Aristotelian preference for the wisdom of the mean as the ideal, as espoused in *The Nicomachean Ethics*,[22] the Friar thus counsels Romeo to avoid the extremes of either excess ('too swift') or defect ('too slow'), and he affirms, quite contrary to the message of today's entertainment industry, 'Therefore love moderately, long love doth so' (2.6.14–15).[23] Even an ardent lover like Portia implores the need for moderation in love (*Merchant*, 3.2.111–14). The ethos of violence stands directly opposed to the ethos of moderation.

Zeffirelli does not cut but rather undercuts the gravity of the Friar's counsel in the marriage scene by having it appear 'rote' because Romeo repetitively completes the Friar's lines (2.6.12–13), as if rehearsing a lesson, and the Friar gently slaps Romeo's face to conclude this mentoring. Presumably the Friar gave similar advice to

Romeo during his courtship of Rosaline, but if he did, it fell on deaf ears, as the advice does now. Several hours later Romeo will need another admonition about immoderate love after he naively but earnestly proclaims that 'love-devouring Death' can do whatever he dares because it is enough for Romeo that he may call Juliet his (2.6.7–8). Several hours after that statement Romeo will contradict himself, as he did with his proclamations regarding Rosaline, when he attempts suicide in return for 'body's banishment' (3.3.11), even though Juliet is now his wife. Instead of 'rote' advice from the Friar in the marriage scene, in Shakespeare's text it is Romeo's earlier love of Rosaline that is proclaimed 'rote', and which is clearly distinguished as 'doting' and not true 'loving'. However, the Friar's specific term 'doting' to describe Romeo's love of Rosaline is adopted by Romeo himself later to describe the extremity of his love for Juliet – 'Doting like

---

'true birth' (2.3.20), or 'true use' (3.3.124) of God's good creations, which have been wounded through the Fall so that it is now more difficult to know and to act on what is true.

19 Novy, e.g., thinks that the Nurse 'has a more positive attitude toward sexuality' and that the Friar should have helped Juliet elope. See Novy, *Love's Argument*, p. 107. However, the Nurse argues for bigamy as if it is 'wisely done' (3.5.234); the Friar, on the other hand, reminds Romeo of how fortunately happy he is to have Juliet as his wife (3.3.128–9, 135–7), he sends Romeo to Juliet for their marital consummation (3.3.146–7), and he conscientiously plans how to keep the marriage viable, despite the reccurring obstacles (3.3.148–54, 166–72; 4.1.113–17). Shakespeare also discards the idea of disguised elopement which does appear in Brooke's poem. Juliet initiates the idea (lines 1619–22), but Romeus refutes its practicality, arguing that her father and kin would angrily pursue them, and death, not life together, would be the reward (lines 1643–86).

20 See *Paradise Lost*, Book VIII, lines 586–93, pp. 199–200.

21 See Tilley, *Proverbs*, N321: 'Nothing violent can be permanent.' Cf. also, 'Such beginning, such end' (B262).

22 See Aristotle, *The Nicomachean Ethics*, trans. H. Rackham, in The Loeb Classical Library (London and New York, 1926), II.vi.9–15, pp. 92–5.

23 See Tilley, *Proverbs*, L559: 'Love me little, love me long (No extreme will hold long).'

me' (3.3.67). Shakespeare literally cultivates the violence of Romeo's and Juliet's love by giving them more wishes, at critical junctures, and actions for death than Brooke does. Unlike Brooke's poem, for example, Romeo has an ominous dream (1.4.106–11), both lovers immediately see death as their only option if they are to be physically deprived of the other (1.5.116–17; 1.5.133–4), and in response to the decree of exile, both announce their suicide intentions, accompanied by on-stage props (rope ladder and dagger) to effect death (3.2.132–7; 3.3.102–8).[24]

The Friar's apt advice for Romeo's idea of love should not be undercut since it is surprisingly Shakespeare's detailed addition to Brooke's poem. Shakespeare has developed the importance of the Friar's role by making him Romeo's 'sin-absolver' and most trusted 'friend' (3.3.50). Critics understandably fault the Friar for his secrecy, but the desired privacy of romantic love begins in the play with Romeo's self-cultivated secrecy. The Friar's secrecy responds both to Romeo's trust and to the tense social atmosphere of distrustful fear created by the existing feud that cloaks open communication. In the poem Romeus confides his unrequited love story in his friend (Benvolio's counterpart); in the play Romeo has chosen to confide in no one but the Friar until the deeply concerned Lord Montague instigates Benvolio's role of confidant, again Shakespeare's addition. Thus, when Romeus seeks the friar's blessing for an immediate marriage, Brooke's friar raises general concerns, and even suggests a delay of a week or two (line 600), but there is no friendly lecture about Romeus's character and his central weakness as a lover. Because the film de-emphasizes what appears to be Romeo's fickleness by deleting the early discussion of Rosaline, the viewer is mystified when the Friar interjects that name and admonishes Romeo for having betrayed his vow to a former love. The film's initially vague presentation of Romeo as a lover is too amorphous for Shakespeare's specific

portrayal of Romeo's love for Rosaline and the dramatic function of that relationship.

Shakespeare, moreover, complicates Romeo's fickleness found in Brooke's poem and weds it to his paradoxical theme of thwarted intents. Shakespeare's reluctant Romeo agrees to Benvolio's advice about viewing other beauties, only in order to prove true to his first (1.1.219–28). Brooke's unrequited Romeus gives up, contemplates leaving Verona (lines 73–6), and agrees to attend the Capulet feast, believing wholeheartedly that he *should* find a new love (lines 141–50). Brooke's lover seems a more typical youth; Shakespeare's is more exceptional in his extreme fervour. Romeo intends to prove himself no heretic in love until the onslaught of raw experience – the vision of another Capulet lady more beautiful than the first – proves him false. This new love at first sight surpasses the former, and Romeo's ardour is also sparked by mutuality – 'Her I love now / Doth grace for grace and love for love allow; / The other did not so' (2.3.85–7), lines deleted in the film. Romeo's role as a lover is even somewhat paradoxical given the play's various perspectives. Romeo is violent in the nature of his love, as the Friar would not have him be, but Romeo is not violent in his physical relationship to Juliet, as the sexual stance of men like Sampson and Mercutio would have him be, that is, thrusting women to the wall (1.1.14–16) or being 'rough with love' (1.4.27).

Zeffirelli undermines Romeo's role within the play's larger tragic patterns by deleting

---

[24] Cf. Brooke, line 325, which Shakespeare intensifies through contractual imagery and debt/death wordplay for Romeo; lines 355–8, in which Juliet has no death announcement, only woe; lines 1159–92, in which Juliet swoons and merely wishes for death but does not plan how to effect it; and lines 1291–352, in which Romeus has 'raging fits' (line 1349) and wishes for death but does not make any attempt to take his life. For Shakespeare's originality in his use of the rope ladder, see my essay, 'Nashe as "Monarch of Witt" and Shakespeare's *Romeo and Juliet*', *Texas Studies in Literature and Language*, 37 (1995), 314–43; pp. 323–5.

Romeo's *reasons* for why he chooses as he does, in the Rosaline affair, in his decision to fight Tybalt, and in his despair over banishment, to say nothing of his use of the Apothecary and his duel with Paris, whole episodes omitted in the film. In his duels Romeo nobly intends not to fight either Tybalt or the yet unidentified Paris, but when he finds himself sufficiently provoked, his good intents in both cases are overwhelmed by 'fury' (3.1.115; 5.3.63). Omitting the opening Rosaline and the closing duel episodes, Zeffirelli delimits the counter perspectives on Romeo as a lover afforded by these episodes that Shakespeare explicitly developed in his alteration of Brooke's narrative.[25] Therefore, as with so many of Shakespeare's contrastive parallels in this play, both similarity and dissimilarity are conjoined in a single character role or episode for the effect of paradox. Romeo's love for Rosaline serves as both contrast and parallel to his love for Juliet. Unlike his love for Rosaline, Romeo's love for Juliet will prove an 'ever fixèd mark' (Sonnet 116, line 5), but like his former love, this love will also exhibit what Elizabethans would recognize as the inherent danger of violence, fuelled now by exacerbating circumstances.

To conclude the initial on-stage encounter between Romeo and the Friar, Zeffirelli directs the Friar's intent gaze to a church crucifix immediately after the Friar responds to Romeo's complaint that he had been earlier advised to bury his love for Rosaline: 'Not in a grave, / To lay one in, another out to have' (2.3.83–4). The near 'resurrection' imagery of the lines, together with the crucifix, symbolizing martyred love, seems to prompt the Friar's resolution to assist his 'pupil', whom he still sees as a 'young waverer' (2.3.82, 89): 'In one respect I'll thy assistant be: / For this alliance may so happy prove / To turn your households' rancour to pure love' (2.3.90–2). From an Elizabethan perspective, Zeffirelli's visual symbolism could be even more provocative than the film itself suggests. Through the image of the crucifix as the symbol of divine

love's triumph over human sin through death, Elizabethans might perceive more than simply the love of the heirs overcoming the hate of their parents. In his Easter sonnet, no less a poet than Edmund Spenser exhorted his bride-to-be that their human love should be modelled ideally on divine love as demonstrated on Calvary: 'So let us love, deare love, lyke as we ought: / Love is the lesson which the Lord us taught'.[26] Closing this scene with Shakespeare's lines, Zeffirelli has Romeo laugh goodnaturedly at the Friar's own physical stumble that suggests he is a well-meaning bungler unable to follow his own advice against the downfall of haste as he hurries after the eager Romeo: 'Wisely and slow, they stumble that run fast' (2.3.93–4). The viewer also smiles as the Friar figuratively 'stumbles' on his own advice through his hasty performance of a clandestine marriage.

Even though the Friar is the most knowledgeable character in the play, he resembles all the others in being limited by tragic ignorance, being ignorant about the Paris match and the miscarriage of his letter to Mantua until late disclosure fosters desperate measures. Unlike the Friar and Romeo, Juliet knows about the potential obstacle of Paris, but overwhelmed by love for Romeo, Juliet has forgotten Paris, along with her dutiful promise to her mother (1.3.98–100), just as quickly and thoroughly as Romeo declares he has forgotten Rosaline's

---

[25] Benvolio seems romantically inclined because, like Romeo, he too is up early seeking privacy, and he speaks knowingly about how to cure unrequited love (see 1.1.109–21, 1.1.156–229, and 2.2.31–2). For a stimulating discussion of Paris as a contrast to Romeo in terms of Elizabethan staging of their scene together, see Alan C. Dessen, 'Much Virtue in As: Elizabethan Stage Locales and Modern Interpretation', in *Shakespeare and the Sense of Performance: Essays in the Tradition of Performance Criticism in Honor of Bernard Beckerman*, ed. Marvin and Ruth Thompson (Newark, London, and Toronto, 1989), pp. 132–8; pp. 135–8.

[26] See Spenser, *Amoretti*, in *Spencer: Poetical Works*, ed. J. C. Smith and E. de Selincourt (1912; rpt. London, New York, and Toronto, 1966), Sonnet 68, lines 13–14, p. 573.

name (2.3.46). Wedding haste ironically frames the play's opening and ending, and the Friar wishes he knew not why the wedding match with Paris should be 'slowed' when he learns of it (4.1.16). On the other hand, the Friar also recognizes love's sinful temptation for such a passionate Romeo (2.3.44), and witnessing the mutual ardour of Romeo and Juliet, he hastens to have 'Holy Church incorporate two in one' (2.6.37). The virtuously well-intentioned but humanly fallible Friar ironically becomes his own paradoxical instance of 'virtue misapplied', using the risky, although honourable, means of marrying strong-willed, young lovers to justify the virtuous end of familial reconciliation.

Although the actors, Leonard Whiting and Milo O'Shea, charm the audience with their endearing portrayal of the relationship between Romeo and the Friar, Zeffirelli's own negative view of the Friar reveals much about why he adapts Shakespeare's text as he does for the Friar's entrance and exit:

The character of Friar Laurence disintegrates and rightly so. He is introduced in the beginning as a man who believes in drugs and spells and magic. He thinks the answer to the problems of life lies in these kinds of solutions. He is a man haunted by a wrong idea ... He's punished at the end because the poison he has given to Juliet hits him like a boomerang ... In fact, he makes one mistake after another. He should have taken the two children to the families, to the Prince, and said, 'This is it. I'll marry them in public in the square.' Everything would have been all right ... The tragedy is these poor kids who believed so genuinely.[27]

If everything had turned out 'all right', the play would be a comedy and not a tragedy. The Friar's goal of Verona's peace is achieved, not comedically, as he intended, but tragically: 'A greater power than we can contradict / Hath thwarted our intents' (5.3.153–4). Earlier the Friar spoke more wisely than he knew when he reprimanded the Capulets regarding Juliet's supposed death: 'The heavens do low'r upon you for some ill' (4.5.94). The Prince also supports the interpretation of 'this work of heaven'

(5.3.261) in his final condemnation of the feuding patriarchs: 'See what a scourge is laid upon your hate, / That heaven finds means to kill your joys with love!' (5.3.292–3). To make the Friar the tragedy's scapegoat is a tempting but unfair solution given Shakespeare's widespread distribution of grief and guilt at the end, the Prince's explicit exoneration of the Friar (5.3.270–1), and the paradoxical interplay of heavenly fate and human free will.[28] Such a condemnatory view also overlooks Shakespeare's greater development of Romeo's need for the good counsel of wisdom, as voiced by the Friar, as well as Shakespeare's emphasis on the very human difficulty of correlating wisdom with action, regardless of one's age.

Indeed, Shakespeare took pains to create a better Friar, although still humanly fallible, than the one he found in Brooke's poem. Evans observes that 'critical reaction to Friar Lawrence ranges from the uneasily ambiguous to the downright hostile'; Brian Gibbons argues that 'the Friar's mode of expression is formulaic and sententious, uncreatively dependent on the stereotypes of proverb lore ...'[29] Although Shakespeare's Friar is less circumspect than Brooke's in hastily agreeing to wed the lovers, the idea of familial reconciliation is wholly his, not originally Juliet's, as is the case in Brooke (lines 427–8); it is for this special reason he decides to marry the lovers, not partly because Romeo has worn him down with persistence, as is the case in Brooke's poem (line 607).[30]

---

27 See Zeffirelli, quoted in *Staging Shakespeare: Seminars on Production Problems*, ed. Glenn Loney (New York and London, 1990), pp. 264–5.
28 For a succinct explanation of fortune as God's agent, exemplified in Boethius' *De Consolatione Philosophiae*, see Cedric Watts, *Romeo and Juliet*, Twayne's New Critical Introductions to Shakespeare (Boston, 1991), pp. 50–5.
29 See Evans, p. 23; cf. 23–5. See Gibbons, *Romeo and Juliet*, p. 66; cf. 75–6.
30 Brooke's friar is also partly won by the idea that the marriage might appease the feud (lines 608–10), but because that idea originates with Juliet, it seems likely that Romeus used this argument to persuade the friar.

Although Shakespeare's Friar is no less secretive than Brooke's, he is unlike Brooke's friar in morally counselling Romeo as a 'lover' *during* his infatuation with Rosaline, *before* his marriage to Juliet, and *before* (not merely after, as in the film) Romeo's first attempted suicide. He also prudently determines that Romeo's man, Balthasar, should be their letter carrier for communication during the Mantuan exile (3.3.169–71), whereas Brooke's friar neglects any such arrangement so that Romeus sends his man as a spy to Verona.[31] Zeffirelli omits the Friar's foresight regarding this communicative strategy and instead falls back on simple bad luck in his presentation of Balthasar's galloping past the ambling Friar John with the latest news about Juliet.

Shakespeare, on the other hand, develops the sense of 'a greater power' (5.3.153) guiding this tragedy in how he handles such seemingly insignificant details, incorporating Balthasar into the poignant pattern of good intents that backfire through haste and ignorance. When Balthasar sees Juliet's burial, he is so moved that he neglects his duty to visit the Friar and be the designated emissary of news to Romeo, instead riding posthaste to Mantua. Romeo has the presence of mind to ask Balthasar for letters from the Friar, and he does so twice, before and after the news of Juliet's 'death'. Balthasar's simple denial (5.1.32) masks his curious reticence about why he bears no letters, a tragic reticence that parallels so many other similar instances in this play when silence, forgoing 'true shrift' (1.1.150), proves fatal. Without Balthasar as go-between, the Friar is forced to rely on a messenger from his own order. Of all the possible accidents that could befall such a mission, it is probably no coincidence that Shakespeare effects its failure by thwarting good intents, those of Friar John as well as those of Verona's searchers (5.1.5–12). Compounding the tragic ironies for the knowing audience, Shakespeare has his Friar conscientiously take time to write again to Romeo with the truth about Juliet, even though he knows Juliet will

awake 'within this three hours' (5.3.24–30). Perhaps as a result, the Friar finds himself imploring St Francis for speed as he stumbles ominously in the graveyard (5.3.121–2), arriving in time for Juliet's awakening but, alas, a 'full half an hour' (5.3.130) after Romeo's hasty appearance.

Thus, Shakespeare makes his Friar Lawrence much less self-interested and more expressly philosophical and providentialist, an Aristotelian advocate of the mean as the ideal and a Boethian advocate of the seeming paradox of divine providence and human will.[32] Although in the final scene both Shakespeare's and Brooke's friars succumb to fear for themselves, lacking the 'strength of will' (4.1.72) of the young lovers, Shakespeare's Friar will humbly admit the ambivalence of his role, intending to 'impeach and purge' himself (5.3.226), offering his own life to the law 'if ought in this / Miscarried by [his] fault' (5.3.266–7). Brooke's friar, however, 'with bold assured voyce' will insist on his thoroughgoing innocence (lines 2825–69). Zeffirelli has the Friar exit the film with an increasingly fearful repetition of 'I dare no longer stay' (5.3.159). He deletes the Friar's final appearance and lengthy speech, evenhandedly complementing his decision to delete all of the Friar's opening speech. But as Bertrand Evans argues, that final speech is essential for the characters on stage.[33] Zeffirelli deprives his

---

On the other hand, the idea could have occurred independently to the friar; Brooke's phrasing is ambiguous.

[31] See Brooke, lines 2526–34. For a fuller analysis of Balthasar's role as well as Shakespeare's paradoxical use of dreams and innovative use of fairy, see my essay, 'No "Vain Fantasy": Shakespeare's Refashioning of Nashe for Dreams and Queen Mab', in *Shakespeare's 'Romeo and Juliet': Texts, Contexts, and Interpretation*, ed. Jay L. Halio (Newark, Delaware, 1995), pp. 42–82.

[32] Brooke's friar is selfishly concerned about his personal safety and reputation (see lines 2045–60, 2833–58), whereas Shakespeare's Friar never articulates a concern for himself until he panics in the vault. Shakespeare gives to Juliet the logical anxiety that perhaps the Friar has ulterior motives, but she, like the Prince, exonerates him as having been 'tried a holy man' (4.3.24–9).

actors of an enlightened, on-stage catharsis as well as acting opportunities for body language that would register their newfound realizations of the unwitting roles they have played in this tragedy.

Thus, as vital as he is to the play's plot, Friar Lawrence is equally important philosophically for Romeo's choices between the play's competing definitions of manhood. Shakespeare also uses the idea of manhood to open the play through his invention of the machismo banter (radically trimmed in the film) and brawl between the servingmen and masters as an introduction to the 'ancient quarrel' set 'new abroach' (1.1.95) that figuratively poisons Verona. The comic-tragic matrix of this opening revolves around what it means to be a 'man', what a man can and cannot endure. The philosophical definitions of manhood and gender roles are Shakespeare's significant developments of Brooke's emphasis on 'manly reason' (line 1355) as the source of 'wisdom in adversitie' (line 1394), which appears in the friar's criticism of Romeus as a 'frantike man' (line 1292) for calling on 'spedy death' (line 1297) in response to the Prince's decree of banishment.[34] Shakespeare's Friar, seconded by the voice of the Prince, defines manly strength as grace and graciousness, the strength of a *gentle*man who exhibits the self-control of right reason in avoiding wilful violence, in tempering courage with wisdom, and in loving properly, himself as well as others. Of the featured young men, only Benvolio, whose name means 'good will', is left alive at the play's conclusion.

Competing with this philosophy is that of 'rude will', the physical and violent view of manliness more frequently practised in Verona. This philosophy perpetuates the fatal feud, and it may be demonstrated through a man's 'naked weapon' (1.1.29), either sword or phallus, a view self-righteously embraced by Sampson, Gregory, Tybalt, Mercutio, and finally even Paris. I have discussed elsewhere the play's three fight scenes that formulate the semiotics of violence, which structurally signal the begin-

ning, midpoint, and end of the play, as well as how Shakespeare develops tragic effects through his characterization of Tybalt, Mercutio, Benvolio, Paris, and Romeo in relation to contemporary views of the duello.[35] Zeffirelli changes Shakespeare's text by turning the duel between Mercutio and Tybalt into a game, and such a change renders Romeo all the more a fool for gravely intervening in what the entire crowd of onlookers perceives to be mere sword*play*. Zeffirelli also sentimentalizes Tybalt who appears dismayed over the sight of Mercutio's blood on his rapier, hardly a man known for his hatred of 'peace' (1.1.61) and his 'wilful choler' (1.5.88). Instead of following Shakespeare's implicit stage direction for the return of a 'furious' Tybalt (3.1.112) who intends to skewer the man he originally targeted, Zeffirelli reverses this direction and has an enraged Romeo pursue a sombrely retreating Tybalt.

What I would like to focus on here is again the significance of Zeffirelli's deletion of Romeo's reasons (3.1.100–6) for abandoning peaceful love for warlike hate, in particular Romeo's self-indictment: 'O sweet Juliet, / Thy beauty hath made me effeminate, / And in my temper softened valour's steel!' Shakespeare has radically changed this duel from the general brawl in Brooke's poem, and his addition of Romeo's self-conviction of effeminacy cultivates greater tragic irony if the nuances of this term and the imagery of tempering steel are contextualized philosophically. If Romeo's lament is taken at face value, then he shamefully regrets how Juliet's beauty has weakened his manly temper, which is naturally steel-like in valour. Now Romeo adopts Mercutio's battle-of-the sexes rhetoric (see, e.g., 1.4.27–8; 2.1.23–

---

[33] See Evans, 'The Brevity of Friar Lawrence', *PMLA*, 65 (1950), 841–65; p. 842.

[34] Cf. Brooke, lines 1352–8, with Shakespeare's 3.3.108–11.

[35] See '"Myself Condemnèd and Myself Excus'd": Tragic Effects in *Romeo and Juliet*', *Studies in Philology*, vol. 88 (1991), 345–62; pp. 351–2, 361–2; '"Draw, if you be men"', pp. 163–89; pp. 178–89.

9; 2.4.13–15) to see his romantic love as weakness, not strength; it has softened his valour that is symbolized by his steel sword, which until now has remained sheathed. Therefore, Romeo's figure of speech likens his own mistemperament to the mistempering of a sword blade which should become tempered (hardened) by being dipped in icy water. Zeffirelli, however, over-romanticizes Romeo by having him appear unweaponed, a strange choice given Benvolio's belief that Romeo will dare to answer Tybalt's challenge (2.4.11–12) and given the self-consciousness of the young men who wish to be seen as men, not boys, bearing rapiers as social signifiers.

Romeo's metaphor, however, is most appropriate for this tragedy; it not only recalls the fatherly concern over Romeo's literal mistemperament (1.1.122–46; 2.3.33–40; 3.3.114–15), but also the figuratively 'mistempered weapons' the Prince initially denounced as 'neighbour-stainèd steel' and 'cankered' because his 'rebellious subjects' have behaved like 'beasts' (1.1.72–86). The film omits the Prince's line about bestiality, but Escalus (whose name derives from 'scala' or 'scale', suggesting the ideas of hierarchy and justice) here anticipates the Friar's philosophy and his disapproval of Romeo's misuse of his nature. In his final hour Romeo, maddened with desperation, will painfully resort to bestial imagery by describing 'the time' and his 'intents' as 'savage-wild' (5.3.37–9), lines also cut in the film. At the vault the Friar will discover Paris' and Romeo's 'discoloured' swords, now 'masterless and gory' (5.3.143–4). Juliet will finally command Romeo's dagger to 'rust' in her bosom, its new 'sheath', so that her father finds 'this dagger his mistane' because its 'house' is properly on Montague's back and not 'mis-sheathed' in Juliet (5.3.170, 203–5). If weapons are not to be 'mistempered', their masters must have mastery over themselves.

Romeo takes an ironically tragic view of his effeminacy when he sees his manhood in light of the violent ethos contrary to that espoused by the Friar. From the Friar's perspective, Romeo's peaceful offers of conciliatory love to Tybalt would be viewed not as evidence of 'vile submission' (3.1.66) or 'effeminate' in the negative sense of 'weak', but rather 'effeminate' in the positive sense of 'tenderhearted, compassionate'.[36] The Friar would approve Romeo's strength to turn the other cheek in his patient endurance of Tybalt's slander, something Sampson and Gregory of the house of Capulet would never be strong enough to do since men of such mind refuse to 'carry coals' (1.1.1), that is, forbear insults, as the play's opening line comically, but also ominously, forewarns. For the Friar well-managed or wise love is strength, not weakness, and it is the foundation of Christian faith, whether Catholic or Protestant, because God is love (1 John 4.8, 16). The Friar indicates this belief when he counsels his 'young waverer' that 'women may fall, when there's no strength in men' (2.3.80). He does not refer here to the brute physical strength of men, which is what Sampson has in mind when he misuses Scripture (1 Peter 3.7) for his mistreatment of women as 'the weaker vessels' (1.1.14), despite the Bible's exhortation for men to honour women.[37] The Friar refers rather to the moral strength of men in proving themselves true lovers. Were Romeo to have persisted in 'effeminate' love, rather than converting to 'fire-eyed fury' (3.1.115), the law would have accomplished Tybalt's death and Romeo would not be banished.

The idea of Romeo's effeminacy in the negative sense of unmanly weakness, however, resurrects itself when Romeo violently confronts the Prince's decree, so that the Friar concludes his homily: 'But like a mishavèd and

---

[36] For meanings presented herein, see the OED, 'effeminate', adj., 1a, 1b, 1c, and 3.

[37] See 1 Peter 3.7, the passage and its gloss. The gloss reads: 'Man oght to loue his wife, because they lead their life together, also for that she is the weaker vessel, but chiefly because that God hathe made them as it were felowe heires together of life euerlasting.'

sullen wench, / Thou pouts upon thy fortune and thy love: / Take heed, take heed, for such die miserable' (3.3.143–5). Zeffirelli begins this scene almost with the Nurse's entrance, deleting the important opening 70 lines in which the Friar delivers the news and attempts to reason against Romeo's 'rude unthankfulness' (3.3.24) for exile instead of death. Romeo reasons that Juliet is 'heaven' (3.3.29); thus, physical separation from her, despite their souls' union, is 'hell' (3.3.18). John Donne's love poem for his wife, *A Valediction Forbidding Mourning*, might have comforted Romeo to endure the lover's pain of physical separation. Instead, the 'armour' the Friar offers is 'adversity's sweet milk, philosophy' (3.3.54–5). But Romeo responds, 'Hang up philosophy' (3.3.57), like disused armour, finding rational disputation meaningless in the face of heartfelt pain: 'Thou canst not speak of that thou dost not feel' (3.3.64). Romeo scores a hit with an observation native to other Shakespearian characters, such as Benedick: 'Well, everyone can master a grief but he that has it' (*Much Ado*, 3.2.26–7). However, some members of an Elizabethan audience would recognize the significance of an important Boethian parallel in the Friar's specific metaphor for philosophy ('sweet milk') and in the basically Boethian situation of a philosophical advocate attempting to comfort a man made distraught by 'the slings and arrows of outrageous fortune' (*Hamlet*, 3.1.60). Boethius' metaphor for philosophy is 'milke' or a restorative drink that proves a sovereign but paradoxical comfort; philosophy may be bitter when first tasted but becomes sweet when inwardly received.[38] Shakespeare's coupling of masculine ('armour') and feminine ('sweet milk') images aptly follows Boethius' presentation of philosophy as a good lady whose refreshments and 'weapons' cure the wounds of that fickle female, the goddess Fortuna.[39] However, Shakespeare's adapted allusion to Boethius presents a paradox of propriety because its obvious situational appropriateness is also invested with tragic irony. Unlike the wiser Boethius who bemoans his 'bannishment', a

similarly banished but dissimilarly effeminate Romeo passionately refuses here to consider philosophically his 'estate' (3.3.63) and to imbibe wisdom, not standing as a man but remaining prostrate 'on the ground, with his own tears made drunk' (3.3.83), precisely in his 'mistress' case' (3.3.84).[40]

The Friar, however, finally wins this debate with his 'good counsel' (3.3.160), but not before Romeo amazes him with a desperate attempt to stab himself: 'I thought thy disposition better tempered' (3.3.115). Romeo's attempt is forestalled, ironically overmastered by a woman's, indeed, a Nurse's, intervention, according to the stage direction in the First Quarto. Zeffirelli, on the other hand, has the Friar disarm Romeo. When Romeo railed earlier against his life, he wondered why the

38 See *Queen Elizabeth's Englishings of Boethius, 'De Consolatione Philosophiae'* ..., ed. Caroline Pemberton (London, 1899), Book I, Prose II, line 3, p. 5; Book II, Prose I, lines 18–20, p. 20; Book III, Prose I, lines 3–13, p. 43. Cf. Geoffrey Chaucer, *Boece*, in *The Works of Geoffrey Chaucer*, ed. F. N. Robinson (2nd edn, Boston, 1957), line 6, p. 322; lines 36–40, p. 329; lines 25–29, p. 341. For the Latin, see Anicius Manlius Severinus Boethius, *De Consolatione Philosophiae*, ed. Georgius D. Smith (New York, 1976), line 3, p. 6; lines 18–20, p. 28; lines 12–14, p. 60. Boethius' text was popular in medieval-Renaissance England, surviving in a significant number of manuscripts and translated by two monarchs, Alfred the Great and Elizabeth I, as well as by Geoffrey Chaucer.

39 See Queen Elizabeth, *Englishings of Boethius*, Book I, Prose II, lines 3–5, p. 5. Cf. Chaucer, *Boece*, 'melk' and 'armures', lines 5–11, p. 322; Boethius, *Philosophiae*, 'lacte' and 'arma', lines 3–6, p. 6. The feminine image of philosophy as 'milk' appears to recall the etymological meaning of 'feminine' as 'woman, properly "the suckling one", or "the sucked one"'. See *The Oxford Dictionary of English Etymology*, ed. C. T. Onions, G. W. S. Friedrichsen, and R. W. Burchfield (Oxford and New York, 1966), 'feminine', p. 350.

40 For 'bannishment', see Queen Elizabeth, *Englishings of Boethius*, Book II, Prose IV, line 53, p. 28; for disputation about one's 'estate', see Book II, Prose IV, line 36, p. 28. Cf. Chaucer, *Boece*, 'exil', line 108, p. 333; 'estat', line 75, p. 333; Boethius, *Philosophiae*, 'exsilium', line 56, p. 40; 'status', line 38, p. 39.

Friar had not provided for him 'poison mixed' or 'sharp-ground knife', some 'sudden mean of death, though ne'er so mean' (3.3.44–5), but in the Capulet vault both mean means are provided by Romeo, the poison intentionally, the dagger unintentionally. Romeo's suicidal attempt midpoint in the play is Shakespeare's addition to Brooke's poem, and it provokes the Friar's sternest lecture on Romeo's manhood and his misuse of it: 'Art thou a man? thy form cries out thou art; / Thy tears are womanish, thy wild acts denote / The unreasonable fury of a beast' (3.3.109–12). For this scene Zeffirelli keeps the most straightforward passages and most of the plot information.[41] He excises, however, the metaphorical comparisons of Romeo to an 'unseemly woman in a seeming man, / And ill-seeming beast in seeming both', a false usurer, a skilless soldier, and a misbehaved wench, all of which the Friar uses to illustrate Romeo's digression from 'the valour of a man' (3.3.127) because he misuses his 'wit' or reason (meant to guide his manly shape and love) for destroying his life and '[his] lady that lives in [his] life' (3.3.117). To Romeo applies Hamlet's insight, 'And reason panders will' (*Hamlet* 3.4.78).

The culminating comparison of Romeo to a misbehaved wench, however, goes beyond his womanish tears to the idea of effeminacy as wilful self-indulgence, and this nuance recalls the Friar's initial caveat about the dominance of rude will as deadly. Shakespeare will later develop this nuance of being effeminate in a most striking juxtaposition of male form and womanish behaviour in his characterization of a brave but nonetheless effeminate Hotspur. Hotspur, that man's man who lives for martial honour, is at least twice presented as womanish in his wilful lack of self-government. This might surprise a modern audience, but Elizabethans would be familiar with the philosophy underlying such an association. As the Friar reprimands Romeo (3.3.52, 61), so also Northumberland scolds his son for listening to no one but himself: 'Why, what a wasp-stung and impatient fool / Art thou to break into this woman's mood, / Tying thine ear to no tongue but thine own!' (*1 Henry IV*, 3.234–6). Hence, Worcester's incisive schooling of Hotspur for being too 'wilful blame' (3.1.173) is juxtaposed with the entrance of the ladies and Glendower's description of his daughter's 'peevish, self-willed harlotry' (3.1.194), which like Hotspur's, is resistant to good 'persuasion' (3.1.195).

Juxtaposing male with female behaviour also characterizes Romeo's situation in two ways: (1) the Nurse reports that Romeo is behaving like Juliet (3.3.84–90), and (2) for the Friar's schooling of Romeo, Shakespeare changes Brooke's poem (cf. lines 1277–84) and keeps the Nurse present to play the man by urging Romeo to measure up, thereby serving paradoxically as a behavioural contrast to an effeminate Romeo. Like the lovers, Glendower's daughter is 'desperate' over her husband's departure, and the husband, like Romeo, is advised to set an example of strength for his wife or 'then will she run mad' (3.1.207). Even Lady Percy teases her devilishly 'humorous' (3.1.227) Hotspur who complains he 'cannot choose' (3.1.144): 'you are altogether governed by humours' (3.1.230), although his capriciousness is not due to romantic love. Lovers, however, are notoriously humorous as Mercutio's conjuring asserts, 'Romeo! humours! madman! passion! lover!' (2.1.7). Despite Henry IV's initial view of Hal as 'effeminate' (*Richard II* 5.3.10), Hal will prove more manly than Hotspur in his ability to rule 'all humours' (2.5.93–6), which is the witty point of his juxtaposed parodies of Francis (2.5.33–81) and Hotspur (2.5.99–109), both of whom are overruled by their weaknesses. Hotspur's bravery is genuine, although misguided by 'ill-weaved ambition' (5.4.87), so that his valour is not criticized but rather his

---

[41] The film keeps lines 108–11 plus the first half of line 114 ('Thou hast amazed me'), but it omits the subsequent 21 lines plus lines 143–5, resuming with the last half of line 135 through line 142 and keeping lines 146–58.

lack of rational self-discipline that comprises moral manly strength. Hotspur foolishly asserts: '... for I will ease my heart, / Although it be with hazard of my head' (1.3.125–6). If Romeo is to 'stand' and 'be a man; / For Juliet's sake' (3.3.88–9), he will have to rise above rude will and not make a hazard of his head in order to ease his heart, although we have great sympathy for the play's aborted music of ' "Heart's ease" ' (4.5.100–4).

In accord with the play's paradoxical perspectives, the cross-gendering of an effeminate man is matched on occasion with its opposite, the manly woman. Given the philosophy of Elizabethan patriarchy, Romeo bears a greater responsibility for wise government of the spousal relationship. However, in several instances Juliet appears less effeminate than Romeo. Juliet, unlike Romeo, wisely recognizes that their contract is too sudden, like the stormy violence of lightning, and that the bud of their love needs the blessing of time for ripening; Juliet, however, does not enact this wisdom, returning moments later to propose marriage (2.2.116–22, 143–8). Unlike Romeo, Juliet comforts herself regarding Romeo's slaying of Tybalt, rationally calming her rage, after she is provoked by the Nurse's 'slander' against her husband (3.2.90–107). However, she too would commit suicide, ironically with the instrument originally intended for love and life (the rope ladder), if the Nurse did not promise to bring Romeo to her that night (3.2.132–41), and her deadly intent, deleted by Zeffirelli, parallels Romeo's more actively violent love in the next scene which the film does show. In her soliloquy before drinking the Friar's potion (a speech omitted in the film), Juliet's manlike valour is underscored in her rational deliberation about this act and its possible consequences (4.3.24–54), unlike her passionate proclamations in the Friar's cell when she was desperate with near despair (4.1.77–86). The Friar cautioned her then that she would have to be very daring to enact this 'remedy' (4.1.76) which would deliver her

from the shame of bigamy if no 'womanish fear, / Abate [her] valour in the acting it' (4.1.119–20). Deliver her it would if Romeo had not arrived a half hour too soon. Juliet's courage to risk awakening in her family's tomb is emphasized by contrast with the fear of a man, Paris' page, who is 'almost afraid' simply to 'stand alone' in the dark churchyard (5.3. 10–11). 'Love' does give Juliet 'strength' to conquer fear (4.1.125). But despite her initiatives, Juliet will end by following the example of suicide set for her by her spouse, tragically enacting the Friar's earlier 'sentence': 'Women may fall, when there's no strength in men' (2.3.79–80).

Juliet's comedic drinking of the Friar's medicine, not 'poison' as Zeffirelli states, in order to live and to love her 'lord, ay husband, friend' (3.5.43) contrasts with Romeo's tragic drinking of poison in order to die and lie with her. Romeo's deadly use of poison, unlike Juliet's use of a medicinal potion, recalls through dramatic imagery the Friar's verbal imagery for the weak flower's 'medicine' and 'poison' analogous to man's 'grace' and 'rude will' (2.3.23–8). So also the Friar's life-oriented intention for using his crowbar (5.2.21) to open the tomb contrasts with Romeo's death-oriented intention for the use of his crowbar (5.3.22). But 'death's the end of all' (3.3.92) one's earthly hopes and chances. The very act of suicide becomes a paradoxical performance of strength and weakness, love and hate. The lovers demonstrate the strength of will to overcome the basic instinct for self-preservation, committing an act of 'hate' of the self (3.3.118) for 'love' of the other (5.3.293); they also evince weakness of will in order to escape 'world-wearied flesh' (5.3.112) rather than 'forbear, / And let mischance be slave to patience' (5.3.220–1). Shakespeare's contrastive parallels in dramatic actions and stage props reminds us of the Friar's philosophical emphasis on the difficult duel between grace and rude will within the paradox of human nature, that marriage of 'heaven' (soul) and 'earth' (body) (3.3.120) so intricately bonded that virtue can stumble and vice rise depending on one's use or abuse of that complex nature.

Zeffirelli's omissions streamline the play in order to idealize and idolize the romantic lovers and to create a relevant youth movie for the sixties by highlighting the theme of the generation gap, and by emphasizing the play's emotional, at the expense of its intellectual, power. If the blind Gloucester's line about worldly perception, 'I see it feelingly' (*Lear, History*, 20, 144; *Tragedy*, 4.5.145), might be figuratively applied to the purpose of Shakespearian tragedy, we would have to acknowledge the poignant interplay of both 'seeing' and 'feeling'. Zeffirelli's substantive changes enlarge what we 'see' in a visual sense, but diminish it in a perceptual sense. Should one element be sacrificed at the expense of the other? The hybridity of Shakespeare's text poses a greater challenge for response, one that is still unresolved for the play's vigorous afterlife in the vaults of literary criticism. Critics no longer debate whether or not the play is a tragedy, but rather what kind of tragedy is it, how does it achieve its effects, and what is the measure of its success. Over half the play's criticism focuses on the problem of tragic responsibility, a persistent issue that perhaps will always rankle for those who wrestle with it. A comparative analysis of some of Zeffirelli's omissions in light of Shakespeare's commissions illuminates part of this problem as well as what is lost, despite the technological gains, in the process of translating the 'brawling love' and 'loving hate' (1.1.167) of this paradoxical tragedy, which even concludes with the paradoxical image of an irradiation of gloom – a morning sun that mournfully sheds dark light.

'LAWFUL DEED': CONSUMMATION, CUSTOM, AND LAW IN *ALL'S WELL THAT ENDS WELL*

SUBHA MUKHERJI

Having wed Helena at the king of Rossillion's behest, Bertram, the king's ward, refuses to bed her and flies to Italy with her dower, leaving a conditional letter for her: 'When thou canst get the ring upon my finger, which never shall come off, and show me a child begotten of thy body that I am father to, then call me husband; but in such a "then" I write a "never"' (*All's Well That Ends Well*, 3.2.57–60).[1]

Bertram's marriage, overseen by king and priest, counts as a solemnized *de praesenti* union for all practical purposes. And as Henry Swinburne confirms in his *Treatise of Spousals*, 'Spousals *de praesenti*, though not consummate, be in truth and substance very Matrimony, and therefore perpetually indissoluble.' This treatise, written around 1600 but published in 1686, is the only systematic exposition of marriage laws and the first handbook of canon law to be written in England.[2] According to Swinburne, the use of long absence as a legal means for escape applied only to *de futuro* spousals.[3]

What, then, is Bertram resisting by refusing to sleep with Helena? What is the status of his apparently impossible condition? This moment in the action has been interpreted by critics as the transformation of a legal possibility into a 'fairy-tale' one, Bertram's stipulation being read as a purely fantastic setting of tasks in the romance mode.[4] But such readings fail to account for Helena's meeting of his terms as though they were an actual legal impediment, and her final securing of him in what is, effectively, a court of law. Bertram's instinctive

belief that 'not bed[ding] her' somehow counteracts the effects of 'wed[ding] her' (3.2.21–2) does not stem simply from his own wrong-headedness, but from factors actually present in contemporary English society.

My point of entry into the play's engagement with law will be marital consummation as it figures in Bertram's conduct and Helena's response. I will interpret the concept of consummation in terms of its contrasting roles in Christian marriage and Christian divorce. But

---

1 Though I use the Oxford Shakespeare, I retain the traditional name for the heroine. I should like to thank Ben Griffin for assistance with references.
2 Henry Swinburne, *A Treatise of Spousals, or Matrimonial Contracts*, ed. Randolph Trumbach (London, 1985) (hereafter, *Spousals*).
3 For influential examples of the critical opinion that Bertram's resistance is a legal escape route, see M. L. Ranald, 'The Betrothals of *All's Well That Ends Well*', *Huntington Library Quarterly*, 26 (1962–3), 179–92; p. 186, and Howard Cole, *The 'All's Well' Story From Boccaccio to Shakespeare* (Urbana, 1981) (hereafter, Cole), passim. Enforcement could be a ground for nullification, but only if it was raised by a party in court; Bertram's failure to do so at the relevant moment suggests the impracticality of this provision in a situation of authority and dependence. The one technically permissible objection a ward could raise – that against disparagement – is brought up by him but not sustained. On wardship, see Joel Hurstfield, *The Queen's Wards: Wardship and Marriage under Elizabeth I* (London, 1958).
4 See Madeleine Doran, *Endeavors of Art: A Study of Form in Elizabethan Drama* (Madison, 1954), pp. 251–2, and W. W. Lawrence, *Shakespeare's Problem Comedies* (New York, 1960), pp. 32–77.

the act of sex in the social experience of marriage confounds these two functions, even as it conflates law and customary ritual. Its peculiar status in the play will be shown to hinge on its legal function as evidence. The problems of evidentiary procedure in English church courts provide an important focus for the play's treatment of marriage law. The two main forms of evidence that I will look at are the exchange of rings and pregnancy. My analysis of the ambiguities of evidence will refer to larger theoretical issues of motive and intention that are legally unresolvable but particularly conducive to exploration in drama.

In reconstructing the relevant legal history, I shall use Swinburne's treatise, which I will refer to as *Spousals*. This represents an attempt to codify as well as interpret the law, since Swinburne was dealing with an area of legislation that was not only supposed to discipline and punish but also to provide moral guidance for social and personal behaviour. *Spousals* seeks to mediate between legal theory and practice, the written word and the spoken, the spoken word and the sign, all of which constituted marriage as social practice. I shall also be drawing upon a draft fragment, preserved in Durham, which follows the completed *Treatise of Spousals* in what seems to be the authorial manuscript. Entitled 'Of the signification of divers woordes importing Matrimonye, etc.', this is, I take it, the beginning of the second part of what Swinburne originally intended to be a three-part treatise on spousals, marriage and divorces. I will refer to it henceforth as *Matrimony*.[5]

My other group of primary materials consists of surviving records of spousal litigation from contemporary church courts, mainly Durham, Chester, Norwich and Canterbury. Together, these two sets of texts provide a comprehensive picture of law as human action, and the contradictions in such action are dramatized in Shakespeare's *All's Well*.

The clue to our understanding of the nature of Bertram's conduct lies in the status of sexual consummation in popular custom, which

derived elements from the theology, rituals and attitudes surrounding marriage, and its relationship with law. Among the many factors that constituted the overall sense of the accomplishment of a marriage, consummation had a role of special interest and curious standing. Theologically, a sacramental symbolism and sanctity attached to it, as reflected in *The Book of Common Prayer*. 'For this cause shall a man ... be joined unto his wife, and they two shall be one flesh. This mystery is great.'[6]

In law, however, intercourse was not strictly a factor in the formation of marriage in sixteenth- or early seventeenth-century England. The church, which was in charge of matrimonial litigation, held, from the twelfth century onwards, that present consent, and not the sexual act, makes a valid and completed marriage.[7] This position was marked by Pope

---

5 Durham University Library, Palace Green, Mickleton and Spearman Manuscript 4, fol. 115–24. I am indebted to Sheila Doyle of the Durham University Law Library for drawing my attention to this manuscript volume.

6 *The Book of Common Prayer 1559: The Elizabethan Prayer Book*, ed. by John E. Booty (Charlottesville, 1976), p. 297. Though, by this time, both the reformers and the bishops were clear that scripture did not provide sanction for the sacramental status of marriage, its desacramentalization remained largely a matter of theological definition in England. To prevent it from being divested of dignity and solemnity in popular perception – an effect that was distinctly possible, and would threaten exactly the regularization sought by the reformers – the service was made to stress that marriage was a 'holy ordinance', and further, was coupled with the receiving of Holy Communion, at the same time as the sacramental language and claim were dropped. This was enough to preserve the sacramental sanctity of marriage for the common people, who did not pause to work out the technical distinctions of the reformers. See Eric Joseph Carlson, *Marriage and the English Reformation* (Oxford, 1994) (hereafter, Carlson), pp. 36–49.

7 On church courts, see Ralph Houlbrooke, *Church Courts and the People during the English Reformation 1520–1570* (Oxford, 1979) (hereafter, Houlbrooke). For accounts focusing on marriage litigation, see Martin Ingram, *Church Courts, Sex and Marriage in England 1570–1640* (Cambridge, 1987) (hereafter, Ingram); R. H. Helmholz, *Marriage Litigation in Medieval England*

Alexander III's promulgation of consent as the basis of the institution, irrespective of either solemnization or consummation. In England, where the pre-Tridentine canon law of marriage survived the Reformation and did not change till 1753, informal or private contracts continued to have claim to legal recognition since consent was still the ultimate and sole criterion of validity. So, consummation was as irrelevant in 'law' as solemnization; hence the frequent clubbing together of the two by contemporary writers such as Swinburne as well as by legal historians in our own times.[8]

But given the inevitable confusions, uncertainties, and difficulties of proving consent, unsolemnized marriages were increasingly disapproved of by state and church. Certain 'legal effects' – property rights and benefits (*Spousals*, 15) – were made conditional upon solemnization, and Tudor and Early Stuart England floundered through the curious doubleness of a situation where validity and illicitness could coexist in the same union.[9] There was tightening pressure from both Protestant and Catholic reformers to regularize marriage, and one of its manifestations was an effort to impress on people that ecclesiastical solemnization alone made sexual union licit.[10] The denunciation of intercourse before or without the public ceremony implied, firstly, that solemnization was seen by many as being connected with, indeed, guaranteeing and sanctioning consummation. Secondly, it suggests the association of intercourse with the social acceptance of a lawful union. Even among legal thinkers, there were those who, as Swinburne writes in *Matrimony* (120-1), made a distinction between 'matrimony initiate' or 'begunne' and matrimony 'consummate', between 'true' and 'perfect' marriage. 'This word *Nuptiae*, Marriages', he writes in *Spousals*, is not necessarily used to mean solely 'the Substance and indissoluble knot of Matrimony only, but doth often signifie the Rites and Ceremonies observed at the celebration of Matrimony' (*Spousals*, 8-9). It is in terms of a society where 'rites and ceremonies' were an essential constituent of the customary view and practice of marriage that Bertram's holding out against 'the great prerogative and rite of love' (2.4.41) has to be understood.

However, though it could not normally constitute a marriage in itself, there were a few specific circumstances in which sexual consummation could have a legal function. When a spousal was contracted between infants or between minors, it could be ratified and made into an indissoluble knot by willing cohabitation after attainment of the age of consent.[11] Sexual relations could give *de futuro* spousals between adults the effect of *de praesenti* marriage; they could also turn conditional spousals into matrimony.

If custom and ritual are major contributors to Bertram's perspective, these situations where intercourse has a proof-value form the other, more distinctly legal influence. Indeed, custom itself must have been conditioned by such legal associations. The witness depositions and the personal responses in contract suits of the period communicate a sense of how the specific legal functions of copulation led to a more general and undifferentiating notion of sex as being a

---

(Cambridge, 1974) (hereafter Helmholz); and Carlson, pp. 142–180.

8 See, for example, Helmholz, p. 27; Martin Ingram, 'Spousal Litigation in the English Ecclesiastical Courts, *c.* 1350–1640' in R. B. Outhwaite, ed., *Marriage and Society: Studies in the Social History of Marriage* (London, 1981) (hereafter, Ingram, 'Spousal'), pp. 35–57; pp. 37, 45; *Spousals*, p. 14.

9 See G. E. Howard, *The History of Matrimonial Institutions chiefly in England and the United States* (Chicago, 1904), 3 vols., vol. I, p. 339. The interplay of attitudes to Claudio and Juliet's sexual involvement in *Measure for Measure* turns exactly on this duality. For an incisive exposition of this point, see A. D. Nuttall's '*Measure for Measure*: The bed-trick' in Nuttall, *The Stoic in Love* (London, 1989), pp. 41–8.

10 See James A. Brundage, *Law, Sex and Christian Society in Medieval Europe* (Chicago, 1987), pp. 551–74.

11 See *Spousals*, pp. 21, 36–41; Sir Edward Coke, *The First Institute of the Lawes of England* (London, 1628), section 104.

factor that could make an otherwise uncertain match conclusive. In a Durham suit of 1570 for restitution of conjugal rights, cohabitation figures centrally in all the depositions. Isabel Walker's witness Richard Bell, keen to stress the validity of her marriage to William Walker and, thereby, *her* claims, says that they 'dwelte in house here in Durham togither, as man and wyfe by the space of one yere, or more'. On the other hand, William's witness emphasizes the finality of Isabel's marriage to her reportedly precontracted husband Robert Stathan; he deposes that 'he hath known ... [them] ... dwell to gyther in one house as man and wyfe, as this examinate and neighbours thereabouts dyd take ytt'.[12]

A different legal channel that influenced the way consummation was viewed proceeded from the laws regarding annulment, by which divorce could be obtained by proof of non-consummation in cases of precontract, duress, consanguinity, affinity or impotence. The divorce of Lady Frances Howard from the Earl of Essex came through in 1613 when her allegation of his incompetence was confirmed by his admission that 'he could never know his said wife'.[13] The background to this law lies in the canonical tradition which associated indissolubility with the 'becoming one flesh' of married partners.[14] The question whether a man who, after his betrothal, feels a call to enter religious life was free to do so was met by Pope Alexander III with the answer that he could first marry and then leave off to become a monk if he did not follow up the marriage with carnal coupling. His premise was that the Christian prohibition against putting asunder those whom God had joined applied only to incorporated couples; his precedent, St John's turning to religion from a virginal marriage. But this contradicted the fundamental canonical assumption that consent, not coitus, is the substance – a position he himself upheld. His circumvention of this problem is described by J. T. Noonan as resembling 'a legal trick, of a lawyer's way of satisfying contradictory purposes by keeping

form and sacrificing substance, of nominally honoring the oath to marry while permitting the actual subversion of the oath.'[15]

One way of reconciling the canonical contradiction is to make, as canon law obviously did, a distinction between the model of Christian divorce, provided by St John, and the example of Christian marriage, provided by Mary and Joseph.[16] The notion that mutual consent was the essence and physical union was the substance of marriage could thus be kept from a direct conflict and be channelled into two separate legal procedures. But this separation proved all too artificial in social practice. For consummation could function both as a constituent of marriage and as a sign of it. Originally, the constitutive function came into play mostly in clandestine or disputed marriages, while the signifying role was predominant in unions accomplished through the full formalities, being, as it were, an ultimate expression of the marriage. In a court of law, however, the two were easily conflated because in both capacities, the fact of consummation was required to establish certainties, to prove a status. Thus, in a Durham case of 1587, the doubts about the reality of the solemnized marriage of Sir Thomas Gray with Lady Catherine Neville arise because they have 'not cohabited continually'. That the marriage

---

[12] James Raine, *Depositions and other Ecclesiastical Proceedings from the Courts of Durham, extending from 1311 to the Reign of Elizabeth* (London, 1845) (hereafter, Raine), pp. 218–26.

[13] See J. O. Halliwell, ed., *The Autobiography and Correspondence of Sir Simonds D'Ewes* (London, 1845), vol. 1, pp. 87–9.

[14] See James A. Coriden, *The Indissolubility Added to Christian Marriage by Consummation: A Historical Study from the End of the Patristic Period to the Death of Pope Innocent III* (Rome, 1961), pp. 7–23.

[15] J. T. Noonan, *Power to Dissolve: Lawyers and Marriages in the Courts of the Roman Curia* (Cambridge, Massachusetts, 1972), p. 80.

[16] For Swinburne's reference to the marriage of Mary and Joseph as the authority behind the notion that 'carnall knowledge' is not essential for 'perfect matrimony', see *Matrimony*, p. 120.

emerges as being viable and valid in court is due to the establishment of the fact that since a certain day they have 'nightly laid in one bed, as becometh man and wife'.[17] Anne Yate and George Johnson of Cheshire go through a very different event – a plebeian trothplight match, possibly *de futuro*, contracted through a witnessed handfast, but unsolemnized. But in the legal dispute over it in 1562, as in the previous case, the deponents confirm the marriage with reference to sexual union, and the causal relation suggested by their phrasing indicates the inseparability of consummation as sign of status and as proof of contract. Oliver Foxe asserts that they were 'reputid and taken for man and wief amonge their neighboures' 'for they did lye in one house, and nothinge betwix them but a broken wall and a paintid clothe'. Cecilia Key confirms, 'the neighboures ... did take them as man and wief, in somuche that they have laine together in bed, and so vsed them selves as man and wief'.[18] Does the importance of consummation here derive from its status as the criterion of indissolubility in the divorce paradigm? Or, from its assimilation into the formalities of making a marriage, and so its association with solemnization instead of consent? It is impossible to tell. What one can perhaps tell is that the deponents did not pause to work out such distinctions before giving testimony.

Thoughts about marriage and related legal actions covered and intertwined the issues of formation and validation of matrimony, as well as of the making and unmaking of marriage. The status of sexual union continued to be a focus of some of the dualities in marriage law, and Bertram's refusal is both a response to, and an expression of this doubleness. On the one hand, Bertram is holding out against the one formality that is left him to resist, having been rushed through the paraphernalia of 'contract' and 'ceremony'. From this point of view it is a token non-completion of the *ritual* stages of marriage in society. Marital non-cohabitation did draw considerable social attention in early

modern England, was on occasions a ground for presentment in court,[19] and could even be disallowed by court decree.[20] A Yorkshire parochial presentment of 1568 states that 'They say all is well saving that John Pennye and his wif lyveth not to geither.'[21]

But on the other hand, the resisted consummation is not, for Bertram, a mere external formality. Given that the legal validity of a marriage depended on mutual consent, he is exploiting the one remaining channel through which he can express his own consent or lack of it. Thus it comes to represent the substance of marriage, the indissolubility that it stands for in the canonical law of divorce. Here is a reconcilement of the apparently opposite standings of intercourse in the marriage and divorce paradigms that is less sophistical and more instinctive than the one offered by Alexander III. If the rationale behind granting importance to copulation is the idea that it expresses volition, the conflict is resolved. Especially in formally solemnized marriages like Bertram's, where the legally constituent elements are taken up in the self-generating momentum of ceremonies, the contract becomes more clearly an organized event than an expression of individual will; consequently, the post-legal stage of consum-

---

17 Raine, pp. 322–6.
18 Furnivall, *Child-Marriages, Divorces, and Ratifications, &c. In the Diocese of Chester, A.D. 1561–6* (London, 1897) (hereafter, Furnivall), p. 58.
19 See, for example, the 1623 case against John Cocke of Tillington and his wife, cited in P. Hair, ed., *Before the Bawdy Court: Selections from church courts and other records relating to the correction of moral offences in England, Scotland and New England, 1300–1800* (London, 1972) (hereafter, Hair), p. 107, or the Yorkshire presentment cited in n. 21 below.
20 See E. D. Stone and B. Cozens-Hardy, eds., *Norwich Consistory Court Depositions 1499–1512 and 1518–1530*, Norfolk Record Society 10 (1938) (hereafter, Stone and Cozens-Hardy), no. 90.
21 See T. M. Fallow, 'Some Elizabethan Visitations of the Churches belonging to the Peculiar of the Dean of York', *Yorkshire Archaeological Journal*, 18 (1905), 197–232.

mation becomes the clearer site of consent. 'I have wedded her, not bedded her, and sworn to make the "not" eternal', he writes to his mother, making a statement about the distinction, in his mind, between what has been achieved by legal form, and a voluntary and meaningful entry into the married state. The duality of the situation is further underlined by Bertram's language; the riddling and the cautious precision in his letters even while at one level he has committed himself – swearing 'to make the "not" eternal' – translates the sense of a lacuna written into the very language of the marriage ritual. The irony remains, of course, that Bertram's very defiance of law takes the form of an action prompted by legal instinct, neither custom nor social attitude being independent of law any more than law can function apart from these.

The transition of 'consummation' from its link with solemnization to its connection with intention is not peculiar to Bertram's psychology. Depositions from the period suggest that men and women did frequently associate the sexual act with 'consent'. The most telling example is that of Mawde Price alias Gregorie whose means of preventing her enforced and solemnized marriage to Henry Price from becoming real was to refuse to let him 'have ... his pleasure apon her', and instead, having regular sexual relations, and two children, with her precontracted husband, Randall Gregorie. This becomes the single focus of each of the depositions in this Chester case of 1562, and is clearly regarded by the witnesses as being directly related to consent. Alice Dood's phrasing actually identifies copulation and matrimonial intention; she says that Henry and Mawde did not 'cohabete voluntarie together, nor did consent together as man and wiff'. Matilda Broke's testimony reinforces this equation; 'verelie they neuer consented together'. To Henry Price himself, Mawde's resistance to sex is a sign of the non-reality of the marriage, and moves him finally to seek judicial annulment. Randall, the precontracted husband,

considers Mawde's refusal to have 'carnall dole' with Henry a sure indication of her 'not [accepting] hym as her husband'.[22]

Swinburne stresses the legal weight of 'voluntary Cohabitation' in converting child-marriages into 'true substantial Matrimony' and draws attention to the similarity of this criterion to the one that turns *de futuro* spousals into marriages. He goes on then to distinguish 'other more feeble Conjectures of kissings, ... etc.' from those that 'are evident and urgent, and equivalent to the presumption of Carnal copulation' because it is required 'that this Consent, whereby Spousals are turned into Matrimony, do appear *evidenter*, evidently' (*Spousals*, 40–1). Talking of conditional contracts, he says that if the parties know each other carnally 'before the event of the condition', they are 'deemed to ... yield their mutual Consents to Contract and Consummate pure and perfect Matrimony' (121). Swinburne, we must remember, was a legal practitioner, familiar with custom as well as legal theory. It is significant that his explicit association of consent with consummation is made problematic, if not contradicted, by his resorting to the law of presumption elsewhere. Discussing complicated conditional spousals, he prescribes the 'favourable Presumption' that 'is to be preferred in all doubtful Cases' regarding the purpose of any sexual involvement that may have followed (219). If a man bound upon oath to marry one of three sisters lies with any one of them, 'he is presumed to have made choice of her as his Wife' (221). The difficulty of ensuring that this presumption is also the truth of intention arises most clearly in the marshalling of proof. The law of evidence, for all its safeguards against getting the intention wrong, can, more than any other legal endeavour, make 'consummation' an absolute tool, disjoined from its motive. So Swinburne says, 'Spousals do become Matrimony by carnal knowledge, albeit the Man were constrained, through *fear of death*

---

[22] Furnivall, pp. 76–9.

to know the Woman' (226).[23] The process by which Bertram's condition is met in *All's Well* dramatizes the way in which the contradiction in Swinburne, which is also a contradiction in law, is produced by the peculiar demands of 'evidence'. This is paradoxical, given that the theoretical importance of sex in marriage law was based so largely on the belief that it could be, potentially, the surest proof of consent.

This is not the only way in which Bertram's instinctive 'use' of law rebounds on him. When, desperate not to let the marriage materialize, but powerless, as a ward, to prove duress, he resolves to 'End ere [he] [does] begin' (2.5.26), he is making a mental demarcation between public ritual and a private counterpart in consummation. Neither Helena nor anyone else has doubts about what law vouches to be hers (2.4.41–2; 2.5.79–82). What Bertram denies is the *relationship* that the contract is presumed to guarantee. He is reclaiming sexual union for the sphere of the personal from the sphere of legal validation. But he does not simply protest through inaction; he further makes consummation the condition for a fuller acknowledgement of the marriage. By himself positing sex as an evidence for Helena to establish the rights of love, he forfeits his rights to a personal scale of criteria. As Helena sets about to realize his condition, consummation becomes more public than ever, and more sharply distinguished from personal consent, by the very virtue of being used as proof, and hence being required 'to appear *evidenter*' in a legal space.

These reversions are the subject of the following section which will also make clear how Helena emerges as a defendant seeking to validate her marriage, while Bertram corresponds to the unenthusiastic party fumblingly attempting a sort of annulment. Seen within this structure, Bertram's preoccupation with non-consummation is entirely appropriate, and fulfils the legal expectation of a divorce suit. Helena's attainment and use of carnal union is equally appropriate to her own legal purpose. The meeting of the two 'causes' demonstrates schematically the

coming together of sign and proof, of formation and validation, and with these, of the principles of union and those of annulment in the practised legality of marriage.

The process by which Helena earns the right to be acknowledged by Bertram as his wife is quasi-legal, but by the time it is completed, it looks like a proper legal validation. That is largely because this development is crossed with another, truly legal pattern of events consisting of the interaction between Bertram and Diana, leading to an actual trial where Bertram has to defend himself against Diana's claim of marriage and her allegation of marital disacknowledgement. These legal events, of course, are instrumental to the successful accomplishment of Helena's project, and stems from the plan to use Diana to set the stage for the bed-trick. A Shakespearian creation,[24] Diana stands at the intersection of the legal and the quasi-legal structures, and represents the inextricability of the one from the other. The Bertram–Diana part of the play illuminates the nature of Helena's use of evidence by exploring the ambiguities of proof in a more clear-cut legal framework.

The relationship between Bertram's condition and its fulfilment is also one between a promise and its performance, terms and their enactment, and so, between word and deed. In contract law, a bond, the common device to secure contractual settlements, was finalized by using a 'deed' – the term describing a document under seal. By the beginning of the seventeenth century, the notion of contract had already begun to extend from its original sense of 'a transaction ... which transferred property or generated a debt' to include the modern sense

---

23 See also *Spousals*, p. 225.

24 See Joseph Jacobs, ed., *The Palace of Pleasure: Elizabethan Versions of Italian and French Novels From Boccaccio, Bandello, Cinthio, Straparola, Queen Margaret of Navarre, And Others, Done into English by William Painter* (New York, 1966) (hereafter, Painter), 'The thirty-Eigth Nouell' – Shakespeare's immediate source for the story of *All's Well*.

of a consensual pact, an exchange of promise between individuals – a meaning formerly borne by the word 'covenant'.[25] Such agreements being transient events, the 'deed' is what made them concrete and gave them legal validity.

An examination of the principle underlying this importance of the 'deed', however, reveals its origins in evidentiary problems. In medieval town courts, a contract that had not been observed could be proved by the oath of the plaintiff. This inevitably began to be felt as inadequate: the very need of proof in this matter was prompted by an awareness of the elusive and indeterminate nature of words. This is what led to law's sharp distinction between mere words on the one hand and action or deeds on the other. By 1321 it was legally prescribed that 'the only acceptable evidence of a covenant in the royal courts was a deed'.[26] In its original sense of an exchange of property, a contract had to be executed in order to be effected – there was no notion of sueing an unperformed contract. When its sense expanded, the function of performance was taken on by the act of sealing the document of contract in front of witnesses – something done, and hence a deed. From this, its original meaning in law, the word 'deed' came to be applied by transference to the product of the event – the document itself. Thus, a deed was both what made a contract in the legal sense, and what proved it. As well as being often signified by gestures such as a handclasp, it was itself a sign of the agreement.

The particular relevance of the word-deed hierarchy in marriage law is brought out through the liaison between Diana and Bertram. Persistent in his efforts at overcoming Diana's maidenly resistance, Bertram remonstrates, 'How have I sworn!' (4.2.21). Diana retaliates immediately that his oaths 'are words and poor conditions', and insists on a seal. This is not simply a metaphorical way of disputing Bertram's sincerity but a legal argument; an attempt to steer Bertram's private declarations

into a contract that can be proved later in a legal event which, as she knows and he does not, has already been planned.

The explicit use of terms from contract law in connection with professed commitments of love dramatizes an actual link between spousal and contract litigation. Actions against breach of faith that came up as part of the church courts' bulk of marriage litigation were allied in principle to common law actions for breach of contract. Besides, there actually existed a common law action for breach of promise of marriage.[27] Likewise, contract suits formed a sizeable portion of the church courts' business in the sixteenth and seventeenth centuries, and the practice of settling for cash was comparable to the common law action.[28] The law of contract, after all, is essentially the 'law of obligations', as Baker puts it, one that 'governs those expectations of good faith which arise out of particular transactions between individual persons'.[29] This is exactly the issue in many spousal cases surviving from Tudor and Stuart times. Baker goes on to explain that this type of obligation could be dealt with either in terms of 'the right to performance of the contract or of the wrong of breaking the contract and thereby causing loss'. Helena's performance and validation of a conditional contract in the shape of Bertram's letter, and Diana's sueing Bertram for denying marital obligation dramatize these two complementary processes. The demarcation of the spheres of common law and canon law, thus, is among the several polarities that the play breaks

---

25 Baker, p. 360. See also pp. 361 and 375.
26 Ibid., p. 362.
27 See S. F. C. Milsom, *Historical Foundations of the Common Law* (London, 1983), pp. 88–90 and 289.
28 Ingram, 'Spousal', p. 52. On the reciprocal influence between common law, and canon law as practised in the church courts, see R. H. Helmholz, *Canon Law and English Common Law*, Selden Society Lecture, 1982 (London, 1983), esp. pp. 15–19.
29 Baker, p. 360.

down, in representing overlapping spheres of social experience.

When Diana expresses her misgivings about the 'unsealed' nature of a verbal promise, Bertram's reply supplies the possible nature of the deed that can seal it –

> Change it, change it.
> Be not so holy-cruel . . .
> Stand no more off,
> But give thyself unto my sick desires.
>
> (4.2.32–6)

It is the act of sex, tacitly agreed upon thereafter, that Diana refers to when she talks of the need to 'token to the future our past deeds' (64). It is this, again, that Helena has in mind when she anticipates the 'lawful deed' planned for the night.

The marriage contract in Renaissance England can be seen as having consisted of a word component – the expression of present and mutual consent, and a deed component – the physical act of consummation. Like the written document in contract law, then, sexual intercourse is, potentially, what will clinch the private and unwitnessed agreement between Bertram and Diana as well as provide the evidence which Diana cynically suggests will be needed; it will draw his unsealed words into a legal 'deed' and ratify the verbal contract of espousal by performance.

The identification of the promissory and sexual components of a spousal pact with the verbal and the performative respectively, and of these, in turn, with the initial and legalizing aspects of a contract, was an element in the contemporary perception of the legality of marriage. This comes across in such court records as Matilde Price's personal response in the case of Price *v.* Price discussed earlier:[30] 'necque habuit carnalem copulam cum dicto Henrico, nec quia ex parte sua necque ratificauit hoc matrimonium re aut verbo . . .' [(she) neither had carnal copulation with the said Henry, nor on her part ratified this marriage by word or fact]. This is a case where the validation of an unsolemnized precontract and the invalidation of a solemnized marriage turn on the establishment of the fact of non-consummation in the latter; where *verba* becomes entirely secondary as the dispute in court diverts all attention to the superior ratifying power of *res*, which in this instance is 'carnal copulation'.[31] One of the meanings of the word 'ratify' in the sixteenth century was in fact 'to consummate' (*OED*, sense 3).

The 'deed' that is accomplished in *All's Well* through Diana's intervention, however, ratifies Bertram's earlier conditional contract with Helena, not his present one with Diana. It is the bed-trick in which all three senses of 'deed' – action, sealed contract and copulation – come together. The instrumentality of the subplot for the main plot, and their analogical relation highlight the fact that their distinctness is symptomatic of deeper divisions within the legal action in the main plot. One of the demonstrable instruments of the interlacing of plots is the pair of rings set in circulation by Diana. In serving this function, the rings as tokens of marriage and of intercourse alternate between two configurations in their relation to 'deed'.

While Bertram suggests sex as the seal called for by Diana, Diana demands his ring. This is the first ring to draw the audience's attention. Bertram's giving of it is analogous to a deed or to the signing of a 'deed', either of which can be a seal on an agreement. This takes us right back to Swinburne's discussion of the role of the verbal formula. It is in asserting the assumed function of words in making a marriage that Swinburne is faced with their potential inadequacy, even treacherousness. He does ultimately hold up the validity of the *de praesenti* formula, but in the very process of confirmation, he has to concede that

---

30 See p. 186 above.
31 Cp. Humphrey Winstanley *v.* Alice Worsley, a 1561 divorce suit from Chester, Furnivall, pp. 2–4.

mortal man cannot otherwise judge of Mens meanings, than by their sayings for the Tongue is the Messenger of the heart; and although it sometimes deliver a false message, yet doth the Law accept it for true, when as the Contrary doth not lawfully appear.

(*Spousals*, 87)

As court records show, the contracting parties were the least likely, especially at the moment of spousal, to be verbally precise, and not sure to be conversant with legal formulae; the witnesses were often uneducated and were mostly reliant on memory. Moreover, spousal disputes brought to court frequently involved secret contracts, with no witnesses to testify.

It is in recognition of such inadequacies or unavailability of the 'word' as evidence that Swinburne offers the exchange of rings as a possible solution (*Spousals*, 86). Moreover, he grants the ring a special position among the non-verbal signs that take on a demonstrative or validating function – deserving to be spoken of 'before all other signs' (207).[32] The giving and receiving of a ring was, indeed, one of the commonest gestures invested with special matrimonial significance in the period. The surviving depositions convey a vivid sense of why rings had such a hold on the popular imagination and how the imperatives of certain actual situations harnessed their symbolic importance to a legal one.[33]

Typically, rings assumed the greatest legal significance in settling disputes concerning un-witnessed and unsolemnized contracts, where material proofs were often the only available evidence.[34] In the case of Thomas Allen *v*. Alice Howling of Norfolk (1562), the determining factor is a 'Ring of gould'. In her personal response to Thomas's claim of matrimonial rights, Alice denies her alleged receipt of this ring 'in the waye of matrimony'. But her attempt at freeing herself is thwarted by John Smith and William Walker, who testify, in almost identical terms, that Thomas gave and Alice accepted the ring as an acknowledged token of present marriage.[35]

The popularly perceived value of ring-giving

as a symbolic and integral ceremony in a matrimonial context derived, paradoxically, from its traditional association with solemnized weddings *in facie ecclesiae*; thus it almost lent a semblance of formality to clandestine marriages. The formalizing and mnemonic qualities of the ring come together in George Haydock's deposition about the runaway Sothworth couple of Chester (1565): 'what wordes were spoken betwene the parties, he certenlie cannot declare, biecause he did not marke them well'; what he does remember, though, is that 'gold and silver was put on the boke' and 'a ringe [was] put on her finger'.[36]

In Southern dioceses too, the Puritan challenge does not seem to have revolutionized custom.[37] In the Canterbury case of Wanderton *v*. Wild (1582), the ring clinches a contract – much in the manner prescribed by the pre-

---

[32] See also *Spousals*, pp. 71, 101, 206–12.

[33] On the various symbolisms of the ring, see *Spousals* pp. 207–9; A. H. Bullen, *An English Garner: Some Shorter Elizabethan Poems* (Westminster, 1903), p. 296, posy no. 15; J. E. Cirlot, *A Dictionary of Symbols and Imagery*, tr. J. Sage (London, 1971), p. 273; G. F. Kunz, *Rings for the Finger* (Philadelphia, 1917), pp. 193–248; Shirley Bury, *An Introduction to Rings* (London, 1948), pp. 15–17; Stith Thompson, *Motif-Index of Folk Literature* (Copenhagen, 1958), vol. 6, pp. 650–1.

[34] See Houlbrooke, 58, esp. n. 14; Peter Rushton, 'The Testaments of Gifts: Marriage Tokens and Disputed Contracts in North-East England, 1560–1630', *Folk Life* 24 (1985–6), 25–31. See also *Spousals*, Sections XII–XV.

[35] Norfolk and Norwich Record Office diocesan records (hereafter, NNRO), DN/DEP (deposition books of the consistory court) 9, bk. 8, 158v, 162–3v; DN/ACT (Act books) 9, bk 10.

[36] Furnivall, pp. 65–6.

[37] For attacks on the ring in Puritan writing, see Anthony Gilby, *A Pleasaunte dialogue, Betweene a Souldier of Barwicke, and an English Chaplaine* (Middleburg, 1581), M5r; Dudley Fenner, *Certain Learned and Godly Treatises* (Edinburgh, 1952), p. 96; Andrew Kingsmill, *A View of Mans Estate* (London, 1576), sig. K2r. Also, Donald McGinn, *The Admonition Controversy* (New Brunswick, 1949), pp. 218–19; Richard L. Greaves, *Society and Religion in Elizabethan England* (Minneapolis, 1981), pp. 184–5.

Reformation order of matrimony[38] – and gives a *de futuro* spousal the sanctity of present marriage, at least in the eyes of the deponents. After the parties uttered words of pledge to each other which, predictably, 'he remembreth not', Michael Haell, a witness to the contract, said to them, 'If you receaue any such thing as you pretend conclude the matter as it myght to be done els I will not medle in it.' 'Then the said Wanderton took the said Agnes by the handes', and they uttered what was, roughly, the formula of a *de futuro* contract. 'Then they losed ther handes, and Wanderton gaue her a Ring gelt saying to her take this as a token that you have confessed and I the like to you, you to be my wife and I to be your husband [...] and she receaued the same Ring thankfully' (176). Haell's claim is that they are well and truly married.[39] This bears out the popular currency, in some places at least, of the legal provision set out but qualified as being practically unsound by Swinburne – that in spousals *de futuro*, 'When as on[e] and above the words, there is an Accumulation of some Act joyned therewithal ... For example: ... the Man delivereth to the Woman a Ring, ... hereby the Contract is presumed Matrimonial' (*Spousals*, 71). The delivery of a ring here has the status of an act or deed.

This is the function made to serve by Bertram's 'subarration' to Diana, which, in conjunction with his words, would technically count as a promise of marriage:

> Here, take my ring.
> My house, mine honour, yea my life be thine,
> And I'll be bid by thee.   (4.5.52–4)

We have, here, not only an evocation of the familiar situation of a private contract, and its characteristic method of establishing a formal context, but also the associated possibility of later dispute already present in the inception.

What Diana engineers, however, is an exchange of rings. This accords an altogether more complex set of values to the rings by the time they resurface together at the end, to constitute the comic and legal resolutions.

While the course of Bertram's ring gets deflected from its original path through the introduction of Diana, a new ring is imported by her dark promise to Bertram:

> And on your finger in the night I'll put
> Another ring that, what in time proceeds,
> May token to the future our past deeds.
>   (4.2.62–4)

In its promised exchange with the first ring, it has already become associated with Diana's virginity – 'Mine honour's such a ring. / My chastity's the jewel of our house' (4.2.46–7). This is the jewel Diana pledges in return for Bertram's family jewel. In deed, though, it is Helena's chastity that is going to be its operative but invisible counterpart. The bawdy sense is reinforced by the verbal echo of Bertram's letter to Helena which posited, by linguistic juxtaposition, a cause-and-effect relationship between getting the 'ring upon [his] finger' and showing 'a child begotten of [her] body' (3.2.57–9).

Bertram's language is deliberately rendered ambiguous by Shakespeare to suggest an unmistakeable sexual meaning; 'the ring ... which never shall come off' (3.2.57–8), with its multiple suggestion of a spousal ring with its eternal associations, Bertram's heirloom and the yet uncracked ring of Helena's virginity. It was, in Painter, far more clearly and singly the specific ornament belonging to Beltramo: 'I do purpose to dwell with her, when she shal have this ring (meaning a ring which he wore) vpon her finger, and a sonne in her armes begotten by mee.'[40] The change from 'her finger' to 'my finger' and from 'this ring' to 'the ring ... which never shall come off' not only permits but invites a sexualized reading, and strengthens the

---

[38] *The Sarum Missal*, tr. A. H. Pearson (London, 1844), p. 552. See also 'The Form of Solemnization of Matrimony' as given in *The Book of Common Prayer*, pp. 290–3.

[39] Canterbury Cathedral Archives (hereafter, CCA), X.10.20, 173–6.

[40] Painter, p. 174.

syntactical link between the two conditions. It is this metaphorical connection that is taken up by Helena and literalized during the bed-trick.

The literal and bawdy meanings of 'ring' in Bertram's statement of his first condition are, however, taken apart and met separately, even as Helena's agency is divided between herself and Diana. Thus, the actual ring on Bertram's finger that Helena has to get in spite of his resolution that it 'never shall come off' (3.2.58) has already been obtained by Diana. But while its procurement was meant to be a proof of Helena's cohabitation with Bertram, it becomes an alleged token of his marriage to Diana in the scene of arbitration, and a confessed token of his supposed sexual deeds with her. Meanwhile, Helena's pregnancy takes on the role of signifying his actual 'deed' with Helena. This splitting of functions foregrounds the separation between the woman Bertram thinks he sleeps with, and the woman he actually penetrates. His ring gets reconnected with Helena's conception only at the very end, a connection that is explicitly underlined by Helena's words:

> There is your ring.
> And, look you, here's your letter. This it says:
> 'When from my finger you can get this ring,
> And are by me with child', et cetera. This is done.
>
> (5.3.312–15)

This is at once a realization and restatement of the implied connection between ring and sex in Bertram's letter, and a reuniting of divided agencies in the figure of Helena – a covering up of the many divisions through which her husband has had to be 'doubly won'.

Meanwhile, the second ring, the actual jewel that Helena has put on Bertram's finger 'in the night', spotted by Lafew as Helena's and by the king as his own gift to her, is defined ultimately as a proof that Bertram 'husbanded [Helena's] bed at Florence', since it is clear that 'this ring was ... hers' (5.3.126–7). Part of the *raison-d'être* of this ring is its necessary role of providing additional support for Helena's claim of Bertram's paternity of her yet unborn child.

Without this token of intercourse between Helena and Bertram, it would be less clear that Helena's conception followed from Bertram's night of pleasure in Florence.

Thus, if the first ring was initially analogous to the action or 'deed' that seals an oral contract, its later use as a sign of Bertram's supposed activities with Diana, and the use of the other ring as a seal and token of his actual congress with Helena, point to yet another relation between ring and deed in the play. 'Deeds', as what the rings, with their spousal and sexual associations, will help make evident, becomes clearly the act or acts of sex. Originally posited as a more reliable expression of intention than words, 'deeds' have now themselves become something to be proved; they, no less than words, are signs to be interpreted.

The special position given to rings by Swinburne and their centrality in the popular perception of marital obligations are borne out by their importance in the final episode. A scene of reconciliation and spousal negotiation quickly darkens into one of arraignment, as the 'amorous token for fair Maudlin' (5.3.69) is recognized by the king as the 'token' by which he would have relieved Helena, and as Bertram stakes all on it:

> If you shall prove
> This ring was ever hers, you shall as easy
> Prove that I husbanded her bed in Florence
>
> (125–7)

The trial structure of this scene is officially established upon the delivery of Diana's letter. Stating with legal precision her claim of marriage, and clearly setting out the charge against Bertram, this letter takes the place of a libel which is defined by Henry Consett as 'a Writing which containeth the action' in his account of the practice of the church courts in Renaissance England.[41] Here, of course, the court is presided over by the king, instead of a doctor of law, but

---

41 Henry Consett, *The Practice of the Spiritual or Ecclesiastical Courts* (London, 1685), p. 76.

the royal presence itself is another factor which defines the legality of the space in the disclosure scene.[42] Diana's very phrasing – 'and a poor maid is undone' (141–8) – evokes the ambience of the sex-related litigation of the church courts – recalling numerous pleas by women claiming to be used, deceived or abandoned. The legal situation gets wholly formalized with the king's declaration of his suspicion and the countess's call for 'justice' (152–6).

In this set-up, the rings become the *exhibita* or material objects produced in court to support allegations. Diana's presentation of the first ring – the one given her by Bertram – is clearly accorded a higher truth value than other forms of evidence such as witness testimony. When Bertram casts aspersions on Parolles's personal credibility, the king points out, 'She hath that ring of yours' (212).

The terms in which the characters respond to the rings suggest at least one of the reasons behind their evidentiary impact. The entire drama around the first ring starts when it catches the king's eye – 'for mine eye, / While I was speaking, oft was fastened to 't' (82–3). Bertram's denial that it ever was Helena's is met with the Countess's assertion, 'Son, on my life / I have seen her wear it' and is corroborated by Lafew's 'I am sure I saw her wear it' (90–2). One remembers depositions like Christabell Andro's, who recounts the contract between William Headley and Agnes Smith, as well as registers its reality entirely in terms of images – 'she ... *sawe* the parties contract and gyve ther faith and trewth to gither ...; and the said William gave the said Agnes one pair of glowes and a bowed grote, and she gave unto ... William one gold ring'.[43]

It is the impact of 'ocular proof' that Diana exploits when she presents this ring dramatically in court – '... O behold this ring' (5.3.194). The Countess immediately notes, 'he blushes and 'tis hit' (198). But Diana has hit the mark in more senses than one. Everyone else in the assembly reacts as much as Bertram does, and the Countess declares at this point, 'That ring's

a thousand proofs.' (202) As Swinburne puts it, 'Not to be, and not to appear, is all one in Construction of Law' (*Spousals*, 181). The function of proof, therefore is to make the truth apparent or visible. *Enargaeia* was defined by Aristotle as an exercise which represents an object before the eyes of the viewers, and the Latin word for *enargaeia*, suggestively, is *evidentia*.[44]

Significantly, however, most of the deponents one encounters do not – and cannot – actually reproduce the incident or the facts they are seeking to ascertain. Rather, they attempt to narrate them vividly. Evidence, thus, involves an exercise in re-presentation and hence, inevitably, a metonymic relation between the truth sought to be proved, and the sign that is meant to evoke it. Even exhibits – be they letters, handkerchiefs, deeds or rings – are legal tokens. The way they make things evident is by symbolically or associatively evoking an entire situation before the eyes of the judge. The necessary translocation involved in evidentiary practice is dictated by the fact that the action or the intention to be proved cannot literally be shown in court, and yet has to be somehow made apparent. The inadequacies and ambiguities of this process gain a specially concise focus in the context of marriage law in which the crucial events and factors to be established were

---

[42] On the relation between the definition of a 'court' of law and the presence of the monarch, see J. H. Baker, *The Legal Profession and the Common Law* (London, 1986), pp. 153–69.

[43] Raine, pp. 238–40. See also Furnivall, pp. 187–96 (Edmund *v.* Bird) and pp. 65–7 (Sothworth *v.* Sothworth); Raine, p. 243 (Grynwill *v.* Groundye).

[44] *Rhetoric*, 3.11.1, 3.11.4, and 3.10.6, in *The Rhetoric and Poetics of Aristotle*, tr. W. Rhys Roberts and Ingram Bywater, ed. Friedrich Solmsen (New York, 1954). The potential of the image for being an instrument of proof is a well established concept in Aristotle and emerges from a collateral reading of the *De Anima* and *Nichomachean Ethics*. On the provenance of this notion in Renaissance England, see Kathy Eden, *Poetic and Legal Fictions in the Aristotelian Tradition* (Princeton, 1986), pp. 69–111.

usually private acts and utterances, and very often the specific act of sex. *All's Well*'s dramatization of this area of law highlights a condition common to the theatre and the church courts. Both are faced with the task of often having to represent and legislate a realm removed from the public space of the stage or the court. Both, therefore, have to devise their own enargaeic modes to show what must necessarily be absent from this space but what is, at the same time, central to their motives of representation. The ring, here, inscribes this phenomenon, by virtue of its metaphoric valencies and its role as a 'monumental' token (4.3.18). Legally as well as theatrically it bodies forth what must lie outside the limits of representation.

This is part of the larger problem of an uneasy relation between intentionality and legal truths revealed by adventitious proofs. When the king confronts Bertram with the evident truth that Diana 'hath that ring of [his]', what Bertram denies in self-defence is not the fact that he gave it to her, nor indeed the implied fact of intercourse, but the matrimonial intention that is assumed and alleged to have informed both these acts (5.3.213–22). Exactly this argument is given by many defendants in debates over love tokens, especially rings, in disputed contract suits from the period. Alice Cotton of Canterbury says she received Thomas Baxter's gifts as 'mere gift' and not 'in ... waie of marriage' (1574).[45] What comes closest to Bertram's disclaimer is perhaps John Smith's distinction between the use of tokens for a sexual contract and for a marital one in his personal response against Christian Grimsdiche's libel in a Chester trothplight case of 1562: 'beynge askid, for what intent' he gave her tokens, 'he sais, because he had, and wold have, to do with her, & knew her Carnally; & not for that he wold mary her'.[46] Such disputes highlight the difficulty of assessing the intention of the giver through the perception of the receiver and of others. From their position of privilege over the spectators or the judge at a law court, a theatre audience would have seen enough of Bertram and heard

enough from him by the time he is brought to trial, to be clearly struck by the fallacy of a 'reasonable inference' of 'Wedlock' from the fact of Diana's possession of his ring.

The 'second' ring – the one that has travelled from the king to Bertram via Helena and Diana respectively, to surface in court as a proposed gift for Maudlin – turns out to be no less dubious a proof of intercourse and identity than the first ring is of spousal subarration. It is, of course, established that this ring was Helena's at one time, something that Bertram was confident could never be proved; but law's natural conclusion from this contingency, that Bertram 'husbanded her bed in Florence', completely eschews the question of intention in applying the formula for a valid marriage. Bertram thinks he sleeps with Diana, and if that act is to seal any marriage, it is his with her – as indeed it legally would – since the 'news' of Helena's death, arriving before the bed-trick, has met the stipulation of Bertram's *de futuro* spousal to Diana (4.2.72–3). The fact that he is 'quit' (5.3.301) is due to an arbitrary separation of fact and meant truth in the 'deed of darkness' in Florence.

The connection between this legal fiction and evidentiary law's reliance on what is visible is something Swinburne's *Spousals* is aware of: 'for proof is not of the Essence of Matrimony' (*Spousals*, 87).[47] But 'although ... he which is the searcher of the heart doth well know their deceit and defect of mutual Consent', yet the 'judgement of Mortal man' must pronounce them married since 'the contrary doth not lawfully appear' (85). Hence such paradoxes as 'this deceit so lawful' 'Where both not sin, and yet a

---

[45] CCA, X.10.17, 152v. See also ibid., X.10.12, 182–v.
[46] Furnivall, p. 57.
[47] 'Legal fiction' may be roughly defined as a lie perpetrated with official or institutional authorization, in the interest of the commonweal. On 'legal fiction', see Ian Maclean, *Meaning and Interpretation in the Renaissance: The Case of Law* (Cambridge, 1992) (hereafter, Maclean), pp. 138–42.

sinful fact' (*All's Well*, 3.7.38, 47). Hence, too, the irony that though 'not bedding but consent makes marriages' (*Matrimony*, 120), it is the bedding that, in this instance, proves it. The darkness and the silence that are the conditions for the bed-trick come to stand for the limits to the vision of the mortal judge, for what cannot be made evident either visually or by narration in a temporal court of law. Bertram's conditional pledge of love – 'If she, my liege, can make me know this clearly' – touches precisely on the discomfort surrounding the knowledge law brings, but it is immediately forestalled by Helena's assertion – 'If it *appear* not plain and *prove* untrue ...' (*All's Well*, 5.3.317–19). Helena's answer, in collapsing the gap between cognition and legal certification, articulates the rules that operate in the world of the play, as in law.

The Swinburnian unease around error and the inadequacy of law to accommodate its moral implications lies at the core of the bed-trick. In *Matrimony*, he states clearly and unproblematically that marriage contracted by those who 'doe not consent ... for that they be ... seduced by Error mistaking one person for another' 'is of no moment or effect in Lawe' since matrimony must be a 'coniunction of ... myndes' (121–2). But where the issue is not mere definition but ascertainment of status in the case of a complex human situation, law and its agents have to face a dilemma. Thus, the bed-trick cannot be 'lawful meaning in a lawful act', since the act is joint, and involves two meanings.[48]

The bed-trick is a fictional situation that singles out a potential for fiction in law itself, by which the difference between the singleness of fact and the plurality of truth is collapsed, and a status is presumed. Its likeness to a legal fiction is highlighted by the mendacious means it adopts to achieve an ostensibly ethical end. It is no surprise that Helena, law's most self-aware user, should embody some of the dualities that the play's movement, largely through her energies, seeks to harmonize. To claim the honour that is

hers, she has to 'steal' it surreptitiously (2.5.81) by becoming, as it were, a 'girl' of Italy, to make Bertram 'captive' to her service (2.1.21–2). The law trick that is the specific instrument of Helena's design turns on a logic familiar to a Renaissance English audience, but it acquires a specific status by being used in the context of subtle and strategic double-dealing by the heroine at her most 'Machiavellian' in the very land of plots and policies.[49]

But Helena's Italianate plotting does not ultimately create a simply negative sense of unsavoury cunning; nor is law reduced to a sceptic's quarry. Her character is in many senses Machiavellian in a positive way, and, paradoxically, her use of law and its particular literary location, even while they demystify law, result in a configuring of it as a peculiarly human and contingent measure. Her very first soliloquy (1.1.78–97) signals a transition in her attitude to fate, from passive resignation to a belief in the space it allows for individual enterprise – 'The fated sky gives us free scope.' The only hindrance to exploiting such 'scope' – a concept akin to Machiavelli's *occasione*[50] – is our 'slow

---

[48] On Swinburne's upholding of legal presumption in 'such a favourable matter' as marriage, see *Spousals*, pp. 88, 98, 103 and 149.

[49] On the contemporary English stereotype of Italy, see Roger Ascham's interpolation at the end of the first part of his *Scholemaster* (c. 1570), quoted in Jacob's introduction to Painter, p. xix. See also Thomas Nashe, *The Unfortunate Traveller* in R. B. McKerrow, ed., *The Works of Thomas Nashe* (Oxford, 1958), vol. II, pp. 301–2.

[50] See Quentin Skinner and Russell Price, ed., *Machiavelli: 'The Prince'* (Cambridge, 1988) (hereafter, *The Prince*), Chap. XXVII for the discussion of Caesar Borgia's prudence and ability (*prudentia* and *virtú*) manifested by his alertness to *occasione*, i.e. his recognition of the right opportunity and his acting upon it. See also Chap. XXI. Also relevant to this discussion is Machiavelli's stress on flexibility and adaptability to a particular circumstance or *fortuna* with all its limitations – see *The Prince*. Chap. XXV, pp. 85–7. This recipe for success is exactly what Helena's compromises are based on. Its link with prudence in Machiavelli, as stated in Chap. XV, is also an element in Helena's personality.

designs'. Her tough-minded confidence in possibilities and the expedient and inventive effort with which she sets about to achieve these brings her in line with the prudent protagonists – often heroines – of the *novellae*, whose *industria* is usually their main capital.[51]

The dual associations gathered by law in the course of the play lend the ending its distinctively mixed flavour. After the rapid escalation of legal dangers and implications in the final scene, Helena's spectacular entry must seem a relief in the immediate context, indeed some sort of a salvation. Back in Rossillion, Helena has shed her Italian character, and apparently displaces the world of sexual intrigue and precise legal wrangles as she steps into Diana's place to take over the limelight. She is not to be seen as one of those 'clamorous and impudent' women litigants that the likes of Lord Keeper Egerton and Chancery counsel Anthony Benn were, at the time, denouncing and attempting to keep out of the courts.[52] As in the bed-trick, so here, the status of an event is transformed by the replacement of one woman by the other: the lustful defiling of the 'pitchy night' and its legal and obligatory consequences are taken on by the Bertram–Diana sub-plot, while the central relationship of the play is strategically cleansed of its more degrading associations, and prepared for the 'renown' of the 'end'.

The moment that registers this change is when Helena and Bertram are brought to face each other for the first time in the scene, through Bertram's voluntary interposition. In response to the king's wonder at what seems to him an apparition – 'Is't real that I see?' – Helena says,

> No, my good lord,
> 'Tis but the shadow of a wife you see,
> The name and not the thing.   (5.3.308–10)

Even as the teasing, paradoxical mode of speech gets sublimated here into a medium that brings romance to the verge of anagnorisis, Bertram remonstrates, 'Both, both. O, pardon!' (310). If the bed-trick was the symbolic moment of the split between meaning and action, 'the name' and 'the thing', the present exchange between Bertram and Helena marks, no matter how fleetingly, the healing of these divisions in an act of forgiveness. An appropriate atmosphere is provided by Helena's self-presentation, aided by Diana, which creates an aura of miracle heightened by the regenerative associations of pregnancy. This sense of the wondrous is the main constituent of the romance mode which acts here as an equivalent of the social rituals that transform marriage from a contract into a mystery.

Yet the transition is not seamless. Even while status is attained, the contractual basis of marriage is not let out of sight. The particular instrument for sustaining this awareness is the continued and insistent mooring of the scene in the details of marriage law. Helena's achievement is to have foiled Bertram's attempt at seeking a divorce by establishing the fact of cohabitation: this is the specific significance of her staking 'deadly divorce' on the indisputability of the proofs of having met his terms (320). Thus, in the indistinct but comprehensive area covered between the two, both the marriage and the divorce paradigms behind their 'legal' actions get taken up and pursued till the end of the play where, finally, they are tied together.

Sex having been in *All's Well* the very site of a radical absence of volition, its centrality to the sacramental notion of indissoluble matrimony,

---

[51] See Cole, chap. II, esp. pp. 19–20, on the honour accorded to human effort, ability, and ingenuity in Boccaccio. See also Lorna Hutson, 'Fortunate Travelers: Reading for the Plot in Sixteenth-Century England', *Representations*, 41 (1993), 83–103, on the 'transformative virtues' of prudence, enterprise and pursuit of occasion in Italian *novellae* and in Machiavelli, esp. pp. 88–90, 97, 99.

[52] See W. Baildon, *Les Reportes del Cases in Camera Stellata 1593–1609* (1849), pp. 39 and 161; Bedfordshire Record Office, L28/46. See also W. R. Prest, 'Law and Women's Rights in Early Modern England', *The Seventeenth Century*, 6 (1991), 169–87; 182.

which ostensibly contributes to the magic of the final reunion, extends the paradox of the earlier action. Swinburne's explanation of why 'Marriage is that great Mystery' is germane to what the pregnant wife's appearance relies on for its 'miraculous' impact: 'By Marriage the Man and the Woman are made one Flesh, so they are not by Spousals.' It is in the absence of such a union that he declares 'Spousals' to be 'utterly destitute of ... mystical effect: And ... Marriage is greater than Spousals ...' (*Spousals*, 16). In *All's Well*, 'making one flesh' is in a sense what turns a spousal into matrimony, but the mystery around the incorporation of man and wife is at least partly replaced by consummation as an instrument of law and custom.

As the external symbol and visible outcome of this incorporation, Helena's pregnancy plays a crucial role in foregrounding the contractual basis of the revalidated union. While its procreational and promissory implications introduce a sense of romance quickenings, the function it serves in the resolution of the plot is legal. It is framed as an 'ocular proof' of the sexual consummation stipulated in Bertram's letter: 'one that's dead is quick − / And now behold the meaning!' (5.3.305–6).[53] This is in many senses a scene of remarriage − a familiar scenario, where the fact of intercourse acts as the single validating seal that at once proves and forms matrimony. Bridal pregnancy by itself was common enough in Elizabethan England;[54] and though prenuptial fornication was a punishable offence, in practice, judicial attitudes to it varied according to local custom, and were often quite tolerant where honourable intentions were clear or marriage had already followed.[55] But the remarriage in *All's Well* takes place not in church but in a virtual court. The visual resonances of a pregnant woman turning up in open court would evoke associations of incontinence and fornication − charges often spurred by illicit pregnancy. 'Pregnancies', Ralph Houlbrooke asserts, 'always figured prominently among the presentments made'; and, as he further puts it, 'rather more women than men were normally

presented, because a pregnant woman was bound to be more conspicuous than her partner'.[56] As far as Bertram's conscious intention defines the deed that Helena's pregnancy proceeds from, the result is indeed symptomatic of the typical situation; only, it is transformed here by Helena's intention and her triumphant use of 'occasion'. What lends the legal connection of the scene its specific dubiousness is the combination of the marital and the evidentiary purposes behind Helena's action. As often in disputed suits of this kind, what is still at stake, implicitly, is Bertram's agency in the conception. In Shakespeare's time, determination of paternal identity was a troubling legal issue.[57] We have Swinburne's own pronouncement on the matter, in his discussion of why 'wedlock [is] called Matrimonye rather than Patrimonye': 'the mother is alwaies more certein than the father and truthe is stronger than opinion' (*Matrimony*, 118).

It is interesting to note one of Shakespeare's modifications of this source story. In Painter − as in Boccaccio − Giletta was 'brought a bedde of twoo sonnes, which were very like vnto their father ...'. She enters Beltramo's banquet not pregnant but with these two, their resemblance to their father being posited and accepted as manifest evidence of paternity, strengthening the implication of her possession of his ring: 'for beholde, here in myne armes, not onely one sonne begotten by thee, but twayne, and likewise thy Ryng. ... the Counte hearing this, was greatly astonned, and

---

53 Cp. the function of Juliet's 'plenteous womb' in *Measure for Measure*, which 'expresseth [Claudio's] full tilth and husbandry' to the public gaze (1.4.42–3).
54 See Ingram, pp. 219–23, esp. p. 219.
55 Ibid., 223–6.
56 Houlbrooke, p. 76.
57 See L. A. Montrose, ' "Shaping Fantasies": Figurations of Gender and Power in Elizabethan Culture', *Representations* 1:2, Spring, 1983, 61–94 (72–3). For a historical study of the evolution of embryology, see J. Cole, *Early Theories of Sexual Generation* (Oxford, 1930).

knewe the Ryng, and the children also, they were so like hym.'[58] If Shakespeare had left this episode unchanged, he would still have had the opportunity to evoke legal associations, for facial similarity has been known to have been a factor in establishing the father's identity in church courts.[59] But pregnancy as a presence in court was potentially more scandalous because there was an unavoidable uncertainty surrounding paternity and, by implication, a potential for the use of pregnancy for manipulation. It was not unknown for women to claim marital rights by offering their conception as proof of cohabitation. The motives could be various – as Martin Ingram puts it, women resorting to law to pressurize men into marriage could be 'naive, scheming, or … desperate'.[60] Among them, pregnant women not only had a stronger incentive but were 'in a better moral position to attempt coercion' than others.[61] They were also likely to receive local backing, not least owing to a concern about the threat of bastardy to the poor rates.[62] In the Salisbury case of Diar *v.* Rogers (1609), Henry Rogers is said to have promised that 'yf he did beget the said Alice with childe, that he would marry with her'. The witnesses for the manifestly pregnant plaintiff Alice Diar keep harping on the obligation that her conception has placed him under; as Alice Tante (?) puts it, it is 'in the respect of the said Henry Roger's faythfull promise [that] the said Alice offered her selffe to be begotten with child by … Henry'.[63] Even unconfirmed claims of pregnancy could create enormous pressure and a climate of opinion hard to cope with.[64] Not only can such a situation, irrespective of the truth or spirit of the alleged promise, be conducive to enforcement; the pressures incumbent on the defendant of such a suit are even known to have tempted women to have 'deliberately sought to become pregnant to induce the man to marry her'.[65] Such is the lingering sense of uncertainty that Bertram articulates, when he takes a faltering step back from his

spontaneous 'Both, both. O pardon!' to qualify his acceptance of the situation:

> If she, my liege, can make me know this clearly
> I'll love her dearly, ever ever dearly. (5.3.317–18)

In a play where comic law operates through actual legal means, and recognition is arrived at through a trial, the incertitude surrounding the legal knowledge undercuts the absolute nature of the anagnoristic moment. This marriage, for all that the providential emplotment of Helena's 'course' suggests, is made not in heaven but in the bawdy court. Where the king is overwhelmed into a typical romance reaction (307–9), the audience would be aware that the inevitable outcome of the discovery has as much to do with legal logic, by which the church court arbiter would probably order Bertram to take her back and live with her as married people should.[66]

As ever, though, it is in the figure of Helena, the employer of the legal tricks for the 'miraculous' ending, that the comic energy of the play as well as its use of law acquires a more complex status than mere stratagem can lay claim to. In her, policy and genuineness, simulation and

---

[58] Painter, vol. I, pp. 178–9.

[59] See NNRO Dep. 4B, 30v; Dep. 5B, 173v; both cited in Houlbrooke, p. 77 (n. 74).

[60] Ingram, 'Spousals', p. 47.

[61] Ingram, p. 210.

[62] Ibid., 210–11. See also G. R. Quaife, *Wanton Wenches and Wayward Wives: Peasants and Illicit Sex in Early Seventeenth-Century England* (London, 1979), pp. 218–20.

[63] Salisbury Diocesan Records, deposition books preserved in the Wiltshire Record Office (hereafter, WRO), D1/26, 136v–137v; 140r–141v.

[64] See, for instance, J. T. Fowler, ed., *Acts of Chapter of the Collegiate Church of St. Peter and Wilfred, Ripon, 1452–1506*, Surtees Society 64, 1875, p. 31ff.

[65] Ingram, p. 225. See, for example, Office v. Rowden, WRO (1612), AS/ABO 11; and Office v. Greene (1621), WRO, AW/ABO 5.

[66] See W. Hale Hale, *A series of precedents and proceedings in criminal causes extending from the year 1475 to 1640; extracted from act-books of ecclesiastical courts in the diocese of London* (1847), p. 44; Stone and Cozens-Hardy, p. 90.

sincerity, power and powerlessness have been inextricably compounded from the very beginning: 'I do affect a sorrow indeed, but I have it too' (1.1.51). It is this spirit that she infuses into the final scene. When she appears in court, big with child, her condition – betokening the triumph of her initiative – becomes a means for the strategic adoption of a traditional image of the obedient wife whose pleasure lies in being acted upon by her husband, a calculated evocation of domestic sanctities, so 'that man [can] be at woman's command, and yet no hurt done!'[67] Yet, as with the women 'who', in the words of *The lawes resolutions of women's rights* (1632), could 'shift it well enough' in the legal world of early modern England,[68] this is not simply a camouflaging of Helena's agency. It is also a pointer to her real vulnerability and, in an odd sense, passivity in the emotional transaction contained in the quasi-legal one. When she says, 'O, my good lord, when I was like this maid / I found you wondrous kind', her utterance is a gentle reminder to us that her active plotting has had to be executed through a virtual loss of identity in the act of sex; its humour lies in her acknowledged sexual enjoyment of even this imperfect emotional experience (5.3.311–12). As far as she is concerned, the seamier aspects of what has passed are not simplemindedly forgotten but deliberately put behind: 'This is done', she says, after curtailing her recitation of Bertram's conditional letter with a significant 'et cetera' (315). Peter Hall's 1992 production, appropriately, made Helena tear up the letter – which is also the contract – as she spoke these words.

Through her, then, law is finally felt to acquire a more positive value than merely being a sceptical alternative to either the *vera philosophia* or the perfect science that it was considered to be in some of the most prominent humanist traditions of jurisprudence. It emerges, rather, as an art of the probable, that involves prudence rather than wisdom – a perspective that was actually emerging in the Renaissance, questioning the more idealistic view of law.[69] Law is not in itself a transformative principle, but a pragmatic means of working through the essentially contingent human condition towards achievements that are necessarily provisional. It is for the individual to renounce and go beyond the legal devices to build on the possibilities made available to her by them. Over and above the obvious irony of the play's title, there is a sense in which it is felt to encapsulate the peculiar and hard-bought wisdom of the play. All one can begin with, in a sense, is this 'end'. This is not a romance, like *Pericles* or *The Winter's Tale*, where the children have been born and the regeneration has visibly begun. Helena's pregnancy, among its other expressive functions, suggests the play's projecting of fulfilments in the future. To take up the possibilities afforded by legal means is what the function of romance is posited as. Nor need the value of law necessarily lie in the discovery or assertion of certitudes; probability itself can be its gift to the human condition, and indeed a positive step towards knowledge. The king's words, as he accepts Helena's offer of her improbable 'medical' services, capture a perspective which the play ultimately invites the audience to accommodate:

---

[67] *All's Well*, 1.3.90–1.

[68] T. E. *The lawes resolution of women's rights: or, the lawes provision for women* (London, 1632), p. 4.

[69] On the jurisprudential debate on whether law was a science or an art, the conflicting visions of the status of law, and the argument for law emerging as an 'unphilosophical mixture of the necessary and the contingent in jurisprudence' that was 'in fact superior to that of philosophy', see Maclean, pp. 20–9. See also Donald Kelley, 'Vera Philosophia. The Philosophical Significance of Renaissance Jurisprudence', in *History, Law and the Human Sciences: Medieval and Renaissance Perspectives* (London, 1984), pp. 267–79. On the history of the idea of probability, see Ian Hacking, *The Emergence of Probability: a Philosophical Study of Early Ideas about Probability, Introduction and Statistical Inference* (Cambridge, 1975), and Douglas Lane Patey, *Probability and Literary Form: Philosophic theory and literary practice in the Augustan age* (Cambridge, 1984), esp. pp. 3–74.

More should I question thee, and more I must,
Though more to know could not be more to
    trust:
From whence thou cam'st, how tended on – but
    rest
Unquestioned welcome, and undoubted blessed.
    –   (2.1.205–8)

Like a promise, marriage, happy endings to stories and happiness itself, are all, in a sense, absolute and ignorant – like Pascal's wager with God, a leap of faith.

'HAVE YOU NOT READ OF SOME SUCH THING?' SEX AND SEXUAL STORIES IN *OTHELLO*

EDWARD PECHTER

Why does Othello suddenly abandon his affectionate trust in Desdemona for a conviction of betrayal? This question, by placing the protagonist's understanding at the play's centre, takes us back to Bradley's first words about the play in *Shakespearean Tragedy*: 'the character of Othello is comparatively simple, but ... essentially the success of Iago's plot is connected with this character. Othello's description of himself as "one not easily jealous" ... is perfectly just. His tragedy lies in this – that his whole nature was indisposed to jealousy, and yet ... unusually open to deception'.[1] Bradley has long been discredited – a story with which we are all familiar. In 1933 L. C. Knights's 'How Many Children Had Lady Macbeth?' repudiated the notion of treating dramatic characters as the authors and origins of their own histories, autonomous agents with lives outside the dramatic action.[2] Knights's essay coincided with a redirection of Shakespeare studies from character to language, from the 'whole nature' of the protagonist to the coherent artifice of the play itself. Wilson Knight's 'spatial hermeneutics' figures notably in this move away from Bradley, as part of a 'modernist paradigm';[3] psychological integrity is fragmented into linguistic patterns that re-achieve wholeness in a self-reflexive rather than representational text. If a play begins to resemble *Les Demoiselles d'Avignon*, it makes more sense to speak of the structural relation of geometric forms – image patterns contributing to symbolic coherence in a dramatic poem – than about which if any of the characters has a noble nature.

We no longer indulge in the Bradley-bashing that was routine during this period; we ignore him now, the consequence of yet another shift that has rendered his kind of commentary apparently irrelevant. In Richard Rorty's view, there is no such 'thing as "human nature" or the "deepest level of the self" ... socialization, and thus historical circumstance, goes all the way down'.[4] Rorty wants to collapse the distinctions between depth and surface, inner and outer.[5] If modernists reconceived representation, renouncing the mirror of nature for an abstract and self-referring aesthetic text, a view like Rorty's seems to abandon the concept of representation altogether, denying that there is

---

[1] A. C. Bradley, *Shakespearean Tragedy: Lectures on 'Hamlet', 'Othello', 'King Lear', 'Macbeth'* (1904; rpt. London, 1964), p. 151.

[2] This essay is available with some minor revisions in Knights's *Explorations: Essays in Criticism Mainly on the Literature of the Seventeenth Century* (1947; rpt. New York, 1964), pp. 15–54.

[3] The phrases are taken from Hugh Grady, *The Modernist Shakespeare: Critical Texts in a Material World* (Oxford, 1991), esp. chapter 2.

[4] *Contingency, Irony, and Solidarity* (Cambridge, 1989), p. xiii.

[5] More precisely, Rorty wishes to displace these distinctions from the status of ontological categories, where they inscribe a foundational difference between Reality and Appearance, and put them into service for a rough-and-ready pragmatist use, specific to a particular context.

any stable substance out there (or in here) to be imitated, and that the aesthetic text itself exists with any authority beyond that given by a contingent historical process. From another angle, however, current critics have not abandoned representation but universalized it. If everything is a text, then nature (including the 'whole nature' of Othello's 'character') and art (including *Othello*) are just different cultural constructs or discursive practices – of many, two. As a consequence, we cash in the question of Othello's jealousy for an enquiry into the sex-gender system; and *Othello* as an object of interest leads us not to Shakespeare or heroic tragedy, authors or theatrical genres, but to the literary system and its contribution to the production and reproduction of cultural value. Hence Valerie Traub, in her state-of-the-art book about *Circulations of Sexuality in Shakespearean Drama*: 'I am less interested in the ways works of art are empowered than in the ways characters are represented as negotiating and struggling *for* power, the extent to which they are granted or denied agency – in short, the ways their subjectivity is constructed through representational means [and] the "processes whereby sexual desires are constructed, mass-produced, and distributed"'.[6]

In conducting this breathless Cook's Tour, I have bypassed some picturesque complications. As W. B. Worthen points out, the typical 'actorly reading' of Shakespeare remains, in contrast to academic criticism, 'notably trained on questions of "character" [as] integrated, self-present, internalized, psychologically motivated'.[7] As with acting, so with teaching Shakespeare: drop into most Shakespeare classes and you will hear Bradley-speak. Since academic criticism is a different mode of understanding from teaching or acting, we should not expect an identity of interests and assumptions. At the same time, the remoteness of academic discourse from two such influential ways of representing Shakespeare as pedagogy and theatre is remarkable. Even more remarkable are the residues of Bradley surviving in academic

criticism itself. As Margaret Mikesell points out, the 'renewed criticism of Bradleyan traditions in the early 1950s' often rested in the very methods that were being repudiated, treating 'Othello and Iago as characters [with] the personalities of real people'.[8] This is still the case. 'It is important, of course', Ania Loomba declares, 'to guard against reading dramatic characters as real, three dimensional people'; but these words follow a description of Othello as shedding his alienated 'insecurity' for a 'conception of his own worth' that 'slowly comes to centre in' and then depart from Desdemona's choice – a description that would sit comfortably in the pages of *Shakespearean Tragedy*.[9]

Why does Bradley haunt us, like a half-remembered, maybe even unread text? In one of the first attempts to recuperate Bradley for critical practice, A. D. Nuttall, pointing to an odd discrepancy between the frequently non-sensical claims of Knights's attack and the general acceptance of his claims as self-evidently true, remarked that 'the whole debate may be complicated by the presence of unacknowledged historical factors', a 'pre-rational historical reaction' against 'the over-heated Victorian age'.[10] This shrewd suggestion allows us to understand Bradley-bashing as an over-determined gesture by which Shakespearians could assert their authentic modernity, liberated from the naiveties of eminent Victorianism. But the 'unacknowledged historical factors' may extend deeper than Victorian sentiment. Con-

6 *Desire and Anxiety: Circulations of Sexuality in Shakespearean Drama* (New York and London, 1992), p. 4.
7 'Invisible Bullets, Violet Bears: Reading Actors Reading', in Edward Pechter, ed., *Textual and Theatrical Shakespeare: Questions of Evidence* (Iowa City, 1996), pp. 210–29, p. 212.
8 Margaret Lael Mikesell, Introduction, Part 1, in Mikesell and Virginia Vaughan, eds., *'Othello': An Annotated Bibliography* (New York, 1990), pp. xi–xxiv, p. xvii.
9 *Gender, Race, Renaissance Drama* (Manchester, 1989), pp. 54–8.
10 'The Argument about Shakespeare's Characters', *Critical Quarterly*, 7 (1965), 107–20, p. 109.

sider Michael Bristol who, after proposing recently that audiences should 'efface their response to ... Othello, Desdmona, and Iago as individual subjects endowed with personalities and with some mode of autonomous interiorized life', has to admit the difficulty of such an effacement, 'not least because the experience of individual subjectivity as we have come to know it *is* objectively operative in the text'.[11] From this perspective, an interest in Othello's character is not merely a hangover from Bradley or nineteenth-century novels, some recently acquired detritus to be jettisoned, but part of a continuing engagement going back to the origins, as best we can determine them, of our interest in the Shakespearian text.

The explanatory narrative I synopsized earlier has a lot going for it: by accounting for Bradley's irrelevance in terms of a naive representability underwritten by an old-fashioned assumption of personal integrity, it makes use of powerfully central concepts in the development of modern thought – 'master-problems', in Perry Anderson's phrase.[12] At the same time, these concepts may be serving as screens in the composition of a story generated out of wish-fulfilment as well as disinterested analysis, motivated by a desire to bring about the disappearance we claim to be describing as an accomplished fact. Bristol's 'efface', in concert with 'unacknowledged' and 'pre-rational' in Nuttall, suggest that the uncanny residual presence of Bradley in current criticism is the consequence of denial. We need to reconsider our relation to Bradley, and to the long tradition of commentary which lies behind *Shakespearean Tragedy*, not in order to restore his eminence but to understand our own situation.[13] And *Othello* seems like a particularly appropriate play on which to base this reconsideration, for as Edward Snow has argued, from its irascible inauguration ('Tush, never tell me! ... 'Sblood, but you'll not hear me!') to its agonized terminal gesture ('The object poisons sight; / Let it be hid'), 'repression pervades the entire world' of the play.[14]

Once more, then: how to explain Othello's reversal of feelings about Desdemona, from 'Perdition catch my soul / But I do love thee' to 'O curse of marriage' within only a few minutes time (3.3.91–2, 272)? I am quoting from the Temptation Scene which, parading before us familiar ideas and feelings from the play's opening, suggests that Othello's alteration should be understood as part of a lucid sequence. At the beginning of the play, Othello speaks self-confidently of his marriage: 'my demerits / May speak unbonneted to as proud a fortune / As this that I have reached' (1.2.22–4);

11 'Charivari and the Comedy of Abjection in *Othello*', in Linda Woodbridge and Edward Berry, eds., *True Rites and Maimed Rites: Ritual and Anti-Ritual in Shakespeare and His Age* (Urbana and Chicago, 1992), pp. 75–97, p. 85 (Bristol's emphasis). For a powerful argument that Shakespeare not only sustains but originates modern notions of subjectivity, see Joel Fineman, *Shakespeare's Perjured Eye: The Invention of Poetic Subjectivity in the Sonnets* (Berkeley and Los Angeles, 1986).

12 'It is clear', Anderson tells us, writing about theory since World War Two, 'that there has been one master-problem around which *all* contenders have revolved[:] the nature of the relationships between structure and subject in human history and society'. See *In the Tracks of Historical Materialism* (Chicago, 1984), p. 33 (Anderson's emphasis).

13 I am hardly the first to try to bring either Bradley or the concept of character back into consideration. In addition to Nuttall, see the discussions in John Bayley, *The Characters of Love: A Study in the Literature of Personality* (London, 1960), chapter 1, esp. pp. 33–47; and the chapters in S. L. Goldberg, *An Essay on 'King Lear'* (Cambridge, 1975), pp. 34–67; and E. A. J. Honigmann, *Shakespeare: Seven Tragedies: The Dramatist's Manipulation of Audience Response* (London, 1976), pp. 4–15. For more recent discussion, coming at the question from widely divergent positions, see Christy Desmet, *Reading Shakespeare's Characters: Rhetoric, Ethics, and Identity* (Amherst, 1992); Alan Sinfield, 'When Is a Character Not a Character? Desdemona, Olivia, Lady Macbeth, and Subjectivity', in *Faultlines: Cultural Materialism and the Politics of Dissident Reading* (Berkeley and Los Angeles, 1992), pp. 52–79, esp. p. 62; and Bert O. States, *Hamlet and the Concept of Character* (Baltimore and London), 1992.

14 1.1.1 and 4; 5.2.374–5. See Edward A. Snow, 'Sexual Anxiety and the Male Order of Things in *Othello*', *English Literary Renaissance*, 10 (1980), 384–412, p. 384.

now he begins to doubt 'mine own weak merits' (3.3.191). This acknowledgement, trivial in itself, precipitates a rush of startling reversals. Brabantio's warning, 'Look to her, Moor, if thou hast eyes to see. / She has deceived her father, and may thee', had prompted a secure dismissal early on: 'My life upon her faith' (1.3.292–4). Now in the face of Iago's reiteration, 'She did deceive her father, marrying you', Othello becomes worried: 'And so she did' (210, 212). In the scene's turning point a moment later, Othello suddenly takes the initiative, 'And yet how nature, erring from itself – ' and Iago, himself cautious so far, spots an opportunity so desirable that he interrupts Othello to seize it:

> Ay, there's the point; as, to be bold with you,
> Not to affect many proposèd matches
> Of her own clime, complexion, and degree,
> Whereto we see in all things nature tends.
> Foh, one may smell in such a will most rank,
> Foul disproportions, thoughts unnatural!
>
> (232–8)

At the end of this speech, a shaken Othello dismisses Iago, but too late to reverse the process that will lead to catastrophe.

Nature is the crucial idea here, and again we hear echoes of the beginning: 'and she in spite of nature, / Of years, of country, credit, everything, / To fall in love with what she feared to look on!' (1.3.96–8). For Brabantio, nature should have drawn Desdemona to young Venetians of her own rank, 'the wealthy curlèd darlings of our nation' (1.22.69), and her attraction to Othello, 'against all rules of nature' (1.3.101), must be the perverse consequence of witchcraft. The perplexing questions and ambivalent feelings raised by this claim,[15] unresolved in themselves, migrate into a narrative conclusion: Othello denies witchcraft, Desdemona acknowledges she was half the wooer, Brabantio drops the case. But the question returns here in its own conceptual terms, moving Othello to adopt the same cultural stereotypes articulated earlier by Brabantio and

now reiterated by Iago as defining his own nature.

> Haply for I am black,
> And have not those soft parts of conversation
> That chamberers have; or for I am declined
> Into the vale of years – yet that's not much –
> She's gone. I am abused, and my relief
> Must be to loathe her. (3.3.267–72)

As Arthur Kirsch says, 'Othello eventually internalizes Iago's maleficent sexual vision and sees himself with Iago's eyes', repellent in 'his age and color', thus 'becom[ing] convinced that Desdemona's manifest attraction to him is itself perverse'.[16] Kirsch's story represents something like a current consensus,[17] but if the meaning of Othello's transformation is thus clear, the motive remains mysterious. Why should Othello, against all evidence and self-interest,

---

[15] The perplexing questions centre on the competing claims of nature and culture. The ambivalent feelings can be located in terms of the contradictory generic signals many commentators have associated with this play (Susan Snyder, for instance, in *The Comic Matrix of Shakespeare's Tragedies: 'Romeo and Juliet', 'Hamlet', 'Othello', and 'King Lear'* (Princeton, 1979)): if we are watching a comedy, then we are on the side of young love in general and female desire in particular; if tragedy, then the claims of established patriarchal authority demand our primary allegiance. In 'Othello and Colour Prejudice', G. K. Hunter suggests that the play provokes racist feelings only to require their repudiation (*Dramatic Identities and Cultural Tradition: Studies in Shakespeare and His Contemporaries: Critical Essays* (Liverpool, 1978), pp. 31–59). A. J. Cook describes a similar change in our feelings about Desdemona in 'The Design of Desdemona: Doubt Raised and Resolved', *Shakespeare Studies*, 13 (1980), 187–96.
[16] *Shakespeare and the Experience of Love* (Cambridge, 1981), p. 32.
[17] See Edward Berry, 'Othello's Alienation', *Studies in English Literature*, 30 (1990), 315–34; and David Bevington, 'Introduction' to his edition of *Othello* (1980; rpt. Toronto and New York, 1988), p. xxviii. For a version of this argument written before materialism and constructionism became generally current and including some astute commentary on the question of character, see G. M. Matthews, 'Othello and the Dignity of Man', in Arnold Kettle, ed., *Shakespeare in a Changing World: Essays* (New York, 1964), pp. 123–45.

buy into the view Iago offers of himself and Desdemona? Othello himself sees the foolishness – 'Exchange me for a goat / When I shall turn the business of my soul / To such exsufflicate and blowed surmises' (3.3.184–6) – but proceeds to make the investment nonetheless.

All this, however, assumes what is at issue – namely, that Othello is free to make up his mind, not just about Desdemona but about himself, as though he has secure possession of a stable core of autonomous being. The play seems to encourage our current scepticism about such an assumption, drawing attention to the way belief rests on and is shaped by cultural clutter – stories, superstitions, social stereotypes, clichéd aphorisms, vague memories, dreams, the immediate influence of overheard aimless chatter and snatches of old songs.[18] Such influences are particularly potent in times of stress. Brabantio's jump to the witchcraft conclusion is a good example: 'Have you not read, Roderigo, / Of some such thing?' (1.1.175–6). Iago is the source of this clutter, Burke's voice whispering at the ear,[19] burrowing under the threshold of conscious reflection and lodging the vinous poison of mistrust, disgust, abhorrence. He represents what we now call ideological interpellation, or what Renaissance commentators, describing the world from inside a theological rather than a sociological lexicon, understood as diabolical possession. As such, Iago is the origin and the content of Brabantio's dream ('This accident is not unlike my dream'), which Brabantio has no choice but to believe ('Belief of it oppresses me already' [1.1.144–5]), because Iago's white (or is it black?) noise subtends and determines belief. He has already turned Cassio inside out by the time of the Temptation Scene; Othello is a more ambitious project, but Iago's success should seem predictable as well as amazing.

Othello's alien status gives us a familiar current context to understand his story: the immigrant novel. Othello's metaphorical transformation happens literally to Saladin Chamcha in *The Satanic Verses*: he turns into a goat.

His thighs had grown uncommonly wide and powerful, as well as hairy. Below the knee the hairiness came to a halt, and his legs narrowed into tough, bony, almost fleshless calves, terminating in a pair of shiny, cloven hoofs, such as one might find on any billy-goat. Saladin was also taken aback by the sight of his phallus, greatly enlarged and embarrassingly erect, an organ that he had the greatest difficulty in acknowledging his own.[20]

Finding himself in a kind of asylum along with other embodied clichés of an exotic colonial domain – a manticore, some water-buffalo, slippery snakes, 'a very lecherous-looking wolf' – Chamcha asks, ' "But how do they do it?" ' ' "They describe us" ', the manticore tells him. ' "That's all. They have the power of description, and we succumb to the pictures they construct." '[21] Rushdie's description of *The Satanic Verses* – 'the move from one part of the world to another and what that does to the various aspects of one's being-in-the-world'[22] – can make Othello's transformation the centrepiece of an altogether plausible narrative. First he has the power to describe himself, inhabits his own narrative, but moving to Christian Europe he becomes displaced from his 'perfect soul' (1.2.31) and begins to occupy a different

---

18 In this regard, Lisa Jardine comments brilliantly on Iago's misogynist clichés at the beginning of Act 2. See 'Cultural Confusion and Shakespeare's Learned Heroines: "These are old paradoxes" ', *Shakespeare Quarterly*, 38 (1987), 1–18.

19 See Kenneth Burke, '*Othello*: An Essay to Illustrate a Method', *Hudson Review*, 4 (1951), 165–203. I am profoundly indebted to Burke both for local detail and the general argument I am making here. See also Joel Altman, ' "Preposterous Conclusions": Eros, *Enargeia*, and the Composition of *Othello*', *Representations*, 18 (1987), 129–57; and Patricia Parker, 'Preposterous Events', *Shakespeare Quarterly*, 43 (1992), 186–213.

20 Salman Rushdie, *The Satanic Verses* (New York, 1988), p. 157.

21 Ibid., p. 168. The *Othello* subtext in Rushdie is clearly intentional. See Paul A. Cantor, '*Othello*: The Erring Barbarian among the Supersubtle Venetians', *Southwest Review*, 75 (1990), 296–319.

22 John Banville, 'An Interview with Salman Rushdie', *New York Review of Books* (4 March 1993), 34–6, p. 34.

story, until finally his blackness serves to figure not a royal-heroic self but bestial sexuality.

But should we be reading Othello as the abject victim at the centre of an immigrant novel? The play was produced in an early colonialist culture, substantially ignorant of much that we have come to know of colonial and postcolonial experience. More to my formalist purposes here, *Othello* lacks the accumulation of finely attenuated nuance required to work in the manner of an immigrant novel, the sense of 'dilatory time' (2.3.363) that Iago, a master narratologist, understands as necessary for such a mode. This problem is insoluble (plays are not novels), but *Othello* goes out of its way to exacerbate it, compressing Cinthio's expansive narrative into an action that seems to occupy a mere two days, beginning at night with the elopement, arriving the next day at Cyprus, proceeding to the Temptation Scene on the day after, and concluding with the murder that night. We have bumped into the famous 'double-time' problem – 'the gap', as John Bayley puts it, 'between the swift dramatic time of the plot and the lingering fictional time of the domestic psychology ... between the impact of the *coup de théâtre* on our emotions, and the effect of the analysis of love and jealousy upon our minds'.[23] It is easy to demonstrate that the impact of swift time is misleading, but the impression remains, and in Morgann's famous adage, 'In Dramatic composition, the *Impression* is the *Fact*.'[24] We must understand Othello's transformation not as the 'eventual internalizing' of Kirsch's narrative, nor as something that '*slowly*' or '*finally*' comes about, as in Loomba's or my own rewriting of the play, but as issuing from his experience in the very brief interval that seems to elapse since the beginning of the action.

According to Stanley Cavell, *Othello* makes us think 'not merely generally of marriage but specifically of the wedding night. It is with this that the play opens.'[25] 'Even now, now, very now, an old black ram / Is tupping your white ewe' (1.1.88–9). This coupling, the first concrete image we are offered upon which to load (or lodge) the play's matter, may not describe what really happened, or even what happened at all. As many critics have argued, the uncertainty when or even whether Othello and Desdemona consummate their marriage serves to generate anxious speculation on our part, sustained by the pressure of a highly eroticized language which enacts to the mind's eye various images of the deed about whose actual performance we remain unresolved.[26] This

[23] Bayley, *The Characters of Love*, p. 134.

[24] *Morgann's Essay on the Dramatic Character of Sir John Falstaff*, ed. William Arthur Gill (1912; rpt. Freeport, 1970), p. 4. Harley Granville-Barker tries to demonstrate that double time solves a problem of audience belief, but since it is Shakespeare who creates the problem, Granville-Barker's argument winds up going round in circles. See *Prefaces to Shakespeare* (1946; rpt. Princeton, 1963), vol. 4, pp. 141–7. Graham Bradshaw has tried to explain away the problem, but his claims, which depend upon a hefty investment in Bianca's pre-dramatic career in Venice, are implausible. See *Misrepresentations: Shakespeare and the Materialists* (Ithaca and London, 1993), pp. 147–68.

For versions of the distinctions at work in the double time of *Othello*, consider Paul Valéry's discussion of the way 'our poetic pendulum travels from our sensation toward some idea or some sentiment, and returns toward some memory of the sensation and toward the potential act which could reproduce the sensation'. See *The Art of Poetry*, trans. Denise Folliot in Jackson Mathews, ed., *The Collected Works of Paul Valéry* (London, 1958), vol. 7, p. 72. See also Kenneth Burke's distinction between plots driven by lyrical associationism and by rational extension in *The Philosophy of Literary Form* (1941; rpt. Berkeley and Los Angeles, 1973), pp. 30–2.

[25] *Disowning Knowledge in Six Plays of Shakespeare* (Cambridge, 1987), p. 132.

[26] For critics (many of them following in Cavell's wake, as I am) who claim that *Othello* 'refers us to a hidden scene of desire that ... is a focus of compulsive fascination for audience and characters alike', see (in alphabetical order): Janet Adelman, *Suffocating Mothers: Fantasies of Maternal Origin in Shakespeare's Plays, 'Hamlet' to 'The Tempest'* (New York and London, 1992); Lynda E. Boose, '"Let it be hid": Renaissance Pornography, Iago, and Audience Response', in Richard Marienstras and Dominique Guy-Blanquet, eds., *Autour d' 'Othello'* (Paris, 1987), pp. 135–43; and 'Othello's Handkerchief,

irresolution lasts until Othello's invitation on the first Cyprus night: 'Come, my dear love, / The purchase made, the fruits are to ensue. / The profit's yet to come 'tween me and you' (2.3.8–10); but even as Othello's disarmingly ingenuous couplet gives rest to one kind of anxious uncertainty, *have they or haven't they?*, its alarming specificity creates another: *what now will it be like?* This interest is displaced by the flurry of business with Iago, Cassio, Roderigo, and Montano; but Cassio's violent story sustains as well as displaces our interest in Othello and Desdemona's lovemaking, occurring (presumably) 'even now, now, very now'; especially when Iago's astounding simile to describe the disturbance re-evokes that opening image:

> Friends all but now, even now,
> In quarter and in terms like bride and groom
> Devesting them for bed; and then but now –
> As if some planet had unwitted men –
> Swords out, and tilting one at others' breasts
> In opposition bloody.   (2.3.172–7)

The Temptation Scene follows and the play gives us the dramatic impression – the fact – of its occurring the next morning. By means of *post hoc ergo propter hoc*, a mode of narrative understanding implicit in Morgann's Law of Dramatic Composition, we are encouraged to locate the origins of Othello's transformation in his sexual consummation: it is the cause, it is the cause.

The impression is powerfully confirmed at just this pivotal point of the Temptation Scene when Othello's sudden loathing situates itself with specific reference to Desdemona's body:

> O curse of marriage,
> That we can call these delicate creatures ours
> And not their appetites! I had rather be a toad
> And live upon the vapour of a dungeon
> Than keep a corner in the thing I love
> For others' uses. Yet 'tis the plague of great ones;
> Prerogatived are they less than the base.
> 'Tis destiny unshunnable, like death.
> Even then this forkèd plague is fated to us
> When we do quicken.   (3.3.272–81).

The 'corner in the thing I love' directs us to Desdemona's genitals. The forkèd plague alludes to the cuckold's horns, but its demonstrative specificity, '*this* forkèd plague', so soon after 'keep a corner', summons the groin to the mind's eye, like the 'bare, forked animal' in *Lear* (3.4.101). And like the 'simp'ring dame, / Whose face between her forks presages snow' later in the same play (4.5.116–17), Desdemona's whole being seems for a bizarre moment drawn down and compressed into her private part: she is both the thing and the thing in the thing.[27] Similarly graphic details inform Othello's speech to and about Desdemona later on:

"The Recognizance and Pledge of Love"', *English Literary Renaissance*, 5 (1975), 360–74; Arthur Little, Jr, '"An essence that's not seen": The Primal Scene of Racism in *Othello*', *Shakespeare Quarterly*, 44 (1993), 304–24; Katharine Eisaman Maus, 'Horns of Dilemma: Jealousy, Gender and Spectatorship in English Renaissance Drama', *ELH*, 54 (1987), 561–83; and 'Proof and Consequences: Inwardness and Its Exposure in the English Renaissance', *Representations*, 34 (1991), 229–52; Michael Neill, 'Changing Places in *Othello*', *Shakespeare Survey 37* (1984), pp. 115–31; '"Hidden Malady": Death, Discovery, and Indistinction in *The Changeling*', *Renaissance Drama*, 22 (1991), 95–121 (from which the quotation about the 'hidden scene of desire' at the beginning of this note is taken (p. 98)); and 'Unproper Beds: Race, Adultery, and the Hideous in *Othello*', *Shakespeare Quarterly*, 40 (1989), 383–412; Patricia Parker, 'Dilation, Spying and the "Secret Place" of Woman', *Representations*, 44 (1993), 60–95; 'Fantasies of "Race" and "Gender": Africa, *Othello*, and Bringing to Light', in Margo Hendricks and Parker, eds., *Women, 'Race', and Writing in the Early Modern Period* (New York and London, 1994), pp. 84–100; and 'Shakespeare and Rhetoric: "Dilation" and "Delation"', in Parker and Geoffrey Hartman, eds., *Shakespeare and the Question of Theory* (London, 1985), pp. 57–74; and Peter L. Rudnytsky, 'The Purloined Handkerchief in *Othello*', in Joseph Reppen and Maurice Charney, eds., *The Psychoanalytic Study of Literature* (Hillsdale, N.J., 1985), pp. 169–90.

27 Cf. Neill: Desdemona is 'not merely the precious "thing", the stolen treasure of love's corrupted commerce, but herself the lost place of love' ('Changing Places', p. 128).

OTHELLO But there where I have garnered up my
    heart,
  Where either I must live or bear no life,
  The fountain from the which my current runs
  Or else dries up – to be discarded thence,
  Or keep it as a cistern for foul toads
  To knot and gender in! Turn thy complexion there,
  Patience, thou young and rose-lipped cherubin,
  Ay, here look grim as hell.
DESDEMONA I hope my noble lord esteems me
    honest.
OTHELLO O, ay – as summer flies are in the
    shambles,
  That quicken even with blowing. O thou weed,
  Who are so lovely fair, and smell'st so sweet,
  That the sense aches at thee – would thou hadst
  ne'er been born!   (4.2.59–71)

As Kittredge points out,[28] *thence*, the repeated
theres and finally *here* emphatically situate our
attention; the sequence reduces Desdemona to
an 'it' at once vague and grotesquely specific,
especially when the rose-lipped cherubin now
looks out, his face between the forks, from the
place he was looking *at* a moment earlier. The
proliferating evocative power of these passages
performs a similar compression upon Othello's
life story. 'When we do quicken' in the first
passage conflates birth and desire (quickening as
tumescence) and locates both in the place of
betrayal – the place in the second passage where
life is both given and denied ('discarded'), and
where desire is at the same time awakened and
repelled (the summer flies that quicken with
blowing); as though birth, desire, and betrayal –
the entire trajectory of any male's affective career
in the tragic (or satiric) mode – are simultaneously
present in this same loved and loathed thing.

    Writing about 'the thing *denied our sight*
throughout the opening scene',[29] Cavell described an image of sexual coupling; but as
Patricia Parker notes, the focus in these passages
is much more concentrated upon 'the "priv-
ities" of woman opened simultaneously to
scientific "discovery" and the pornographic
gaze'.[30] Like many recent critics for whom
Othello enacts a primal scene (see note 26),
Parker suggests that the play entices its spectator

into the quasi-erotic pleasures of a dominant
position from which to determine meaning; but
we can be sceptical about 'the gaze', both
generally and as an approach to this play.[31] Rich

---

[28] George Lyman Kittredge, ed., *Othello* (Boston, 1941),
   p. 211.
[29] *Disowning Knowledge*, p. 132.
[30] 'Fantasies of "Race"', p. 87.
[31] Laura Mulvey, who established the idea of 'the gaze'
   ('Visual Pleasure and Narrative Cinema', *Screen*, 16
   (1975), 6–18), twice subsequently cautioned against applying it to all movies ('Afterthoughts on "Visual Pleasure
   and Narrative Cinema" Inspired by *Duel in the Sun*',
   Framework, 15–17 (1981), 12–15; and 'Changes', *Discourse*, 7 (1985), 11–30. All this material is now conveniently available in *Visual and Other Pleasures* (Bloomington
   and Indianapolis, 1989).) We should be even more
   sceptical about transferring 'the gaze' to theatre, and even
   more sceptical yet again when the theatre was produced
   in such a remote period. Notions of ocular proof associated with experimental science were developing in the
   Renaissance, as were notions of true perspective in
   painting and a single privileged vantage point in the
   masque. These ideas, however, had not achieved anything like their subsequent authority. They competed
   with other ideas about perception and different epistemological theories. Renaissance ideas about poetry and
   theatre, moreover, often repudiated the primacy of the
   visual, an integrated objective stage *gestalt*, and a single
   controlling point of view. In support of these claims, see
   Desmet, *Reading Shakespeare's Characters*, pp. 112–13;
   Barbara Freedman, *Staging the Gaze: Postmodernism, Psychoanalysis, and Shakespearean Comedy* (Ithaca, 1991);
   Terence Hawkes, *Shakespeare's Talking Animals: Language
   and Drama in Society* (London, 1970), p. 43 and p. 130;
   James R. Siemon, *Shakespearean Iconoclasm* (Berkeley and
   Los Angeles, 1985); Wylie Sypher, *The Ethic of Time:
   Structures of Experience in Shakespeare* (New York, 1976),
   pp. 116–20; Rosemond Tuve, *Elizabethan and Metaphysical Imagery: Renaissance Poetic and Twentieth-Century
   Critics* (Chicago, 1947); and Robert Weimann, *Shakespeare and the Popular Tradition in the Theater: Studies in the
   Social Dimension of Dramatic Form* (Baltimore and London,
   1978). There have been others, apart from Mulvey
   herself, who have warned against overinvesting in the
   idea of the gaze (see Edward Snow, 'Theorizing the Male
   Gaze: Some Problems', *Representations*, 25 (1989), 330–
   41; and Stephen J. Greenblatt, *Learning to Curse: Essays in
   Early Modern Culture* (New York and London, 1990), pp.
   175–81); nonetheless, critics carry on with the gaze
   sometimes in full knowledge of Mulvey's disclaimers. Its
   power seems to be irresistible.

as they are in vivid detail, these passages multiply and condense incompatible images and contradictory significances to produce an effect not of mastery – a privileged vantage from which to fix meanings, as in a stable visual field – but of giddiness verging on nausea. The 'mind now floods', as Graham Bradshaw says of the rapid sequence of images in the second passage – 'fountain', 'cistern', 'it' – unarrestably until we are allowed (or required) to pause at the climactic image of the copulating toads.[32] They are the most memorably vivid presence here, as was the solitary toad in the earlier passage, but in neither do the toads function primarily in terms of visual representation. In the dungeon of the Temptation Scene, 'that dank corner of the emotional prison',[33] you are less likely to see anything than to feel what Othello later describes as 'the slime / That sticks on filthy deeds'[34]; or to smell the damp and stagnant air, 'the vapour', as he says here, we must breathe in to sustain life. With the cesspool and the slaughterhouse, the cistern and shambles, this evocation of malodorous fumes intensifies into the overwhelming specificity of excrement and rotting flesh – the aroma that seems to generate Flaubert's curious question about one of his whores: 'Have you ... sniffed at the fog of her clitoris?'[35]; what Eliot, in the pre-Pound version of *The Waste Land*, called 'the good old hearty female stench'.[36]

Following a long line back to Plato, Renaissance commentators on the senses designated sight and hearing as the higher faculties, consigning smell, along with taste and touch, to the carnal modes of knowledge.[37] In *Civilization and Its Discontents*, Freud imagines a primal scene in which primitive humanity stands upright, discovers its nakedness, and transfers its sensory allegiance from smell to sight.[38] Such stories underwrite Hans J. Rindisbacher's claims about smell as 'strongly connected with sexuality', the 'very animal function', the 'oldest unsublimated medium', within which we experience the 'force of individual attraction

[32] Bradshaw adds that '*flooded* seems the right word [until] the images smash against *dries up*, and reform into the wrenchingly gross, unhinging image of "it" – "it!" – as a foul *cistern*' (*Misrepresentations*, p. 179). Lawrence Danson talks about the 'fluid metaphors ... suggested by Othello's figuring Desdemona as either "fountain from which [his] current runs" or "cistern for foul toads to knot and gender in". In *Cymbeline* the idea of the wife as a watery site is complexly joined with the idea of the wife as property – the one idea, as we would expect, confounding the other, since you can't *keep* things that flow like a fountain or breed like a cistern' ('"The Catastrophe is a Nuptial": The Space of Masculine Desire in *Othello*, *Cymbeline*, and *The Winter's Tale*', *Shakespeare Survey 46* (1994), pp. 69–79, p. 75).

[33] Neill, 'Changing Places', p. 130.

[34] 5.2.155–6. For remarks on the powerful sense of sexual disgust in 'this appalling line', see William Empson, *The Structure of Complex Words* (London, 1964), pp. 226–7; and Snow, 'Sexual Anxiety', p. 388.

[35] Quoted by Francine du Plessix Gray in 'Splendor and Miseries', *New York Review of Books* (16 July 1992), 331–5, p. 334.

[36] Valerie Eliot, ed., *The Waste Land: A Facsimile and Transcript of the Original Drafts Including the Annotations of Ezra Pound* (London, 1971), p. 23.

[37] 'Love regards as its end the enjoyment of beauty; beauty pertains only to the mind, sight, and hearing. Love, therefore, is limited to these three, but desire which rises from the other senses is called, not love, but lust or madness.' Sears R. Jayne, ed. and trans., *Marsilio Ficino's Commentary on Plato's Symposium* (Columbia, Missouri; 1944), p. 130.

[38] According to Freud, the civilizing of human sexuality since prehistory, said to reside in the stability of family arrangements, involved 'the diminution of the olfactory stimuli by means of which the menstrual process produced an effect on the male psyche. Their role was taken over by visual excitations, which, in contrast to the intermittent olfactory stimuli, were able to maintain a permanent effect ... The diminution of the olfactory stimuli seems itself to be a consequence of man's raising himself from the ground, of his assumption of an upright gait; this made his genitals, which were previously concealed, visible and in need of protection, and so provoked feelings of shame in him.' *Civilization and its Discontents*, trans. James Strachey (New York, 1962), p. 46. For a suggestive discussion of Freud and of various associations, especially in the nineteenth century, between smell and the primitive, see Hal Foster, '"Primitive" Scenes', *Critical Inquiry*, 20 (1993), 69–102.

between the sexes'.[39] The play's evocation of smell may be understood as a way around the problem Iago describes:

> But how, how satisfied, my lord?
> Would you, the supervisor, grossly gape on,
> Behold her topped? . . .
> It were a tedious difficulty, I think,
> To bring them to that prospect.   (3.3.399–403)

Ocular proof may be impossible, but it is olfactory proof, anyway, that provides the most powerfully convincing testimony about what really happened on the wedding night. This evidence finally allows us to answer my original question why Othello reverses his feelings about Desdemona: it is *because of her nasty smell.*

This conclusion is even sillier than Rymer's: if not 'the *Tragedy of the Handkerchief*',[40] then of the vaginal douche – the 'clyster-pipes', as Iago says, blowing reechy kisses from his fingers into the air (2.1.179). Like Rymer – unresponsive to the handkerchief's symbolic resonances: the wedding sheets, stained with blood and sexual fluids[41] – we are being too literal. The smells do not tell us what really happened in Othello and Desdemona's consummation, but what Othello thinks happened. Smells are notoriously transient – as here: the stench of the shambles does not prevent Othello's registering her 'smell . . . so sweet', nor the sweetness the stench of her deed ('Heaven stops the nose at it' [4.2.79]) a moment later.[42] And smells are notoriously subjective. As Marston's Cockledemoy says, 'Every man's turd smells well in his own nose.'[43] But this is not to say that the meanings of smell are determined uniquely by an autonomous individual sensorium. Any somatic base for smell is located beneath the semantic threshold of meaning or consequence. Since all sensory experience belongs to the moment, we need, as Rindisbacher says, 'acculturation and particularly language' in order to 'give it a temporal dimension, add past and future, loss and longing, hope and despair'.[44] This dependence is particularly strong in the case of smells, whose very evanescence seems capturable only

[39] *The Smell of Books: A Cultural-Historical Study of Olfactory Perception in Literature* (Ann Arbor, 1992), p. 13, p. 160 and p. 231.

[40] *A Short View of Tragedy*, in Curt A. Zimanky, ed., *The Critical Works of Thomas Rymer* (New Haven, 1956), p. 160.

[41] Cf. Boose, 'Desdemona's Handkerchief'. Rymer, though, seems to have taken the point almost despite himself; consider the following remarks, intended to make fun of the play's concentration on such a trivial thing as the handkerchief: '*Desdemona* dropt the Handkerchief, and missed it that very day after her Marriage; it might have been rumpl'd up with her Wedding sheets: And this Night that she lay in her wedding sheets, the *Fairey* Napkin (whilst *Othello* was stifling her) might have started up to disarm his fury, and stop his ungracious mouth' (p. 162). Or, just earlier: 'Had it been *Desdemona's* Garter, the Sagacious Moor might have smelt a Rat; but the Handkerchief is so remote a trifle, no Booby, on this side *Mauritania*, cou'd make any consequence from it' (p. 160). One might say that, though blind, Rymer could register the meaning well enough as taste and smell. Rudnytsky argues that 'Rymer's comparison of the handkerchief to a "Garter" comes to seem particularly inspired' as suggesting its fetish-like quality ('The Purloined Handkerchief', p. 185). Peter Davison is picking up similar olfactory resonances in his remark that Rymer's point about the garter and smelling a rat is very '*pungently*' put (*Othello*. The Critics Debate Series (Basingstoke, 1988), p. 83 [my emphasis]). Davison, who remarks on the 'surprising . . . *personal* acrimony' in *Othello* criticism (p. 10), suggests that 'the peculiar viciousness that animates some critics . . . may stem from what in *Othello* subconsciously disturbs them' (p. 53). This suggestion seems plausible, especially in conjunction with all the anecdotes from the play's theatrical history of audiences so upset that they felt moved in some way to intervene in the action. In this context, Rymer's tone of furious resistance is interesting and revealing. He may not be a good critic, but he is not the perverse anomaly he is sometimes taken to be.

[42] By contrast, the primary visible qualities can be fixed in a quantitatively determinate space (this tall, that shape, even such-and-such a colour). As a consequence of its greater stability, ocular proof may seem like a more realistic and even worthwhile project than olfactory proof. It was, arguably, beginning to acquire such authority in the Renaissance – but only beginning to, and not for everybody (my point in note 31).

[43] John Marston, *The Dutch Courtesan*, ed. M. L. Wine. Regents Renaissance Drama Series (Lincoln, Nebraska; 1965), 3.3.45.

[44] *The Smell of Books*, p. 4.

through the memories and historical associations which language can evoke.[45] The transience and subjectivity of smell thus bring us back to the verbal or cultural constructedness of the subject itself. The 'foul and the fragrant' qualities detected by an individual's nose are the product, as Alain Corbin says, of the 'social imagination'.[46]

From this perspective, the meaning of Cockledemoy's words matters less than their aphoristic tone. He sounds as though he is quoting, and so he is – Montaigne, Erasmus, perhaps on back to Aristotle.[47] Eliot implies a similarly general familiarity as with 'the good old hearty female stench'; *oh, that stench*, we are asked to respond; *of course*. Cassio's description of Bianca, "Tis such another fitchew! Marry, a perfumed one!' (4.1.143) works the same way. The polecat is 'noted for its rank odour and lechery', Sanders tells us, and the phrase *such another* is 'a common idiom meaning "one just like all the others"'.[48] Eliot may have had a private waste land and individual talent, Shakespeare his secret sorrows and period of sex nausea, but language like this derives its authority elsewhere. 'Love has pitched his mansion in / The place of excrement.'[49] Crazy Jane's words to the bishop may recall her particular sexual experience, but like the 'saws of books' Hamlet tries to wipe from the tables of his memory after meeting the ghost (1.5.100), they resonate a sententious generality. *Has she not read of some such thing?* Perhaps the good old hearty male tag, *inter urinas et faeces nascimur*, we are born between piss and shit. The aphorism is sometimes attributed to St Augustine – wrongly, it seems, and unlike Cockledemoy's, its origins cannot be determined; but the very anonymity helps to produce the sense of an impersonal authority, independent of any particular author or individual source: 'True he it said, what ever man it sayd'.[50]

Othello's disgust in the Temptation Scene is embedded deeply in the same aphoristic generality. "Tis the plague of great ones', he says and, describing the curse of marriage, affirms the

---

[45] The 'auratic phenomenon' of smell 'is almost purely linguistic, despite its evident lack of terminological grounding, in fact precisely because of it. The connectors in the "smell *like* ..." or the "smell *of* ..." are the true linguistic places of the olfactory, empty of sensual quality themselves, functional particles, providers of linkage, connections, bonds. [The] shortcoming of language for the olfactory thus turns out to be the true reflection of the liminal and transgressive qualities of that sensory mode' (Rindisbacher, *The Smell of Books*, pp. 330–1).

[46] *The Foul and the Fragrant: Odor and the French Social Imagination* (Cambridge, Mass.; 1986). The book was originally called *Le Miasme et la Jonquille*, so the phrase is actually the translator's, perhaps thinking of 'l'imaginaire'.

[47] In an unpublished essay, 'The Adverse Body: John Marston', Ronald Huebert points out that Marston found the adage in Florio's Montaigne, 'where it appears as a bathetically unheroic couplet: "Ev'ry mans ordure well, To his own sense doth smell."' According to Huebert, Florio would have found it 'not in Montaigne's racy French', but in a Latin epigram, 'Stercus cuiusque suum bene olet', itself a mistranslation of Erasmus's Adage 2302, 'suus cuique crepitus bene olet'. For the presumed origins in Aristotle, see John Weightman, 'How Wise Was Montaigne?' *New York Review of Books* (5 November 1992), 32–5, p. 33.

The idea still commands belief. Freud claimed that the social factor in the repression of anal erotism is 'attested by the circumstance that, in spite of all man's developmental advances, he scarcely finds the smell of *his own* excreta repulsive, but only that of other people's' (*Civilization and its Discontents*, p. 47, Freud's emphasis). And Weightman reports that 'When, quite recently, I heard it said of a world-famous but rather self-righteous musician, "He thinks his own shit doesn't smell", I took the expression to be a typically rude Australianism' ('How Wise?' p. 33). Its current authority has a different rhetorical register – or two different registers – from the aphoristic mode. For Freud, inhabiting a culture more respectful of scientific empiricism than of familiar topoi, the authority is represented not as a maxim but as data – something 'attested by circumstance'. Weightman seems to imply that a bumptious colonial's language may be more authoritative, closer to the true core of tradition, than the polite diction of the metropolitan centre.

[48] Norman Sanders, ed., *Othello*. New Cambridge Shakespeare (Cambridge, 1984), p. 147.

[49] 'Crazy Jane Talks with the Bishop'. *The Collected Poems of W. B. Yeats* (New York, 1959), pp. 254–5.

[50] *Spenser's 'Faerie Queene'*, ed. J. C. Smith (Oxford, 1909), vol. 2, p. 121 (Book 4, Canto 10, 1). The misattribution

collective wisdom of the plural pronoun, speaking for all married men ('that we can call these delicate creatures ours') and for all heroes ('even then this forkèd plague is fated to us / When we do quicken'). This is the tone of the canny insider, and though new to Othello's speech, it is not new to us. This is Iago's tone. His speech has been from the beginning a tissue of sententious topoi – as here: 'I know our country disposition well' (3.3.205). This is Hamlet's pun on 'country matters', 'a fair thought to lie between maids' legs' (3.2.111, 113), and it may be said to originate the explicit focus upon female sexual parts. The double meaning – I know how our Venetian women dispose of their cunts; I know how our Venetian cunts dispose of themselves – substantiates the gross synecdoche realized a moment later in Othello's speech: transforming women into the things that make them women. But if Othello assimilates Iago's innuendoes, it is through the suave confidence with which they are communicated: 'This fellow . . . knows all qualities with a learned spirit / Of human dealings' (3.3.262–4). Iago speaks from the cultural centre. The manticore was right. Iago has 'the power of description', and Othello 'succumbs to the pictures' Iago constructs. As Kirsch said, Othello comes 'eventually' to 'see . . . with Iago's eyes' – or smell with his nose, or (as in Rushdie's Heideggerian phrase) to reconstitute his 'being-in-the-world' to accord with Iago's.

Whatever the play's impressions upon us, it seems we cannot escape from an understanding in which Othello's sexual knowledge of Desdemona is not the origin but the consequence of his transformation, not the cause but the effect – specifically, an effect of discourse. 'It is not words that shakes me thus', Othello says later in a spastic trance that seems to re-enact his lovemaking with Desdemona (4.1.40). But it is words, the story woven of social, racial, and sexual stereotypes in which his knowledge – of himself, Desdemona, everything – is embedded. How it came to be embedded thus we are not told; the play does not record the process of this

transformation. It provides a beginning, up to and including 'Perdition catch my soul / But I do love thee', and an ending, starting with 'O curse of marriage', separated by only a few minutes playing time. In lieu of an extended narrative middle, the play gives us intensely charged erotic images, requiring us to imagine Othello's lovemaking with Desdemona; but whatever (and however) we can register disperses itself into stories about sexual feelings and actions, and still other stories (about military promotions, for instance) to which sexual feelings and actions do not seem immediately relevant. The cause for Othello's transformation must be there, in these hints of an immigrant novel the play requires us to invent.

Like Bradley's kind of criticism, the problem I have been struggling with has been relegated to the status of error, and then to oblivion. This story begins with Eliot's charge of '*bovarisme*' in Othello's final speeches.[51] Leavis projected this

---

may originate with Freud, to infer from Traub, who passes it along in *Desire and Anxiety* (p. 58 and p. 156). St Augustine is a likely candidate, considering how frequently he participated in this traditional repugnance for the female body. The aphorism can serve also to celebrate the carnivalesque body ('Fair and foul are near of kin' – the main tone in Yeats's poem). For recent commentators who have appropriated the maxim without any attribution, see Greenblatt, *Learning to Curse*, p. 60; Norman Mailer, *Tough Guys Don't Dance* (New York, 1984), p. 116; and Gail Kern Paster, *The Body Embarrassed: Drama and the Disciplines of Shame in Early Modern England* (Ithaca, 1993), p. 210. Mailer is a particularly interesting writer in this context. He writes obsessively about different excremental–sexual smells and has developed a whole metaphysics about the proximity of female orifices (Mailer's Manichaenism is a subject about which doctoral dissertations are presumably being written even now, now, very now). He even invented a witty neologism for the perineum (employing the plural pronoun whose rhetorical power I shall be describing in a moment): 'we boys out on Long Island used to call [it] the Taint' – presumably for its suggestions of rotten meat, like Othello's 'shambles', but explicitly because ''taint vagina, 'taint anus, ho, ho' (*Tough Guys*, p. 93).

[51] 'Shakespeare and the Stoicism of Seneca', 1927; rpt. in

view backward to reveal an Othello who 'has from the beginning responded' with a self-dramatizing egotism: 'the essential traitor is within the gates'. As a consequence, Bradley's view of a not-easily-jealous Othello becomes 'sentimental perversity'.[52] For current critics too, Othello is vulnerable from the beginning – not, though, because of some peculiar (and presumably corrigible) failure on his part but as the necessary consequence of a general condition. The essential traitor is now 'always already' within the gates. In one version of the current story, we focus on the inherent vulnerability of Othello's alien status, Loomba's 'insecurity', or the 'self-doubt of this displaced stranger' which, according to Neill, 'opens him so fatally to Iago's attack'.[53] From another angle, Othello suffers not from his cultural background but his gender. According to Janet Adelman, male desire 'inevitably soils that object' in which it invests itself and therefore 'threatens to "corrupt and taint" [Othello's] business from the start'.[54] In the Lacanian description, Othello's fate is determined by desire itself, irrespective of gender. 'If language is born of absence', Catherine Belsey tells us, 'so is desire, and at the same moment. This must be so ... Desire, which invests the self in another, necessarily precipitates a division in the subject.'[55] In Stephen Greenblatt's strong and influential version, Othello's transformation is simply the 'clearest and most important' example of social construction as a general condition: 'In *Othello* the characters have always already experienced submission to narrativity.'[56]

Greenblatt builds from a perception of Othello's Senate speech as 'a narrative in which the storyteller is constantly swallowed up by the story'. This anxiety is then displaced onto Desdemona, as in the lovers' ecstatic Cypriot reunion:

OTHELLO O my fair warrior!
DESDEMONA   My dear Othello.
OTHELLO It gives me wonder great as my content
   To see you here before me. O my soul's joy,

If after every tempest come such calms,
May the winds bellow till they have wakened
   death,
And let the labouring barque climb hills of seas
Olympus-high, and duck again as low
As hell's from heaven. If it were now to die,
'Twere now to be most happy, for I fear
My soul hath her content so absolute
That not another comfort like to this
Succeeds in unknown fate.
DESDEMONA   The heavens forbid
But that our loves and comforts should
   increase
Even as our days do grow.   (2.1.183–96)

Like many others, Greenblatt recognizes in this passage two distinct registers for experiencing pleasure.[57] Othello's speech describes violent movement building to a climax so intense, 'content so absolute', that an intuition of disappointment follows: maybe never again, a sort of *post coitum tristis*. By contrast Desdemona registers pleasure not as the short sharp shock of termination, but as a slow and gradual increase, unfolding without any evident anxiety or much differentiation into an indefinite future. But does it follow from this, as Greenblatt claims, that Desdemona's promise of a daily increase is actually a threat because it 'denies the possibility

---

Selected Essays. New Edition (New York, 1950), pp. 107–20, p. 111.

52 'Diabolic Intellect and the Noble Hero', 1937; rpt. in *The Common Pursuit* (Harmondsworth, 1969), pp. 136–59, p. 139, p. 141.

53 'Changing Places', p. 127.

54 *Suffocating Mothers*, p. 63 and p. 65. Adelman's generously detailed notes indicate the depth and range of this object-relations approach among current critics.

55 'Desire's Excess and the English Renaissance Theatre: *Edward II, Troilus and Cressida*, and *Othello*', in Susan Zimmerman, ed., *Erotic Politics: Desire on the Renaissance Stage* (London and New York, 1992), pp. 84–102, p. 86 and p. 95.

56 *Renaissance Self-Fashioning: From More to Shakespeare* (Chicago, 1980), p. 237. Adelman uses the same phrase about 'the impossible condition of male desire, the condition always already lost' (*Suffocating Mothers*, p. 69).

57 Adelman makes the point and provides references to five others who interpret the passage in similar ways, ibid., pp. 72–3 and p. 278.

of [Othello's] narrative control' and 'devour[s] up his discourse' in a way that eventually drives him to murder?[58] Whatever ominous premonitions we may sense, the lovers' greeting in Cyprus ends in blissful fulfilment. 'Amen to that, sweet powers!' he says in response to her prayer for an endless daily increase of love and comfort, thereby accepting her version; but with 'I cannot speak enough of this content. / It stops me here, it is too much of joy', he immediately reaffirms his own. Then finally – 'And this (they kiss) and this, the greatest discords be / That e'er our hearts shall make' (196–20) – he transforms their 'discords' into kisses, as though unresolved differences, far from disrupting the pleasure of their union, become the source of its security.

So too with the Senate speech. Like all life stories, Othello's describes displacement: growing up, leaving home, enslavement, religious conversion; but these potential traumas are represented (if at all) not as rupture but as continuity, the accumulation of undifferentiated experience. That his journey goes from 'boyish days / To th' very moment' of the telling (1.3.131–2) suggests not the risk of engulfment but the confident assumption of a capacious future, an unperturbed sense that he will continue to assimilate and structure the material of his life into the daily increase Desdemona later describes. (Indeed, one reason why Desdemona's later words fail to threaten Othello is that he can already experience his life in this female-gendered register.) On the first page of the 'personal history' that bears his name, David Copperfield acknowledges uncertainty whether he will 'turn out to be the hero of my own life', deferring to a text behind his own control: 'these pages must show'.[59] But Othello seems somehow to have eluded this problematic split between narrator and narrative subject. 'Such was my process', he says (141), referring at once to his experience and his relation of that experience, his life and his life story. He cannot be swallowed up by his narrative, because he and

his narrative are perfectly identical. How can we know the storyteller from the story?

A protagonist of 'perfect soul' such as this or one anxiously vulnerable and radically flawed from the beginning, as in Greenblatt and other recent accounts of the play: what is at stake in this disagreement? Consider Hazlitt, who opens his commentary on *Othello* by declaring that 'tragedy purifies the affections by terror and pity. That is, it substitutes imaginary sympathy for mere selfishness. It gives us a high and permanent interest, beyond ourselves, in humanity as such. ... It makes man a partaker with his kind.'[60] Hazlitt, writing in a book called *The Characters of Shakespeare's Plays*, helped develop the tradition that culminated in Bradley.[61] By treating Othello's character as the play's motivational centre, and by emphasizing Othello's 'perfect soul' at the beginning, I have been trying to reconnect with this tradition; but I have no wish to reaffirm Bradley's apparent faith as such in the transcendent humanity of heroic individuals, or to imitate the methods apparently generated out of that faith. By

---

58 *Renaissance Self-Fashioning*, p. 238 and p. 243.
59 For an interesting discussion of Dickens's opening, see A. D. Nuttall, *Openings: Narrative Beginnings from the Epic to the Novel* (Oxford, 1992), pp. 172ff.
60 In P. P. Howe, ed., *The Complete Works* (London, 1930), vol. 4, p. 200.
61 Of course this tradition does not vanish abruptly with Bradley. Helen Gardner's 1955 British Academy lecture gave it perhaps its purest expression (the clarity of after-life – Minerva's owl flies at twilight): *The Noble Moor* (rpt. Folcroft, Pa., 1969). And there continue to be generously responsive acknowledgements of Othello's romantic-heroic stature in Jane Adamson, *'Othello' as Tragedy: Some Problems of Judgment and Feeling* (Cambridge, 1980); Bayley, Cavell, Kirsch, and Mark Rose ('Othello's Occupation: Shakespeare and the Romance of Chivalry', *English Literary Renaissance*, 15 (1985), 293–311). In one recent commentary in this mode, Thomas Clayton's tone of bemused disaffection from current critical norms fairly reflects the view that such celebratory criticism has become, like Bradley himself, self-evidently obsolete. See ' "That's she that was myself": Not-so-famous Last Words and Some Ends of *Othello*', *Shakespeare Survey 46* (1994), pp. 61–8.

abstracting dramatic characters from their relationship in the dramatic action to produce individualized portraits, Bradley sought to guarantee that our fascination with Iago never interferes with our admiration for Othello.[62] This strategy, however, systematically sanitizes and diminishes the play's power, for while it assures a full measure of pity for Othello's collapse, it avoids terror and any intuition of our own complicity in the events leading to the catastrophe – a guilty complicity that must underlie all the testimony from critical and theatrical traditions of this play's intolerable experience.

On the other hand, consider the tone of normative certainty in the current view: 'always already', 'inevitably', 'necessarily', 'this must be so'. *Così fan tutte*. These critics are worldly and insouciant; they know their culture disposition well. As I am by no means the first to remark, the anti-heroic reading of the play winds up sounding like Iago.[63] This is not a bad thing. The play writes us into Iago's perspective at the beginning and in one way or another succeeds in sustaining this alliance, no matter how unholy we understand it to be, up to the end. Current versions should help to account for precisely that sense of guilty complicity Bradley refused; but by moulding the protagonist to conform to a normative shape, they manage to make an equal (though opposite) refusal. For by treating Othello as an exemplary subject, trapped in the prisonhouse of language or the impossible condition of male desire, current versions leave only his alien status as extraordinary; and once this status is defined as the immigrant protagonist's inherent and necessary vulnerability, we are left with nothing more than abjection: *l'homme moyen sensuel* – not a transcendent 'humanity as such' but a derisory 'human, all too human'.

A fall from this height, like Gloucester's from what he supposes to be Dover Cliff, evokes some pity, perhaps, but no fear, and (since we see it coming) not even much surprise. That Bradleyan and anti-Bradleyan assumptions arrive at similar conclusions might suggest that

differing beliefs about character are less than fully determining. It matters, of course, whether we come to the play as humanists or constructionists, but watching *Othello* does not require us to solve conceptual problems, like the relative weight of nature and culture, from a position of absolute ontological conviction.[64] To the extent that such conviction commits us to

---

[62] Bradley clearly knows what he is doing and why. About Iago he asks, 'How is it then that we can bear to contemplate him; nay, that, if we really imagine him, we feel admiration and some kind of sympathy? ... Why is the representation tolerable, and why do we not accuse its author either of untruth or of a desperate pessimism? To these questions it might at once be replied: Iago does not stand alone; he is a factor in a whole; and we perceive him there and not in isolation, acted upon as well as acting, destroyed as well as destroying. But, although this is true and important, I pass it by and ... regard him by himself' (pp. 190–1).

[63] For others who make this point, see Bayley (pp. 129–30) and Kirsch (p. 31). Calderwood is particularly given to the canny insider's tone, as witness the words I emphasize in the following passages from *The Properties of 'Othello'* (keyed to the order of the four versions of contemporary criticism as I described them above): (1) The alien's abject dependency and Iago's inevitable triumph: 'But *after all what should we have expected?* The Moor is a stranger' (p. 68). (2) The impossible condition of male desire: 'This masculine appropriation of women in Venice helps explain why Othello's faith in Desdemona succumbs with such surprising ease to Iago's beguilements.. He loses faith in part because he never really had any. Though he endows his wife with heavenly qualities, deep down he suspects, *like any other husband*, the sorry truth' (p. 31). (3) Lacan: 'To see yourself in another, as he does – *as we all do* in our psychological extensions of Lacan's mirror stage – is to divide as well as unify the here/thereness of the body/self' (p. 105). (4) The submission to narrativity: '*Normally* the speaking subject is enormously in excess of the grammatical subject; we *are* [Calderwood's emphasis] far more than we can say' (p. 58).

[64] The play leaves the question open. Though asking us to credit Othello's nobility, it does not insist that we understand this nobility as necessarily self-generated. Maybe he is formed by his birth, social position, family and early environment. 'I fetch my life and being / From men of royal siege', he tells us early on (1.2.21–2). Maybe he is climatologically constructed (not a ridiculous notion in the Renaissance), as Desdemona suggests explaining his temperamental indisposition to jealousy:

stability and consistency of understanding, it may be the last thing we need. Consistency led Bradley into a maundering pathos, but at least he knew where to start. For unless we are prepared to respond to Othello's existence at the beginning with 'imaginary sympathy', responding with affection and wonder to a marvellous strangeness emanating from a different bodily place, black or tawny, and a world elsewhere – unless, that is, we can see Othello's visage in his mind, we will never be able to acknowledge the play's tragic power.

Theatrical impressions, heroic tragedy, pity and terror: all these acknowledge a major investment on my part in mode, genre, and above all artistic effect. Unlike Valerie Traub, who in the passage I quoted early on declares a relative lack of interest 'in the ways works of art are empowered', I have been writing from inside the traditional vocabulary of literary aesthetics. Traub's diminished interest represents a strong claim often made in current criticism that the sceptical scrutiny of this vocabulary – seeing through aesthetics to the literary system of which it is part, and finally to the cultural system that is said to generate and contain it (as well as everything else) – produces powerful results. According to Traub, since sexual taboos, 'prohibitions on incest or homosexuality, for instance', are 'arbitrary political constructs and thus open to transformation', then 'by deconstructing and refiguring the anxieties that regulate and discipline erotic life', we can 'contribute modestly to the project of carving out space within the social structure for greater erotic variety'.[65]

This is not a very plausible story; it is hard to believe that a politically inflected deconstruction, or any other way of studying Shakespeare, can contribute, even modestly, to a greater erotic variety. How, then, can we account for the proliferation of such claims on the current critical scene? Here, by way of an answer, is one story: in these austere times, we inhabit an increasingly production-driven research culture, characterized by the felt need to pursue socially useful projects. The functional value of these projects is defined by the functionaries who hold us accountable to themselves in the name of their own accountability to a construct called 'the public' or 'the taxpayer'. In this environment of 'targeted research', we are all cultural workers – willy nilly, though some of us do make love to our employment. As such, we experience submission to the relentlessly instrumental narrativity of the regulators and so find ourselves pointing to imaginary profits on the bottom line. It would be quixotic to inveigh against such strategic claims; after all, the regulators control the purse strings, and they have the power of description. Now, however, it seems we have succumbed to their pictures, promising such payoffs not just strategically to our administrators, but with genuine conviction to each other and even to ourselves.

Hazlitt too was doing targeted research, aiming at 'a high and permanent interest, beyond ourselves, in humanity as such'. In returning to Hazlitt and to Bradley, I am not suggesting that Hazlitt's target is inherently superior, or any more accessible to literary study. Responding with 'imaginary sympathy' to *Othello*'s power will not lead us necessarily to realize humanity as such, erotic variety, or any of the other goals in our various agendas (at least not without the anguished self-disgust Burke described as 'our filthy purgation'[66]). The relation between literary study and ethics, Richard Lanham's ' "Q" question', has gone without satisfactory answer since Plato, because there is no single answer.[67] Stanley Fish is right: like virtue, literary study is its own reward.[68] With a masterpiece like *Othello*, this is more than enough.

'the sun where he was born / Drew all such humours from him' (3.4.30–1).
[65] *Desire and Anxiety*, p. 8.
[66] 'Othello', p. 200.
[67] See 'The "Q" Question', *South Atlantic Quarterly*, 87 (1988), 653–700, modified and incorporated in *The Electronic Word: Democracy, Technology, and the Arts* (Chicago, 1993).
[68] 'Why Literary Criticism is Like Virtue', *London Review of Books* (10 June 1993), 11–16.

FRENCH LEAVE, OR LEAR AND THE KING OF FRANCE

R. A. FOAKES

Most of the variants between the two texts of
King Lear can be explained as cuts or expansions;
those who think the Quarto is the better text
see the Folio as weakening Shakespeare's intentions; those who think the Folio is a revision,
possibly by the author, of the Quarto see the
Folio as improving on the Quarto. The larger
changes, as represented in the 300 or so lines
found in the Quarto but not in the Folio, and
the 100 or so lines found in the Folio but not in
the Quarto, appear to be purposeful, but in the
absence of external evidence debate continues
about the nature of the purpose, and whose
purpose is in question. Allowing for possible
errors by printer or scribe, minor corrections or
sophistications, and possible indifferent variants
such as 'vncleane' (Q) or 'vnchaste' (F; 1.1.223)
and 'respects' (Q) or 'regards' (F; 1.1.234), the
majority of the smaller changes also seem to be
purposeful, and like the larger cuts or additions,
may be regarded as modifications of the Quarto
in the Folio. The basic structure of the play
remains the same in both texts, and 'virtually no
speech of any length seems to have been either
wholly reworked or replaced by a different
one'.[1] There are one or two places, such as the
scene of the duel between Edgar and Edmund,
and the ending with the death of Lear, both in
5.3, where the dramatic action is radically
altered, but the only substantial speech that
appears to offer two different versions in Quarto
and Folio is Kent's general commentary on the
state of affairs addressed to a Gentleman in 3.1.

The changes in Kent's speech relate to differences between the Quarto and Folio texts a few
lines earlier at the end of Act 2, where there is no
break in the Quarto. Here, in his anger at his
treatment by Goneril and Regan, Lear rushes out
of Gloucester's house into the storm accompanied by Kent, Gloucester and the Fool according
to the Quarto (F simply has '*Exeunt.*'), and editors
reasonably assume that the Knight (Q) or Gentleman (F) who attends on Lear in the scene
leaves at the same time. Gloucester returns to
report to Cornwall and Goneril that Lear is 'in
high rage', and the Folio inserts an extra line here:

GLOUCESTER The king is in high rage.
[F only] CORNWALL   Whither is he going?
GLOUCESTER He calls to horse, [Q and F] but will I
  know not whither.

Regan and Cornwall each give the order, 'Shut
up your doors' to Gloucester, who remains
with them at the end of the scene. The inserted
words are consistent with and echo Lear's call
for horses at 1.4.254 and 260, and again at
1.5.48, though he never appears on horseback.
Gloucester's words have a point, for if Lear has
charged off on horseback, it could explain why
Kent, who enters in the next scene, has to ask a
Gentleman 'Where's the king?' The Gentleman
knows Lear has the Fool with him, but, like
Kent, has lost touch with him. By the time

---

[1] Richard Knowles, 'Revision Awry in Folio *Lear* 3.2',
Shakespeare Quarterly, 46 (1995), 32–46, citing p. 32.
Knowles provides a comprehensive historical survey of
debate about this scene, so I have made no attempt to
duplicate it here.

Kent catches up with Lear, at 3.2.26, they are all on foot. The insertion of two half-lines in the Folio carefully preserves the metre here.

Within a few lines of this passage the Folio equally neatly excises eight lines describing Lear, again so as to preserve the metre:

[Q and F] KENT I know you. Where's the king?
GENTLEMAN Contending with the fretful
  elements;
  Bids the wind blow the earth into the sea,
  Or swell the curled waters 'bove the main
  That things might change or cease [Q only] tears
    his white hair,
  Which the impetuous blasts with eyeless rage
  Catch in their fury and make nothing of,
  Strives in his little world of man to outscorn
  The to-and-fro-conflicting wind and rain;
  This night wherein the cub-drawn bear would
    couch
  The lion and the belly-pinched wolf
  Keep their fur dry, unbonneted he runs,
  And bids what will take all.
  [Q and F] KENT But who is with him?

The image of Lear hatless and tearing his white hair has been suggestive for actors, and the idea of the 'little world of man' as a microcosm or epitome of the external world establishes the link between the storm in nature and the storm in Lear's mind that is dramatized in the following scenes in Act 3. But the lines may have been cut as unnecessary, since they describe what we shortly are to see Lear do, and merely expand what the Gentleman says in his first four lines. Also they perhaps were thought to give undue emphasis to Lear in a short scene that shifts attention from him to a larger context, and makes a bridge between his exit into the storm, and appearance confronting the winds and rain in 3.2.

It looks as though some deliberate editing of this sequence was being undertaken in whatever copy lies behind the Folio text. What follows therefore is surprising, for the next alteration appears at first sight to be a clumsy substitution of a different speech by Kent in the Folio for that in the Quarto. The text runs as follows:

Quarto:

Folio:

Until the 1970s most editors routinely conflated these two passages, printing the Folio lines first, and adding 'But true it is . . .', etc., after 'furnishings', to give Kent a long, somewhat disconnected and unwieldy speech. Some of the difficulties with these two speeches had been noted, as when Dr Johnson complained that in the Folio Kent gives the Gentleman no commission, but sends him off 'he knows not why, he knows not whither'.[2] Indeed, in this text it seems that the Gentleman somewhat rudely interrupts his superior in the middle of his utterance. In the Quarto text Kent's initial

---

[2] Cited by Knowles, 'Revision Awry', p. 36.

remarks about a 'division' between Albany and Cornwall break off suddenly at 'But true it is', and seem unconnected with his announcement that the French have invaded Britain. The editorial habit of conflating the passages helped to obscure these difficulties, since Kent was presented as breaking off his account of Albany and Cornwall at 'furnishings' – to turn to the topic of a French invasion with the words 'But true it is, from France there comes a power'.

Those who were troubled by the apparent contradictions between the two texts proposed a variety of explanations for the changes, none of which achieved wide acceptance, and it was in the 1980s that debate intensified, when the idea gained currency that Shakespeare or someone else might have revised the play between the printing of the Quarto and the Folio versions. In particular, Gary Taylor forcefully argued that the Folio lines here showed a deliberate revision of the Quarto, designed, together with a number of other changes or omissions elsewhere in the Folio text of the play, to remove or obscure references to a French invasion of England, and emphasize instead the idea of possible civil war.[3] This explanation of the differences between the Quarto and Folio seemed at first persuasive, but, as E. A. J. Honigmann showed, it cannot be accepted, if only for the good reason that other references to a French invasion later in the play, as at 3.7.2–3, 'the army of France is landed', appear in both texts, and were not omitted from the Folio.[4]

Once it was seen that an explanation in terms of the war with France was unsatisfactory, other explanations began to be offered or revived. One reformulates an old idea that the passages may be seen as showing a difference between the Quarto and Folio 'in which the same speech by a prominent character has been differently cut'.[5] This way of accounting for the changes ignores the loose ends in the Quarto and Folio versions, and seems to me implausible. Censorship has been invoked as another way to account for differences between the texts, both

in relation to the Quarto lines, because of their reference to war with France, and in relation to the Folio passage, because of its reference to corruption in court. In the absence of external evidence, both texts can be suspected of being tampered with in this way, so that I find unconvincing the argument for local censorship.[6] Those who regard the passages as alternatives generally prefer the Quarto, claiming that it is more coherent and stylistically superior. However, value judgements in such cases are notoriously unreliable, and both versions have been accepted as by Shakespeare, the more complex syntax of the Folio being in a 'style more typical of Shakespeare's later work'.[7] In the theatre the Quarto text has more frequently, though not always, been preferred in recent productions.[8]

Such theories attempt to explain the absence of the Quarto lines from the Folio, or the absence of the Folio lines from the Quarto text, and focus on Kent's speech as presented in the two texts. They ignore the evidence of the context in the Quarto and Folio, which shows that deliberate editing was being undertaken, with the addition of two half-lines in the Folio,

---

3 'The War in *King Lear*', *Shakespeare Survey 33* (1980), pp. 27–34.

4 'Do-it-Yourself *Lear*', *New York Review of Books*, 25 October 1990, pp. 58–60; see also R. A. Foakes, *Hamlet versus Lear* (Cambridge 1993), pp. 106–7, and Knowles, 'Revision Awry', p. 42.

5 *King Lear: A Parallel Text Edition*, ed. René Weis (1993), p. 30.

6 For discussion of such theories, and a forceful refutation of them, see Gary Taylor, 'Monopolies, Show Trials, Disaster, and Invasion: *King Lear* and Censorship', in *The Division of the Kingdoms*, ed. Gary Taylor and Michael Warren (Oxford, 1983), pp. 77–119, especially pp. 80 and 112–13.

7 *King Lear*, ed. Jay Halio (Cambridge, 1992), p. 269; see also E. A. J. Honigmann, 'Shakespeare's Revised Plays: *King Lear* and *Othello*', *The Library*, 6th series, 4 (1982), p. 153.

8 See Robert Clare, '"Who is it that can tell me who I am?"': The Theory of Authorial Revision between the Quarto and Folio Texts of *King Lear*', *The Library*, 6th series, 34–59, especially pp. 45–7.

and the omission of seven full and two half-lines found only in the Quarto, in such a way as to preserve neatly the metrical pattern. It would thus appear most probable that the differences between Kent's speeches originate in further editing of the text from which the Folio was printed, but that for some reason the compositor was confused by the markings he saw, and failed to carry out the editor's intentions.

But if so, what were those intentions? The newest explanation, proposed by Richard Knowles, ingeniously argues that the eight lines added to the Folio 'are not in fact a consecutive block of text but are two passages intended for two different locations in the Q text'.[9] He thinks that the first three and a half lines of the Folio passage were meant to follow '*Cornwall*', as they do in the Folio, and argues that Kent's claim that the French have spies in Britain makes more plausible the news of a French invasion. The remaining four and a half lines he would insert in the Quarto after 'The King hath cause to plaine', so that the speech would end as follows:

> you shall find
> Some that will thanke you, making iust report
> Of how vnnaturall and bemadding sorrow
> The King hath cause to plaine, What hath bin
> seene
> Either in snuffes, and packings of the Dukes,
> Or the hard Reine which both of them hath
> borne
> Against the old kinde King; or something deeper,
> Whereof (perchance) these are but furnishings.
> I am a gentleman of blood and breeding,
> And from some knowledge and assurance,
> Offer this office to you.

Knowles supposes that two passages for insertion on the same page in the prompt-book of *King Lear* were written on one slip, and were mistakenly treated, by a scribe making a transcript to serve as printer's copy, as a single passage to be substituted for what was in the original. Thus in spite of his contempt for the Folio lines as incoherent and 'stylistically awkward if not unintelligible',[10] Knowles ends

by proposing an arrangement that preserves almost all the lines in Quarto and Folio, and gives Kent a very long speech indeed. This arrangement would cut out the Quarto phrase 'But true it is', and produce instead a clumsy line, 'Intelligent of our State. From *France* there comes a power.' It also inserts Folio lines in the passage cited above in a way that I find puzzling, since there is no direct connection between the 'bemadding sorrow' felt by Lear and the 'snuffes, and packings', i.e., resentments and intrigues, of Cornwall and Albany. Furthermore, one might expect Kent to end with the message he wants the Gentleman to convey, as in the Quarto.

What Knowles argues for is another form of conflation of Quarto and Folio, one which is more coherent than the usual patching together created by the insertion of all of the additional Folio lines after '*Cornwall*', but which solves some problems only to create other difficulties.

The idea that the Folio lines might represent two passages derives from Peter Blayney,[11] who, however, thought the first three and a half lines were intended as a revision to replace the statement in the Quarto that a French force has landed in England. It seems to me that he was right to feel that the Quarto lines about invasion and the Folio lines about spies were not meant to coexist in one speech. Others have thought likewise, but the reasons offered have usually been censorship or Gary Taylor's idea that the Folio substitutes the idea of a civil war for a foreign one. The problem here is not with the idea of substitution, but with the reasons suggested for it. If the speech is considered in relation to the rest of the action in the play, a simpler explanation for the difficulties emerges, one that neither depends on the elaborate

---

[9] Knowles, 'Revision Awry', p. 42.
[10] Ibid., p. 37.
[11] As Knowles generously acknowledges in 'Revision Awry', p. 42, where he refers to notes prepared for the as yet unpublished vol. 2 of Blayney's *The Texts of King Lear and their Origins* (Cambridge, 1982).

supposition that two passages marked for insertion were treated as one, nor amalgamates Quarto and Folio to produce a very long and still not very coherent conflation.

Assuming that the Folio lines about spying were designed to replace the reference to a French invasion in the Quarto, what might be the reasons for such a change? In the first place, a reference to the French is premature in terms of the action. Lear has just gone off into the storm, and Kent has lost touch with him (possibly because he is on foot and the king left on horseback, according to the Folio). Meeting the Gentleman in 3.1 Kent asks him to convey to Dover news of the harsh treatment the king has suffered. The French (Cordelia among them) therefore cannot yet know of what has just happened, and there is no reason as yet for them to have invaded England. The report of a French landing is also premature in relation to the announcement made by Cornwall at the beginning of 3.7 that 'The army of France is landed' (Quarto and Folio), an announcement made on the basis of a letter stolen by Edmund from Gloucester's closet at 3.5.11. When Gloucester advises Edmund to 'incline to the king' in 3.3, he says, 'There is part of a power already landed' (Quarto), or 'footed' (Folio), a change that is consistent with the omission of the reference to a French invasion in Folio 3.1; here 'footed' could refer to the forces of Albany or Cornwall.[12] If the references to a French invasion are left out of 3.1 and 3.3, as in the Folio, the action becomes more coherent, as Kent sends the Gentleman off to Cordelia, who presumably informed Kent, in the letter he displays and reads at 2.2.162, that she was planning to return to England.

The news that the French army has landed then comes appropriately in 3.7 after Lear has been sent on a litter to Dover, and after Edmund has betrayed his father to Cornwall as 'an intelligent party to the advantages of France' (3.5.9). The word 'intelligent' echoes and adds meaning to Kent's use of it in Folio 3.1 with reference to spies passing intelligence to France;

Gloucester is revealed as the known spy among the 'Seruants' of Albany and Cornwall, and is punished as a 'traitor' in 3.7. The Folio clarifies and makes more consistent the flow of the action here. Why then do references to a French invasion occur as early as 3.1 in the Quarto, and why were some, but by no means all, such references omitted from the Folio? It is possible to answer this question by considering an ambiguity in the meaning of the term 'France'.

Shakespeare's 'principal source'[13] for his play was the old play of *King Leir*, in which, after Cordella is reconciled to her father, the King of Gallia invades England to defeat in battle Cambria and Cornwall and their British forces, and restore Leir to his throne. In Shakespeare's play the King of France has quite a strong presence in the opening scene, where he takes Cordelia to be his queen, and does not appear on stage again. In this scene, as also at 1.2.23 ('France in choler parted'), and 2.4.208 ('the hot-blooded France that dowerless took / Our youngest born'), he is referred to as 'France'. Three later references to him survive in the Quarto, all of which were omitted from the Folio text. In 4.2 Goneril pours scorn on her husband for his inactivity in the face of the French invasion:

> Where's thy drum?
> France spreads his banners in our noiseless land ...

Here 'France' means the King of France rather than the country, as is made clear in the next scene, 4.3, which is altogether absent from the Folio, and which begins with Kent asking the Gentleman, 'Why the King of France is so suddenly gone back, know you no reason?' Affairs of state have caused him to return to

---

[12] The word 'footed' is used again at 3.7.46 with explicit reference to 'traitors' who have arrived from France, whereas Gloucester's statement, 'There is part of a power already footed' (3.3.11) leaves unclear whose 'power' is on the march.

[13] Citing Halio's Introduction to his edition of *King Lear*, p. 3.

France, leaving his marshal behind; but it seems as though Albany thinks of him as again in England in Quarto 5.1, where he leads on his army protesting that his concern is not to fight Lear:

> For this business,
> It touches us as France invades our land,
> Not bolds the king with others whom I fear
> Most just and heavy causes make oppose.
>
> (5.1.24–7)

As 'the king' means Lear, so 'France' would seem to refer to the King of France.

Other references to France remain in the Folio text, but only one that specifically relates to the king, when Cordelia reports in 4.4 that 'great France' has been moved by her tears to provide an army to aid her father. The effect of this scene, however, differs in the Folio from that in the Quarto. In both texts she appears here for the first time since the opening scene, but in the Quarto she comes on after two references to the king of France landing in England, and after a Gentleman's description of her as a saintly emblem of pity in 4.3, and she is accompanied at her entrance by a 'Doctor, and others'. There is no suggestion that she is leading the army provided by her husband. In the Folio, by contrast, the omission of references to France and the King of France from 3.1, 3.5, 4.2, and 4.3, together with the cutting of about 35 lines in 4.2 and the whole of 4.3, means that Cordelia appears abruptly, with no preparation, after scenes of the meeting between the blind Gloucester and Edgar as Poor Tom (4.1), and of Albany and Goneril quarrelling (4.2). In the Folio she enters in the next scene 'with Drum and Colours' and 'Souldiours', and is apparently herself at the head of an invading army.

The differences between the entries at the beginning of 5.2 in the Quarto and Folio are also relevant. The Quarto has 'Enter the powers of France over the Stage, Cordelia with her father in her hand', an entry that suggests that the French forces are led by someone other than Cordelia

and Lear, who appear to be bringing up the rear. The Folio by contrast has 'Enter with Drumme and Colours, Lear, Cordelia, and Souldiers, ouer the Stage, and Exeunt', so putting Lear and Cordelia at the head of their (French) army. The Folio is consistent in removing any hints of an intervention by the King of France. The Quarto, on the other hand, seems uncertain and ambiguous about the role of the French king. The references to him suggest that Shakespeare may have had an early conception of his play that was closer to the old Leir, and envisaged an action in which French forces led by the King of France invaded England to rescue Lear. The references to the King of France in the Quarto, which include the puzzling indication in 4.3 that he has just returned there from England, may thus be residual traces of a conception of the play that underwent modifications that eventually resulted in the Folio version. If so, the Quarto would probably represent an intermediate stage in the evolution of the play, not a first draft.

To return then to 3.1: the evidence I have outlined seems to me to strengthen the case for thinking that the changes in the Folio were intended to replace the reference to a French invading force in the Quarto. The Folio lines, however, do not make very good sense as they stand, since Kent does not tell the Gentleman where to take his message. I suggest that the markings made by the reviser were misunderstood, and that more was omitted from the Folio than was intended; the simplest solution to the problems of the two texts here is to suppose that the eight lines added in the Folio were designed to replace the four irregular lines (nearly five if set out as blank verse) that relate to France, and that the rest of the speech in the Quarto was meant to be kept in the Folio. I assume that the punctuation is erratic, as often in both texts, that the period after 'State' is no more reliable than the semi-colon after 'set high', and that both should be commas in modern punctuation. I suppose that Kent's message in the Folio is intended to be mysterious, hinting at civil turmoil, webs of intrigue, spying, and something worse; the passage beginning 'What hath been seen' I take to be in direct apposition with 'Intelligent of our state', speculating on the nature of the intelligence conveyed to France. Kent then changes the subject on the word 'furnishings' to give directions to the Gentleman, whose main function is to report on the harsh treatment meted out to Lear by his daughters and sons-in-law. Kent's speech then reads as follows when modernized:

KENT   Sir, I do know you,
  And dare upon the warrant of my note
  Commend a dear thing to you. There is division,
  Although the face of it is covered
  With mutual cunning, 'twixt Albany and
    Cornwall,
  Who have, as who have not that their great stars
  Throned and set high, servants, who seem no less,
  Which are to France the spies and speculations
  Intelligent of our state, – what hath been seen
  Either in snuffs and packings of the dukes,
  Or the hard rein which both of them hath borne
  Against the old kind king; or something deeper,
  Whereof (perchance) these are but furnishings. –
  Now to you:
  If on my credit you dare build so far
  To make your speed to Dover, you shall find
  Some that will thank you, making just report
  Of how unnatural and bemadding sorrow
  The king hath cause to plain.
  I am a gentleman of blood and breeding,
  And from some knowledge and assurance
  Offer this office to you.

This arrangement has the advantage of making Kent's speech consistent with the action. He speaks of 'division' between Albany and Cornwall, ironically echoing Gloucester's

comment about the 'division of the kingdom' at 1.1.4. He refers to spies reporting on English affairs to France, using the word 'intelligent', which anticipates Edmund's use of it at 3.5.12 to denounce his father. Kent also sends the Gentleman off to report at Dover the sufferings of Lear. The speech thus deals with three matters, quarrels between Albany and Cornwall, spies passing intelligence to France, and the cruel way Lear has been treated. In the Folio the Gentleman reappears with Cordelia in 4.4, and may be presumed to have delivered Kent's message earlier, a message which provided reasons for the arrival of an invading force from France reported in 3.7. The Folio text puts that force under the command of Cordelia, and dismisses the King of France from the action after the opening scene. He lingers in the Quarto, hinting that Shakespeare may in his initial conception, as in earlier versions of the story, have contemplated a different ending, in which the King of France played a part. This is, of course, speculation, but all interpretation must be speculative, since the only direct evidence we have is in the texts as printed in Quarto and Folio.[14]

---

[14] It is possible that censorship of a larger kind affected the Folio text, not in order simply to remove the reference to a French invasion in Quarto 3.1, but rather to cut out any suggestion in the last three acts that a French army under the King of France defeated the British on their own soil; but *The True Chronicle History of King Leir*, published in 1605, shows the Gallian king successfully doing just that in order to restore Leir to his throne. It seems to me, as I have argued, that the changes in the Folio clarify a conception of the action different from that found in the Quarto.

THE ACTOR AS ARTIST: HAROLD HOBSON'S SHAKESPEARIAN THEATRE CRITICISM

DOMINIC SHELLARD

Harold Hobson, the first recipient of a knighthood for theatre criticism (in 1977) and the drama critic of *The Sunday Times* from 1947 to 1976, is best remembered today for his discovery of Harold Pinter's *The Birthday Party*, his critical jousting with his great rival, Kenneth Tynan of the *Observer*, and his championing of Absurdist drama, notably the work of Beckett. This article aims to demonstrate that these well-known preoccupations were less important for Hobson's critical practice than his belief that it was his critical duty to provide a historical record of what he had witnessed and that the actor was the pre-eminent member of the theatrical triumvirate of actor, director and playwright. These two critical edicts are most evident in Hobson's review of performances of Shakespeare.[1]

Hobson's first actual review of a Shakespearian production, submitted as a freelancer to the *Christian Science Monitor* in 1930, shortly after coming down from Oriel College, Oxford, provides an early indication of his desire to elevate the importance of the performer above that of the director and even the playwright. The review, blandly entitled ' "Macbeth" at Oxford', is a formulaic account of the Easter production of the Oxford University Dramatic Society, which commences with an extensive listing of all the participants. As tentative as Hobson's very first published review, a bald description of Pirandello's *Lazzaro* at the Huddersfield Repertory Theatre, starring Donald Wolfit and published in the

Christian Science Monitor on 30 July 1929, ' "Macbeth" at Oxford' is significant for its one moment of passion, when the reviewer turns to the performance of Lady Macbeth. Having complimented the producer, Brewster Morgan, on the elaborate arrangement of steps that comprised the set, Hobson continues:

The second outstanding feature was the astonishing performance of Lady Macbeth given for the society by Gwen Ffrangcon-Davies. Flouting all the recent traditions of acting this part as a woman of impressive presence and savage and commanding temper, Miss Davies emphasized all the feminine and quiet aspects of the character. In doing so she gave a performance that was throughout effective, and in the sleep-walking scene, positively electrifying.[2]

The restrictions of space regrettably prevent Hobson from amplifying his observations, but they demonstrate how his attention was more likely to be drawn to theatrically effective acting performances which enhance rather than suffocate the ensemble of fellow actors, instead of a rigid, directorially conceived drama, that subjugates actors to the whims of a controlling force external to the performance. This suspicion of the over-dominant director was to harden by the mid-thirties and it became a recurrent critical motif to be applied equally to

---

[1] For a complete list of every article that Hobson wrote about Shakespeare, see D. M. Shellard, *Harold Hobson: The Complete Catalogue 1922–1988* (Keele University Press, 1995), pp. 307–8.

[2] ' "Macbeth" at Oxford', *Christian Science Monitor*, 12/4/1930.

the perceived excesses of Hall, Barton and Brook in the nineteen sixties. In response to Stanley Bell's 1934 production of *The Merchant of Venice* at the Alhambra, for example, Hobson commented that the performance was 'crammed with little incidents, some amusing, some dull, which are not in the play's text, and, what is perhaps more important, which do not appear to have been devised to illustrate any single unified emotional aspect of the drama'. This recourse to directorial tricks was seen by Hobson as a prevalent and regrettable trait in recent productions of the playwright:

In the old days Shakespeare was pulled about to make an actor-manager's holiday, and the play was stuffed with all sorts of 'business' not warranted by the text. Today, he is made a producer's hobby-horse, or a convenient mouthpiece through which Komisarjevsky or Tyrone Guthrie may deliver to the world whatever they consider the world is in need of hearing.[3]

Hobson had begun reviewing plays as a profession at a time when the London theatre was facing the twin external threats of the new media (radio and the 'talkies') coupled with the world economic down-turn, and the internal challenge of the realignment of the power-balance between the actor, dramatist and director. One of the ways in which the London theatre attempted to counter these problems was through a revival of Shakespearian productions, which Hobson had first applauded during the summer of 1930, with the three separate productions of *Hamlet*, starring Henry Ainley, John Gielgud and the German, Alexander Moissi, and a production of *Othello*, featuring Paul Robeson. This reawakening of interest in Shakespeare had stimulated a fresh debate, however, as to whether Shakespeare was 'better appreciated when read in the study than when seen on the stage'.[4] In an editorial for the *Christian Science Monitor* (by now, his main employer), 'Shakespeare on Trial', Hobson had offered an explanation as to why it was attractive but erroneous to perceive Shakespeare as a paper playwright:

Many productions of Elizabethan drama have of late been disappointing, because the quiet, naturalistic type of acting fostered by an endless succession of drawing-room comedies has proved quite inadequate to the abounding eloquence and rhetoric in which they are so rich. This stricture does not apply, however, to the acting of either Mr Gielgud or Mr Ainley. Both are capable of reciting verse as it should be recited, rhythmically, musically, and with gusto, and so are giving London the best Shakespearian performances that it has seen for years.[5]

It was a theme that the newly appointed London Drama Critic of the *Christian Science Monitor* was to return to on a number of occasions, because it alluded to his evolving belief that drama was a fluid, vibrant entity, rather than a static, measured discipline. In 'Shakespeare for Repertory',[6] for example, Hobson expresses support for the formation of a permanent Shakespearian repertory company, since

The principal enemies of Shakespeare have often been neglect and the star actor. When Shakespeare has not been put fairly constantly upon the stage, a generation of players grows up that is more or less incapable of speaking verse properly, so that when a stray revival is put on, the actors bring to it a technique based on the naturalistic prose dialogue of modern drama, with the consequence that a dull and utterly unsatisfactory performance results, and Shakespeare is immediately voted a tedious fellow who, for entertainment value, cannot compete with the talkies or the latest revue.[7]

Significantly, in the light of Hobson's subsequent enthusiasm for the Christian Verse Drama of T. S. Eliot and Christopher Fry in the early forties, and the poetic allusiveness of Samuel Beckett in the early fifties, it is as early as 1933 that he can be seen to be evincing a desire for drama that is provocative and suggestive, rather than safe, well constructed and readily compre-

---

3 ' "The Merchant of Venice" ' , *CSM*, 14/4/1934.
4 'Shakespeare on Trial', *CSM*, 10/6/1930.
5 Ibid.
6 'Shakespeare for Repertory', *CSM*, 5/3/1932.
7 Ibid.

hensible, in addition to choosing to see Shakespeare as an incentive to future playwrights, rather than a historical impediment which they need to throw off. The best example of this, and in particular, of Hobson's belief that poetic drama could move new British playwrighting on from its obsession with middle-class trivia, comes in the piece, 'Toward a New Tragedy'. Having quoted several lines from *King Lear*, *Macbeth* and *Othello*, Hobson observes:

It is not sufficient nor fair to say that the modern dramatist does not write lines like these because he cannot; he would not be allowed to if he could; for the convention of today is that he must write in prose. That is, perhaps, his chief difficulty. Is it possible, in the rhythms of conversational prose, such as the twentieth-century playwright might use, to sound the accent of majesty which tragic drama demands? Some critics say that it is not. But I think that it is. For, after all, the thing has been done. It is true that most of Shakespeare's prose occurs in scenes of low emotional pressure, thus indicating that he himself thought verse to be the better medium for his great effects. Undoubtedly verse is the better medium for scenes of that kind; but the question is not whether prose is as good as verse for high tragic matters, but whether it is any good for them at all. Here Shakespeare himself answers the question by writing Lady Macbeth's last scene in prose. Again, the prose of Shylock's: 'Hath not a Jew eyes? Hath not a Jew hands, organs, dimensions, senses, affections, passions?' or of Hamlet's 'What a piece of work is man' is equal to any demands that can be made upon it. It is prose like this, strong, nervous, eloquent, and not the colorless speech of everyday existence, that tragedy must use today if it is to survive.[8]

The true significance of Hobson's consideration of Shakespeare in his first decade of critical writing is that it increased his receptivity for any new drama which eschewed the temptation to imitate the well-constructed play written in insipid modern prose, and aimed instead to appeal through a suggestive and allusive discourse. Hence, Hobson's delight in the work of Auden and Isherwood, whose *The Dance of Death* he described as a 'brilliant, and ... entirely

successful attempt to work out for the theater a new, significant art-form'.[9] This immersion in the delight of verse and poetic drama did much to prepare the ground for Hobson's empathy with Absurdist theatre.

In May 1939, Hobson encountered one of the many incredible strokes of luck that characterized his career. Worried that his wife, Elizabeth, a teacher, was on the verge of being evacuated from London along with her school, Hobson telephoned the Board of Education and was astounded to be informed by a civil servant not only of her destination, but of the general plans for evacuation. Realizing that this was a scoop of the first order, Hobson wrote up the information and submitted the article to *The Sunday Times*. The story, entitled 'Families Who Will Make Their Own Evacuation Plans',[10] duly appeared on the front page the following Sunday, and Hobson's fifty-year connection with the newspaper had begun.

From July 1945 until July 1947, Hobson was considered to be the permanent substitute of James Agate, *The Sunday Times*' current and renowned theatre critic. Initially, Hobson's occasional substitute reviews were disappointingly derivative, caught between aping Agate's distinctive style and attempting to draw attention to his own less coruscating approach. During his first year as deputy he was rarely able to write reviews, but in September 1946, whilst Agate was attending the Cannes Film Festival, Hobson was granted a series of three consecutive articles. Given Hobson's pre-war interest in Shakespearian verse and the importance of the actor, it was perhaps inevitable that the piece which would first alert his superiors to his suitability to inherit Agate's mantle should comprise an account of Laurence Olivier's performance as King Lear.

Laurence Olivier's Lear, like his 1944 Oedipus and Richard III, is generally acknowl-

---

[8] *CSM*, 23/5/1933.
[9] 'The Dance of Death', *CSM*, 22/10/1935.
[10] *The Sunday Times*, 14/5/1939.

edged to be one of the most masterly theatrical performances of the twentieth century. The contemporary acclaim for the entire company was instantaneous and Olivier himself was greeted with adulation – Alan Dent claimed that 'Olivier's Lear is nothing short of a tremendous achievement',[11] Peter Fleming wrote of a 'superb performance of which London has every right to be proud',[12] and Philip Hope-Wallace commended the 'great ease and mastery' with which Olivier both directed and acted.[13] It is perhaps Hobson's article, 'Mr Olivier's Lear',[14] however, that most evocatively conveys the actor's achievement. In Hobson's favoured 'touchstone' style, he begins by relating that Irving started the play 'in noise and tumult and barbaric war' but doubts that this impressive opening could have been finer than Olivier's, for the production team and the actor have solved the problem of making Lear's division of the kingdom appear plausible. They make the preliminary conversation between Kent and Gloucester 'a thing of easy and supple comedy' so that 'when the King himself appears, white-haired, white-bearded, yet swift and eager and active, we recognize him at once for what he is, a humourist, a man of infinite fecundity of wit, choleric maybe, but resilient and alert, ready in sheer intellectual energy and physical well-being for any jest or experimental escapade ...'

Hobson conveys the unpredictability of Lear at the start, as well as the coiled energy with which Olivier wanted to invest the part, by marrying a relation of the scene to an interpretation of the actor's intent: '[Lear] is bursting with overflux of vital forces: from his brain at any moment may spring some plan, some scheme, half joke, half earnest, which, born on the inspiration of a moment, may, in sudden change of mood, have consequences to wreck kingdoms and ruin lives.'

The brilliance of this review lies in the fact that it exploits rather than capitulates to the restrictions of space. The dynamic energy of the prose exactly parallels the suppressed energy of

Lear which Hobson feels is an integral part of Olivier's performance. Hobson maintained that the most dramatic work that he had ever read was Thucydides' *History of the Peloponnesian War*, and he was to return to it throughout his career.[15] Noted for its balance between compression and breadth, its maintenance of pace, its scientific method, its elegant style and its analysis of the causal link between events, it has clearly influenced Hobson in accomplished reviews such as this, where personal observation, theatrical evaluation, historical information and the depiction of atmosphere are all blended into a distinctive and perfect whole. Even by this stage of the review, Hobson has referred to a historical precedent, considered a question of academic interpretation, conveyed a sense of occasion (so often lost in reviews of famous performances), mentioned by name the production team, described Olivier's physical presence, emotional depth and dramatic intent and alluded to Dr Johnson's confusion about the work – all with no loss of pace, no irrelevant digression and no discordant phrase. The perfection of Olivier's depiction is honoured by the craftsmanship of Hobson's prose.

Having dealt with the play's opening, Hobson dispenses with the artificially elevated tone he had adopted in his two earlier September reviews and proceeds to compliment the actor on avoiding a well-laid trap:

Mr Olivier's Lear is very old: he is also strong. There is about him none of that senility which many great actors have affected. In poetic truth undoubtedly this is right. Under one aspect this play presents man as the plaything of the gods: they kill us for their sport. Where the quarry is lame or feeble or impotent, surely the sport is poor? It was said of the great Duke of Marlborough that he could be bought, but that he was worth buying. Mr Olivier's Lear is a man who

[11] 'Royal Lear', *News Chronicle*, 27/9/1946.
[12] 'The Theatre', *The Spectator*, 27/9/1946.
[13] 'Theatre', *Time and Tide*, 5/10/1946.
[14] ST, 29/9/1946.
[15] Harold Hobson, *Indirect Journey* (London, 1978), pp. 164–5.

by temperament is capable of being tortured: but he is worth torturing. The cries and the lamentations, the curses and the threats that are torn out of his breast are like the crash of thunder and the stab of lightning. They are not the whimpering of a weak old man: they are the groaning and the weeping of the universe. This is a cosmic grief.

Indeed, Olivier's utterance of

> I will do such things –
> What they are, yet I know not; but they shall be
> The terrors of the earth   (*Lear* F (1623), 2.2.454–6)

when confronted by Regan, reminds Hobson of Olivier's anguished cry as Oedipus, which rang round the rafters of the New Theatre like 'the echo of the crack of doom'.

The penultimate paragraph of the review hints that this Lear is the result of the distillation of the very best elements of Olivier's previous roles:

There was once a time when Mr Olivier was all violence, all extreme passion; like Kean, he was constantly upon the rack. But, as his passion has strengthened and his expression of it ripened, so has it grown more controlled. There are moments in his performance of Lear that are of utter stillness and of quiet pathos. The same power that can set the storm in motion can now calm it by the lifting of a hand.

And so, after the effusive rhythm of the previous four paragraphs, the review, too, comes to a full close by highlighting two other noteworthy performances, Alec Guinness as the Fool and Peter Copley as Edmund, and then authoritatively proclaiming that 'there is no weakness anywhere'. The genius of Olivier's performance has inspired and suffused Hobson's own writing to the extent that the reader is inclined to accept the validity of the momentous last phrase, that 'the central performance must stand among the very greatest things ever accomplished upon the English stage'. As 'evidence' of Olivier's achievement, this review is one – albeit very important – testimony amongst several. As confirmation of Hobson's desire, at the earliest point in his career as a full-time critic, to be enthused by memorable acting performances, passages of mellifluous verse and

productions of suggestive, instead of explicit, sentiment, this piece is a marker against which his earlier and his subsequent criticism – most notably on Absurdist drama – should be read.

Hobson's growing critical confidence whilst Agate's deputy, engendered by articles such as 'Mr Olivier's Lear', was further demonstrated by his consideration of another Shakespeare play, *Othello*, the following year. He had often considered the play in his *Christian Science Monitor* columns, and as recently as April 1946, had written that one of the four stage performances he would most like to have witnessed had been Kean's Othello.[16] A week later he reported why Gielgud did not feel that he would make an effective Moor: 'he considers his voice to be wholly of tenor quality, while he maintains that Othello's speeches should have running through them a bass undertone that suggests the warrior and statesman'.[17] The occasional *Sunday Times* column gave Hobson a chance to move beyond stage gossip and consider matters of analysis – the readership was intelligent and expected more than reportage – so on 6 April 1947 Hobson decided to consider whether the role of Othello 'was beyond the compass of an actor'.

The article, entitled 'Iago's Fault',[18] is not an academic treatise, but raises an interesting point with regard to the principal character. Having seen Jack Hawkins's adequate but unexceptional performance in the title role at the Piccadilly a week before, Hobson wonders – in spite of Hazlitt's delight in Kean's portrayal – whether the part is capable of being played. He himself has 'never seen an Othello who affrighted and dominated the eye', and he agrees with one unidentified actor to whom he had spoken that the character demands an actor of giant physical stature and a booming voice, qualities which are rare in great contemporary performances. A second anonymous actor, however, suggests

---

16 'Conversation at Luncheon', *CSM*, 16/4/1946.
17 'Mr Gielgud Wants a New Play', *CSM*, 20/4/1946.
18 *ST*, 6/6/1947.

that the difficulty in playing Othello lies not in the physical demands of the role, but in his overshadowing by Iago. It is this which intrigues Hobson and he concludes that it is Iago 'who sets the plot in motion, and controls the action', with Othello only enjoying two significant moments: 'when he delivers his speech to the Senate about his wooing of Desdemona, and when he stills the brawl in the streets with the astounding "Keep up your bright swords, for the dew will rust them".' The article then ends with three rhetorical questions: 'Would our Othellos then be better if our Iagos were worse? Has Shakespeare here written a play of which the effect is greatest when one of the chief characters is less than perfectly played? And if so, is this a defect in craftmanship?'

The Sunday Times received a deluge of letters in response to this piece, mostly listing recent praiseworthy Othellos, including Matheson Lang, Paul Robeson, Baliol Holloway, Louis Calvert, Lewis Waller, Giovanni Grasso and Godfrey Tearle.[19] Hobson had discovered his audience.

Six weeks after this article appeared Hobson was appointed theatre critic of *The Sunday Times* upon James Agate's death.[20] He was to occupy this post from 1947 to 1976, becoming the most notable British theatre critic of the third quarter of the twentieth century. The passion of his Shakespearian observations, his delight in memorable acting performances and his ability to provoke and intrigue in equal measure were to become critical traits and although it is his championing of new writing by playwrights such as Beckett, Pinter and Osborne for which he is most renowned, it is in his writing on Shakespeare that his intuitive love of performance continued to be most evident. An important example of this is provided by his response to Olivier's Old Vic Richard III in 1949:

From the moment when Sir Laurence's malign hunchback first hobbles across the stage, after entering through a door whose lock he avariciously fingers as if to see that decency and generosity have

been shut out, this performance amuses, delights and astonishes. Mark how, in that opening soliloquy, by a waving of the arms, and a swaying of his crooked body, a mad nodding of his monstrously nosed head, and a rapid quickening of his speech, he creates a choking, snaring forest: and mark, too, the effect at once pitiful and revolting, when he drops on one knee to court the Lady Anne, and falls to one side in his deformity. These things prepare one for the greater achievements to come.

This infectious enthusiasm for new insights conveyed by actors into old texts is also seen in his response to the young Richard Burton's Prince Hal in 1951, where the quizzical, faintly bemused tone of Hobson's review suggests a performance notable for its thought-provoking originality and rare in its fresh interpretation of a familiar text:

The production of the first half of 'Henry IV' offers what must be one of the rarest of theatrical experiences: namely, a performance in a principal part which, in the light of the text and the received notions of the author's intentions, cannot be accorded even the moderate praise of being called good, yet which gives the deep and ordered emotional release that is among the actual marks of greatness. Moreover, this suggestion of greatness is not a thing of flashes merely, coming only at the crises of the play, though that in itself would be sufficiently memorable. It is in the bone and sinew of the performance, and is as evident in the actor's stillness when other players are speaking as when he is sailing the full flood of his mistaken inspiration.

The originality of Burton's interpretation lay in his depiction of Prince Henry not as a joyous libertine, but as a 'man who had a private vision of the Holy Grail, and was as determined to say nothing about it as he was incapable of forgetting it'. Hobson, demonstrating his unique understanding of the actor's craft – remarkable even in someone who has had practical experi-

---

19 See *ST*, 20/4/1947 and 18/5/1947 for some examples.
20 For a more detailed account of Hobson's accession to the post and his difficult relationship with Agate, see D. M. Shellard, *Harold Hobson: Witness and Judge* (Keele University Press, 1995), pp. 57–72.

ence of the stage – and with a perfect use of metaphor that is reminiscent of Hazlitt and Agate at their most incisive, maintains that, although this interpretation is hard to justify textually, it is permissible given the new dimension that it gives to the work: 'An actor, it cannot be too often said, is not merely an embodiment of other men's ideas. He has a flame of his own to light, and to get it going he sometimes burns the paper his author has written on. Instead of a light-hearted rapscallion Mr Burton offers a young knight keeping a long vigil in the cathedral of his mind. The knighthood is authentic, the vigil upheld by interior exaltation.'

If Burton has gone wrong, Hobson is claiming, then he has gone wrong magnificently. He ends his notice with a neat utilization of his diminishing newspaper space: 'But, like Mr Burton himself, I am short of inches, and the catalogue of praise must end long before it is exhausted'[21] – a notice that has reiterated Hobson's high regard for this actor's contribution to drama.

This emotionally subjective approach to criticism (a critical leitmotif for Hobson) allowed him later to explain away the generally acknowledged poor performance of his favourite actor, Ralph Richardson, as Timon of Athens in March 1956:

Sir Ralph cannot understand the wickedness and bitterness of men; of all our players, his is the eye that is most perceptive of goodness and nobility. And so, probably unconsciously, driven by the force of his compulsive personality, he plays Timon, in the later scenes, not as a screaming, lesser Lear, but as a resigned, misfortune-accepting Edward II. Each Shakespearian viciousness of phrase is transformed into a threnody, a lamentation. Borne along by the music of the verse, blandly kicking the meaning out of the window, he presents a Timon on whom there falls at last 'a silence luminous and serene, a shining peace.'[22]

In Hobson's view, Richardson's idiosyncratic approach to the part was valid because it was an act of original creation that added a new per-

spective to the work. As if aware of the controversy that the production would create, Hobson sought to defend it with a similarly passionate intensity:

This kind of acting may be, and is, hotly disputed. Let the academic and the narrow-minded call it a flagrant betrayal of the intentions of the author, or the product of slipshod reading. I don't care: neither, I imagine, does Sir Ralph. It is, quite simply, creative acting of the highest kind, in which the actor as artist presents to the world his own vision, and thereby enriches it.

To this Romantic critic, the actor as artist presenting the world with his own vision, a revelation of his own personality, represented the height of theatrical achievement for a performer.

Kenneth Tynan, on the other hand, despised the Old Vic performance of Timon of Athens, terming it 'the ghastly norm' for London and ridiculing Richardson's highly eccentric interpretation: 'To the role of the scoutmaster Sir Ralph Richardson brings his familiar attributes: a vagrant eye, gestures so eccentric that their true significance could only be revealed by trepanning, and a mode of speech that democratically regards all symbols as equal.'[23]

There is a fitting irony, therefore, in the fact that Hobson's first encounter with the young Kenneth Tynan, the scourge of iconography, who was to become his critical sparring partner on the Observer in the late fifties, was also at a performance of Shakespeare. Towards the end of January 1949, Hobson witnessed a performance by the Oxford University Dramatic Society (OUDS) in the Rudolf Steiner Hall, London, of the First Quarto Hamlet, a production which bore the flamboyant student's unmistakable stamp. The play, Hobson wrote, was:

under the direction of Ken Tynan of Magdalen, a long, lean, dialectically brilliant young man who

---

21 'Henry IV', ST, 8/4/1951.
22 'Here's Glory', ST, 9/9/1956.
23 'Edinburgh and London', Observer, 9/9/1956.

seems to occupy in the contemporary University a position pretty similar to that of Harold Acton when I was up. In other words, Mr Tynan appears to be the mascot of, as well as the driving force behind, those cultural experiments of which Oxford, when at its best, is usually full. Undoubtedly he is a man of ideas, several of which he has crammed into this production of a 'Hamlet' which, travestied as it is by its own text, he does not hesitate high-spiritedly to travesty still further by the lively pranks of his direction.[24]

These 'pranks' include an eighteenth-century setting, a king dressed in a coloured waistcoat and a queen wearing a green riding-cloak, and Hobson concludes that the evening, in which Tynan took the role of the Second Player, was 'memorable, irreverent, and highly interesting' – adjectives which could all be applied to the best of Tynan's subsequent criticism.

As has become clear Hobson was infinitely more interested throughout his career in actors' conceptions of Shakespeare than directors', and only Peter Brook's *Titus Andronicus* in 1955, with its parallels with the holocaust, drew a focus on the director: 'There is absolutely nothing in the bleeding barbarity of "Titus Andronicus" which would have astonished anyone at Buchenwald.'[25] He did, however, give valuable public support to Peter Hall's work at the Royal Shakespeare Company during the nineteen sixties, having greatly admired Hall (if not all his productions) since the climactic Arts production of *Waiting for Godot* in 1955.

For too long, Hobson's reputation has been based on a perception of an idiosyncratic and inconsistent approach to theatre criticism. Penelope Gilliatt's devastating survey of contemporary critics in the November 1959 edition of *Encore* contained the memorable sentence that 'It would be unfair to suggest that one of the most characteristic sounds of the English Sunday is the sound of Harold Hobson barking up the wrong tree' and it was accompanied by a caricature by James Bucknill of a canine Hobson straining at the leash and yapping at a tree-trunk. This formidable combination of witty cartoon and provocative comment quickly passed into theatrical folklore, with its influence in formulating a view of Hobson's criticism far outstripping its relevance or accuracy. Later in her article, Gilliatt makes a much more perceptive claim: 'To put it more charitably, which is one of the qualities he values, his judgement is that of a lover rather than a critic – enraptured, intuitive, and open to attacks of sudden irrational suspicion.'[26]

It is as a lover of thrilling acting that this intuitive critic, guided by his own emotional reaction and intelligence of perception, and consistently adhering to the critical manifesto he had set out in the 1933 article for the *Christian Science Monitor*, entitled 'The Actor as Artist',[27] that Hobson should best be assessed. This approach was always apparent in his writing on important Shakespearian performances and its zenith was reached in Hobson's reaction to Laurence Olivier's Macbeth in 1955.

Whenever Hobson went to review a play, he generally sat in an aisle seat for easy access – he had been stricken by polio when he was eight years old – and was accompanied by someone to help him if necessary. These theatrical companions were most frequently his first wife (theatre managers would breathe a sigh of relief if they saw Elizabeth accompanying her husband because this increased the chances of a favourable review);[28] Edward Sutro; and, particularly during the last ten years of Hobson's career, Richard Jackson, the theatrical agent. A further practical consideration that resulted from Hobson's disability was that he rarely left his

[24] 'First Quarto "Hamlet"' *CSM*, 22/1/1949.
[25] 'A Modern Play', *ST*, 21/8/1955.
[26] Penelope Gilliatt, 'A Consideration of Critics', *Encore*, November 1959.
[27] 'The Actor as Artist', *CSM*, 20/3/1933.
[28] A belief to which Richard Jackson and Michael Billington testified in two interviews with D. M. Shellard – (25/3/92) and (23/4/92) respectively. Richard Jackson felt that Hobson's dislike of American musicals was in part influenced by Bessie's refusal to go to see them.

seat at the interval and never went to the bar to fraternize with the other critics – the only way that he discovered the views of his colleagues, aside from a brief conversation at his seat, was by reading them when published.

While critic of *The Sunday Times*, Hobson was remarkably sanguine about the effect of his disability. As for any effect it had on his critical approach, it only increased his admiration for feats of athletic prowess and physical exertion.[29] As he moved from Sheffield to Oxford in the twenties, his passion for football and Sheffield Wednesday was matched and exceeded by his interest in cricket. He followed it with the quiet fanaticism that only devotees of the game can manifest and not only based his one novel, *The Devil in Woodford Wells*, on the intricate details of a scorecard, but became a member of the MCC and a repository of knowledge on batsmen, bowlers and averages. His first theatrical idol in the nineteen thirties was Jack Buchanan, the epitome of the energetic, all-action performer (to whose show, *Stand Up and Sing*, in 1931 he had been given free tickets by Roscoe Drummond of the *Christian Science Monitor*, launching him on his career as a critic)[30] and he was frequently to admire similarly slick performers. One actor who radiated a mesmerising physicality on stage was Laurence Olivier and it is an indication of the impressiveness of his performance as Macbeth that Hobson should attempt to convey a feature of his interpretation by means of an analogy that had great personal resonance for the critic. The famous 'Sunderland' analogy indicates both how Hobson's style owed much to his journalistic flair, sensing the dramatic effect of an original yet appropriate metaphor, and how of all the twentieth-century theatre critics Hobson is the most consistently autobiographical, always insisting that his subjective emotional response is conditioned by the shaping effects of his life. He is the High Romantic critic par excellence.

Having baldly stated that Olivier's opening scenes as Macbeth are bad, Hobson proceeds to explain that this is because the actor is simply not interested in the business of deposing Duncan. He throws away the 'Is this a dagger ...' speech and appears to be bored during the actual murder. This was disconcerting for the audience who felt that they were about to witness the humbling of a once-great actor into the 'Second Division'. However, the moment of peripeteia that normally occurs in the best of Hobson's reviews, actually occurs in this instance on the Stratford stage, for there then 'almost immediately began the superb leap upwards into glory which confounded the wicked, and made the righteous cheer'. When Olivier utters the 'Methought I heard a voice cry, "Sleep no more"' speech, Hobson identifies the heart of the actor's interpretation of the role, namely 'not Macbeth's imagination of Duncan's murder, but his conscience after it' – and herein lay the basis of Olivier's great triumph:

His 'multitudinous seas incarnadine' is tremendous; it is greasy and slippery with an immense revulsion. As distress and agony enter into him, the actor multiplies in stature before our eyes until he dominates this play, and Stratford, and, I would say, the whole English theatre. When, after the knocking on the door, he reappears in a black monkish gown tied with a rope, he looks like Judas, like a character in a greater drama than Macbeth's, a Judas who, in his dark brooding silence, has begun already to think of the potter's field and the gallows.

Having identified Olivier's approach to the part, Hobson now turns to the second act, an act that was 'full of unforgettable things'. This Macbeth 'briefs the murderers of Banquo with a contempt for their trade which is exceeded by his contempt for himself', a contempt the more arresting because it is tinged with a bitter amusement.

It was a moment of extreme tension and Donald Spoto, in his biography of Olivier, explains how the actor created this:

---

[29] Harold Hobson, *Indirect Journey* (London, 1978), p. 39.
[30] Ibid., p. 177.

In the scene with the murderers ... there are three words often tossed aside and sometimes even cut – 'well, then, now' – but Olivier made sense of them. He stopped, eyed the two killers mockingly, pointed with both index fingers at them and said 'Well' enquiringly. After a pause he said 'Then' in a tone suggesting he wanted them to approach him. But they remained still and his 'Now', after a pause, was a terrifying imperative.[31]

Just as Olivier was able to invest single, unpromising lines with great significance, Hobson too could imbue simple stage events with a tremendous, almost overpowering relevance. Whereas this technique of exaggeration was later to invite ridicule when it was excessively applied, in 'Nonpareil' it accords perfectly with Hobson's tone of unlimited enthusiasm. He marvels at the scene where the ghost of Banquo appears – 'At the feast Sir Laurence slides into the seeing of Banquo's ghost and a subsequent cry with a gradual ease that has not been equalled on the English stage since his sensational lamentation in "Oedipus Tyrannus"'[32] – and he reserves his greatest admiration for a facet of Olivier's interpretation that complements Hobson's own Christian attitude to life. If his belief that *Waiting for Godot* contains a positive Christian dimension is debatable, his identification of the spiritual malaise of *Macbeth* being the source of the work's tragedy is entirely appropriate:

... the finest element in his performance here is that, in the midst of all this remorse and terror, he never forgets that despair is the greatest of sins. Macbeth's life has been such that he ought to despair; his fortune is such that he must despair; but despair he does not. In this refusal he discovers a terrible grandeur, so that when he reminds his wife that his enemies are still assailable, one's heart rises to him, both to the pathos of a man who will not recognise an inevitable destruction, and to a courage that may be evil but is certainly unquenchable.

This grandeur is maintained to the end of the work because although Hobson feels that the play collapses after the feast, 'Sir Laurence remains astoundingly aloft':

When he says that his way of life is fallen into the sere and yellow leaf, you would swear that Macbeth, for all his wickedness, has a right to feel that the universe has monstrously betrayed him. And nothing more beautiful than his speaking of 'She should have died hereafter' will be heard in England till the golden-crested wren becomes a nightingale.

Many elements of this production had concurred with the strongest personal and critical interests of Hobson – the emphasis upon an aspect of Christian theology, the sin of despair; a depiction of the beauty of marriage, ironically implicit in Olivier's tender delivery of the 'She should have died hereafter' line; the unexpected recovery of the main actor that permits an eventual victory for the slow starter and almost made Olivier support Sunderland instead of Chelsea;[33] and a gripping theatricality that would always appeal to a critic whose style was rooted in a subjective, emotional response. As in his 1946 review of Olivier's King Lear, Hobson's exposure to genius had again had a catalytic effect upon his writing, enabling him both to record Olivier's achievement and convey an impression of its substance – the goal of all the finest critics. Hobson's success can be measured by the fact that when he ends his review by stating that 'Macbeth is notoriously one of the most treacherous parts in the entire realm of drama; but Sir Laurence's performance is such that I do not believe there is an actor in the world who can come near him' – we are inclined to consider his judgement plausible.

---

[31] Donald Spoto, *Laurence Olivier* (London, 1991), p. 221.

[32] This is an error on Hobson's part. He is actually referring to *Oedipus Rex*.

[33] Olivier revealed in a 1963 interview that this particular facet of the review made a great impression on him: 'It nearly made me support Sunderland instead of Chelsea ... In the arts generally, but perhaps especially in the theatre, the mighty are always in danger of falling. It is good to know that there are some people who are not glad about it', 'Olivier – My Life, My Work, My Future', *ST*, 3/11/1963.

SHAKESPEARE PERFORMANCES IN ENGLAND, 1994–1995

PETER HOLLAND

A PAIR OF *HAMLETS*

The year's two productions of *Hamlet* came with such hype that they provoked the postponement of a third, Sam Mendes's planned production with Simon Russell Beale. Both were sharply defined by their choice of theatre. To mark the renaming of the Globe in Shaftesbury Avenue as the Gielgud Theatre in honour of Gielgud's ninetieth birthday, Peter Hall directed *Hamlet* with his own company, starring Stephen Dillane, Horatio to Mel Gibson's Hamlet in Zeffirelli's film. It was the obvious choice of opening production, both a tribute to the greatest Hamlet of his generation and a way of defining a distance from the romantic, poetic Prince Gielgud made so emphatically his own between the wars. Jonathan Kent's production for the Almeida company starring Ralph Fiennes, which must have been originally planned for the small scale of the Almeida, needed, in the aftermath of Fiennes's huge success in *Schindler's List*, to find a larger space before moving to New York where Fiennes's performance won a Tony award. This *Hamlet* moved east, using the Hackney Empire, a decaying, once splendid and undeniably enormous theatre designed by Frank Matcham, now more commonly the home of Music Hall, the only theatre I have been in for some time that positively encourages the audience to take their drinks into the auditorium after the interval.

Dillane's performance negotiated brilliantly with the ghosts of memories of Gielgud. While his Hamlet foregrounded its modernity, it did so only after emphasizing Dillane's ability to offer a lyrical Hamlet in the Gielgud mould. Indeed initially, in the first court scene (1.2), Dillane surprised by his attention to old-fashioned virtues of line and eloquent verse-speaking, as if Hall's long-standing obsession with the beat of the verse and the force of line-endings had created a new Gielgud. But the trauma of the encounter with the ghost of his father generated in this Hamlet a startlingly new mode, a bitter jokiness and a harsh modernity that, immediately and irrevocably, made him disjunct from the rest of the characters. Dillane's Hamlet was consistently funny, more willing to enjoy the wit than is currently fashionable. But the humour had an edge that was precisely defined by the reactions of those at whom it was directed: the accuracy of Dillane's mimicry of Sinden's rich and fruity pronouncements and *sotto voce* mutterings as Polonius did not, as usual, pass Polonius by; instead the audience was made insistently and disturbingly aware of the irritation and anger the mimicry caused its object.

Sinden's Polonius was certainly not a figure to anger lightly. Dressed, like the other courtiers, in red frock-coat and breeches, black stockings and black top-hat, Polonius looked laughably like some rare variety of beetle but behind the brilliance of the comedy which one might have expected Sinden to achieve were clear markers of something very different: his comment to Ophelia, 'I do know / When the

14 *Hamlet*, 2.2, The Peter Hall Company at the Gielgud Theatre, 1995: Claudius (Michael Pennington),
Polonius (Donald Sinden), Ophelia (Gina Bellman), Gertrude (Gwen Taylor).

blood burns' (1.3.115–16) was a sudden and very personal memory cutting through the facade of the busy, efficient, harsh old man. But Sinden's Polonius was also still an astute and powerful politician, gazing as intently as Horatio and Hamlet at Claudius's reactions to the murder of Gonzago, as if he knew what had happened or now realized the truth about the death of old Hamlet, or making his recommendation to Claudius, 'confine him where / Your wisdom best shall think' (3.1.189–90), into an explicit suggestion of imprisonment in a dungeon.

The processes of this court were defined by its paperwork, as Laertes offered his petition to return to France and Hamlet his written request to return to Wittenberg, the former first toyed with by Claudius before being accepted, the latter firmly rejected before Claudius passed the paper to Gertrude who tore it in two as Hamlet helplessly acquiesced. Though Michael

Pennington's Claudius was often drunk, always reaching for the drinks table for a glass of whisky or red wine, his aggressively male physical presence was insistently dangerous, corrupt and as politically astute and pragmatic as his chief counsellor. He was also sexually charismatic, inducing in Gwen Taylor's Gertrude both a painfully inappropriate girlishness in the intensity of her desire for him and an appearance of sheer stupidity as she grinned far too much throughout the court scenes, making her rejection of Claudius after the closet scene a transforming moment for her. As Claudius tried to close in on her, Gertrude firmly kept her distance, as if the 'rank sweat of an enseamèd bed' (3.4.82) which Hamlet had forced her to smell face-down in the sheets had been transferred to the once overwhelming object of her sexual desires. Reappearing after the interval (taken after the Fortinbras scene, 4.4), Gertrude had changed costume to a dignified and matronly black, now, as it were, being her age, rejecting her sexuality at precisely the moment that Ophelia would most fully express hers.

Gina Bellman's Ophelia, no worse than most, carefully laid out Polonius's clothes on the ground to suggest his corpse and then obscenely rode on them, like a parody of sex, echoing the feigning of sex with which Hamlet had assaulted Gertrude. It was with great difficulty that, later in the scene, Laertes held Ophelia away to avoid the full, open-mouthed kiss she was trying to give him. Hall was centrally concerned with the characters' finding of their own sexuality: his talk to the company at the start of rehearsals (printed in the programme) argued that 'shifting sexuality, uncertain sexuality, is at the heart of the play' and that 'for the Renaissance ... there wasn't heterosexuality or homosexuality, there was just sexuality'. The ease with which Dillane's Hamlet could discard Ophelia suggested that, far from being abstracted, the nature of Hamlet's sexuality was defined by his repression of it, his placing it as insignificant in the context of isolation in which he found himself. It was of a piece with the questioning of Rosencrantz and Guildenstern: 'what make you at Elsinore?' (2.2.272) was a weary question in the full knowledge of the inevitability of yet one more betrayal to add to the world's stock.

Reviews of the production inevitably drew attention to the moment at which Hamlet stripped naked on the stage but there was nothing remotely sexual about it. In 4.2, as a direct consequence of lugging out Polonius's corpse, Hamlet was covered in blood (and who would have thought Polonius to have had so much blood in him?). Calmly and neatly, he took off his clothes and stuffed them in a laundry-bag until, as he was led off to Claudius, his naked body became a comic robot, the residual flesh almost a machine. For the confrontation with Claudius Hamlet was now dressed in a very silly nightgown, his nakedness clothed but in such a way as to ridicule Claudius, especially as he tried to hop off to England

like a pantomime fairy waiting for the flying wire to work. The act of stripping was comic but also logical, a rational response to the bloodstains rendered absurd and humorous by its transposition to an inappropriate place and moment, a climactic moment in Dillane's presentation of the character as a figure who, in the aftermath of the encounter with the Ghost, now found himself consistently in the wrong place at the wrong time. Hamlet's response to this displacement was to use all his intelligence, his immense powers of thought, but without ever finding in the thought a solution or a resolution. The isolation produced in this Hamlet actions that were entirely logical for him but, equally completely, bound to appear madly illogical to everyone else, as the rest of the cast stayed in the social world Hamlet had been forced to abandon.

The different facets of Dillane's performance came together magnificently on Hamlet's return to Denmark. His encounter with Alan Dobie's wry and precisely real Gravedigger was a game of two equal wits, enjoyed by both of them. For the first time Hamlet's comedy was matched, for the Gravedigger and Hamlet were similar outsiders to Claudius's court. The wit was not at this moment an act of patronizing and hurtful superiority, as it had been and would be again when he forced Laertes at dagger-point face down into Ophelia's grave so that he could sweep the mound of earth on all three of them. His entry into the funeral scene (5.1.250–4) allowed the re-emergence of the full-throated lyrical and heroic style, the Gielgud voice, unheard for hours in this long production (running close to four hours); but in its new context, so completely changed from its earlier resonances, this too came over as only another mockery, a vicious, pained reaction to Laertes's grief.

By this stage, Hamlet was in remarkable control, able, it seemed, almost to prevent the play's continuation. His response to the proposed duel, 'How if I answer no?' (5.2.131), completely floored Osric who took a long pause as he tried to find an answer. In the duel, Laertes was obviously more skilful, as Hamlet kept falling out of the arena, but Laertes's reluctance to kill Hamlet kept the bout going. Once he had stabbed Hamlet, Laertes tried to escape but was stopped by Osric and the other courtiers for Hamlet to stab him. Hamlet then thrust Claudius through the leg to render him immobile before killing him with a lunge vertically down through his back, an act of extreme brutality, leaving Claudius slumped like a drunk in the gutter as the wine poured down from a very large goblet. Only death now left Hamlet surprised.

Throughout, the production had brilliant details and insights, modestly stated and pursued. In the closet scene, for instance, Hamlet set up two large court portraits as if to give his mother a lesson in art history, before he slashed at Claudius's portrait, turning the picture into a thing 'of shreds and patches'. Most satisfying of all was a double that is so obvious I wonder why I have never seen it before: Michael Pennington played both Claudius and his brother. The latter's torments and immense agony were explored in an eloquent lyrical voice, the huge verse paragraphs effortlessly placed. The degeneration from old Hamlet to Claudius, the move from the heroic to the cruel and bloat king, was all the sharper, the comparison all the keener as it played across the actor's own appearance.

As Claudius stormed out of the play-scene, throwing down a purse for the players contemptuously, Dillane's Hamlet grabbed a prop crown and seated himself in Claudius's place, neatly suggesting an ambition that Hamlet could perform but never feel. He was still holding the crown as he saw Claudius at prayer and put it down, stopping only to consider the murder on his way out. The crown was a small touch, unforced and unemphatic. At the parallel moment at the Hackney Empire, Ralph Fiennes's Hamlet played with various pieces from the players' costume skip, trying on an orange robe and a mask, experimenting with heroic postures and strange walks. Hamlet the performer is a familiar trope but here, with the prayer scene played in front of a drop like a front-cloth scene in a nineteenth-century melodrama, the costume became Hamlet's necessary disguise, a way of freeing himself into a new form of existence, experimenting with the role of an active avenger. But when, in the closet scene, Hamlet's orange robe was echoed by Gertrude's dressing-gown, the effect lost meaning, the logic of the disguise no longer followed through.

Jonathan Kent's production was full of such inconsequentialities. But what marked it above all was its sheer pace. An almost obsessive concern with speed was a remarkable feature of a number of productions this year. Here it produced the effect of lines and scenes rattling by as if the determinant on the production was a three-hour time-limit. As Matt Wolf suggested (*Herald Tribune*), Kent's was an 'impetuous yet uninfected staging' in which Fiennes's was a Hamlet 'for whom events cannot happen fast enough'. There could be no pause here for reflection. The soliloquies were gone through at a speed which left the audience marvelling at Fiennes's technique but never engaging with Hamlet's processes of thought: for John Peter in *The Sunday Times* 'To be or not to be' 'sounds, not like thought moulding itself into speech, a subtle intelligence grappling with a problem, but like an obsession that has already been rehearsed more than once' and, while he was prepared to read this back into the character as 'the spiritual equivalent of probing and probing an open wound', I found it only a demonstration of an actor's skills, a superficial effect that damagingly disengaged actor from character.

Where Dillane's Hamlet had been emphatically modern, Fiennes's was a throwback to a romantic tradition of aristocratic Hamlets. As he shouted 'My fate cries out' (1.4.58) he struck a yearning diagonal pose as if waiting for a nineteenth-century engraver to capture the moment. It was all of a piece in its placing in

15 *Hamlet*, The Almeida Theatre Company at the Hackney Empire, 1994: Hamlet (Ralph Fiennes).

Hamlet history with the definition in set and costumes of Claudius's court as a nineteenth-century world of frock-coats, where, for instance, both the play-scene and the duel were after-dinner entertainments for an audience in evening-dress clutching their brandies. It also provided a firmly established context for Terence Rigby's First Player who could appear as a consummately professional actor-manager, tossing his trilby to another actor as he began the Pyrrhus speech, but holding onto his cigar which, after he had finished speaking with sobbing emotion, he calmly puffed on again.

Lucy Hall's set for Peter Hall's production had been disappointing: a raked disc surrounded by dangling red ropes with a cloud-scape projected onto a disjointed cyclorama behind. Peter J. Davison's design for Hackney was dominated by the odd angle at which the back wall and front edge of the stage had been constructed, an effect that deliberately and effectively distorted all the perspectives of the set. In front of the back wall (again of clouds) various wood panels dropped, creating a series of fully walled rooms, a country house that could suddenly, for example for Hamlet's first soliloquy (1.2.129f.), take on the eerie emptiness of a deserted mansion, powerfully mimicking Hamlet's isolation.

The fixed world of an establishment smugly pleased with itself provided a firm context for the most startling and intriguing performance in the production: Francesca Annis's Gertrude. Beginning as a fashion-plate, with her stylish elegance and careful, almost china-doll make-up, Gertrude proved to have created for herself a brittle facade. The closet scene was the turning point: opening in a warm glow of autumnal light, the scene transformed as the dying Polonius pulled down a long curtain to allow a cold, dawn light to fill the stage and remove all traces of romantic lighting. Hamlet's sexual violence had been clear in the nunnery scene where he had poked at Ophelia's crotch with his hand, spat on his shirt-tail and used it to smear her lipstick across her face and finally pulled up her skirt to rape her, very quickly, from behind. Through the play scene Ophelia (Tara FitzGerald) had been a traumatized rape victim, perched on the edge of her chair as she suffered the physical pain consequent on Hamlet's actions.

Now, in the closet scene, Gertrude would receive similar treatment and with similar consequences. If Gertrude was not actually raped, Fiennes's Hamlet certainly imitated rape. On Claudius's touch she shrieked and pulled away in revulsion, weeping but also traumatized, pulling the covers around her in a parody of decorum as Rosencrantz and Guildenstern entered. Through the second half of the play, Gertrude's ability to keep control of herself collapsed and she quivered on the edge of madness. By the final scene she sat with her head twitching, her make-up a terrible mask, her suffering ignored by all about her. I have never seen the consequences of Hamlet's treatment of Gertrude so graphically and horrifyingly exposed, counterpointed by the aggressive sexuality of the mad Ophelia, who hacked off locks of her hair to distribute as flowers and sang of 'St Valentine' while eyeing Claudius's crotch. By comparison with the women's suffering, Hamlet's madness seemed only an actor's performance and his treatment of them unmistakably brutal, callous and self-regarding.

A COUPLE OF *ROMEO AND JULIETS*

The year's two productions of *Romeo and Juliet* both typified the problems of artistic directors and their companies. Neil Bartlett, the artistic director of the Lyric Hammersmith, is best known for his experimental work with the company he created, Gloria, and for a series of fine productions of French classical drama; his *Romeo and Juliet* was his first Shakespeare production in England, a co-production with the West Yorkshire Playhouse. For Adrian Noble, on the other hand, *Romeo and Juliet* was a play that had come round yet again in the RSC cycle.

The twin promptings for Bartlett's production both deserve respect: a desire to create a style of Shakespeare stripped to its essentials and a wish to work with Emily Woof, a young actor who had quickly established a reputation for her work in solo performance theatre. Bartlett wanted a production that was the antithesis of the extravagances of the immediately preceding show at the Lyric, a version that emphasized narrative pace, removed the accretions of the play's stage history and left a bare acting-space. The opening music mixed echoes of musical transformations – Prokofiev, Tchaikovsky, Leonard Bernstein – as if to summon them up and then firmly discard them. What would stay behind would be the empty space.

Bartlett's intentions derived from a respect for the text: 'it is only in the movies or at the ballet or the opera that Shakespeare acquires landscapes, scenery, the baggage of "period"'. Instead he aimed to 'honour the pace of its storytelling, because it is in the pace that sex turns out, frighteningly, to have the same urgency, the same rhythm and the same speed as destruction'. The 'stripped' staging that he described would then be as much interpretative as a means of revealing the narrative beneath. The production's slogan, taken from Bartlett's programme-note, was 'twelve actors, five knives, one rope ladder and an empty stage'. The source of this derived from Bartlett's hard look at the 'Bad' quarto, its staging requirements, its effects and even its punctuation. Responding to what he saw as Q1's actor-oriented editing of the longer Shakespeare text,

16 *Romeo and Juliet*, Lyric Theatre, Hammersmith, 1995. Stuart Bunce (Romeo) and Emily Woof (Juliet).

Bartlett created a text that 'uses the lines of the "Good Quarto" arranged into the shape of the "Bad Quarto"', cutting firmly and effectively, 'removing, shifting or transforming into physical business any words whose late sixteenth-century beauty cannot rescue them from their late sixteenth-century incomprehensibility'. The result, sleek and efficient, was a performance whose drive was unavoidable as scene-changes vanished and whose losses were rarely glaring or disturbing.

The only disappointment was the design's transformation of the play into a modern street world. Bartlett may have argued that Italy was

Shakespeare's 'shorthand evocation of sex, violence, glamour and religion' but by dressing the young men in sharp suits and ties he made them into stereotypes of Italian style, giving the actors too glib a manner, offering a convention of cool macho behaviour that was too easily distanced from the audience. If it was a sop to the Lyric's young audience, it was an unnecessary one, as was the production's recurrent interest in teasing explorations of homosociality, as Mercutio, for instance, grabbed Tybalt's testicles and kissed him on the mouth. The effect was usually too Italianate, too ready a recourse to stock images of Italian street life. But there was also a series of reappearances for Mercutio late in the play as Balthasar, Apothecary, Friar John and finally as a ghost who disarms Paris, enabling Romeo to kill him, a directorial intervention at odds with the narrative simplicity and directness elsewhere aimed at.

The production slogan managed to avoid mentioning the centrality the design accorded Juliet's bed, the focal point of the set, on or in which Juliet was usually to be seen as the rest of the action unfolded around her. This was less a statement about the significance of Juliet as a reference point for the play's action than a desire to leave Emily Woof onstage. Woof's Juliet, young, waif-like but full of real strength and energy, belonged firmly in the production's concept of style, checking her hair in mirrors, clutching copies of *Vogue* or *Marie Claire* from which she seemed to have learned all she knew about the emotional problems of adolescence. With a Nurse (Roberta Taylor) who was strikingly unfunny – the cuts eliminated much of her glorious ramblings – but young and deeply concerned for her charge, this Juliet was less the gauche adolescent than a young woman whose world made perfect sense until her passion for Romeo destroyed it.

There were problems in the performance: as Michael Billington commented in the *Guardian*, 'such a spirited girl, you feel, would follow Romeo to Mantua rather than surrender to his banishment'. Even more problematically, Woof found it difficult to work with the other actors whenever she was not immured in her bed, as if her experience of solo theatre had disabled her from responding to, feeding off other performers. Stuart Bunce's disappointing Romeo may have offered her little but Bartlett's concentration on his Juliet did nothing to help his Romeo find a role for himself in the production. Bartlett and Woof may have concurred in their recognition of the play as 'large-scale, passionately physical work focused around adolescent dreams of sexuality' but it was a recognition that concentrated only on Juliet's dreams, making Romeo only an insignificant element in her world.

However, they certainly succeeded in exploring the centrality of sexual desire to Juliet's dreams. It was clear, for instance, just how important it would be to this Juliet that she was 'sold' but 'Not yet enjoyed' (3.2.27–8) when, in the balcony scene, she had asked Romeo 'What satisfaction canst thou have tonight?' (2.1.168), inserting a teasing pause before 'tonight'. The effect reappeared, with far more complex meaning, when, after Tybalt's death, she told her mother 'I never shall be satisfied / With Romeo till I behold him' and again leaving a long pause before 'dead' (3.5.93–4), a reading derived from Q1's punctuation.

If the production was undeniably limited in its achievements, with some conspicuously poor acting in the minor roles, there was a scrupulous theatrical intelligence at work in achieving and maintaining the energy of the performance. At Stratford, by contrast, Adrian Noble's production flagged from beginning to end. Noble too had cut hard at the text: according to the programme, 'approximately 564 lines have been cut' but the performance still ran three hours. One might have expected that what had been left would have been thoughtfully considered but there were few actors who made me hear a line afresh. When the waiter, in the onstage café (the focus for piazza life in this Verona), fed up with Benvolio and the others standing on the chairs and the tables, shouted 'Get off' it was not only the rather feebly unShakespearian language that made me pay attention but also that he made the line matter. Even more strikingly, at the discovery of Juliet's supposed death on her wedding morning, Gary Taylor as Peter, slumped in profound grief on the side of the stage and then unable to joke with the musicians in his distress, registered the pain of loss more effectively than the overlapping laments of parents, groom and Nurse.

But Noble's severest problem was stylistic. On the morning after the Capulet ball, as the waiter was setting up the tables at the café, Mark Lockyer's Mercutio staggered on upstage, nursing a painful hangover, entering down one of the long vistas of Kendra Ullyart's set. The waiter dropped his metal tray with a clang and Lockyer winced, clutching the ice-pack ever more firmly to his head. The gag can be, for the audience, a pained memory of such feelings. But why did the waiter drop the tray? It could, I suppose, be an accident: busy with his chores, he had let the tray slip from his grasp; he could have been annoyed and thumped it down on the table in irritation. But in this performance the waiter dropped the tray only so that Mercutio could wince and Lockyer gain an easy laugh. The action was solely conditioned by its immediate effect.

The night before, in the middle of the crowded party, Juliet's debut ball, Mercutio was to be seen at the kids' table, playing cards with them. Later, searching for Romeo, he ventriloquized through a glove puppet, with which one of the children had earlier been playing. I found myself wondering why Mercutio had stolen the puppet. Again the realist detail, the action that provoked the possibility of the gag, was inadequately grounded. The realist method of the production, its firm stylistic base as well as its sense of period (Italian risorgimento, a nineteenth-century world), suggests a novelistic resource for its detailing. The materials of such stage business have, in Noble's chosen technique for the production, to emerge out of the panoply of the dense, lived world of the social life of Verona, a world where, for instance, Capulet talked with Paris in 1.2 on his way home with a cake-box, which he carefully handed to Peter, precisely so that there would be a grand cake at the party to be cut and distributed to the guests.

Noble's choice of style meant that the realist detail could not simply be a pretext for a laugh, for then the moment and the character would have become far less interesting. Lockyer is a fine clown but Mercutio is not only a clown: his strange, idiosyncratic imagination was never glimpsed. The Queen Mab speech became a species of verbal diarrhoea that quickly bored the others as they drank at the café. Mercutio's confrontation with the Nurse had none of the misogyny that has become common in other productions but no threat of violence either, nothing but a genial teasing that was too gentle to make much effect. Lockyer's performance never engaged with the social reality and the complexity of relationships in which Mercutio is so profoundly embedded. A comic young man about town, this Mercutio never justified the fury of Romeo's reaction to his death, never hinted at the complex movement, the difficult transition from male world to love world that Romeo has to make. It exemplified the production's passionlessness.

Many of the reviewers blamed this on the weakness of Zubin Varla's Romeo. It was bold of Noble to cast such a young actor in the role but Varla was quite simply overparted. But my emphasis on the shortcomings of Lockyer's Mercutio suggests that the fault did not solely lie in the technical limitations of a young actor. Rather, Noble's production left the actors isolated, failed to find a means for them to build connections and patterns, to create a character. The apparent dramatic demands of the social world conjured up on stage were not followed through. Far too often it was as if the lines had not been heard, their meaning not considered. When, for instance, Lady Capulet tries to turn her daughter's thoughts towards marriage, she comments 'By my count / I was your mother much upon these years / That you are now a maid' (1.3.73–5). Though Lucy Whybrow's 'Alice in Wonderland' Juliet was certainly not thirteen, she looked very young indeed. But Darlene Johnson's Lady Capulet had not seen her twenties for a while. There is no reason why Lady Capulet should be, say, twenty-eight, as the line suggests, but the gap between the performer's age and the clear statement in her lines ought, surely, to have produced a slight look, a little reaction, something that registered the point. Here it skated by, unremarked and unremarkable.

Ullyart's mobile set pitted black buildings against a white sky, all marbled and hence cold

17 *Romeo and Juliet*, 2.2, RSC, 1995: Friar Laurence (Julian Glover) has an espresso before he gathers 'baleful weeds'.

and implacable. As oppressive as the tomb it would become by the end of the play, its alleys all narrowed disturbingly so that the space crowded and confined the characters who bustled inside it. It was a demanding space for the actors, a space of visibility, as when Romeo, at his first entrance, had to pretend not to notice his parents before being able to come forward, down the alley, to talk to Benvolio. It was a very public arena in which to explore the people of the play but the production never did so.

Few emerged with credit. Julian Glover's Friar Laurence, most at home at his laboratory bench, gleefully mixing up Juliet's potion with the enthusiasm of an amateur chemist, thoughtfully built up a portrait of a well-meaning man whose actions were controlled by his cowardice. But it was only too characteristic that, at his first appearance, he was seen stopping off at the café for his morning espresso, apparently intending to 'up-fill this osier cage of ours / With baleful weeds and precious-juicèd flowers' (2.2.7–8) from the vase of freesias on the café table. Lucy Whybrow's Juliet, so vulnerably young at the start, hinted at the growth to appalling isolation, the demands of a precocious maturity, but her voice lacked range and no Juliet can be expected to make the language of 'Gallop apace' do its work when she is stuck on a swing.

Noble's current approach to Shakespeare has been to step back from the actors, giving them a context within which to play without seeking to predetermine the results through a sharply angled directorial line. It is a risky method that here produced only a bland world where I yearned for an incisive intervention from the director to generate the power and intelligence that the actors were having such difficulty finding for themselves. The clashes and jars of the play only too rarely made a flourish; it was there, briefly and belatedly, when a troupe of singing bridesmaids burst in on the sight of the 'dead' Juliet but by then the production had gone as cold as its set.

A BRACE OF *TEMPESTS*

Both the year's productions of *The Tempest* were designed for touring: David Thacker's, for the RSC's small-scale tour, and Silviu Purcarete's, for Nottingham Playhouse in a co-production with the Hebbel Theater in Berlin and the Amsterdam company Offshore.

Small-scale touring productions have their own necessary limitations which the best turn to strengths. It was good to see, in Thacker's production, a *Tempest* without much in the way of set except a few trunks and boxes, good, too, to see the Swan stage stripped back to the bare back wall, an open platform for the action to unfold on. But precious little then unfolded. Undercast, underpowered, underimagined, this *Tempest* was little more than perfunctory.

The production had opened in London and had changed markedly by the time I saw it in Stratford. At first, as Paul Taylor put it in *The Independent*, Paul Jesson played 'an isolated Prospero who remains on stage throughout, brooding over his magic book' or, as Robert Hewison phrased it in *The Sunday Times*, 'Jesson spends a lot of time sitting at a wonky little table with a huge book on it, looking more like a worried manager than a magician.' But this was the first *Tempest* I have seen in which not a single one of the books which Prospero prized above his dukedom was to be seen onstage.

But the change was much more emphatic than that: it had become a *Tempest* less dominated by Prospero than any other I can recall. It was partly the consequence of the generally low-key style of Jesson's performance, a genial father, a benign aristocratic castaway but with no glimmering of energy or imagination. There was nothing to hint at the magus, the duke, the plotter, the embittered victim. Jesson's Prospero was a thoroughly nice chap, most sharply defined as he comforted and cradled the exhausted Ferdinand who was still moving logs at the start of Act 4. It was too easy to forget, as one looked sympathetically at this caring

18   *The Tempest*, 3.1, RSC at the Swan Theatre, 1995: 'I'll bear your logs the while': Miranda (Sarah-Jane Holm) offers to help Ferdinand (David Fahm) carry a log (Bonnie Engstrom as Ariel).

gesture, that it was Prospero's enslavement that had exhausted Ferdinand in the first place.

But the diminution of Prospero was mostly the consequence of the spirit-centredness of the production, for the nearly bare stage was always cluttered by the onstage presence of Ariel (played by Bonnie Engstrom with wide staring eyes) and her three attendant apprentice spirits. It was neat enough to have them play the logs for Ferdinand to carry or the clothes that Trinculo and Stefano were distracted by. But they also responded to much else in the action, so that Caliban's freedom-song induced in them mental torment as they held their hands in agony to their heads like sufferers with acute migraines. If, as rather literal-minded directors tend these days to insist, Ariel has to appear in the storm, then Thacker's solution was a good one with Ariel as the Ship's Master creating a storm in the minds of passengers and crew before literally 'flaming amazement' with little shafts of fire flicked over the stage.

Engstrom's Ariel was clearly envious of Miranda, always ready to dart angry, jealous looks at her (especially during the masque) and she turned 'Where the bee sucks' into a sad anticipation of parting from her beloved Prospero, before spending much of the last scene downstage, sitting with her head up, contemplating the sky with longing and loneliness intermixed, balancing Antonio who sat at the other downstage corner, head down. Once released, Ariel took a yearning step towards Prospero as he turned upstage and walked away from her. If a female Ariel seemed like a throwback to an old theatre tradition long out of fashion, Engstrom at least made something adequately significant of it, using her gender to create an additional layer to the master–servant relationship.

Ariel's rival, Dominic Letts's Caliban, emerged from an onstage trunk, a shipwrecked castaway himself in rags and tatters rather like old Ben Gunn in *Treasure Island*. Rarely upright, his triumphant moment came as the spirits performing the masque danced with their audience

and, with Caliban increasingly controlling the action standing on the trunk, Prospero found that the dance was moving out of his control, as most of the other characters, especially the lords, joined in, making the dance less and less a vision of order and harmony and more a wild, dangerous, subversive carnival. This was a thoughtful moment, taking the masque further through its archetypal sequence than is usually the case or than the text demands, making its disruption Prospero's angry and necessary reclaiming of power over his device. But with the lords as dull as usual and a noticeably unfunny and uninteresting Stefano and Trinculo, large swathes of the play unfolded with nothing to intrigue. I am all in favour of clean and uncluttered Shakespeare, in which the language does the work but the effect has to be one in which the play is constantly illuminated interestingly and afresh: there was little that seemed to want to engage with the play's demands. When a play as difficult as *The Tempest* appears a little banal, then something has gone seriously wrong.

Silviu Purcarete, a Romanian director, has established a reputation for himself as one of the most exciting of European directors. His production of *Titus Andronicus*, first seen in 1992, was still touring Europe in 1995, visiting the Avignon Festival.[1] The international collaboration for his production of *The Tempest* at Nottingham exemplifies a newly inter-cultural strand of current Shakespeare production, the phenomenon of the international show freely transmitted from culture to culture, an item in a structure of global cultural exchange.[2] Strikingly, this production followed immediately on his production of the same play in Portugal at the Teatro S Joao, Oporto.

---

[1] The production was reviewed alongside Gregory Doran's production of *Titus* for the Market Theatre of Johannesburg by Jonathan Bate, *TLS*, 28 July 1995, pp. 18–19.

[2] See Dennis Kennedy, 'Shakespeare and the Global Spectator', *Shakespeare Jahrbuch*, 131 (1995), 50–64.

19   *The Tempest*, Nottingham Playhouse, 1995: Prospero (Michael Fitzgerald) and the Spirit Orchestra.

The Nottingham *Tempest* was, however, the first time Purcarete had directed Shakespeare in English. Though he spoke eloquently in the programme note of his discovery of the English text, of 'the magic of the words' and the 'very special' quality of 'breathing in the English language', Purcarete's vision of the play was dominated by music and visual effect, never by the uncovering of moments of the language. Spoken for the most part extremely slowly and with actors clearly instructed never to be quick on their cues, the scenes of *The Tempest* unfolded with an aural monotony in which actors became pawns in a director's imaginative vision, a form of directorial dictatorship that is sharply opposite to the English tradition of actor prominence even within strongly conceptual director's theatre. For all the attention the performance paid to the possibilities of language, this production might as well have been in a foreign language, as, for the director, it was.

Purcarete's brutal treatment of the text was most apparent at the play's opening. The audience was kept out of the auditorium as Alonso and his court slowly processed through the foyer, Alonso wearing a red crown and pushed in a wheelchair, the others in suits and bowler-hats waving white fans. The procession ended at the auditorium doors which opened to fierce noises and a torrent of red light; the court screamed, entered, the doors shut behind them and that was all the production ever offered of the first scene.

As the audience, by this time a little bemused, entered, they found a set, designed by José Manuel Mela, of an empty revolve across which light played to suggest the sea, while above it stretched a series of steel chords suggesting a musical stave and which, in the course of the evening, would be raised and lowered without apparent meaning. Upstage stood Prospero (Michael Fitzgerald), bewigged and robed as an eighteenth-century figure, turning every so often as the audience settled.

Visually striking, the effect clearly and over-emphatically defined the island as a space of dream and of music. This Prospero, a figure of the Enlightenment, was unambiguously Mozart, the genius of the place. The island's spirits were a masked string quintet who wandered on and off playing, initially as accompaniment to Miranda's singing of Barbarina's cavatina at the opening of Act 4 of *The Marriage of Figaro*, a text that evoked childhood love and the sense of loss. The aria would be heard throughout the performance until, at the very end, as Prospero spoke the epilogue almost to himself as the revolve took him away from the audience, Caliban sat playing the melody on a violin, initially as hideous scratchings but metamorphosing magically and movingly into beauty.

Purcarete's vision of Caliban denied the fashionable view of him as the 'savage' victim of colonialism. Instead Caliban is 'the weak mind, but the mind of the child before society'. Like a child, there is in his behaviour 'a mixture of non-comprehension, fear leading to violence, but also extreme sensitivity'. Played by Gheoghe Ilie, a huge bald figure, wearing only a nappy, Caliban erupted onto the stage from under Prospero's bed, a frightening monster but also a frightened child, shouting and screaming and waving his arms in his terror that was at the same time terrifying, pulling out of his nappy clothes-pegs which he fixed all over his body as self-tormenting punishment. Disturbingly vulnerable, this Caliban seemed never to have warranted Prospero's treatment of him, deserving tenderness and education, at least until, when encouraging Stefano to 'knock a nail into [Prospero's] head' (3.2.62) he produced a hammer and metal spike to give the plot an awful reality. The mixture was unnerving as when the dance to accompany the catch moved from a wild stamping to delicate tiptoeing and back again. For Purcarete, Caliban 'is partly animal, but perhaps he is closer to God', a view which could be seen but not heard since Ilie's English was mostly incomprehensible.

Throughout, music was the locus for beauty and horror, a quality Purcarete found peculiarly acutely mixed in Mozart (used in his *Titus* to accompany the Thyestean feast 'because the moment had to have splendour and horror'). Ferdinand's log was a massive metal skeleton of a double-bass which he kept carrying into 4.1. Disappointingly Purcarete ducked the masque, playing it behind a curtain while Prospero as prompter mouthed his script from the wings, until he pulled the curtain back to reveal the spirits holding up an enormous skeleton, the same one that Caliban had carried on in 2.2 and tenderly arranged on the ground. The skeleton suggested a monstrous Sycorax, now defined as the horror entered into the splendour, a reminder of what lay outside Prospero's eighteenth-century rational and musical universe.

Within this strange dream-world, Prospero's confrontation was less with his enemies now within his power than with the fact of death. *The Tempest* is, for Purcarete, 'about time before death. Death as something final, closed ... Prospero is the artist. Like all artists he has to face a paradox: the extreme strength of art and simultaneously its weakness, uselessness.' The concern with death was particularly intriguing given the age of this Prospero: Fitzgerald looked still in his thirties, a man who ought to be too young to be preoccupied with death. Found first in his bed, Prospero tottered to his feet, needing Miranda's shoulder to lean on until, putting on his magic robe and his wig, he acquired an energy. Empowered, Prospero dominated his world, until the ending consigned him back to the limited world of bodily fragility and the imminence of death. Unlike Thacker's Prospero, there was here no threat to that dominance posed by Ariel for Purcarete took the typically extreme route of denying Ariel an onstage presence at all, leaving him merely a literally disembodied voice, heard but unseen.

The production has seemed in retrospect a cruel paradox. My notes and thoughts create a memory of a richly visual world, a beautiful and striking imagination, a sustained and intelligent view of the play. Yet in execution the experience of the production was dull, the actors so subordinate to the vision that they became celebrants of a religiose ritual, not the ritual of *The Tempest* but of the director's power. Purcarete's production was a perfect mixture of the best and worst sides of the stereotype of the European director's Shakespeare, antagonistic to language and the actor but revelling memorably in the visual beauty of the theatre.

TWO HIGH-SPEED ROMANS

I referred earlier to the speed-addiction of Jonathan Kent's *Hamlet*. It was the merest dawdle beside Peter Hall's *Julius Caesar* in Stratford. While I plead guilty to exceeding the speed-limits as I drive to and from Stratford, I do not see a particular virtue in breaking the sound barrier onstage. Speed, as classical musicians always emphasize, is not the same thing as pace and one performance of a presto finale can feel faster than another while actually being slower on the clock, as the conductor breathes vitality and energy into every note while keeping the metronome marking ticking more slowly.

Hall's *Caesar* was about speed, not pace, the exact inverse of his *Hamlet*. It will be remembered for its timing: two and a quarter hours without an interval. As Irving Wardle wryly commented in *The Independent on Sunday*, 'For once, nobody can say that the play falls off in the second half.' As the play whizzed by, I found myself applauding the vocal virtuosity that enabled the actors to keep going at that pace. But, rather like listening to a virtuoso pianist whose thrilling fingerwork can just occasionally make one forget that a piece of Liszt is much more than the sum of its passagework, these pleasures pall. As, in the middle of the quiet, eerie storm Hall created, Julian Glover's taut, tense and interestingly honourable Cassius belted through his conversation with Michael Gardiner's overly camp Casca, the language became meaningless at this speed, sound

20 *Julius Caesar*, 1.2, RSC, 1995: Caesar (Christopher Benjamin) and Antony (Hugh Quarshie).

without fury signifying very little indeed. No wonder then that when he first began to work on John Nettles' Brutus, Glover's Cassius generated precious little response, Brutus facing away from him, out towards the audience, musing introspectively rather than finding matter for his thoughts in Cassius's words. It would be intriguing if the effect were isolating for the characters, unable to connect with each other from their separate worlds, but instead the effect was isolating for the actors, a feature that did not help the play at all.

John Gunter's set for *Caesar* was a tired recycling of old ideas. I have seen too many productions by now where the stage is dominated by a statue of Caesar. This particular looming head seemed to have been carved out of a giant bar of white chocolate and when the blood ran down it as it hovered over the battle-field of Philippi it looked as though Caesar had a runny nose that needed wiping with a giant tissue. The alarming appearance of segments of animal statues, like the horse that reared through the upstairs window of Caesar's house, hinted at the conventional bestiary of Roman iconology but without doing more than dwarf the characters beneath them. That the characters are dwarfed by the oppressive burden of the history of Rome is a truth about the play but one that a production needs to work with, not merely state. The definition of Rome as alien as well as modern-seeming in its politics is not best served by what Paul Taylor dubbed 'the introduction here of symbols, or rather Symbols'.

Trying to listen to a production moving at this pace was tiring on the ears. The almost unremitting reds and blacks of the costumes and the gloomy set darkly lit were tiring on the eyes. The sense of sprinting a marathon was not helpful. The actors became increasingly off-hand and unconcerned as the play unreeled. Hugh Quarshie, usually a fascinating actor, made the merest sketch of Antony, his switches unmotivated so that the genuine tears with which he began the forum scene turned into the machiavel using the will without ever making clear how the transition came about. Nettles' Brutus was a predictable and conventional portrait of the difficulties of liberalism. Only Christopher Benjamin contributed something new, a Caesar who was frightened and fatalistic, desperately using the pomposity of the language to try to convince himself that 'always I am Caesar' (1.2.213) might become somehow true through emphatic statement and repetition. But the tyrannical anger with which he confronted Metellus Cimber was lost beside the very stagey theatrical effects of the death, the sudden spurt of blood as Casca stabbed him from behind, and the sound of a thunderclap which would be heard again for the deaths of Brutus and Cassius later like some Chekhovian breaking string. The spraying blood here and at the murder of Cinna the poet had their own silly after-echo as, for the rest of the evening, the characters' shoes kept sticking to the residue on the stage-floor and squeaking in an embarrassing way that suggested Epihodov's problems in *The Cherry Orchard* more than the awesome consequences of a tyrannicidal blood-bath.

Beside the principals, the other characters flowed past as a largely undifferentiated mass. No one could possibly remember which of Cassius's and Brutus's officers at Philippi was which. But Shakespeare's small roles are not pieces of verbiage or scene-filling; they deserve and repay sustained attention, detailed characterization, honest acting. But to do that an actor needs time and the speed of this production

defeated them. Occasionally an actor tried to impress himself on the memory by doing something deeply eccentric, like Paul Bentall's hysterical Artemidorus or his insane Poet, but the effect was peculiar, not interesting. For the most part the named Romans were as unremarkable as the unnamed plebeians.

Hall notoriously failed, in his 1984 production of *Coriolanus* at the National Theatre, in his attempt to use paying members of the audience as the crowd, clutching their raincoats and shopping. After the success of Stephen Pimlott's use of the citizens of Stratford to play the male establishment of Vienna in his production of *Measure for Measure* in the previous season, it must have seemed like a good idea to use the citizens of Stratford again for the people of Rome. But crowds are fickle things: onstage and off, they need careful training. It was disastrous to have them, as Hall did, rhubarbing away, mouthing comments to each other at the start and then allow a few professional actors, career plebeians as it were, to dominate them. Hall's citizenry filled the edges of the stage but they never looked remotely interesting. They were not theatrical, merely awkward. Where Nemirovich-Danchenko famously gave each citizen a personal history in his production for the Moscow Art Theatre, Hall left them as a bland mass, occupying space. They were also oddly unaffected by what happened around them, able to turn their backs on the corpse of Caesar covered in a blood-soaked sheet which Antony had so carefully brought in and placed downstage behind them.

Pandarus ends his interminable tale to Cressida about the hair on Troilus's chin: 'and all the rest so laughed, that it passed'. 'So let it now', replies Cressida, 'for it has been a great while going by' (1.2. 162–5). No one could complain that Hall's *Caesar* was a great while going by, but it was a pity that all one was left with was a feeling 'that it passed'.

Where Hall's *Caesar* was all speed and no pace, Barrie Rutter's production of *Antony and Cleopatra* for Northern Broadsides was a fine balance of the two. Never losing its impetus, this *Antony* had all the qualities of freshness and energy I have come to associate with the company's work. This was Northern Broadsides' fourth Shakespeare production and their appearance on the English Shakespeare scene has come to seem the most important intervention during my period of reviewing for *Survey*.

Mike Poulton, in his programme note, wrote of Shakespeare's *Antony and Cleopatra* as 'vigorously and noisily alive, up and running, kicking and screaming' and the same epithets can easily be applied to the production. Theatrical energy can be imposed freneticism, a busy-ness that has little to do with the play's language and dramaturgy. Here the energy was being generated by the play moment by moment, line by line. All the characters – not only the title-figures – were vigorously alive; it was not only in the spectacular drumming for the battle scenes nor only in competition with the wide-open spaces and overtly resonant acoustic of the Cambridge Corn Exchange (where I saw the production) that this *Antony and Cleopatra* was noisily up and running. It achieved what Bartlett's *Romeo and Juliet* or Thacker's *Tempest* could not: a stripped-down Shakespeare that never had to apologize for any supposed limitations of cast-size or scenic extravagance.

Deliberately eschewing any hint of the play as a spectacle of set-design, Rutter created the opposition of Rome and Egypt in the simplest terms, primarily as an opposition of costume: comfortably flowing trousers and sandals for men and women in Egypt against formal suits and lace-up shoes in Rome. Where Octavius (Andrew Cryer) strutted, Ishia Bennison's Cleopatra ran. Yet, if one allowed one's theatrical imagination to be fired, the fragmentary metonymy fully implied the alternative worlds behind.

The performance opened with the most startling contrast. A bare-chested comic spoke as Philo, acting as Master of Ceremonies, as a trolley was wheeled out with a parodied Antony and Cleopatra on it, both male, both sharp mockeries of the lovers, speaking their opening dialogue in 1.1. Watched by a single onstage spectator, Caesar, the action aggressively offered the image that Cleopatra later envisages: we saw the 'quick comedians' and 'some squeaking Cleopatra boy [her] greatness / I'th' posture of a whore' (5.2.212–17). Then, without a break, the 'real' Antony and Cleopatra bounded onto the stage and, in a single line, the parody was shown up for its lying fictionality, fully vanquished by their power and resonance.

If the parodic could be so swiftly overcome, the production consistently explored the very different threat posed by the characters' own predisposition to undercutting their heroic, mythic image. Bennison's Cleopatra was rarely regal, a Northern 'lass' whose wryly sharp style could show up Antony's posturing, mockingly applauding his rhetoric in parting in 1.3. It was a risky manoeuvre, having, as Jeffrey Wainwright suggested in *The Independent*, 'no regard for queenliness in the high English fashion' but threatening all the time to make Cleopatra a figure whose coquettish wit was trivial. Yet by her deliberately restrained use of the regal style, Bennison made its occasional appearances all the more powerful and moving so that, as she offered Scarus 'An armour all of gold' (4.9.27), one saw instantly why Scarus was more overwhelmed by her voice and pose than by the generosity of the reward.

The effect was most dangerous in Antony's death scene where her insistent kisses and voluble speech drew from him a repetition of 'I am dying, Egypt, dying' (4.16.43) with the comic exasperation of a man whose girl-friend just will not shut up. But, at his death, her switch of register for 'The crown o'th' earth doth melt' (65–70) redeemed all and Bennison followed the devastating image of emptiness with a wild, animal howl of grief, again the contrast all the more startling because completely unexpected.

21 *Antony and Cleopatra*, Northern Broadsides, 1995: Antony (Barrie Rutter) and Enobarbus (Dave Hill).

Unafraid, the production allowed the audience to make apparently superficial analogies: Octavia (Deborah McAndrew), in her neat blue suit, as an employee of the Halifax Building Society perhaps or the dirty orange work-jackets of Antony's army suggesting dustmen from the local town council. But the resonances were never able to diminish the action as the characters' language and the staging's power soared above the realist implications. At Actium, Antony, wearing a Herculean lion-skin, and Cleopatra, in a horned headdress of Isis, took their places at the oil-drums and plastic canisters on which their army drummed, confronting the neat blue of Rome. When Cleopatra put down her drum-sticks and walked off and Antony threw down his to run after her, the betrayal was powerfully visualized. The subsequent defections of Antony's men were equally strong as Camidius

walked across the stage to join the Roman drummers, an orange-costumed figure now amongst the blue.

In a cast of fifteen doubling and trebling up efficiently, Dave Hill's magnificent Enobarbus stood out, the rich tones of his voice easily matching the eloquence of his description of Cleopatra's barge and his death a deeply moving consequence of his clear-sighted comprehension of his betrayal. But no performance took undue prominence. At the end, robed in white and with a wreath of flowers on her head, Cleopatra sat on a bench, lit by candles, as, in one of the production's characteristically restrained lighting effects, the stage darkened and the action achieved its image of stasis. *Antony and Cleopatra* is a frighteningly difficult play to stage well: by the simplest means and the utmost trusting of the text, Northern Broadsides achieved far more than most.

TWO STRATFORD EXPERIMENTS

Experimental productions on the main stage in Stratford are not common sights. The restrictions of conventional expectation inhibit radical experiment. Both Gale Edwards's *The Taming of the Shrew* and Stephen Pimlott's *Richard III* were marked by their radical approach to the play's endings, endings which demanded to be read back across the rest of the production.

Productions of *Shrew* necessarily demand that they are defined by their treatment of Kate's final speech but Edwards's production was particularly defiant in its approach to the play's opening. The programme here had an especial usefulness: it is not often that I need a synopsis in a programme for a Shakespeare play to explain to me what is happening onstage. The RSC seems to have an objection on principle to playing the Induction using anything remotely approximating to the words Shakespeare wrote. Edwards, the first female director of a production of *Shrew* that I have seen, took a predictably and perhaps necessarily radical look at the Sly scenes. Her *Shrew* was more completely Sly's dream than any other.

The production began, not with a drunken Sly arguing with 'Marian Hacket, the fat alewife of Wincot', but with an aggressively drunken Sly arguing with one of those intriguing unseen figures in Shakespeare, Mrs Sly. The Lord and the huntsmen, the whole plot of the Induction, became part of the dream itself with the Lord as a dream-master, summoning up the figures of the dream-world, as with a grand gesture he caused a little proscenium arch to rise up out of the stage floor through which came the troupe of players, including Mrs Sly, who will play out the dream of wish-fulfilment with Mrs Sly as Kate, the dream of male power that Sly clearly wants. Edwards took an imaginative step and found a worthwhile way of setting up the misogyny and female oppression that is for us such a troubling feature of the play.

For the rest of the first half of the performance the production seemed to have forgotten its starting-point completely. On Russell Craig's mobile set, the town of Padua became a farce world of brash and garish devices. Indeed a cynical and xenophobic part of me put its coarseness down to the director's being Australian. This part of the production was typified by Mark Lockyer's Tranio, overacting shamelessly and scene-stealing maliciously. This Tranio, given the power to be his own master, was transformed from harlequin in diamond-patterned trousers into the rock star Prince. With Timothy Davies's Hortensio as a lounge lizard modelled on Kenny Everett's Frenchman, Tilly Blackwood as a very funny and thoroughly repellent Bianca, adroit at manipulating her father and her suitors, and assorted other grotesques and caricatures, the play seemed to be heading for the broadest, brashest treatment ever, typified by the arrival at the wedding – where the guests, sheltering from the rain, wore black as if it were Kate's funeral – of a bright red baby Fiat containing a groom in feathers and with one boxing glove and a servant in a pink tutu. The only actor who seemed to be comfortable in this chaos was Michael Siberry as Sly metamorphosed into Petruccio. This Petruccio, much given to speechifying (Grumio had heard it all before), may have been shaken by the sight of Hortensio and the broken lute but went into round one of his encounter with Kate with boundless confidence, buoyed up by his game-plan worked out in soliloquy.

Beside Siberry's Petruccio, Josie Lawrence's Kate looked and sounded as though she was in a different play or rather as if Mrs Sly were an unwilling participant in Sly's dream. Her voice deep and portentous as if she was uncomfortable playing Shakespeare comedy and was in training for tragedy, Lawrence played Kate as a woman playing out a role someone else has defined, a male fantasy of the kind of woman who deserves dominating. The two were clearly smitten from the first time they looked in each other's eyes and the farce seemed to be unfolding genially and happily. By the interval, taken after Tranio and Bianca kissed passionately as Lucentio

22 *The Taming of the Shrew*, 5.2, RSC, 1995: 'My hand is ready, may it do him ease': Petruccio (Michael Siberry) and Katherine (Josie Lawrence).

looked helplessly on, it seemed as though the frame had been used to simplify the play mercilessly.

But all changed in the second half. Now, with an increasingly diabolic Lord in control, Kate's torments began to become darker and far more painful. A starving ghost, a degraded woman in the madness of Petruccio's house inhabited by an array of grotesque servants, Kate was a pitiable sight, not remotely comic at all. As she sat slumped on a chair, even Petruccio, as he left the stage after his soliloquy of power ('Thus have I politicly begun my reign', 4.1.174), was about to caress her tenderly, and she stayed as mute victim behind the following scene for Bianca, the gap between the sisters' experiences now painfully wide. In the scene with the tailor she ended up on the floor in the centre of the stage, cradling a piece of the dismembered gown, a tearful, lonely image of

suffering while Petruccio and Grumio argued about the order to the tailor on one side of the stage. Petruccio, victorious, could now afford to be generous to this battered and defeated bride and his tenderness increased her tears.

Smiling, loving, eating and happy in the next few scenes, Kate had found a joy in marriage though it was difficult to see why she should have done. This was, in effect, the climax of Petruccio's plot and Sly's dream. Docile and affectionate, Kate happily canoodled – there is no other word for it – with Petruccio on the side of the stage while they watched the plot of Lucentio's two fathers unfold. It was in the last scene that the production took its last and most savage twist. As Kate squared up to the Widow, she was clearly unnerved by Petruccio's readiness to bet on her, 'A hundred marks my Kate does put her down' (5.2.37), distressed by his easy retreat to the male world of wagers as she would be later by her father's flourish of his chequebook to give her husband 'twenty thousand crowns, / Another dowry to another daughter' (118–19). She was now closely aligned with Tranio, who had entered stripped of his finery, a servant in an apron carrying black rubbish bags, humiliated and back in his real place, as Kate was now discovering the limits of hers.

Before he began his wooing of Kate, Petruccio had collected up the money offered by Hortensio, Gremio and the false Lucentio, scooping it into his hat. Now the wager money on the wives was gathered into his hand. Kate's mute pleas not to have to trample on her hat were overborne and she delivered the speech he demanded of her as a remarkable mixture of emotions: the orthodox language of female submission seemed to be spoken through her, rather than by her, forced to acknowledge that this is how the world is. Her words angered her but she was also close to a breakdown, her hands pulling at her hair. She ended on the floor, her hand offered to 'do him ease', an action that was both more threatening and more despairing than any of her earlier violence, and Siberry's Petruccio backed away, dropping the money. The programme helpfully explained that 'Petruccio slowly realises what he has been attempting to do to Katherina in the name of love. By the end of the speech his dream has become a nightmare.'

When a Stratford programme announces that '175 lines have been cut', it is rarely cause for alarm. I was sorry to have lost Biondello's marvellous description of Petruccio's arrival for the wedding but none of the other cuts to this point troubled me. But this is the first Shrew I have seen that cut 'Why, there's a wench! Come on, and kiss me, Kate' (5.2.185). Now, with hands to head, Petruccio could hardly bear to look at his bride. The scene dissolved, the dream mechanism was unwound and Sly woke to find his wife standing over him as he, still on his knees, embraced her, anxiously and, at least for the moment, repentantly.

I have needed to describe this movement at length because it is as radical a reinterpretation of the last moments of this troubling play as any I can recall, even if it has clear connections with Michael Bogdanov's 1978 RSC production with Jonathan Pryce. But I have also had to reconstruct it because it was only in retrospect that I felt any confidence in having followed the meaning that was unfolding. I came to respect the thoughtfulness of Edwards's production, the way it allowed the garish simplicity of the first half to be re-read in the light of the second, the way it used the dream-structure to make the action move beyond Sly/Petruccio's control, into consequence and result, its own logic producing a mode of female subjection that made even Sly aware of its devastating cost, to himself as much as to the woman he wishes to control. The production was intellectually demanding, even if it could only be so through rewriting the play, producing a commentary on the play, reading over it rather than through it.[3] If that interpretative mode left me worrying about whether audiences who did not know the play would appreciate what had been done it seemed a price worth paying. This was the fifth time the RSC had produced Shrew in the previous thirteen years and the production justified yet another look at the play. But, significantly, my high opinion of its intellectual rigour only came *after* the event. As I left the theatre after the performance I felt cheated.

This tension between the experience of watching a production and the post-performance thinking-through of its argument can make a production improve in the memory, the immediate response buried in the pleasurable hard work of analysis. As with Purcarete's Tempest and Edwards's Shrew, so Stephen

---

[3] For an attack on the production see John Peter's fulminating review in The Sunday Times: 'how many liberties can you take with a play in order to interpret it? What is the difference between interpreting a play and making it say what *you* want it to say? Do dead playwrights have rights?'

Pimlott's *Richard III* has taken on a warmer glow as it has positioned itself in my theatre memory. Again, the logic of the interpretation has come to dominate over the problem of production.

Yet there were production problems, most of them consequent on Tobias Hoheisel's set. Many of the court scenes were played on a platform which glided out from the space revealed under the well, with a useful gallery, which was set upstage. But even at its fullest extent the platform kept the action far from the audience, a distance which the playing of the scenes did not seek to build on. At that distance the events seemed unimportant, disengaging the audience when the playing encouraged engagement.

In an interview,[4] David Troughton, Pimlott's Richard, spoke of the need to construct the character by working backwards from the soliloquy at Bosworth (5.5.131–60), the need to find a reason for that outbreak of conscience. In a director's programme-note, a rare phenomenon in RSC programmes these days, Pimlott identified the speech as the discovery of despair, placing it in 'the same tradition as the final soliloquy of Faustus': 'Conscience has brought Richard to this point of realization. He looks within himself and finds only emptiness … Richard, utterly alone, facing the truth of who and what he is and deciding his course: "I *shall* despair" – that is the decision he takes, to condemn himself.' It suggests a strongly psychologistic reading of character, not a devil or a vice but a man at the limit of his mental strength.

The cause, the motivation for Richard's actions, was here firmly located as the product of his relationship with his mother (Diana Coupland) and that, in turn, identified as the result of his birth. Troughton had consulted an obstetrician and learned that a breech-birth could produce a hip injury so that Richard's spinal deformity was seen as the result of compensating for the continual hip pain. If that sounds too exact in its medical provenance, it allowed Richard to play on the injury, to use it

when he wished rather than being continually in thrall to it. His costume suggesting a child in short trousers, Troughton's Richard yearned for his mother's love and found only her hatred. After the exit of the court with the dying King Edward in 2.1, Richard found the crown and tried it on, sitting on the throne when, at his mother's entrance, he became sheepish at her glare of disapproval. Significantly, once crowned king, Richard found the throne uncomfortable, unable to sit properly on it.

His meeting with his mother in 4.4 had him, with great awkwardness, place himself on the ground, his head in her lap. Wanting her blessing he received only her curse, following her appalling account of his childhood (4.4.166–75), a speech which came from her loathing of her own son ('Thou cam'st on earth to make the earth my hell', 167). Pimlott identified it as 'a peculiarly terrible scene, a mother cursing her child in a way that is unique in Shakespeare'. Though his mother's hatred does not 'exonerate him … . [it] presents reasons why he is as he is'. Open-mouthed with horror, Richard hurled himself away from her and towards the crown which he had placed on the ground. The brutality of the scene with Elizabeth which follows came directly from the horror and despair, ending with a 'true love's kiss' (361) planted aggressively on Elizabeth's mouth.

The viciousness of this wooing contrasted all the more sharply with the playing of the wooing of Lady Anne (1.2), where Troughton avoided most of the opportunities for cynicism and wit to create a thoroughly convincing lover, with a long and passionate kiss at 'both of them are thine' (193). Yet here too the relationship harped on Richard as abandoned son, playing the sulky child as he asked her 'Bid me farewell' and she responded as a benignly mocking mother with ''Tis more than you deserve' (210). His reaction to the wooing, 'I'll have her', was a wondering triumph of sexual

---

4 'Kaleidoscope', BBC Radio 4, 7 September 1995.

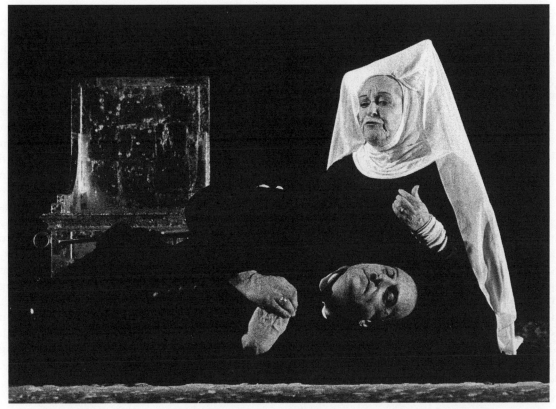

23   *Richard III*, 4.4, RSC, 1995: Mother and son, Duchess of York (Diana Coupland) and King Richard III
(David Troughton).

power ('have' spoken as clearly meaning 'have sex with' her), before he broke the mood with the off-hand cynicism of 'but I will not keep her long' (217).

The coherent detail of this psychological reading of character was set against the emphasis on Richard as actor. At his first entrance, he came to the front edge of the stage, waving at his shadow as he spied it 'in the sun' (1.1.26), raised an expectant finger, opened his mouth to begin his speech when, with a blast of trumpets, the whole court entered on the gallery dressed for a masquerade. Richard grumpily limped offstage, reappearing with jester's cap and bauble, to perform the first thirteen lines as a comic party-piece of welcome for the court, before they froze as the lighting switched to the inner hatred at 'But I' (14). Elsewhere Richard

controlled the stage with mysterious efficiency, asking 'who comes here?' (122) with his back to the entrance through which Hastings came. To meet the citizens in 3.7, Richard turned his attendants into clerics and the three robed up from costumes in a wicker props-basket in the space under the gallery, while the citizens gathered above, unable to see the preparations for the performance of piety.

This performative mode defined the play's ending. There was no battle, no fighting. As the ghosts of his victims entered on the gallery, a pageant to echo the court in the first scene, Richard made his way towards them. His speech drew on Richard's soliloquy in *3 Henry VI* (3.2.174–81), an image of Richard's long search through the 'thorny wood'. As he put down the sword and the crown, he offered, as

PETER HOLLAND

his climactic realization, a phrase divorced from its context early in *Richard III*, 'all the world to nothing' (1.2.225), the full comprehension that all the world had dwindled to meaninglessness and emptiness. The withered arm shook down to its full length, the actor gave up his part and ambled to the corner of the stage and sat down, gazing up at Richmond in the gallery and, when Richmond had completed his long speech of healing, Richard clapped his performance, slowly and hollowly.

Alongside these two perceptions of Richard – son and actor – Pimlott placed a third structure: the ghosts of the dead. The corner where Richard ended his performance, downstage audience left, had, through the course of the production, become identified as the ghosts' place, a space with its own door through which Richard's victims made their final living exit and in which the ghosts frequently gathered to watch the action unfold. The nightmare of the ghosts' curses (5.5) followed Richard's placing of bread and a goblet of wine beside his dagger planted on the ground so that its hilts became a cross and the scene a diabolic parody of communion while Richmond prayed. Richmond himself became a figure in Richard's dream, the ghosts' blessings on him something which horrified Richard even more than their curses.

Margaret, finely played by Cherry Morris who had played the same role in Sam Mendes's production for the RSC, was from the start associated with the ghosts' corner, defining herself through her stage placing as the link with all the dead of the tetralogy so that she became the play's memory of the longer sweep of history. But her first cursing (1.3.193–211) had her enemies writhing in slow-motion agony, a cheaply theatrical effect. Indeed the production gave most of the cast little opportunity to develop their characters. Michael Siberry contributed an eloquently lyrical Clarence, John Nettles an astute but restrained Buckingham, Paul Bentall a Hastings found romping in bed with Jane Shore. But too often

the characters were subordinated to the director's will, so that, for instance, the three citizens in 2.3 became a bland chorus speaking their *sententiae* in unison and dividing the scrivener's lines in 3.6 between them, while the large crowd of Stratford amateurs recruited to play the citizens of London stood immobile on the gallery in 3.7, until the women screamed as Richard's guards forced them back to hear Richard's acceptance of the crown, the crowd no more effective here than they had been in Hall's *Julius Caesar*.

What was consistently missing in the production's careful detailing and its strong reading was an edge of danger. Only when Richard smashed to pulp the Archbishop's bag of strawberries as if it contained Hastings's head was there the violent passion so completely missing elsewhere. The very strength of the director's interpretation, for all its coherence and harmony, had partly buried the actors (though less than Purcarete's *Tempest* had), leaving strong effects but without the individual energies the actors could have provided.

OLD AND NEW AT THE NATIONAL THEATRE

Watching Terry Hands's production of *The Merry Wives of Windsor* on the Olivier stage at the Royal National Theatre was like meeting up with an old friend whom you never expected to see again: the reunion is full of nostalgia but you cannot help thinking that the world has moved on since you last met. Hands directed the play for the RSC in 1968 and the production was a revelation; it was his first Shakespeare production for the company and stamped him as a brilliantly talented young director. He wrote a sharp and intelligent introduction for the Folio Society edition of the play in 1974 (reprinted at length in the National Theatre programme). His 1968 production was revived in 1975 to take its place with Hands's explorations of both parts of *Henry IV* and *Henry V*, creating a cycle of Falstaff plays. This

24   *The Merry Wives of Windsor*, 2.1, RNT, 1995: Mistress Page (Maureen Beattie) reads Falstaff's letter.

year Hands chose the same play to mark his debut at the National, working again with the same designer, Timothy O'Brien. Even the casting had its own echo of his earlier thoughts: Brenda Bruce, Mistress Page in 1968, re-appeared transformed into Mistress Quickly; Tim Wylton, Bardolph in 1985, was now Doctor Caius. In many ways it was as if the National had simply borrowed the RSC for the event: by Michael Billington's count, seventeen of the twenty main parts were played by ex-RSC performers.

It was certainly worth telling the new generations of theatre-goers just what it was that Hands had uncovered in 1968, the richness of his depiction of a small Elizabethan town. For Windsor is not London and the court characters, Falstaff and Fenton, do not fit into this society, belonging to Windsor Castle perhaps but certainly not Windsor Town: they are

patronizing arrivals, initially contemptuous of the provincial bourgeoisie and overweening in their self-confident assumption that the wealth of Windsor is theirs for the taking. Gerard Logan's matinée idol of a Fenton had to work hard to convince Anne Page, as well as her parents, that he has genuinely fallen in love and abandoned his earlier aims of repairing his squandered fortune.

But it was the life of the town that filled the stage. All through the production, Hands covered scene-changes with the town band processing across the stage, while troops of Sir Hugh's schoolchildren played leapfrog or catch, chanting playground rhymes. Mistress Page and Mistress Ford compared Falstaff's letters at the market, while other townsfolk were buying cauliflowers or turning over the clothes on the Renaissance equivalent of an Oxfam stall. Bardolph was no sooner turned tapster than he could be seen at the back of the stage, serving beer to a table of workingmen.

All of this detailing, finely in place, suggested the busy, bustling density of town life against which the action was played. Yet, where O'Brien's sets in 1968 had put a town street on stage, Windsor had now become much more rural. Backed with a field of ripe corn and with a Thames ketch moored upstage, with its characteristic sails hoisted, the play's houses were vestigial frames in a pastoral landscape. The play's contrast of town and surrounding fields had collapsed into a vision of Merrie England closely modelled on Hofnagel's painting of *A Fête at Bermondsey*, used for the production's publicity. The first scene was played in an orchard, as if Justice Shallow had brought his with him from Gloucestershire and from *Henry IV Part 2*. All the characters apart from Falstaff and Fenton now spoke in a rustic accent, setting off the Received Pronunciation of the newcomers all the more sharply but also prone to sound too like stage Mummerset, voices for the audience to mock affectionately for their strange sounds.

O'Brien and Hands were of course right to remind us that an Elizabethan town like Windsor is little larger than a modern village but their choice of autumnal colourings, however much justified by the play, took on its own overtones of nostalgia. The Windsor of Hands' *Merry Wives* now looked disconcertingly like a living museum, part of a Shakespeare theme-park, a stop-off on the 1990s Heritage Trail. In the warm glow of the production's benign enjoyment of others' folly, the audience could relish the comedy but lost sight of that firm and validated sense of community without which the play's strata have no meaning.

Yet the production was richly enjoyable in its exploration of what Hands sees as 'Shakespeare's warmest and richest comedy'. If some of the minor roles were overfull of comic mugging and if some of the business was tired and predictable, Hands was clearly trying scrupulously to avoid the easy options in search of cheap gags. The audience laughed at lines and situations, not at extraneous pratfalls. When, for instance, Alan David's Sir Hugh, a gentle Welsh parson, sang to himself to keep up his spirits while nervously waiting for his duel with Dr Caius, it was gloriously right that he should end up conducting an enormous imaginary Welsh male-voice choir. Denis Quilley's Falstaff, huge of girth and orotund of voice, would naturally attempt press-ups (his arms on a stool, not of course on the ground) as he anticipated his strenuous encounters with the two wives. Quilley's preening vanity was one of the production's pleasures, a man so sure of himself that it took little for Mistress Quickly to massage his shoulders and his ego until he agreed to visit Mistress Page again, even after his watery experiences in Datchet Mead.

But beside the gallery of expectedly comic characters both play and production set the far more troubling figure of Ford. Richard McCabe started as a melancholic man, dressed in tightly buttoned-up customary suits of solemn black like some Puritan Hamlet. The jealousy churning within him always risked exploding as words were spat out with venom and the grimace became increasingly like a manic rictus. Shedding both clothes and dignity, Ford in his obsessions twisted his body into the representation of what he feared, wrenching his hair into two huge cuckold's horns, his tongue also taken over by his imaginings. His search of the buck-basket – a word that he could barely manage to get past his lips – produced the usual flurry of dirty linen but McCabe catapulted himself into it so that it ended upside down on top of him as he crawled around the stage like some bizarre tortoise. His matter-of-fact statement, 'Well, he's not here I seek for' (4.2.145), both superbly counterpointed the preceding freneticism and served to underline the mad rationality of his search. It also predicted the moving calm with which he would finally balance love and jealousy. Once he had heeded Page's warning, 'Be not as extreme in submission / As in offence' (4.4.10–11), McCabe's

25   *Richard II*, 1.1, RNT, 1995: Enter the King (Fiona Shaw).

Ford could settle into a trusting and loving embrace of Geraldine Fitzgerald's bright-eyed Mistress Ford, at last calm of mind, all passion spent.

Hands's *Merry Wives* was a comforting return to the old; Deborah Warner's *Richard II* had the brilliant shock of the new. As the audience entered the Cottesloe theatre for *Richard II*, they found the action already under way: down the length of the rest of the playing-area stood a series of pedestals, each surmounted by a small and enigmatic object, guarded by an eerie figure in black who, as the moment of performance approached, collected the objects, storing them in a reliquary, and carefully took all the pedestals. It is not common for the set to be

dismantled before the play has properly begun and the effect here was bemusing, the only moment in the whole production where the production's intentions were unclear.

Meanwhile, behind a light gauze at one end of the theatre, in a space lit by wall-mounted candles, servants were robing Richard in his royal regalia; underneath the robes, Richard's body was wrapped in bandages like some medieval mummy. Somewhere above the audience's heads, a group of female singers began an ethereal, haunting requiem which would punctuate the performance throughout its four-hour length. Only at the end, as Exton single-handedly dragged onto the stage a rough wooden coffin and tipped off the lid to reveal

26   *Richard II*, 3.4, RNT, 1995: The playing area during a dress rehearsal.

the corpse of Richard would the bandages and the music (as the choir sang 'dona nobis pacem') make final and complete sense: from first to last Warner's *Richard II* was an elegy for the loss of Richard and with Richard his entire world, a medieval world of ceremony and order, of religion and mystery, now irrevocably lost, replaced by the banal *realpolitik* of Henry IV. By the interval, the candles on the wall had all guttered and died and were not replaced in the second half, an effect of great simplicity and immense power, a symbol suggesting the dying of Richard's rule.

As a view of the play there is nothing radical in this. Indeed, it opens a space for a certain suspicion about its overly benign view of Richard's world. Behind the steel-hard clarity of Deborah Warner's directing, a style which suggested a superficial sympathy with Boling-broke's cold rational pragmatism, the pro-

duction revealed an unexpected nostalgia for a different, lost way. While most of the immediate responses to the production inevitably concentrated on the cross-gender casting of Fiona Shaw as Richard II, it is the production's politics that now seem most surprising, tinged with a reactionary mood that teetered on the edge of but never crossed over into sentiment-alism, overborne by its deeply humane concern, a concern for individuals, all disturbingly lost in the political world, that underpinned every moment of the performance.

The theatre itself had been transformed by Hildegard Bechtler's rigorous design into a traverse, a narrow playing area of light wooden floor and low walls that stretched the full depth of the theatre with the audience ranged along the two long sides, facing each other. It suggested and encouraged confrontation, characters set oppositionally, unable in its tight width to pass each other. Most obviously ideal for the lists at Coventry, where, with immensely detailed and powerfully ritualistic ceremony, Bolingbroke and Mowbray prepared for their fight, kept apart by Richard and his court who occupied the middle of the theatre, the stage-space proved itself, over and over again, to offer each scene the energizing dynamic it needed. In 1.2, for instance, the entire scene was controlled and shaped by the slow progress of the aged and crippled Duchess of Gloucester down the theatre, leaning heavily on two sticks, while John of Gaunt stood immobile. Indeed the staging of this scene precisely enabled what was, quite simply, the most brilliant and perfect Shakespeare performance I have seen: Paola Dionisotti's Duchess, brutally hard in her vindictive grief, spitting out her words with frightening power and the utmost lucidity, confronting Graham Crowden's Gaunt, as every step of her progress and every movement of her body underlined the words with the utmost intensity.

The shape of the playing area also encouraged multiple perspectives. In 3.3, for instance, Struan Rodger's Northumberland, a figure dangerously manic in his aggressive pursuit of Richard, stood isolated in the middle of the empty, darkened stage, far in advance of Bolingbroke and the others, while Richard, Aumerle and his attendants clustered at a distance on a small golden balcony. The moment of connection between the two was not Richard's own descent; instead, at 'down I come' (177), he draped a sheet over the edge of the balcony, threaded the crown onto it and let it slide slowly down the sheet which he then let go so that it dropped to the ground to strange music heard in the air as the others stood shocked at the sight and sound – an image, as so often in the production, of devastating simplicity and power.

Reviewing this production has been extremely difficult: every scene contained details of speech or movement, of blocking or effects, that seemed to demand recording, moments

that marked the language, emphasized spoken thought, in a fashion that is necessarily rare, for staging of this quality cannot but be unusual. The style may have been emphatically simple but it was based on a full comprehension of the flexibility and rapidity of transitions in Shakespeare's language so that the action coloured but never covered the lines, revealing the meaning of speech, never denying its sinuous effect. Playing a full text – at least I failed to note any significant cuts – Warner demonstrated the coherence and inner necessity of every line, its demandingly intense accumulation of argument across the vast expanse of the play. The rigour of her work, always in service of the play, always demonstrating its profoundly considered respect for the playwright, was a humbling object-lesson.

Warner's scrupulous intelligence was supported by her cast, each playing to their limits. If I single out Michael Bryant's York it is only because his performance was a startling representation of an actor achieving such comfortable ease with the language that, at moments, it took on edges of a reality that made the others appear to be only acting. Whatever we may mean by that strange sense of life in Shakespeare's characters was perfectly present in Bryant's York, a man wandering through the play's political confusions with his personal integrity intact, his values completely internalized into his being so that, after berating Bolingbroke for the rebellion in 2.3, he cannot help himself from turning back and becoming host ('So fare you well – / Unless you please to enter in the castle', 158–9), embarrassed by his own hospitality but totally incapable of suppressing his generosity and social obligations. Such consummate playing took the domestic comedy of Aumerle's conspiracy in its stride: the 'boots' scene (5.2) allowed all its farce without for a moment losing sight of the threat to Aumerle's life and to the throne, the clash of family and state fully and appallingly present.

As Richard was carried in for the lists, the production music took on a rare irony as the choir sang 'Rex tremendae maiestatis'. Shaw's Richard was here appealingly boyish, the child-king, desperately unsure what to do. As the preparations for the duel reached fever-pitch and the drums and trumpets thundered, Richard could be seen in complete panic, desperate to find something to save Boling-broke. He threw his warder down as a last-second reaction, surprising himself as much as anyone else by his action. There was no trace here of a pre-planned strategy, only a terrified bid to protect the object of his desire. Reviewers were troubled by Shaw's performance but, alarmingly, it was a female critic who was most vituperative, as Rhoda Koenig complained in *The Independent* that 'Shaw's Richard is a stereotyped girlie', that Richard was 'unlikely to be such a giggling prat' and, as her culminating insult, complaining that 'Shaw doesn't have enough maleness to play Peter Pan'. But the absence of 'maleness' in Shaw's performance had nothing to do with her own gender. Instead her Richard was precisely Peter Pan, a child forced unbearably to have to grow up, until, in the scene of the murder, Richard had finally and agonizingly matured to the furthest reaches of experience. The earlier playfulness had now become a distant memory but from the start it had been accompanied by a febrile gaucheness, trying to make jokes ('Our doctors say this is no time to bleed', 1.1.157) but using the mirror, in which he was forever checking his appearance, to cool his face and neck. The jokes could be inordinately light-hearted, as, for instance, the sudden idea to lead the army into Ireland produced a fake 'Oirish' brogue (doubly funny, given that Shaw's natural voice has an Irish accent) and had Richard leading his followers in a mocking Irish jig. But the wit could take on darker hues: Richard arrived too early at Gaunt's deathbed, wearing a black armband and clutching a funeral wreath which he tried to hide behind his back before dumping it on a servant. At the lists, after Mowbray's dignified exit, Richard darted to the door to check Mowbray had gone

before he cut the length of Bolingbroke's exile, the cheeky little gesture in itself enough to justify Gaunt's anger. Such joking was still there late in the play, in the cheery little wave to Bolingbroke after Richard had descended from the balcony in 3.3.

In the deposition scene (4.1), Richard entered with the crown in a shopping-basket and placed it on the floor between himself and Bolingbroke, undercutting the solemnity of the ritual by trying to play pat-a-cake with him. But the game was now excruciatingly painful and he responded to Bolingbroke's question, 'Are you contented to resign the crown?' (190), with an off-hand 'Aye', then turned and buried his head in the lap of the seated York and screamed 'No'. Miming the reverse coronation through tears, Richard prostrated himself full-length before the crowned King Henry, then punched at him until Henry embraced him and calmed him. The childishness was an adult's retreat from the awareness of uncontrollable circumstance and ineradicable pain. From then on, the joking was lost, especially after 5.1, when Richard was dragged in on a blanket, filthy, thirsty and cowering from his tormentors. In his last scene, tied to a rope in the centre of the stage, Richard killed two of his executioners but, with a wry irony, he reached the literal end of his tether and Exton, out of Richard's reach, could stab him.

Richard's desire for Bolingbroke, his mirror-image, was held within this framework. Never explicitly homoerotic – since Richard did not here have the maturity to contain an adult sexuality – the depth of emotion was effectively naturalized by Shaw's gender so that the embraces, stroking, kisses and other gestures of affection were both between two male characters and between a male and female actor, the latter removing any of the frisson that displays of homosexual emotion produce for a mostly heterosexual audience. It gave the scenes with Queen Isabel (Brana Bajic, affecting in her grief) a certain distance as the two were kept apart by the performers' gender, evading a lesbian embrace of performers but also keeping the married couple strikingly apart. But Shaw's gender was never an intervention: rather, her femaleness and Richard's boyishness combined to create a character who was in so many ways 'not-male', as, Shaw has argued, kings are 'not-male' in renaissance political thought, their gender invisible behind their regality.

Beside the intensity of Shaw's performance, David Threlfall's Bolingbroke was deliberately underplayed, so that his take-over of power was a shift to an emptier state, ruled by a remarkably benign man who no longer wore the splendid robes of kingship and whose elaborate throne was now covered with a simple green baize cloth. The contrast was acute with Richard, who, when he sat on the throne, found that his legs did not reach the ground and left his feet dangling, again like a child.

This is the end of my sixth and final review of productions for *Survey*. There is no need for a retrospective conclusion: Deborah Warner's *Richard II* sums up all the virtues of Shakespeare production that I have tried to value highly throughout my reviews. Its consistent intelligence, its refusal to accept tradition for its own sake, its creation of a particular and flexible space for actors and audience to share, and, above all, its unfailing understanding of and respect for the complexity and power of Shakespeare's writing – all these strengths exemplify the very best in English productions of Shakespeare. It provides – I trust not too neatly – a triumphant ending for my extremely enjoyable stint.

PROFESSIONAL SHAKESPEARE PRODUCTIONS IN THE BRITISH ISLES, JANUARY–DECEMBER 1994

compiled by

NIKY RATHBONE

Most of the productions listed are by professional companies, but a number of productions with mixed amateur and professional casts have been included. Information is mainly taken from newspaper reviews held in the Birmingham Shakespeare Library. Notable this year has been the increasing number of professional or semi-professional companies performing at open-air sites such as National Trust houses and Oxford and Cambridge college gardens, exploiting the link between Shakespeare and the tourist industry. There is also an increasing number of small touring companies, probably a response to the effect of the recession on professional theatre: an interesting twentieth-century version of the strolling players tradition.

ANTONY AND CLEOPATRA

The Court Theatre Company at the Courtyard Theatre, King's Cross, London: May 1994
Director: Adrian Brown
Antony: Hayward Morse
Cleopatra: June Abbot

The Berliner Ensemble and Wiener Festwochen at the King's Theatre, Edinburgh: August 1994
German translation by Elisabeth Plessen
Director: Peter Zadek
Designer: Wilfried Minks
Antony: Gert Voss
Cleopatra: Eva Mattes

First performance, Berlin, May 1994; also performed in Vienna and Amsterdam.

AS YOU LIKE IT

Cheek by Jowl, tour continues.
See *Shakespeare Survey 48*. The production also toured Europe and New York.

Box Hedge Theatre, tour, performing in the gardens of country houses: July–September 1994

Dream-Makers, Cannizaro Park Open Air Theatre, Wimbledon: August 1994
Director: Leo Dolan
Performed by a mixed amateur and professional cast.

Eye Theatre, London: July 1994
Director: Tom Scott
Set in the 1930s, to Gershwin and Cole Porter music.

Hot Air Productions performing in Oxford college gardens: July 1994
Part of the Oxford Shakespeare Festival
Producers: Aaron Simpson and Michael Cohen
Aaron Simpson and Michael Cohen, the producers, put on four shows in two Oxford locations in 1993. In 1994 ten plays were produced in Oxford college gardens and three in Cambridge. The cast and backstage staff are undergraduates, but the producers intend to develop the venture professionally.

TAG, Glasgow, tour: September 1994
Director: Tony Graham
Designer: Kate Borthwick
Music: Iain Johnstone

English Touring Theatre, Crewe, tour: September 1994–
Director: Stephen Unwin
Designer: Bunny Christie
Rosalind: Kelly Hunter.

Adaptations

My Sweet Rose
The Custard Factory, Birmingham, tour: April 1994–
A revival of the adaptation toured in 1991 under the title *Wicked Bastard of Venus*.

THE COMEDY OF ERRORS

Illyria Theatre Company, tour of National Trust and English Heritage open-air sites: June 1994–
Director: Billie Reynolds.

Nottingham Playhouse: September 1994–
Director: Paul Clayton
Designer: Kevin Knight
Adriana: Paula Wilcox.

Perth Theatre, Perth, Scotland: November 1994
Director: Richard Baron
Designer: Craig Hewitt
A minimalist production played on a re-creation of an Elizabethan stage, using an all-Scottish cast.

CORIOLANUS

Seventh Seal Theatre Company at the Theatre Royal Studio, Norwich: April 1994.

The RSC at the Swan Theatre, Stratford: May 1994–
Director: David Thacker
Designer: Fran Thompson

Music: Adrian Johnston
Coriolanus: Toby Stephens
Aufidius: Barry Lynch

CYMBELINE

Rented Space Theatre Company at Etcetera, London (Fringe): September 1994–
Director: Ajay Chowdhury
Designer: David Oldman
Cymbeline: Jaron Yaltan
Set in India under the Raj, with Posthumus portrayed as an English orphan brought up at the court of one of the independent Indian states.

HAMLET

The Hamlet Project. Schools working on the project in 1993 continued their work. Eventually about sixty schools were involved, from Britain and Ireland, Denmark, Germany, Norway, Poland. Some attended a weekend *Hamlet* Festival in Bremen in March, and the finale was held on 30 April at the Globe site in London, when Danish and German schools performed.

The Brewery Players at the Studio Theatre, Brewery Arts Centre, Kendal, and tour of India: March 1994–
Adapted and directed by Nigel Banks.

Kaos Theatre, Cumbernauld Theatre, Gloucestershire and tour of Scotland
Director: Phil Morle
Hamlet: Richard Crawford
The performers initially entered blindfold, and made considerable use of dance and mime.

Scapegoat Theatre Company, Norwich Arts Centre and tour: March 1994–
A new company, with the remit: 'To breathe new life into old and classic texts.'

The Young Vic, May 1994
Director: Julia Bardsley
Hamlet: Rory Edwards

Gertrude/Ophelia: Natasha Pope

The New Shakespeare Company at the Open
Air Theatre, Regent's Park: June 1994–
Director: Tim Pigott-Smith
Designer: Tanya McCallin
Hamlet: Damien Lewis
Advertised as the first production of *Hamlet* at
the Open Air Theatre.

Stafford Shakespeare Company, Stafford Castle:
July 1994
Producer: Nick Mowatt
Director: Rob Swinton
Hamlet: Jason Riddington

The Peter Hall Company at the Thorndike
Theatre, Leatherhead; British and foreign tour:
July 1994–
Director: Sir Peter Hall
Designer: Lucy Hall
Hamlet: Stephen Dillane
Claudius: Michael Pennington
Polonius: Donald Sinden
Ophelia: Gina Bellman
Gertrude: Gwen Taylor

Birmingham Stage Company, The Old Rep
Theatre, Birmingham: September 1994–
Director: Richard Dreyfuss
Assistant Director: Graeme Messer
Designer: Alice Purcell
Hamlet: Russell Boulter

Chester Gateway Theatre: October 1994–
Director: Michael Crompton
Designer: Michael Vale
Hamlet: Dominic McHale
Cut to two hours, with Fortinbras omitted,
eclectic costuming and set in no particular
period.

Adaptations

Hamlet, a ballet version, performed by the Cape
Ballet, South Africa, at Sadler's Wells Theatre,
London: April 1994
Director and choreographer: Veronica Paeper

Designer: Peter Cazalet
Music: Peter Klatzow.

Horatio's Tale, by Nick Hennegan
Maverick Theatre Company, at the Midland
Arts Centre, Birmingham and tour: May 1994–

I Hate Horatio by Paul Rudwick
Tower Theatre, Canonbury, London: August
1994
Director: Nan Webber
First performance, Broadway, 1991. Plot: The
ghost of John Barrymore helps Andrew Rally to
play Hamlet in Joseph Papp's Shakespeare
Festival.

HENRY V

The RSC at the Royal Shakespeare Theatre,
Stratford: May 1994–
Director: Matthew Warchus
Designer: Neil Warmington
Henry: Iain Glen

HENRY VI

York Theatre Royal: October 1994–
Director: John Doyle
Designer: James Merifield
Henry VI: Edward York
Richard, Duke of Gloucester, later Richard III:
David Leonard
An adaptation of *Henry VI Parts 1–3*, mainly
drawn from *Part 3*, played in repertory with
Richard III as an exploration of the development
of Richard.

*Henry VI: The Battle for the Throne; Henry VI
Part 3*
The RSC at The Other Place, Stratford, UK
regional tour and Los Angeles: July 1994–
Director: Katie Mitchell
Designer: Rae Smith
Henry VI: Jonathan Firth
Queen Margaret: Ruth Mitchell
Adapted from *Henry VI Part 3*.

JULIUS CAESAR

The RSC production directed by David Thacker, having completed its tour of the UK, toured Holland, Denmark, Japan and Germany. See *Shakespeare Survey 48*.

The English Shakespeare Company, tour continues. See *Shakespeare Survey 48*.

Breach of the Peace Theatre Company at the Bridewell, London: January 1994
Performed in repertory with *The Merchant of Venice*. The Bridewell is a new theatre, converted from a former swimming baths, and now advertised as showing Shakespeare regularly.

Manchester Royal Exchange: September 1994
Director: Robert Delamere
Designer: Rob Howell
Antony: Danny Sapani
Caesar: Denys Hawthorne
A production which strongly contrasted the private and public words of politicians.

KING LEAR

Kaboodle Theatre Company, tour continues. See *Shakespeare Survey 47*.

Talawa at the Cochrane Theatre and tour: March 1994–
Director: Yvonne Brewster
Lear: Norman Beaton, later replaced by Ben Thomas
Fool: Mona Hammond
Billed as Britain's first contemporary black Lear.

The RSC at the Barbican Theatre, London: May 1994, and tour.
Transfer from Stratford.
See *Shakespeare Survey 48*.

Adaptations

Gorbelly by Richard Harford
Sheffield Crucible Theatre in Education at the Merlin Theatre, Sheffield: July 1994

An adaptation for young audiences, set in a restaurant and concerned with jealousy and inter-generational strife in families.

The Tale of Lear
The Suzuki Company of Toga, Japan at the Everybody's Shakespeare Festival, Barbican Theatre, London: November 1994
Directed and adapted by Tadeshi Suzuki
Lear/Old Man: Uichiro Fueda
Nurse/Fool: Hirohisa Hasegawa
Performed by an all-male cast, in Japanese with English surtitles.

LOVE'S LABOUR'S LOST

The RSC at the Barbican Theatre, London: May 1994–
Transfer from Stratford.
See *Shakespeare Survey 48*.

MACBETH

The RSC production shown at the Barbican Theatre, London, in December 1993 transferred to the Royal Shakespeare Theatre, Stratford in March 1994, followed by a national tour.
See *Shakespeare Survey 48*.

Soho Group, London, in association with Kent Shakespeare Project at Deal Castle. National and European tour: May 1994–
Director: Lake Dixon
An all-women professional company of five working on a development from Deal Theatre Project's educational work. The production explored issues of gender.

Sherman Theatre Company, Cardiff, and tour: February 1994–
Director: Jamie Garven
Macbeth: Russell Gomer

Edinburgh Theatre Arts at the Church Hill Theatre, Edinburgh and tour: March 1994–

The Waterside Theatre Company, Stratford: May 1994–

A severely cut version, played by a company of five.

Hot Air Production Company at the Oxford Shakespeare Festival: July 1994–

London via Stoke productions at the Lyric Studio Theatre, Hammersmith: August 1994
Directors: Elle Lewis and Tony Longhurst
Set in 1960 London gangland with the witches played as down and outs.

Cannizaro Park Open Air Theatre: July 1994–
Director: Leo Dolan
Lady Macbeth: Linda Regan, from the cast of a television show, *Hi-de-Hi*.

Project Theatre, Dublin: July 1994
Director: Gerard Sternbridge
Designer: Harry Harris
Macbeth: Darragh Kelly
Lady Macbeth: Ann Callanan
Macbeth and Lady Macbeth inhabited a cage-like hemisphere over which the evil spirits crawled, impersonating almost all the other characters in the play, and manipulating the minds of Macbeth and his wife.

Albion Shakespeare Company, Norwich, tour of open-air venues, with *Romeo and Juliet*: July 1994–
Director: Barry Halloren
A traditional production.

Livespace Theatre Company, London, tour of open-air sites: July 1994–

Theatre Clwyd, Wales: September 1994
Director: Helena Kaut-Hawson
Designer: Pamela Howard
Macbeth: Timothy West

Second Age at the Riverbank Theatre, Dublin: October 1994
Director: Alan Stanford
Designer: Trevor Knight
Macbeth: Simon O'Gorman
The parts of the witches were developed and extended to include additional cast who remained on stage during much of the action.

Sturdy Beggars at the Bridewell Theatre, London: November 1994
Director: Stephen Jameson
Designer: Andrew Marsland
Macbeth: Andrew Jarvis
The production was set in a primitive stone circle.

Adaptation

Macbeth, the musical, Atelier Productions, Sofia, Bulgaria at the Hen and Chicken, Bristol: November 1994
Macbeth: Krassy Damianov
Highlights from the play, performed with mime and clowning witches, and set to rock music.

MEASURE FOR MEASURE

Cheek by Jowl, University of Warwick Arts Centre and world tour: February 1994–
Director: Declan Donnellan
Isabella: Anastasia Hille
Angelo: Adam Kotz
A modern-dress production.

Logos Theatre Company at the Mermaid Studio Theatre, London: May 1994
The company was formerly called Sharers and Hirelings. Played in repertory with *The Merchant of Venice*.

The RSC at the Royal Shakespeare Theatre, Stratford: October 1994–
Director: Stephen Pimlott
Designer: Ashley Martin-Davies
Isabella: Stella Gonet
Angelo: Alex Jennings

THE MERCHANT OF VENICE

The Bridewell, London: January 1994
In repertory with *Julius Caesar*.

West Yorkshire Playhouse, Leeds: March 1994–
Director: Jude Kelly
Designer: Paul Andrews

Music: Jason Carr
Antonio: Michael Cashman
Shylock: Gary Waldhorn
Portia: Nicola McAuliffe
Jude Kelly cast extras representing the Jews of Venice from the Leeds Jewish community's amateur dramatic society and the actors playing Shylock and Tubal were also Jewish. The production also addressed the problem of mixed marriages and considered homosexuality.

The RSC at the Barbican Theatre, London: April 1994–
Transfer from Stratford.
See *Shakespeare Survey 48*.

Logos Theatre Company at the Mermaid Studio Theatre, London: May 1994–
Director: Dermot O'Brien
Portia: Elizabeth Rees
Played in repertory with *Measure for Measure*, the production had strong elements of farce.

Bruton Theatre, Musselburgh: September 1994
Director: Eve Jamieson
Designer: Graham Hunter
Antonio: Joe Gallagher
Shylock: Don Crerar

Harrogate Theatre: October 1994
Director: Andrew Manley
Shylock: Damian Myerscough
Set in a concentration camp with the guards as audience. Shylock was eventually shot.

The Goodman Theatre of Chicago at the Barbican Theatre, London: November 1994
Director: Peter Sellars
Costume design: Dunya Ramicova
Lighting design: James F. Ingalls
Sound design: Bruce Odland
Antonio: Geno Silva
Shylock: Paul Butler
Portia: Elaine Tse
TV monitors were hung from the auditorium roof, showing close-ups of the actors' faces. During the trial scene, newsreel footage of the Los Angeles riots was shown.

THE MERRY WIVES OF WINDSOR

Northern Broadsides, tour continues.
See *Shakespeare Survey 48*.

Hot Air Production Company, open-air production at the Oxford Shakespeare Festival: July–August 1994.

A MIDSUMMER NIGHT'S DREAM

The Worcester Theatre Company at the Swan Theatre, Worcester: February 1994
Director: Pat Trueman
Designer: Jill Cresswell

Durham Theatre Company, tour: March 1994–
Director: Cliff Burnett
A small-scale touring production, set in a civil war zone.

The New Victoria Theatre, Newcastle under Lyme: March 1994
Director: Rob Swain
Bottom: Richard Hague

The New Shakespeare Company, Regent's Park Open Air Theatre: May 1994–
Director: Deborah Paige
Designer: Geraldine Pilgrim
Music: Jonathan Goldstein
Titania: Estelle Kohler
Bottom: Robert Lang

Attic Theatre, open-air production at Hazelwood House, Bath: June 1994
Director: Jonathan Kay
The actors played different parts in each show, and their moves were improvised.

Box Hedge Theatre Company, open-air production touring stately homes: June 1994–
This is their third national touring production of a Shakespeare play.

Lincoln Shakespeare Company at the Bishop's Palace, Lincoln: June 1994
Director: Simon Clark.

PROFESSIONAL PRODUCTIONS IN THE BRITISH ISLES

Open-Hand Productions, open-air production in Cambridge college gardens: July 1994
Artistic Director: Dr David Crilly

The RSC at the Royal Shakespeare Theatre, Stratford: July 1994–
Director: Adrian Noble
Designer: Anthony Ward
Music: Ilona Sekacz
Theseus/Oberon: Alex Jennings
Hippolyta/Titania: Stella Gonet
Puck: Barry Lynch
Bottom: Desmond Barrit
The sets derived from twentieth-century Surrealism, particularly the paintings of René Magritte.

Bedford Theatre Company, Bedford Park: August 1994
A newly formed company.

Broomhill Opera, Tunbridge Wells: August 1994
A production of Benjamin Britten's opera and Shakespeare's play
Director for the play version: Mark Dornford-May
Director for the opera: Stephen Langridge
Claimed to be the first professional joint staging in Europe of both the opera and the play. Broomhall Opera has recently been founded by Kit Begley of the English National Opera, as a training opportunity for young professional opera singers.

Northern Broadsides, the Manor Mill, Oldham and tour: September 1994–
Director: Barrie Rutter
Oberon: Barrie Rutter
Titania: Ishia Bennison
Bottom: John Branwell
The rustics became a mill maintenance team, doubling as macho fairies, with Bottom as a shop steward.

Compass Theatre Company, Sheffield, tour: October 1994–
Director: Neil Sissons

Bottom: Nick Chadwin
The forest became an industrial wasteland in this production, and Puck an Artful Dodger with bowler hat and brolly.

The Georgian Film Actors' Studio, Tblisi, Georgia, at the Pit, the Barbican Theatre, London: November 1994
Director: Mikhail Tumanishvili
Designers: George Alexi-Meskhishvili and Keti Alexi-Meskhishvili
First produced, Georgia, 1992, Edinburgh Festival Fringe, 1993, Everybody's Shakespeare Festival 1994. Played in Georgian with English subtitles.

Adaptations

Dream
Theatre on the Podol, Kiev, Ukraine at the Edinburgh Festival: August 1994
An exaggeratedly sexual production in which *Pyramus and Thisbe* becomes a parody of Titania's dream.

If We Shadows, a Midsummer Night's Dream for the twenty first century
Insomniac Productions at Dancehouse Theatre, Manchester: November 1994

MUCH ADO ABOUT NOTHING

Walkington Productions at the Liverpool Everyman Theatre: July 1994
Director: Andrew Walkington
A semi-professional company.

Wales Actors Company, tour of open air sites in Wales: July 1994–
Director: Ruth Garnault

Hot Air Productions, open-air productions in Oxford college gardens: August 1994
Oxford Shakespeare Festival

Adaptations

Much Ado About Nothing, adapted and directed by Derek Killeen and Michael Cross

A rock musical at the Key Theatre, Peterborough: August–September 1994
Music: Simon Pearce
Choreography: Liz Hill.

OTHELLO

Fast Intent Theatre company at the Railway, London (Fringe) March 1994
Director: Oliver Godfrey
Othello: Nick Monu
Desdemona: Ruth Gemmel
Iago: Ben Wheatley

Open-Hand Productions, open-air production in Cambridge college gardens: July 1994.

Hot Air Productions, open-air production in Oxford college gardens: August 1994
Oxford Shakespeare Festival.

Two Way Mirror Theatre Club, Kentish Town, London: November 1994
Director: Richard Pinto
Advertised as part of a Shakespeare season, to be followed by *The Comedy of Errors* and *Twelfth Night*.

Adaptations

Othello, Arc Dance company at Sadler's Wells Theatre, London: February 1994
Choreographer: Kim Brandstrup
Music: Ian Dearden
Othello: Irek Muhkamedev
A new ballet version.

Othello
The Custard Factory, Birmingham, tour: March 1994
Director: Julie-Anne Robinson
Othello: Clinton Blake
Iago: Michael Glen Murphy
Desdemona: Jacqui O'Hanlon
An original interpretation of Desdemona as a flirtatious woman who delights in her power over men.

Goodnight, Desdemona (Good morning, Juliet)
Turtle Key Productions, Fulham, London: June 1994
A comedy based on *Othello* and *Romeo and Juliet*. Constance, an academic, finds herself in a position to change the course of the action.

Othello
Theatre on the Podol, Kiev, Ukraine at the Edinburgh Festival: August 1994
Set, literally, in a swimming pool, with the actors swimming around in the water, which apparently symbolized the protagonists' powerlessness against the force of sexuality. Othello was played by a puny white actor, and Iago by a sexually attractive hulk.

PERICLES

The Rose Theatre Company, Rudolph Steiner House and tour of the UK and Europe: January 1994–
Director: Christopher Marcus
The company also gave educational workshops on the play.

The Royal National Theatre at the Olivier Theatre, London: May 1994
Director: Phyllida Lloyd
Designer: Mark Thompson
Music: Gary Yershon
Pericles: Douglas Hodge
Narrator: Henry Goodman
King Antiochus / Cerimon / Bawd: Kathryn Hunter
The production treated the play as a fairy tale and spectacular costumes were used to suggest the different locations.

RICHARD III

Northern Broadsides at the Tower of London: April 1994
Director: Barrie Rutter
Richard: Barrie Rutter
Queen Elizabeth: Ishia Bennison
The company toured *Richard III* in 1992.

Third Party Productions, tour: Spring 1994
Director: Mark Knight
Richard: Patrick Knox
Played against a backdrop of banners which doubled as doors and tents. Third Party Productions were previously known as the Medieval Players.

Odeon Theatre of Bucharest, Romania, tour organized in connection with Manchester City of Drama Year: May 1994–
Translation into Romanian by Mihai Maniutiu
Director: Mihai Maniutiu
Designer: Constantin Ciubotariu
Richard: Marcel Iures
First performed, Romania, 1993. A production with some very striking theatrical effects played as black comedy and incorporating a wolf, symbolizing Richard's alter ego. The part of Henry was omitted.

Bare and Ragged Theatre Company: at the Edinburgh Festival: August 1994
Director: John Burrows

York Theatre Royal: October 1994
Director: John Doyle
Designer: James Merifield
Richard: David Leonard
Played in repertory with *Henry VI*, as a study in the development of Richard. David Leonard regularly plays the villain in York Theatre Royal pantomime. A huge crown of pikes hung over the stage for both productions.

Lincoln Shakespeare Company, Lincoln Cathedral: November 1994
Music: Colin Walsh

ROMEO AND JULIET

ESC tour continues.
See *Shakespeare Survey 48*.

The Civic Theatre, Leeds: January 1994
Director: Michael Brooksbank
Romeo: Philip Astley
Juliet: Sarah Oldknow

Millfield Theatre Company, London: March 1994
Director: Graham Bruce
Designer: Zoe Castle
Romeo: Dominic Frisby
Juliet: Tanya Roach
A modern-dress production set in New York. Millfield are a new professional company based in north London.

Theatre of the Learned Monkey, Moscow, Russia at the Theatre-in-the Mall, Bradford University: June 1994
Director: Anatoly Fourmantchouk
Romeo: Maxim Razuvgen
Juliet: Stanislav Klassen
Performed mainly in Russian by an all-male cast, supposedly of strolling players.

Heartbreak Productions, Leamington, tour of Warwickshire open-air sites linked with Shakespeare: June 1994–
Director: Jeremy James
Romeo: Daniel Hopkins

The Duke's Theatre Company, Lancaster Park open-air promenade production: June 1994–
Director: Han Duijvendak
Romeo: Rupert Wickham
Juliet: Lucy Slater

Open Hand Productions in Cambridge college gardens: July 1994

Hot Air Productions in Oxford college gardens: July 1994–
Part of the Oxford Shakespeare Festival.

The Oxford Stage Company, tour of the UK and Japan: July 1994–
Director: John Retallack
Designer: Julian McGowan
Music: Karl James
Romeo: Stephen Moyer
Juliet: Tara Woodward
A fast-moving production, reduced to two hours' playing time, which developed the theme of lack of communication between youth and age.

Albion Shakespeare Company, tour of London parks and other open air venues, with *Macbeth*: July 1994

Babel, the Tron Theatre, Glasgow, tour with *Twelfth Night*: September 1994
Babel is a new theatre company.

The Stephen Joseph Theatre, Scarborough: September 1994
Director: Steven Hirst
Designer: Kate Marriott
Romeo: Shaun Parkes
Juliet: Cathy Sara
Played in the round and designed to appeal to younger audiences.

Sheffield Crucible: October 1994
Director: Michael Rudman
Romeo: Jonathan Wrather
Juliet: Nicola Buckingham
A traditional production set in the Italian Renaissance.

Romeo und Julia
Düsseldorfer Schauspielhaus, Germany, Everybody's Shakespeare Festival, the Barbican Theatre, London: November 1994
Translator: Frank Gunther
Director: Karin Beier
Set design: Florian Etti
Music: Thomas Witzmann
Romeo: Matthias Leja
Juliet: Caroline Ebner
Performed in German with English surtitles. A fast, often very comical production in which modern youngsters seek out the emotional thrills and adventure denied them by the controlled, formal world of their parents.

Adaptations

Sex and Suicide
Durham Theatre Company, tour: September 1994
A modern-dress production, using video screens to present the actors in close-up and repeat significant images.

Spin Off Theatre Company, Humberside, tour of local schools: November 1994
Highlights from the play, performed in a traditional way for schools audiences.

Itim Theatre Ensemble, in association with the Cameri Theatre of Tel Aviv, Israel. Everybody's Shakespeare Festival, The Pit, the Barbican Theatre, London: November 1994
Translator: Raphael Eliaz
Adapted and directed by: Rina Yerushalmi
Set design: Moshe Sternfeld
Performed in Hebrew with English surtitles. The use of multiple Romeos and Juliets allowed the production to move through time and space, and to represent different aspects of emotional experience. First performed, Tel Aviv, 1993.

The Punk and the Princess
Film version scheduled for release in December 1994
Producer: Mike Sarne
Set in Notting-hill Gate, London, in the 1960s. Juliet becomes Rachel, a Jewish American whose father makes erotic films. Romeo is the son of a policeman. Shakespeare appears briefly as an actor-manager interested in staging Shakespearian adaptations; the Friar is a drug dealer known as Monk.

THE TAMING OF THE SHREW

The Lyric Theatre, Belfast: March 1994
Director: Robin Midgley
Katherine: Paula McFetridge
Petruchio: Ian Beattie
The Prologue was re-written to present Sly as a Belfast drunk.

Mappa Mundi, tour: April 1994–
Director: Lynne Seymour
Katherine: Lloyd Llewellyn-Jones
An all-male group of actors, with a female director.

Theatre Set Up, tour: June 1994
Director: Wendy McPhee

A Commedia dell'Arte production played in eighteenth-century Harlequinade masks and costumes.

Ludlow Castle, the Ludlow Festival: June 1994–
Director: Val May
Katherine: Prunella Gee
Petruchio: Michael Simkins
Presented as 'The Great Shrew-Taming Show', with burlesque and slapstick.

Open Hand Productions, Cambridge college gardens: July 1994

Hot Air Productions, Oxford college gardens as part of the Oxford Shakespeare Festival: July 1994–

Kent Repertory Productions, the Lakeside Theatre, Hever Castle: July 1994

The Sherman Theatre, Cardiff at Dyffryn Open Air Theatre Festival: August 1994–
Director: Jamie Garven

THE TEMPEST

The Cygnet Theatre at Exeter New Theatre and tour: March 1994–
A presentation of new acting talent.

Oddsocks Productions, tour: June 1994–
A fast, lively production, played as presented by Pembroke's Players, a group of Elizabethan strolling players including Will Shakespeare.

Greenwood Festival Theatre, open-air production in Rufford Country Park: July 1994
Director: Pam Morgan
Three actors played Ariel, to represent the spirit's different aspects; hot, wet and windy. The company is new, and plans to present a Shakespeare play each year in one of Nottingham's country parks.

The RSC at the Barbican Theatre, London: July 1994
Transfer from Stratford.
See *Shakespeare Survey 48*.

Hot Air Productions, open-air production in Oxford college gardens, the Oxford Shakespeare Festival: August 1994.

Birmingham Repertory Theatre, September: 1994
Director: Bill Alexander
Designer: Ruari Murchison
Music: Jonathan Goldstein
Prospero: Jeffery Kissoon

Changeinspeak Productions at Studio One, Battersea Arts Centre, Battersea, London: October 1994
Director: Simon Blake
Prospero: Kevin Molloy
Caliban: David Fisher
Set in 1930s Hollywood, Prospero playing the Director, Caliban played to epitomize black stereotypes of the time.

TIMON OF ATHENS

Ursa Major Theatre Company, Whiteleys' Store, Bayswater, London
Director: John Longenbaugh
The art nouveau setting of Whiteleys' atrium was very suitable for this production set in the 1920s.

TROILUS AND CRESSIDA

Strathclyde Theatre Group and Focus Theatre, Ramshorn Kirk Studio Theatre, Glasgow: November 1994
Designer: Ed Wardle
Set on a world map featuring major twentieth-century war zones, with eclectic costumes and props from Norman helmets to Russian Kalashnikovs, representing war in various periods.

TWELFTH NIGHT

The RSC at the Royal Shakespeare Theatre, Stratford: May 1994–
Director: Ian Judge
Designer: John Gunter

Music: Nigel Hess
Viola: Emma Fielding
Malvolio: Desmond Barrit

Babel: The Tron Theatre, Glasgow and tour
with *Romeo and Juliet*: August 1994
This new company intend to present classic
drama in a simple, uncluttered way.

Bristol Old Vic: September–October 1994
Director: Andy Hay
Designer: Mick Bearwish
Music: John O'Hara
Viola: Robin Weaver
Malvolio: Richard Frost
A white cube set with a maze of doors and
windows for sudden entrances and exits.
Seamen abseiled from helicopters and a fridge
full of cans of beer rose through a trapdoor in
this present-day production.

Salisbury Playhouse and Edinburgh Royal
Lyceum, joint production touring the UK and
China: November 1994–
Director: Deborah Paige
Designer: Isabella Bywater
Music: Matthew Scott
A richly costumed production, with a simple
abstract set.

THE TWO GENTLEMEN OF VERONA

The RSC/Royal Insurance tour continues.
See *Shakespeare Survey 46*.

THE WINTER'S TALE

The RSC production toured Wellington, New
Zealand, Tokyo, New York and Washington.

See *Shakespeare Survey 47*.

Centre Dramatique National Orléans and
Loiret-Centre Théâtre-Machine at the Royal
Lyceum Theatre, Edinburgh: August 1994
Director: Stéphane Braunschweig
Designer: Giorgio Barberia and Stéphane
Braunschweig
Music: Gaultiero Dazzi
French translation: Jean-Michel Déprats
The set moved spectacularly to express Leontes'
jealousy and the wrath of Apollo.

ATTRIBUTED PLAYS

Edward III: The Savoy London: 16 October
1994
A rehearsed reading by leading RSC actors
including Owen Teale and Daniel Massey
Director: Loveday Ingram
Presented with *Shakespeare in Love*, scenes from
the plays, songs and sonnets.

MISCELLANEOUS

Shakespeare's Apprentice, by Andy Rashleigh
The Unicorn Theatre, London: February 1994

The King's Player, by Trevor Gare: May 1994–
A one-man touring show, based on the experience of an actor at Elsinore in Elizabethan
times.

The Shakespeare Revue, devised by Christopher
Luscombe and Malcolm McKee, and played by
a small group of RSC actors: Everybody's
Shakespeare Festival, the Barbican Theatre,
London: November 1994.

THE YEAR'S CONTRIBUTIONS TO SHAKESPEARE STUDIES

1. CRITICAL STUDIES *reviewed by* DAVID LINDLEY

GENERAL

'The study of literature has clearly changed profoundly in many ways during the last twenty years or so, and all of us have perforce participated in these changes with varying degrees of delight, resistance, confusion, excitement and so on.' Edward Pechter's summary is undeniably accurate, and over the last five years it has often been convenient to use the varying responses to this changing landscape as a means of structuring the first section of this annual survey. But in this, my final year, there seems to have come something of a change of temper. In place of often acrimonious confrontation there seems to be more interest in modes of accommodation between different critical perspectives. Edward Pechter's book, *What Was Shakespeare?*, is, indeed, founded upon an attempt not to reconcile conflicting positions, but to accept the fact of disagreement as necessary, inevitable and irresolvable, and to characterize it as something to live with and through. In a series of rewritings of already published essays he gives his grounds, often wittily, for a belief that 'the fundamental conflicts within Shakespeare criticism cannot be resolved'. But his response is neither despair, nor an embattled espousal of one or other critical position, but a Rorty-inspired pragmatism, so that the answer to the question 'What is to be done?' turns out to be 'business as usual'. We will, in Pechter's view, continue to debate, and yet to recognize the provisionality of all critical positions, without thereby forfeiting strength of purpose. For some, despite its clear-headed and wittily expressed demonstration of the limitations of the more authoritarian brands of historicism, Pechter's book will seem like a cop-out; others will see its preoccupation with the debate between historicism(s) and 'traditional' criticism as missing out rather too much of the current critical firmament (there's little on feminism, and even less on psychoanalytic criticism, for example). But whatever one's response to its argument, the book is a significant symptomatic statement at a time when battle-fatigue seems to be setting in.

Three books, in very different ways, negotiate with historicist modes of thinking. The opening chapter of Katherine Eisaman Maus's *Inwardness and the Theatre in the English Renaissance*, with wide-ranging reference to philosophical, historical and, especially, religious writing of the period, elegantly and effectively challenges and qualifies the potent assaults on notions of 'subjectivity' by cultural materialists and new historicists, in particular their insistence that the self is constructed relationally and publicly rather than deriving from some essential inner self. In the chapters which follow she focuses on particular areas where the relationship between the public and the private, the knowable external and unknowable inner is especially significant. The machiavel is discussed with particular reference to *Richard III*; Marlowe is the dramatist upon whom the problematic nature of the establishing of heresy in religious controversy is shown to press;

Bibliographical details of works reviewed are listed alphabetically by author at the end of each review article.

281

Othello manifests the uncertainties in legal processes and indeterminacy in the interpretation of evidence. In the longest and most powerful chapter of the book Jonson and Shakespeare are set side by side in their interrogation of sexuality. *Volpone*, *Epicoene* and *Measure for Measure* are considered in the light of the procedures of the ecclesiastical court, where the attempt to make private sexual conduct public generates two problems. 'The first dilemma, with which Jonson is deeply concerned, involves the epistemological puzzles in ascertaining physical facts to which no disinterested party can possibly be a witness. The other problem – Shakespeare's main concern in *Measure for Measure* – is that the material terms in which the ecclesiastical courts construe sexuality may be entirely inadequate to an accurate understanding and evaluation of erotic desires and behaviors.' This contrast is developed persuasively and forcefully. In all this is a book very well worth reading for its balanced and carefully nuanced negotiation with texts and theories.

Strange Attractors, sadly Harriett Hawkins's last book, does not so much challenge as circumvent historicizing approaches. Paradoxically she uses up-to-date scientific chaos theory to find a way of reinstating and legitimating some much older approaches to literary texts. She sees the accounts of the dynamics of 'deterministic chaos', which insist 'that randomness, irregularity, unpredictability [are] not just occasional', but are 'the context, the medium we inhabit in everyday life' as enabling the liberation of 'some formidable literary dinosaurs from their designated pens in criticism's methodologically ordered Jurassic Parks'. Hawkins celebrates the resistance to linear narratives that chaos theory enables as she charts her way through the canonical literary texts and popular modern fictions and films alike with characteristic verve, rescuing and revising, for example, Coleridge's view of Shakespeare's 'organic' forms on the way. I especially enjoyed the section on *The Tempest* and its subsequent metamorphoses, described here as 'fractal forgeries', since 'the dynamics operative in the artistic tradition itself could, in the case of wildly different adaptations and interpretation of complex non-linear works, be seen as cognate to the iterations, recursions, self-similarities, symmetries and asymmetries operative in the non-linear systems of nature'. It's a hugely enjoyable book to read.

But the most powerful of these three books is Robert N. Watson's *The Rest is Silence*. His argument that 'the fear of death as annihilation produced a crisis in Renaissance culture' depends upon an approach informed by psychoanalysis which 'presumes a substantial continuity in human sensibilities over nearly four centuries' and itself constitutes a challenge to characteristic historicist positions, but it is conjoined with a firmly historically founded questioning of the widely circulated argument that denies the possibility of meaningful Renaissance atheism. In his introduction he cogently demonstrates the inadequacy of this last proposition, and asserts the value of seeing much Early Modern discourse on death, including Christian consolation, as 'an elaborate cultural construction designed to block our view of nothingness'. Believing that annihilation was not only a thinkable but a frighteningly persuasive presence in Early Modern England, he suggests that: 'in the absence of a salvational theology, there are two usual ways of participating in the ancient human quest for immortality. One is to die for the ancestor's cause ... the other way is to renew the ancestor's likeness through procreation.' The first possibility is explored in *The Spanish Tragedy* and *Hamlet*, the second in *Measure for Measure* and *Macbeth*. In all these plays, he contends, consolatory strategies are relentlessly questioned, and he concludes that: 'Shakespeare evidently recognized that these secular solutions would not bear the new load.' The analyses of the plays are rich and powerful, especially perhaps that of *Measure for Measure*, which generates 'a tragic and parodic attack on our fundamental hopes for individual survival'. The latter part of the book, offering extended analyses of Donne and Herbert, is, if anything, even more persuasive and valuable – and, appealingly, the process of this analysis seems itself to generate a modification of the underlying perspective. At the book's opening Watson's purpose is relentlessly demystifying, and his ethical thrust arises from 'the suspicion that … the knots of repression are still being tied, in order to sustain and conceal the conspiracy of faith', whereas by the time we reach a final 'Retraction' he records a sense that 'the denial of death may be a narrative necessarily imposed on the unmanageably infinite concept of personal annihilation'. It seems, then, that – both for writer and reader this book does more than offer a fixed hypothesis – there is, instead, a vital sense of exploration and discovery. This is a powerful, humane and important book.

At first sight, Ned Lukacher's *Daemonic Figures: Shakespeare and the Question of Conscience* might seem to be setting out on a quest analogous, or complementary to, Watson's. It is, he tells us, 'an attempt to tell two closely linked stories: the first concerns Shakespeare's place in the history of conscience; the second focuses specifically on Shakespeare's relation to, and his effect on, the interpretations of conscience by Heidegger and Freud'. After that, however, things become considerably less clear. A hundred pages trace the history of conscience from Plato to Heidegger; when Shakespeare finally appears, his texts (principally *Merchant*, *Hamlet* and *Macbeth*) are read from what seems to me a bewildering mixture of perspectives in which some rather reach-me down history and speculative biography are uneasily combined with Freudian psychology, Heideggerian mystification, and deconstructive teasing. I simply do not believe that Shakespeare's name is 'strewn like an acrostic' through the lines: 'and with a hideous cra*sh* / T*ake*s prisoner Py*rr*hus' *ear*'. (The cue for three pages of word-spinning.) Nor am I persuaded that the '*cl*' sound in Macbeth is: 'neither a word nor a concept but rather the *différantial* band between them and from which they both arise, the residue of a

primordial temporality'. It is no doubt my regrettable lack of familiarity with the philosophical work and languages that Lukacher deploys, and my lack of sympathy for the wilder shores of deconstruction that in part make me find this book so baffling.

It would, of course, be wrong to suggest that cultural materialism (or new historicism) have had their day. Peter J. Smith's *Social Shakespeare* begins by advertising itself as a further contribution to the process begun by *Political Shakespeare*, though he aims at 'a distinct refocusing of political criticism upon the Shakespearian text as realized in production'. Unlike the earlier book, this is the work of one writer – though it scarcely aims at the cumulative building up of a single case. Instead we get rather disconnected chapters of varying force and subtlety – the best, perhaps, on *Merchant of Venice* and *Jew of Malta*, the anti-Semitism they embody and the problems they pose in the modern theatre. Though written with some energy, a good deal of the book goes over pretty familiar ground, espousing the multiplicity of the Shakespearian text, bashing away at 'traditional critics', complaining at the heterosexist capture of the Bard, and so on. There are a number of questionable, and sometimes mutually contradictory assertions – it seems odd, for example, that he should speak of Lady Macbeth as the 'one notable exception' to the rule that 'women in Shakespeare's plays are linguistically and politically impotent' in the chapter that precedes his discussion of *Antony and Cleopatra*. His essay on this play is founded on consideration of the nature of 'sexual geography' in the Renaissance. The representation of the female body as territory to be conquered is, of course, 'demeaning' – and this rather tired assertion is not strengthened by some careless reading of the poems he cites. More seriously, perhaps, his claim that water is the male element, and earth the female is wildly oversimplified. But perhaps what irritates most about the book is the contradiction between its claims for the plural possibility of the Shakespearian text on the one hand, and its censorious dismissal of productions that refuse to politicize on the other.

The strongest essay in *Weyward Sisters: Shakespeare and Feminist Politics* is by Dympna Callaghan, and is also avowedly Marxist in its approach, demonstrating the ways in which *Romeo and Juliet* manifests its implication in social transformation at a time when feudalism gave way to absolutism and capitalism, and the ideology of love and the family was refashioned in response. In the course of the essay she argues with those historians who have attacked Stone's thesis about the transformation of attitudes to love and marriage in the period, asserting that 'essentialist social historians' miss the point that 'historical materialism is not about amassing historical detail; it is about history as structured material conflict'. I'm old historicist enough to find this a dangerous proposition – but the essay is useful particularly in highlighting the role of the Prince in his arrogation to himself of the power of the fathers, and more generally in suggesting ways in which the play participates in 'the project of the marriage treatises'. The other two essays are less successful, both operating from a version of the familiar pedagogic request to 'imagine you are the first murderer/second servant/lady-in-waiting and tell the story from your point of view'. Jyotsna Singh offers readings of both parts of *Henry IV*, *Measure for Measure* and *Othello* from the prostitute's angle, suggesting that this reveals 'a complex relation between the economic practice of prostitution and masculine fear of male sexuality'. In the long opening section she is, however, continually compelled to acknowledge that there is very little evidence of the prostitutes' point of view in the documentary record. In an altogether more ludic piece Lorraine Helms examines ways in which a feminist player might negotiate with and contest the 'women's parts' the plays offer, and, taking her cue from Eagleton's (in)famous assertion that 'positive value in *Macbeth* lies with the witches', imagines a performance/rewriting of the play performed by a female troupe, The Weyward Sisters.

The strategies adopted by Singh and Helms in this book are akin to those which Martha Tuck Rozett recounts and celebrates in *Talking Back to Shakespeare*. She begins from an account of her pedagogic practice, detailing the ways in which she encourages her students to interrogate Shakespeare's texts through journals and rewritings which explicitly foreground their own personal and cultural positions. This leads to a series of chapters which describe a wide variety of transformations of Shakespearian texts in adaptations and rewritings which more or less explicitly evade, challenge or subvert the authority of the Bard. It's a gentle book, clearly the work of a committed teacher, and makes some persuasive connections between student criticism and other rewritings of the plays. Its guiding assumptions about the need for teachers to meet the students on their own ground are reflected also in the 1995 issue of *Shakespeare Quarterly* devoted to pedagogy. The editor comments that 'this teaching issue is less theoretical than the 1990 one, and the philosophical unruliness of that earlier issue has been replaced by a focus on specific techniques' – perhaps bearing out the sense of a changing critical world I noted at the beginning of this review. The collection deals with the problems of negotiating the increasing unfamiliarity of many students with some of the most basic information and reading habits necessary to approach the plays (Martha Rozett); maintains a desire to enable students to work from where they are rather than imposing an authoritarian view from the lecture podium (especially pointed in Michael Yogev's account of teaching Shakespeare in Israel), and discusses the need to embrace film and video as teaching material (the subject of essays by Michael J. Collins and Stephen M. Buhler). One of the strongest essays in the volume, by Milla C. Riggio, tackles the question of the importance of history and recognition of historical distance, focusing on questions of deviance and cultural identity through an account of teaching *Othello*. These essays record teaching strategies developed throughout a course. *Teaching with Shakespeare*, edited by Bruce McIver and Ruth Stevenson, arises from a series of one-off lectures with follow-up workshops given by distinguished scholars at Union College (though Patricia Parker's witty exploration of wordplay in *Merry Wives* and subsequent account of a discussion of Pyramus and Thisbe was 'prepared for this volume' since the actual event was published elsewhere). The lectures themselves have much value in setting out basic critical issues for a student audience – particularly R. A. Foakes's clear and lucid account of the current state of critical controversy and Annabel Patterson's summary of the ways in which *Henry V* has been accommodated to different political purposes. The reports of workshops (presumably edited and tidied up though they are) sometimes serve to indicate how far the ambitions of the teacher are curtailed in the practice of the classroom – avowedly so in the case of Annabel Patterson who chose not to reproduce the workshop because she felt it did not go well enough (a twinge of sympathy here!). Perhaps the pairing that works most triumphantly well is Helen Vendler's lecture on reading the *Sonnets*, and her teasing out of the implications of Sonnet 129 with her class. Annabel Patterson's 'Palinode', an overview of the collection as a whole, raises a series of important and pertinent questions, as she reviews the gains and losses that 'the fresh air that came rushing into the field of literary studies' with the explosion of theory has brought. I share her sense that issue-driven criticism risks blotting out both the skills of close reading and the possibility of inclusive response to the richness of text, but am also struck by the ways in which, taking all these three books together, there is a danger that, driven by the indifference of students and the need to accommodate their perspectives on the one side, and the fashionable tendency to privilege indeterminacy and contestatory reading on the other, we run the risk of failing to communicate the sense of dispassionate scholarly and intellectual effort necessary to validate the study

of literature at University level as a challenging and rigorous discipline. These three studies are important in raising questions that ought to be central to our experience as both scholars and teachers, questions that acquire an obvious urgency in an exchange between Alan Brimer and Martin Orkin in the journal *Shakespeare in Southern Africa* (1993), with the former defending the history of Shakespeare criticism in the country, suggesting that it was not as inert and complicit as the latter claims it to have been.

The afterlife of Shakespearian texts, central to Rozett's book, is the subject of two chapters of Peter Conrad's *To be Continued: Four Stories and their Survival*. In the first he looks at musical representations, chiefly of *Romeo and Juliet*, and in a wonderfully agile essay considers Bellini, Berlioz, Gounod, Prokofiev and Bernstein, amongst others. He persuasively argues that 'because the characters of Shakespeare's play are devotees of language, they resist the mollifications of music ... [the play] must be romanticized against his will', and charts the successive, differently motivated transformations that composers have effected. Paradoxically, of course, his own enterprise is to turn music back into words – a job he essays with wit, dexterity and aphoristic sleight of hand. If the Conradian style seems rather more irritating and the argument less focused in the second essay, treating of *Lear*'s migration outside Britain, to Balzac's France, Turgenev's Russia and Kurosawa's Japan amongst many others, it may be my own regrettable lack of familiarity with a number of the texts he discusses which is to blame. Julian Rushton's study of Berlioz's *Roméo et Juliette*, though primarily devoted to musical analysis, offers some useful supplementation and historical particularity to Conrad's treatment of the work, especially in directing attention to the way in which the composer was influenced by Garrick's and Kemble's adaptations of Shakespeare's text.

Rawdon Wilson's *Shakespearean Narrative* isn't quite what one assumes it is going to be from the title. For he is explicitly not interested in the plays in the theatre, and the term 'narrative' is used to describe the moments in the plays when different characters 'halt the action ... and start telling stories'. These inset stories are compared to the narrative poems, and considered in the light of narrative theory, with chapters on 'Conventions', 'Voice', 'World', 'Character' and 'Boundaries'.

In producing this annual survey a reviewer has to attempt to be open to a variety of approaches and perspectives. Occasionally, however, one encounters a book where one feels simply incompetent to arrive at any sort of informed verdict. This is the case with Dirk Delabastita's *There's a Double Tongue*. It is a contribution to translation theory, focused on and through the particular problems of representing wordplay in translation. Lengthy opening chapters set up theoretical approaches to translation and to puns, and are followed by a more detailed investigation of translations of *Hamlet* in several languages. The exhaustive taxonomy of problems and possible responses to them runs to over 300 pages, with a further 150 pages of examples of puns and ambiguities in *Hamlet* and its translations. Translation studies is a growing area – and this seems to be a major contribution to the field.

HISTORIES

Not directly on Shakespeare, though a very important book for students of the history plays, is Annabel Patterson's study of Holinshed. She attempts to rescue the historical compilation (considering both the 1577 and 1587 versions) from the twin attacks commonly visited upon it – that it is on the one hand an indiscriminate heaping up of materials, on the other simply an instrument of the Tudor myth – as well as from the oft-repeated notion that it is a text only rendered significant by the fact that Shakespeare used it. Her careful readings develop characteristic concerns. She claims that the compilers cultivated a deliberate, dispassionate objectivity

before the competing accounts they synthesized, and that though they were writing for a middle-class audience, they showed considerable sympathy for the dispossessed poor, and for women. Though her revisionist account will, no doubt, be open to challenge, the perspective she offers on the nature of Shakespeare's most important historical source must in future be taken into account by any student of the plays. Indeed the questions she raises, about the constructedness of the chronicle history, its ambivalent points of view, and its preoccupation with issues of legitimacy and authority, run through many of the articles I have encountered this year.

What kind of historical narrative *Richard II* offers is considered by Paul Budra, who suggests that when Richard asks to 'tell sad stories of the death of kings', 'he is moving towards a construction of an historical self around a popular vision of the form of history' – the *de casibus* tragedy. Budra usefully, I think, questions the historical sophistication of Shakespeare's audience and suggests therefore the importance of popular forms of historical narrative, such as ballads, or *Mirror for Magistrates*, in providing the shapes by which history could be recognized. More contentiously, and in complete contrast, John Halverson considers that the label of 'tragedy' given to the play in the quartos has misled readers over the centuries. In his view Richard himself cannot be regarded as a tragic figure, and, instead, the 'real, radical power of the drama lies primarily in its comic, absurdist perspective, which pervades, sometimes subtly, sometimes egregiously, the whole fabric of the play'. It all depends on how one responds to Richard's rhetorical energy.

The remaining essays all attempt to contextualize the plays they consider. In *Tudor Political Culture*, edited by Dale Hoak, Peter C. Herman advances the thesis that '*Henry V* reflects the widespread distrust of authority in the 1590s', basing it partly on the treatment of the common soldiers, partly on the belief that the play invites an ironic distancing from the rhetoric of the Chorus. There is little that is new or compelling in the evidence offered to support this by now rather familiar reading of the play. A rather more complex effort is made by Charles Whitney to situate *1 Henry IV*, 4.2 in the political climate of 1596–7. He suggests that Falstaff's leading of a ragged army into battle, seen through a Bakhtinian lens, contains savagely festive elements that generate the possibility of its being read by different sectors of the audience in different, even contradictory ways. In the course of his essay Whitney mentions the fact that the Martin Marprelate tracts 'are carnivalesque disputations'. For Kristen Poole, in what to me is the most suggestive of these essays, the connection between the dramatic representation of Falstaff and the anarchic satire of the tracts is central. She argues that: 'if Oldcastle was widely identified as an early puritan, and stage puritans were widely expected to be comically grotesque figures, then the depiction of Oldcastle as the grotesque Falstaff was not only natural but even expected'. She recognizes that her view 'may at first seem counterintuitive', but builds her argument that Falstaff can be both satirist and satirized through comparison with the Marprelate tracts and the official reaction to them, concluding that the plays in which he appears re-enact 'issues of discursive and political control presented by the Marprelate controversy'. It's a persuasive argument. Ellen C. Caldwell's article on Jack Cade exhaustively documents the history of Cade's rebellion, then surveys the response of sixteenth-century historians (whom she views in a very similar way to Annabel Patterson) before turning to the play which she asserts was open to a variety of responses.

TRAGEDIES

If quantity were the sole measure of the current status of plays in the critical league table, then *Hamlet* is perhaps recovering its position at its head. Of the three books on the play this year the most interesting is *New Essays on Hamlet* (the first of a promised series entitled 'The Hamlet Collection'). The essays are sectioned under headings such as 'Politics and Performance', 'Psychoanalysis and Language', 'Renaissance Feminisms' – and there is, perhaps inevitably, some pushing of familiar pieces round the board, though the general level is high. The 'selfhood' of the play's hero occupies a number of writers, and if I found Andrew Mousley's 'Hamlet and the Politics of Individualism', considering the relationship between the hero's 'antic self-irony' and 'a version of self still actively engaged with problems of agency', more persuasive than psychoanalytic perspectives offered by Joanna Byles then that probably says as much about me as them. Essays considering the historical production of readings of *Hamlet* – by Martin Wiggins on the coercive force of a character-based tradition, and by Heiner O. Zimmerman on German appropriations of *Hamlet* from the late eighteenth century to the present day – were especially enjoyable. It's a lively collection, and every reader will find something of value in it.

Two contrasting book-length studies are, I think, only for *Hamlet* enthusiasts. If one accepts that 'the deep action of Shakespearean tragedy resonates with the great themes of psychoanalytic science', then John Russell's study of *Hamlet* will no doubt have its interest. Using the theories of Margaret Mahler and Heinz Kohut to revise the classic Freudian formulation, he argues that Hamlet's delay is caused by bad parenting, in that Gertrude and King Hamlet, because of their own narcissistic agendas, have failed to permit their son's proper development and escape from paternal omnipotence. Robert E. Wood's study examines the theatrical dimension of the play, including its use of space and time, soliloquy, and generic frameworks of expectation brought to it by the audience. More suggestive to me is Jonathan Baldo's essay on the play, which opens up an interesting perspective not only on this text, but on others. Arguing that the figure of synecdoche was both central to the political culture of the period, and fundamental to the processes of theatrical characterization, he sees Shakespeare's later tragedies, and pre-eminently *Hamlet*, as betokening 'a falling confidence in the various kinds of social, psychological, and aesthetic forms of integration promised by synecdoche'.

Historicism of an older sort is represented by Garry Wills's book on *Macbeth*. In a series of short and breezily written chapters he sketches potential relationships between the Gunpowder Plot, the Jesuits, witchcraft, equivocation and the play, using the similarities between *Macbeth* and other plays produced in response to the events of 1605 to suggest that at this particular historical juncture such a collocation had an especial force. One can accede to a good deal of this, without feeling that Wills has quite sorted out what he is doing with it. It is not just that he skims swiftly over the problematic textual status of the Hecate scenes, which are significant to his argument that Macbeth himself becomes 'one of the great male witches of drama', or that he becomes sidetracked into rather unpersuasive textual detail in the reading of Macbeth's soliloquies. For in his reading of the ways in which the Gunpowder Plot might interact with the play he seems to me to adopt a rather straightforward line, accepting the government propaganda at face value, and assuming that *Macbeth* simply replicates its purposes. Especially if one were to accede to Gary Taylor's proposition that Shakespeare was himself a Catholic (advanced in his contrasting of Shakespeare and Middleton as oppositional figures), but even if one simply brought a little new historicist scepticism to the conjuncture, then things might seem rather more complex.

No such complaint could be levelled at Terence Hawkes's brief and punchy study of *King Lear*. Its second chapter is devoted to an explication of the critical processes of Cultural Materialism and New Historicism, the final chapter to a restatement of his oft-repeated formula that the play (and its author) exist only in the meanings that we mean by them. In between these (perhaps predictable) gestures are telling readings of the play's dealings with

reason and madness, mapped on to questions of gender; of the plight of the 'masterless man', translated into larger questions of employment and unemployment in a changing social and economic fabric; and of language and its limitations. The polemic critical purpose of the book gives it an edge, and it will certainly be attractive to the students for whom the series is intended. It is, however, a pity that, in a familiar move, the openness to multiple appropriation which is an avowed tenet of Hawkes's critical position does not extend to so-called traditional or humanist readings, disqualified by their presumed ahistoricism (and notably underrepresented in the bibliography).

A significant moment in the history of this survey is signalled by mention of Ben R. Schneider's essay in the first issue of a new electronic journal, *Early Modern Literary Studies*. It's a pity that the rather loosely structured essay setting *King Lear* in the context of Stoic attitudes to death is rather overtaken by Robert Watson's book. But it undoubtedly seems that electronic publication will very swiftly take an important place in the work of my successors in compiling this review. It can only be a guess, but I would anticipate that this essay has probably been read by more individuals than most of the other publications mentioned in this survey.

As the proliferation of criticism continues (whether electronic or printed), so perhaps there is more and more need for books which, like Virginia Mason Vaughan's study of *Othello*, acknowledge that 'most of the contexts provided are already familiar to Shakespearean scholars' yet act usefully 'to bring a broad range of texts together in an intertextual framework'. The first part of the book sets the play in four of its contemporary contexts – of 'global discourse', 'military discourse', 'racial discourse' and 'marital discourse'. Each of these chapters elegantly synthesizes a good deal of information, and enables the student to see the multiple possibilities the play holds. The second, and much longer part of the book considers successive stagings of the play, from the Restoration to Robeson as well as two films (Welles and Nunn) to chart the different ways in which those issues have been perceived and represented. If no very surprising conclusions are reached, all students and scholars will find this book enormously useful.

They will find Hugh Grady's essay a much more difficult text. 'Iago's discourse', he suggests, 'acts out a logic that presciently recapitulates that dialectic of enlightenment defined in the twentieth century by Horkheimer and Adorno as well as key components of the disciplinary society described by Foucault'. Iago exhibits in this argument the 'dangerous mentality of instrumental reason', a 'desacralizing' force, which 'is instrumental to no final end than instrumentality itself'. It's a politicized and theorized version of Coleridge's 'motiveless malignity', and for those willing to struggle through its linguistic thickets has much to offer. A straightforward consideration by Rochelle Smith of Desdemona's singing of 'The Willow Song' as 'the fullest expression of her chaste and mature sexuality' usefully sets it in an account of women's singing in drama. She claims that it marks a significant watershed in being the first song by a virtuous woman rather than a courtesan.

Three very different essays on *Julius Caesar* exhibit some of the best and worst of critical practices. Barbara L. Parker attempts to persuade us that the subtext of *Julius Caesar* is constructed by the association of maleness, sexuality and religion in the figure of the Roman church as the whore of Babylon. The argument is founded upon relentless pursuit of double entendre at the verbal level, which culminates in the suggestion that the scene of Caesar's funeral is 'the play's sexual climax ... The action subtextually replicates all the stages of the sex act, from arousal to coitus to orgasm'. I find this risibly unpersuasive. Barbara J. Bono sets out on a very ambitious project in little scope. Her argument that this play 'exorcises as stage tragedy contemporary fears about the transition of power that Elizabeth's death would bring,

and prophetically argues the need for a not-necessarily benevolent Jacobean imperial authority' is interesting, and persuasively presented. But the essay's opening claim that it will move between two kinds of critical activity, 'a retrospective criticism seeking to recover cultural ideals and a prospective criticism open to the forces of history' is not, I think, fulfilled – indeed its theoretical anxiety is actually an unnecessary burden. The most successful of these essays for me is Cynthia Marshall's exploration of the 'necessity of seeing dramatic character as an unstable mixture of actorly body and textual meaning'. She examines the ways in which the theatrical spectacle of Portia's wound and the accuracy of Calphurnia's dream of Caesar's fate raise a series of questions about the stable significance afforded to character as political symbol both within the play and by subsequent readers of it.

Again I note three essays on *Antony and Cleopatra*, each pursuing a different agenda. The tamest is Christopher Wortham's rehearsal of some fairly familiar material about *Antony and Cleopatra* and the emblems of Mars/Venus and Hercules, arguing that the play's preoccupation with temperance made it particularly suitable to the ideology of the court. The most tendentious is Maurice Hunt's proposition that 'The concepts and terminology of modernism and postmodernism form metaphors especially effective for grasping Elizabethan and Jacobean writers' struggle to arrest and contain flux in paradigms true to shifting perceptions of the world', a proposition he supports through a consideration of the play's lack of geographical fixity, and its preoccupation with images of dissolution and transformation which are then accommodated to postmodern perceptions of the collapse of all dichotomies. Much the most substantial is Jonathan Gil Harris's essay – which like Wortham's examines the importance of a classical subtext – but here the tale of Narcissus – and like Hunt's wishes to dissolve the familiar, stable dichotomy of Egypt and Rome. In a complex but stimulating argument he begins with an unusual version of the Narcissus myth in a 1595 poem by Thomas Edwards, where Narcissus perceives his own reflection as female, then builds up a persuasive picture of the Roman construction of desire as fixed upon 'a reflection, or projection of itself', in order to suggest that Cleopatra is very much constructed by and through this Roman perspective. In the process he has interesting things to say about the homo-erotic elements in the play. It's a valuable piece.

As I remarked last year, *Coriolanus* seems to be becoming ever more significant in the critical world. It is, then, perhaps a timely gesture which sees the *Garland Critical Essays* series reach *Coriolanus* in a volume edited by David Wheeler. Material is included from the seventeenth century to the present, reflecting the interest in the play both as political drama and as psycho-sexual exploration, together with a substantial number of theatre reviews. The collection ends with three new essays. The first, by the editor, explores the treatment of the play in the Restoration and the eighteenth century, looking at four adaptations/versions of the play (Tate, Dennis, James Thomson and Thomas Sheridan). He argues that they chart a movement from political preoccupation towards an emphasis upon the brilliant performer. The second, a rather lumpenly written piece by Karen Aubrey, contends that attention to the play as satire rather than (or as well as) tragedy gets round the difficulties many critics have historically had with it; the third is a detailed consideration of Peter Hall's 1984 production by S. K. Bedford. As a whole it is a serviceable collection – though I do not think the new essays quite earn their place over others that might have been included.

COMEDIES

The influence of the New Comedy of Plautus and Terence, staples of the grammar-school curriculum, on Shakespeare has often been discussed, but never with the comprehensive thoroughness that Robert S. Miola brings to the task in his *Shakespeare and Classical Comedy*. For he is interested not only in the direct recollection of the classical originals, but with their mediation through Italian writers, and with the ways in which they are brought to productive play with other comic, romance and moral traditions. In each chapter Miola highlights one particular aspect of classical comedy, and explores its use in two Shakespearian texts. In the process he shows the playwright engaging in 'a sophisticated critical response to New Comedy' – and in the final chapter looks at the way ingredients from the classical stock are redeployed in *Hamlet* and *Lear*. At times the sheer weight of Miola's learning, the collection of parallel and analogue, threatens to bury the reader under detail, and sometimes he is perhaps inclined to suggest too easily that attention to the traditions will 'correct' modern misreadings (as in the sympathetic response to Malvolio, for example) but throughout he has many positive insights to offer into the creativity of Shakespeare's imitative processes. It will be an important reference point for all students of the comedies.

Comic metamorphosis is the subject of two strong, but interestingly contrasting books. Michael Shapiro's *Gender in Play* begins: 'Because of our own fascination with sexual identity and gender roles, contemporary scholarship has devoted considerable attention to various forms of cross-dressing in other historical periods.' His scholarly and comprehensive study places the five Shakespearian texts in which a female character masquerades as a man in the context both of contemporary attitudes to cross-dressing and of dramatic tradition, and adds useful appendices of cognate plays, sources and analogues, and transcriptions of court records of prosecutions of cross-dressed women. His basic argument is that the 'layering of gender identities, when cross-gender disguise was superimposed on cross-gender casting' produced a 'theatrical vibrancy' which, amongst other things, 'underscored the actor's presence' thereby involving the audience 'more deeply in playful complicity in games of illusion-making'. After fairly brief consideration of the social realities of cross-dressing in the period, Shapiro turns to each of the plays in sequence, framing each discussion with consideration of dramatic precedents and successors. His concentration is on the ways in which the plays function in the theatre; and in contradistinction to most of the existing work on this topic he eschews any attempt to ask 'what the various theatrical treatments of gender reveal about the larger culture because I think these theatrical treatments need more detailed study as works of theatrical art before they can be made to yield insights into attitudes toward sexuality and gender in early modern England'. As individual readings of the plays, categorizing and tracing the evolution of Shakespeare's use of a dramatic motif, from the 'cheeky page' of *Two Gentlemen of Verona* through the 'anxieties of intimacy' occasioned by Viola's duet scenes with Orsino and Olivia to the marginalization of the cross-dressed Imogen in the romance mode of *Cymbeline*, each of the chapters has insightful comment to make. But the deliberate self-containment of the project inside the walls of the theatre, whilst a useful and timely caution against too ready a translation of the theatrical into the larger cultural world, does perhaps curtail the ambition of the book, and limit its intervention in the critical debate which is succinctly outlined in the opening chapters.

For Shapiro the invocation of ideas and ideals of androgyny is mistaken, and strikes him as 'an anachronistic reading of the play-boy/female page'. Grace Tiffany takes exactly the opposite view. Her *Erotic Beasts and Social Monsters* argues that Shakespeare's comic world celebrates precisely the mythic, transformative ideal of androgyny, and sets his vision against the satiric condemnation offered by Ben Jonson. After an introduction setting out the history of the androgyne figure in the classical world, she devotes a chapter to Shakespeare, traversing virtually all his Elizabethan comic output, to suggest multiple ways in which 'the androgy-nous beast ... figured and supported by an animal imagery as well as transvestite stage incarnations, operates to connect isolated selves, bridging their separated worlds'. This is contrasted with Jonson's negative vision, where feminized males and masculine women are threats to stability and defined identity. She then suggests that Shakespeare in *The Merry Wives* and Jonson in *Bartholomew Fair* and *The New Inn* each 'tried out' the other's position, and concludes with an interesting reading of *As You Like It* as a play involved in the 'war of the theatres', explicitly as an answer to *Every Man Out of His Humour*. In attempting to set up the 'mythic' and 'satiric' responses to androgyny as an explanatory model Tiffany perhaps tries to tidy things up a little too cleanly – in particular, I think, she tends to underplay the sense of peril and danger in Shakespearian comedy. But it is a very suggestive study, lucidly written and with many felicitously observed details. As a coda to these two books may be noted Robert Weimann's essay, discussing the question of disguise more generally, which arrives at a conclusion not unlike Shapiro's, that 'disguise in the Elizabethan theatre constituted a highly concentrated site of heteroglossia where one type of speech or discourse was permanently in danger of being contradicted by other cultural and theatrical practices'.

Not the least of the virtues of both Shapiro's and Tiffany's books is the clarity of their argument and prose style. Jonathan Hall's *Anxious Pleasures* is heavily theorized, and frequently produces sentences like this: '*The Merchant* is an enigmatic play because, while it does represent a major historical transition from feudal usury to mercantile capitalism in terms which offer analysable gratifications to the subjects of the new polity, it also represents the discursive production of the gratifying historical narrative out of an intense dialogism which undoes the fixity of the opposing narrative agents themselves.' Throughout the book big abstractions clank. But yet within the verbiage lies an argument that is interesting, and which can at times produce readings of the plays under discussion that are both thoughtful and thought-provoking. One of the book's central propositions – that 'the subject who laughs is a subject divided against his/her own internalized ideological commitments', and therefore that laughter offers 'a moment of potentiality' – is profitably used to question the notion of clarifying closure at the end of comedy. So, for example, in his discussion of *The Taming of the Shrew* he concludes that Katherina's apparent submission at the end can be read as her acquisition of the possibility of ironic speech, which then puts in question Petruchio's control since it 'makes the nature of the surrendered self forever problematic'. A very similar conclusion is reached in Wayne Rebhorn's essay on the play. He considers Petruchio as a representative of male rhetoric, points to the links between rhetoric, power, and rape, but suggests that the play dramatizes the failure of rhetorical power in that it is not by words that Katherina is persuaded. Instead, he suggests, it is Katherina's acquisition of rhetorical arts which serve 'not as an invincible offensive weapon ensuring the male ruler's power and authority, but as a potent defensive weapon by which his female subject can resist him even in the act which makes her seem to confirm his triumph'.

It is *The Merchant of Venice* which figures most prominently in discussion of the middle comedies this year, and the problem of Shylock to which most attention is given. Avraham Oz's book concludes with an epilogue in which he discusses performances of the play in Israel since 1936 and the various responses to them as a case-study to illustrate 'the unbridgeable gap between alleged intention and subjective interpretation'. It is a fascinating conclusion to a difficult and elusive study, which asserts early on that 'Shakespeare's plain anti-Semitism is ... basically redundant.' For Oz the play may be read 'as a continuous process whereby the characters are attempting to transform their political experience, in the broad sense of the term, into what seems to be, from the stance of

official ideology, creative spiritual unions; and this transformation is done by propounding, and responding to, prophetic riddles whereby the signifiers attached to given dramatic subjects are creatively transgressed and dislocated'. The two long chapters which discuss 'modes of riddle and prophecy' and 'riddles of identity' draw on a wide range of Shakespearian and other texts, as well as upon contemporary theorists and psychoanalysts. They are not an easy read, and their overall drift is not easily summarized. The most immediately striking idea in the book is that of Shylock as 'terrorist' in that he 'subverts the soul of Venetian order, namely, its book of laws, and turns it upon itself'. But there is much else – including for example his sympathetic account of Bassanio's solving of the riddle of the caskets as manifesting an 'openness to grasp new meanings', and betokening a 'conversion from the calculating Venetian to Portia's wise lover' that readers of the play will find interesting.

A very different reading of the play is offered by Robert Zaslavsky. Noting the problems of the play, and the problems of audiences in finding a response to it, he suggests that Shakespeare might feel the desirability of an open, multicultural society, but doubt its feasibility. For him, the figure of hope in this play is Launcelot Gobbo who 'represents the possibility of peaceful coexistence between Christian and Jew'. A much more complicated reading is offered by Charles Spinosa, who seeks to read the trial scene as a dramatization of the cultural tensions embodied in the contemporary *Slade's Case* between traditional customary practice in matters of obligation (embodied in Shylock) set against newer contractualist notions (embodied in the Venetians) which are resolved by Portia's 'hyper-rational skepticism'. In the end the effort of allegoresis seems to me less than compelling. In contrast to these essays on the overall shape and tendency of the play Julie Hankey considers the Victorian treatment of Portia, on stage and (principally) in written sources in a useful study of the ways in which the character resisted easy categorization, and could therefore serve women writers especially as a figure which 'allowed them to incorporate into their picture of perfect womanhood all the qualities that orthodoxy regarded as threats'.

Brief mention may be made of a scatter of other articles on the comedies. Frederick Keifer trawls representations of the seasons in contemporary woodcuts, to come up with the suggestion that in the final dialogue song of *Love's Labour's Lost* 'Spring' should be performed by Jacquenetta, 'Winter' by Dull. Leslie S. Katz argues that *Merry Wives* puts the audience of the 'real' Garter feast in Windsor at the centre of its action, expressing through Falstaff their transgressive desires, and draws attention to various relationships between the Falstaff of this play and that of the histories. In a rather flimsy article, David Thatcher argues that the traditional reading of Vincentio's explanation to Friar Thomas of why he left Vienna as implying a deliberate 'testing' of Angelo is mistaken. One might agree with the argument – but wonder where it leads. Claudio in *Much Ado* and Bertram in *All's Well* are both problematic figures. Noting that 'at the end of both plays, the dialogue allots more discursive space to the reconciliation between the hero and his male associates than to the reunion of the count and his wife' Michael D. Freidman argues that the sense of comic closure 'derives from the hero's return to the male social order, which occurs when he ultimately accepts marriage to the proper woman'. In this interesting essay, Freidman teases out the implications of the problem for performance of both plays, remarking how frequently modern performances supply business of different kinds to persuade audiences that in fact the romantic attachment is what really matters, underplaying in the process 'the preservation of male bonds as a motive for the characters' actions'. Rather different is David McCandless's view of *All's Well* (drawing on folk-tale and psychoanalytic feminist theory) as one which destabilizes gender, and his suggestion that actually staging the bed-trick 'by fetishizing the male body and empowering a

female gaze, could underline the instability of the genders that Helena and Bertram seek to stabilise' might appeal to some director – though I wonder if the effect of such a strategy on the audience would be quite what McCandless hopes.

An overview of the late plays is offered by Fred Parker. He argues that a 'sense of the passage into the "madness" of romance as both desirable and dangerous' animates them all, and points in particular to the way in which fairy tale's capacity to speak of fundamental psychological states involves 'a dangerous kinship between romance and regression' and 'reflects upon an essential ambiguity of romance, which commonly enacts the journey toward maturity in a form which serves the wish-fulfillment of the child'. So, for example, Leontes's idealization of the time of childhood is a malign regression, but dangerously close to the process of healing that Paulina prescribes. Only in *The Tempest*, he points out, is the reunion between father and daughter renounced, and he suggests that this refiguring is symptomatic of a deeper renunciation of 'a magic which has been active within all four of the plays'. It is a clear and powerful piece.

That *Cymbeline* is a play engaged in important though problematic ways with the pressing question of British nationalism is by now generally accepted. Jodi Mikalachki gives an interestingly gendered account of the growth of nationalism, which she sees as predicated on the erasure of militant females like Bonduca, and symbolized in a number of plays by the masculine embrace of Roman and Briton. She suggestively accounts for the presence of the Queen's nationalist speech in the play, and offers a nuanced reading of Imogen, especially in her relationship to Lucius. One would perhaps want to ask how the Bonduca liberally praised and represented in the train of Queen Anne in Jonson's *Masque of Queens*, almost exactly contemporary with *Cymbeline*, complicates the picture – but it is a significant essay.

Mythic backgrounds for the romances are

invoked in three articles. Carmine di Biase suggests that Ovid's account of the myth of Cephalus and Procris is evoked in *Cymbeline*, and that Shakespeare also knew and used the version of the fable in Pettie's *Petite Pallace*. Sarah Annes Brown makes a not very convincing attempt to claim that the influence of Ovid on *The Tempest* extends further than the familiar adaptation of Medea's speech – exhibiting perhaps some of the dangers in too facile an adoption of a notion of intertextuality, where the less obvious a recollection is, the more valuable the critic deems it to be. More persuasively Peggy Muñoz Simonds offers a characteristically comprehensive survey of emblems of Orpheus and of music relevant to *The Tempest* in the service of a benign view of the play, which sees Prospero 'as a type of Orpheus in bringing harmony to his garden kingdom, controlling his own passions, and civilizing the wild man'.

B. J. Sokol's book-length study of *The Winter's Tale* is an important contribution, combining exposition of the iconology of Renaissance art, social history, herbal lore and modern psychoanalytic theory in a fascinating discussion. Psychoanalysis supplies the suggestion that Leontes suffers from 'couvade syndrome' – a phenomenon he demonstrates was known during the Renaissance – and argues that this accounts for his extremity of passion in the play's opening. Herbal lore complicates the message of Perdita's catalogue of flowers; detailed discussion of the old-fashionedness of painted sculpture by the time of the play's composition and consideration of what was known and thought of Romano are brought to bear upon the statue scene. In more general terms Sokol explores the play's uncertainties, demonstrating that the second half of the play – far too easily characterized as curative and idealized – is riddled with anxieties of various sorts, about sexuality, about marriage and about art itself. In his treatment Paulina and Camillo, as well as Perdita, emerge as more complex figures, and Autolycus becomes crucial to the difficult balancing act Sokol sees the play as

performing. The book is well-written, wide-ranging and consistently interesting. Also investigating Renaissance contexts, but coming up with a much odder reading of the play is Daryl W. Palmer who, starting from Hermione's invocation of her Russian parentage, explores the possible significances for the play as a whole of Elizabethan and Jacobean perceptions of Russia as a land of winter and of tyranny. Thoroughly documented though his essay is, and suggestive as are some of the parallels he draws, I do not find the argument as a whole persuasive.

Peter Holland's essay on *The Tempest* is full of insightful observations about staging, costume and props and their significance and effect. The continuing process of rewriting *The Tempest* in a postcolonial context is the subject of Thomas Cartelli's elegant essay on Michelle Cliff's *No Telephone to Heaven*. The problem he outlines is that in responding to and rewriting the play an author risks reinscribing the dominance of the 'master texts', and suggests that the effort must now be 'to work through and master the impulse to write back to the centre'. He sees Cliff's novel as at least in part achieving this purpose, especially through her reconfiguration of Miranda to produce 'a thoroughly creolized and womanized novel in which the new, New World Miranda effectively replaces both Prospero and Caliban as an agent of self-determination and cultural change'.

POEMS

The *Sonnets* have a peculiar opacity. The characteristic response to their elusiveness in recent years has been to concentrate on what they might be held to say about their poet/speaker. This is the line followed by James Dawes who concludes, after examining the poems' fixation on decay, that: 'the sequence as a whole, then, dramatizes the mind's endurance of love, its struggle over time between desire and disgust, between philosophical idealism and the dictates of the corporeal'. But two other essays attempt to reinstate questions of implied audience as significant for a reading of the *Sonnets*. Christopher Martin's long, close reading of the *Sonnets* in his *Policy in Love* sets Shakespeare beside Ovid and Petrarch. He considers their different negotiation between the lyric poet's purpose in speaking of private matters, set against the larger audience of which he is in some way conscious and concludes that 'whatever self-discovery the sonneteer manages in these poems is rooted primarily in his acute, almost obsessive sensitivity to public witness. For this speaker, all articulation of independent subjectivity itself remains subject to (that is, ironically dependent upon) communal critical approval'. The study valuably focuses attention upon the problematic relationship of the poet with 'the world' in general, and with the rival poet in particular – these poems becoming more readily integrated within the sequence as a whole from this perspective. David Schalkwyk suggests that 'in our treatment of the Sonnets we take a cue from the necessary embodiment, both in physical terms and in terms of the represented situation of political and economic relations, that is inescapable in the theater'. His comparison of the *Sonnets* to *Love's Labour's Lost* and *Twelfth Night* is suggestive in many details, though the essay, I think, loses its way rather, and struggles with the problem that no matter how one might want to reinstate the importance of the addressee to a consideration of the poems at a theoretical level, lack of material evidence (unlike the material bodies of the stage) forever curtails the enterprise.

Last year it was *Rape of Lucrece* that excited most interest; this year it is the turn of *Venus and Adonis*. A. D. Cousins elaborates on the ways in which Shakespeare's Venus embodies, but also parodically subverts a whole series of conflicting iconographical traditions. Sayre Greenfield discusses allegory and allegorical reading in both Spenser and Shakespeare's representation of the myth, suggesting that allegoresis tends to be invoked when the disrupted and/or disruptive nature of a text is felt to need explaining (away).

The essay is better on the history of readings of the poem than in anything new it offers. Pauline Kiernan in effect uses a kind of allegoresis in which Venus becomes the poet forever turning the object of her adoration into linguistic conceit, stifling even as she describes the bodily reality of Adonis. But the most interesting and persuasive essay on the poem is that by Catherine Belsey, who sees its indeterminacy about the legitimacy of love as reflecting its particular historical moment, when the replacement of ideals of celibacy with ideals of matrimony necessitated a renegotiation of concepts of love and lust and their differentiation. In this context critics' tendency to focus on Adonis's clear distinction between love and lust as a moral centre of the poem becomes a symptom of the triumph of a particular, normative view that the poem itself continuously resists.

CODA

After five years spent compiling this survey, it is tempting to proffer some magisterial statement about the current scene in Shakespeare criticism, to adjudicate on what's in and what's out at the theoretical high table. It is a temptation I shall resist, not only because it is too diverse and plural a world to be neatly summarized, but because it seems that, after a decade or more of dog-fights, critics are increasingly able without strain to draw on different critical perspectives in fruitful ways. To me, this is a positive development – to others, no doubt, a worrying abandonment of principle in pursuit of an elusive middle-ground and a sorry reflection of the realignment of the political landscape currently developing at least in Britain.

Similarly, it is tempting to repeat the complaint that there is simply too much criticism for any individual to be able to encompass. I am only too aware of books that have passed me by, and articles that I have overlooked. But if that is a problem now, the growth of electronic

DAVID LINDLEY

media and data retrieval systems (let alone the ever-increasing institutional pressure to publish in quantity and at speed) threaten only to multiply it further, so that studies will groan ever more under the freight of footnotes, and merciful forgetting will become inexcusable laziness. Undoubtedly there *are* too many books published that are a couple of rewrites short of an argument, too many journal articles that attempt to compensate for lack of substance with glossy theoretical packaging, or which tamely refigure the already well known. And it is certainly true that the horror expressed by my predecessor, R. S. White, at the barbarous tongue in which much criticism is couched is a feeling I share all the more strongly after five years of compelling myself to struggle through material that I might otherwise have abandoned. But therein, perhaps, lies the value of this experience. For the experience of such intensive reviewing is at the same time humbling and energizing, both in exposing the limitations of my own knowledge and in forcing me to confront as sympathetically as possible alien perspectives. In this respect, perhaps, my own experience enacts and confirms what, in this year's work at least, seems to me the possibility that tribal affiliation to this or that critical camp can be and is being supplanted by a more inclusive open-mindedness. There are too many enemies of literary studies gathered at the gate to waste unnecessary time on internecine squabbles.

WORKS REVIEWED

Baldo, Jonathan. 'Ophelia's Rhetoric, or Partial to Synechdoche'. *Criticism*, 37 (1995), 1–36.

Belsey, Catherine. 'Love as Trompe-l'oeil: Taxonomies of Desire in *Venus and Adonis*'. *Shakespeare Quarterly*, 46 (1995), 257–76.

Biase, Carmine di. 'Ovid, Pettie, and the Mythic Foundation of *Cymbeline*'. *Cahiers Elisabéthains*, 46 (1994), 59–67.

Bono, Barbara J. 'The Birth of Tragedy: Tragic

Action in *Julius Caesar*'. *English Literary Renaissance*, 24 (1994), 449–70.

Brown, Sarah Annes. 'Ovid, Golding and *The Tempest*'. *Translation and Literature*, 3 (1994), 3–27.

Budra, Paul. 'Writing the Tragic Self: Richard II's Sad Stories', *Renaissance and Reformation*, 18.4 (1994), 5–16.

Burnett, Mark Thornton and John Manning, eds. *New Essays on Hamlet*. New York: AMS Press, 1994.

Caldwell, Ellen C. 'Jack Cade and Shakespeare's *Henry VI, Part 2*'. *Studies in Philology*, 92 (1995), 18–79.

Callaghan, Dympna, Lorraine Helms and Jyotsna Singh. *Weyward Sisters: Shakespeare and Feminist Politics*. Oxford UK and Cambridge USA: Blackwell, 1994.

Cartelli, Thomas. 'After *The Tempest*: Shakespeare, Postcoloniality and Michelle Cliff's New, New World Miranda'. *Contemporary Literature*, 36 (1995), 82–102.

Conrad, Peter. *To be Continued: Four Stories and their Survival*. Clarendon Press, 1995.

Cousins, A. D. 'Venus Reconsidered: the Problem of Love in *Venus and Adonis*'. *Studia Neophilologica*, 66 (1994), 197–207.

Dawes, James. 'Truth and Decay in Shakespeare's *Sonnets*'. *Cahiers Elisabéthains*, 47 (1995), 43–53.

Delabastita, Dirk. *There's a Double Tongue: An Investigation into the Translation of Shakespeare's Wordplay with Special Reference to Hamlet*. Amsterdam: Rodopi, 1993.

Freidman, Michael D. 'Marriage Bonds and Marriage in *All's Well* and *Much Ado*'. *Studies in English Literature*, 35 (1995), 231–50.

Grady, Hugh. 'Iago and the Dialectic of Enlightenment: Reason, Will and Desire in *Othello*'. *Criticism*, 37 (1995), 537–58.

Greenfield, Sayre. 'Allegorical Impulses and Critical Ends: Shakespeare's and Spenser's Venus and Adonis'. *Criticism*, 36 (1994), 475–98.

Hall, Jonathan. *Anxious Pleasures: Shakespearean Comedy and the Nation-State*. Madison: Fairleigh Dickinson University Press; London: Associated University Presses, 1995.

Halverson, John. 'The Lamentable Comedy of Richard II', *English Literary Renaissance*, 24 (1994), 343–69.

Hankey, Julie. 'Victorian Portias: Shakespeare's

Borderline Heroine'. *Shakespeare Quarterly*, 45 (1994), 426–48.

Harris, Jonathan Gil, '"Narcissus in thy face"': Roman Desire and the Difference it Fakes in *Antony and Cleopatra*'. *Shakespeare Quarterly*, 45 (1994), 408–25.

Hawkes, Terence. *William Shakespeare: King Lear* (Writers and their Work). Plymouth: Northcote House, 1995.

Hawkins, Harriett. *Strange Attractors: Literature, Culture and Chaos Theory*. New York and London: Prentice Hall/Harvester Wheatsheaf, 1995.

Hoak, Dale, ed. *Tudor Political Culture*. Cambridge: Cambridge University Press, 1995.

Holland, Peter. 'The Shapeliness of *The Tempest*'. *Essays in Criticism*, 45 (1995), 208–29.

Hunt, Maurice. 'Elizabethan "Modernism", Jacobean "Postmodernism": Schematizing Stir in the Drama of Shakespeare and His Contemporaries'. *Papers on Language and Literature*, 31 (1995), 115–44.

Katz, Leslie S. 'The Merry Wives of Windsor: Sharing the Queen's Holiday'. *Representations*, 51 (Summer 1995), 77–93.

Keifer, Frederick. 'Spring and Winter in *Love's Labor's Lost*: An Iconographic Reconstruction'. *Comparative Drama*, 29 (1995), 91–107.

Kiernan, Pauline. 'Death by Rhetorical Trope: Poetry Metamorphosed in *Venus and Adonis*'. *Review of English Studies*, 46 (1995), 475–501.

Lukacher, Ned. *Daemonic Figures: Shakespeare and the Question of Conscience*. Ithaca and London: Cornell University Press, 1994.

Marshall, Cynthia. 'Portia's Wound, Calphurnia's Dream: Reading Character in *Julius Caesar*'. *English Literary Renaissance*, 24 (1994), 471–88.

Martin, Christopher. *Policy in Love: Lyric and Public in Ovid, Petrarch and Shakespeare*. Pittsburgh: Duquesne University Press, 1994.

Maus, Katharine Eisaman. *Inwardness and Theater in the English Renaissance*. Chicago and London: University of Chicago Press, 1995.

McIver, Bruce and Ruth Stevenson, eds. *Teaching with Shakespeare: Critics in the Classroom*. Newark: University of Delaware Press; London and Toronto: Associated University Presses, 1994.

Mikalachki, Jodi. 'The Masculine Romance of Roman Britain: *Cymbeline* and Early Modern English Nationalism'. *Shakespeare Quarterly*, 46 (1995), 301–21.

Miola, Robert S. *Shakespeare and Classical Comedy: The Influence of Plautus and Terence*. Oxford: Clarendon Press, 1994.

Oz, Avraham. *The Yoke of Love: Prophetic Riddles in The Merchant of Venice*. Newark: University of Delaware Press; London and Toronto: Associated University Presses, 1995.

Palmer, Daryl W. 'Jacobean Muscovites: Winter, Tyranny and Knowledge in *The Winter's Tale*'. *Shakespeare Quarterly*, 46 (1995), 323–39.

Parker, Barbara L. 'The Whore of Babylon and Shakespeare's *Julius Caesar*'. *Studies in English Literature*, 35 (1995), 251–70.

Parker, Fred. 'Regression and Romance in Shakespeare's Late Plays'. *The Cambridge Quarterly*, 24 (1995), 112–32.

Patterson, Annabel. *Reading Holinshed's Chronicles*. Chicago and London: University of Chicago Press, 1994.

Pechter, Edward. *What Was Shakespeare? Renaissance Plays and Changing Critical Practice*. Ithaca and London: Cornell University Press, 1995.

Poole, Kristen. 'Saints Alive! Falstaff, Martin Marprelate, and the Staging of Puritanism'. *Shakespeare Quarterly*, 46, 47–75.

Rebhorn, Wayne A. 'Petruchio's "Rope Tricks": *The Taming of the Shrew* and the Renaissance Discourse of Rhetoric'. *Modern Philology*, 92 (1994–5), 294–327.

Rozett, Martha Tuck. *Talking Back to Shakespeare*. Newark: University of Delaware Press; London and Toronto: Associated University Presses, 1994.

Rushton, Julian. *Berlioz: Roméo et Juliette*. Cambridge: Cambridge University Press, 1994.

Russell, John. *Hamlet and Narcissus*. Newark: University of Delaware Press; London and Toronto: Associated University Presses, 1995.

Schalkwyk, David. '"She never told her love": Embodiment, Textuality and Silence in Shakespeare's Sonnets and Plays'. *Shakespeare Quarterly*, 45 (1994), 381–407.

Schneider, Ben Ross. 'King Lear in its Own Time: The Difference that Death Makes'. *Early Modern Literary Studies*, 1.1 (1995). URL http://unixg.ubc.ca:7001/0/e-sources/emls/emlshome.html.

Shakespeare in Southern Africa, 1993.

Shapiro, Michael. *Gender in Play on the Shakespearean Stage: Boy Heroines and Female Pages*. Ann Arbor: The University of Michigan Press, 1994.

MARK THORNTON BURNETT

Simonds, Peggy Muñoz. '"Sweet Power of Music": The Political Magic of "the Miraculous Harp" in Shakespeare's *The Tempest*'. *Comparative Drama*, 29 (1995), 61–90.

Smith, Peter J. *Social Shakespeare: Aspects of Renaissance Dramaturgy and Contemporary Society*. London: Macmillan; New York: St Martin's Press, 1995.

Smith, Rochelle. 'Admirable Musicians: Women's Songs in *Othello* and *The Maid's Tragedy*'. *Comparative Drama*, 28 (1994), 311–23.

Sokol, B. J. *Art and Illusion in The Winter's Tale*. Manchester and New York: Manchester University Press, 1994.

Spinosa, Charles. 'The Transformation of Intentionality: Debt and Contract in *The Merchant of Venice*'. *English Literary Renaissance*, 24 (1994), 370–409.

Taylor, Gary. 'Forms of Opposition: Shakespeare and Middleton'. *English Literary Renaissance*, 24 (1994), 283–314.

Thatcher, David. 'Questionable Purpose in *Measure for Measure*: A Test of Seeming or a Seeming Test'. *English Literary Renaissance*, 25 (1995), 26–44.

Tiffany, Grace. *Erotic Beasts and Social Monsters: Shakespeare, Jonson, and Comic Androgyny*. Newark: University of Delaware Press; London and Toronto: Associated University Presses, 1995.

Vaughan, Virginia Mason. *Othello: A Contextual History*. Cambridge: Cambridge University Press, 1994.

Watson, Robert. N. *The Rest is Silence: Death as Annihilation in the English Renaissance*. Berkeley, Los Angeles and London: University of California Press, 1994.

Weimann, Robert. Textual Authority and Performative Agency: The Uses of Disguise in Shakespeare's Theater'. *New Literary History*, 25 (1994), 789–808.

Wheeler, David, ed. *Coriolanus: Critical Essays*. New York and London: Garland Publishing, 1995.

Whitney, Charles. 'Festivity and Topicality in the Coventry Scene of *1 Henry IV*'. *English Literary Renaissance*, 24 (1994), 410–48.

Wills, Garry. *Witches and Jesuits: Shakespeare's Macbeth*. New York and Oxford: Oxford University Press, 1995.

Wilson, Rawdon. *Shakespearean Narrative*. Newark: University of Delaware Press; London and Toronto: Associated University Presses, 1995.

Wood, Robert E. *Some Necessary Questions of the Play: A Stage-Centered Analysis of Shakespeare's Hamlet*. Lewisburg: Bucknell University Press; London and Toronto: Associated University Presses, 1994.

Wortham, Christopher. 'Temperance and the End of Time: Emblematic *Antony and Cleopatra*'. *Comparative Drama*, 29 (1995), 1–37.

Zaslavsky, Robert. '"Which is the Merchant here? and which the Jew": Keeping the Book and Keeping the Books in *The Merchant of Venice*'. *Judaism*, 44, 181–92.

2. SHAKESPEARE'S LIFE, TIMES, AND STAGE
reviewed by MARK THORNTON BURNETT

In the recent crop of Renaissance studies, Eric Sams' *The Real Shakespeare* must surely stand as one of the more contentious titles. With the recovery of the first thirty years of Shakespeare's life as his stated aim, Sams presents a quirky case, erecting a thesis about the chronology and authenticity of the dramatist's early productions on the basis of speculation and uncertain seventeenth-century biographical statement. The claim that Shakespeare came from an illiterate Catholic background, the observation that he left school to help on the family farm, the view that he was clearly named and identified in the

Parnassus plays, and the conviction that the Earl of Southampton was a powerful presence behind the 1594 novella, *Willobie his Avisa*, are among the most surprising aspects of Sams' argument. Equally problematic is the insistent conflation of biographical fact and textual detail, as revealed in the parallels drawn between imagery of blood in Shakespeare's drama and his supposed experience of the butcher's trade. For Sams, texts constitute codes to be deciphered or puzzles to be resolved through authorial identification, and to this end he asserts (unconvincingly) that *Edmund Ironside*,

298

Fair Em, *Locrine*, *The Taming of a Shrew*, the *Ur-Hamlet* and other unassigned plays are all from the pen of the dramatist. If this is not sufficient to rock most sensibilities, throughout there runs an irritated dialogue with critics, which is clearly demonstrated in the bibliography: those studies of which Sams disapproves are accompanied by an asterisk, and he even has the confidence to list his own unpublished work. Towards the end he castigates Peter Alexander for an *idée fixe* (p. 161), but the term also typifies the opinions entertained by Sams himself.

While provoking and frustrating in equal measure, Sams' book does have the merit of drawing attention to a number of key questions. What importance should be attached to plays which do not boast a canonical status? How pronounced a pressure does context exert on text? To what extent can the wisdoms of older critical traditions be incorporated or revised? Is the 'real' Shakespeare to be found in a fresh appreciation of early printed materials, or does his 'reality' inhere in later and more diffuse languages and practices? Such questions, which only arise incidentally from *The Real Shakespeare*, touch upon associated issues such as original theatrical conditions, cultural transactions, editorial conventions, and the role of contemporary theory in literary studies. The 'real' Shakespeare, it emerges, belongs less to an Elizabethan moment than to a range of peculiarly modern appropriations and performances, and it is with adaptations of his work and the political applications of the dramatist that much current criticism is occupied.

I

As several editions suggest, an endeavour to make texts from the Shakespearian period available, in ways which shed light on influences and interconnections, is still critically active. Their unique contribution is to identify a network of distinctive political orientations, and to broaden an awareness of the rivalries and patronage systems in operation among contemporary play-wrights. Tom Cain's edition of Ben Jonson's *Poetaster*, which is usually dated 1601, partly situates the play in terms of the 'War of the Theatres', unravels personal and satirical allusions, and contrasts an Augustan ideal of wise rule with the dramatist's vision of a polity dominated by malice and intrigue. The editor is to be applauded in that he is alert to changes introduced to avoid censorship, corrects folio and quarto placements of speeches, begins to shift attention away from the Poetomachia, and (confronting the mystery of 'Captain Hanham') forwards two possible candidates. It is not entirely clear why Cain has confined his collation of the 1616 folio to copies in England, and the remark that Jonson displays 'sympathy towards [the Earl of] Essex' (p. 44) might be challenged, since *Cynthia's Revels* contains contrasting critical comment. But this remains a solid, sensitive and worthwhile edition, which underscores contests between writers as well as the impact of an independent dramatic achievement.

The editorial recovery of Renaissance texts is similarly shown to advantage in the continuing publications of scholarly societies. A fine example of this work is John Pitcher's edition for the Malone Society of Samuel Daniel's *Hymen's Triumph*, a play usually dated 1614 and surviving (in one copy) as MS De. 3. 69 at Edinburgh University Library. Impressively up-to-date with recent criticism, Pitcher presents a soundly realized reconstruction of the play's compositional circumstances, reflecting on blanks in the manuscript, pointing to connections with the Roxborough wedding, and locating (in Additional Manuscripts in the British Library) early versions of the songs. Pitcher identifies three hands in the manuscript (A, B and Daniel's italic) and offers the intriguing suggestion that Lady Roxborough herself may have appended corrections. In almost every respect, Pitcher has put together a polished volume, and it is only a matter of slight regret that questions about the identity of the scribes and the processes whereby they consulted are not always fully addressed.

The Real Shakespeare and fresh editorial investigations illustrate (with varying successes) a popular critical imperative – to uncover the points of contact between material forces and literary production, and to develop a nuanced appreciation of the working conditions which Renaissance dramatists experienced. In this respect, the liveliest studies are concerned with the possibilities and limitations of contemporary playhouses. Gail McMurray Gibson's *The Theater of Devotion* represents a finely researched reflection on intersections between secular imagery, spiritual discourses and late medieval drama, with a particular concentration on Norfolk, Suffolk and the N-town cycle. Proceeding from the thesis that the incarnation of Christ was a justification of and a model for much fifteenth-century art, Murray combines archival scholarship with an analysis of the theatre, religious devotion, sculpture and ecclesiastical architecture, and thereby highlights emergent commercial forces as well as the shared concerns of complementary cultural practices. The best chapter centres on Margery Kempe, and weaves together meditations, wills, relics and folk magic with exemplary delicacy. It is gratifying to see this sumptuously illustrated volume in paperback, even if the bibliography omits a comprehensive list of archival sources.

The wide-ranging researches of Murray have eloquent counterparts in three related volumes, which aim to reveal a number of aspects of the 'reality' of the Renaissance theatrical experience. The first is Alan H. Nelson's *Early Cambridge Theatres*, a remarkable attempt to describe university colleges, halls and chapels as playing spaces, which follows in the steps of the recent Globe and Rose excavations. Unfortunately Nelson never quite confronts the plays themselves, and references to Walter Hawkesworth's *Labyrinthus*, William Johnson's *Valetudinarium*, Thomas Legge's *Richardus Tertius* and Thomas Tomkis' *Albumazar* are frustratingly brief. If Nelson's interests do not always extend to literary exploration, however, his archaeological brilliance is refreshingly evident in his com-

ments on the intricacies of joinery and carpentry, on heights and dimensions, on windows, doors and tiring chambers, and on the sale and volume of candles. Aided by his previous participation in the 'Records of Early English Drama' project, Nelson has produced a model work of painstaking architectural restoration.

The two remaining volumes similarly provide a wealth of new information and detail in their efforts to reclaim the characteristics and conventions of playing and playhouses in the English Renaissance. Fascinating glimpses into the circulation of scurrilous verses, profanations of the Sabbath, payments to players and the place of popular amusements are afforded by Alan B. Somerset's edited two-volume collection on *Shropshire* for the 'Records of Early English Drama' project, which also furnishes a context for a richer understanding of Corpus Christi celebrations and more general seasonal customs. Like the travelling players he resurrects, Somerset has ranged widely among the record repositories, and he completes his labours with an excellent appendix essay on patrons and travelling companies. There are, nevertheless, one or two minor disappointments. The handwritten typographical symbols are rather unsightly (pp. 274, 618), and it would be helpful to have the Latin translations next to the English transcriptions. In addition, Somerset is occasionally somewhat misleading in his adjudication between manuscript and printed sources: we have to wait until page 430 to learn that the letters of Lady Brilliana Harley are available in an 1854 edition, and it is never mentioned that 'Dr Taylor's History', a manuscript chronicle at Shrewsbury School, was substantially edited in an 1880 article, although the article is referred to (without appropriate comment) in the 'Select Bibliography' (p. 491). With a rather greater emphasis on the play in Elizabethan and Jacobean performance comes Alan C. Dessen's *Rediscovering Shakespeare's Theatrical Vocabulary*. Despite sidestepping a number of considerations – such as a play's different versions and the genesis of stage directions in particular theatrical circumstances – Dessen writes with admirable mastery, continually returning to the question of what the Shakespearian playgoer might have witnessed. Paragraphs of examples and odd repetitions sometimes slow the prose, but this does not spoil Dessen's argument that images constituted a dictionary of theatrical codes, that meanings could be generated by properties left on stage, that nightgowns, sick-chairs and keys were enlisted as thematic devices, and that open hands and dishevelled hair could connote insanity. Theatrical language and stage directions are pressed to yield unexpected depths of signification in this book, which is enhanced by a thorough knowledge of selected modern performances.

II

The 'real' Shakespeare would therefore appear to be an amalgam of different tendencies and preoccupations, a prompt for assessments of the playhouse as an institution, connections between diverse areas of artistic activity, and the historical specificity of the dramatist's craft. These reconstructions have as a central component the role played by culture, a focus of interest which is more explicitly stated in journals, monographs and recent anthologies. Current criticism subsumes the text to larger developments, and reads that process in terms of the multiple guises that culture assumes.

The Ben Jonson Journal, according to the 'Editor's Page', is 'an annual review devoted to the study of Ben Jonson and the culture in which his manifold literary efforts thrived'. The assembled articles (on Jonson's masques and poetry, John Donne's satires, Aemilia Lanyer's patronage, Andrew Marvell's politics and Shakespeare's tragedies) are uneven in quality. Some (William Kerrigan's piece on 'Shakespeare and Splitting' is a notable example) neglect important research on prostitution (by Ian W. Archer, Paul Griffiths and Jyotsna Singh), while others unnecessarily rehearse a

familar play's plot (as in Thomas Clayton's essay on *Coriolanus*). The best studies belong to David McPherson who writes on numerology and Sara Van Den Berg who finds in literary metaphors and realizations of coronation entries inscriptions of London's symbolic power. More generally, the superficially attractive presentation masks dreadful typographical errors, which include 'Dom' for 'Don' (p. 6) and '*Johnson*' for '*Jonson*' (pp. 28, 30). The notation system is inconsistent, and some of the books reviewed are five years old. *The Ben Jonson Journal* has excellent promise, but it has not yet settled on a clearly defined identity.

A more magisterial attempt to unravel the forms that culture inhabits is Lawrence Manley's *Literature and Culture in Early Modern London*. At over six hundred pages, the book claims a comprehensiveness of coverage to which a journal can only aspire, and Manley is certainly generous in the kinds of texts explored. His interest is in the relationship between the development of the metropolis and new literary possibilities and, to mount his thesis, he considers embodiments of collective urban experiences, humanism and civic complaint, Stow and his contemporaries, poetic emblems of London, mayoral shows and satirical pamphlets. Throughout Manley refers to the recent work of historians to estimate population growth, the economic contributions of the guilds and the impact of print. One chapter ('From Matron to Monster') is an energetic elaboration of anxious efforts to make sense of an unprecedented urban phenomenon; the remaining chapters, although characterized by bright local observations, are less satisfactory. A major difficulty resides with the fitful theoretical appurtenances: Mikhail Bakhtin, Michel de Certeau, Karl Marx and Raymond Williams jostle with each other uncomfortably, and a number of different theoretical positions are entertained without being adequately dovetailed. All too frequently Manley relies on secondary sources (the phrase 'quoted in' is a staple of the footnotes), and several chapters strike one as summaries rather than interpretations in their own right. It is a pity that the final chapters on the drama do not sparkle (as much as they might) with freshly minted insights.

The broad scope of Manley's book is one of its shortcomings (and can possibly be listed among its virtues), and it is therefore welcome to find more focused studies of culture in the period, which combine close readings with discursive comment. In electing to concentrate on Spenser and Milton, Linda Gregerson in *The Reformation of the Subject* takes up authors only partially discussed in Manley's *Literature and Culture in Early Modern London*, and her argument that the English Protestant epic refracted a debate about the shaping power of representation is dynamically sustained. Following the break with Rome, poetry was forced to contemplate its idolatrous potential, a claim which Gregerson illustrates with reference to Spenserian characters who attempt to reform each other, to imagery of mirrors in his epic, and to new uses of allegorical functions and figures. Through Malbecco, who resists collapsing into a merely allegorical status, Spenser examines his own symbolic method, staging contests for 'scriptive dominion' (p. 137) and examining the means whereby subjectivity was constituted. In these discussions, Gregerson is subtle and persuasive, speaking in an arrestingly original voice, and her expertise is no less apparent in the Milton chapters. Eve's exposition of her own narcissistic consciousness is excitingly linked to the Reformation theme, as is the psychologically informed analysis of various creative gestures, acts of remembering and idolatrous tendencies.

In Gerald MacLean's edited book, *Culture and Society in the Stuart Restoration*, Milton also figures prominently, mainly in essays by Blair Worden and Steven N. Zwicker on *Samson Agonistes* and literary controversy respectively, although the second is more successful than the first. Worden's piece, for instance, notes parallels between the poem and 'Roundhead' writings of the 1660s without offering much in the way of concluding statement. As a whole, however, this is an absorbing and enlightening volume, which reads the Restoration in terms of nationalist ambitions, republican ideology and the growth of a more secular culture. Those chapters by Andrew R. Walkling on representations of the collapse of ancient constitutional structures in Purcell and Tate's masques, by Nancy Klein Maguire on rewritings of Shakespeare in response to the political crisis of 1678–83, by James Grantham Turner on intersections between Pepys' sexual practice and court culture, and by Elaine Hobby on the epistolary and romantic conventions infusing the work of Hannah Wolley are particularly fine. Thanks to the contributions of Elaine Hobby and Moira Ferguson, the crucial part played by women in late seventeenth-century culture is finally being granted a long overdue attention.

By shifting the axis towards the relationship between women and print, *Culture and Society in the Stuart Restoration* is characteristic of a group of studies that seeks to understand gender-related questions in terms of their cultural specificity and historical moment. In dictionaries, anthologies and monographs, male constructions of women are being subjected to informed scrutinies, as are efforts made by women themselves to escape conventional calumnies and speak in their own voices. Typical of the development to read 'Shakespeare' as a cultural signifier, a contextual tool and a set of patriarchal attitudes is Gordon Williams' three-volume *A Dictionary of Sexual Language and Imagery in Shakespearean and Stuart Literature*. Priced at an exorbitant £350, this is not a publication to be bought on a whim; the cost notwithstanding, Williams has assembled a first-class resource, which is brim-full with sprightly observations and scholarly instances. Obviously in such a collection there are likely to be points at which a different citation or Shakespearian emphasis would have seemed appropriate. Under 'Antlers', for example, Falstaff might have been mentioned; Bottom is curiously missing from the definition of 'Ass's Ears'; Thomas Dekker and Thomas Middleton's *The Roaring Girl* is oddly absent from the section on the 'Hermaphrodite'; the analysis of 'St Valentine' neglects to consider Ophelia's songs; and the discussion of the 'Whirligig' would surely have benefited by taking into account Edward Sharpham's play, *Cupid's Whirligig*. The bibliography is not entirely accurate, since 'Oxford' is confused for 'Durham' (p. 1581), 'Shakespeare Head' for 'Blackwell' (p. 1581) and 'Conyl' for 'Coryl' (p. 1609). An index of places, names and subjects might also have been useful. Laying to one side the possibility of minor modifications, *A Dictionary of Sexual Language and Imagery in Shakespearean and Stuart Literature* is a triumph, a splendid labour of love (or lust). Early printed books as well as manuscripts from the Additional and Harleian collections have been combed to bring to life an enormous body of familiar and unfamiliar meanings, and additionally attractive features are the volumes' twentieth-century applications: the introductory materials relate sexual language to modern debates about censorship, while a capacious definition of 'Stuart' allows Williams to trace through usages to their more modern incarnations.

It is difficult to be as enthusiastic about the poorer anthology compiled and edited by N. H. Keeble, *The Cultural Identity of Seventeenth-Century Woman*. The stated intention is to exemplify constructions or, as Keeble puts it in his introduction, 'ways of conceptualizing, describing, characterizing and presenting women and their experiences' (p. xi). Faulting one book for failing to be another may not be fair, but the very limited space given to women's own voices in this book does force one to wonder about the usefulness of the undertaking. Women, of course, conceptualized themselves as well as being described by their male counterparts, and thus the absence from these pages of such seventeenth-century writers as Hannah Allen, Hester Biddle, Mary Carleton, Sarah Cheevers, Sarah Davy, Katharine Evans,

Mary Penington, Anna Trapnel, Jane Turner and Joan Vokins (to name only a few of non-aristocratic rank) seems regrettable in the extreme. (Even the bibliography of secondary sources is partial in that important studies by Patricia Crawford, Ann Rosalind Jones, Barbara Lewalski, Mary Prior and Linda Woodbridge do not appear.) Keeble organizes his book according to sections, some of which are entitled 'Beauty', 'Vices' and 'Virtues', which begs the question of whose beauty is the object of interest. The opinions of Richard Baxter and John Milton would seem to occupy too much space; the subtle effects of the discourses of witchcraft are represented hardly at all; and comments such as Margaret Cavendish was a 'remarkable and individualistic woman' (p. 44) tend to grate. Only two extracts concern women's roles in the religious sects (pp. 201–2), and 'authorship' is reflected in a very brief section at the close.

Turning from collections and anthologies to monographs, a more favourable impression is made by authored studies, which profitably examine the relationship between women and culture from a variety of perspectives. The majority of studies of this kind are invigorating and innovative, but this does not apply to Marliss C. Desens's *The Bed-Trick in English Renaissance Drama*, which disappoints as a rather limp account of the substitution convention. As Desens's title indicates, she explores those plays in which women take other women's places in the boudoir; from this tantalizing beginning, however, the book soon falls into formalist and essentialist description. Too often Desens appears to take the oppressive nature of patriarchy at face value, and the impact of her prose is further dulled by such remarks as 'the bed-trick … allowed … dramatists … to probe some of the complexities of human behavior' (p. 17); 'The abbot's words show … the world of social reality' (p. 57); 'there are no easy answers' (p. 85); and 'the use of a Moor … suggests an underlying racism' (p. 100). The class inflected nature of partner substitution remains unacknowledged (maidservants, for instance, were the most common types employed in the bed-trick), and several rich expressions of the convention deserve mention, such as the sixteenth-century pamphlets, *The Cobbler of Canterbury* and *The Deceit of Women*, and John Fletcher's play, *Women Pleased*. While the subject is fruitful, the treatment Desens accords it leaves open more questions than are ever properly resolved.

In a more cogently theorized category is Laura Levine's *Men in Women's Clothing*. Attracted, like Desens, to situations which throw into doubt the binarisms of gendered identities, Levine argues that fears of effeminization were discharged on the Shakespearian stage, that the masculine self was vulnerable, and that a supernatural component was an inevitable part of the theatrical project. In a series of concise chapters, Levine suggests that *Troilus and Cressida* countenances the possibility of men shading into women at any moment; maintains that *Antony and Cleopatra* realizes masculinity as a hollow performance; claims that *Bartholomew Fair* enacts a process whereby gender difference disappears altogether; and reads *Newes from Scotland* as a contradictory meditation on infernal interventions, the precariousness of power, and the transformatory effects of rape. Once or twice Levine blurs her conclusions in an urge to go beyond the New Historicist chiasmus, and the fictive pleasures of effeminization are arguably as relevant as the terrors; eventually, however, there is little with which to quarrel. *Men in Women's Clothing* is an invaluable work: a corrective to some New Historicist definitions of and locations for power, a keen assessment of anti-theatricality within the drama and without, and a shrewd recognition of the partnership shared by playing spaces and diabolical practice.

Two of the features selected for comment in criticism of the relationship between women and culture (representations of women and women's writing) are successfully fused in Warren Chernaik's *Sexual Freedom in Restoration Literature*. Taking his cue from the impetus of new approaches to the English Renaissance, Chernaik sets out to contextualize the Restoration pursuit of sexual freedom and its political, philosophical and practical implications. Tensions inherent in the ideology of individual liberty are detected, and attention is directed to the ambivalence with which claims of freedom and autonomy, rebelliousness and security are treated. The theoretical framework has its anchorage in the work of Michel Foucault and Eve Kosofsky Sedgwick, which permits informed remarks on the Earl of Rochester's indebtedness to Thomas Hobbes and Epicureanism as well as the role played by John Locke's philosophical experiment. When he moves in the second part to Aphra Behn, Chernaik's practised nimbleness begins to falter, although he is adept at rehearsing the dismantlement of blazon traditions. Larger historical shifts are generally passed over in this book, whose chief strength resides in its careful unpacking of clusters of poetic meaning, and 'masculine' and 'feminine' are perhaps too diagrammatically employed as ideological concepts. One wonders, too, if Behn's writing is rather more complex than simply '[pandering] to dominant patriarchal values' as well as '[challenging] them' (p. 194), as Chernaik insists. If Chernaik periodically slips into a subversion and containment impasse, however, his book still impresses with its individual readings, bold contrasts and effervescent enthusiasm.

The revision of canonical assumptions, the currents of exchange running between literary texts and cultural contexts, and the challenge posed by marginalized voices – these are the pursuits and preoccupations of the Shakespearian critic, and they are demonstrated in abundance in Alison Findlay's *Illegitimate Power*, a study of bastards in Renaissance drama. Although Findlay smoothes over some shades of meaning (in her rehearsal of puritan ideology, for instance), is hesitant to ascribe motives to apprentices' rebellions, and does not clearly identify how representations of bastards changed over the period, she writes with fluency, imagination and scholarship, and her book contains readings to engross and materials to stimulate. Bastards emerge as indicators and instigators of a crisis of authority, as illegitimacy was encoded as a threat to the tenets of patriarchy. Findlay shines in the ways in which she maps legal niceties, unfolds social constructions, highlights connections with other discourses (such as witchcraft) and elaborates a mainly conceptual approach to her theme, which does not prevent more detailed comment on particular playtexts. Surprising numbers of plays feature bastard characters, and they are selected to cast meaning on a range of subjects, from established religion to political expediency and Platonic ideals. An eloquent final chapter considers the bastard type in relation to issues of theatrical space and audience response.

III

Despite the wealth of information which recent studies uncover, the pursuit of the 'real' Shakespeare is necessarily a quest for a chimera. For Shakespeare now signifies culture, rather than (as was the case for an earlier generation of critics) culture signifying the playwright. As an author, Shakespeare has been consigned to a postmodern extinction, since 'reality' is only another fiction, one more construction. But as a testing ground for competing definitions of culture and theoretical enquiry, Shakespeare thrives, and now actively connotes the ideological place of the early modern playhouse, the society to which it belonged and the subsequent forms that theatrical and textual practice could adopt. With one foot in the later medieval period and the other in the Restoration, Shakespeare serves as a vehicle with which to address conflicts and correspondences, developments and discontinuities. It should not appear surprising, therefore, that Shakespeare's nineteenth- and twentieth-century manifestations have come to represent a field of a critical

activity as well as a source of anxiety. In this respect, Shakespeare, while still part of a theatrical institution, can also be seen to belong to a curiously liminal and cross-cultural territory, which finds its imaginative expression in the medium of cinema, the corridors of Eastern Europe and the consulting room of the psychiatrist.

The 'Shakespeare in Performance' series represents only one example of a move to understand the dramatist in relation to trends in twentieth-century culture, and two new volumes in the collection are quite successful in establishing the sensitivity of modern productions to social change and political upheaval. Following a knowledgeable appraisal of staging difficulties and Victorian revivals, Geraldine Cousin, in her volume on *King John*, discusses the RSC productions of the early 1970s (which were dominated by a sombre vision of a battered and maimed England), the BBC version of 1984 and Deborah Warner's 1988–9 realization at Stratford-upon-Avon and London. Cousin is surely right to highlight the Warner production's confrontation with issues of nationhood, dispossession and the legitimacy of authority, but her powers of perception are less forcefully reflected in the chapter on *King John* on television. With Leonard Rossiter in the title role and employing a variety of cardboard cut-out sets and self-consciously artificial devices, the BBC production might well be regarded as a purposefully anti-naturalistic meditation on the psychologically alienating faces of kingship, which draws its inspiration from absurdist and Brechtian theatrical conventions. That Cousin interprets the production as no more than 'effective' (pp. 86, 87) – a term which she over-uses – and 'fundamentally ... conservative' (p. 100) is arguably to her book's detriment. In *A Midsummer Night's Dream*, Jay L. Halio has rather more material on which to base an argument and, while reluctant to pass judgement on the play itself, is quick to detail its performative dimensions. Although the continual recourse to the 'illusion and reality' formulation can irritate, Halio nevertheless manages to meet the requirements of a survey at the same time as offering a number of densely elaborated case studies. He provocatively associates the 1935 film by Max Reinhardt and William Dieterle with the disillusioned mood of the capitalist 1930s; is perceptively mixed in his assessment of Peter Brook's celebrated 1970 *A Midsummer Night's Dream*; pertinently recognizes themes of harmony and completeness in Bill Alexander's 1986 production; and writes refreshingly about the muddy pool metaphor in Robert Lepage's 1992 version of the play at the National Theatre. In Halio's volume an attentiveness to detail and a breadth of coverage work together to illuminate the manifold readings and reactions that *A Midsummer Night's Dream* engages.

In contrast, H. R. Coursen's *Reading Shakespeare on Stage* is rushed in delivery, and lacks the care and thought which mark some volumes in the 'Shakespeare in Performance' series. This is an uncertain book, a collection of reviews from various newsletters and a flawed attempt to provide a set of instructions for the novice playgoer. As a result, Coursen, who chooses Shakespearian productions staged in Ontario, London and Stratford-upon-Avon mainly during the early 1990s as his sample, is mixed in his messages, at once writing in a general way and with all the theoretical baggage of the specialist. It is easy in this book to lose one's path in a welter of secondary critical opinions, to the extent that Coursen's own views of the productions run the risk of disappearing beneath a mass of extracts from critics' reviews. The intermittent discussion of theatrical space lends *Reading Shakespeare on Stage* some coherence (particularly in the account of *Twelfth Night* at the Open Air Theatre, Regent's Park, in 1989), but the book cannot boast many such virtues. There are unfairly carping references to cultural materialists; Margreta de Grazia's name is continually misspelt Margaret de Gratzia (p. 47); Bernard Bresslaw's appears as Bernard Breeslaw (p. 98); the stills vary in quality; and this reviewer, at least, took exception to the remark that 'youngsters [who] live in Belfast or Brooklyn' (p. 71) are starved of theatre. The Belfast Festival at Queen's is obviously too peripheral to influence Coursen's analysis.

The performance of Shakespeare, however, is in some ways only marginal to the place of the dramatist in nineteenth- and twentieth-century culture. Since his presence haunts the studios and theatres of Victorian artists and actor-managers, the collaborations of modern singers and musicians, and the articulation of radical ideologies in the former communist countries, Shakespeare embodies not so much a corpus of dramatic material as a repository of ideas which can be put to various uses. Far from being an unchanging locus for transcendent values, Shakespeare is a shifting entity in the process of being continually rewritten to suit the needs of particular historical junctures, as studies mainly concerned with appropriations of the dramatist suggest. Edwin Austin Abbey (1852–1911) was a prolific and inventive artist known for his Shakespearian subjects, and his work is granted a generous appreciation in Lucy Oakley's *Unfaded Pageant*, which lavishly reproduces quick sketches, designs for books and magazines, costume ideas and major oil paintings. Oakley situates the artist in the context of Victorian constructions of Shakespeare, reading his comments in relation to contemporary moral attitudes, the influence of the pre-Raphaelite movement, and the spectacular productions of theatrical associates. Meticulously arranged discussions explain Abbey's use of emblematic animals, his predilection for foreshortened perspectives, and his reworking of compositions in response to a sometimes hostile popular press. If Oakley's account hesitates to plumb dangerous interpretative depths, it still pleases as a colourful reminder of the magnificence of Victorian versions of Shakespeare and as a fitting memorial to Abbey's achievement.

Of the Victorian actor-managers who commissioned work from artists such as Abbey, Sir Henry Irving is probably the most celebrated.

Jeffrey Richards has collected and edited his major writings in *Sir Henry Irving*, the four sections of which reinstate the challenging aspects of his ideas about the philosophy of acting and the social role of the theatre. The first edition of its kind, *Sir Henry Irving* contains a plethora of intuitive reflection on 'the exaltation of sensibility' (p. 35), the naturalistic tradition, and the actor's professional responsibilities, in ways which anticipate Shakespeare as a construction and the more psychologically plausible orientations of modern performances. The introduction addresses the contemporary view that drama constituted a history with moral lessons (p. 10); rather more pointing of this nature, however, would have been facilitative in the book as a whole. A tighter overview of Irving's biography is an unhappy omission; the orotund abstractions of Irving's pronouncements invite some editorial clarification; and there are points at which an indebtedness to other nineteenth-century writers calls for comment.

Its shortcomings notwithstanding, *Sir Henry Irving* is a significant addition to the reconstitution of the Victorian Shakespeare; in contrast, one is obliged to ask if the autobiography of Robert Atkins, the late Edwardian actor-manager, is sufficiently remarkable or substantial to merit publication in a book-length format. In a career which stretched from 1906 to 1963, Atkins spent five years as Director of Productions at the Old Vic, founded the Open Air Theatre at Regent's Park, and had a spell as Director of the Shakespeare Memorial Theatre, Stratford-upon-Avon. George Rowell performs his editorial task competently, but the supplementary contributions by J. C. Trewin and A. C. Sprague only draw attention to the fact that the autobiography, started in 1952 and chronologically confused even in the sections which do survive, only covers the very early years. Opportunities for editorial intervention are generally avoided, so that the early productions alluded to by Atkins remain tantalizingly unidentified. The labour of a disciple, *Robert Atkins* wants a critical perspective on its subject, particularly as the autobiographical tone is alternately awe-struck and offensive: Atkins' family is barely mentioned (p. 76); curious remarks on '"Gypos"' (p. 98) inform the prose; and there are references to the 'chatter ... of the negroes in Baltimore' (p. 85) and to 'humans of many races' (p. 95). In the absence of the complete text, Atkins' story is incidentally interesting but too fragmentary to demand a sustained engagement.

From artistic adaptation to theatrical invention and operatic experiment, appropriations of Shakespeare run across a gamut of cultural categories. William H. L. Godsalve's *Britten's 'A Midsummer Night's Dream'* provides an analysis of the 1959–60 libretto by Benjamin Britten and Peter Pears based on Shakespeare's play. It is clear that Godsalve is well versed in musical accomplishment, but his book has far more to excite the Britten scholar than the Shakespearian critic. He details Britten's role as an eclectic assimilator and innovator; does a good job in tracking down the editions used; and prudently presents the cuts, additions and changes made by the composer to the text. The dialogue between music and play rarely ventures beyond the confines of noting intriguing parallels, however. The opera's post-war contexts surely deserve a fuller treatment, and the eventual conclusions amount to no more than statements of the obvious: changes were introduced, Godsalve observes, 'to produce an aesthetically successful opera' (p. 87), adding 'Britten matches the textual dramatic events with musical meanings' (p. 204).

As far as his Victorian, Edwardian and immediately post-war realizations are concerned, Shakespeare represents a powerful presence in theatrical experiment and more heterogeneous cultural exchanges. The representation of the dramatist points to essentially conservative estimations as well as to an awareness that successive generations respond to and employ his work in innovative and unpredictable ways. Whether the same can be said for

Shakespeare in the 1990s is debatable. From one perspective, the Shakespeare of today has been robbed of his authorial agency but blessed with the ability to sharpen the techniques of other disciplines, to generate new texts and mediums, and to shape a history which is still in the making. In *Shakespeare as Prompter*, Murray Cox and Alice Theilgaard, a practising psychotherapist and psychologist respectively, are 'sacred healers' who argue for the partnership shared by therapy and theatre. 'Our purpose', they state, 'is to show how Shakespeare has an inherent capacity to prompt the clinical work of psychotherapists when movement comes to a standstill, and to demonstrate the relevance of the aesthetic imperative within therapeutic space, when narrative begins to fail' (p. 8). The authors' procedure entails rehearsing a patient's case and then leaping to an apposite Shakespearian instance, although it is never established quite how the dramatist's work functions in practice. Consequently, the eclectic use of Shakespeare tends to have a reifying effect as very different texts all serve as grist to the therapeutic mill. That any creative metaphor might work as well is inadequately recognized. *Shakespeare as Prompter* is only partly about Shakespeare, and the reader looking for an intervention in materialist appropriations, for instance, will be disappointed. The book tells us more about therapeutic applications and languages but, even in this respect, there are striking lacunae in the argument. Given Cox and Theilgaard's interest in object-relations theory and commitment to interpersonal and intrapersonal experience, it is curious that Jacques Lacan is quickly dismissed (p. 283) and that Peter Rudnytsky features neither in the text nor in the bibliography. This book will confuse Shakespearians; for therapists, its aims and methods may be no less difficult to assimilate.

Two final collections underscore the phenomenon that Shakespeare in the 1990s is only partly constructed in terms of the stage, since his work is now broadcast in alternative media and in a range of cultural and national locations. In this sense, a wedge has been driven between the dramatist and the theatre, and the very 'English' sentiments with which he has been associated have been emptied of their traditional meanings. Anthony Davies and Stanley Wells's edited collection, *Shakespeare and the Moving Image*, is a robust and informative appraisal of Shakespeare in relation to his cinema and television manifestations. Previous scholarship is surveyed, and one of the fourteen articles (by Graham Holderness and Christopher McCullough) constitutes an invaluable filmography. Alive to colour, tone and narrative possibility, the contributors examine opposing and complementary Shakespearian incarnations, and the best essays unravel the complexities of spatial strategies used on screen (Anthony Davies), the 'theatrical' nature of film (Peter Holland), the absent television spectator (Michèle Willems), the ruthless vision of Kenneth Branagh's *Henry V* (Michael Manheim) and the appeal of Russian versions of *Hamlet* (Neil Taylor). Other essays push Shakespearian film studies in new directions by attending to Shakespeare and the Hollywood treatment, the partnership shared between drama and opera, and the competing interpretations of rival directors. One might have wished for longer and more theorized engagements with Kenneth Branagh's *Much Ado About Nothing* and Peter Greenaway's *Prospero's Books*, although the decision to sidestep these productions takes nothing away from the book's successes. *Shakespeare and the Moving Image* impresses with its dense discussions and breadth of example, in such a way as to establish the dramatist's central place in new visual media and to rewrite his relevance for a modern audience.

What one culture finds relevant, another may choose to see as baffling and obscure. The very different appearance of Shakespeare in Eastern Europe is testified to in an anthology edited by Michael Hattaway, Boika Sokolova and Derek Roper, *Shakespeare in the New Europe*. Generated by the fall of some Eastern

European nations in 1991 and an interdisciplinary conference held in 1993, the collection revitalizes Shakespeare through the medium of translation, and stresses intersections between multi-culturalism and dramatic craft. Questions concerning social integration, geographical displacements, historical progress, the German Romantic spirit, dissident adaptations, postcolonial appropriations and the impact of queer theory are fruitfully aired in twenty-one fully illustrated and contrasting contributions. There are also provocative studies of Shakespeare in relation to Elizabethan and Jacobean notions of fellowship, honour and surveillance, although Robin Headlam Wells' piece on *Hamlet* and honour could benefit from taking into account the work of Karen Coddon on the same play. Similarly, the recent research of Michal Kobialka on *Hamlet* might precisely complement the essay of Marta Gibińska on the play's fortunes in Poland. It is to be regretted, in addition, that Thomas Rymer's *Short View of Tragedy* is dated 1962 (p. 282) and that Derek Roper, one of the editors, is missing from the list of contributors. To write properly about the past, there also needs to be a critical engagement with the political present, however, and in the context of the ongoing struggles in the former Yugoslavia, *Shakespeare and the New Europe* makes a forceful and apposite statement. The book also demonstrates that the 'reality' of Shakespeare, in its traditional sense, has been superseded by an assembly of fictions and illusions, fractured, transforming and amorphous.

WORKS REVIEWED

Atkins, Robert. *Robert Atkins: An Unfinished Autobiography*. London: The Society for Theatre Research, 1994.

Chernaik, Warren. *Sexual Freedom in Restoration Literature*. Cambridge: Cambridge University Press, 1995.

Coursen, H. R. *Reading Shakespeare on Stage.* Newark: University of Delaware Press, London and Toronto: Associated University Presses, 1995.

Cousin, Geraldine. *Shakespeare in Performance: 'King John'*. Manchester and New York: Manchester University Press, 1994.

Cox, Murray, and Alice Theilgaard. *Shakespeare as Prompter: The Amending Imagination and the Therapeutic Process*. London and Bristol, Pennsylvania: Jessica Kingsley Publishers, 1994.

Daniel, Samuel. *Hymen's Triumph*. Ed. by John Pitcher. Malone Society. Oxford: Oxford University Press, 1994.

Davies, Anthony, and Stanley Wells, eds. *Shakespeare and the Moving Image: The Plays on Film and Television*. Cambridge: Cambridge University Press, 1994.

Desens, Marliss C. *The Bed-Trick in English Renaissance Drama: Explorations in Gender, Sexuality, and Power*. Newark: University of Delaware Press/ London and Toronto: Associated University Presses, 1994.

Dessen, Alan C. *Recovering Shakespeare's Theatrical Vocabulary*. Cambridge: Cambridge University Press, 1995.

Findlay, Alison. *Illegitimate Power: Bastards in Renaissance Drama*. Manchester and New York: Manchester University Press, 1994.

Gibson, Gail McMurray. *The Theater of Devotion: East Anglian Drama and Society in the Late Middle Ages*. Chicago and London: University of Chicago Press, 1994.

Godsalve, William H. L. *Britten's 'A Midsummer Night's Dream': Making an Opera from Shakespeare's Comedy*. Madison and Teaneck: Fairleigh Dickinson University Press/London and Toronto: Associated University Presses, 1995.

Gregerson, Linda. *The Reformation of the Subject: Spenser, Milton and the English Protestant Epic*. Cambridge: Cambridge University Press, 1995.

Halio, Jay L. *Shakespeare in Performance: 'A Midsummer Night's Dream'*. Manchester and New York: Manchester University Press, 1994.

Harp, Richard, and Stanley Stewart, eds. *Ben Jonson Journal: Literary Contexts in the Age of Elizabeth, James, and Charles*. Volume 1. Reno: University of Nevada Press, 1994.

Hattaway, Michael, Boika Sokolova and Derek Roper, eds. *Shakespeare in the New Europe*. Sheffield: Sheffield Academic Press, 1994.

Irving, Sir Henry. *Sir Henry Irving: Theatre, Culture*

and Society. Ed. by Jeffrey Richards. Keele: Ryburn Publishing, 1994.

Jonson, Ben. *Poetaster*. Ed. by Tom Cain. Manchester and New York: Manchester University Press, 1995.

Keeble, N. H., ed. *The Cultural Identity of Seventeenth-Century Woman: A Reader*. London and New York: Routledge, 1994.

Levine, Laura. *Men in Women's Clothing: Anti-Theatricality and Effeminization, 1579–1642*. Cambridge: Cambridge University Press, 1994.

MacLean, Gerald, ed. *Culture and Society in the Stuart Restoration: Literature, Drama, History*. Cambridge: Cambridge University Press, 1995.

Manley, Lawrence. *Literature and Culture in Early Modern London*. Cambridge: Cambridge University Press, 1995.

Nelson, Alan H. *Early Cambridge Theatres: College, University, and Town Stages, 1464–1720*. Cambridge: Cambridge University Press, 1994.

Oakley, Lucy. *Unfaded Pageant: Edwin Austin Abbey's Shakespearean Subjects*. Seattle: University of Washington Press, 1994.

Sams, Eric. *The Real Shakespeare: Retrieving the Early Years, 1564–1594*. New Haven and London: Yale University Press, 1995.

Somerset, J. Alan B., ed. *Records of Early English Drama: Shropshire*. 2 vols. Toronto, Buffalo and London: University of Toronto Press, 1994.

Williams, Gordon, ed. *A Dictionary of Sexual Language and Imagery in Shakespearean and Stuart Literature*. 3 vols. London and Atlantic Highlands, N.J.: Athlone, 1994.

3. EDITIONS AND TEXTUAL STUDIES

reviewed by JOHN JOWETT

ARDEN 3

A development that will already be known to every Shakespeare scholar is that the Arden Shakespeare has entered a new cycle. The erstwhile 'new' Ardens, now to be known as Arden 2s, are beginning to be replaced with even newer Arden 3s. Arden thus affirms its position as the only Shakespeare series that has maintained a leading position throughout the century, and sets its sights firmly on the next millennium. The new cycle opens with *Henry V*, edited by T. W. Craik, *Titus Andronicus*, edited by Jonathan Bate, and *Antony and Cleopatra*, edited by John Wilders. Every aspect of general editorial policy has been scrutinized and many details have been carefully rethought. The scope of these changes is sufficient to ensure that the Arden 3 series will succeed as a constructive modernization of its predecessors.

The Arden general editors have successively adapted the edition to the needs of the moment while sustaining its corporate identity. On the verso of the first batch of Arden 3 title-pages we are reminded, as before, of the genealogy of general editors from W. J. Craig and R. H. Case to the present team, Richard Proudfoot, Ann Thompson, and David Scott Kastan. Craik's edition of *King Henry V* is dedicated to the memory of three Shakespeare scholars: amongst them are a former general editor, H. F. Brooks, who perhaps did more than anyone to establish Arden 2 as a fresh edition for post-war readers, and A. R. Humphreys, one of Arden 2's best editors. To point out these details is to highlight the continuity of the Arden series, and its ability to survive through evolutionary change. Paradoxically, it must be this adaptability if anything that justifies the assertion, on the paperbacks' back cover, that Arden is 'the definitive edition of Shakespeare's plays'. Whereas one might have assumed that to be definitive is to be conclusive, fixed and final, the Arden claim seems to be based on its potentially infinite capacity to redefine itself for new generations. The Arden's survival skills seem to be based on a Protean and even Shakespearian kind of definitude.

Introductions are printed in a much larger type-face than their predecessors; they vary in length between 84 pages (Wilders) and 121 pages (Bate). The tone of the introductions is typically less scholarly – or should one say 'scholastic'? – than that associated with Arden 2, or, for that matter, most Oxford and Cambridge editions. It would seem that the publishers have the sixth-form and lower undergraduate market firmly in view, and the general editors' commitment 'to maintain the quality and general character of its predecessors' might in this respect be questioned. The same comment applies to the disappearance of a standard feature of Arden 2, the appendices which presented generous selections from the source materials. Commentaries are a little less severe than those of the earlier Ardens. The old sub-variorum style, with its extensive citation of parallels and quotation from earlier editors, has been on the wane for some time, but now is finally abandoned, creating more space for discussion of matters such as staging. This brings the scope of commentaries much more into line with current practice in the rival series.

Arden joins with the Oxford and Cambridge series in other ways, including the provision of illustrations. As might be expected, illustrations from performance figure prominently, but a particularly good feature of the Arden illustrations is the regular provision of photofacsimiles of Quarto and Folio pages. Hence we have parallel texts of Q and F *Henry V* 4.6.4–38, part of a Folio column illustrating the confusion over messengers in *Antony and Cleopatra* 1.2.92–130, which is the sort of tangle that no collation can adequately represent, shorter photoquotations from the same play exemplifying the problems of lineation, a parallel text showing part of Q1 *Titus* on the left-hand page and the edited text facing – though the latter, presumably through some coding error, appears with

spurious angled brackets that should not have been printed – and an illustration showing the 'fly' passage in the Folio text of the same play. In every case the illustration is integrated with the textual discussion and illuminates it. In no two cases is the presentation or purpose of the textual illustration the same. Apart from the glitch in *Titus*, this is one respect in which the three editions are an effective showpiece for the series.

Arden 3s do not include a list of critical reading, though all references are gathered together under the heading 'Abbreviations and References'. This brings together a helpful body of information and keeps the Introduction clean from footnotes. Instead of a glossarial index there is an index to the Introduction and commentary: a valuable feature in its own right, even if largely restricted to proper names. A student interested in Deborah Warner's production of *Titus* will be able to locate all twenty-six of Bate's references to it, most of which are to be found in scattered commentary notes on how particular pieces of business were handled.

A problem that faces all editions of Shakespeare that aim to be both competent works of scholarship and intelligible presentations of the work to non-specialist readers is how to document the textual editing. The collation line for all but the most straightforward text can quickly become filled with impenetrable clutter. Part of the reason is that a single consolidated collation simply performs too many distinct functions. This is why the New Penguin series presents separate tabulations of readings, and one reason why the Oxford *Complete Works* prints a separate list of control-text stage directions.[1] These matters have not been reconsidered to any effect in Arden 3, but instead the collation notes have been shifted from mid-page, between text and commentary, to the foot of the page. Who

---

[1] Alongside the other textual apparatus in Stanley Wells and Gary Taylor, with John Jowett and William Montgomery, *William Shakespeare: A Textual Companion* (1987)

was it that observed or jested that the usual page layout recapitulates the Saussurian sign, with the collation line occupying the position of the bar between signifier (text) and signified (commentary)? A more traditional and pragmatic view would be that one logically needs to record the establishment of the text before going on to explicate and comment upon it. It is all too easy to surmise from the Arden 3 layout that the collations are a dumping ground for information regarded as necessary but ignorable, an impression to some extent confirmed in the three editions by variability in accuracy and format. Even as it literally downgrades the collation line, the new series continues the example set in the Oxford and Cambridge series of bringing forward the significance of textual matters to the more general reader, both in the commentary and the Introduction. Gone is the sense, so marked in some of the Arden 2s, that the Textual Introduction provides a special reserve for primary scholarly investigation of the printing and transmission of the text. But the collation line is reinforced as a ghetto, and part of the challenge of presenting textual documentation satisfactorily has not been met.

The publishers Routledge have made a point of seeking accolades from actors and directors, and the edition's self-descriptions are so keen to highlight the theatrical dimension that they repeatedly neglect the fact that Arden has included and will continue to include non-dramatic works. Editors respond to the theatrical mandate in different ways. Wilders offers a useful if conjectural account of *Antony and Cleopatra* in Jacobean performance; he includes a partial stage history in his section called 'The Question of Unity', and interweaves references to the play in performance elsewhere. Craik condenses the very full performance history of *Henry V* into a survey of twelve type-pages: a paragraph on original performances, about a page per century on the years up to 1900, and a fuller account of twentieth-century stagings and film versions. Only Jonathan Bate makes a really positive virtue of his treatment of the play in

performance. He does so spectacularly well, putting a vigorous account of *Titus* on stage at very stage-centre in his Introduction. Using this section (pp. 37–69) as a means for raising fundamental questions as to the play's style, coherence, and meaning, Bate achieves a remarkable fusion between performance history and criticism.

Editors are similarly variable in response to their general editors' mandate that they should address 'a new generation's encounter with Shakespeare'. If Craik gives a brief summary of work on *Henry V* by Stephen Greenblatt, Alan Sinfield, and Jonathan Dollimore, his edition as a whole is meagerly responsive to the strands in criticism they represent. Wilders makes frequent reference to Janet Adelman's study of *Antony and Cleopatra*,[2] but neglects feminist and gender-based criticism to an astonishing degree. Again, Bate does conspicuously better, reacting at least briefly to critics such as A. R. Braunmuller, Suzanne Gossett, Stephanie Jed, Stephen Orgel, and Nancy Vickers, whilst keeping a firm perspective on the cultural milieu of the 1590s and never faltering in a critical advocacy that is both distinctive and itself very much of a 'new' generation.

In his *Henry V*, Craik provides an accurate text, except that its 'Dat it is not de fashion' at 5.2.259 omits 'be' after 'not'. The collation is occasionally vague or misleading to the point that it could be called inaccurate. Craik's commentary is particularly ample and detailed, with careful attention to the play's language, textual problems, the interpretation of stage directions, and Shakespeare's handling of source material. A section of the introduction on 'the play' offers a description of the text realized as stage action. It is most effective when it senses the play's unpredictable brilliance, as where Craik highlights its sudden broadening of perspective as the King talks to the common soldiers. Craik could scarcely be said to offer a neutral account;

---

2 *The Common Liar: An Essay on 'Antony and Cleopatra'* (1973).

rather, he builds up a distinct though traditionalist reading which, critically sympathetic and undogmatic, finds the play at once simple and subtle. The epic heroism remains relatively unperturbed by the potential shocks of subversion and disintegration.

Craik describes the 1599 Quarto and 1623 Folio texts from the point of view of a man purchasing them as new editions. A fictional young woman reader of Craik's edition might realize, when she becomes a postgraduate, that Craik's young man of 1599 had limitations as her mentor. One must wonder whether the summary of the action in Q1 can be as uninfluenced by consideration of F as the fiction presupposes. But few readers will check Q1. A major and substantive reform in the Arden 3 series is the provision of complete photofacsimiles of 'bad' quarto texts. It is perhaps unfortunate that they are offered merely as an alternative to full collation in situations where, to quote the general editors, 'the divergences from the present edition are too great to be recorded in full in the notes'. The justification rather warns off the student from *reading* these texts even as they are made available. Craik's account of Q1 similarly provides no line-references or signature references such as might relate it to the facsimile, and so fails to encourage the reader to do what his young man is doing. Well he might, for his tone is firmly dismissive: Q1 is unlikely to tempt this young man to go and see the play on stage. The following section gives a firm restatement of the orthodox view of 'bad' and 'good' quartos that conveys little impression that the categorizations have recently been subjected to sceptical scrutiny.

Craik accepts that Q1 derives from a script that has been theatrically adapted as well as memorially contaminated. He finds no clear indication as to whether the adaptation preceded or followed from the reconstruction, though here he might have considered Kathleen Irace's arguments that major and deliberate cuts in Q, and perhaps other theatrical changes,

came after memorial reconstruction.[3] Her case applies with special urgency to the Quarto's adaptation of the roles of the Dauphin and Bourbon. Disagreeing with Gary Taylor, Craik finds the Quarto's methods of alteration in any case too perfunctory to be Shakespearian.[4] On this matter Taylor's and Craik's discussions are both unavoidably impressionistic at key points.

Craik is equally unpersuaded by Q at 1.2.146–7: 'For you shall read, neuer my great grandfather / Vnmaskt his power for *France*'. F more feebly has: 'For you shall reade, that my great Grandfather / Neuer went with his forces into France'. E. A. J. Honigmann has described 'unmasked his power for France' as 'magnificent',[5] but Craik is sufficiently suspicious of the idiom in Q for him to fend off the verb by suggesting, implausibly, that 'Vnmaskt' may be an error for 'Embarkt'. I am not convinced that there is a deficiency of sense in Q1, nor that its short line is metrically objectionable. Taylor, otherwise following F, reads 'unmasked his power unto'. An editor accepting Q's capacity to include occasional minor authorial improvements might go further, and risk accepting both of the Quarto lines.

In other cases, even on occasion where F is entirely coherent in its own right, Craik is prepared to adopt readings from Q. On Quarto authority Falstaff is said to have described Bardolph's nose as 'a black soul burning in hell-fire' (2.3.39–40) rather than the Folio's less explicit '… in Hell'. There are a number of readings, 'hell-fire' being one of them, where Craik justifies parting from the most authoritative text by positing that it was locally corrupted by readings from Q3. He adduces a few of Andrew

---

3 In 'Reconstruction and Adaptation in Q *Henry V*', in *Studies in Bibliography*, 44 (1991), 228–53, as well as in the more recent study reviewed below.

4 In 'We Happy Few: The 1600 Abridgement', in Stanley Wells and Gary Taylor, *Modernizing Shakespeare's Spelling, with Three Studies in the Text of 'Henry V'*, 72–111, pp. 105–8, and Taylor's Oxford Shakespeare edition (1984), pp. 24–6.

5 *The Stability of Shakespeare's Text* (1965), p. 133.

Cairncross's more suggestive examples of apparent Q3 influence,[6] but inexcusably ignores Taylor's study refuting both Cairncross's hypothesis in general and the significance of these examples in particular.[7] The most significant consequence is that the Governor of Harfleur's entry, which Quartos and Folio alike place after King Henry's threatening 43-line speech 'How yet resolves the Governor of the town?', is relocated to before the speech. Unless one can be confident that a quarto did indeed impinge upon the Folio, this editorial change must plainly be wrong. There is therefore a strong onus on the editor to demonstrate any quarto influence before acting on it. Without a reaffirmation in the light of Taylor's points the matter must, to say the least, remain in doubt.

Assessment of Craik's edition, more than most, needs to take account of the editor's emendations where neither Q nor F is followed. A particularly elegant emendation is Craik's 1980 conjecture, already accepted in substance by Taylor and Andrew Gurr, 'I owe God a death' for Jamy's contextually odd 'ay, or goe to death' (3.2.117),[8] though why Craik prints 'God' rather than 'Got' as in Taylor and Gurr is unclear. In lines 31–2 of the Prologue to Act 2 there is another difficulty to which Craik finds a fresh solution. F prints:

> Linger your patience on, and wee'l digest
> Th'abuse of distance; force a play.

Alexander Pope and Taylor both treated the Folio as primarily deficient in metre, but Craik suspects further that F's use of 'digest' is un-Shakespearian. The distinction in sense that he makes is hard to follow, but one might well be disconcerted by the way F's 'force a play' seems simultaneously to suggest stuffing a sausage, cramming a stomach, and forcing a hard stool, none of which follows at all conformably or comfortably from 'digest'. Craik offers:

> Linger your patience on and well digest
> Th'abuse of distance, and we'll force our play.

Against this reading, the near-repetition 'and well ... and we'll' raises doubts, the emendation

of 'a' to 'our' is hard to justify, and one would like a good explanation for the remaining double error posited in F.[9] The emendations do help with the sense, however. They put the leisurely 'Linger' and 'digest' into effective parallel, and create some dissociation between the sequentially difficult 'digest' and 'force', so that it is the audience that can now at ease 'digest' what the actors strenuously 'force'.

In some other cases Craik's new reading addresses imaginary difficulties:

> They know your grace hath cause, and means, and might;
> So doth [F 'hath'] your highness.   (1.2.126)

> To look [F 'booke'] our dead and then to bury them;   (4.7.72)

The second example actually weakens the text, as does 'my full eyes' (4.6.34) for F's 'mixtfull eyes'. At both 4.7.37 ('intoxicates') and 4.7.96 ('Maiesties') Fluellen's characteristic ungrammatical terminal '-s' is emended away. Similarly, where Fluellen says that Gower 'is good knowledge and literatured in the Warres' (F, 4.7.148), Craik corrects the past participle to 'literature', influenced by Q's 'hath good littrature'. Here 'literatured' is, as Gurr engagingly says, 'A vivid polysyllable to pronounce in Llewellyn's voiceless consonants.'

With Wilders in his edition of *Antony and Cleopatra*, as with Craik, Shakespeare appears as a sufficiently fascinating writer and play-maker, but rather short on those brave translunary things that Michael Drayton found in Christopher Marlowe and that many readers find in Shakespeare. Wilders writes rather like a good professional teacher addressing a class of first-year undergraduates who are half-wondering

---

[6] 'Quarto Copy for Folio *Henry V*', in *Studies in Bibliography*, 8 (1956), 67–93.
[7] 'Quarto Copy for the Folio Text: A Refutation', in Wells and Taylor, *Modernizing*, pp. 41–71.
[8] In Taylor's Oxford Shakespeare edition (1984) and Gurr's New Cambridge edition (1992).
[9] Perhaps in terms of a misunderstood marginal addition of 'and well digest / Th'abuse of distance'.

about their exam questions. Indeed many students will no doubt value the orderliness of Wilders's introduction, its directness, its lack of hyperbole. There are convenient sub-headings: for instance *'Instability of characters'*, *'Images of instability'*, *'The philosophy of instability'*, and, finally in the section, *'The desire for stability'* (this last a good hint to those students), a firm page or so on each.

The only authoritative text for *Antony and Cleopatra* is the Folio, so in this respect at least the play is relatively stable. Wilders is less than Roman, however, in accidentally allowing 'this' for 'the' at 1.5.47; 'have praised' for 'ha' praised' at 2.6.76; 'has' for 'is' at 2.6.105; and 'CHARMIAN' for 'IRAS' at 5.2.192. At 1.4.9 the article in F's 'th'abstracts' is silently expanded to 'the'. At 4.8.20 a note might have been offered to explain why F's 'ha we' has been expanded to 'have we'. This looks like a spurious sophistication on Wilders's part, but as the type-line is justified, Compositor B just might have contracted his copy to save space. The collation has been sensibly tidied up by deferring to an appendix the lineation notes, of which there are necessarily many for this play. Nevertheless, as with Craik, the collation sometimes sulks at the foot of the page looking a bit unwanted;[10] and the lineation appendix omits to record a number of relineations.[11]

In the text, Wilders preserves Scarus' description of Cleopatra, in F, as a 'ribaudred' nag (3.10.10). Michael Neill (in the Oxford edition) and Wilders resist the Oxford *Complete Works*'s graphically plausible reading 'riband-red', on account of its odd way of expressing 'having red ribbons', its uncertain application to Cleopatra, and the awkwardness of speaking it in the line. It is surprising that no favour has been shown to adjectival 'ribaldry', which might have been spelt 'ribaudrey' or 'ribaudrie' in the copy, and would mean 'obscene, indecent', and indeed 'debauched'. As far as I know the reading has not even been conjectured. Of course it's pleasant to have the luxury of floating an emendation without the responsibility of adopting it,

but one reason for doing so here is that it demonstrates that the established menu of editorial readings is not exhaustive. Wilders does make a couple of new emendations. 'Hoo' in place of Folio 'How' at 3.2.11 scarcely counts, as it could be considered a spelling variant.[12] Wilders's Caesar 'cannot *lean* / To be ungentle' (5.1.59), which corrects F's 'leaue', and is a good alternative to the usual 'live' or 'learn'. Elsewhere Wilders tends to confine himself to the set menu. He selects judiciously; one might at least make question, though, of following F's 'abstract' at 3.6.62: 'Which soon he granted, / Being an abstract 'tween his lust and him'. To make sense of this one has to construct a clause for which F provides the merest skeleton, something like: '... *the granting of it* being a removal

---

[10] At 1.2.0.1 the lemma ought to read 'Soothsayer' instead of '*Officers*'. At 1.2.119 the note needs to refer also to lines 120 and 126. At 2.6.81 SD '*Manent*' should read '*Manet*'. At 2.7.29 SD '*and drink*' is wrongly attributed to '*Oxf subst.*'. At 2.7.111 'beate', the reading attributed to Theobald, should read 'bear'. At 3.13.97 SD '*Servant*' should read '*Seruant*'. At 4.6.11 SD the record of F's reading needs to be deleted. At 4.7.3 SD there is a spurious semi-colon. I have also noted stage directions silently reworded (2.2.180.1 and 3.7.66.1), speech-prefixes silently altered in form, and inconsistency over the recording of misprints. A number of changes that should probably be regarded as modernizations are recorded as emendations: for example, Folio 'Scicion' (a characteristic Shakespearian spelling) for *Sicyon*, 'browes' for possessive *brows*', 'wand' for *waned*, 'Mesena' (as in North's Plutarch) for *Misena*, 'disgested' for *digested*, 'Sidnis' for *Cydnus*, 'gloue' for *glow*, 'Ventigius' for *Ventidius*, 'Cicelie' for *Sicily*, 'liue' for *lief*, 'stroke' for *struck*, 'Archilaus' for *Archelaus*, 'Adullas' for *Adallas*, possibly 'Brandusium' for *Brundusium* (perhaps Shakespeare posited a semi-Italianate 'Brandisium'), 'Leaders leade' for *leader's led*', 'Iusteus' for *Justeius*, 'Celius' for *Caelius*, 'Caesarian' for *Caesarion*, 'Towrus' for *Taurus*, 'cease' for *seize*, personified 'Death' for 'death', possibly 'dislimes' for *dislimns*, 'A' for *Ah*, 'in' for *e'en* (as the commentary note recognizes), 'Marble constant' for *marble-constant*.

[11] For instance on 1.2.91, 2.3.11, 2.3.16–17, 2.7.30, 3.3.41, 3.7.6–9, 3.13.16–19, 4.8.18–19, and 5.2.203–4.

[12] As is suggested by F's 'how' at 4.14.105, emended 'ho'. The two readings might have been treated in the same way.

of that which stood between his lust and him' (my pointedly literal gloss). The elided subject of 'Being' is tolerable, but 'abstract 'tween' is almost impossibly compressed, and Theobald's 'obstruct' has much to commend it.

A casual flick through Jonathan Bate's edition of *Titus Andronicus* reveals that something unusual has happened to the act-scene-line referencing system in Act 2. Recognizing that there is not even a scene-break in the undivided Quarto at the point where F and editors mark the end of Act 1, Bate continues the already long opening scene into what is usually 2.1. This creates a difficulty because the edition as a whole adheres to the act-scene system. The standard 2.2 becomes Bate's 2.1, and 2.3 falls back to 2.2. That is to say, Bate makes his revised numbering the basis for his reference system, so that the usual 2.1.90, for example, becomes 1.1.589 in Bate's edition. But in the scene traditionally identified as 2.1 there is a double line-numbering system, with the standard system indicated in square brackets. The traditional act-scene numbering is similarly preserved in square brackets in the following scenes, where there is a rather messy double scene-marker, as '2.1 [2.2]'. The reorganization of Act 2 arises because the Folio act divisions have been imposed on an undivided text retrospectively. Bate's initial sense that F's act marking should be ignored has much to be said for it, but his relocated act division is a fictional convenience that corresponds to no reality. Quite simply, a continuous-performance text is ill at ease with act divisions, and preferably should not retain them. Arden 3 could have done worse than introduce through scene-numbers where appropriate, as have a number of editions in the Revels series of non-Shakespearian drama.

Bate marks off alleged 'false starts' in the Quarto text by enclosing them within braces. These are inserted at 1.1.35–8, 3.1.36, and 4.3.94–100. In each case Bate acknowledges possible defences of the full text as it stands in Q. In the second passage, where the Folio confirms a duplication in the Quarto by omitting the words 'And bootless unto them', Bate might have made a point about the Folio reading, but he does not discuss this crucial information. He might also have mentioned that the Folio omits the previous half-line, 'yet plead I must', words that he does not separate off in brackets. With false starts, as with act-scene divisions, Bate uses typography to allow him to sit a little uncomfortably on the fence. This accords imperfectly with his incisive and occasionally reckless willingness to emend in other situations. For instance where editors usually take Titus' 'thou has made it [the letter] like an humble suppliant' (4.3.116) as an address to Marcus, Bate takes the line to be spoken to the Clown and emends 'hast made' to graphically dissimilar 'must hold'. Q's 'hast made', though probably correct, vanishes, where lines that probably should have been deleted are printed conspicuously.

The most obvious example of typographical intervention is 3.2, the passage usually referred to as the 'fly scene', which is printed in F alone. The scene is usually regarded as Shakespearian, and there is ample evidence that it is an afterthought. Bate has the passage printed in a distinct typeface that shows its independence of Q, the usual control text. This simple and elegant expedient is complicated when the same typeface is used for Marcus' line at 1.1.403, 'Yes – and will nobly him remunerate' and the following '*Flourish*'. Bate claims that he marks the line out because he suspects that it is unShakespearian. Thus the treatment of 1.1.403 is keyed to a question of suspect authorship, whereas the identical treatment of the fly scene is keyed to a question of integrity of version in full acceptance that there is no real doubt as to authorship. Moreover, the highlighted '*Flourish*' further destabilizes the cogency of Bate's distinction. If this particular flourish is in some way suspect, inauthentic, or even merely additional, is not the same true of other stage directions, some of them flourishes, that Bate introduces from F without distinguishing them in any special way? Bate might have applied the special typeface to dialogue unique to F, and to the speech-prefixes and stage directions supporting that dialogue, without any initial reference to the question of authorship. The '*Flourish*' then might have been printed in the regular typeface because it is a routine elaboration of the following entry and does not appear as a consequence of the added line.

Notwithstanding its limitations, and though it will not please all readers, Bate's attempt to distinguish versions typographically has value. All editing is at some level inconsistent and improvisatory, and most editing is driven by pragmatic considerations as to what is of help to the reader. Bate draws important information about the text into the reader's more immediate view. Future editors should not, however, be lulled into thinking that his solution will be adequate where there are two versions of a play that vary in more radical and complex ways.

Bate's text has the immediate and considerable virtue of being, as far as I have noticed, accurate.[13] In the collation, emendations that originated as conjectures are not attributed to the first edition to accept the reading. At 3.1.282 we are told rightly that F substitutes 'things' for 'Armes' at the end of the line, but wrongly that it also deleted 'And' from the beginning of the line. Idiosyncratically, Bate puts location notes in the collation, recording the first editor to insert the information.

As one might expect of Bate, there is a fine attention in his commentary to resonances from classical sources that extends beyond the explication of Latin phrases, quotations, and paraphrase. When Titus is presented with the heads of his two sons, Bate amplifies Shakespeare's verbal focus on the implied stage direction in Marcus' 'Why art thou still?' (3.1.264) by noting, 'Ovid's Hecuba also has a moment of silence at the height of grief ...'. Thus Bate quietly establishes that here is a primary scene of suffering revisited and rewritten. In such cases the reader is given concrete, pertinent, and connotatively enriching information. The expressivity of the text is sometimes also brought out through intelligent and apt editorial stage directions. At 4.1.51–5 Titus says:

> Lavinia, wert thou thus surprised, sweet girl,
> Ravished and wronged as Philomela was,
> Forced in the ruthless, vast, and gloomy woods?
> See, see! Ay, such a place there is where we did
>   hunt ...

As with Titus' silence, the unguided reader may not notice any particular import in those unremarkable words 'See, see'. Bate prints them as a separate part-line preceded by the stage direction '[*Lavinia nods.*]' Here he has made constructive use of a 1620 German acting version which supplies the direction '[*She sighs deeply and nods her head*]'. This unusually early independent documentation of performance supports what might otherwise be seen as a vivid but arbitrary explication of the action. Bate is often helpful in this sort of way even where there is no such early testimony to the action. So for example in 5.3 Titus '[*Unveils Lavinia*]' so that she can be publicly recognized before he stabs her. He shares, however, the general and squeamish reluctance of editors to specify the critical information in the same scene that Tamora eats the pie. This must count as the great Repressed amongst editorial stage directions. Titus' retrospective assertion that the mother has eaten, and 'daintily' indeed, comes as a disconcerting surprise, especially in an edition such as Bate's that is usually so informative.

OTHER EDITIONS

The Arden 3s have been given detailed treatment as new arrivals, but the Oxford and Cambridge Shakespeares have had an active year too. The latter series is represented by another *Titus Andronicus*, edited by Alan

---

13 One might quibble at 'Hallo' for Q's 'Hollo' at 1.1.524; at 2.2.144 'suckst' should have an apostrophe; at 5.3.193 the disyllabic value of 'closed' is not noted (which, as a datum of Q1, is a textual matter even if Arden 3 does subordinate it to the commentary).

Hughes. In establishing his text, Hughes is conservative both in emendation and modernization. He prints 'shipwrack' (shipwreck), 'scrowl' (scrawl), 'stanch' (staunch), 'sounded' (swoonèd), all of which readily modernize. He retains 'Lavicious' (2.3.110), 'satisfice' (2.3.180) and 'successantly' (4.4.112), all of which look very much like misprints or misreadings. The text has, however, a handful of serious errors. In the opening direction for 2.2 the words 'making a noise' have inexplicably disappeared. At 4.1.77 'you' should read 'ye'. At 4.2.155 'to' has been omitted after 'like'. At 5.2.29 'thine' is an error for 'thy'. At 5.3.150 'all' is omitted after 'Stand'. The collation too has moments of weakness.[14]

Like other editors, Hughes makes use of the stage directions in F, which are taken to derive from a theatrical manuscript consulted in the printing-house. F, for example, is the source for a number of music directions that are regularly imported into the edited text. In several places Hughes goes further. He favours formulaic 'Flourish' over the more specific and presumably authorial wording of the control text, 'sound trumpets', a decision that touches on a number of editorial dilemmas and calls for careful justification. Hughes's receptiveness to Folio stage directions certainly goes too far at 5.2.165, where F's 'Exeunt' is incorporated, without brackets (in contrast with an absolutely certain and necessary Folio amplification upon Q at 3.2.286 which is printed in square brackets). In Q and F alike, two of the characters involved in F's exeunt have their throats cut on stage during Titus' ensuing speech; they can scarcely have left beforehand. A little later, after 5.3.15 and 25, there are two misconceived attempts to combine Quarto and Folio directions. In the second case F interestingly replaces trumpets with hoboyes. As Andrew Gurr has noted, the private theatres regularly preferred woodwind to brass.[15] This is therefore a variant that is nicely consistent with F's provision of act divisions in suggesting a late revival for the indoor Blackfriars theatre, where act intervals would be observed and trumpets might be deafening.

Hughes's 'Hoboyes. A table brought in. Trumpets sounding ...' accords with neither Q nor F, and is most implausible.

Hughes's discussion of the origins of the play, hedged in as it is with many an 'if' and 'but', lacks the breezy confidence of Bate. Hughes thinks Shakespeare may have written a draft of the play before coming to London. This accounts for the stylistically crude writing that he identifies most particularly in Act 1, but Hughes goes on to recognize a theatrically assured technique in that same section of the play. Quite apart from the wholly hypothetical nature of the idea, it is difficult to see how Shakespeare would have acquired this technical proficiency before immersion in the London theatre. Further difficulties come into view over the eighteenth-century prose History of Titus Andronicus. Hughes sees it as originating in a lost chapbook of 1592 or earlier, claiming that the first item in John Danter's entry in the Stationers' Register of 'a booke intituled a Noble Roman Historye of Tytus Andronicus' and 'the ballad thereof' is for the chapbook, not the play. He cites the wording of the entry, though 'Roman Historye' is not notably closer to 'History', or the History's half-title 'Tragical History', than the play-quarto's 'Romaine Tragedie'. Undeterred by this tenuous case (for there is otherwise no evidence to link the 'History' with Danter or even with the sixteenth century), Hughes points out that there would have been very little time between Henslowe's 'ne' production of 'titus & ondronicus' at the Rose on 23 January 1594 and the Stationers' Register entry on 6 February:[16] too little time, he supposes, for a prose history

---

14 For instance it records a non-existent variant at 1.1.69.3 SD, at 5.1.0 SD.1 misrecords Quarto 'Drum s' as 'drums', misattributes the reading 'swart' at 2.4.72.

15 The Shakespearean Stage, 1574–1642, 3rd edition (1992), p. 176.

16 Hughes does not note, as Bate does (p. 70), that Henslowe's date of 23 January is probably an error. As Titus was the fourth play of the week, it would have been performed on Thursday 24 January.

THE YEAR'S CONTRIBUTIONS TO SHAKESPEARE STUDIES

deriving from Shakespeare's play and a ballad deriving from the prose account to have been written and handed over to Danter. Hughes is wrong to force a choice between this fictional scenario and the preferred alternative, an earlier manuscript or lost edition of the *History* such as might have acted as the play's source. MacD. P. Jackson's arguments for seeing the chapbook as, at the earliest, a late seventeenth-century production seem to me much more persuasive,[17] but Hughes does not cite them.

Hughes presents a full and relatively detailed account of the play's fortunes on the stage, a task simplified by the nineteenth century's distaste for it. As he moves to the twentieth century he relinquishes the chronological method and sets up a more thematically organized dialogue between critical viewpoints and the play's fortunes on the stage. It is described as 'the work of a brilliant stage craftsman, exploring the resources of his trade: the visual potentialities of human form and movement, the spatial dynamics and mechanical resources of the playhouse'. Hughes is aware that this does not explain the play's strange juxtapositions of butchery and precious language. He emphasizes Peter Brook's production of 1955 as crucial for revealing *Titus* as an effective work of tragedy, a case of theatrical practice leading the way towards critical reappraisal. He himself remains uneasy with the play on the page, but confident that performance is unusually significant towards making aesthetic and emotional sense of it.

w>Roger Warren and Stanley Wells have collaborated to prepare a pleasant and enriching edition of *Twelfth Night* for the Oxford series that achieves considerable homogeneity of editorial purpose. The text is based on the one Wells prepared for the Oxford *Complete Works*. It is accurate, though at 2.1.38 a Folio exit direction has presumably been taken to be contentious and has been printed in brackets with no explanation, as in the parent edition. In Warren and Wells's collation I would have liked to see record of some modernizations

where *OED* has two headwords, such as 'coroner' (1.5.128; F 'Crowner'), 'swathes' (2.3.138; F 'swarths'), 'all ready' (3.1.89; F 'already'), and 'haply' (4.2.52; F 'happily'). There are a few minor unrecorded lineation changes,[18] though in some cases it is difficult to be sure whether the Folio setting indicates verse or prose.

The introduction is constantly alert to nuances of language and tone. Warren and Wells are ever responsive to the play's theatrical potential and informative about its realizations on the stage. Yet they have avoided a dutiful long march from the Globe (and in this case the Middle Temple) to the latest production at the RSC, giving instead a brief and sharply etched formal stage history. Even as the introduction moves through sections on the play's title, the setting in Illyria, the source, and the play's position within Shakespeare's writing of comedy, there is a strong sense that the purpose is always to illuminate our response to the play, and details of productions enliven the discussion at every turn. And this is equally or more true of the central part of the introduction that addresses the dramatic action itself. By avoiding systematic documentation, Wells and Warren are able to offer a series of vivid clarifications and edifications that implicitly look forward to future real and imaginary productions by their book's readers. It is an approach that is especially effective for this play.

The editors are particularly successful in addressing what they call 'the emotional realities of the characters' (p. 60), a task they perform with critical rigour and an avoidance of sentimentality. They give careful consideration to the way those emotional realities find their way

---

[17] '*Titus Andronicus*: Play, Ballad, and Prose History', in *Notes and Queries*, 234 (1989), 315–17.
[18] For instance at 3.4.45–6 (verse-line), 3.4.84–5 (verse: sir/), 3.4.165–6 (verse: cannot/) 4.2.50–1 (verse?), 4.2.99–100 (verse), 4.2.119–20 (verse), 5.1.9 (verse), 5.1.28–9 (verse), 5.1.30–1 (verse??), 5.1.2284–5 (verse), 5.1.197 (prose).

319

through the play's poetic artifice. It must be admitted that Warren and Wells's reliance on the comments and actions of actors and directors could be seen as overemphasizing the psychologically realist perspectives on character such as are assumed in the methods of Stanislavski. In their discussion of Viola's 'willow-cabin' speech the editors focus on what Olivia hears: they quote Harold Jenkins's astute observation that she 'starts to listen'. But this doesn't explain why the speech can be moving to us when it is based on hyperbolic conventions and is, theoretically, empty of sincere emotional content on Viola's part. The question 'Who is speaking?' is here an urgent enigma. If the enigma is beyond untangling, it might say something about the play's emotional texture whilst opening onto more indeterminate notions of self.

A third collaborator, James Walker, has written an Appendix that provides settings for all of this unusually tuneful play's music. Sometimes actual Elizabethan or Jacobean settings can be reproduced, in other cases Walker proceeds by analogy, as when he supplies the play's need for opening music with a pavan by Orlando Gibbons that contain a double 'dying fall', or by composing an original pastiche score of his own. This pragmatic approach ensures that the performer will never be without a score when one is needed.

The introduction to Peter Holland's Oxford edition of *A Midsummer Night's Dream* opens with a fascinating and learned section on dreams. This might well become a first port of call for those who need a summary account of Renaissance dream-lore, performing something of the same function in this respect as John Kerrigan's New Penguin edition of the Sonnets does on the subject of time. The play itself sometimes seems temporarily forgotten, though the idea of dreaming is so central to the *Dream* and the critical practices of interpreting the play that it is perhaps as well to set the essential features of medieval, Renaissance and even

modern dream-theory in place from the beginning.

The rest of the introduction is largely organized around dramatic roles: there are sections on '*Robin*', '*Theseus and Hippolyta*', '*The Lovers*', and so on. Holland responds positively to recent criticism that has stressed questions of gender, power, and mythology, though he keeps the play firmly in view and is keen that it should not be falsified. He writes (p. 73): 'What is so remarkable about Titania's night with Bottom is not a subdued, suppressed sexual bestiality that has only been properly uncovered in the twentieth century but rather the innocence which transforms something that might so easily have been full of animal sexuality into something touchingly naïve.' This formulation leaves the reader pondering on a rather fine distinction between something suppressed and something that might have been. Actually though, what Holland objects to is the practice of turning the scene into a 'phallic celebration' that in some productions is neither subdued nor suppressed. The objection is anti-permissive in more than one way. Though I can concur with Holland's sense of the text, I am not sure that an editor should disallow a vision that finds a different theatrical emphasis and a wilder energy.

Holland's commentary is excellent on matters of staging and matters theatrical. His text is accurate on the whole, though I noted a spurious article 'a' before 'darkness' at 5.1.377. Holland accepts where possible F's alterations and elaborations of Q's stage directions, even where, as with Robin Goodfellow's entry at 3.1.49.1 instead of 3.1.71.1, he retains a 'nagging suspicion' that F is wrong. There are few editions that will discuss difficulties and possibilities of staging in such detail as does Holland's, or with such an informed sureness of touch. On language too the commentary is powerful and perceptive, as when Holland notes that the 'observed immediacy' of the gossip's 'dewlap' at 2.1.50 is later metamorphosed into an Ovidean image when Theseus' hounds are described as 'dewlapped like Thessalanian bulls' (4.1.121).

There are moments when an extra editorial touch might have reassured the reader, as some examples from a fifty-line passage will suggest. In what sense is the Amazon 'bouncing' (2.1.70)? Are 'floods' (2.1.103) tides or the results of excessive rainfall? If the latter, as is suggested by 'washes all the air', what control is their 'governess' the moon thought to have over them? Is there an Edenic hint in 'We are their parents and original' (2.1.117)? In cases such as these only the sophisticated reader will be grateful to be left pondering.

Holland confines his excerpts of source material to brief quotations in his introduction, but valuably rounds off the edition with an appendix headed 'Shakespeare's Revision of Act 5'. This deals first with the crucial new material including the lines on imagination that was evidently added in the Q1 copy manuscript, and then with variants between Q1 and F. Q1's additions are shown in parallel texts, modernized and edited, of 'Q1 Lined as Printed' and the 'Hypothesized Original Version'. A purist might prefer these texts to be less heavily mediated, but the advantage of Holland's presentation is that it cuts through to the essential feature of an important textual argument.

For this year's review I have at hand one new title in the 'Shakespearean Originals' series of reprints of first editions, Graham Holderness and Bryan Loughrey's edition of *The Chronicle History of Henry the fift*. Their evaluation of the text's worth contrasts startlingly with Craik's: the Quarto 'can be addressed in its own right as a vigorous and powerful instance of Elizabethan comic-historical drama' (p. 13). This is indeed a sound and sufficient basis in itself for presenting the text, but they go on to assert that the hypotheses of memorial reconstruction and adaptation have 'far less claim on our attention than the authority of a historical document' such as the Quarto (p. 15). By 'historical' the editors presumably mean 'existing in the present'. The comparison of 'hypotheses' with the unqualified and undefined 'authority' of the Quarto effects a puzzling correlation. And one begins to wonder whether the point is that any 'historical' document has authority as a document or that this particular one has authority because it houses 'an extremely good play' (p. 13). The attacks on critics who have identified memorial error and adaptation in the text suggest the latter, in that arguing against such alleged 'corruption' becomes the corollary of arguing for the virtues of the script. Holderness and Loughrey do not dismantle the often-despised dichotomy of 'good' and 'bad' texts; they vary it. Surely, however, a sub-Shakespearian reconstruction might, on its own terms, prove an effective piece of theatre, in which case memorial transmission and theatrical adaptation would not of necessity preclude a 'good' play. To assume otherwise would take the series title 'Shakespearean Originals' too seriously, and ultimately would embrace the same position as the most eager vilifiers of this 'bad' quarto.

In their edition the play is headed with a half-title that erroneously substitutes a rearranged text of the title-page for the Quarto's actual half-title. The text that follows is inaccurate. On pp. 67–75 alone I noted a couple of errors per page.[19] A spectacular carelessness of this edition is that an appendix of 'Photographic facsimile pages' provides facsimiles not of the Quarto at all, but of the New Shakspere Society reprint of 1875. Here the commitment to the authority of the document collapses in tatters.

FOLIOS AND EARLY EDITIONS

Anthony James West's 'Provisional New Census of the Shakespeare First Folio' is the first

---

19 'reckoning' for 'rekconing', 'blood.' for 'blood,', 'thing,' for 'things', 'today' for 'to day', 'crasing' for 'crasing,', 'mortailitie' for 'mortalitie', 'slovendry' for 'flovendry', 'die' for 'dei', 'appelles' for 'apelles', *Fer* for 'Fer', 'il' for 'ill', 'plaines' for 'plaines,', *Suffoke* for *Suffolke*, 'Whereupon' for 'Wherupon', '*Captain*' for 'Captain', '*the*' for 'the', '*of*' for 'of', 'displeasures.' for 'displeasures,', and 'not' for 'no'. Some of these readings correct misprints, but the editors claim not to emend the text.

such systematic listing of locatable and reported copies of the Folio since Sidney Lee's of 1902. West establishes a new but provisional numbering system based on location: 'USA 26', 'Germany 3', and so on; the numbering within each nation-group is based on alphabetical order of place, with the chauvinistic exception that London comes before Arundel and Birmingham. Listed copies have either been seen by West himself or confirmed as present by a librarian or reliable third party. Also provided are a concordance of Lee numbers and West's numbers, notes on copies recorded by Lee but not now found, and copies untraced in Lee and still untraced. West plans eventually to replace his location-plus-number identifier with a through-number. There may be good reasons for this, but the present system is both more immediately informative and more sharply distinguished from Lee's numbering. Further, it seems a pity to publish an identifying system that will shortly be rendered inoperative.

Simon Jarvis's *Scholars and Gentlemen* has the advantage over other recent studies of eighteenth-century editing that it surveys editions from Alexander Pope to Samuel Johnson rather than focusing on the contribution of a single editor. This is in accordance with his view that there is no single exemplary editor who, as Peter Seary suggests of Lewis Theobald,[20] heroically anticipated methodologies ahead of his time or, as Margreta de Grazia suggests of Edmond Malone, embodies the epistemological break that initiates the Enlightenment.[21] Jarvis's emphasis is on the emerging credibility of scholarly labour itself. He examines in detail what editors did and what they said they were doing, as gradually, unevenly, and still by Malone's edition incompletely, the *textus receptus* lost its grip as editorial copy.

The narrative is perhaps more Whiggish than Jarvis would care to admit. He identifies the 'professed Pedant' who pursues minute scholarly criticism and enjoys low social prestige, in contrast with the more leisurely 'Gentleman of Letters' who disdains such drudgery (p. 12),

whilst recognizing that individual editors cannot be partitioned into one category or the other. It would, he suggests, be even more meaningless to label each editor as a Whig or Tory of his field. The subtlety of Jarvis's study lies in his identification of conflicting tendencies in all the major editors he considers. Thus Pope's self-declared but only theoretical 'religious abhorrence of all Innovation' should lead to a conservative treatment of his copy, Nicholas Rowe's 1714 edition, but is compromised by his actual recourse to early quarto readings and, contrastingly, to an editorial approach that sometimes 'approaches the condition of adaptation' (p. 61). At face value, Pope's procedures may seem illogical, but Jarvis relates them to his position as on the one hand anti-pedantic gentleman of letters and on the other hand paid professional editor. Jarvis finds Theobald less systematic in his bibliographical methods than Seary proposes, and locates a conflict in his principles: Theobald appreciated the need to preserve feature of Shakespeare's language that had come to seem incorrect or barbarous, yet desired that textual criticism should establish models for the further improvement of the national language. William Warburton attempted to unite 'broad taste with minute learning' (p. 108), but found himself caught in a chicken-and-egg dilemma that 'The provision of a canon of correct texts of good authors is intended to obviate disagreement about the correctness or otherwise of particular expressions, but such a canon, and the details of its texts, are themselves determined by those who wish to refer to such authorities in case of dispute' (p. 127). It was Johnson, of course, who took on the challenge of lexicography before attempting to edit Shakespeare. His philological and editorial labour expresses 'tensions between Johnson's unprecedentedly blunt refusals to dissimulate the professional character of his work,

---

[20] *Lewis Theobald and the Editing of Shakespeare* (1990).
[21] *Shakespeare Verbatim: The Reproduction of Authenticity and the 1790 Apparatus* (1991).

on the one hand, and the claims to a public authoritativeness which persist ... both in the *Dictionary* and in the edition of Shakespeare' (p. 181).

Jarvis's own tendency towards minute criticism can detract from the overall argument. There is much reference to 'tensions between on the one hand ...' as though these were socially and politically significant contradictions. But the representations of Jarvis's title are usually editors' self-representations, or at least emanate from within the circle of textual scholars. Despite a useful first chapter on 'The Culture of Scholarship in Early Eighteenth-Century England', the larger cultural and socio-political spaces are usually filled only sketchily. Detail prevails most strikingly over coherence in an Appendix called 'Collations', which features a table I just cannot understand. Nevertheless, Jarvis's book as a whole shows clearly how the social position of scholarly labour was related to the establishment of a national language and culture. One is made aware that to undertake to edit was not to engage in a self-evident practice but to seek out an unstable position within evolving discourses surrounding the function of scholarship.

AUTHORSHIP

The Oxford Shakespeare *Complete Works* claims that *1 Henry VI* is 'By William Shakespeare and Others'.[22] Gary Taylor's 'Shakespeare and Others' provides us, at last, with the basis for that authorship claim. Taylor adroitly points out that the leading case for Shakespeare's authorship of the whole depends on a textual hypothesis that has been decisively rejected by recent critics. Those who dismiss Andrew Cairncross's heavily reconstitutive emendations have not acknowledged that in doing so they fatally injure his vindication of the play's consistently Shakespearian textual quality. Acceptance of Shakespeare's sole authorship is left hanging on two vulnerable threads: the false assumptions that the Folio editors would not have included a collaborative play and that Shakespeare would not have collaborated in the first place. *All is True* (*Henry VIII*), and *Timon of Athens* are both widely recognized as Folio texts of joint authorship, and Shakespeare evidently collaborated further in *Pericles*, *Two Noble Kinsmen*, *Sir Thomas More*, and *Cardenio*. As Taylor notes, Heminges and Condell might not have known whether a play was entirely by Shakespeare or not if it had been written before they knew Shakespeare and a full thirty years before it was set for the Folio. Any doubts might have been resolved in favour of inclusion because it allowed them to construct an impressive trilogy of Henry VI plays.

Taylor draws together a wide variety of criteria by which to establish split authorship, including the spellings 'O/Oh', the inconsistent ranking of Winchester as cardinal and bishop, the spelling of 'pucelle', the presence of scene division, the use of 'here' in stage directions, the prevalence of the verbal inflections 'eth' and syllabic '-ed', the contraction 'ne'er', the frequency of brackets, the preference for 'ye', 'among', and 'betwixt' as against 'you', 'amongst', and 'between', the proportion of verse-lines with feminine endings, the position of caesuras, the frequency of compounded adjectives, and the choice between 'Henry' and 'Harry'. Most of these are binary choices, but clusters of preferences establish, with varying degrees of certainty, the presence of four hands. Taylor makes a strong case for contributions from Shakespeare, who wrote 2.4 and 4.2–4.7.32, and Thomas Nashe, who wrote Act 1; the other hands remain unidentified. The authorial characteristics of Shakespeare's collaborators are given as follows (p. 168):

z [Nashe] (act 1): O, Puzel, -ed, -eth, ne'er, no brackets, *here* [in stage directions]
y (act 3, most of act 5): Oh, Pucelle, Burgonie, scene divisions, ye
w (II.i–II.iii. II.v, IV.i): O/Oh, Puzell, *Joane.*, Burgundie

---

[22] See also *Textual Companion*, pp. 112–13.

JOHN JOWETT

'w' is most similar in profile to Shakespeare, but can be differentiated from him as follows:

> w (II.i–II.iii. II.v, IV.i): O/Oh, brackets frequent, infrequent feminine endings, caesura after fifth syllable, trisyllabic Orleans, Henry
>
> Shakespeare (II.iv, IV.ii–IV.vii.32): O, brackets rare, frequent feminine endings, caesura after sixth syllable, frequent compound adjectives, disyllabic Orleans, Harry

It is above all the idiosyncratic 'here' in stage directions, found with a similar frequency in *Summer's Last Will and Testament*, that singles out 'z' as Nashe. The identification of Nashe is properly grounded in mechanical and quantifiable traits, but Taylor ices his cake by noting that R. B. McKerrow himself, who was sceptical of 'disintegrationist' theories and 'probably knew Nashe's work better than any scholar in this century' (p. 177), accepted on stylistic grounds that Nashe was the most likely dramatist to have shared with Shakespeare in the play.

Taylor's work invites further investigation into the possible identities of 'w' and 'Y'. He intriguingly suggests that the latter might be the author of *Locrine* and perhaps parts of *Edward III*. Another line for further enquiry lies in the possible connection between Shakespeare's apparent collaboration with three other dramatists in about 1592 and the attack on Shakespeare as a thief of others' work in *Greene's Groatsworth of Wit*, published the same year. In the meantime Taylor has given us plenty to digest in his strongly argued hypothesis that a play in the Shakespeare canon is actually for the most part by others.

A steady and clear account of the procedures that go into stylometrics appears in Thomas B. Horton's 'Distinguishing Shakespeare from Fletcher through Function Words'. Horton is well aware of the objections that have been raised against stylometric studies, and he explicates procedures that are designed to avoid the obvious pitfalls. He works from original-spelling electronic texts of Shakespeare's and Fletcher's plays, rejecting multiple-text plays, and regularizing only the forms he is testing. What is quietly impressive about the article is its avoidance of statistical jargon, and Horton avoids too the unlikely claims of probability that assault the common sense in some earlier studies. He is interested in seeing how his findings square with those derived from other methods. Stylometry according to Horton is a method that has no intrinsic right to call other studies and common sense alike in doubt. Though an effective instrument, it is itself fallible.

Horton assesses his own stylometric investigation into Shakespeare's and Fletcher's shares in *Henry VIII* and *Two Noble Kinsmen* against the findings of G. R. Proudfoot and Cyrus Hoy.[23] He sets aside scenes of less than 500 words as too short to be reliably tested. Other scenes are described as 'like' or 'very like' Shakespeare or Fletcher, or are found to be of uncertain similarity. His findings disagree with Proudfoot and Hoy over 2.3 ('like Sh') and 4.3 ('very like Sh') in *Two Noble Kinsmen*. He admits a number of explanations for 2.3, including a third hand, but interprets his own findings as much more convincing than the rather meagre linguistic evidence Hoy found in 4.3. The results for *Henry VIII* are less clear in that much more of the play proves indeterminable. As against seven scenes of agreement with Hoy there are four scenes of disagreement: 1.3 ('like Sh'), 4.1 ('very like Sh', where Hoy finds Fletcher as well), 4.2 ('like Sh'), and 5.4 ('very like Sh'). Horton notes that his findings confirm Shakespeare's responsibility for the scenes most widely thought to be his, and support the suggestions of R. A. Foakes,[24] Hoy, and others that in scenes where the evidence conflicts Fletcher revised Shakespeare's work. The revision theory works well for 2.1–2 and the first section of 3.2, and can be extended

---

[23] In Proudfoot's Regents Renaissance Drama edition of *Two Noble Kinsmen* (1970), and Hoy's 'The Shares of Fletcher and his Collaborators in the Beaumont and Fletcher Canon (VII)', in *Studies in Bibliography*, 15 (1962), 71–90.

[24] In his Arden 2 edition of *Henry VIII* (1957).

to 1.3 and 5.4. More controversially, Horton claims that Fletcher probably had little or nothing to do with Act 4. He concludes that 'scholars should re-evaluate the relation between the copy text of *Henry VIII* and the various internal evidence that it contains' (p. 334).

SPELLING AND PUNCTUATION

Even Fredson Bowers, that most committed of old-spelling editors, was ready to acknowledge that the punctuation in early printed texts would usually bear limited resemblance to that in the original printer's copy manuscript. Few in recent years have spoken of the expressivity of punctuation in the Shakespeare quartos and Folio. Anthony Graham-White's *Punctuation and Its Dramatic Value in Shakespearean Drama* does so. The strength of his book is that it is judiciously aware of the various factors that influence the pointing of a given text. It is helpful too that Graham-White discusses punctuation from the point of view of its effect rather than authorial intention, though as the emphasis is on *dramatic* effect the compositor question will not go away, and indeed intentionality too is not quite banished.

What emerges is a richly informative study of punctuation in early modern theory and practice, and specifically in dramatic manuscripts and the printed texts of plays. Graham-White builds his study on the basis of a number of useful distinctions. As other commentators have noted, though the period saw rapid developments towards more logical and standardized systems of pointing, punctuation in Shakespeare's day remained based primarily on the rhythms of spoken speech rather than the grammatical logic of sentence structure. Graham-White shows how the use and value of particular punctuation marks were at variance with modern practice, and draws attention to a number of distinctive forms that have no modern equivalent.

Graham-White looks particularly closely at the punctuation of *Gammer Gurton's Needle*, Quarto *Richard II*, and plays by Marston and Jonson. Despite the book's concern with 'Shakespearean' drama, the Shakespeare example is perhaps the least convincing in its own right, even though the choice of text is influenced by its reputation for cleanness and rhetorically sensitive pointing. Graham-White notes a colon at the end of one of Bullingbroke's speeches:

> *Richard.* Set on towards London, Cosen is it so?
> *Bullingbroke.* Yea my good Lord:
> *Richard.* Then I must not say no.   (sig. G2v)

He comments, 'one might infer from the colon that Bullingbroke, with ironic courtesy, invites him [Richard] to have the last word'. It is a subtle and interesting observation, even if the open-ended 'might' invites a strong riposte that one might well find it prudent to avoid such inferences. How does one weight the possibility of manuscript show-through against the possibilities of foul case or compositorial whim? Despite his awareness as a matter of principle that compositors could overwhelmingly influence the punctuation of the text, Graham-White does not attempt to evaluate the extent to which Simmes's compositors could be responsible for traits of punctuations. Neither of those who worked on *Richard II* seems to have been particularly faithful to copy even when dealing with substantives, and Simmes's Compositor A, who set most of the play including the passage quoted, can be observed making changes to punctuation at will even when setting from printed copy.[25] Graham-White himself cites the example of the 1622 edition of *A Fair Quarrel* where two different compositors accidentally set the same four pages from printed copy. The pages show that a considerable amount of variation could be introduced, even when the copy had already been standar-

---

[25] See W. C. Ferguson, 'The Compositors of *Henry IV Part 2, Much Ado about Nothing, The Shoemakers' Holiday*, and *The First Part of the Contention*', in *Studies in Bibliography*, 13 (1960), 19–29, p. 25.

dized to the requirements of print. When Graham-White writes of the need for 'a meaningful and intended pattern of usage' in a play (p. 82), he is clearly not thinking of compositors as the bearers of that intention. Recognition of the rhetorical structure of early modern pointing, though valuable in itself, cannot break down the barrier between performance-oriented manuscript and reader-oriented book.

Nevertheless, there is much in this book that will be salutary to the old-spelling editor, who has a special responsibility to retain punctuation that is not clearly erroneous. It will also set challenges to the modern-spelling editor, whose pointing works on different principles entirely. Grahham-White succeeds at the polemical level in pleading for greater respect towards the period's non-grammatical punctuation.

The case for old spelling editions is always stronger for non-dramatic poetry than for plays, which helps Katherine Duncan-Jones make a comparable plea for the original spellings of the Sonnets in 'Filling the Unforgiving Minute: Modernizing SHAKE-SPEARES SONNETS (1609)'. Developing objections to modernizing outlined, for example, by Philip Gaskell,[26] she concentrates on forms that might be modernized in more than one way. 'Fild', for example, might be realized as 'filed' or 'filled'. But in the examples Duncan-Jones cites there tends to be a clear primary sense, and the secondary sense might be disputed:

> Who will beleeue my verse in time to come
> If it were fild with your most high deserts?

> When houres haue dreind his blood and fild his
>   brow
> With lines and wrincles

As regards the latter, *OED* does not support Duncan-Jones's suggestion that *filed* might apply here in the sense 'incised with a filing instrument', for the action of filing is to make smooth, not to etch or score. Her second case-study is the unusual form 'mynuit', which she takes to be a distinctive Shakespeare spelling. The suggestion is that

there is a possible pun between the usual modernization *minute* and the French *minuit*, for 'midnight', and the resonances of the midnight hour are affirmed with reference to *Doctor Faustus* and Donne's nocturnal on St Lucy's Day. Duncan-Jones's alertness as editor allows her to uncover new riches. Yet she properly admits a sense of exploration and conjecture. The question therefore arises: if she, as editor, can open up only tentative and debatable new readings by attending to old spellings, what can reliably be produced by a reader less well versed in Shakespeare's language and the poetics of the period, less alert to the history of language, less well trained in perceiving the relevance of printing-house practices? Duncan-Jones's readings demonstrate the need for editorial commentary, but that commentary might be applied either to the printed form 'fild' or 'filled', 'mynuit' or 'minute'. Still, there is some force in her ingenious concluding remark: 'A modernized text, in which the unforgiving "minute" has been either "filed" or "filled", but not both, prohibits many such richly complex associations.'

LATE INNOVATIONS

A number of studies challenge what can be rather too easily packaged as 'old' narratives about composition and early performance, and ring in 'new' alternatives. Whether 'new' implies 'better' or, more relativistically, 'more appropriate for us to accept', the old/new dichotomy has the potential to be as coercive as, to cite an example from an 'old' narrative, Alfred W. Pollard's distinction between good and bad quartos. It is of even less categorical value.

Roslyn L. Knutson's reconsideration of the 'War of the Theatres' uses this rhetoric. Its substance as textual criticism and theatrical history lies in Knutson's review of the various

---

[26] In *From Writer to Reader* (1978), pp. 7–8.

accounts in *Hamlet* Q1, Q2, and F of the players' arrival at out-of-town Elsinore. Q2 and F share Rosencrantz's explanation that 'their inhibition, comes by the meanes of the late innouasion' and his comment that they are not held in the same estimation as they were when Hamlet was in the city. F goes on to add the passage on 'an ayrie of Children, little Yases, that crye out on the top of question'. Q1's equivalent passage for all this is:

> *Gil.* No my Lord, their reputation holds as it was
>   wont.
> *Ham.* How then?
> *Gil.* Yfaith my Lord, noueltie carries it away,
> For the principall publike audience that
> Came to them, are turned to priuate playes,
> And to the humour of children.

Q1 thus shares a reference to 'children' actors with F but not Q2. Conventional wisdom would have it that in this respect Q1 shows affinities with F that place the Q1 version later than the copy for Q2. Knutson proposes instead that Q1 gives the first version of the passage. She dates it at 1599–1600, and takes it to refer to the reopening of the St Paul's playhouse. The Q2 script belongs to 'after May 1603' (p. 13). Knutson sees the Q2 lines as a replacement for the Q1 passage, which had lost its topicality. The 'inhibition' is the closure of the theatres as a consequence of the 1603 plague, and the 'innouasion' is not the Essex rebellion of 1601, as often thought, but the crowning of the new monarch. As for the Folio passage, Knutson points out that the boy players were not performing 'on the top of question', that is, with maximum contention, around 1600. That came later, between 1604 and 1608, with the Children of Blackfriars. The Folio is therefore seen as giving a third topical gloss relating to those years, in which the 'children' make a textual come-back.

This account presents a number of difficulties. Q2's wording 'comes by the meanes of' suggests that the innovation actually caused the inhibition on acting. There was no such

causality between the coronation and the closing of the theatres; it would be especially strange for Shakespeare to suggest such a consequence just after his company had received the royal livery; and indeed few would have believed him as the theatres were closed *before* the accession of James. It is highly unlikely that the Q1 text can in fact antecede the Q2 text, for, quite apart from its relative proximity to F in the passage under discussion, its structural features are persistently closer to F. Furthermore, the postulate that Q2 stems from a 1603 production would have to dispose of other indications of earlier authorship.

Barbara Freedman is another critic who believes that allusion studies have been hampered by old narratives. Her rather grand title 'Shakespearean Chronology, Ideological Complicity, and Floating Texts: Something is Rotten in Windsor' heads an article that seeks to unfix *The Merry Wives of Windsor* of its occasionalist anchor – though she is by no means the first critic to do so. Freedman makes a number of points against the assumption that the play was written for performance at Lord Hunsdon's Garter election in 1597. She claims that the case for any other Shakespeare play having been written to mark a special event lacks serious credibility, making *Merry Wives* potentially a unique case. Perhaps so, though debate will certainly continue over the possibility that plays such as *The Tempest* were written for a specific place and time. Freedman is right to point out that there is no known example of topical satire or of any specific full-length play performed at a Garter ceremony. Nor do we know of Lord Hunsdon or anyone else commissioning a play for Queen Elizabeth; nor is *Merry Wives* entirely credible as a compliment to her.

Freedman recognizes that the strong point of Leslie Hotson's argument in *Shakespeare versus Shallow* (1931) for a Garter occasion lies in the link he set in place between the patron of the Chamberlain's Men and Frederick, Count of Mömplegard, both of whom were elected to the Order of the Garter in 1597. If, Freedman surmises, it is questionable whether the play can credibly be seen as a work commissioned by Lord Hunsdon for the Garter feast, the play's allusions to Mömplegard become more free-floating. Freedman finds echoes of the Mömplegard affair as it developed over a number of years; some are more convincing than others. She also puts forward Hans Jacob Breuning von Buchenbach as in some respects a better object of allusion than Mömplegard, and recognizes too a glance at Monsieur de Chastes, who stole post-horses in September 1596 in order to return from England to attend a celebration of Henri IV's election to the Garter in France. Thus she proposes a composite satire of foreigners involved with Garter elections over a sustained period of time.

A discussion of date will be most convincing as an argument against an occasionalist dating if it produces a coherent alternative. It is a curious feature of Freedman's argument that although many of her findings seem to indicate, where they discriminate, a pre-1597 date for the play's composition, she finally comes into agreement with Gary Taylor's suggestion of early 1598.[27] Taylor's determinate date, and implied determinate place of first production (the Globe theatre), are used puzzlingly to sustain a conclusion as to the play's 'topical indeterminacy'. Inexactitude in the perceived date of allusions and multiplicity of satirical referent are put into a loose and dubiously tenable constellation with the play's perceived popularism and its existence in two versions, all children of Indeterminacy as, ironically, an organizing abstraction.

The inception of Merry Wives is also considered in Giorgio Melchiori's Shakespeare's Garter Plays. In the first half of the book, however, Melchiori draws together a number of theories that he has presented elsewhere, particularly in his edition of 2 Henry IV, on the writing and supposed revision of the Henry IV plays.[28] A number of critics have suspected, plausibly enough, that when Shakespeare began to write Part 1 he had no plans for a sequel, and that the material at his disposal was subsequently redis-tributed so as to allow the banishment of Falstaff to be deferred from the end of Part 1 to the end of Part 2. Melchiori takes this hypothesis further by claiming that Shakespeare originally wrote and completed the one-part play ending with the banishment, which he refers to as the ur-Henry IV. He argues the point in extraordinary detail, even offering a scene-by-scene synopsis of the lost original.

Though Melchiori closely probes unconformities in Part 2 such as the duplication in name between Corporal Bardolph and Lord Bardolph, the textual tangle over the ghost-character Umfrevile, the stage direction giving Bardolph's original designation as Sir John Russell, the speech-prefix for Oldcastle, he never quite demonstrates that any of them is resolved with discernible advantage by supposing it was caused through the expansion of an ur-Henry IV. Let me take one instance, the Oldcastle prefix 'Old.' at 1.2.122. Melchiori notes that in the scene in question speech-prefixes stipulate 'John' or 'Sir John' up to 1.2.94, 'Falstaff' from there to l. 165, and then 'John' again. The inference made from the occurrence of 'Old.' amidst the 'Falstaff' prefixes is that the latter have been systematically altered from 'Oldcastle' and belong to a section of the scene that appeared in the ur-Henry IV. Unfortunately, however, there simply is not an identifiable mid-scene section that separates off from the rest of the scene, on two counts. First, the sequence of prefixes for Falstaff over 1.2.67–109, namely 'Iohn', 'Falst.', 'Iohn', 'Iohn', 'Falst.', 'sir Iohn', 'Falst.', with its five changes of mind, presents a thoroughly blurred boundary between the two sections. This strongly suggests

[27] In Textual Companion, p. 120.
[28] New Cambridge edition (1989); see also 'Sir John Umfrevile in Henry IV, Part 2, I.i.161–79', in Sonderdruck aus Real 2 (1984), 199–209, 'The Corridors of History: Shakespeare the Remaker', in Proceedings of the British Academy, 72 (1986), 67–85, 'Reconstructing the ur-Henry IV', in Essays in Honour of Kristian Smidt, edited by P. Bilton, L. Hartveit, S. Johansson, A. O. Sandved, and B. Tysdahl (1986), pp. 59–78.

a sequential transition, not a clean break between a *2 Henry IV* expansion and an ur-*Henry IV* antecedent. Secondly, the putatively revision-stage prefixes for 'Sir John' overlap with putatively ur-*Henry IV* prefixes for the Justice between the latter's entry after 1.53 and the beginning of the 'Falstaff' run which Melchiori puts at 1.95. Setting these objections aside, even if the middle section of the scene were to have been written earlier than the rest, it would not follow that Oldcastle was the name used throughout. After all, even in this exceptional scene over half the scene's prefixes call the character Falstaff rather than (Sir) John, so the proximity of the '*Old.*' prefix to Falstaff prefixes is not remarkable. And if the '*Falst.*' prefixes in 1.2 are seen as alterations from the ur-text's 'Oldcastle', if (Sir) John characterizes the new writing in the scene, it is strange that it is '*Falst.*' that becomes the standard prefix in the rest of the Quarto. Even if, notwithstanding, Oldcastle was named throughout the section of 1.2 with 'Falstaff' prefixes, one is still left a considerable way short of arriving at the conclusion that the passage must have appeared in an ur-*Henry IV*, for even after Lord Cobham's insistence that Oldcastle be banished from the stage Shakespeare's 'Old' habits might, in a rough draft at least, have died hard. I press the point because Melchiori's argument has a considerable editorial consequence: if Oldcastle, along with Russell and Harvey, belong to the irrecoverable ur-*Henry IV* they were never present in *1 Henry IV* as we have it, and the Oxford Shakespeare's emendation to the pre-censorship text would be untenable. But, however fascinating Melchiori's reconstruction might be, I can see no evidence whose interpretation must favour the supposition of an ur-*Henry IV* conjecture over other, less conjectural, accounts of the texts.

It is the second part of the volume that brings us closer to Freedman's discussion. Like Freedman, Melchiori is unimpressed with the idea that *Merry Wives* was commissioned for performance at the 1597 Garter feast. Instead he proposes that Shakespeare wrote a shorter entertainment for that occasion that became incorporated into the eventual stage-play. The theory is not new, in that G. R. Hibbard suggested that the final scene might have constituted such an entertainment,[29] but Melchiori describes a much more substantial lost precursor. It would have comprised a love plot (Fenton and Anne Page), an unworthy knight plot (perhaps requiring no more than two characters, Falstaff and the Host of the Garter), a German Duke plot (more elaborately woven into the action than in the play texts), and the Garter masque proper (essentially the final scene as in the Folio but without recourse to Mistress Quickly, Evans, and Pistol for acting the parts). As Hibbard also envisaged, Shakespeare developed the full-length play only after writing *Henry V*, borrowing the comic characters Bardolph, Pistol, Nym, Shallow, and Mistress Quickly from history plays that had already reached the stage. The case for a short Garter entertainment in 1597 followed by a full-length play in 1600 has more to be said for it than the ur-*Henry IV*, but the apparent flesh on the hypothesis is again actually made up of ghostly conjecture.

The Garter is a kind of metaphorical support upholding all Melchiori's ideas. Unfortunately that institution remains practically invisible even when Melchiori turns to *Edward III*. He takes it as a matter of 'general consensus' that Shakespeare had a hand in the play, whilst seeing the play as more substantially by Shakespeare than is usually accepted. Melchiori develops an argument made in his *Shakespeare's Dramatic Meditations* (1976) to the effect that Sonnet 94 distils the political ideas of a passage in 2.1 of *Edward III*, and finds in the play a prefiguration of the structure of the whole Henriad. Thus *Edward III* enters the sequence to make up, along with *Merry Wives*, what Melchiori calls Shakespeare's 'Garter cycle'. Critical ingenuity, like textual-

---

[29] In his New Penguin edition (1973), pp. 49–50.

critical ingenuity, is hard pushed to fill the silence of the plays in question on Garter matters. Melchiori offers a half-page paragraph highlighting the significance of honour in these plays. The perception that honour is a significant theme is as old as Shakespeare criticism itself. The conclusion that the plays in question are in some meaningful sense Garter plays rests on a tenuous basis; indeed, one might be tempted to recall Falstaff's, or Oldcastle's, reductive view of honour as 'Air'.

DISPUTED QUARTOS

The Contention, *Richard, Duke of York*, and the first quartos of *Romeo and Juliet*, *Henry V*, *Hamlet*, and *Merry Wives* are the subject of Kathleen Irace's *Reforming the 'Bad' Quartos*. On the first page Irace recognizes two simultaneous properties of Q1 *Hamlet*: it restructures the more familiar and longer text in ways that suggest theatrical adaptation, yet it also alters the local verbal texture in a way that is hard to reconcile with the usual processes of adaptation. She is unapologetically quick in imposing value judgements on these processes: words such as 'muddled', 'flawed' and 'garbled' are fit to describe the dialogue, whereas the theatrical alterations are often 'clever', 'valuable' and 'effective' (p. 12). These descriptions, by refusing to praise or damn the overall quality of the text, provide a healthy starting-point, though even a dichotomy between structural virtue and verbal vice is unlikely to offer a consistently comfortable *modus vivendi* with these insistently variable texts.

Irace finds the six texts clearly demarcated from all others, yet within this distinct territory she finds room for considerable variation in the character of each text. One characteristic they do share is relative brevity, and so Irace usually adopts the designator 'short' as her reformation of the opprobrious 'bad'. If one wants a non-peremptory label, 'short' will do for the six, even though it would be confusing in the cases of a non-Shakespearean text such as *Doctor*

Faustus, where the shorter text is the one now accounted 'good'. I shall borrow the epithet myself in the remainder of this review.

The revision theory, at least in its usual strong form, specifies that the short quarto text must be earlier in origin than its longer alternative. Irace identifies Steven Urkowitz as the one critic who has argued strongly for seeing the short quartos as pre-revision texts, and catches him badly off-balance when she notes, 'Among the passages copied from the short quartos as compositors set the longer texts are the key stage directions in the *Contention* that Urkowitz ... believed should have "proven terminally embarrassing" to the theory of memorial reconstruction. Instead, the likelihood that these nearly identical stage directions were copied from Q to F in the printing house very seriously undermines Urkowitz's own case for Shakespearean revision as applied to the short quartos' (p. 97).[30] Q1 *Romeo and Juliet* and Q1 *Hamlet* were likewise consulted during the setting of the second quartos, and this opens up a similar possibility that these texts too contain localized variation introduced in the printing house that will flow in the opposite direction from the sequence of underlying versions. In such plays the adaptation/reconstruction theories can accommodate a certain amount of two-way variation between the first quarto and its successor; by Urkowitz's reading, in contrast, and in conflict with what numerous critics have observed most clearly in the three-text play *Hamlet*, the development should uniformly proceed from the first quarto onwards.

In five of the six short-quarto plays, the longer counterpart shows strong signs of having been printed from some kind of authorial draft. Folio *Merry Wives* is exceptional, and indeed seems to derive indirectly from a prompt-book. Irace recognizes late theatrical expurgation in F,

---

[30] Irace here quotes Urkowitz, '"If I mistake in those foundations which I build upon": Peter Alexander's Textual Analysis of *Henry VI Parts 2 and 3*', in *English Literary Renaissance*, 18 (1988), 230–56, p. 253.

but moots that in this case at least Shakespeare could have introduced in Q 'limited, finite changes, designed for certain performances, while the slightly longer version might have been retained for court performances' (p. 107). What is particularly in question here is the variant script for the final scene. Irace is perhaps over-generous to a hypothesis she rejects for the other texts. Indeed it is a paradox that she admits the possibility of local authorial alteration in a short quarto where the overall verbal correspondence between Q and F is extraordinarily low and the general level of apparently non-Shakespearian re-origination in Q is therefore most high: as she notes on p. 123, only about 40 per cent of F's lines appear in any form whatsoever in Q. *Merry Wives* happens also to be the short quarto that has a corresponding longer text that could itself most plausibly be put forward as an authorially revised version without violence to her understanding of its origin.

For Irace, nothing refutes the early-draft explanation of the short quartos as decisively as the positive evidence for memorial transmission. At the heart of her study lies an attempt to verify or disprove the assumption that the varying level of verbal correspondence between short and long texts depends on the varying reliability of actor-reporters. Ignoring spelling and word order, Irace labelled every line as having entirely the same words in both texts, or most of the same (over 50 per cent), or merely some; where there was no verbal correspondence a line could be identified as having variant forms describable as paraphrase or as standing in one text only. This classification of lines is perhaps a blunt instrument, perhaps necessarily. Nonetheless, Irace is able to affirm what has often been claimed more impressionistically: that there is a high level of verbal correspondence between texts within the speeches of particular characters, and that there is a lower but still enhanced level of correspondence when the same characters are on stage but silent.

The results are more convincing for some plays than others. The low level of textual correspondence between Q and F *Merry Wives* as a whole allows for high correlations where things get better in the parts of Falstaff and the Host, and in the passages where they are present on stage. Whereas these parts stand out with particular clarity, the situation is notably less distinct with *The Contention* and *Romeo*. Variability between the texts is only to be expected, but it is a potential weakness of Irace's study that she makes only casual attempts to assess the statistical significance of her results.

Irace emphasizes that the short quartos typically combine memorial transmission with theatrical adaptation. In the cases of *Hamlet, Richard, Duke of York*, and *Henry V* the major cuts would seem to be no earlier than the reconstruction. Irace finds it hard to determine whether adaptations were constructed for provincial tours. Only two short quartos, *Henry V* and *Hamlet* (which is advertised on the Q1 title page as having toured to Oxford and Cambridge), have a small enough cast for most estimates of the size of touring companies, though those estimates vary, and it has been questioned whether either quarto effectively reduces the number of actors.

In her conclusion Irace reveals that she had initially imagined that her study of actors' roles would overturn the theory of memorial reconstruction. This is believable, because Irace's study is throughout careful and fair-minded. The book has two major virtues. First, it refuses to be satisfied with the complacent scepticism that claims that the historical determination of these texts is irrelevant or entirely unknowable. Secondly, even as it reinforces the case for memorial reconstruction it works as a strong piece of advocacy for the interest and theatrical effectiveness of the short quartos. Irace has presented a more comprehensive and competent account of the short quartos than anyone to date who denies memorial reconstruction. She teaches us to read these texts without embarrassment, and equally without a moral imperative to approve of them as in some way 'alternative' Shakespeares.

A text too good – or too long – for the purposes of Irace is considered in Peter Davison's presidential address to the Bibliographical Society, which reflects on editing the First Quarto of *Richard III*. Davison has conducted a systematic evaluation of variants using the techniques developed by George Thomson and George Kane; the detail of that study is not presented here, but some of the conclusions are. He notes, for example, that the degree of variability in the correspondence between Q and F is consistent for certain dramatic roles: Richard, Hastings, and Richmond vary little, but Buckingham's speeches in Q and F are usually divergent. One is left wondering whether these variations are quantifiable by the sort of technique Irace adopts. Davison upholds the view that the Quarto is based on a memorial reconstruction by the Lord Chamberlain's Men put together while the company was away from London, probably on the recorded tour of 1597 that ended shortly before the play was printed. Noting that the Master of the Revels's licence for performance in other situations seems to have stood as an alternative or equivalent to a specific licence for printing, Davison observes that *Richard III* was the first Shakespeare play to have been printed on the authority of a licence from the Revels Office. The inference he draws is that the Stationers' Company took this step because the manuscript contained no licence to perform, as would be inevitable if it had been compiled in the provinces.

These are suggestive consolidations of previous work on *Richard III* by David L. Patrick and others.[31] I am less convinced by some of the details that arise from a casting chart designed to show that the Quarto text could have been performed on tour by ten men and two boys. Admittedly by way of conjecture, Davison attributes the roles of Hastings and Richmond to Shakespeare, on the basis that their speeches are accurately preserved. We cannot, however, be at all sure that it would be a characteristic of Shakespeare as actor–author to remember the lines he performed with greater accuracy than his mere-smear actor colleagues. Indeed the very opposite might be the case: Shakespeare might have asserted a special right to tinker and improve; his mind might have been especially open to the previously unwritten possibilities of the text; there might have been no hard and fast line between recall and recreation.

Davison's assumption has a consequence that is sufficiently odd to call it in question. In 5.3 when the ghost of Hastings appears to Richmond, an actor other than the actor of Hastings (Shakespeare) has to play the ghost of Hastings. It is odd too that Davison has Grey played by a boy actor, especially as a man plays his ghost. In this case the discontinuity is needed to uphold Davison's suggestion that no more than ten men and two boys constituted the touring company. If Grey is a man, one needs an eleventh man, but if his ghost is a boy, one needs a third boy. As so often with casting charts, arbitrary presuppositions can shape the conclusion. Davison notes that the ghosts appear out of the order established by the earlier sequence of the play's action when the figures were alive. The doubling chart purports to show how this arrangement might accommodate the scene to the small company. Evidently Davison has in mind particularly the two boy actors, as the out-of-sequence appearance of the ghost of Hastings might allow the boys to do a quick costume change – a very quick one in fact, as Hastings's ghost has only five lines to say. Thus Q3's correction to sequential order, though unauthoritative, restores what Shakespeare would have written. It is a vulnerable line of argument. Davison assumes that the Duchess of York, Queen Margaret, and Queen Elizabeth would all be played by men. This is possible, but so much a matter of conjecture that it supplies no basis on which to delimit the number of boys to two, and therefore no basis on which to posit that the order of the ghosts

---

[31] Patrick, *The Textual History of 'Richard III'* (1936).

has been altered to enable the scene to be played by these two boys.

Davison ranges attractively between textual scholarship and theatre history, he is anecdotal as well as learned, and in his opening and conclusion he tacks usefully towards the *teaching* of bibliography. Although one can see why a hardened bibliographer might jib at some of his methods, Davison enriches our sense of Q1 *Richard III* – and leaves us wanting to know more about this enigmatic text.

KING LEAR

In 'Revision Awry in Folio *Lear* 3.1' Richard Knowles intriguingly plays oracular mouthpiece to Peter Blayney. That is, he offers what seems to be a modification of an unpublished suggestion outlined in notes that Blayney made available to him and elaborated in private correspondence. Blayney and Knowles attend to Kent's account in 3.1 of the French intervention, which Knowles claims to be the only passage in the play that, by the revision theory, has been substantially rewritten rather than cut or expanded. He concurs with those who find the Quarto version superior both to the Folio alternative and to the historically usual editorial conflation of the two. Knowles acknowledges revision in the passage, but posits that additionally the Folio incorporates two serious faults: two revisions have been run together as one, and a Quarto passage has been excised by accident. Perhaps the best way to bring a complex textual discussion into focus is to compare the disliked Folio passage with part of the Blayney-Knowles recombination. In modernized, edited form the Folio says, of Albany and Cornwall:

> Who have – as who have not that their great stars
> Throned and set high – servants, who seem no less,
> Which are to France the spies and speculations
> Intelligent of our state. What hath been seen,
> Either in snuffs and packings of the Dukes,
> Or the hard rein which both of them hath borne

> Against the old kind King; or something deeper,
> Whereof perchance these are but furnishings –

At which point the Gentleman interrupts. To be sure, this does not make easy reading, but the convoluted syntax and the elliptical anxiety on matters political are strongly reminiscent of passages such as Prospero's account of his deposition in *The Tempest* 1.2. If the speech is clouded, there might be sound reasons for avoiding specific details of the French activities and of Kent's commission to the Gentleman, on aesthetic as well as political grounds. As Kent says, 'Few words'. What is particularly to be stressed in view of Knowles's rearrangement is the overall coherence of the passage: 'the *spies* and *speculations* / Intelligent of our state' leads directly into 'What hath been *seen*'. The caesura here is the point where Knowles, following Blayney's suggestion, splits the passage into two fragments. Of these, the first precedes the Quarto-only passage, as in the erstwhile conflated text, and the second is inserted towards the end of the Quarto-only passage thus (here I quote Knowles's old-spelling reconstruction on p. 43):

> you shall find
> Some that will thanke you, making iust report
> Of how vnnaturall and bemadding sorrow
> The King hath cause to plaine, What hath bin
> seene,
> Either in snuffes, and packings of the Dukes,
> Or the hard Reine which both of them hath borne
> Against the olde kinde King; or something deeper,
> Whereof (perchance) these are but furnishings.
> I am a Gentleman of blood and breeding,
> And from some knowledge and assurance, / Offer
> this office to you.

Blayney and Knowles have created a strong discontinuity in the new combinate line 'The King hath caused to plaine, What hath bin seene'. The difficulty persists whether one follows Blayney in taking 'What' as equivalent to 'whatever' and beginning a new sentence that continues to the end of the speech, or follows Knowles in seeing the extended clause beginning 'What' as a continuation of the just report that the Gentleman will receive. By the criterion of elegance, this emendation is not convincing. And the case for assuming error in the first place remains very much in doubt.

In Robert Clare's 'The Theory of Authorial Revision between Quarto and Folio Texts of *King Lear*', as with Davison's article in the same issue, the journal of the Bibliographical Society embraces an approach to texts informed by an awareness of the theatre. Clare begins by surveying the contributions of the revisionists, observing that their arguments 'depend more upon cross-referenced interpretative commentary than upon any conclusive bibliographical scrutiny' (p. 37), which indeed is true of much textual criticism. Clare joins in the interpretative party when he disputes the theatrical cogency that the revisionists claim for the Folio text. He points out that the role of Albany, which revisionists argue to have been purposefully revised, turned out to be too inconspicuous to merit any comment at all in most reviews of Nicholas Hytner's 1990 Folio-based RSC production. It has to be said, of course, that many of the changes between Q and F do not appear designed to be conspicuous. The Folio's more substantial cuts are especially likely to alter the shape and theatrical dynamic of the play, but Clare argues that they are often to be regretted; 'conflation should continue to provide a basis for rehearsals, and ultimately for performance' (p. 54). He strongly defends the mock-trial scene in theatrical terms. Some of Clare's points seem persuasive, and yet they can be at least as impressionistic as the arguments of Steven Urkowitz and Roger Warren that they counter.[32] 'Most Lears would argue that the journey to 4.6 is only made possible by playing the mock trial first' he says (p. 49). Perhaps; but then perhaps not. Though he deplores the loaded vocabulary of the revisionists, he embraces some loaded vocabulary himself: the mock trial is 'too important' for a 'responsible' author to have cut it (p. 51).

When he contests the status of Folio alterations to Edgar's role, Clare cites what he properly takes to be the theatrical appeal of Edgar as witnessed by his prominence on the Quarto title-page. The Folio changes give him further prominence, 'but hardly in a way that could be said to be consistent with positive "strategies of revision"' (pp. 58–9). Whereas the theatrical effectiveness of the Quarto's mock-trial scene argues for its necessity in performance, the theatrical effectiveness of Edgar's enhanced role in the Folio text argues for its redundancy. The theatre is cited with approval only when it is the modern theatre: modern actors and directors are allowed to speak with an authority that transcends the here and now and puts them in alliance with Shakespeare, whilst the practice of the company with whom Shakespeare performed is found lacking.

Ann R. Meyer's 'Shakespeare's Art and the Texts of *King Lear*' is another recent publication that seeks to sew together some of the seams that were unpicked in the Oxford Shakespeare's two-text editing of *King Lear*. She first accuses the Oxford editors – primarily Taylor – of introducing Folio readings to the Quarto text in contradiction of the stated policy 'as far as possible, to emend Q – where emendation seems desirable – as though F did not exist'.[33] She gives the example of 3.4.6, where Q describes the storm as 'crulentious' (uncorrected) or 'tempestious' (corrected), and F alters to 'contentious'. Blayney, who argued for the use of the copy manuscript in correction, produced a subtle argument to show how the Quarto corrector here corrupted the text further.[34] Whether or not one accepts the mechanics of Blayney's account, the graphical dissimilarity between the Quarto alternatives suggests that the manuscript did not read 'tempestious'.

---

32 Urkowitz, *Shakespeare's Revision of 'King Lear'* (1980), especially pp. 80–128; Warren, 'The Folio Omission of the Mock Trial: Motives and Consequences, in *The Division of the Kingdoms: Shakespeare's Two Versions of 'King Lear'*, edited by Gary Taylor and Michael Warren (1983), pp. 45–57.

33 Quoting *Textual Companion*, p. 510.

34 *The Texts of 'King Lear' and Their Origins*, vol. I, *Nicholas Okes and the First Quarto* (1982), pp. 248–9.

Correspondingly, the similarity between 'cru-lentious' and 'contentious' suggests that the former is an error for the latter. This is the view Taylor accepted.[35] As Meyer too agrees that 'contentious' is the correct reading, her one substantive point over this crux depends on her not perceiving or not accepting that Blayney's and Taylor's line of reasoning could be developed without reference to F, but I suspect that most competent textual editors would be able to work it out even if the Folio were not at hand.

Switching her angle of attack, Meyer goes on to support Paul Hammond's argument that the uncorrected Quarto reading 'come on bee true' should be emended, on the basis of F's 'Come, vn-/button heere' (3.4.102–3), to 'come, un-button'.[36] Admittedly, although 'come on, be true' can be defended, 'come, unbutton' makes stronger sense and could possibly be corrupted to the original Quarto reading. The soft under-belly of two-text editing of *Lear* and comparable works is the impossibility for an editor to guard effectively against both of two diametric charges: of making excessive use of the non-copy-text, or of failing to select the best reading available. Though Meyer tries to make both charges stick, Taylor's editing for the Oxford text emerges consistent with its principles. Emendation of 'come on bee true' would not be desirable if F did not exist. Meyer would have found stronger ammunition if this defensible reading had been dropped in favour of the Folio.

When she considers Lear's death, Meyer rejects revision as an explanation for the Q/F variants, and instead suggests that lines were omitted by the Quarto compositor to save space. This is, at first sight, an intriguing possibility, especially as, citing Blayney,[37] Meyer can establish that the last page, L4, was set after the outer forme had been printed. Objections that might be raised are: (a) the signs of space-saving independent of the supposed shortening of the text are routine in this quarto; (b) as composition was, we are told, *seriatim*, the decision

exceptionally to print the outer forme first, which excludes the possibility of printing text on L4v, would have been effected when only L4 remained to be set, and therefore almost immediately before the compositor supposedly realised the exceptional need to save space; (c) the compositor was left with the equivalent of three type-lines for the '*FINIS.*', which is actually set in larger type than in many other play quartos; (d) space-saving can account for by no means all the significant Q/F variation. Apart from minor verbal variants in the Quarto page that are of no significance as space-saving measures, the passage also contains two crucial speech-prefix alterations. One of these, the Folio reattribution of Lear's 'Break, heart, I prithee break' to Kent, is logically related to the Folio addition or Quarto omission of the words 'Look on her. Look, her lips. / Look there, look there!' just before it. The changes work together to give Lear a potentially if equivocally hopeful death that is uncountenanced in the Quarto. Especially in view of this strong indication of artistic reshaping, it is implausible instead to suppose a relatively serious compositorial error following hard on extravagant compositorial space-saving. What further undermines Meyer's case is that she has to suppose that the compositor guiltily inserted 'O, o, o, o' as a substitution for the dying words he had omitted. Not only is it inconvenient to have to envisage that the compositor made an insertion in a passage where he was trying to save space, but also Meyer seems to have forgotten that the protagonist dies with exactly the same 'O, o, o, o' in Folio *Hamlet*.

Meyer anticipates Clare in arguing that Q is the better text for its inclusion of the mock-trial scene, but she regards F as having the advantage

---

[35] *Division of the Kingdoms*, pp. 455–6.

[36] In Hammond's review of the Oxford *Complete Works*, in *Seventeenth Century Journal*, 3 (1988), 85–107, p. 103. Taylor and Meyer agree in rejecting the corrected Quarto's shortened reading 'come on'.

[37] *Nicholas Okes and the First Quarto*, pp. 217–18.

for its version of the play's ending. Thus she, like Clare, eclectically picks out best readings in order to demonstrate that such eclecticism should be installed as an editorial method. The assumptions that permit such choices predicate the conclusion. Yet this method is quite typical of the new eclecticists. A new general theory for thinking in terms of a single-text non-versional *Lear* needs establishing before localized best-text arguments can properly begin to be advanced. Until then, each text bears best witness to one of two versions, and what remains for an editor is to define the extent of error in each text. Editors will naturally differ as to how they patrol the frontier between the texts. But I use a misleading metaphor: editors do not stop variants from migrating, but they relocate otherwise indigenous variants themselves. Obviously – at least, one would have thought obviously – one should refrain from identifying error where the text can plausibly be defended. This does not apply with much force to the Quarto variant 'crulentious'/'tempestious', where the nature of the corrected reading in relation to the uncorrected reading seriously undermines its apparent credibility in its own right. The principle applies forcefully, however, to the last page of Q, where, in advance of her permissive but inconclusive explanation of error, Meyer makes a presupposition of error that is virtually groundless.

The eclecticists may not deny authorial revision absolutely; rather they seek to delimit it, and are sometimes hostile to it as an explanation. Many of the analytic techniques are borrowed from the revisionists themselves, but where the revisionists tend to be convergent to the point of the monolithic, the new eclecticists are local historians of the text whose findings remain unsynthesized and perhaps beyond synthesis. In the General Introduction to the Oxford Shakespeare *Textual Companion* Taylor pointed out that where Shakespeare did not himself initiate a change that helped bring the text into performance, he can only be assumed to have acquiesced in such a change (p. 19).

Several critics have responded to the two-text *King Lear* by attempting to disengage once again an innocent authorial text from the Folio song of experience. The new eclecticists of *King Lear* therefore tend to mistrust the theatre in which Shakespeare himself worked and to see it as a contaminating influence. To oppose the 'theatrical' to the 'authorial' will always readily problematize the Folio. But if the Oxford Shakespeare's limited socialization of the text is at issue, that issue needs confronting more directly than is attempted in the studies under review. Furthermore, such studies repeatedly rely on a flawed assumption. A cut that leaves a slight scar cannot be affirmed as non-authorial on that account, and the attempt to distinguish authorial cuts on the basis that they are successful cuts will always be on shaky ground practically as well as theoretically.

The two-text *King Lear* rehabilitated a 'doubtful' quarto and presented the effects of textual difference to the reader. It seemed a few years ago that the attempt to rehabilitate the 'bad' quartos might be positioned as a further development in the same direction. One has only to think of the work of Urkowitz. It now looks otherwise: whilst recent work on the short quartos tends to insist on their viability as texts in their own right, recent work on *Lear*, paradoxically, takes us away from Quarto and Folio as distinct entities and begins to re-merge them. If there is a symptomatic contradiction within the field of studies here, an attempt to account for it might come to interesting conclusions as to the state of Shakespeare textual criticism today.

WORKS REVIEWED

Clare, Robert. ' "Who is it that can tell me who I am?": The Theory of Authorial Revision between Quarto and Folio Texts of *King Lear*'. In *The Library*, VI, 17 (1995), 34–59.

Davison, Peter. 'Bibliography: Teaching, Research and Publication. Reflections on Editing the First Quarto of *Richard III*'. In *The Library*, VI, 17 (1995), 1–33.

Duncan-Jones, Katherine. 'Filling the Unforgiving Minute: Modernizing SHAKE-SPEARES SONNETS (1609)'. In *Essays in Criticism*, 45 (1995), 199–207.

Freedman, Barbara. 'Shakespearean Chronology, Ideological Complicity, and Floating Texts: Something is Rotten in Windsor'. In *Shakespeare Quarterly*, 45 (1994), 190–210.

Graham-White, Anthony. *Punctuation and Its Dramatic Value in Shakespearean Drama*. Newark: University of Delaware Press, and London: Associated University Presses, 1995.

Horton, Thomas B. 'Distinguishing Shakespeare from Fletcher through Function Words'. In *Shakespeare Studies*, 22 (1994), 314–35.

Irace, Kathleen O. *Reforming the 'Bad' Quartos: Performance and Provenance of Six Shakespearean First Editions*. Newark: University of Delaware Press, and London and Toronto: Associated University Presses, 1994.

Jarvis, Simon. *Scholars and Gentlemen: Shakespearian Textual Criticism and Representations of Scholarly Labour, 1725–1765*. Oxford: Clarendon Press, 1995.

Knowles, Richard. 'Revision Awry in Folio *Lear* 3.1'. In *Shakespeare Quarterly*, 46 (1995), 32–46.

Knutson, Roslyn L. 'Falconer to the Little Eyases: A New Date and Commercial Agenda for the "Little Eyases" Passage in *Hamlet*'. In *Shakespeare Quarterly*, 46 (1995), 1–31.

Melchiori, Giorgio. *Shakespeare's Garter Plays: 'Edward III' to 'Merry Wives of Windsor'*. Newark: University of Delaware Press, and London and Toronto: Associated University Presses, 1994.

Meyer, Ann R. 'Shakespeare's Art and the Texts of *King Lear*'. In *Studies in Bibliography*, 47 (1994), 128–46.

Shakespeare, William. *Antony and Cleopatra*. Ed. by John Wilders, Arden 3. London and New York: Routledge, 1995.

King Henry V. Ed. by T. W. Craik, Arden 3. London and New York: Routledge, 1995.

Titus Andronicus. Ed. by Jonathan Bate, Arden 3. London and New York: Routledge, 1995.

Titus Andronicus. Ed. by Alan Hughes, The New Cambridge Shakespeare. Cambridge: Cambridge University Press, 1994.

A Midsummer Night's Dream. Ed. by Peter Holland, The Oxford Shakespeare. Oxford: Clarendon Press, 1994.

Twelfth Night. Ed. by Roger Warren and Stanley Wells, The Oxford Shakespeare. Oxford: Clarendon Press, 1994.

Taylor, Gary. 'Shakespeare and Others: The Authorship of *Henry the Sixth, Part One*. In *Medieval and Renaissance Drama in England* 7 (1995), 145–205.

The Chronicle History of Henry the fift, With his battell fought at Agin Court in France. Togither with Auntient Pistoll. Ed. by Graham Holderness and Bryan Loughrey, Shakespearean Originals: First Editions. Lanham, Maryland: Barnes and Noble, 1993.

West, Anthony James, 'Provisional New Census of the Shakespeare First Folio'. In *The Library*, VI, 17 (1995), 60–73.

BOOKS RECEIVED

This list includes all books received between September 1994 and September 1995 which are not reviewed in this volume of *Shakespeare Survey*. The appearance of a book in this list does not preclude its review in a subsequent volume.

Adams, Martin. *Henry Purcell: The Origins and Development of his Musical Style*. Cambridge: Cambridge University Press, 1995.

Aronson, Alex. *Shakespeare and the Ocular Proof*. New York: Vantage Press, 1995.

Bains, Y. S. *Making Sense of the First Quartos of Shakespeare's 'Romeo and Juliet', 'Henry V', 'The Merry Wives of Windsor' and 'Hamlet'*. Shimla: Indian Institute of Advanced Study, 1995.

Basch, David. *The Hidden Shakespeare: A Rosetta Stone*. West Hartford, CT: Revelatory Press, 1994.

Berg, Frederic. *ATHE Directory of Theatre Periodicals*. Evansville, Indiana: Association for Theatre in Higher Education, 1994.

Clark, J. C. D. *Samuel Johnson: Literature, Religion and English Cultural Politics from the Restoration to Romanticism*. Cambridge: Cambridge University Press, 1994.

Edelstein, T. J., ed. *The Stage is all the World: The Theatrical Designs of Tanya Moiseiwitsch*. The David and Alfred Smart Museum of Art. The University of Chicago in association with the University of Washington Press, 1994.

Gira, Catherine, and Adele Seeff. *'Henry IV Parts I and II': An Annotated Bibliography*. New York: Garland, 1994.

Harvey, Nancy Lenz. *'The Taming of the Shrew': An Annotated Bibliography*. New York: Garland, 1994.

Kolin, Philip C., ed. *'Titus Andronicus': Critical Essays*. New York: Garland, 1995.

Luxon, Thomas H. *Literal Figures: Puritan Allegory and the Reformation Crisis in Representation*. Chicago and London: University of Chicago Press, 1995.

Mirsky, Mark J. *The Absent Shakespeare*. Madison, Teaneck: Fairleigh Dickinson University Press; London and Toronto: Associated University Presses, 1994.

Shakespeare, William. *King John*. Ed. by Pat Baldwin and Rex Gibson, Cambridge School Shakespeare. Cambridge: Cambridge University Press, 1994.

Shakespeare, William. *The Two Gentlemen of Verona*. Ed. by Rex Gibson and Susan Leech, Cambridge School Shakespeare. Cambridge: Cambridge University Press, 1994.

Shakespeare, William. *The Tempest*. Ed. by Rex Gibson, Cambridge School Shakespeare. Cambridge: Cambridge University Press, 1995.

Slights, William W. E. *Ben Jonson and the Art of Secrecy*. Toronto, Buffalo, London: University of Toronto Press, 1994.

Trussler, Simon. *The Cambridge Illustrated History of British Theatre*. Cambridge: Cambridge University Press, 1994.

BOOKS RECEIVED

Water, D. Douglas. *Christian Settings in Shake-speare's Tragedies.* Rutherford, Madison, Teaneck: Fairleigh Dickinson University Press; London and Toronto: Associated University Presses, 1994.

Whalen, Richard F. *Shakespeare: Who Was He? The Oxford Challenge to the Bard of Avon.* Westport, Connecticut and London: Praeger, 1994.

INDEX

The index does not include titles of books referred to in the review articles. These books are listed alphabetically by author at the end of each review article.

INDEX

INDEX

INDEX

INDEX

INDEX